Between Facts and Norms

Studies in Contemporary German Social Thought (partial listing)
Thomas McCarthy, General Editor

Between Facts and Norms

Contributions to a Discourse Theory
of Law and Democracy

Jürgen Habermas

translated by William Rehg

The MIT Press, Cambridge, Massachusetts

First MIT Press paperback edition, 1998

This edition ©1996 Massachusetts Institute of Technology
This work originally appeared in German under the title *Faktizität und Geltung. Beiträge zur Diskurstheorie des Rechts und des demokratischen Rechtsstaats*, ©1992 Suhrkamp Verlag, Frankfurt am Main, Germany.

This book was set in New Baskerville at MIT Press and was printed and bound in the United States of America.

Library of Congress Cataloging-in-Publication Data

Habermas, Jürgen
    [Faktizität und Geltung. English]
    Between facts and norms : contributions to a discourse theory of
law and democracy / Jürgen Habermas ; translation by William Rehg.
        p.   cm. — (Studies in contemporary German social thought)
    Includes bibliographical references and index.
    ISBN 0-262-08243-8 (hardcover : alk. paper), 0-262-58162-0 (paperback)
    1. Sociological jurisprudence. 2. Democracy—Social aspects.
3. Rule of law—Social aspects. I. Title. II. Series.
K372.H3313 1996   95-40229
340'.115—dc20   CIP

Contents

Contents

Translator's Introduction
William Rehg

Both legal theory and the theory of democracy stand at a crossroads today. In the long-standing democratic regimes of the postindustrial West, problems of social complexity, pluralism, and the welfare state have been putting aged constitutional frameworks under tremendous stress. Such challenges are only intensified with the spread of democratic impulses across the globe, to areas where the cultural and infrastructural conditions for democracy and the rule of law must still be consciously constructed. In this context, one of the more fertile and optimistic theoretical developments has been associated with ideas of "deliberative democracy." These ideas reflect a concern that citizens' participation in the democratic process have a rational character—that voting, for example, should not simply aggregate given preferences but rather follow on a process of "thoughtful interaction and opinion formation" in which citizens become informed of the better arguments and more general interests.[1] Jürgen Habermas's *Between Facts and Norms*, with its emphasis on the role of public discourse in democracy, certainly contributes to this intellectual trend. But it would be wrong to view it simply as one more argument for deliberative democracy. In many respects the culminating effort in a project that was first announced with the 1962 publication of his *Strukturwandel der Öffentlichkeit*,[2] *Between Facts and Norms* offers a sweeping, sociologically informed conceptualization of law and basic rights, a normative account of the rule of law and the constitutional state, an attempt to bridge normative and empirical approaches to democracy, and an account of the social context required for democracy. Finally, it frames and caps these arguments with a bold proposal for a new paradigm of law that goes beyond the dichotomies that have afflicted modern political theory from its inception and that still underlie current controversies between so-called liberals and civic republicans.

An undertaking of such scope, which pulls together three decades of reflection and interdisciplinary research, which is immersed in both German and American debates, and which moves at a number of different levels, places considerable demands on its readers. The primary goal of this introduction is to lighten that burden. If one is to understand Habermas's particular approach to law, one has to have some sense of the basic features of his conceptual framework. After elucidating these in section 1, I briefly sketch the key arguments of the book in section 2. Section 3 notes certain terminological points.

1

Anglo-American philosophical treatises on law often begin with a definition of the concept of law itself. In *Between Facts and Norms*, the basic concept of law as a system of rights does not make its full appearance until chapter 3. The ambitious scale of Habermas's undertaking requires considerable preparation, and thus the first two chapters set a rather elaborate stage that features both his own conceptual architectonic and the surrounding landscape of debate. The conceptual apparatus was most fully expounded in his two-volume *Theory of Communicative Action*,[3] and one might read the present work as drawing out the legal, political, and institutional implications of this earlier endeavor. In this first section, I want to introduce the reader to the broader conceptual apparatus and motivate its appropriateness for the analysis of modern law and democracy. I begin by saying something about the puzzle that Habermas starts with, the paradoxical duality of modern law. We can then understand the theory of communicative action as particularly well suited to acknowledge this tension in law and deal with it constructively.

The Duality of Modern Law

To approach the analysis of modern law in terms of a tension "between facts and norms"—or between "facticity and validity," to translate the German title of the book more literally—is not so surprising. The legal sphere has long been characterized by theorists in terms of a duality of this sort. As we shall see, this tension resides at several levels, but at each level we find a social reality on the one side and a claim of reason (which is sometimes belied by the reality) on the other. Consider, for example, compulsory laws backed by sanctions. On the one hand, such laws appear as the will of a lawgiver with the power to punish those who do not comply; to the extent that they are actually enforced and followed, they have an existence somewhat akin to social facts. On the other hand, compulsory laws are not simply commands backed by threats but embody a claim to legitimacy. Oliver Wendell Holmes's insistence that we must understand law as the "bad man" does—that is, look at laws only in view of the possible negative consequences of being caught at lawbreaking—cannot be the whole story. In fact, many citizens are not consistently "bad" in this sense, and it is doubtful whether a system of law could long endure if everyone took this external approach all the time. At least some portion of a population, indeed the majority, must look at legal rules as standards that everyone *ought* to follow, whether because they reflect the ways of ancestors, the structure of the cosmos, or the will of God, or because they have been democratically approved or simply enacted according to established procedures. What H. L. A. Hart has termed the "internal aspect" of law is a function of its legitimacy or social recognition.[4] Exactly how such legitimacy should be construed is a further question, of course. The important point is this: law is a system of coercible rules and impersonal procedures that also involves an appeal to reasons that all citizens should, at least ideally, find acceptable.

Habermas is heavily indebted to Immanuel Kant's concept of legitimacy, which brings out this tension in law particularly well. Consider, for example, the basic equal rights of individual liberty, such as property and contract rights. Kant grounded their legitimacy in a universal principle of law (the *Rechtsprinzip*, often translated as "principle of right"), which can be interpreted as summarizing the conditions under which it is possible for a morally oriented subject to universalize coercible limits on the external behavior of strategically oriented individuals. According to Kant, the "moral conception" of law is "the sum of those conditions under which the free choice (*Willkür*) of one person can be conjoined with the free choice of another in accordance with a universal law of freedom."[5] This analysis of rights brings out the *internal tension* between facticity and validity inhabiting law in general: as actionable and enforced, such rights (and legal norms in general) represent social facts demarcating areas within which success-oriented individuals can choose and act as they wish; as linked with a universalizable freedom, rights deserve the respect of moral subjects, and thus carry a claim to legitimacy.

However, Kant's account of legitimacy, as Habermas reads it, ultimately subordinates law to morality. Kant also relied on a metaphysical framework that is no longer plausible: on his account, the possibility of universal rational acceptability depends on a preestablished harmony of reason beyond the empirical world. Whereas subordinating law to morality oversimplifies the rational bases of legitimacy, invoking a transcendentally unified reason presumes consensus prior to actual public discourse. Nonetheless, Kant's appeal to rational consensus as a regulative ideal captures an important part of the tension in law. If law is essentially constituted by a tension between facticity and validity—between its factual generation, administration, and enforcement in social institutions on the one hand and its claim to deserve general recognition on the other—then a theory that *situates* the idealizing character of validity claims *in* concrete social contexts recommends itself for the analysis of law. This is just what the theory of communicative action allows, without the metaphysical pretensions and moralistic oversimplification we find in Kant.

A Postmetaphysical Theory of Reason

The theory of communicative action is primarily a theory of rationality, an attempt to rescue the claims of reason that were once advanced within encompassing metaphysical systems (such as that of Thomas Aquinas), philosophies of history (such as G. W. F. Hegel's), or philosophies of consciousness (such as Kant's). According to Habermas, the growth of empirical science, the pluralization of worldviews, and other developments have rendered such grand philosophical approaches generally implausible—and have in the process given rise to impoverished views of reason as merely instrumental. Hence if one is to salvage a comprehensive concept of reason today, one must take a "postmetaphysical" approach. As Habermas uses it, the term "postmetaphysical," which should not be confused with "postmodern," covers a number of different philosophical theories. As specific examples, one might point to John Rawls's "political not metaphysical" theory of justice and Ronald Dworkin's theory of "law as integrity."[6] In any case, for Habermas a postmetaphysical vindication of reason is possible only insofar as philosophy—in an interdisciplinary cooperation with empirical inquiries of various sorts—can show how the use of language and social interaction in general necessarily rely on notions of validity, such as truth, normative rightness, sincerity, and authenticity.[7] This necessitates not only a philosophical analysis of communication but also an attention to debates within a range of disciplines.

Postmetaphysical philosophy thus need not surrender all ambitions of its own. This is already evident in the focus on validity. On Habermas's view, claims to validity involve an idealizing moment of unconditionality that takes them beyond the immediate context in which they are raised. This is clearest with certain types of truth claims, as they are commonly understood. For example, when we assert today that the earth is a sphere (approximately), we do not simply mean that it is "true for us" that the earth is spherical. Rather, we are also saying that anyone, of whatever generation or culture, who believes otherwise is mistaken. To be sure, the universalist understanding of truth has come under fire even in the philosophy of the natural sciences, and thus it should be no surprise that a philosopher who defends a universalist concept of normative validity in the practical domain—the domain of morality, politics, and law—faces rather imposing hurdles. The crux of the challenge is constructively to maintain the tension between the strongly idealizing, context-transcending claims of reason and the always limited contexts in which human reason must ply its trade. It is thus quite understandable that the tension "between facts and norms" should stand at the very center of Habermas's attempt to bring his theory of communicative action to bear on the existing institutions of law and democracy. A legal-political theory based on a theory of communicative action cannot avoid this tension, which in fact appears at every level of the analysis, as Habermas takes pains to demonstrate in the first chapter: within the use of language itself, within modern law, and between law and social reality. I turn now to Habermas's application of the theory of communicative action, first to social coordination in general and then to modern law.

The Communicative Structures of Social Coordination

The first chapter can be read as Habermas's own highly theoretical reconstruction of the paradoxical character of law and the special role of law in modern society. This reconstruction has a number of densely interwoven strands: not just an abstract theory of validity but an ambitious theory of modernity as well, it attempts to reconstruct the rise of modern law with its dual structure. Rather than trace its intricacies step by step, in what follows I will illustrate the basic categories necessary to follow Habermas's account.

One should first be aware that the theory of communicative action involves a particular view about how social coordination is effected through language. Drawing on insights from American pragmatism and the speech-act theories of J. L. Austin and John Searle, Habermas considers a "formal-pragmatic" approach to language as most adequate for social theory. This approach goes beyond semantic and syntactic analyses of meaning and grammar to examine the general structures that enable competent speakers actually to engage in successful interaction, which involves more than simply knowing how to form grammatical sentences.[8] Specifically, competent speakers know how to base their interactions on validity claims that their hearers will accept or that could, if necessary, be redeemed with good reasons. As already mentioned, this involves a tension between facticity and validity insofar as a claim to validity raised here and now, and perhaps justified according to local standards, ultimately points beyond a particular community. At least this is the case with truth claims and moral claims. As understood by participants engaged in interaction and discourse, truth claims are claims about the objective world that all human beings share, and moral claims have to do with norms for interpersonal relationships that any autonomous adult should find rationally acceptable from the standpoint of justice and respect for persons. If such claims are valid, then any competent speaker should, under suitable conditions, be able to accept the claim on the basis of good reasons. When a claim is contested, actually bringing about such rational acceptance requires actors to shift into a *discourse* in which, the pressures of action having been more or less neutralized, they can isolate and test the disputed claim solely on the basis of arguments.[9]

To be sure, not all types of claims anticipate the agreement of a universal audience. The differences between types of discourse can be quite important in this regard. For example, claims about what is good for a particular group (or person), or about a particular group's authentic self-understanding, may be addressed only to the individuals concerned and those who know them well. Such discourses, which Habermas labels "ethical," differ both in theme and scope of audience from the "moral" discourse concerned with universal norms of justice.[10] But even these more limited ethical claims presuppose an orientation to mutual understanding, which for Habermas is constitutive of communicative action. The orientation to reaching understanding about validity claims serves as a mechanism for social integration inasmuch as it grounds shared expectations, ways of interpreting situations, and so forth.

To illustrate Habermas's approach further, imagine that a dispute arises within a group and that its members wish to resolve it consensually on the basis of validity claims. According to Habermas, conflict resolution on the basis of reasoned agreement involves at least three idealizing assumptions: members must assume they mean the same thing by the same words and expressions; they must consider themselves as rationally accountable; and they must suppose that, when they do arrive at a mutually acceptable resolution, the supporting arguments sufficiently justify a (defeasible) confidence that any claims to truth, justice, and so forth that underlie their consensus will not subsequently prove false or mistaken. No local, spatiotemporally finite consensus can fully realize these idealizations; yet if they should subsequently prove false—if members discover that a crucial term was understood in two different ways or that they were seriously self-deceived or that they were mistaken about certain facts or norms—then there are grounds for questioning the original agreement and reopening the discussion. That is, these idealizations imply a tension between the de facto social acceptance (*soziale Geltung*) of a group consensus and the idealized validity (*Gültigkeit*) that such a consensus must claim for itself if members are to accept it as reasonable. Communicatively achieved agreements are in principle always open to challenge, and thus are at best a precarious source of social integration. If a community is to be a stable one, then, it requires more than explicit agreement as a basis for social cooperation.

Conflict resolution will be rendered easier the more the members of the group can limit their discursive efforts to a few problematic validity claims. For example, if they are at odds over how best to manage a particular environmental threat—one might imagine a city council debating how to deal with an imminent flood—they have a better chance of reaching agreement if they only have to resolve an empirical question about the effectiveness of two competing strategies, and do not also have to argue over fairness criteria, or what would count as a successful outcome. In short, reaching agreement communicatively requires a large background consensus on matters that are unproblematic for group members.

The implicit agreement represented by such a *lifeworld* background stabilizes a communicatively integrated group insofar as it removes a large body of assumptions from challenge—as it were, fusing validity with the facticity of a given cultural background. This is because the background not only provides its members with shared resources for managing conflict; as a source of shared identities, it also lessens the number of issues that are likely to be contested at any given time, so that large areas of social interaction rest on a stable basis of unquestioned consensus.[11]

If members cannot agree on how to resolve a specific conflict, say on the aforementioned question of how to deal with an impending flood, they can attempt to bargain. As Habermas understands this mode of conflict resolution, it involves a certain shift in perspective on the part of the conflicting parties from communicative to *strategic action*. Rather than attempting to convince one another of a validity claim regarding the intrinsically better strategy, each party begins to bargain with threats and promises in the hope of inducing the other to cooperate with it in pursuing a given flood policy. In more general terms, an actor who adopts a strategic attitude is primarily concerned with getting his or her way in a social environment that includes other actors. In many contexts it is understood by those involved that such an attitude is appropriate. In fact, the need for modern law partly arises because, with the growth of capitalist market economies, contexts dominated by strategic action become increasingly important for social coordination.

The Need for Positive Law

To understand modern law within the framework provided by Habermas's theory of communicative action, we need to introduce some complications that the above illustration provisionally set aside for the sake of clarity. First, because modern societies are pluralistic, conflict resolution must occur across a number of subgroups, each of which has a somewhat different self-understanding and set of shared background assumptions. Second, modern pluralization has engendered a process that Max Weber called the "disenchantment of the world." For our purposes, this refers to the loss of the "sacred canopy," the fact that pluralization has undermined, or at least fragmented, common religious authorities and worldviews.[12] Third, modern societies have developed a complex differentiation of functional spheres defined by specific tasks of social reproduction (economy, educational system, politics, and so on).

Pluralization and disenchantment undermine the ways in which communities can stabilize themselves against shared backgrounds and authorities that removed certain issues and assumptions from challenge. Modern societies witness an increasing variety of groups and subcultures, each having its own distinct traditions, values, and worldview. As a result, more and more conflicts must be settled by reaching explicit agreement on a greater range of contestable matters, under conditions in which the shared basis for reaching such agreement is diminishing. Areas of life in which facticity and validity were once fused come under increasing critical scrutiny—facticity and validity increasingly split apart, as it were—setting in motion a process of societal rationalization. That is, members are increasingly forced to separate different spheres of validity, for example, to distinguish scientific questions from those of faith, those of justice and morality from aesthetic judgments, and so forth, a development that Weber attempted to capture with his concept of the differentiation of "value spheres."

This increasingly differentiated use of communicative reason at the level of the lifeworld is associated with the third of the above aspects of modernity, the functional differentiation of semi-independent subsystems in which strategic action acquires greater importance for social coordination.[13] The capitalist economy is perhaps the most obvious example of this. Buyers and sellers act "strategically" rather than communicatively inasmuch as they make decisions according to their own interests and external market conditions. The social coordination that arises on this basis is achieved not by reaching agreement on validity claims but "behind the actors' backs," through anonymous market mechanisms created by the intermeshing of largely unintended consequences of action. In functionalist parlance, the economy represents a level of social integration that occurs through the "nonlinguistic steering medium" of money. This medium relieves market participants of the need to reach a substantive consensus, so that—in theory, at least—they can simply pursue their own personal advantage and trust to the overall aggregate effect of the market to distribute goods and services evenly and efficiently.[14]

Besides money and the economic reproduction it steers, "system integration" is also effected through the medium of power in formally structured organizations. In bureaucratic administrations, for example, the hierarchically stratified power of superiors over subordinates effects a coordinated realization of collective goals. The authority to issue binding commands means that the superior does not have to convince subordinates of the advisability of each task assigned to them, thus reducing the need for explicit consensus. Although this is by no means the whole story of how bureaucratic organizations actually function,[15] it does indicate how hierarchical organization at least reduces *some* of the burdens involved in reaching explicit agreement.

Modern law is meant to solve social coordination problems that arise under the above conditions, that is, where, on the one hand, societal pluralization has fragmented shared identities and eroded the substantive lifeworld resources for consensus and, on the other, functional demands of material reproduction call for an increasing number of areas in which individuals are left free to pursue their own ends according to the dictates of purposive rationality. The solution is to confine the need for agreement to general norms that demarcate and regulate areas of free choice. Hence the dual character of law: on the one hand, legal rights and statutes must provide something like a stable social environment in which persons can form their own identities as members of different traditions and can strategically pursue their own interests as individuals; on the other hand, these laws must issue from a discursive process that makes them rationally acceptable for persons oriented toward reaching an understanding on the basis of validity claims.

We now have the basic elements in Habermas's concept of modern law: (a) an account of certain features of modern societies; (b) a distinction between communicative and strategic action; and (c) an account of communicative action in terms of validity claims that must be vindicated in discourses of different types. Note how this last feature goes beyond Kant's account, which ultimately subordinated law to morality. Whereas Kant took universalizable moral validity as the model for legitimate law, Habermas proposes a more complex set of discourses that underlie legitimate lawmaking. In fact, this discourse approach is the key to his argument that democracy and the rule of law are internally related.

Before taking up this argument in section 2, though, we should note that there is also an *external tension* between facticity and validity, specifically a tension between the claims of the constitutional-democratic legal order and the ways in which forms of social power actually intrude on and undermine the conditions for legitimate lawmaking. For theorists with Habermas's sociological awareness, no plausible concept of modern law can ignore this external tension between facts and norms, and it is precisely the failure to appreciate this tension that leads to a certain one-sidedness in many contemporary political theories. The second chapter gives us a sense of Habermas's course by charting the shoals on which some leading alternatives have run aground. To close this first section, then, I briefly indicate Habermas's path between the two main alternatives.

Between Rawls and Luhmann

Many Anglo-American readers will already be familiar with one of these alternatives, John Rawls's theory of justice.[16] As much as he agrees with Rawls, Habermas finds that the highly normative theory of justice does not sufficiently appreciate the social facticity confronting constitutional ideals. To be sure, Rawls's concern with overlapping consensus and the social stability of his conception of justice does attempt to show how this conception can find acceptance within a particular *cultural* context. Rawls's theory can plausibly appeal to the fact that constitutional democracies have flourished in societies in which certain political traditions and ideas of fairness are widely shared. But this still ignores the problem of how legal *institutions* can realize such ideals in contexts shaped by powerful interests and complex functional requirements. And, to judge from the pessimism of many sociological observers of democracy, appeals to cultural ideals alone will not answer the problems posed by welfarism, bureaucratization, powerful corporate interests, an apathetic citizenry, and so forth.

The other main alternative, the systems theory of Niklas Luhmann, will probably be less familiar to English-speaking readers. In fact, Luhmann is one of the most influential social theorists in Germany today (along with Habermas himself) and, judging by translations of his work, he is not completely unknown to English-speaking audiences.[17] Nonetheless, a lengthier introduction to his approach, beginning with some historical background, is called for.

In the social-contract tradition going back to Thomas Hobbes, which Habermas also refers to under the umbrella of "rational" or "modern" natural law,[18] the legal constitution of society on the basis of individual rights appeared as a plausible extension of the contract relationship that governed the bourgeois economy. The economic institutions of contract and ownership already entailed a view of legal persons as free and equal, and thus as bearers of equal rights. Karl Marx's critique of capitalism turned this normative intuition inside out. Marx viewed the economy as a system of anonymous relations oriented not toward the freedom and equality proclaimed in 1789 but toward a humanly alienating self-reproduction of capital. Law—and more generally, the consciously accepted norms and ideals behind law—was no longer seen as the key element in social coordination; the focal point of social analysis shifted to the depersonalizing economic system whose integrating achievements proceeded behind the participants' backs. Coming out of the tradition of political economy (Adam Smith, David Ricardo, James Mill, et al.), this theoretical approach requires one to adopt an external-observer perspective, or what Habermas calls an "objectivating perspective" on social relations. The "performative perspective" of the participants themselves tends to be viewed with some suspicion, as subject to illusions, and it may even be dismissed as irrelevant. For Marx, the participant perspective still retained theoretical relevance inasmuch as the awareness of systemic mechanisms of capitalist integration had a critical, revolutionary power: even as he relied on an observer perspective, he addressed his theoretical analysis to participants who took the bourgeois norms of freedom and equality seriously. Contemporary systems theory, however, drops this normative involvement altogether for a thoroughly objectivating, technocratic approach to society. With its rigorous restriction to the observer perspective, systems theory takes an approach the very opposite from that of Rawls, with his commitment to the normative self-understanding of constitutional democracy.

In broad terms, systems theory has a certain appeal because of its ability to conceptualize forms of complex social organization that are effected more at an anonymous macrolevel than through the direct intentions of individual participants. I have already briefly described two such forms of organization, the market economy and bureaucratic organizations. As a "system," society (or its subsystems, such as the political system or economy) is not just the sum of individual beliefs and decisions but a set of functionally interdependent elements whose coordinated operation maintains the whole system or subsystem. Which elements are selected and how their functioning is conceived varies with the particular version of systems theory, but mechanistic equilibrium models and biological homeostasis models have provided two of the more influential metaphors for early systems theory.[19] Though heavily indebted to Talcott Parsons, Luhmann has radicalized systems theory by drawing on a concept of "autopoiesis" that was originally intended for living organisms.[20] Systems are "autopoietic" in the sense that "the states of the system are exclusively determined by its own operations. The environment can eventually destroy the system, but it contributes neither operations nor structures. The structures of the system condense and are confirmed as a result of the system's own operations, and the operations are in turn recursively reproduced by structural mediation."[21]

This implies that systems are "operationally closed." One should not confuse this with causal independence from the outside world. The legal system, for example, could not exist without the psychological systems of its judges, lawyers, clients, and so forth. Rather, systems are operationally closed in the sense that the communication of meaning within the system is defined solely in terms of the system's own language. As a result, a system can register events outside itself only insofar as they can be "translated" into its own language. An exchange of property, for example, can be "observed" by the legal system only insofar as it is mediated by an appropriate legal mechanism, such as a deed or valid will. Conversely, legal actions, such as a suit for damages to property, have meaning in the economic system only insofar as they impinge on monetary transactions. Inasmuch as the system's language, or "code and programming," determine what, and how, external events are observed, a system reproduces not only itself but its environment as well. Conversely, there is no central, overarching perspective on society as a whole but only a multiplicity of perspectives corresponding to the different subsystems. On Luhmann's systems approach, society is "polycentric."

If we examine the structure of the systemic language of law, however, we can see that such closure is compatible with a certain kind of "cognitive openness." Programs and codes are the means by which a system solves its basic problem, that of selecting possibilities in environments that are both complex and contingent.[22] In virtue of its binary code of legal versus illegal (where "illegal" has a broad sense that includes "not legally binding"), law selects certain actions and omissions as expectable within the legal community. Thus actors can expect that others will expect them to do action A in situations of type X, or not to do B in situations of type Y, and so forth.[23] To handle disappointments of these expectations, the law attaches sanctions to their violation. Normative expectations thus have the property that disappointments of the expectation do not lead to "learning"; that is, one does not adjust one's expectation as one does in the case of a disappointed cognitive expectation, say, about how nature will behave. Rather, one punishes the violator so as to reinforce the original expectation. Learning, or development in law, occurs in virtue of its "programming," which allows the legal system to adapt to new situations by developing new "programs," that is, by creating new norms. In this way, law is "cognitively open" to its environment.

Since the environment is itself an internal construct of the system, however, cognitive openness does not break social subsystems out of their operational self-enclosure. The turn to autopoiesis has thus forced systems theorists to search for ways to account for intersystemic effects.[24] This problem also turns up in Gunther Teubner's modifications of systems theory, modifications that in Habermas's view either are empirically untenable or tacitly presuppose the very kind of communicative action that systems theory must exclude. Habermas argues that such problems cannot be resolved if theory is closed to the participant perspective that governs the everyday use of language. It is from the perspective taken in communicative action, and thus through the flexibility provided by ordinary language, that legal "communications" are able to mediate between functional subsystems and the lifeworld.

The lesson of Habermas's reading of Rawls and Luhmann is this: if an account of modern law is to be neither sociologically empty nor normatively blind, then it must incorporate a dual perspective. The theorist of law can ignore neither the participants' own normative understanding of their legal system nor those external mechanisms and processes that are accessible to the sociological observer. The need for this dual perspective explains Habermas's continuing respect for such thinkers as Weber and Parsons, who attempted to combine internal and external perspectives in their analyses. To be sure, neither thinker succeeded in consistently maintaining both perspectives. But their failures are at least instructive, and in fact lie behind the complexity and multiperspectival character of Habermas's own analyses. More specifically, to do justice to the dual character of law, Habermas proposes to examine it from *both* normative and empirical perspectives, both as a "system of knowledge" (or set of public norms) and as a "system of action" (or set of institutions) embedded in a societal context. He thus devotes chapters 3 through 6 to the normative self-understanding of constitutional democracies, whereas chapters 7 and 8 take up issues connected with empirical sociology: how the normative model relates to empirical investigations of democracy and how it must be situated in regard to social-power processes. Chapter 9 then caps off the investigation by proposing a new paradigm for approaching the rule of law and democracy.

2

Having set forth the basic parameters of modern law in chapter 1 and charted various theoretical pitfalls in chapter 2, Habermas is ready to reconstruct the normative understanding of the modern rule of law—how legitimate law is possible—in chapters 3 and 4. In analyzing modern law as a system of rights, chapter 3 supplies the basis for the central thesis of the book: the rule of law, or constitutional state, is internally related to deliberative democracy.[25] Because some of the most important debates in political and legal theory arise between these two conceptual poles, showing how they are internally linked together promises to represent a considerable theoretical advance. To see what Habermas is up to, it helps to position his thesis between two opposed views, which are admittedly somewhat stylized for purposes of presentation.

On the one side are classical "liberal" views. Stemming from such thinkers as John Locke, this approach emphasizes the impersonal rule of law and the protection of individual freedom; democratic process is constrained by, and in the service of, personal rights that guarantee individuals the freedom to pursue their own goals and happiness.[26] On the other side, one finds traditions of "civic republicanism" stemming from Plato and Aristotle and later reshaped by, among others, Jean-Jacques Rousseau. This approach gives pride of place to the democratic process as a collective deliberation that, at least ideally, leads citizens to reach agreement on the common good. On this view, human freedom has its summit not in the pursuit of private preferences but in self-governance through political participation.[27] Consequently, republican views tend to ground the legitimacy of laws and policies in notions of "popular sovereignty," whereas liberal views tend to define legitimate government in relation to the protection of individual liberty, often specified in terms of human rights.

This split is not entirely surprising if one recalls the features of modern law noted in section 1 above. Modern legal norms require only outward compliance regardless of individual motivation, but they should, at the same time, have a rational basis that also makes it possible for persons to accept them as legitimate and thus deserving of obedience. The need for legitimation is acute, because such norms must be positively enacted without appeal to a higher source of justification, such as a shared religious worldview. In view of this duality, one can see that coercible law can be accepted as legitimate insofar as it guarantees two things at once. On the one hand, as demarcating areas in which private individuals can exercise their free choice as they desire, law must guarantee the *private autonomy* of individuals pursuing their personal success and happiness. On the other hand, because its enactment must be such that reasonable individuals could always assent to its constraints rationally, legitimate law must also secure the *public autonomy* of those subject to it, so that the legal order can be seen as issuing from the citizens' rational self-legislation, as it were. The two broadly construed approaches, liberal and republican, tend to stress either one side of autonomy or the other as the basis of legitimacy.

In arguing for an "internal relation" between private and public autonomy, Habermas wants to do justice to both sides, that is, provide an account of legitimate law in which both human rights and popular sovereignty play distinct, irreducible roles. Before giving this account, it helps to note the twin pitfalls Habermas wants to avoid: one must be careful to locate the legitimacy of law at the proper level, neither subordinating law to morality nor conflating it with a community's assertion of shared values and traditions of the good life. This is not to deny that both moral considerations and "ethical" reflection on substantive values are pertinent to law: laws regulate interpersonal relations in a manner similar to moral norms, but they do so only within a concrete community having a particular history and, pluralization notwithstanding, probably at least some shared understanding of the common good. Moreover, both issues of justice and the determination of policies and collective goals form important parts of law and politics. It is not surprising, then, that attempts to explain legitimacy often turn to one type of discourse or the other, depending on whether private or public autonomy receives greater emphasis.

Habermas sees a general tendency in modern natural-law theory, Kant's included, to understand basic liberties in overly moralistic terms, merely as the legal expression of the mutual respect that persons ought to show one another as morally autonomous agents. By contrast, Rousseauian civic republican accounts, by emphasizing the importance of shared traditions, civic virtue, and agreement on the common good, run the risk of reducing deliberative democracy to the ethical discourse in which a concrete community reflects on its substantive values and traditions in order to determine what course of action is good for it in a given social situation. Neither moral respect nor ethical reflection, however, can by itself account for the legitimacy of law in complex pluralistic societies.

To deal with these problems, Habermas centers his account of legitimacy on a discourse principle (D) that lies at a different level than the distinction between moral and ethical discourse. As a principle for the impartial justification of norms in general, (D) also underlies both morality and law: "Only those norms are valid to which all affected persons could agree as participants in rational discourses."[28] By anchoring the legitimacy of law in a discourse principle that is conceptually prior to the distinction between law and morality, Habermas hopes to avoid a moralistic interpretation of law and consequent favoring of private autonomy in the form of human rights. At the same time, the discourse principle points to a model of legitimation that undercuts the liberal-republican split. Legitimate law must pass a discursive test that potentially engages the entire range of different types of discourse. These include not only moral and ethical discourses but also "pragmatic" discourses in which alternative strategies for achieving a given aim are assessed; in addition, insofar as an issue involves conflicting particular interests and values that do not permit consensus, a legitimate legal regulation of the issue must involve fair compromise.

With this framework in place, Habermas can argue that the internal relation between private and public autonomy requires a set of abstract rights that citizens must recognize if they want to regulate their life together by means of legitimate positive law. This "system of rights," which each concrete democratic regime must appropriately elaborate and specify, delineates the general necessary conditions for institutionalizing democratic processes of discourse in law and politics. To summarize, these rights fall into five broad categories. The first three are the basic negative liberties, membership rights, and due-process rights that together guarantee individual freedom of choice, and thus private autonomy. The fourth, rights of political participation, guarantees public autonomy. Habermas argues that each side is indispensable and cannot simply be reduced to the other: without the first three sets of rights, there is no private autonomy (and thus no free and equal subjects of law), but without the fourth set the laws and rights guaranteeing private autonomy are merely paternalistic impositions rather than expressions of self-governance. Rights of political participation, that is, enable citizens themselves to shape and further define the rights they enjoy as "privately autonomous" and thus to become "the authors of the laws to which they are subject as addressees." Finally, a fifth category of social-welfare rights becomes necessary insofar as the effective exercise of civil and political rights depends on certain social and material conditions, for example, that citizens can meet their basic material needs.

As conceived so far, the system of rights regulates only the interactions among equal citizens; it is only in chapter 4 that Habermas introduces the role of state authority, whose police power is necessary to enforce and thus stabilize the system of rights. This introduces a further step in the institutionalization of discourse and, with it, a further dimension of the tension between facticity and validity that is internal to the rule of law, namely, the tension between state power and legitimate law. To capture this tension, one must keep two things in view at once. On the one side, law and political power fulfill certain systemic functions for each other: the law authorizes some exercises of power and disallows others and, in addition, provides the procedures and forms that define various governmental powers and competences to begin with; government power, meanwhile, provides a threat of sanctions that makes law socially effective. On the other side, the law employed by the state in its various offices and activities must itself be legitimated through a broader discourse of citizens and their representatives. Hence, pace Luhmann, a functionalist analysis of bureaucratic power and legal procedures cannot stand on its own but must be tied to an account of public reason. For Habermas, this latter account must ultimately refer to democratic processes of "opinion- and will-formation" in the public sphere. As a formation of opinion *and* will, public discourse is not merely a cognitive exercise but mobilizes reasons and arguments that draw on citizens' interests, values, and identities. Political discourse thus brings in the citizens' actual sources of motivation and volition. It thereby generates a "communicative power" that has a real impact on the formal decision making and action that represent the final institutional expression of political "will."

In this further step in his analysis of law, then, Habermas is concerned to link the informal discursive sources of democracy with the formal decision-making institutions that are required for an effective rule of law in complex societies. The constitutional state represents the crucial set of legal institutions and mechanisms that govern the conversion of the citizenry's communicative power into efficacious and legitimate administrative activity: law "represents . . . the medium for transforming communicative power into administrative power."[29] It is from this perspective that one must account for the various principles, tasks, and institutions of the constitutional state, such as the separation of powers, majority rule, statutory controls on administration, and so forth.

Having sketched a philosophy of law in chapters 3 and 4, Habermas turns in chapters 5 and 6 to jurisprudence proper, or legal theory. Hence these chapters should be of special interest to jurisprudential and constitutional scholars. There Habermas tests the philosophical analysis of the previous two chapters against specific legal theories that are (or have been) influential in two particular legal systems, those of the United States and Germany. The argument thus represents a further step toward actual legal practice, for now the self-understandings of two existing legal orders are at issue. Once again, further dimensions of the internal tension between facticity and validity organize the presentation, which is now focused primarily on judicial decision making and the role of the Supreme Court (in Germany, the Federal Constitutional Court). In chapter 5, the major concern is the jurisprudential tension between, on the one hand, the need for judicial decisions to conform to existing statutes and precedents and, on the other, the demand that decisions be right or just in light of moral standards, social welfare, and so forth. This tension has long been felt in American jurisprudence, as shown by the early critique of "mechanical jurisprudence" by such theorists as Roscoe Pound, and it defined the context for Hart's influential *Concept of Law*.[30] In developing his own position on this issue, Habermas not only surveys legal realism, legal hermeneutics, and positivism but also devotes considerable attention to Ronald Dworkin's theory of judicial decision making.

Chapter 6 takes up issues involved in the separation of powers and the role of constitutional courts. Specifically, Habermas examines the apparent competition between legislature and judiciary in the welfare state; the "value jurisprudence" of the German high court (which tends to dissolve the difference between collective goods and constitutional rights); and American debates over the nature of constitutional review. In the course of this last-mentioned discussion, he takes up John Hart Ely's proceduralism, Frank Michelman's and Cass Sunstein's civic-republican proposals, and Bruce Ackerman's distinction between "normal politics" and "higher" constitutional lawmaking.[31] In his treatment of these issues in chapters 5 and 6, various features of a new kind of proceduralist understanding of law and democracy begin to emerge. These features are, inter alia, the intersubjective, dialogical aspect of judicial legal argumentation; the deontological character of basic rights in contrast to other values; and a nonpaternalistic understanding of the role of the Supreme Court in safeguarding the discursive quality of legislative decision making. The result is a proceduralist conception that incorporates the insights of the aforementioned theorists but also criticizes and attempts to go beyond them.

Before elaborating this proceduralist understanding of law more completely, Habermas shifts his perspective in the next two chapters. The account of democracy and law thus far has been normative in character. It will be empirically plausible, however, only if it confronts the challenges posed by social power and societal complexity. Thus, having dealt in chapters 3 through 6 with tensions between validity and facticity that are internal to constitutional democracy, in chapters 7 and 8 Habermas takes up issues bearing on the external tension between social facts and law. The central question is whether one can still meaningfully speak of constitutional democracies in light of rather disheartening empirical studies of power and complexity. Sociological theories of law and politics draw attention to the multifarious ways in which various social interests and powerful organizations attempt to instrumentalize the political process for strategic purposes; or else they point out how the functional complexity of contemporary societies no longer permits direct democratic control but rather requires indirect administrative measures guided by expert knowledge. In either case, the normative ideal of a self-organizing society, with law and politics as the site of an encompassing social integration, can appear hopelessly out of touch.

As one might anticipate from chapter 2, Habermas's response employs a dual theoretical perspective. Specifically, his new "proceduralist concept of democracy" acknowledges how the constitutional state is subject to social forces and functional demands most evident to the sociological observer. At the same time, it insists on the empirical relevance of deliberative democratic ideals accepted by the citizens themselves as engaged participants. This dual perspective thus enables one to spot the deficiencies in one-sidedly empiricist conceptions. In addition, it provides a standpoint from which to criticize overly narrow interpretations of democratic participation (as found, for example, in rational choice theory).

Habermas's proceduralist view is also predicated on the rejection of two opposed conceptions that can be stylized, once again, as "liberal" and "civic republican." In this context, the important question is how one should understand the roles of state and society in political action. On the one hand, politics must involve more than the minimal government of liberalism, a government restricted to preserving an unencumbered market economy under the rule of law. On the other hand, it must be less than the collective action of a homogeneous political society—the community envisioned by classical republicanism. Whereas the liberal view overlooks the public, deliberative side of democratic institutions, the republican view suggests an overly unitary "popular will" inhering in the citizenry as a subject writ large. On a proceduralist view, only the state, as a political system invested with decision-making powers, can "act." But its action is legitimate only if the formal decision-making procedures within the constitutional state have a discursive character that preserves, under conditions of complexity, the democratic sources of legitimacy in the public at large.

In chapter 7 Habermas both draws on and criticizes different sociological theories of democracy in order to outline, in broad terms, a proceduralist approach that can handle societal complexity. In chapter 8 he then goes on to examine the central challenges of social power and systemic complexity. The unsuccessful attempts to account for democratic politics solely in terms of either rational self-interest or functional systems show that an empirically viable theory of democracy cannot dispense with the communicative sources of legitimacy. Thus Habermas's proceduralist account must show how the political system, though one functional subsystem among many, can nonetheless be tied to broader societywide communicative processes that have a democratic, legitimating quality.

More specifically, in this "two-track" view of democratic lawmaking, formally institutionalized deliberation and decision must be open to input from informal public spheres. This means that the political system (and the administration in particular) must not become an *independent* system, operating solely according to its own criteria of efficiency and unresponsive to citizens' concerns; nor must it become too subservient to particular interests that have access to administrative power through unofficial paths of influence that bypass the democratic process. Conversely, the public sphere must not itself be "subverted by power," whether that of large organizations or of the mass media. Habermas's model places considerable normative responsibility for the democratic process on those public forums, informal associations, and social movements in which citizens can effectively voice their concerns. Chapter 8 closes with an analysis of the various conditions under which the public sphere can fulfill its democratic function. These conditions include channels of communication that link the public sphere to a robust civil society in which citizens first perceive and identify social issues; a broad range of informal associations; responsible mass media; and agenda-setting avenues that allow broader social concerns to receive formal consideration within the political system.

In the final chapter, Habermas undergirds his investigation with a fuller account of the paradigmatic dimensions of the proceduralist approach. His argument thus moves to a deeper level, that of competing "paradigms of law and democracy." Here "paradigm" refers to the basic assumptions about society that inform efforts to realize constitutional-democratic ideals. Precisely because such efforts must come to grips with real social contexts, they presuppose some idea, even if a tacit one, of a historically specific social facticity. Not only judges, lawyers, and legislators, but citizens in general tend to share broad background assumptions about their society, its challenges and possibilities, and how the law should respond to these. Such assumptions can be loosely organized around different legal paradigms. In chapter 9, then, Habermas argues for the superiority of the "proceduralist paradigm" over two inherited paradigms whose opposition has stalemated a number of current discussions. The liberal paradigm of "bourgeois formal law," which dominated the nineteenth century, privileges individual freedom under the banner of minimal government, formal equality before the law, and legal certainty. Meanwhile, however, social inequalities and other problems related to complexity and unrestrained capitalism have, especially in the twentieth century, motivated attempts to instrumentalize law for substantive purposes of social utility. Behind such attempts one can discern a social-welfare paradigm of "materialized" law, so called because of its emphasis on the realization of substantive social goals and values (such as welfare provisions, social security, and regulation of commerce). The problems arising from this paradigm, such as unchecked administrative discretion and intrusive welfare bureaucracies, are also quite familiar by now.[32]

The women's struggle for equality illustrates these paradigmatic issues quite well. The call for equal voting rights, demands for equal access to education, and so on, rest on notions of formal equality emphasized by the liberal paradigm. By contrast, efforts to accord specific benefits to women, such as provisions for maternity leave, special aid to women with children, child-care services, and the like, embody the social-welfare paradigm. As feminist critics have noted, a concern simply with formal legal equality ignores the real inequalities that can arise from contingent social conditions and gender differences, whereas government aid programs often define such differences inappropriately, besides fostering welfare dependency and overintrusive bureaucracies. On a proceduralist approach, the legitimate regulation of such issues requires that women themselves take part in public discussions that determine which gender differences are relevant to definitions of equality. The proceduralist paradigm thereby imparts a dynamic quality to the idea of equal rights.

Habermas's proceduralist approach demonstrates its usefulness for other issues as well, such as regulating the workplace and labor politics. The general lesson, however, is this: the proceduralist paradigm allows one to see further implications of the internal relation between private and public autonomy—thus between equal individual liberties and political self-determination—that was first proposed in chapter 3. One thereby gains a better handle on the difficult notion of equal treatment. In addition, one sees how administrations can meet the demands of complexity and social welfare without undermining constitutional democracy. Here Habermas, going beyond his earlier critique of the welfare state, suggests that a proceduralist approach demands a new way of thinking about the separation of powers; it requires, for example, a more democratic, participatory form of administration.[33]

The argument of *Between Facts and Norms* is both lengthy and complex. It is also pitched at a very abstract level. Readers should, however, find some additional help from the postscript and two appendices. The appendices provide more succinct statements of the key conceptual developments that preceded the book; in the postscript one finds a summary, written with the advantage of hindsight and critics' reactions, of the central conceptual arguments.[34] In any case, it is this very complexity and abstractness that promise to make this book a rich and suggestive source of insight for reflection on the problems facing contemporary constitutional democracies.

3

In closing, some brief remarks on the translation itself are in order. Besides the usual difficulties of translation, there are challenges stemming from the fact that *Between Facts and Norms* deals with two different legal orders. In the American legal system, influenced as it is by the English common-law tradition, case law has always occupied a central position. As a result, the law tends to be perceived as a dense and complicated thicket—or, to borrow Karl Llewellyn's term, a "bramble bush"—that grows precedent by precedent, often in a less than orderly fashion. By contrast, German legal thought has been heavily influenced by Roman civil law, with its emphasis on systematic codification. Moreover, the current German private law came into being by a single act of legislation, when the Reichstag formally adopted the Civil Code—the *Bürgerliches Gesetzbuch* or BGB—that had been drafted by experts at the end of the nineteenth century. This focus on unity and coherence goes hand in hand with the dignity that civil-law traditions reserve for scholarly commentary and analysis—*Rechtsdogmatik* or "legal doctrine"—as opposed to judicial opinion and precedent.[35] However, one should not overemphasize such differences. Since the adoption of the German Civil Code, judicial interpretation and adaptation have become an important part of the code itself, so that differences between the German and American systems have lessened. Nonetheless, the differences that do remain, even if only in the background, sometimes pose translation problems. Most of these problems lie at the level of specialized terms and technicalities that are best dealt with in translator's notes or simply by bracketing the German. But one occasionally notices the broader difference in spirit. The central term *Rechtsstaat* is itself an example of this. When contrasted with the English equivalent, "rule of law," *Rechtsstaat*—which literally means "law-state"—reveals the greater emphasis that the German legal tradition places on the state. Depending on the context, I translate *Rechtsstaat* either as "rule of law" or "constitutional state." I also use "government by law," as a way to split the difference.

The translation of the various types of rights can also pose occasional difficulties stemming from differences between the German and American legal orders. To begin with, German legal theory draws a strong distinction between the "subjective rights" due the individual and "objective" law, whereas Anglo-American usage speaks simply of "rights" and "law."[36] I normally follow the latter usage, unless the context calls for an emphasis on the subjective-objective distinction. As far as particular types of rights go, I have generally taken a fairly literal approach for the sake of precision. *Privatrechte*, for example, I translate as "private rights," whereas *Freiheitsrechte* is "rights of liberty" or "liberty rights," or even simply "liberties." *Abwehrrechte* I translate as "rights against the state," or with similar circumlocutions, though "negative rights" is sometimes appropriate as a shorter form. *Grundrechte* include the "basic" or "fundamental rights" protected by the Constitution, and so may also be translated as "constitutional rights."

The term "civil rights" poses more of a problem. In a few places, Habermas uses "civil rights" (in English) in the narrow sense of T. H. Marshall, as referring to those "rights necessary for individual freedom—liberty of the person, freedom of speech, thought and faith, the right to own property and conclude valid contracts, and the right to justice."[37] In this sense, civil rights are distinct from rights of political participation and welfare rights. In the few places where "civil rights" has this narrower meaning, the context should make it quite clear that Marshall's sense is intended. Otherwise "civil rights" renders terms such as *Staatsbürgerrechte, staatsbürgerliche Rechte*, and *Bürgerrechte*, which include the full range of citizenship rights.

For many other terms, fidelity to Habermas's own style requires a greater flexibility. Terms that mark an important distinction in certain contexts—such as the difference between *Geltung* (factual acceptance) and *Gültigkeit* (ideal validity)—may be used more or less interchangeably elsewhere, so that the same English word suffices for both. In other cases, the German is both rich and fluid enough to make a rigid adherence to one-to-one correlations neither possible nor desirable. This is the case, for example, for the broad range of German words having to do with power and authority. In such cases, the demands of context and readability are decisive. Where a particular distinction is important for Habermas's argument, I rely on the context itself and choice of English terms to make this clear; if necessary, the different German terms are parenthetically noted. But where an exact distinction is less important, broad associations can suffice.

Finally, for the sake of a more American idiom I use both " state" and "government" to translate *Staat. Regierung*, by contrast, tends to have a narrower meaning, referring to the leadership or party in office (in Germany, *Bundesregierung* refers to the Chancellor and Cabinet; in the United States, one typically refers to "the Administration," for example, the Roosevelt Administration). However, I use "administration" to translate *Verwaltung*, which denotes the functional aspect or branch of the state as a bureaucratically organized implementing power. Thus, to keep *Regierung* distinct from these other terms, I translate it with capitalized circumlocutions, such as "incumbent Administration," "Government leaders," and "Government in office."

The reader should be aware that Habermas himself has had a considerable hand in the translation, in some cases adapting and rewriting the text for the Anglo-American audience. As a result, the English occasionally departs from the German original, for example by adding clarifying phrases, dropping cumbersome and unnecessary insertions, or simply by finding another way of wording things.

In order to avoid sexist language, I have (with Habermas's assent) alternated the use of feminine and masculine pronouns from chapter to chapter.

This translation would not have been possible without the help of a number of people. Of these, some contributed considerable time and effort. I want especially to thank Thomas McCarthy and James Bohman for reading and commenting on multiple drafts; Jürgen Habermas for his extensive, and very helpful, suggestions on the penultimate draft; and Larry May and David Ingram for their careful reading of an early version of the translation. Thanks also go to Günter Frankenberg, Klaus Günther, Jed Donelan, Vic Peterson, Paul Shupack, Joseph Heath, R. Randall Rainey, Richard Dees, G. O. Mazur, Joel Anderson, Robert Stalder, Steve Snyder, Matthew Carr, David Fleming, Thomas Schwarz, and Ian Boyd. I am grateful to Thomas McCarthy, James Bohman, Jürgen Habermas, Larry May, Michel Rosenfeld, R. Randall Rainey, John Griesbach, Pauline Kleingeld, William O'Neill, Mark Burke, and Timothy Clancy for providing feedback on my introduction. Finally, I thank the employees of University Copiers, Etc., for their consistently friendly, high-quality photocopying services.

Preface

In Germany the philosophy of law has long ceased to be a matter just for philosophers. If I scarcely mention the name of Hegel and rely more on the Kantian theory of law, this also expresses my desire to avoid a model that set unattainable standards for us. Indeed, it is no accident that legal philosophy, in search of contact with social reality, has migrated into the law schools.[1] However, I also want to avoid the technical jurisprudence focused on the foundations of criminal law.[2] What could once be coherently embraced in the concepts of Hegelian philosophy now demands a pluralistic approach that combines the perspectives of moral theory, social theory, legal theory, and the sociology and history of law.

I welcome this as an occasion to display the often unrecognized pluralistic approach of the theory of communicative action. Philosophical concepts no longer constitute an independent language, or at any rate not an encompassing system that assimilates everything into itself. Rather, they provide a means for the reconstructive appropriation of scientific knowledge. Thanks to its multilingual character, if philosophy simply keeps the basic concepts clear it can uncover a surprising degree of coherence at a metalevel. Hence, the basic assumptions of the theory of communicative action also branch out into various universes of discourse, where they must prove their mettle in the contexts of debate they happen to encounter.

The first chapter treats in rather cursory fashion a few aspects of the relation between facticity and validity that touch on the basic assumptions of the theory of communicative action. Naturally, this problem that arises "between facts and norms" (as the title puts it) requires a more extensive philosophical clarification than I can accomplish here. The second chapter sketches an approach that spans the gap between sociological theories of law and philosophical theories of justice. The two following chapters then reconstruct parts of the modern contractarian approaches to natural law within the framework of a discourse theory of law. Here I draw on a discourse ethics that I have developed elsewhere.[3] However, I now characterize the complementary relation between morality and law differently than I once did, even as recently as the Tanner Lectures.[4] In the fifth and sixth chapters, I test out the discourse-theoretic approach on central issues of legal theory. Specifically, I refer to current discussions in the Federal Republic and the United States, the two countries whose legal traditions are familiar to me. In the seventh and eighth chapters, I clarify the normative concept of deliberative politics and examine, from a sociological perspective, the conditions for constitutionally domesticating the circulation of power in complex societies. Here I treat democratic theory mainly under the aspects of legitimation. The last chapter brings legal theory and social theory together in the concept of the proceduralist paradigm of law.

I also hope that the argument outlined above will performatively refute the objection that the theory of communicative action is blind to institutional reality—or that it could even have anarchist consequences.[5] Of course, the potential of unleashed *communicative* freedoms does contain an anarchistic core. The institutions of any democratic government must live off this core if they are to be effective in guaranteeing equal liberties for all.

I had to get more involved in technical legal discussions than I wanted to as a layman. In the process, my respect for the impressive constructive accomplishments of this discipline has grown even more. My proposals for clarifying the paradigmatic background understanding of the law and the constitution are intended as a contribution to an ongoing discussion. Specifically, this contribution is directed against the growing skepticism among legal scholars, above all against what I consider a false realism that underestimates the empirical impact of the normative presuppositions of existing legal practices. Moreover, a moral-practical self-understanding of modernity as a whole is articulated in the controversies we have carried on since the seventeenth century about the best constitution of the political community. This self-understanding is attested to both by a universalistic moral consciousness and by the liberal design of the constitutional state. Discourse theory attempts to reconstruct this normative self-understanding in a way that resists both scientistic reductions and aesthetic assimilations.[6] The three dimensions of cognitive, evaluative, and normative validity that have been differentiated within the self-understanding of modernity must not be collapsed. After a century that, more than any other, has taught us the horror of existing unreason, the last remains of an essentialist trust in reason have been destroyed. Yet modernity, now aware of its contingencies, depends all the more on a procedural reason, that is, on a reason that puts itself on trial. The critique of reason is its own work: this double meaning, first displayed by Immanuel Kant, is due to the radically anti-Platonic insight that there is neither a higher nor a deeper reality to which we could appeal—we who find ourselves already situated in our linguistically structured forms of life.

Three decades ago I criticized Marx's attempt to transpose the Hegelian philosophy of right into a materialist philosophy of history:

With his critique of ideology applied to the bourgeois constitutional state and with his sociological dissolution of the theoretical basis for natural rights, Marx so enduringly discredited... both the idea of legality and the intention of natural law, that the link between natural law and revolution has been broken ever since. The parties of an internationalized civil war have divided this heritage between themselves with fateful clarity: the one side has taken up the heritage of revolution, the other the ideology of natural law.[7]

After the collapse of state socialism and the end of the "global civil war," the theoretical error of the defeated party is there for all to see: it mistook the socialist project for the design—and violent implementation—of a concrete form of life. If, however, one conceives "socialism" as the set of necessary conditions for emancipated forms of life about which the participants *themselves* must first reach an understanding, then one will recognize that the democratic self-organization of a legal community constitutes the normative core of this project as well. On the other hand, the party that now considers itself victorious does not rejoice at its triumph. Just when it could emerge as the *sole* heir of the moral-practical self-understanding of modernity, it lacks the energy to drive ahead with the task of imposing social and ecological restraints on capitalism at the breathtaking level of global society. It zealously respects the systemic logic of an economy steered through markets; and it is at least on guard against overloading the power medium of state bureaucracies. Nevertheless, we do not even begin to display a similar sensibility for the resource that is *actually* endangered—a social solidarity preserved in legal structures and in need of continual regeneration.

In contemporary Western societies governed by the rule of law, politics has lost its orientation and self-confidence before a terrifying background: before the conspicuous challenges posed by ecological limits on economic growth and by increasing disparities in the living conditions in the Northern and Southern Hemispheres; before the historically unique task of converting state socialism over to the mechanisms of a differentiated economic system; under the pressure of immigration from impoverished southern regions—and now eastern regions as well; in the face of the risks of renewed ethnic, national, and religious wars, nuclear blackmail, and international conflicts over the distribution of global resources. Behind the hackneyed rhetoric, timidity reigns. Even in established democracies, the existing institutions of freedom are no longer above challenge, although here the populations seem to press for more democracy rather than less. I suspect, however, that the unrest has a still deeper source, namely, the sense that in the age of a completely secularized politics, the rule of law cannot be had or maintained without radical democracy. The present investigation aims to work this hunch into an insight. In the final analysis, private legal subjects cannot come to enjoy equal individual liberties if they do not *themselves*, in the common exercise of their political autonomy, achieve clarity about justified interests and standards. They themselves must agree on the relevant aspects under which equals should be treated equally and unequals unequally.

I have no illusions about the problems that our situation poses and the moods it evokes. But moods—and philosophies in a melancholic "mood"—do not justify the defeatist surrender of the radical content of democratic ideals. I will propose a new reading of this content, one appropriate to the circumstances of a complex society. If defeatism were justified, I would have had to choose a different literary genre, for example, the diary of a Hellenistic writer who merely documents, for subsequent generations, the unfulfilled promises of his waning culture.

I have appended two works already published in German. One of these places the procedural concept of democracy in a larger historical context; the other explains the continually misunderstood concept of constitutional patriotism under three different aspects.

In the 1985–86 academic year, the Leibniz Program of the *Deutschen Forschungsgemeinschaft* (German National Science Foundation) gave me, rather unexpectedly, the opportunity to start a five-year research project of my own choosing. This fortuitous constellation provided the occasion for starting a research group on legal theory. This group formed the unusually stimulating and instructive context in which I could tease out the several threads I had taken up at the same time in my lectures at the University of Frankfurt. This cooperative endeavor fared especially well, producing not only a series of monographs but many other publications besides.[8] Without the productive support afforded by competent coworkers, I would have lacked the courage to tackle the project of a legal philosophy; I also would have been unable to appropriate the jurisprudential arguments and knowledge necessary to carry out such a project. In addition, I am grateful to the permanent members of the group—Ingeborg Maus, Rainer Forst, Günter Frankenberg, Klaus Günther, Bernhard Peters, and Lutz Wingert—for their helpful comments on earlier versions of my manuscript. I would also like to thank Thomas McCarthy for his suggestions. I am indebted to Klaus Günther's legal expertise for so much instruction that I almost hesitate to relieve him of responsibility for my mistakes, but relieve him I do, just as I relieve the others of such responsibility. Finally, I thank Mrs. Heide Natkin for her help in the process of repeatedly correcting the manuscript.

J. H.
Frankfurt, July 1992

1

Law as a Category of Social Mediation between Facts and Norms

The concept of practical reason as a subjective capacity is of modern vintage. Converting the Aristotelian conceptual framework over to premises of the philosophy of the subject had the disadvantage of detaching practical reason from its anchors in cultural forms of life and sociopolitical orders. It had the advantage, though, of relating practical reason to the "private" happiness and "moral" autonomy of the individual. That is, practical reason was thenceforth related to the freedom of the human being as a private subject who could also assume the roles of member of civil society and citizen, both national and global. In the role of world citizen, the individual fuses with the human being in general, is an "I" both unique and universal. To this eighteenth-century conceptual repertoire the nineteenth century added the dimension of history. The individual subject is involved in its life history in a manner similar to the way that states, as subjects of international law, are caught up in the history of nations. G. W. F. Hegel expressed this point in his concept of objective spirit. Naturally, Hegel remained convinced, just like Aristotle, that society finds its unity in the political life and organization of the state. The practical philosophy of modernity continued to assume that individuals belong to a society like members to a collectivity or parts to a whole—even if the whole is only supposed to constitute itself through the connection of its parts.

However, modern societies have since become so complex that these two conceptual motifs—that of a society concentrated in the state and that of a society made up of individuals—can no longer be applied unproblematically. This circumstance led Marxist social theory to forego a normative theory of the state. To be sure, traces of practical reason could still be discerned, as a philosophy of history, in the Marxist concept of a democratically self-governing society in which both the bureaucratic state and the capitalist economy were supposed to disappear. Systems theory erased even these last traces, renouncing any connection with the normative contents of practical reason. The state forms just one subsystem alongside other functionally specified social subsystems; these stand in system-environment relations with one another, similar to the relation between persons and their society. Starting from Thomas Hobbes's naturalistic conception of the struggle for self-assertion among individuals, the rigorous elimination of practical reason has taken a path that leads to Niklas Luhmann's autopoietic conception of self-referential systems. Neither attenuated empiricist approaches nor efforts at rehabilitation appear capable of restoring the explanatory power practical reason once possessed in the contexts of ethics and politics, modern natural law and moral theory, philosophy of history and social theory.

The philosophy of history can only glean from historical processes the reason it has already put into them with the help of teleological concepts. By the same token, norms for a reasonable conduct of life cannot be drawn from the natural constitution of the human species any more than they can from history. No less than philosophy of history, philosophical anthropology à la Max Scheler or Arnold Gehlen succumbs to the critique coming from the very sciences it ineffectually attempts to employ for philosophical ends—the two approaches display analogous weaknesses. Not much more convincing is the contextualist renunciation of all justification. Although this is an understandable response to the failures of the philosophy of history and philosophical anthropology, it never gets beyond the defiant appeal to the normative force of the factual. The development of constitutional democracy along the celebrated "North Atlantic" path has certainly provided us with results worth preserving, but once those who do not have the good fortune to be heirs of the Founding Fathers turn to their own traditions, they cannot find criteria and reasons that would allow them to distinguish what is worth preserving from what should be rejected.

The traces of modern natural-law normativism thus get lost in a trilemma: neither in the teleology of history nor in the constitution of the human species can we find the content of practical reason, once its philosophical foundation in the knowing subject has been shattered, nor can we justify such content simply on the basis of the fortuitous resources of successful histories and traditions. This explains the attractiveness of the only option that seems to remain open: the brash denial of reason altogether, whether in the dramatic form of a post-Nietzschean critique of reason or in the more sober variety of a systems functionalism that neutralizes anything that, from the participant perspective, appears obligatory or at all meaningful. Anyone in the human sciences not absolutely committed to a counterintuitive approach will find this solution rather unattractive as well. For this reason, I have taken a different approach with the theory of communicative action, replacing practical reason with a communicative one. This involves more than a change in terminology.

In the classical modern tradition of thought, the link between practical reason and social practice was too direct. This meant that the sphere of social practice was approached entirely from the angle of normative or—once filtered through a philosophy of history—cryptonormative issues. Just as practical reason was supposed to orient the individual's action, so also natural law up to Hegel wanted to single out normatively the only reasonable social and political order. But a concept of reason transposed into the linguistic medium and unburdened of the exclusive relationship to moral issues plays a different role in theory construction; it can serve the descriptive purposes of a rational reconstruction of competences and structures of consciousness hitherto operative in history. The work of reconstruction can then link up with functional approaches and empirical explanations.[1]

Communicative reason differs from practical reason first and foremost in that it is no longer ascribed to the individual actor or to a macrosubject at the level of the state or the whole of society. Rather, what makes communicative reason possible is the linguistic medium through which interactions are woven together and forms of life are structured. This rationality is inscribed in the linguistic telos of mutual understanding and forms an ensemble of conditions that both enable and limit. Whoever makes use of a natural language in order to come to an understanding with an addressee about something in the world is required to take a performative attitude and commit herself to certain presuppositions. In seeking to reach an understanding, natural-language users must assume, among other things, that the participants pursue their illocutionary goals without reservations, that they tie their agreement to the intersubjective recognition of criticizable validity claims, and that they are ready to take on the obligations resulting from consensus and relevant for further interaction. These aspects of validity that undergird speech are also imparted to the forms of life reproduced through communicative action. Communicative rationality is expressed in a decentered complex of pervasive, transcendentally enabling structural conditions, but it is not a subjective capacity that would tell actors what they *ought* to do.

Unlike the classical form of practical reason, communicative reason is not an immediate source of prescriptions. It has a normative content only insofar as the communicatively acting individuals must commit themselves to pragmatic presuppositions of a counterfactual sort. That is, they must undertake certain idealizations—for example, ascribe identical meanings to expressions, connect utterances with context-transcending validity claims, and assume that addressees are accountable, that is, autonomous and sincere with both themselves and others. Communicatively acting individuals are thus subject to the "must" of a weak transcendental necessity, but this does not mean they already encounter the prescriptive "must" of a rule of action—whether the latter "must" can be traced back deontologically to the normative validity of a moral law, axiologically to a constellation of preferred values, or empirically to the effectiveness of a technical rule. A set of unavoidable idealizations forms the counterfactual basis of an actual practice of reaching understanding, a practice that can critically turn against its own results and thus *transcend* itself. Thus the tension between idea and reality breaks into the very facticity of linguistically structured forms of life. Everyday communicative practice overtaxes itself with its idealizing presuppositions, but only in the light of this innerworldly transcendence can learning processes take place at all.

Communicative reason thus makes an orientation to validity claims possible, but it does not itself supply any substantive orientation for managing practical tasks—it is neither informative nor immediately practical. On the one hand, it stretches across the entire spectrum of validity claims: the claims to propositional truth, personal sincerity, and normative rightness; to this extent it reaches beyond the realm of moral-practical questions. On the other hand, it pertains only to insights—to criticizable utterances that are accessible in principle to argumentative clarification—and thus falls short of a practical reason aimed at motivation, at guiding the will. Normativity in the sense of the obligatory orientation of action does not coincide with communicative rationality. Normativity and communicative rationality *intersect* with one another where the justification of moral insights is concerned. Such insights are reached in a hypothetical attitude and carry only the weak force of rational motivation. In any case, they cannot themselves guarantee that insight will issue in motivated action.[2]

One must keep these differences in view when I continue to use the concept of communicative reason in connection with a reconstructive social theory. In this new context, the received concept of practical reason also acquires a different, more or less heuristic status. It no longer provides a direct blueprint for a normative theory of law and morality. Rather, it offers a guide for reconstructing the network of discourses that, aimed at forming opinions and preparing decisions, provides the matrix from which democratic authority emerges. From this perspective, the forms of communication that confer legitimacy on political will-formation, legislation, and the administration of justice appear as part of a more encompassing process in which the lifeworlds of modern societies are rationalized under the pressure of systemic imperatives. At the same time, such a reconstruction would provide a critical standard, against which actual practices—the opaque and perplexing reality of the constitutional state—could be evaluated.

In spite of the distance from traditional concepts of practical reason, it is by no means trivial that a contemporary theory of law and democracy still seeks to link up with classical concept formations at all. This theory starts with the socially integrating force of rationally motivating, hence noncoercive processes of reaching understanding. These provide a space for distance and recognized differences within a sustained commonality of convictions. Moral philosophers and philosophers of law adopt this perspective in the normative discourses they still carry on, indeed with greater vigor than ever before. Because they specialize in dealing with questions of normative validity in the performative attitude of participants, they usually remain inside the limited horizon of lifeworlds whose spell has been broken by the objectivating observations of social scientists for some time now. Normative theories are open to the suspicion that they take insufficient notice of the hard facts that have long contradicted the contractarian self-understanding of the modern constitutional state. From the objectivating viewpoint of the social sciences, a philosophical approach that still operates with the alternatives of *forcibly* stabilized versus *rationally* legitimated orders belongs to the transitional semantics of early modernity. Such terminology seemingly became obsolete once the transition from stratified to functionally differentiated societies was complete. Even when we adopt a theoretical approach that accords a central role to a communicative concept of "practical reason," we must, so it seems, single out a special and particularly demanding form of communication that covers only a small part of the broad spectrum of observable forms of communication: "using such narrow channels one can hardly succeed, in the new paradigm of reaching understanding, in once again filling out a sufficiently complex theory of society."[3]

Tossed to and fro between facticity and validity, political theory and legal theory today are disintegrating into camps that hardly have anything more to say to one another. The tension between normative approaches, which are constantly in danger of losing contact with social reality, and objectivistic approaches, which screen out all normative aspects, can be taken as a caveat against fixating on one disciplinary point of view. Rather, one must remain open to different methodological standpoints (participant vs. observer), different theoretical objectives (interpretive explication and conceptual analysis vs. description and empirical explanation), the perspectives of different roles (judge, politician, legislator, client, and citizen), and different pragmatic attitudes of research (hermeneutical, critical, analytical, etc.).[4] The following investigations stretch over this wide field.

Discourse theory was hitherto tailored to individual will-formation and has proven itself in the areas of moral theory (in the narrow Kantian sense) and ethics (in the broader Aristotelian sense). However, from a functional point of view it can be shown why the posttraditional form of a principled morality depends on positive law as its complement.[5] From the very start, then, questions of legal theory explode the framework of a purely normative way of looking at things. The discourse theory of law and democracy must break away from the conventional paths of legal and political philosophy, even as it takes up their issues. In chapters 1 and 2, I pursue the dual goal of explaining how the theory of communicative action accords central importance to the category of law and why this theory in turn constitutes a suitable context for a discourse theory of law. Here my concern is to work out a reconstructive approach that encompasses two perspectives: the sociology of law and the philosophy of justice. In chapters 3 and 4, I reconstruct the normative content of the system of rights and of the idea of the rule of law from the perspective of discourse theory. In connection with questions raised by modern natural law, I attempt to show how the old promise of a self-organizing community of free and equal citizens can be reconceived under the conditions of complex societies. I shall then test and elaborate the discourse concept of law and democracy in the context of contemporary discussions. Chapter 5 treats in general fashion the problem of the rationality of adjudication, and chapter 6 deals with the problem of the legitimacy of the Supreme Court. Chapter 7 develops the model of deliberative politics by challenging theories of democracy that rely on an empiricist concept of power. In chapter 8, I investigate how the constitutional channeling of social and political power functions in complex societies. Finally, in connection with these insights gained from social theory, the discourse theory of law serves to introduce a proceduralist paradigm of law. As I show in the concluding chapter 9, this model can take us beyond the opposition between the social models that underlie the formalist and the welfarist concepts of law.

***

In legal theory, sociologists, lawyers, and philosophers disagree over the appropriate characterization of the relation between facticity and validity. Depending on the position one takes on this problematic relation, one accepts different premises and arrives at different theoretical strategies. For this reason, I want to begin by explaining the issue in social theory that grounds my interest in legal theory. The theory of communicative action already absorbs the tension between facticity and validity into its fundamental concepts. With this risky decision it preserves the link with the classical conception of an internal connection, however mediated, between society and reason, and hence between the constraints and necessities under which the reproduction of social life is carried out, on the one hand, and the idea of a conscious conduct of life, on the other.[6] Admittedly, with this comes the problem of having to explain how the reproduction of society can possibly proceed on such fragile ground as that of context-transcending validity claims. The medium of law, particularly in the modern form of positive (or enacted) law, offers itself as a candidate for such an explanation. Legal norms of this type make possible highly artificial communities, associations of free and equal legal persons whose integration is based simultaneously on the threat of external sanctions and the supposition of a rationally motivated agreement.

With the concept of communicative action, the important function of social integration devolves on the illocutionary binding energies of a use of language oriented to reaching understanding. I thus begin by recalling how the classical view of the relation between facticity and validity, first developed in the Platonist tradition, changes with the linguistic turn, when language is conceived as a universal medium for embodying reason (section 1.1). The tension between facticity and validity, which then enters into the mode of action coordination itself, sets high demands on the maintenance of social orders. The lifeworld, naturally emergent institutions, and law must offset the instabilities of a mode of sociation that is effected through taking yes/no positions on criticizable validity claims (section 1.2). In modern economic societies, this general problem becomes especially acute where the strategic interactions cut loose from the bonds of traditional ethical life (*Sittlichkeit*) have to be normatively constrained. This explains, on the one hand, the structure and meaning of individual rights and, on the other hand, the idealist connotations of a legal community—as an association of free and equal citizens, this community determines for itself what rules should govern social interactions (section 1.3).

1.1 Meaning and Truth: On the Immanent Tension between Facticity and Validity

Recasting the basic concepts of "practical reason" in terms of a "communicative rationality" has the advantage of not cutting social theory off from the issues and answers developed in practical philosophy from Aristotle to Hegel. In fact, it is far from clear that the price we have to pay for the premises of postmetaphysical thinking must be an indifference to such questions, which in any case continue to be felt within the lifeworld. As long as theory does not itself block its access to the fund of everyday intuitions available to laypersons, methodological grounds are enough to prohibit it from ignoring the problems that objectively impose themselves on participants. To be sure, practical philosophy has taken its basic questions ("What ought I do?" or "What is good for us in the long run and on the whole?") from everyday life in an unmediated way, treating these questions without the objectivating filter of social science. The renunciation of the basic concept of practical reason signals a break with this naive normativism. But even the successor concept, that of communicative reason, still retains portions of the idealist heritage. In the context of an explanatory theory, these idealist elements are by no means an unmixed blessing.

However far removed today's concept of reason is from its Platonic origins, and however much it may have been changed by paradigm shifts, it is still constituted by a reference, if not to ideal contents (let alone to Ideas), then to idealizing, limit conceptions. No idealization remains satisfied with concepts that are merely mimetic adaptations to reality as given. When this operation with the concept of communicative reason is even ascribed to social reality itself—incorporated in it, as it were—the empiricist's suspicions against any kind of confounding of reason and reality perk up. In what sense could something like communicative reason be embodied in social facts? And what forces us to adopt such an assumption, which seems entirely counterintuitive? Although I do not want to recapitulate the basics of formal pragmatics, I must briefly recall how the relation between facticity and validity presents itself *after the linguistic turn.*

1.1.1

By the late nineteenth century, Immanuel Kant's metaphysical background assumptions about the abstract opposition between the noumenal and the phenomenal were no longer convincing. Still less plausible by then was Hegel's speculative account of the dialectical dynamics of essence and appearance. As a result, empiricist views gained the upper hand. These views gave priority to a psychological explanation of logical—or, more generally, conceptual—relations: internal relationships between symbols were assimilated to empirical relationships between mental episodes. This psychologism was countered with nearly equivalent, or at least similar, arguments by C. S. Peirce in America, Gottlob Frege and Edmund Husserl in Germany, and finally G. E. Moore and Bertrand Russell in England. They set the stage for philosophy in the twentieth century by opposing the attempt to make empirical psychology into the foundational science for logic, mathematics, and grammar.

Frege summarizes the central objection in this thesis: "We are not owners of thoughts as we are owners of our representations."[7] Mental representations (*Vorstellungen*) are, in each case, my representations or your representations; they must be ascribed to a representing—either perceiving or imagining—subject who can be identified in space and time. Thoughts, on the other hand, overstep the boundaries of an individual consciousness. Even if in each case they are apprehended by a variety of subjects in various places and at various times, in the strict sense thoughts remain the *same* thoughts in regard to their content.

The analysis of simple predicative sentences, moreover, shows that thoughts have a more complex structure than the objects of representational thinking. By means of names, designations, and deictic expressions, we refer to individual objects, whereas sentences in which such singular terms occupy the subject position usually express a proposition or report a state of affairs. If such a thought is true, then the sentence that expresses it reports a fact. The critique of the view that thinking is representational consciousness rests on these straightforward considerations. Objects alone are given in the mental representation; we apprehend states of affairs or facts in thoughts. With this critique, Frege takes the first step in the linguistic turn. From this point on, thoughts and facts can no longer be located immediately in the world of perceived or imagined objects; they are accessible only as linguistically "represented" (*dargestellt*), that is, as states of affairs expressed in sentences.

1.1.2

Thoughts are propositionally structured. One can get a clear sense of what this means by considering the grammatical form of simple assertoric sentences. I do not need to go into this here. The important point is that we can read the structure of thoughts from the structure of sentences; sentences are those elementary components of a grammatical language that can be true or false. Hence, if we want to explain the peculiar status that distinguishes thoughts from mental representations, we must turn to the medium of language. Both moments—that a thought overshoots the bounds of an individual consciousness and that its content is independent of an individual's stream of experience—can only be described in such a way that linguistic expressions have *identical meanings* for different users. At any rate, the members of a language community must proceed on the performative assumption that speakers and hearers can understand a grammatical expression in identical ways. They assume that like expressions keep the same meaning in the diverse situations and speech acts in which they are employed. Even at the level where meanings have their substrate in signs, the sign-type must be recognizable as the same sign in the variety of corresponding sign-events. The logical relationship between the general and the particular that philosophical idealism conceived as a relation of essence and appearance is reflected in this perceived relation of type and token. The same is true for the concept, or the meaning of a term and its various expressions. What distinguishes a symbolically expressed thought as something general, identical with itself, and publicly accessible—as something transcending the individual consciousness—from the always particular, episodic, and only privately accessible, hence consciousness-immanent representations is the ideal status of linguistic signs and grammatical rules. These rules are what lend linguistic events—at the phonetic, syntactic, and semantic levels—their determinate form, which is constant and recognizable throughout all their variations.

1.1.3

The ideal character inherent in the generality of concepts and thoughts is interwoven with an idealization of a wholly different sort. Every complete thought has a specific propositional content that can be expressed by an assertoric sentence. But beyond the propositional content, every thought calls for a further determination: it demands an answer to whether it is true or false. Thinking and speaking subjects can take a position on each thought with a "yes" or a "no"; hence, the mere having of a thought is complemented by an act of judgment. Only the affirmed thought or the true sentence expresses a fact. The affirmation of a thought or the assertoric sense of a statement brings into play a further moment of ideality, one connected with the validity of the judgment or sentence.

The semantic critique of representational thinking holds that the sentence "This ball is red" does not express a particular representation of a thing, that is, a red ball. Rather, it is the linguistic representation of *the fact that* the ball is red. This means that a speaker who utters 'p' in an assertoric mode does not refer with her affirmation to the existence of an object but rather to the corresponding state of affairs. As soon as one expands 'p' into the sentence "*There is* at least one object that is a ball, of which it *is true* that it is red," one sees that the truth of 'p' and the being-the-case of a corresponding state of affairs or circumstance must not be understood by analogy to a thing's existence. Veridical being or being-the-case must not be confused with the existence of an object.[8] Otherwise one is misled, along with Frege, Husserl, and later even Popper, to a Platonic conception of meaning, according to which thoughts, propositions, or states of affairs enjoy an ideal being-in-themselves. These authors considered it necessary to supplement the two-world architectonic of the philosophy of consciousness with a "third world" of timeless, ideal beings. This sphere of ideal objects is set off against reality or the objective world of objects and events we can perceive or manipulate, on the one hand, and against the mind or subjective world of inner episodes to which each individual has a privileged access, on the other.

This three-world doctrine of meaning-Platonism is, however, no less metaphysical than the two-world doctrine of subjective idealism. It remains a mystery how the three worlds can enter into contact with one another: "Even the timeless . . . must somehow be implicated with the temporal," Frege conceded.[9] Once meanings and thoughts have been hypostatized into ideally existing objects, the relations among the worlds pose stubborn questions. It is hard to explain how sentence meanings and thoughts reflect events in the world and how they enter persons' minds. Formal semantics has slaved away in vain on these questions for decades.

1.1.4

The stable propositional structure of thoughts stands out from the stream of experiences in virtue of an ideal status that furnishes concepts and judgments with general, intersubjectively recognizable and hence identical contents. This ideality intrinsically refers to the idea of truth. But grammatical invariance alone, that is, the linguistic rule structures that account for the ideal generality of concepts and thoughts, cannot explain the idealization connected with the *unconditional meaning of truth claims*. And because formal semantics, in line with Frege, operates only with a concept of language that relegates all aspects of language use to empirical analysis, this approach cannot explain the meaning of truth within the horizon of linguistic communication. Formal semantics recurs instead to the ontological relationship between language and world, sentence and fact, or thought and intellect (as the subjective capacity to apprehend and judge thoughts). C. S. Peirce, on the other hand, took the logical next step in the linguistic turn by applying formal analysis to the use of language.

As Wilhelm von Humboldt viewed conversation, so Peirce considered communication, and the interpretation of signs in general, as the heart of linguistic achievements. Using the practice of reaching understanding as his model, he can explain not only the ideal moment of concept formation, which establishes generality, but also the idealizing moment of forming true judgments, which triumphs over time. In place of the dyadic concept of a linguistically represented world, Peirce installs a triadic concept: the linguistic representation of something for a possible interpreter.[10] The world as the sum total of possible facts is constituted only for an interpretation community whose members engage, before the background of an intersubjectively shared lifeworld, in processes of reaching understanding with one another about things in the world. "Real" is what can be represented in true statements, whereas "true" can be explained in turn by reference to the claim one person raises before others by asserting a proposition. With the assertoric sense of her statement, a speaker raises a criticizable claim to the validity of the asserted proposition, and because no one has direct access to uninterpreted conditions of validity, "validity" (*Gültigkeit*) must be understood in epistemic terms as "validity (*Geltung*) proven for us." A justified truth claim should allow its proponent to defend it with reasons against the objections of possible opponents; in the end she should be able to gain the rationally motivated agreement of the interpretation community as a whole.

Here the reference to some *particular* interpretation community settled in its own particular form of life does not suffice, however. Even if we cannot break out of the sphere of language and argumentation, even if we must understand reality as what we can represent in true statements, we must not forget that the relation to reality contains a reference to something independent of us and thus, in this sense, transcendent. With each truth claim, speakers and hearers transcend the provincial standards of a particular collectivity, of a particular process of communication localized here and now. Thus Peirce, drawing on the counterfactual concept of the "final opinion," a consensus reached under ideal conditions, constructs something like a transcendence from within: "The real, then, is that which, sooner or later, information and reasoning would finally result in, and which is therefore independent of the vagaries of me and you. Thus, the very origin of the conception of reality shows that this conception essentially involves the notion of a community, without definite limits, and capable of a definite increase of knowledge."[11] Peirce explains truth as ideal assertability, that is, as the vindication of a criticizable validity claim under the communication conditions of an audience of competent interpreters that extends ideally across social space and historical time.

1.1.5

With this pragmatic explanation of the idea of truth, we touch on a relation of facticity and validity that is constitutive of the very practice of reaching understanding and is hence relevant for social reality as well. This social reality, which includes Peirce's "community of investigators," is more complex than the aspects of nature objectified in instrumental action or scientific research. With the ideal character of general concepts, we face the problem of explaining, in terms of the rule structure of language, how meanings remain identical in the diversity of various linguistic realizations. The idealization built into truth claims confronts us with the more ambitious task of explaining, in terms of the pragmatic conditions of argumentation, how the validity claims raised *hic et nunc* and aimed at intersubjective recognition or acceptance can, at the same time, overshoot local standards for taking yes/no positions, that is, standards that have become established in each particular community of interpreters. Only this transcendent moment of unconditionality distinguishes the argumentative practices of justification from other practices that are regulated merely by social convention. For Peirce, the reference to an *unlimited* communication community serves to replace the eternal moment (or the supratemporal character) of unconditionality with the idea of an open but ultimately cumulative process of interpretation that transcends the boundaries of social space and historical time from within, from the perspective of a finite existence situated in the world. On Peirce's view, it is within time that the learning processes of the unlimited communication community build the bridges that span all local and temporal distances; it is within the world that such learning realizes the conditions that must be presupposed as sufficiently satisfied for the unconditionality of context-transcending validity claims. Here a certain degree of satisfaction counts as "sufficient" when it qualifies our current practice of argumentation as an exemplary local embodiment of the (unavoidably assumed) universal discourse of an unbounded community of interpretation. With this *projection*, the tension between facticity and validity moves into the presuppositions of communication. Even if these presuppositions have an *ideal* content that can be only approximately satisfied, all participants must de facto accept them whenever they assert or deny the truth of a statement in any way and want to enter into argumentation aimed at justifying this validity claim.

Peirce, who is primarily interested in the semiotic transformation of epistemology and the philosophy of science, develops the above model with the argumentative practice of a republic of letters in view. What applies to processes of reaching understanding within the community of investigators, however, holds mutatis mutandis for everyday communication as well. That is, speech-act theory demonstrates the presence of entirely similar structures and presuppositions in everyday communicative practice. Here, too, participants, in claiming validity for their utterances, strive to reach an understanding with one another about something in the world. Of course, unlike argumentation-guided research processes, the everyday use of language does not turn exclusively or even primarily on its representational (or fact-stating) functions; here *all* the functions of language and language-world relations come into play, so that the spectrum of validity claims takes in more than truth claims. In addition, these validity claims, which also include claims to subjective sincerity and normative rightness, are initially raised in a naive manner, thus *intentione recta*, even if they implicitly depend on the possibility of discursive vindication.

The fact that this expanded spectrum of validity is situated in the lifeworld makes it necessary to generalize Peirce's concept of the unlimited communication community beyond the cooperative search for truth on the part of scientific investigators. The tension between facticity and validity that Peirce uncovered in the inescapable (*nicht-hintergehbaren*) presuppositions of research practices can be pursued even beyond the communicative presuppositions of various types of argumentation, into the pragmatic presuppositions of individual speech acts and the contexts of interaction such acts link together.[12]

1.2 Transcendence from Within: Managing the Risk of Dissension through Lifeworld Backgrounds

Regardless of what position we take on the details of this controversial conception, which requires further clarification, we can say this much: in explicating the meaning of linguistic expressions and the validity of statements, we touch on idealizations that are connected with the medium of language. Specifically, the ideal character of conceptual and semantic generality is accessible to a semantic analysis of language, whereas the idealization connected with validity claims is accessible to a pragmatic analysis of the use of language oriented to reaching understanding. These idealizations inhabiting language itself acquire, in addition, an *action-theoretic* meaning if the illocutionary binding forces of speech acts are enlisted for the coordination of the action plans of different actors. With the concept of communicative action, which brings in mutual understanding as a mechanism of action coordination, the counterfactual presuppositions of actors who orient their action to validity claims also acquire immediate relevance for the construction and preservation of social orders; for these orders *exist* through the recognition of normative validity claims. This means that the tension between facticity and validity built into language and its use turns up again in the dynamics of the integration of communicatively socialized individuals. What is more, this tension must be worked off by the participants' own efforts. In the social integration achieved through enacted law, this tension is, as we shall see, stabilized in a special way.

1.2.1

Every social interaction that comes about without the exercise of manifest violence can be understood as a solution to the problem of how the action plans of several actors can be coordinated with each other in such a way that one party's actions "link up" with those of others. An ongoing connection of this sort reduces the possibilities of clashes among the doubly contingent decisions of participants to the point where intentions and actions can form more or less conflict-free networks, thus allowing behavior patterns and social order in general to emerge. As long as language is used only as a medium for transmitting information, action coordination proceeds through the mutual influence that actors exert on each other in a purposive-rational manner. On the other hand, as soon as the illocutionary forces of speech acts take on an action-coordinating role, language itself supplies the primary source of social integration. Only in this case should one speak of "communicative action." In such action, actors in the roles of speaker and hearer attempt to negotiate interpretations of the situation at hand and to harmonize their respective plans with one another through the unrestrained pursuit of illocutionary goals. Naturally, the binding energies of language can be mobilized to coordinate action plans only if the participants suspend the objectivating attitude of an observer, along with the immediate orientation to personal success, in favor of the performative attitude of a speaker who wants to *reach an understanding* with a second person about something in the world. Under this condition, speech-act offers can achieve an action-coordinating effect because obligations relevant to further interaction result from the addressee's affirmative response to a serious offer.

Communicative action, then, depends on the use of language oriented to mutual understanding. This use of language functions in such a way that the participants either agree on the validity claimed for their speech acts or identify points of disagreement, which they conjointly take into consideration in the course of further interaction. Every speech act involves the raising of criticizable validity claims aimed at intersubjective recognition. A speech-act offer has a coordinating effect because the speaker, by raising a validity claim, concomitantly takes on a sufficiently credible guarantee to vindicate the claim with the right kind of reasons, should this be necessary. However, with such unconditional validity claims, which point beyond all provincial standards that are locally accepted and established, the ideal tension that Peirce analyzed in the validity of true scientific statements enters into the facticity of the lifeworld. The idea of the redeemability of criticizable validity claims requires idealizations that, as adopted by the communicating actors themselves, are thereby brought down from transcendental heaven to the earth of the lifeworld. The theory of communicative action *detranscendentalizes* the noumenal realm only to have the idealizing force of context-transcending anticipations settle in the unavoidable pragmatic presuppositions of speech acts, and hence in the heart of ordinary, everyday communicative practice. Even the most fleeting speech-act offers, the most conventional yes/no responses, *rely on* potential reasons. Any speech act therewith refers to the ideally expanded audience of the unlimited interpretation community that would have to be convinced for the speech act to be justified and, hence, rationally acceptable.

1.2.2

We have distinguished the ideal character of conceptual/semantic generality from that of validity. These aspects can be clarified by examining, on the one hand, the rule structure of language in general and, on the other, the presuppositions of the use of language oriented to mutual understanding. Both levels of idealization are built into linguistic communication itself and, via communicative action, have a hand in constituting the social reality of networks of interactions spreading out radially through space and time. The ideal character of semantic generality shapes communicative action inasmuch as the participants could not even intend to reach an understanding with one another about something in the world if they did not *presuppose*, on the basis of a common (or translatable) language, that they conferred identical meanings on the expressions they employed. Only if this condition is satisfied can misunderstandings prove to be such. The presupposition that linguistic expressions are used with identical meanings can often turn out to be false from an observer's perspective, and perhaps this is always the case under the ethnomethodologist's microscope. But even as counterfactual, this presupposition remains necessary for every communicative use of language.

Any sociology aware that the route to its object domain lies through the hermeneutic understanding of meaning (*Sinnverstehen*) must reckon with this tension between facticity and validity. This circumstance need not irritate its conventional self-understanding as an empirical science, because it can ascribe to the communicatively acting subjects *themselves* the normal capabilities for managing those disturbances in communication that arise from mere misunderstandings. In a rather harmless way, misunderstandings revoke idealizations that were necessarily assumed. Something similar holds for a further, communicatively unavoidable—and again, idealizing—presupposition. Namely, the interacting participants must consider themselves mutually accountable, hence they must presuppose that they can orient their action according to validity claims. As soon as this expectation of rationality turns out to be false, the participants—just like the sociological observer in the role of virtual participant—drop their performative attitude in favor of an objectivating one.

A different kind of problem results, however, from the demanding counterfactual presuppositions of communicative action that are supposed to secure an unconditional character for validity claims. This *second level of idealization*, that is, determines the constitution of social reality in such a way that every communicatively achieved agreement—which makes possible the coordination of actions, the complex buildup of interactions, and the weaving together of action sequences—takes as its yardstick the intersubjective recognition of criticizable validity claims. In virtue of such communicative agreements, the taking of yes/no positions plays a key role in the functioning of everyday language games. These acts of position taking charge the social facts they create with an ideal tension, because they respond to validity claims whose justification must presuppose the agreement of an ideally expanded audience. The validity (*Gültigkeit*) claimed for statements and norms (as well as for first-person reports of experience) conceptually transcends space and time, whereas the actual claim is, in each case, raised here and now, in a specific context in which its acceptance or rejection has immediate consequences. The validity we claim for our utterances and for practices of justification differs from the *social validity or acceptance* (*soziale Geltung*) of actually established standards and expectations whose stability is based merely on settled custom or the threat of sanctions. The ideal moment of unconditionality is deeply ingrained in factual processes of communication, because validity claims are Janus-faced: as claims, they overshoot every context; at the same time, they must be both raised and accepted here and now if they are to support an agreement effective for coordination—for this there is no "null context." The universalistic meaning of the claimed validity exceeds all contexts, but only the local, binding act of acceptance enables validity claims to bear the burden of social integration for a context-bound everyday practice.

An interpretive sociology that realizes that this second, more radical tension between facticity and validity inhabits its object domain must revise its conventional, more or less empiricist self-understanding and conceive of itself as a social science that proceeds in a reconstructive manner. One needs a reconstructive approach to explain how social integration in general can take shape under the conditions of such an unstable sociation, which operates with permanently endangered counterfactual presuppositions.

1.2.3

The first step in reconstructing the conditions of social integration leads to the concept of the *lifeworld*. The starting point is the problem of how social order is supposed to emerge from processes of consensus formation that are threatened by an explosive tension between facticity and validity. The double contingency that every interaction must absorb assumes an especially precarious form in the case of communicative action, namely, the ever-present risk of disagreement built into the mechanism of reaching understanding, where the costs of dissension are quite high from the viewpoint of action coordination. Normally, only a few options are available: carrying out straightforward "repair work"; putting aside the controversial claims, with the result that the ground of shared assumptions shrinks; moving into costly discourses of uncertain outcome and open to unsettling questions; breaking off communication and withdrawing; and, finally, shifting over to strategic action. To be sure, the rational motivation based on each person's ability to say no has the advantage of stabilizing behavioral expectations *noncoercively*. But the risks of dissension, which are continually fueled by disappointing experiences and surprising contingencies, are high. If communicative action were not embedded in lifeworld contexts that provide the backing of a massive background consensus, such risks would make the use of language oriented to mutual understanding an unlikely route to social integration. From the very start, communicative acts are located within the horizon of shared, unproblematic beliefs; at the same time, they are nourished by these resources of the *always already familiar*. The constant upset of disappointment and contradiction, contingency and critique in everyday life crashes against a sprawling, deeply set, and unshakable rock of background assumptions, loyalties, and skills.

We do not need to go into the formal-pragmatic analysis of the lifeworld here, nor into the place that communicative action occupies in a broader theoretical architectonic (i.e., between rational discourse and lifeworld). The lifeworld forms both the horizon for speech situations and the source of interpretations, while it in turn reproduces itself only through ongoing communicative actions.[13] In the present context, what interests me about background knowledge is its peculiar pre-predicative and precategorial character, which already drew Husserl's attention in his investigations of this "forgotten" foundation of meaning inhabiting everyday practice and experience.[14]

As we engage in communicative action, the lifeworld embraces us as an unmediated certainty, out of whose immediate proximity we live and speak. This all-penetrating, yet latent and unnoticed presence of the background of communicative action can be described as a more intense yet deficient form of knowledge and ability. To begin with, we make use of this knowledge involuntarily, without reflectively knowing *that* we possess it at all. What enables background knowledge to acquire absolute certainty in this way, and even augments its epistemic quality from a subjective standpoint, is precisely the property that robs it of a constitutive feature of knowledge: we make use of such knowledge without the awareness that it *could* be false. Insofar as all knowledge is fallible and is known to be such, background knowledge does not represent knowledge at all, in a strict sense. As background knowledge, it lacks the possibility of being challenged, that is, of being raised to the level of criticizable validity claims. One can do this only by converting it from a resource into a topic of discussion, at which point—just when it is thematized—it no longer functions as a lifeworld background but rather *disintegrates* in its background modality. Background knowledge cannot be falsified as such; no sooner has it been thematized, and thereby cast into the whirlpool of possible questions, than it decomposes. What lends it its peculiar stability and first immunizes it against the pressure of contingency-generating experiences is its unique *leveling out of the tension between facticity and validity*: the counterfactual moment of idealization, which always overshoots the given and first makes a disappointing confrontation with reality possible, is extinguished in the dimension of validity itself. At the same time, the validity dimension, from which implicit knowledge acquires the intuitive force of conviction, remains intact as such.

1.2.4

A similar fusion of facticity and validity that likewise stabilizes behavioral expectations appears in an entirely different form at the level of knowledge that has already passed through communicative action and is thus thematically available, namely, in those archaic institutions that present themselves with an apparently unassailable claim to authority. In societies based on kinship, institutions protected by taboos form a site where cognitive and normative expectations merge and harden into an unbroken complex of convictions linked with motives and value orientations. The authority of powerful institutions encounters actors *within* their social lifeworld. In putting things in such terms, we no longer describe the lifeworld as background knowledge from the formal-pragmatic perspective of a participant, but rather objectify it from the perspective of a sociological observer. The lifeworld, of which institutions form a part, comes into view as a complex of interpenetrating cultural traditions, social orders, and personal identities.

Arnold Gehlen's anthropology of institutions directs our attention to the phenomenon of an original, auratically transfigured normative consensus that can be analytically distinguished from lifeworld certainties. This consensus refers especially to behavioral expectations that are culturally transmitted and rehearsed as explicit knowledge, their deep institutional anchoring notwithstanding.[15] In the interplay of mythical narratives and ritual practices one can show why this knowledge can be thematized only with reservations. Ceremonially fixed patterns of communication restrict challenges to the authoritative validity of the syndrome of intermeshing descriptive, evaluative, and expressive contents. This crystallized complex of beliefs reveals a kind of validity, one equipped with the force of factual reality. In this case, the *fusion of facticity and validity* occurs not in the mode of the always already familiar, not in terms of basic certainties that, so to speak, stand behind us, but rather in the mode of an authority that imperiously confronts us and arouses ambivalent feelings. Emile Durkheim worked out the ambivalence of this mode of validity with respect to the status of sacred objects, which instill onlookers with mixed feelings of terror and enthusiasm and simultaneously trigger in them both reverence and trembling.[16] This symbiosis of conflicting affects is still accessible to us today in the aesthetic experience; it is tamed and rendered repeatable in the surrealistically triggered shock that such authors as Georges Bataille and Michel Leiris have not only produced in their own literary works but described as well.[17]

In the simultaneously frightening and attractive *fascinosum* of such authoritarian institutions, it is striking that two moments we now consider incompatible are fused together. The threat of an avenging power and the force of bonding convictions not only coexist, they spring from the same mythic source. The social sanctions imposed by human beings are secondary: they punish violations of an antecedent, intrinsically *compelling* and at the same time *bonding* authority. Social sanctions borrow their deontological meaning, so to speak, from this authority. Evidently, the social integration of collectivities could originally be secured through communicative action only when the concomitant risk of dissension could be brought under control *within the validity dimension itself.* Even today, our deeply rooted reactions to violations of incest or similar taboos recall the fact that the stability of behavioral expectations at the core of kinship societies had to be secured through beliefs that possess a *spellbinding* authority that is at once bonding and frightening. Moreover, this stability had to be achieved *below* that threshold at which the coercive force of sanctions irreversibly splits off from the forceless force of plausible reasons.

Above that threshold, validity retains the force of the factual. This is true whether such validity takes the form of lifeworld certainties that remain in the background of explicit communication or whether it appears in the form of communicatively available value orientations that are nevertheless subject to the rigid communication patterns of a bewitching authority and withdrawn from challenge.

1.2.5

Only with the third step in this reconstruction do we arrive at the category of law. The embeddedness of communicative action in lifeworld contexts and the regulation of behavior through strong archaic institutions explain how social integration in small and relatively undifferentiated groups is at all possible on the improbable basis of processes of reaching understanding. Naturally, in the course of social evolution the risk of dissension increases with the scope for taking yes/no positions on criticizable validity claims. The more societal complexity increases and originally ethnocentric perspectives widen, the more there develops a pluralization of forms of life accompanied by an individualization of life histories, while the zones of overlapping lifeworlds and shared background assumptions shrink. In proportion to their disenchantment, sacralized belief complexes fall apart, under differentiated validity aspects, into the more or less freely thematizable contents of a tradition set communicatively aflow. Above all, however, processes of *social* differentiation necessitate a multiplication and variation of functionally specified tasks, social roles, and interest positions. On the one hand, this allows communicative action to escape its narrowly circumscribed institutional boundaries for a wider range of opportunities. On the other hand, in a growing number of spheres social differentiation not only unshackles but requires the self-interested pursuit of one's own success.

This brief outline should suffice to indicate the *problem* that emerges in modern societies: how the validity and acceptance of a social order can be stabilized once communicative actions become autonomous and clearly begin to differ, in the view of the actors themselves, from strategic interactions. Naturally, self-interested action has always been fused with, or limited by, a normative order.

In societies organized around a state, legal norms are already superimposed on a mature normative infrastructure. In these traditional societies, however, even the law still feeds on the self-authorizing force of the religiously sublimated sacred realm. For example, the notion of a higher law familiar in the medieval tradition of law was still rooted in the sacred fusion of facticity and validity. According to this idea, the law made by the ruler remained *subordinate* to the Christian natural law administered by the Church.

In what follows, I start from the modern situation of a predominantly secular society in which normative orders must be maintained without metasocial guarantees. Even lifeworld certainties, which in any case are pluralized and ever more differentiated, do not provide sufficient compensation for this deficit. As a result, the burden of social integration shifts more and more onto the communicative achievements of actors for whom validity and facticity—that is, the binding force of rationally motivated beliefs and the imposed force of external sanctions—have parted company as incompatible. This is true, at least, outside the areas of habitualized actions and customary practices. If, as I assume along with Parsons and Durkheim, complexes of interaction cannot be stabilized simply on the basis of the reciprocal influence that success-oriented actors exert on one another, then *in the final analysis* society must be integrated through communicative action.[18]

Such a situation intensifies the problem: how can disenchanted, internally differentiated and pluralized lifeworlds be socially integrated if, at the same time, the risk of dissension is growing, particularly in the spheres of communicative action that have been cut loose from the ties of sacred authorities and released from the bonds of archaic institutions? According to this scenario, the increasing need for integration must hopelessly overtax the integrating capacity of communicative action, especially if the functionally necessary spheres of strategic interaction are growing, as is the case in modern economic societies.[19] In the case of conflict, persons engaged in communicative action face the alternatives of either breaking off communication or shifting to strategic action—of either postponing or carrying out the unresolved conflict. One way out of this predicament, now, is for the actors themselves *to come to some understanding* about the *normative regulation of strategic inter-*

actions. The paradoxical nature of such regulation is revealed in light of the premise that facticity and validity have split apart, for the acting subjects themselves, into two mutually exclusive dimensions. For self-interested actors, all situational features are transformed into facts they evaluate in the light of their own preferences, whereas actors oriented toward reaching understanding rely on a jointly negotiated understanding of the situation and interpret the relevant facts in the light of intersubjectively recognized validity claims. However, if the orientations to personal success and to reaching understanding exhaust the alternatives for acting subjects, then norms suitable as socially integrating constraints on strategic interactions must meet two contradictory conditions that, from the viewpoint of the actors, cannot be simultaneously satisfied. On the one hand, such rules must present de facto restrictions that alter the relevant information in such a way that the strategic actor feels compelled to adapt her behavior in the objectively desired manner. On the other hand, they must at the same time develop a socially integrating force by imposing obligations on the addressees—which, according to my theory, is possible only on the basis of intersubjectively recognized normative validity claims.

According to the above analysis, the type of norms required would have to bring about willingness to comply *simultaneously* by means of de facto constraint and legitimate validity. Norms of this kind would have to appear with an authority that once again equips validity with the force of the factual, only this time under the condition of the polarization already existing between action oriented to success and that oriented to reaching understanding, which is to say, under the condition of a *perceived* incompatibility of facticity and validity. As we have already assumed, the metasocial guarantees of the sacred have broken down, and these guarantees are what made the ambivalent bonding force of archaic institutions possible, thereby allowing an amalgam of validity and facticity in the validity dimension itself. The solution to this puzzle is found in the system of rights that lends to individual liberties the coercive force of law. We can then also see, from a historical perspective, that the core of modern law consists of private rights that mark out the legitimate scope of individual liberties and are thus tailored to the strategic pursuit of private interests.

1.3 Dimensions of Legal Validity

Since Hobbes, the prototype for law in general has been the norms of bourgeois private law, which is based on the freedom to enter into contracts and to own property. Even Kant begins his *Rechtslehre* (*Elements of Justice*) by discussing natural, "subjective" rights that authorize each person to use coercion against violations of his or her legally protected liberties. The transition from natural to positive law transforms these authorizations to use coercion—which may no longer be directly enforced by individual persons after the state has monopolized all the means of legitimate coercion—into authorizations to take legal action. At the same time, private rights are supplemented by structurally homologous rights that protect the individual against the state itself, that is, protect private persons from unlawful infringements of the administration on their life, liberty, and property. It is Kant's *concept of legality* that most interests me here. Taking his start from individual rights, Kant uses this concept to explain the complex mode of validity connected with law in general. In the dimension of legal validity (*Rechtsgeltung*), facticity and validity are once again intertwined, but this time the two moments are not fused together—as they are in lifeworld certainties or in the overpowering authority of archaic institutions withdrawn from any discussion—in an indissoluble amalgam. In the legal mode of validity, the facticity of the *enforcement* of law is intertwined with the legitimacy of a *genesis* of law that claims to be rational because it guarantees liberty. The tension between these two distinct moments of facticity and validity is thus intensified and behaviorally operationalized.

1.3.1

For Kant, the facticity-validity relationship within the dimension of legal validity appears as the internal connection that law establishes between coercion and freedom. Law is connected from the start with the authorization to coerce; this coercion is justified, however, only for "the prevention of a hindrance to freedom," hence only for the purposes of countering encroachments on the freedom of each. The validity claim of law is expressed in this internal "conjunction of the universal reciprocal coercion with the freedom of everyone."[20] Legal rules posit conditions of coercion, conditions "under which the will [*Willkür*] of one person can be unified with the will of another in accordance with a universal law of freedom."[21] On the one hand, legal behavior can be enforced as "the mere conformity . . . of an action with the law";[22] this means it must be open to subjects to comply with the law for reasons other than moral ones. The "conditions of coercion" need only be perceived by the addressees as the *occasion* for norm-conformative behavior; as one can see on analytic grounds alone, acting from duty, that is, morally motivated obedience to the law, cannot be brought about by coercion. On the other hand, however, "unifying" the free choice (*Willkür*) of each with that of all others, that is, social integration, is possible only on the basis of normatively valid rules that would *deserve* their addressees' uncoerced, which is to say rationally motivated, recognition from the moral point of view—"in accordance with a universal law of freedom." Although legal claims are coupled with authorized coercion, they must always be such that subjects can comply on account of their normative validity as well, hence out of "respect for the law."[23] Kant's concept of legality dissolves the paradox of rules of action that, without regard for their moral worthiness, only require a behavior that objectively corresponds to the norm: legal norms are at the same time but in different respects enforceable laws based on coercion and laws of freedom.

The dual character of legal validity, which we have first of all clarified in terms of Kant's legal theory, can also be elucidated from the perspective of action theory. The two components of legal validity, coercion and freedom, leave the choice of action orientation up to the addressees. For an empirical approach, the validity of positive law is in the first instance characterized tautologically, in that the law is considered to be whatever acquires the force of law on the basis of legally valid procedures and retains its legal force for the time being, despite the legally available possibilities of repeal. But one can adequately explain the meaning of such legal validity only by referring simultaneously to both aspects—to de facto validity or acceptance, on the one hand, and to legitimacy or rational acceptability, on the other.[24] The *de facto validity* of legal norms is determined by the degree to which such norms are acted on or implemented, and thus by the extent to which one can actually expect the addressees to accept them. In contrast to convention and custom, enacted law does not rely on the organic facticity of inherited forms of life, but on the *artificially produced facticity* found in the threat of sanctions that are legally defined and can be imposed through court action. On the other hand, the *legitimacy* of statutes is measured against the discursive redeemability of their normative validity claim—in the final analysis, according to whether they have come about through a rational legislative process, or at least could have been justified from pragmatic, ethical, and moral points of view. The legitimacy of a statute is independent of its de facto implementation. At the same time, however, de facto validity or factual compliance varies with the addressees' belief in legitimacy, and this belief is in turn based on the supposition that the norm could be justified. The less a legal order is legitimate, or is at least considered such, the more other factors, such as intimidation, the force of circumstances, custom, and sheer habit, must step in to reinforce it.

Generally, the legal system as a whole has a higher measure of legitimacy than individual legal norms. Ralf Dreier includes the following among the necessary conditions for the validity of a legal system:

First, [the legal system] must by and large be socially effective and, second, by and large ethically justified. The legal validity of individual norms [requires] that these are enacted in accordance with a constitution satisfying the above-mentioned criteria. In addition, norms must individually display, first, a minimum of social effectiveness or the prospects for such and, second, a minimum of ethical justification or the potential for such.[25]

The double reference of legal validity to de facto validity as measured by average acceptance, on the one hand, and to the legitimacy of the claim to normative recognition, on the other, leaves addressees with the choice of taking either an objectivating or a performative attitude toward the same legal norm. For a rationally choosing actor who expects norms to be enforced, the legal precept forms a de facto barrier, with calculable consequences in the case of a violation. On the other hand, for an actor who wants to reach an understanding with others about the jointly observed conditions for each's successful actions, the norm's claim to validity, along with the possibility of critically reexamining this claim, binds the actor's "free will" (*Willen*). Keeping these alternatives open does not imply a fusion of the moments that *continue to be* incompatible from the actor's point of view. Depending on the chosen perspective, the legal norm presents a different kind of situational element: for the person acting strategically, it lies at the level of social facts that externally restrict her range of options; for the person acting communicatively, it lies at the level of obligatory expectations that, she assumes, the legal community has rationally agreed on. Thus the actor, taking in each case a different point of view, will ascribe to a legally valid regulation either the status of a fact with predictable consequences or the deontological binding character of a normative expectation. The legal validity of a norm—and this is its point—means, now, that *two things* are guaranteed *at the same time:* both the legality of behavior, in the sense of an average norm compliance that, if necessary, is enforced by sanctions; and the legitimacy of the rule itself, which always makes it possible to follow the norm out of respect for the law.

We can see this dual perspective on law—legal norms as both enforceable laws and laws of freedom—by looking at private rights. Inasmuch as these norms leave open the motives for rule-conforming behavior, we might say they "tolerate" an actor's strategic attitude toward the individual norm. As elements of a legal order that is legitimate as a whole, they appear at the same time with a normative validity claim that expects a rationally motivated recognition. As such, they at least *invite* the addressees to follow them from the nonenforceable motive of duty. This invitation means that the legal order must always make it *possible* to obey its rules out of respect for the law. This analysis of the mode of validity connected with coercible law thus has implications for lawmaking: positive law, too, must be legitimate.

A legal order must not only guarantee that the rights of each person are in fact recognized by all other persons; the reciprocal recognition of the rights of each by all must in addition be based on laws that are legitimate insofar as they grant equal liberties to each, so that each's freedom of choice can coexist with the freedom of all. Moral laws fulfill these conditions per se, but for legal statutes, they must be satisfied by the political legislator. The process of legislation thus represents the place in the legal system where social integration first occurs. For this reason, it must be reasonable to expect those who participate in the legislative process, whether directly or indirectly, to drop the role of private subject and assume, along with their role of citizen, the perspective of members of a freely associated legal community, in which an agreement on the normative principles for regulating social life either has already been secured through tradition or can be brought about deliberatively in accordance with normatively recognized procedures. We have already clarified the unique combination of facticity and legitimacy in individual rights that equip legal persons with enforceable entitlements to pursue their own interests strategically. This combination requires a process of lawmaking in which the participating citizens are *not* allowed to take part simply in the role of actors oriented to success. To the extent that rights of political participation and rights of communication are constitutive for the production of legitimate statutes, they must not be exercised by persons who act merely as private subjects of civil law. Rather, these rights must be exercised in the attitude of communicatively engaged citizens. Hence, the concept of modern law, which both intensifies and behaviorally operationalizes the tension between facticity and validity, already harbors the *democratic idea* developed by Rousseau and Kant: the claim to legitimacy on the part of a legal order built on rights can be redeemed only through the socially integrative force of the "concurring and united will of all" free and equal citizens.

We will deal with the idea of civic autonomy in detail later. For the moment, note simply that it recalls the fact that coercible laws must prove their legitimacy as laws of freedom in the process—and by the kind of process—of lawmaking. Moreover, in this process of enacting law, the tension between facticity and validity is reproduced yet again, though it takes a different form than it does in established law. To be sure, legal behavior can be described as compliance with norms that have been backed with the threat of sanction and have acquired the force of law through the decisions of a political legislature. But the facticity of lawmaking differs from that of the enforcement of law insofar as the permission for legal coercion must be *traced back* to the *expectation of legitimacy* connected with the decisions of the legislature, which are both contingent and revisable. The positivity of law is bound up with the promise that democratic processes of lawmaking justify the presumption that enacted norms are rationally acceptable. Rather than displaying the facticity of an arbitrary, absolutely contingent choice, the positivity of law expresses the legitimate will that stems from a presumptively rational self-legislation of politically autonomous citizens. In Kant, too, the democratic principle has to fill a gap in a system of legally regulated egoism that cannot reproduce itself on its own but must rely on a background consensus of citizens. However, this *gap in solidarity*, which opens up insofar as legal subjects exclusively pursue their own private interests, cannot be closed again by rights tailored for this kind of success-oriented action, or at least not by such rights alone. Enacted law cannot secure the bases of its legitimacy simply through legality, which leaves attitudes and motives up to the addressees.

Either the legal order remains embedded in an encompassing social ethos and subordinate to the authority of a suprapositive or sacred law (as in the stratified societies and absolute states of early modernity), or else individual liberties are supplemented by rights of *a different type*, rights of citizenship that are geared no longer to rational choice but to autonomy in the Kantian sense. For without religious or metaphysical support, the coercive law tailored for the self-interested use of individual rights can preserve its socially integrating force only insofar as the addressees of legal norms may at the same time understand themselves, taken as a whole, as the rational *authors* of those norms. To this extent, modern law lives off a solidarity concentrated in the value orientations of citizens and ultimately issuing from communicative action and deliberation. As we shall see, the jointly exercised communicative freedom of citizens can assume a form that is mediated in a variety of ways by legal institutions and procedures, but it cannot be completely replaced by coercive law. This internal connection between the facticity of law enforcement and the legitimacy of the lawmaking process imposes a heavy burden on legal systems, which are supposed to lighten the tasks of social integration for actors whose capacities for reaching understanding are overtaxed. For nothing appears less probable to the enlightened sociologist than the claim that the integrative achievements of modern law are nourished solely, or even in the first instance, by a normative consensus, whether already existing or achieved, and hence by the communicative sources of solidarity.

With the functional imperatives of highly complex societies, another kind of facticity comes into play. Unlike the facticity of law enforcement, this social facticity is no longer internally related to the legitimacy claimed for the legal order. The normative self-understanding of law can be negated by social facts that intervene in the legal system from without. Here facticity and validity are *externally* related, for both moments—the normative presuppositions of established legal practices, on the one hand, and the social constraints that actually govern legal decisions, on the other—can be described independently of one another. Before taking up this theme in the next chapter, I will recapitulate the *internal relations* between facticity and validity that constitute the infrastructure of law in modern societies.[26]

1.3.2

Following the linguistic turn taken by Frege and Peirce, the opposition between idea and perceptible reality was overcome. As it came down from the Platonist tradition, this opposition was initially construed in ontological terms; later it was cast in terms of the philosophy of consciousness. Ideas are then considered to be directly embodied in language, so that the facticity of linguistic signs and expressions as events in the world is internally linked with the ideal moments of meaning and validity. The generality of meanings gains its ideal status only in the medium of signs and expressions that stand out, according to grammatical rules, from the stream of sign-tokens and speech events (or written materials) as recognizable types. Furthermore, the difference between the truth of a proposition and its being taken to be true is accounted for by explicating truth as rational assertability under ideal conditions, and hence only in reference to the discursive redemption of validity claims. If "true" or "valid" is understood as a triadic predicate, the unconditionality of truth is expressed only in the idealizing presuppositions of our argumentative practice of justification, and hence at the level of language use. This shows the internal relation between the validity of a proposition and the proof of its validity for an ideally expanded audience. What is valid must be able to prove its worth against any future objections that might actually be raised. As was the case with the ideal character of general concepts and meanings, so is the validity dimension of language constituted by a tension between facticity and validity: truth and the discursive conditions for the rational acceptability of truth claims are mutually explanatory.[27]

With the use of language to coordinate action on the basis of mutual understanding, and thus at the level of communicative action, this tension enters the world of social facts. In contrast to the facticity of sign-tokens and speech events, which we could understand as necessary for the embodiment of meanings, the intralinguistic tension between facticity and validity that enters communicative action along with validity claims must be conceived as a moment of social facticity, that is, as a moment of that everyday communicative practice through which forms of life reproduce themselves. To the extent that action coordination, and with it the formation of networks of interaction, takes place through processes of reaching understanding, intersubjectively shared convictions form the medium of social integration. Actors are convinced of what they understand and consider valid. This is why beliefs that have become problematic can be supported or revised only through reasons. Reasons, however, are not adequately described as dispositions to have opinions; rather, they are the currency used in a discursive exchange that redeems criticizable validity claims. Reasons owe their rationally motivating force to an internal relationship between the meaning and the validity of linguistic utterances. This makes them double-edged from the word go, because they can both reinforce and upset beliefs. With reasons, the facticity-validity tension inhabiting language and its use penetrates society. Insofar as it is supported by shared beliefs, the integration of a society is susceptible to the destabilizing effect of invalidating reasons (and is all the more susceptible to the invalidation of an entire category of reasons). The ideal tension breaking into social reality stems from the fact that the acceptance of validity claims, which generates and perpetuates social facts, rests on the context-dependent acceptability of reasons that are constantly exposed to the risk of being invalidated by better reasons and context-altering learning processes.

These properties of communicative action explain why the symbolically structured lifeworld, mediated by interpretations and beliefs, is shot through with fallible suppositions of validity. They help us see why behavioral expectations that depend on such fallible suppositions acquire at best a precarious kind of stability. This stability depends on achievements of social integration that ward off the ever-present danger of destabilization resulting from rationally motivated dissent. To be sure, reasons count only against the background of context-dependent standards of rationality;[28] but reasons that express the results of context-altering learning processes can also undermine established standards of rationality.

We have dealt with two strategies that counter the risk of dissension and therewith the risk of instability built into the communicative mode of social reproduction in general: on the one hand, circumscribing the communicative mechanism and, on the other, giving this mechanism unhindered play. The risk built into communicative action is *circumscribed* by those intuitive background certainties that are accepted without question because they are uncoupled from any communicatively accessible reasons that one could deliberately mobilize. Entrenched below the threshold of possible thematization, these behavior-stabilizing certainties that make up the lifeworld background are cut off from that dimension—opened up only in communicative action—in which we can distinguish between the justified acceptability and the mere acceptance of beliefs and reasons. We have observed a similar fusion of facticity and validity in those value orientations that were bound to sacred worldviews and to the spellbinding authority of strong institutions. This archaic form of authority was not based on the fact that normative beliefs remained in the background, that they could not be thematized and connected with reasons; it was based rather on a prescriptive choice of themes and the rigid patterning of reasons. By putting a hold on the communicative flux of reasons, and thereby stopping criticism, authoritative norms and values provided a framework for communicative actions that remained withdrawn from the vortex of problematization. The social integration accomplished through values, norms, and mutual understanding comes to depend entirely on actors' own communicative achievements only where norms and values are set communicatively aflow and, with a view to the *categorial* difference between acceptability and mere acceptance, are exposed to the interplay of free-floating reasons.

Under the modern conditions of complex societies, which require self-interested and hence normatively neutralized action in broad spheres, the paradoxical situation arises in which *unfettered* communicative action can neither unload nor seriously bear the burden of social integration falling to it. Using its own resources, it can control the risk of dissension built into it only by increasing the risk, that is, by making rational discourse permanent. What kind of mechanism might allow an unfettered communication to unburden itself of socially integrative achievements without compromising itself? One plausible solution to the puzzle would be to "positivize" the law hitherto based in the sacred and interwoven with conventional forms of ethical life (*Sittlichkeit*), that is, completely transform it into enacted law. In other words, a system of rules could be invented that both binds together and assigns different tasks to the two strategies for dealing with the risk of dissension found in communicative action, that is, the strategies of circumscribing communication and giving it unhindered play.

On the one hand, the state's guarantee to enforce the law offers a functional equivalent for the stabilization of behavioral expectations by spellbinding authority. Whereas archaic institutions supported by worldviews fix value orientations through rigid communication patterns, modern law allows convictions to be replaced by sanctions in that it leaves the motives for rule compliance open while enforcing observance. In both cases, destabilization resulting from disagreement is avoided in virtue of the fact that the addressees cannot call into question the validity of the norms they are supposed to follow. In the case of modern law, this "cannot" admittedly acquires a different, namely purposive-rational, sense, because the mode of validity itself is changed. Whereas facticity and validity fuse together in the kind of validity that characterizes authority-bound convictions, the two moments split apart in the validity of law: the enforced acceptance of the legal order is distinguished from the acceptability of the reasons supporting its claim to legitimacy. This binary coding refers, *on the other hand*, to the fact that the combination of positivity and legitimacy takes into account the unleashing of communication, that removal of restrictions that in principle exposes all norms and values to critical testing. Members of a legal community must be able to assume that in a free process of political opinion- and will-formation they themselves would also authorize the rules to which they are subject as addressees. To be sure, this process of legitimation must be included in the legal system. In view of the contingencies of formless, free-floating everyday communication, it is itself in need of legal institutionalization. Aside from this restriction, however, the permanent risk of contradiction is maintained in ongoing discourses and transformed into the productive force of a presumptively rational political opinion- and will-formation.

1.3.3

If one thus views modern law as a mechanism that, without revoking the principle of unhindered communication, removes tasks of social integration from actors who are already overburdened in their efforts at reaching understanding, then the two sides of law become comprehensible: its positivity and its claim to rational acceptability. Clearly, the positivity of law means that a consciously enacted framework of norms gives rise to an artificial layer of social reality that exists only so long as it is not repealed, since each of its individual components can be changed or rendered null and void. In light of this aspect of changeability, the validity of positive law appears as the sheer expression of a will that, in the face of the ever-present possibility of repeal, grants specific norms continuance until further notice. As we shall see, this voluntarism of pure enactment stirs the imagination of legal positivism. On the other hand, the positivity of law cannot be grounded solely on the contingency of arbitrary decisions without forfeiting its capacity for social integration. Law borrows its binding force, rather, from the alliance that the facticity of law forms with the claim to legitimacy. This connection reflects an interpenetration of fact-grounding acceptance with the claimed acceptability of validity claims—an interpenetration that, as a tension between facticity and validity, had already entered into communicative action and into the more or less naturally emergent social orders. This ideal tension reappears in the law. Specifically, it appears in the relation between the coercive force of law, which secures average rule acceptance, and the idea of self-legislation (or the supposition of the political autonomy of the united citizens), which first vindicates the legitimacy claim of the rules themselves, that is, makes this claim rationally acceptable.

This tension within the validity dimension of law also makes it necessary to organize political power, which is called on to enforce (and authoritatively apply) the law, into forms of legitimate law. This desideratum of transforming the power presupposed by law itself is met by the idea of the rule of law (or constitutional state, *Rechtsstaat*). Within the framework of the constitutional state, the civic practice of self-legislation assumes an institutionally differentiated form. The idea of the rule of law sets in motion a spiraling self-application of law, which is supposed to bring the internally unavoidable supposition of political autonomy to bear against the facticity of legally uncontrolled social power that penetrates law *from the outside*. The development of the constitutional state can be understood as an open sequence of experience-guided precautionary measures against the overpowering of the legal system by illegitimate power relations that contradict its normative self-understanding. From inside the legal system, this appears as an *external* relation between facticity and validity, the familiar tension between norm and reality that again and again provokes a normative response.

Modern societies are integrated not only socially through values, norms, and mutual understanding, but also systemically through markets and the administrative use of power. Money and administrative power are systemic mechanisms of societal integration that do not necessarily coordinate actions via the intentions of participants, but objectively, "behind the backs" of participants. Since Adam Smith, the classic example for this type of regulation is the market's "invisible hand." Both media of systemic integration, money and power, are anchored via legal institutionalization in orders of the lifeworld, which is in turn socially integrated through communicative action. In this way, modern law is linked with all three resources of integration. Through a practice of self-determination that requires citizens to make public use of their communicative freedoms, the law draws its socially integrating force from the sources of social solidarity. On the other hand, institutions of private and public law make possible the establishment of markets and governmental bodies, because the economic and the administrative system, which have separated from the lifeworld, operate inside the forms of law.

Because law is just as intermeshed with money and administrative power as it is with solidarity, its own integrating achievements assimilate imperatives of diverse origin. This does not mean that legal norms come with labels telling us *how* these imperatives are to be balanced. In the different subject areas of law, we can certainly see that the needs for regulation, to which politics and lawmaking respond, have different sources. But in the functional imperatives of the state apparatus, the economic system, and other social subsystems, normatively unfiltered interest positions often carry the day only because they are stronger and use the legitimating force of legal forms to cloak their merely factual strength. Therefore, as a means for organizing state activities related to the functional imperatives of a differentiated economic society, modern law remains a profoundly ambiguous medium of societal integration. Often enough, law provides illegitimate power with the mere semblance of legitimacy. At first glance, one cannot tell whether legal regulations deserve the assent of associated citizens or whether they result from administrative self-programming and structural social power in such a way that they independently generate the necessary mass loyalty.

The less the legal system as a whole can rely on metasocial guarantees and immunize itself against criticism, the less scope there is for this type of self-legitimation of law. Indeed, a law responsible for the brunt of social integration in modern societies comes under the *secular* pressure of the functional imperatives of social reproduction; however, it is simultaneously subject to what we might call the *idealistic* pressure to legitimate any regulations. Even the systemic integration achieved through money and power *ought*, in accordance with the constitutional self-understanding of the legal community, to remain dependent on the socially integrative process of civic self-determination. The tension between the idealism of constitutional law and the materialism of a legal order, especially a commercial law that reflects only the unequal distribution of social power, finds its echo in the drifting apart of philosophical and empirical approaches to law. Before I come back to the facticity-validity tension internal to law, I would like to go into the external relation between social facticity and the normative self-understanding of modern law. Specifically, I will treat this relation as it is reflected in the sociological discourses on law and the philosophical discourses on justice.

2

The Sociology of Law versus the Philosophy of Justice

Through communicative action the rationality potential of language for functions of social integration is tapped, mobilized, and unleashed in the course of social evolution. Modern law steps in to fill the functional gaps in social orders whose integrative capacities are overtaxed. The tension between validity and facticity, already built into informal everyday practice in virtue of the ideal content of the pragmatic presuppositions of communicative action, becomes more acute in the validity dimension of modern law. The ideas of a conscious organization and self-organization of the legal community—initially framed in the language of modern natural law—express an awareness of the ideal content of legal validity. To the extent that this awareness develops and the ideal content of law clashes with functional imperatives of the market economy and bureaucratic administration, the normative self-understanding of law provokes an empirical critique. On the one hand, the law must uphold the strong claim that not even the systems steered by money and administrative power may withdraw entirely from a more or less consciously achieved social integration. On the other hand, precisely this claim seems to fall victim to the sociological disenchantment of law. How society deals with this contradiction is a theme that has long occupied critical approaches to ideology and power. Thus the line of legal criticism that confronts claim and reality must be examined here.[1] I will pursue such criticism to the point where it opens onto the more radical objection that law, peripheral now in any case, must gradually drop even the semblance of normativity if it is still to fulfill its function in the face of growing societal complexity. If this objection were true, it would pull the rug out from under a discourse theory that takes its cue from the normative self-understanding of law; in that case, such an approach would have lost contact from the start with a reality grown cynical. In contrast to sociological skepticism about law, philosophical theories of justice resolutely work out the moral content of modern legal orders. These rational constructions of law serve to justify principles according to which a well-ordered society should be set up. In the process, however, they lose touch with the reality of contemporary societies and thus have difficulties in identifying the conditions necessary for the realization of these principles.

I begin by pursuing one line of the sociological discussions, systems theory, in order to examine the advantages and disadvantages of an objectivistic disenchantment of law (section 2.1). I then refer to John Rawls's theory of justice as an example of the complementary difficulties that confront a philosophical discourse of justice carried out in a purely normative fashion (section 2.2). Finally, following Max Weber and Talcott Parsons, I develop the dual perspective that should allow us to do two things at once: take the legal system seriously by internally reconstructing its normative content, and describe it externally as a component of social reality (section 2.3).

2.1 The Sociological Disenchantment of Law

The significance of the category of law in the analysis of state and society has fluctuated through the last three centuries with the ebb and flow of scientific trends. It represented a key category in modern natural law from Hobbes to Hegel, supposedly mediating all other social relationships. Legal motifs seemed to provide an adequate model for the legitimacy of a well-ordered society. The good society was presented as one erected on the blueprint of a rational law. The social doctrine of the Scottish moral philosophers, however, already cast doubt on the rationalism of natural-law theories, pointing out that established practices, customs, and institutions resisted the conceptions of formal law. Adam Ferguson and John Millar, still standing between classical politics and contemporary political economy, were just beginning the move from Aristotle to Marx.[2] As empiricists, they opposed the *prescriptivism* of a rational law whose normative arguments disregarded historical particularity and sociocultural facts. As early sociologists and anthropologists, they opposed a *rationalism* that would neatly resolve the informal fabric of received social relations, established institutions, deeply anchored interest positions, and class structures in a deliberately constructed system of rules.

To be sure, the model of the social contract found support in the evidence that modern exchange society seemed to secure something like a natural autonomy and equality for private persons through their participation in market transactions. With its spontaneous tendency to guarantee freedom, the only thing bourgeois economic society (or civil society, *bürgerlichen Gesellschaft*) still seemed to lack was establishment in formal legal terms. True, this intuition was explicated only in the liberal versions found in John Locke through Immanuel Kant and Thomas Paine.[3] But in all social-contract theories, the intention of constructing basic institutions along the lines of rational natural law amounted to the view that society as a whole could be understood as the intentional complex of a free association of originally autonomous and equal members.[4] This improbable idea gained a certain plausibility only because modern market societies initially appeared as a natural basis on which parties encounter one another as inherently free and equal. Why "inherently"? Under the egalitarian conditions of an equilibrated, small-scale, commodity economy (as Marx will call it), commodity owners—who were imagined as male heads of household—already seemed *virtually* to occupy the position of privately autonomous subjects of law, prior to all intentionally produced political association. Certainly this background was less important in those authors who characterized the state of nature not in terms of economic relations but of power. Still, Hobbesian constructions of the state of nature were at least equivalent to the supposition that bourgeois society functioned, prior to all legal regulation, as the source of political association. It could serve this function because competitive economic relations already require subjects who conclude contracts and to this extent make law.

Whether it was explicitly developed or tacitly assumed, this premise explains why the economic analysis coming out of Scottish moral philosophy cast lasting doubts on the tradition of rational natural law. With Adam Smith and David Ricardo, a political economy developed that conceived bourgeois civil society as a sphere of commodity exchange and social labor governed by anonymous economic laws. Writing in the wake of political economy, Hegel called this civil society a "system of needs" in which individuals were robbed of all real freedom. Finally, as a critic of political economy, Marx saw in the anatomy of civil society nothing but structures in which the self-valorization of capital proceeded over the heads of alienated individuals in order to bring forth ever more drastic forms of social inequality. The concept of civil society thus underwent a transformation. Having begun as an ensemble of *authorizing* conditions that made freedom possible—conditions under which individuals could voluntarily and consciously join in association and bring the social process under their common control—it became an *anonymous* system independent of the intentions of unconsciously sociated individuals, a system that followed its own logic and subjected society as a whole to the economically decoded imperatives of its self-stabilization.

With this change in perspective effected by both political economy and the critique of political economy, the category of law lost its central role in theoretical analysis. The reproduction of social life was not only far too complex to be comprehended in the meager normative motifs of natural law. The mechanisms of social integration were also, it now seemed, of an entirely different kind, namely, a non-normative one. Comprehending the anatomy of bourgeois society in terms of political economy had an unmasking effect: relations not of law but of production formed the skeletal framework holding the social organism together. Before long the medical image was displaced by the venerable metaphors of construction and architecture: law belonged to the political "superstructure" resting on the economic basis of a society in which the rule of one social class over other classes was exercised in the nonpolitical form of the private disposition over the means of production. The recursive process of the production and reproduction of exchange values thoroughly penetrated the social integration effected by modern law—and reduced this law to an epiphenomenon. With this, the market mechanism that was discovered and analyzed by political economy also took the lead in social theory. The realistic model of an anonymous, unintentional sociation taking place behind the actors' backs replaced the idealistic model of an association that legal subjects intentionally bring about and continuously sustain.

Marx, however, still held to a classical concept whose influence extends from Aristotle to Hegel, that of society as totality. He simply took the apex and center of the social whole, into which individuals are incorporated as parts, and turned them right side up. The manifest unity of a legally constituted political order was replaced by the systemically produced, latent unity of capital's self-valorization. As a negative totality, the latter was still related to its opposite, the preserved classical image of a consciously produced totality. After thinkers from Vico to Condorcet shifted the teleology of nature into the dimension of history,[5] society could be conceived as a developing self-referential totality that realizes its telos of intentional association only in the course of the historical process. Specifically, it realizes its essence in the *future* association of producers who, freed of the commodity fetish, will have brought the conditions of the material life process under their common control.

Other objections aside, this precarious construction could withstand neither the critique leveled against its teleological background assumptions nor the doubts cast on the holistic concept of society. However, the strictly objectivating approach favored by Marx, which examines mechanisms of integration from an external perspective, has successfully worked its way into various theoretical traditions. From this perspective, the image of social integration occurring through values, norms, communication, and even law disintegrates into mere illusion. Once the last hopes of the philosophy of history disappeared from Marxist functionalism, society left behind the dynamics of history and, gripped by the repetition compulsions of a self-accelerating and all-pervasive process of accumulation, became a frozen world of reified social relations.[6] This brand of systems theory owes its *melancholic* sense to the fact that it still secretly refers to a totality, now negatively construed as a matrix of sheer compulsion.[7] As soon as the insight into the inevitable differentiation and growing complexity of society prohibits even this inverted reference to the abstract whole of an over-inflated instrumental reason, systems theory *becomes affirmative*, thus losing its critical sting. In the process it breaks away from the philosophical fixation on a single mechanism of integration through the exchange of economic equivalents.

By conceiving a functionally differentiated society as dispersed into multiple systems and decentered, systems functionalism can even outdo the realism of the Marxian model; the systems approach self-referentially subsumes the sociological observer, who views himself and his science as just one subsystem among others. In this polycentrically fragmented society without base or apex, the many recursively closed, boundary-maintaining subsystems form environments for one another. They meet at a horizontal level, so to speak, and stabilize one another by observing one another and, lacking the possibility of direct intervention, by reflexively adjusting to their mutual environments. The transcendental capacities of the monadic Husserlian ego pass over to systems that, though stripped of the subjectivity of transcendental consciousness, remain monadically encapsulated in themselves.

Niklas Luhmann takes his place among the systems-theoretic successors to transcendental phenomenology and thereby transposes the philosophy of the subject into a radical objectivism. In a different way, the structuralist social theories from Claude Lévi-Strauss to Louis Althusser and Michel Foucault take a similar step. In both cases, subjects who constitute their own worlds or, at a higher level, intersubjectively share common lifeworlds, drop out; consequently, all intentional integrating achievements disappear from view. This wipes out all the hermeneutical tracks that point the way into society for an action theory starting with the actors' own self-understanding. By radicalizing Marxian systems analysis this way, the new type of objectivistic social theories avoid the narrowness and the normative ballast associated with the holistic concepts of a philosophy of history. An unobstructed view is opened up for the wide range of variation, contingency, and diversity in highly complex societies.

Investigations into the sociology of law have likewise profited from the new paradigm. The legal system, or the structures underlying it, regain some of the autonomy they lost in the critique of ideological superstructures. Law is no longer considered merely an epiphenomenon but is given back its own inner logic. To be sure, in a wholly decentered society it occupies a merely peripheral position, forming one system or discourse in a disordered manifold of systems and discourses. The relevant phenomena, legally structured or steered communications, are described in a language that objectivistically disregards actors' self-understanding. This language neither seeks nor gains an entry into the intuitive knowledge of participants. Under the artificially defamiliarizing gaze of the system observer who conceives himself as a system in an environment, or that of the ethnologist who approaches even his own native practices and language games as an uninitiated stranger, every context of social life crystallizes into a hermeneutically inaccessible second nature, about which counterintuitive knowledge is gathered as it is in the natural sciences.

If one follows the path from the eighteenth-century controversies between natural-law rationalism and empiricist social theories up to present-day structuralism and systems theory, it seems that sociological reflection has irreversibly undermined more than just the prescriptivist and rationalist presuppositions of social-contract theory. It seems to devalue law in general as a central category of social theory. Luhmann's sociology of law has currently gone the farthest along this axis.[8] Here his view interests me merely as the most rigorous version of a theory that assigns law a marginal position (as compared with its place in classical social theories) and neutralizes the phenomenon of legal validity by describing things objectivistically.

Luhmann conceives law only from the functionalist viewpoint of stabilizing behavioral expectations. In functionally differentiated societies, law has the special task of generalizing behavioral expectations in the temporal, social, and substantive dimensions in a congruent manner, such that contingently arising conflicts can be decided in a binding manner according to the binary code of legal/illegal. The legal system as a whole encompasses every communication that is oriented by law. In a narrower sense, it embraces in particular those legal acts that change the legal situation in accordance with institutionalized legal procedures, legal norms, and doctrinal interpretations. These rather conventional sociological determinations acquire a more specific meaning if one assumes that the evolution of law can be understood as a process in which positivized law finally gains independence as an autopoietic system. As so described, the legal system is a recursively closed circuit of communication that self-referentially delimits itself from its environment, with which it has contact only through observations. "Autopoiesis" means that the system describes its own components in legal categories and employs these self-thematizations for the purposes of constituting and reproducing legal acts by its own means. The legal system becomes autonomous to the extent that its components are linked together in such a way "that norms and legal acts reciprocally produce each other, and that procedures and jurisprudence bring these relations themselves into relation."[9]

This particular conception of law implies, to begin with, that the legal system, as a monad at once closed and open, is uncoupled from all the other action systems. Once it has become autonomous, the legal system can no longer sustain any *direct* exchange with its intrasocietal environments, nor can it have a regulatory effect on these. Because the system always constructs its own environments, contact through observation with events beyond the system boundaries can only provide *occasions* for the autopoietically closed legal system to act on itself. Macrosocial steering functions are denied it. The law can "regulate" society in a metaphorical sense at best: by altering itself, it presents itself to other systems as an altered environment to which these in turn can "react" in the same indirect fashion. I will come back to this shortly.

The second consequence of interest here is that the last remaining traces of a normative self-understanding of the legal system left behind from classical social theory are obliterated. As soon as one reinterprets normative expectations à la learning theory as counterfactual cognitive expectations, one erases the deontological dimension of normative validity and thus the illocutionary sense of ought-statements and their normative backing. Picking up on this idea, Luhmann explains normative expectations in terms of an immunization against learning: "Here psychologists [think] only of behavior that, unwilling to learn, just persists of its own accord. They do not think of behavior that chooses the same strategy while relying on the prevailing morality, institutions, or law. This sheds light on the fact that nonlearning first loses its pathological character in social norms."[10] The difference between "is" and "ought," between truth and normative validity, is reduced to two possible ways of reacting—learning and nonlearning—which represent alternatives *only* in the area of *cognitive* expectations. Cognitive expectations are then considered "normative" if one is not willing to revise them in the event of their disappointment. By setting up its basic concepts this way, functionalist sociology blinds itself to the meaning of the complex mode of validity found in law.

Only this empiricist reinterpretation of the normative aspects of law makes it plausible to assume that the legal system is detached from all *internal* relations to morality and politics. This approach, moreover, prejudices the analysis in such a way that "law" is reduced to the special function of the administration of law. One thereby loses sight of the internal connection between law and the constitutional organization of the origin, acquisition, and use of political power.

In sum, the decisive move is the objectivation of law into an autopoietic system. Described in this way, legal communication is robbed of its *socially integrative* meaning. Legal norms and legal acts thereby lose all connection with the supposition of rationally motivated processes of reaching understanding within an association of legal consociates. By describing the conflict-resolving capacity of law as a purely *systemic* capacity, social integration through law is assimilated to the model of an objective, unintentional coordination. Even the validity claims and reasons put forth in legal discourses thereby forfeit their intrinsic value. As so described, the meaning of legal arguments is exhausted by their function of reducing the surprise value of court decisions (which find their motivation elsewhere) and increasing the actual acceptance of such decisions by clients. What counts for participants as "justification" shrinks, from the viewpoint of the sociological observer, to necessary fictions: "Because reasons are hard to replace as guarantors for complex legal decisions, it *appears* to lawyers as if reasons justify the decision and not decisions the reasons."[11] In systems theory, legal argumentation—which we will see plays a central role in a discourse theory of law—boils down to those special communications in which conflicting opinions are settled by apportioning the code values legal/illegal through the exchange of reasons. Naturally, what counts from a functionalist point of view are only the perlocutionary effects that can be achieved with reasons: they are the means by which the legal system convinces itself of its own decisions. If, however, reasons no longer command a force intrinsic to rational motivation—if, as Luhmann formulates it, reasons cannot be justified—then the high-priced culture of argumentation developed in the legal system becomes a mystery. One would have to explain why "one needs reasons that are not reasons at all."[12]

At the end of a long process of sociological disillusionment, systems theory has cleared away the last remains of the normativism found in modern natural law. Having withdrawn into an autopoietic system, law stands before the defamiliarizing sociological gaze and is stripped of all normative connotations, which in the final analysis refer to the self-organization of a legal community. Described as an autopoietic system, a narcissistically marginalized law can react only to its own problems, problems that are at most externally occasioned or induced. Hence law can neither perceive nor deal with problems that burden society *as a whole*. At the same time, in accordance with its autopoietic constitution, it must finance all its achievements from resources it produces itself. Law can derive its validity only in a positivistic sense, from the actual existence of law. As Luhmann illustrates with court procedures, it has dropped any further-reaching claim to legitimation. There is no output the legal system could deliver in the form of regulations: interventions in the environment are denied it. Nor is there any input the legal system could receive in the form of legitimation: even the political process, the public sphere, and political culture present environments whose language the legal system cannot understand. Law supplies its environments with the "noise" that can at most induce variations in the internal orders of those systems for which the law in turn represents an environment.

However, this assumed *mutual indifference* between law and other social subsystems does not correspond with empirically observed interdependencies. This is the case even if the impressive results of implementation research lead one to be generally skeptical of the behavior-steering effects of legal interventions.[13] I cannot go into the critique and the avoidance maneuvers in detail here.[14] However, I will note a conclusion that Gunther Teubner draws from the fragmentation of society. He shares Luhmann's view of society as a multiplicity of autonomous subsystems that, conducting their own separate discourses, must get by in each case with their own mutually incompatible constructions of reality. At both the theoretical and the empirical level, legal constructivism faces the problem of what the self-referential closure of the legal system implies for the possibilities of communication with other "epistemic worlds": "Is there something like an epistemic minimum in modern society, i.e., something that serves as a common denominator for social discourses despite all autonomization? Does one find covariation or even coevolutionary trends among autonomous social epistemes? Or can the connection only be established in such a way that one episteme is reconstructed inside the framework of another episteme?"[15] Teubner addresses this question from two sides. On the one side, he examines the receptive processing of alien economic, technical, psychiatric, and scientific "knowledge of facts." This knowledge must be translated into the legal code and reconstructed there without the legal system itself being able to assume "full epistemic authority" for the reliability of the foreign knowledge thus incorporated. On the other side, he addresses the question as it bears on the legal "influencing" of other social spheres, however indirect it may be. For both sides of communication, he considers it necessary to posit a medium of "general social communication." With regard to the regulatory "influence" on foreign subsystems, discourses, epistemes, and the like, he uses the term "interference" between law and society (which he distinguishes from "coevolution" and "interpenetration"), thereby opening autopoietic law for real contacts with the economy, politics, education, family, and so on, that go beyond mere "occasions." Because such subsystems come into contact with one another through the *same* (i.e., identical, *dasselbe*) communicative event, actions that have different system references should be able to "intersect" in the same act of communication.

Thus the legal act connected with a rental agreement, for example, "intersects" with an economic transaction and with processes in the participants' lifeworld: "Through the system interference between law, lifeworld, and economy, subsystems can do more than observe one another or regulate merely themselves."[16] They can communicate with one another, for "all forms of specialized communication . . . are always at the same time—literally *uno actu*— forms of general social communication as well."[17] For systems theory the expression "lifeworld" has a dissonant ring, which reveals that Teubner must assume a shared medium of communication operative throughout society and underlying the special codes of the subsystems: "Social subsystems use the flow of [general] social communication, and extract from it special communications as new elements."[18] In addition, the interferences attached to individual acts of communication can structurally solidify into the role interferences of multiple memberships.

I do not think that this proposal is consistent with the architectonic of systems theory. On the one hand, legal discourse is supposed to be trapped in its self-reproduction, constructing only its own internal image of the external world; on the other hand, it is supposed to use "general social communication" so that it can "influence" general social constructions of reality, and in this way influence those of other discursive worlds as well. It is difficult to reconcile these two statements. If the first statement is correct, then one and the same act of communication can belong to two or more different discourses, but the identity of the corresponding utterances in these discourses would be recognizable only from an objective standpoint, and not from the perspectives of the involved discourses. Otherwise one must postulate the possibility of a translation between them—a hermeneutic relation that would explode the closure of each of the mutually impenetrable circuits of communication. This interpretation finds support in an odd formulation:

Any legal act is at the same time—*uno actu*—an event of general social communication. One and the *same* [i.e., similar, *gleiche*] communicative event is linked to two different social discourses—specialized (and institutionalized) legal discourse and diffuse general communication. Interference between law and other social discourses does not mean that they merge into a multi-dimensional superdiscourse, nor does it imply that information is "exchanged" between them. Rather, information is constituted anew within each discourse, and interference adds nothing to the whole process besides the *simultaneity* [*Gleichzeitigkeit*] of two communicative events.[19]

Now, "simultaneity" alone cannot guarantee the "identity" of an utterance that has different meanings depending on the reference language. The identity of the sign-event would have to be perceived once more (in spite of its different meanings) and fixed from the viewpoint of some observer. However, because the presuppositions of systems theory no more permit an observer of this sort than they allow for a general social subject at the center of society as a whole, a communicative event must be identifiable as *the same* (*dasselbe*) from at least one of the discourses. This problematic achievement can be ascribed at best to the medium of the general communication circulating throughout society. In that case, however, this medium would have to function as a natural language that makes translations possible from these "foreign languages" that have solidified into special codes. It would also have to mediate an exchange of information between codes, something that could not occur between them directly. How else could self-referentially closed discourses be submitted to the "test of social coherence" "in ongoing social communication"? However, should Teubner wish to render his second statement plausible this way, he would have to postulate a circuit of communication for society as a whole. Although this circuit would not achieve the level of autopoietic closedness, it would nevertheless function as an interpreter for special discourses by extracting bits of information from them and passing these along.

Empirical evidence forces Teubner to assume things that wreck the theoretical architectonic he desires. In a completely decentered society, no place remains for an encompassing social communication by which society could thematize and affect itself as a whole; for systems theory, society has centrifugally broken up into subsystems, each of which can communicate only in its own language with itself. In place of the lost center of society, Teubner substitutes the "lifeworld." This constitutes itself through an ordinary language that, circulating through all spheres of society, has a reflexive structure of the kind that enables translations from all the codes. If the "mutual interference of systems" is to make "it possible not only for them to observe each other but for there to be real communicative contact between the system and the 'lifeworld,'"[20] then a *general* communication medium must exist below the threshold of functionally specified codes. To all appearances, this medium is the spitting image of ordinary language. It allows the steering media of money or power to separate out but cannot itself be conceived as a systemic mechanism. This proposal, however, does not square well with the conceptualization of law as an autopoietic system. It points rather in the direction of a theory of communicative action, which distinguishes a "lifeworld" bound to the medium of ordinary language from "systems" steered through special codes yet adaptively open to the environment.

This conception does not commit the mistake of considering the codes of closed specialized discourses to be *superior in every respect* to unspecialized ordinary language when it comes to problem solving. Like that other anthropological monopoly, the hand, ordinary language—with its grammatical complexity, propositional structure, and reflexivity—possesses the merit of multifunctionality. With its practically unlimited capacity for interpretation and range of circulation, it is superior to special codes in that it provides a sounding board for the external costs of differentiated subsystems and thus remains sensitive to problems affecting the whole of society. The ways of defining and processing problems in ordinary language remain more diffuse, are less differentiated, and are less clearly operationalized than under the code-specific, unidimensional, and one-sided aspects of cost/benefit, command/obedience, and so on. In return, however, ordinary language is not tied down to just a single code but is inherently multilingual. It does not need to pay the price of specialization, namely, deafness to problems formulated in a foreign language.

If one takes this into consideration, then the functional specifications of the lifeworld proceed in such a way that, briefly stated, its components—culture, society, personality structures—differentiate themselves only *within the boundaries* of a multifunctional language but remain *intertwined* with one another through this medium. This is to be distinguished from the system-building differentiation that proceeds via the introduction of special codes: through such functional differentiation, such subsystems as the money-steered economy and a power-steered administration develop out of, and only out of, the "society" component of the lifeworld.[21] Under these premises, law then functions as a hinge between system and lifeworld, a function that is incompatible with the idea that the legal system, withdrawing into its own shell, autopoietically encapsulates itself. What Teubner describes as an "interference capacity" results from the law's peculiar dual position and mediating function between, on the one hand, a lifeworld reproduced through communicative action and, on the other, code-specific subsystems that form environments for one another. The circuit of lifeworld communication is interrupted at the points where it runs into the media of money and administrative power, which are deaf to messages in ordinary language; for these special codes not only have been differentiated from a more richly structured ordinary language but have been separated off from it as well. True, ordinary language forms a universal horizon of understanding, and it can in principle translate everything *from* all languages. But it cannot in return operationalize its messages in a manner that is effective for all types of addressees. For translations *into* special codes, it remains dependent on the law that communicates with the steering media of money and administrative power. Normatively substantive messages can circulate *throughout society* only in the language of law. Without their translation into the complex legal code that is equally open to lifeworld and system, these messages would fall on deaf ears in media-steered spheres of action.[22] Law thus functions as the "transformer" that first guarantees that the socially integrating network of communication stretched across society as a whole holds together.

2.2 The Return of Modern Natural Law and the "Impotence of the Ought"

The sociological undermining of the normativism of modern natural-law theories has set off a surprising reaction since the early seventies. That is, in the course of a general rehabilitation of issues in practical philosophy, the philosophy of law took a turn that once again made the social-contract tradition of rational natural law respectable, albeit in a rather unmediated way. Since John Rawls's *Theory of Justice* (1971), the pendulum has been swinging in this other direction. Not only among philosophers and legal theorists, but among economists as well, a discourse has gotten under way that unabashedly picks up on theories of the seventeenth and eighteenth centuries, as though one could ignore the disenchantment of law in social science. Lacking metacritical references to the change in perspective brought about by political economy and social theory, the direct resumption of natural-law argumentation has torn down the bridges between the two universes of discourse. In the meantime, however, questions concerning the "impotence of the ought" have again become urgent in the normative discourse. Such questions once motivated Hegel to study Adam Smith and David Ricardo in order to assure himself that the conflict-ridden market society could be conceived as a moment in the actuality of the ethical Idea.[23] In light of this, John Rawls's interest in the conditions for the political acceptance of his theory of justice, a theory first developed in vacuo, likewise appears as the return of a repressed problem. At stake is the old problem of how the rational project of a just society, in abstract contrast to an obtuse reality, can be realized after confidence in the dialectic of reason and revolution, played out by Hegel and Marx as a philosophy of history, has been exhausted—and only the reformist path of trial and error remains both practically available and morally reasonable.[24]

In his *Theory of Justice*, Rawls developed the idea of a "well-ordered" society under the conditions of modern life. This is a system that makes possible the just cooperation of free and equal citizens. The basic institutions of such a society must be set up according to a scheme that *deserves* the rationally motivated assent of all citizens because it can be grounded in justice as fairness. In grounding the two highest principles of justice, Rawls follows the social-contract model. He proposes a procedure that can be understood as explicating the point of view for an impartial judgment of morally substantive questions of political justice. In the "original position," the parties involved in the process of justification are subject to precisely those restrictions (including, inter alia, equality, independence, and ignorance of one's own position in a future society) that guarantee that all arrangements grounded in purposive-rational considerations are at the same time in the interest of all parties, and hence can be accepted as right or just in the normative sense.[25]

At this *first stage* of the normative justification of his model of the well-ordered society—whose features are "liberal" according to Anglo-American usage and "social democratic" from a European viewpoint—Rawls already attends to the problem of self-stabilization. In section 86 of *A Theory of Justice*, he takes pains to demonstrate the "congruence of the right and the good." The parties that agree (*einigen*) in the original position on reasonable principles are artificial entities, that is, constructs; they must not be identified with flesh-and-blood citizens who would live under the real conditions of a society erected on principles of justice. They also are not identical with the reasonable citizens presupposed in the theory, whom one also expects to act morally and thus to subordinate their personal interests to the obligations of a loyal citizen. The sense of justice may ground the desire to act justly, but this is not an automatically effective motivation like, for example, the desire to avoid pain. For this reason, Rawls relies on a "thin theory of the good" to show that just institutions would create circumstances under which it would lie in each one's well-considered interest to pursue one's own freely chosen life plans under the same conditions that also allow other persons to pursue their life plans. In a well-ordered society, it would also always be good for me to satisfy the requirements of justice. Or in Hegel's words, the individual's morality (*Moralität*) would find its ethical (*sittliche*) context in the institutions of a just society. The self-stabilization of a well-ordered society is therefore based not on the coercive force of law but on the socializing force of a life under just institutions, for such a life simultaneously develops and reinforces the citizens' dispositions to justice.

Of course, all this holds only on the assumption that just institutions already exist. It is another question how these can be *established* or at least promoted in present circumstances. For a philosophical theory of justice, this question does not pose itself from a pragmatic point of view. Rather, it first arises in reflection on the political-cultural conditions of the value pluralism under which the theory of justice should meet with a favorable response in the contemporary public of citizens. At this *second stage* of argumentation, we are not dealing with the problem of applying a theory presupposed as valid. We face rather the question of how the normative concept of a well-ordered society can be situated in the context of an existing political culture and public sphere in such a way that it will in fact meet with approval on the part of citizens willing to reach an understanding. In this context, the concept of "reflective equilibrium" assumes an ambiguous role, one Rawls himself has not sufficiently differentiated.

The term "reflective equilibrium" designates a method that is already supposed to work at the stage of theory construction. There it refers to the procedure characteristic of reconstructive theories in general: one draws on a sample of exemplary expressions with the purpose of explicating the intuitive knowledge that subjects use to generate these expressions. The procedure of rational reconstruction assumes a different role at the second stage, where the theory of justice refers reflexively to the context in which it should be embedded. Here the point is to explain how and why its theoretical propositions merely articulate the normative substance of the most trustworthy intuitions of our everyday political practice, as well as the substance of the best traditions of our political culture. By demonstrating that the principles of justice reflect only the most reasonable convictions actually held by the population, the theory of justice is supposed to find its "seat" in political life: "The aim of political philosophy, when it presents itself in the public culture of a democratic society, is to articulate and to make explicit those shared notions and principles thought to be already latent in common sense; or, as is often the case, if common sense is hesitant and uncertain, to propose to it certain conceptions and principles congenial to its most essential convictions and historical traditions."[26] In the course of the seventies, Rawls weakened the strong universalist claim to justification for his theory of justice. This has somewhat blurred the different meanings of his appeal to our best normative intuitions: on the one hand, in the context of the theory's *justification* before philosophical experts and, on the other hand, in the context of the public defense of, and the political *advocacy* for, the theory before citizens of an actual community. The more Rawls believes he should base the theory of justice on the public support for culturally molded intuitions that none "of us" can reasonably reject, the less clear is the boundary separating the task of philosophically justifying principles of justice, on the one hand, from a particular community's enterprise of reaching a political self-understanding about the normative basis of its common life, on the other. In the latter process, which would have to occur in the political forum of a given democratic society, the philosopher's proposed explications can have at most a catalyzing or clarifying function.

A second concept relevant in this context, that of the "overlapping consensus," was initially afflicted with a similar ambiguity. Later, however, Rawls recognized he had to separate the first stage of philosophical justification more clearly from the second stage, which has to do with the issue of acceptance: "In the second stage the idea of an overlapping consensus is introduced to explain how, given the plurality of conflicting comprehensive religious, philosophical, and moral doctrines always found in a democratic society ... free institutions may gain the allegiance needed to endure over time."[27] Admittedly, this text also provides support for competing interpretations. One is not quite sure whether Rawls only intends to deal at a deeper level with a question already treated in the *Theory of Justice*, that is, how a just society can stabilize itself in view of the de facto pluralism of worldviews. Or is the concept of "overlapping consensus" intended rather to answer the question of how one can, in the present circumstances of a democratic society, see to it that the theory finds the measure of well-considered acceptance necessary for a reformist improvement of existing institutions in light of the theory? In the following, I assume the second reading.

In a pluralistic society, the theory of justice can expect to be accepted by citizens only if it limits itself to a conception that is postmetaphysical in the strict sense, that is, only if it avoids taking sides in the contest of competing forms of life and worldviews. In many theoretical questions, and all the more so in practical questions, the public use of reason does not lead to a rationally motivated agreement (*Einverständnis*). The grounds for this lie in the "burdens of reason," burdens that the ideal character of claims to reason impose on finite minds. This is true even for scientific discourses. In practical discourses there is the added factor that questions of the good life, even under ideal conditions, can find reasonable answers only within the horizon of a life project already presupposed as valid. Now, a theory of justice tailored to modern living conditions must reckon with a variety of equally entitled, coexisting forms of life and life plans; from the perspective of different traditions and life histories, disagreement over these is reasonable.[28] As a result, the theory of justice must limit itself to the narrow circle of political-moral questions of principle for which an "overlapping consensus" may reasonably be expected, for these are precisely the questions that concern values included in each of the competing comprehensive doctrines. What one seeks are principles or norms that incorporate generalizable interests.

According to what Rawls has in mind, a postmetaphysical theory of justice that rests on a weak, that is, merely formally defined, concept of the good represents a set of intersecting normative statements. In this set the more comprehensive but context-dependent interpretations of self and world—be they ethical or even religious and metaphysical—"overlap." These competing worldviews must acknowledge the conditions of postmetaphysical thinking at least to the extent that they give themselves over without reservation to public argumentative exchange:

The hope is that, by this method of avoidance, as we might call it, existing differences between contending political views can at least be moderated, even if not entirely removed, so that social cooperation on the basis of mutual respect can be maintained. Or if this is expecting too much, this method may enable us to conceive how, given a desire for free and uncoerced agreement, a public understanding could arise consistent with the historical conditions and constraints of our social world.[29]

It is not entirely clear what Rawls has actually gained with these reflections—and what he has not. He has certainly shown that a normative theory of justice of the sort he proposes can gain entry to a culture in which basic liberal convictions are already rooted through tradition and political socialization in everyday practices and in the intuitions of individual citizens. Rawls not only believes that a milieu with this character can be found today in the pluralist culture of the United States; he also realizes that this pluralism would have to develop and even intensify if the postulated principles of justice assumed a concrete shape in the basic institutions of society. In my view, however, the correspondence between the postmetaphysical theory of justice and the American context in which it arose does not mean that Rawls is "simply trying to systematize the principles and intuitions typical of American liberals."[30] Richard Rorty attributes to Rawls "a thoroughly historicist and antiuniversalistic" attitude.[31] According to Rorty, Rawls has in no way provided a procedural explanation of the impartial judgment of moral-political questions but rather "a historical-sociological description" of the intuitions of justice prevalent in the American population today.

Rorty's contextualistic appropriation of Rawls is not plausible, because such a modest goal would not explain the considerable effort of justification that Rawls has invested in his theory of justice. Rorty collapses the two stages of argument distinguished by Rawls. Moreover, he misses the reconstructive meaning that reflective equilibrium has in the context of justification, mistaking it for an attempt to achieve an existential or ethical self-understanding. The theory of justice could prove suitable for this task, too, once it is able to shed light on its own context of emergence. But if the theory were set up *from the start* as this kind of ethical-existential self-reflection, if it were intended to articulate only *specific* political traditions reflecting the self-image of liberals who have grown up in them, then there would be no need to take a further step beyond the business of theoretical justification—namely, the step in which a reflection on the "fact of pluralism" assures the theory of the necessary conditions for its own acceptability. On Rorty's contextualist reading, Rawls would have avoided the contractarian's chasm between normative theory and reformist practice from the very beginning, albeit at the price of taking back the universalist claim to validity. Then he would have to admit that the two principles of justice do not claim to be valid for, say, Germans, because formative equivalents to the American constitutional tradition cannot be found in German culture and history.[32] I see no indication of such an admission. The lack of an accommodating political culture (which now exists in the Federal Republic of Germany as well) must not be taken to falsify principles of justice that are valid according to the well-considered judgment of parties in the original position. Everyone, even those not among Jefferson's fortunate heirs, should be able to recapitulate this impartial judgment. The presuppositions under which these parties make their agreements elucidate a moral point of view that does not accrue to the privilege of a particular culture but goes deeper, in fact is ultimately anchored in the symmetries of the mutual recognition of communicatively acting subjects in general.

Of course, these abstract conditions that make impartial *judgment* of practical questions possible do not coincide with the conditions under which we are disposed to *act* on moral insight. This leads Rawls to seek out the motivational thrust of an accommodating political culture, which he finds at the privileged site of a continuous constitutional tradition that stretches back over two hundred years. Though certainly challenged again and again by conflicts of class and race, this tradition has constantly been renewed and revitalized by new interpretations. If one takes this relation to tradition literally, though, the theory's *politically* convincing force is limited to a few responsive contexts.

This consequence leads Ronald Dworkin to look for a less contingent way of embedding normative theories. On no account does he want the effectiveness of liberal principles to depend on latent potentials that we can awaken from traditions we just happen to *inherit.* Thus in a recent article Dworkin not only expects theory to take on the burden of justification for abstract principles hanging in midair, as it were. He also sets it the task of providing these principles with an ethical foundation. He opposes uncoupling a postmetaphysical concept of justice from more embracing but concretely structured, and hence motivating, projects of a well-spent life. In place of the deontological priority of the right over the good, Dworkin wants a *liberal ethic* for pluralistic societies. This ethic should be sufficiently formal to go along with the disagreements one can reasonably anticipate in regard to preferred life orientations, yet it should also be substantial enough to constitute a motivational base for implementing abstract liberal principles. This theory, cast as a single whole, is supposed to embed the deontological concept of justice in a consonant ethic:

Liberal philosophers who . . . adopt the restricted view that liberalism is a theory of the right but not the good face the problem of explaining what reasons people have to be liberals . . . : they try to find motives people have, in either self-interest or morality, for setting aside their convictions about the good life when they act politically. I argue that liberals should reject this restricted view of their theory. They should try on the contrary to connect ethics and politics by constructing a view about the nature or character of the good life that makes liberal political morality seem continuous rather than discontinuous with appealing philosophical views about the good life.[33]

In Dworkin's own project, however, we can discern the dilemma in which every ethic claiming universal validity inevitably gets caught today under conditions of postmetaphysical thinking. Namely, as long as such an ethic makes substantive statements, its premises remain confined to the context in which particular historical or even personal interpretations of the self and the world arose. As soon as it is sufficiently formal, however, its substance at best consists in elucidating the procedure of ethical discourses aimed at reaching self-understanding. We do not need to go into this here.[34] In any case, an ethical theory does not lie at the level where it could make up for the weakness of Rawls's attempt to bridge the chasm between ideal theoretical demands and social facts. The resistant reality with which critical reason wants to keep in touch is not just, and not even primarily, made up of the pluralism of conflicting life ideals and value orientations, of competing comprehensive doctrines, but of the harder material of institutions and action systems.

At the first stage of theory construction, Rawls is already concerned with questions of how one can legally implement the principles of justice that were first grounded in abstracto. And he does not fail to recognize the aspect of enforcement by which coercive law is externally coupled with its addressees' behavior—in contrast to morality, which can appeal to the sense of justice alone. But the relation between positive law and political justice stands in need of further clarification. Rawls concentrates on questions of the legitimacy of law without an explicit concern for the legal form as such and hence for the *institutional dimension* of a law backed by sanctions. What is specific to legal validity, the tension between facticity and validity inhabiting law itself, does not come into view. This also foreshortens our perception of the external tension between the claim to the legitimacy of law and social facticity. The reality that contrasts with the norm is reduced in the second stage to a "fact of pluralism" manifested in the cultural conditions for the acceptance of the theory of justice. Rawls asks how plausible the principles of justice are against the background of political traditions and in the *cultural context* of public communication in a pluralistic society. He refers neither to actually institutionalized decision-making processes nor to social and political developments that might run counter to constitutional principles and confront the institutions of the well-ordered society with a rather scornful mirror image.

Rawls's "political" conception of justice responds to a problem that Hegel posed in terms of the relation between morality and ethical life. For the social-contract approach to natural law, the problem of the relation between norm and reality first arose at a different level. Rational natural law, having distinguished law from morality, took into consideration the tension between facts and norms built into positive law itself. This gave it from the start a more realistic focus than a morally oriented theory of political justice. It confronted the reality of the political process, one might say, in its entire breadth. If Rawls wanted to take in *this* issue, he would not stop, at the second stage of his argument, with a reflection on the conditions of an accommodating political *culture*. Rather, he would have to get involved in a normatively informed reconstruction of the historical development of the constitutional state and its *social* basis.

This complex task requires empirical efforts that go beyond the identification of the conditions required for a favorable political culture. The approaches in social theory dealt with thus far, though, are not up to this task. In unmasking the legal system from the observer's perspective, they merely go straight past its normative self-understanding. Only when sociological analyses of law combine external access with an internal reconstruction does it cease to be necessary for normative theory to seek contact with social reality in an *unmediated* way, through the political consciousness of a public of citizens. A normative theory enlisted for purposes of reconstructing the development of the constitutional state in concrete societies can then play a role in a critical description of actual political processes. If one looks to classical social theory running from Emile Durkheim and Max Weber up to Talcott Parsons, one finds interesting starting points for a double perspective of this sort, that is, an analysis equally tailored to the normative reconstruction and the empirical disenchantment of the legal system.[35]

2.3 Parsons versus Weber: Law and Social Integration

The philosophical discourse of justice misses the institutional dimension, toward which the sociological discourse on law is directed from the outset. Without the view of law as an empirical action system, philosophical concepts remain empty. However, insofar as the sociology of law insists on an objectivating view from the outside, remaining insensitive to the symbolic dimension whose meaning is only internally accessible, sociological perception falls into the opposite danger of remaining blind. The broadly neo-Kantian approaches of Weber and Parsons are especially equipped against this danger. They operate with the notion that ideas and interests (Weber) or cultural values and motives (Parsons) *interpenetrate* in social orders. These approaches understand institutionalized action as the selective realization of cultural values under situational constraints. Social orders lend reality to normative patterns of behavior by specifying values with regard to typical situations and by integrating values with given interest positions. Weber takes his cue from a dualistic anthropology, according to which acting subjects, confronted with problems of both "inner" and "outer" need, strive just as much after ideal goods as after material goods. Parsons, too, starts with value orientations and need dispositions that must be coordinated with each other. A similar concept of institution can be developed from the formal problem of action coordination, independent of such assumptions about personality structure.

Each situation offers an actor more possibilities than he can realize in action. If each participant in interaction were to choose, on the basis of his own expectations of success, one alternative from the range of options, a permanent conflict would result from the contingent confluence of such independent selections. This conflict would not be stabilized even if the participants, with their expectations of one another's expectations, reflexively adjusted to each other so that each participant could make his own decisions in the expectation of the other actors' anticipated decisions. No stable social order can emerge from the contingent clashes of different expected interest-positions and competing calculations of success. To explain the formation and stability of behavior patterns, therefore, Durkheim postulated that in every community there exists a preestablished consensus on a set of intersubjectively recognized values, which orient the individual members. In that case, of course, it must be explained how actors who are free in their decisions *bind* themselves to norms at all, that is, let themselves be *obligated* by norms to realize the corresponding values. However gentle it may be, the force of normative claims will be experienced by actors as externally imposed coercion, unless they make it their own as moral force, that is, unless they convert this force into their own motivations. Durkheim concentrated on a sociological translation of the Kantian concept of autonomy. Because this concept grounds the obligation to transpersonal imperatives in personal insight, it is not the same as mere freedom of choice. What is required is a symmetrical relationship between the moral authority of existing social orders and a corresponding self-control anchored in personality systems. Institutionalized values must, as Parsons will say, correspond with internalized values. The addressees of a norm will be sufficiently motivated to comply with norms on the average only if they have internalized the values incorporated in the norms.

The process of internalization that secures a motivational foundation for actors' value orientations is usually not repression-free; but it does *result* in an authority of conscience that goes hand in hand with a consciousness of autonomy. Only in this consciousness does the peculiarly obligating character of "existing" social orders find an addressee who "binds" himself of his own free will.

This corresponds to Weber's view that social orders can only be maintained in the long run as legitimate orders. "The validity of an order means more than the mere existence of a uniformity of social action determined by custom or self-interest."[36] Here "custom" refers to practices based on a dulled, somewhat mechanical habituation, whereas "legitimately ordered action" requires a conscious orientation to a consensus presupposed as valid: "'Consensus' exists when expectations as to the behavior of others are realistic because of the objective probability that the others will accept these expectations as 'valid' for their behavior, even though no explicit agreement was made. . . . Social action that rests on such likely consensus will be called 'consensual action' [*Einverständnis-handeln*]."[37] To be sure, Weber also asserts in this text that the motivations that make it possible to anticipate how others will behave are irrelevant. But the justified supposition of a "legitimate order" must at least *be among* these motivations. Moreover, this order rests on a value consensus to the extent that the ideas or values incorporated in it must be intersubjectively recognized:

> Only then will . . . a social relationship be called an order if the conduct is, approximately or on the average, oriented toward determinable "maxims." Only then will an order be called "valid" if the orientation toward these maxims occurs, among other reasons, also because it is in some appreciable way regarded by the actor as in some way obligatory or exemplary for him. . . . An order which is adhered to from motives of pure expediency is generally much less stable than one upheld on a purely customary basis through the fact that the corresponding behavior has become habitual. The latter is much the most common type of subjective attitude. But even this type of order is in turn much less stable than an order which enjoys the prestige of being considered binding, or, as it may be expressed, the prestige of "*legitimacy*."[38]

In legitimately regulated action, the mutually presupposed consensus is based on the fact that "along with the other motives for conformity, the order also appears to at least some of the actors as exemplary or binding and thus as something that *ought* to be valid."[39] On the other hand, a legitimate order is not based solely on a normative consensus anchored intrapsychically through the internalization of the corresponding values. To the extent that its validity is not grounded through religious authority or in purely moral terms through value-rational belief, and thus is not protected by the corresponding internal sanctions (fear of losing religious benefits, feelings of shame and guilt) and the capacity to bind oneself, it has need of external guarantees. In these cases the expectation of the legitimacy of a social order is stabilized by convention or law. As is well known, Weber speaks of "convention" in cases in which social validity is externally guaranteed by "a general and practically significant reaction of disapproval" toward the deviating behavior; he speaks of "law" if average norm-conformative behavior is guaranteed by the threat of sanctions applied by "a staff engaged in enforcement."[40] The consensus that can be assumed in legitimately regulated action is modified according to the kind of internal and external guarantees that are added to the legitimating reasons. Such consensus rests on an *amalgam of reasons and empirical motives*, where the reasons differ according to whether they derive from mythic narratives, religious worldviews, or metaphysical doctrines, or whether they are of secular origin, springing from the pragmatic, ethical, or moral use of practical reason.

We can see the ambivalent nature of institutions reflected in this mixed validity basis of consensus, which secures social validity for a social order and therewith allows one to expect de facto compliance on the average. Interests can be satisfied through generalized behavioral expectations in the long run only if interests are connected with ideas that justify normative validity claims; ideas can in turn gain broad empirical acceptance only if they are connected with interests that lend them motivational force. This yields the methodological consequence that legitimate orders can be analyzed equally "from above" and "from below"; a reconstructive sociology must do justice to both perspectives. In this way the sociological discourse of law can learn from the philosophical discourse of justice and at the same time transcend the limits of such normative discourse.

The reconstructive analysis undertaken from the participant's perspective of the judge or client, legislator or citizen, aims at the normative self-understanding of the legal system, that is, at those ideas and values by which one can explain the claim to legitimacy or the ideal validity of a legal order (or of individual norms). The empirical analysis undertaken from the observer's perspective aims at the total complex built of beliefs about legitimacy, interest positions, sanctions, and circumstances. It thus aims at the logic of the situation that explains the empirical validity and de facto acceptance of legally institutionalized expectations. Weber draws a corresponding distinction between the *legal* and the *sociological points of view*. The first has to do with the objective meaning contained in legal propositions, the other has to do with a legally regulated practice, for which, "among other things, the subjective ideas that human beings have about the 'meaning' and 'validity' of certain legal propositions also play a significant role."[41]

Weber begins his sociology of law with this distinction. If one takes the legal point of view, one asks,

What is intrinsically valid as law? That is to say: What significance or, in other words, what normative meaning ought to be attributed in correct logic to a verbal pattern having the form of a legal proposition. But if we take [the sociological point of view], we ask: What actually happens in a group owing to the probability that persons engaged in social action [*Gemeinschaftshandeln*] . . . subjectively consider certain norms as valid and practically act according to them, in other words, orient their own conduct towards these norms?[42]

To be sure, Weber relegates the whole of reconstructive, or conceptual, analysis to jurisprudence without properly distinguishing legal doctrine from legal theory and the philosophy of law. Weber's neglect of the philosophy of law might also stem from his skeptical attitude toward cognitivist approaches in moral theory (like those today represented by Rawls or discourse ethics). By confining the reconstruction of meaning and validity within the narrow disciplinary boundaries of legal doctrine, Weber emphasizes the contrast between those two methodological perspectives (i.e., the legal and the sociological) more than their implicit interconnection. As a result, he does not fully grasp what he himself is doing as a sociologist: his own sociological approach in fact includes both perspectives. The conditions for the ideal validity assumed with the belief in legitimacy constitute necessary, even if not sufficient, conditions for the social validity of a legal order. This is because legal orders are "legitimate orders" that, although certainly not fitting ideas seamlessly together with interests, do interpret interests through ideas, thereby making reasons and validity claims factually effective.

Reconstructive analyses assume a distinguished place in Weber's substantive studies of the history and types of law. In accord with studies conducted by Klaus Eder,[43] Rainer Döbert, and me, Wolfgang Schluchter has attempted to work out in detail the internal aspects of legal development analyzed by Weber. Besides the progressive differentiation taking place in substantive areas of law, Weber pursues the rationalization of law from two points of view. He is interested, on the one hand, in the generalization and systematic refinement of legal programs, remedies, and procedures; on the other hand, he examines changes in the cognitive validity bases of law. Schluchter reconstructs the variation in levels of justification of legal decisions by following the model of developmental stages in moral consciousness, a model Lawrence Kohlberg, picking up on Jean Piaget's work, has demonstrated for ontogenesis.[44] Schluchter summarizes the analysis, carried out from viewpoints immanent to law, as follows:

We proceeded from Weber's distinction between revealed, traditional, deduced or natural and enacted (positive) law, on the one hand, and between formal and substantive legal rationalization on the other. Our thesis was that Weber distinguished between the procedural and the substantive aspects of law and treated the rationalization of law from both viewpoints, although he did not give equal weight to them. Therefore, there must be a rationalization of legal procedure as well as of the foundation of law; they are historically related, but must be separated analytically. Whereas legal procedure becomes more logical, the foundation of law becomes more abstract and universal. At the same time the foundation of law shifts from principles that transcend law to ones inherent to law; that is, the foundation of law is secularized.[45]

In the present context, I am concerned only with the methodological point that this kind of sociology of law also depends on a demanding reconstruction of the validity conditions for the "consensus on legality" presupposed in modern legal systems. That is, one can see from this perspective that the positivization of law and the accompanying differentiation between law and morality are the result of a rationalization process. Although this process destroyed the metasocial guarantees of the legal order, it by no means vaporized the noninstrumentalizable quality of the law's claim to legitimacy. The disenchantment of religious worldviews not only has the destructive consequence of undermining the "two kingdoms" of sacred and secular law, and with this the hierarchical subordination to a higher law. It also leads to a reorganization of legal validity, in that it *simultaneously* transposes the basic concepts of morality and law to a postconventional level. With the distinction between norms and principles of action, with the idea that norms should be generated from principles and by voluntary agreement (*Vereinbarung*), with the concept of the lawmaking power of privately autonomous legal persons, and so on, there develops a notion of norms as positively enacted and hence changeable, yet at the same time criticizable and in need of justification. Luhmann does not go far enough when he expresses the positivity of law in the formula "that law is not only *made* by decision (i.e. selected), but is also *valid* by decision (i.e. contingent and alterable)."[46] In fact, the positivity of postmetaphysical law also means that legal orders can be constructed and can continue to develop only in the light of rationally justified, hence universal, principles.

Weber takes this *internal connection between the principles of enactment and justification* into account at the level of action theory. He does so by analyzing legally regulated action—*Gesellschaftshandeln* in contrast to *Gemeinschaftshandeln*—on the model of a voluntary association based on rationally agreed-to enactment. This model assumes a consensus on the legality of rules that combines both moments in an ideal-typical fashion: the enactment is valid because, on the one hand, it has been *positively enacted* in accordance with the existing law of associations and, on the other hand, it has been *rationally agreed to.* The specific rationality of such enactment consists in the fact that members submit to the coercion of state-sanctioned legal provisions only on the basis of a reasonable consensus. Weber believes, of course, that legal orders cannot be considered legitimate solely on the basis of the supposition of such a rationally achieved consensus, but also because "it is imposed by an authority which is held to be legitimate and therefore meets with compliance."[47] This alternative admittedly must still be explained, since legal authority (*legale Herrschaft*) cannot in turn be considered legitimate only in virtue of its legal form or medium through which it is exercised.

The paradoxical basis of the validity of "legal authority" probably stems not only from an unclear use of the concept of rationality[48] but also from Weber's oddly selective treatment of modern law, which he undertakes inside the boundaries of his sociology of domination (*Herrschaft*). It is true that Weber explains the rationalization of law through its internal aspects and has the analytical tools for rationally reconstructing the validity basis of modern law. Nevertheless, this approach is overshadowed by the emphasis that Weber, true to his value-skepticism, places on the *functions* that law fulfills *for* the organization and exercise of political power. The types of law serve Weber only as general guides for investigating the types of legitimate authority; as a result, the functional relation between modern law and the bureaucratic domination of the rational state is emphasized to the point that the *specific contribution of law to social integration* does not receive the attention it deserves. According to Weber, the constitutional state does not, in the final analysis, draw its legitimation from the democratic form of the political will-formation of citizens. Rather, legitimation is premised solely on aspects of the legal medium through which political power is exercised, namely, the abstract rule-structure of legal statutes, the autonomy of the judiciary, as well as the fact that administration is bound by law and has a "rational" construction. (The last feature refers to the state's continuity and written docu-mentation of official business, its organization of competences, its office hierarchies, technical training of civil servants, separation of office and person, separation of the administrative staff from the means of administration, etc.) In Weber we find a specifically German view of government by law, a view quite comfortable with the elitism of political parties.

A quite different picture emerges if one follows Parsons and examines the modern constitutional state from the perspective of the constitutionalization of political power. Structurally constrained by the rational validity bases of modern law, this process fosters the democratic mode of legitimation anchored in civil society, the political public sphere, and modern citizenship. Parsons uses the term "societal community" to designate the core sphere from which each differentiated social system is supposed to have devel-oped. This includes all the mechanisms of social integration: on the one hand, symbolic practices (such as rites, religious cults, and national ceremonies) that secure social solidarity and, on the other hand, second-order institutions like morality and law that regulate typical action conflicts and thus come to the rescue when the stability of institutionalized first-order expectations is in danger. Morality and law represent something like safety nets for the integrative performances of all other institutional orders. As early as tribal societies, this kind of self-referential normative structure developed with archaic legal practices, such as arbitration, oracles, and feuds.[49] Law is a legitimate order that has become reflexive with regard to the very process of institutionalization. As such, it forms the nucleus of a societal community that in turn is the central structure of society in general.

Parsons pursues the social evolution of law in terms of its *own* function of securing social solidarity, and not, like Weber, in terms of its functional contribution to the formation and exercise of political power. In tribal societies law is still interwoven with other normative complexes and remains diffuse. A partially autonomous law develops only with the transition from tribal societies to "civilizations." In this evolutionary step, a form of state organization develops in which law and political power enter into a remarkable synthesis. On the one hand, the state makes possible the institutionalization of procedures for legal adjudication and enforcement that have a prior, superordinate position vis-à-vis the contesting parties; on the other hand, the state first constitutes itself as a legally structured hierarchy of offices, at the same time legitimating itself through the legal form in which political power is exercised. State-sanctioned law and legally exercised political power thus reciprocally require one another. At this evolutionary stage, familiar elements of the legal system can develop for the first time: legal norms or programs that pertain to *possible* future cases and safeguard legal claims *ex ante;* secondary legal norms that authorize the generation and alteration of primary norms of behavior; an administration of justice that transforms legal claims into possibilities for lawsuits; an execution of the law supporting the threat of sanctions, and so on.

Because the specific features of a legal system first appear in state-sanctioned law, there is a certain plausibility to Weber's theoretical strategy of conceiving law as part of the political system. Less plausible is Luhmann's further step of taking modern law out of politics again and giving it independent status as its own subsystem alongside the administration, economy, family, and the like. A different perspective is taken by Parsons, who like Durkheim sees legal development as connected with the evolution of the "societal community." In modern societies this community develops into a civil society (*Zivilgesellschaft*) that frees itself even from the encompassing framework of the capitalist economy (with which it was still fused in Hegel's concept of "bourgeois civil society"). This "civil society" inherits from its forerunner "societal community" the responsibility for the social integration of society as a whole.

The internal features of the shift from traditional law to rational justification and positivity receive a rather casual treatment from Parsons under the headings of "value generalization" and "inclusion"; the successive inclusion of all members of society in the association of free and equal legal persons corresponds to the moral universalism underlying the validity of modern law. Parsons discusses the development of law primarily in terms of its external aspects. The social structures of early modernity are dominated by a process in which an economic system steered through the medium of money differentiates itself from an order of political domination, which for its part takes the shape of a system steered through administrative power. At the same time, the formation of these two subsystems stimulates the separation of civil society from economy and state. Traditional forms of community are modernized into a "civil society" that, under the banner of religious pluralism, also differentiates itself from cultural systems. The need for integration arises in a new way with these processes of differentiation, a need to which positivized law responds in three ways.[50] The steering media of money and administrative power are anchored in the lifeworld through the legal institutionalization of markets and bureaucratic organizations. Simultaneously, interaction contexts are juridically structured—that is, formally reorganized in such a way that the participants can refer to legal claims in the case of conflict—where previously the conflicts arising in them had been managed on the basis of habit, loyalty, or trust. Finally, as the necessary complement to the juridification of potentially all social relationships, democratic citizenship is universalized. The heart of this citizenship is made up of rights of political participation. These are exercised in new public forms of civil society—a network of voluntary associations protected by basic rights—as well as in the forms of communication within a political public sphere produced through the mass media.

The positivization of law necessarily results from the rationalization of its validity basis. As a result, modern law can stabilize behavioral expectations in a complex society with structurally differentiated lifeworlds and functionally independent subsystems only if law, as regent for a "societal community" that has transformed itself into civil society, can maintain the inherited claim to solidarity in the abstract form of an acceptable claim to legitimacy. Modern legal systems redeem this promise through the universalization and specification of citizenship:

A societal community as basically composed of equals seems to be the "end of the line" in the long process of undermining the legitimacy of such older, more particularistic ascriptive bases of membership as religion, ethnic affiliation, region or locality, and hereditary position in social stratification. . . . This basic theme of equality has long antecedents but was first crystallized in conceptions of "natural rights" . . . . The current prominence of poverty and race problems in the United States is largely owing to the deep moral repugnance that the conception of an inherently "lower" class, to say nothing of an inferior race, arouses in modern societies, despite vociferous objections to modern egalitarianism among certain groups.[51]

Finally, in discussing the development of civil society as the social basis for public and inclusive processes of opinion- and will-formation among voluntarily associated citizens, Parsons stresses the significance of equalizing educational opportunities or, more generally, uncoupling cultural knowledge from class structures: "The focus of the new phase is the educational revolution which in a certain sense synthesizes the themes of the industrial and the democratic revolutions: equality of opportunity and equality of citizenship."[52] With this concept of an "educational revolution," Parsons also touches on the political-cultural conditions for a responsive political public sphere. This is the theme that interests Rawls, and rightly so: the more modern legal systems actually redeem their claim to legitimacy in the currency of effective civil rights, the more the criteria for equal treatment come to depend on ever more inclusive processes of public communication.

Parsons understands modern law as a transmission belt by which solidarity—the demanding structures of mutual recognition we know from face-to-face interaction—is transmitted in abstract but binding form to the anonymous and systemically mediated relationships of a complex society. As a point of empirical reference, he uses T. H. Marshall's study of the gradual extension of constitutional rights in England.[53] Marshall's proposed division of "civil," "political," and "social rights" follows a well-known juristic classification. According to this scheme, liberal rights against the state protect the private legal subject against government infringements of life, liberty, and property; rights of political participation make it possible for the active citizen to participate in the democratic process of opinion- and will-formation; and social entitlements grant clients of the welfare state a minimum income and social security. Marshall advanced the thesis that in the last two or three centuries the status of citizens in Western societies has successively expanded and consolidated itself according to this sequence.

In recent discussions attention has turned once again to this concept of citizenship. Marshall studied the progressive inclusion of the citizen primarily in connection with processes of capitalist modernization. But the schema that represents the extension of citizenship rights as the result of a social evolution is obviously too narrow. Anthony Giddens has highlighted the important role of struggles and social movements.[54] Of course, the emphasis on economically motivated class struggles is one-sided. Other kinds of social movements, migrations and wars above all, have also driven on the expansion of citizenship in various dimensions.[55] Conversely, factors stimulating the juridification of new forms of inclusion also affect the political mobilization of the population, thereby helping activate rights that citizens already possess.[56] Finally, the classification of rights has come to include not only cultural rights but also new kinds of civil rights for which feminist and ecological movements today struggle in particular. In the process, a difference that is more evident to an internal, doctrinal approach than to a sociological one has emerged more clearly.

The largely linear development that Marshall and Parsons connect with their concept of citizenship applies at most to the broad trend that sociologists designate by "inclusion." In an ever more functionally differentiated society, an ever greater number of persons acquire ever more inclusive rights of access to, and participation in, an increasing number of subsystems, which include markets, businesses, and workplaces; offices, courts, and the military; schools, hospitals, theaters, and museums; political organizations and mass media; parties, self-governing institutions, and parliaments. This multiplies organizational memberships for the individual; it expands the ranges of options. However, this image of linear progress emerges from a description that remains insensitive to increases and losses in autonomy. It is blind to the large differences in the actual use made of a citizenship that allows individuals to play a role in democratically changing their own status.[57] Only the rights of political participation ground the citizen's reflexive, self-referential legal standing. Negative liberties and social entitlements, on the contrary, can be paternalistically bestowed. In principle, the constitutional state and the welfare state can be implemented without democracy. Even where all three categories of rights are institutionalized, these negative rights and social entitlements are still Janus-faced. Historically speaking, liberal rights crystallized around the social position of the private-property owner. From a *functionalist* viewpoint, one can conceive them as institutionalizing a market economy, whereas from a *normative* viewpoint they guarantee basic private liberties. Social rights signify, from a *functionalist* viewpoint, the installation of welfare bureaucracies, whereas from a *normative* viewpoint they grant compensatory claims to a just share of social wealth. It is true that both individual liberties and welfare guarantees can also be viewed as the legal basis for a social autonomy that first makes it possible to put political rights into effect. But these are empirical, and not conceptually necessary, relationships. In different circumstances negative liberties and social entitlements may well be equally indicative of the privatistic retreat from the citizen's role. In that case, citizenship is reduced to a client's relationships to administrations that provide security, services, and benefits paternalistically.

The syndrome of civil privatism and the selective use of citizenship from the standpoint of client interests become all the more probable the more the economy and state—which have been institutionalized through the same rights—develop systemic logics of their own and push citizens into the peripheral role of mere organization members. As self-regulating systems, economy and

administration tend to close themselves off from their environments and obey only their internal imperatives of money and
administrative power. They explode the model of a legal community that determines itself through the common practice of associated citizens. Built into the very status of citizenship in welfare-state
democracies is the tension between a formal extension of private
and civic autonomy, on the one hand, and a "normalization," in
Foucault's sense, that fosters the passive enjoyment of paternalistically dispensed rights, on the other.[58] Hence, a sociology that would
remain sensitive to tensions of this sort must not renounce a
rational reconstruction of civil rights from the internal perspective
of the legal system. Even Parsons, in the basic concepts of his
systems theory, levels out what Weber reconstructed as the rationalization of law. That is, he treats "inclusion" and "value generalization" as normatively neutral dimensions of system integration; as a
result, the concept of law embodied in the modern constitutional
state loses, in Parsons's approach, both its normative content and
its focus on social integration.[59]

To forestall such levelings, in the two following chapters I first
reconstruct the normative content of citizenship by analyzing the
system of rights and the principles of the constitutional state from
a discourse-theoretic point of view. However, in so doing I try to
avoid an ambiguity prevalent in philosophical discussions of justice. This ambiguity is suggested in the German tradition by the
terms *Recht* (law) and *Rechte* (rights). We speak of "rights" in both
a moral and a legal sense. I would like instead to distinguish law and
morality from the start; unlike Rawls, I am not satisfied with the
distinction between political justice and morality, both of which lie
at the same level of purely normative validity claims. By "law" I
understand modern enacted law, which claims to be legitimate in
terms of its possible justification as well as binding in its interpretation and enforcement. Unlike postconventional morality, law
does not just represent a type of cultural knowledge but constitutes
at the same time an important core of institutional orders. Law is
two things at once: a system of knowledge and a system of action.
It is equally possible to understand law as a text, composed of legal
propositions and their interpretations, and to view it as an institution, that is, as a complex of normatively regulated action. Because

motivations and value orientations are intertwined in law as an action system, legal norms have an immediate effect on action in a way that moral judgments do not. On the other hand, the comparatively high degree of rationality connected with legal institutions distinguishes these from quasi-natural institutional orders, for the former incorporate doctrinal knowledge, that is, knowledge that has been articulated and systematized, brought to a scholarly level, and interwoven with a principled morality.

With this concept of law, philosophical analysis builds bridges to an empirical analysis that has a "dual perspective." On the one hand, in renouncing a systems-theoretic approach, whether Parsonian or Luhmannian, one must also avoid returning to a holistic concept of society. The "people" and the "association of free and equal citizens" are just as unavoidable as legal constructions as they are inappropriate as models for society in toto.

The communicative concept of the lifeworld breaks with the idea of a whole composed of parts. The lifeworld is constituted from a network of communicative actions that branch out through social space and historical time, and these live off sources of cultural traditions and legitimate orders no less than they depend on the identities of socialized individuals. Thus the lifeworld is not a large organization to which members belong, it is not an association or a union in which individuals band together, nor is it a collectivity made up of members. Socialized individuals could not maintain themselves as subjects at all if they did not find support in the relationships of reciprocal recognition articulated in cultural traditions and stabilized in legitimate orders—and vice versa. The everyday communicative practice in which the lifeworld is centered issues *equiprimordially* from the interplay of cultural reproduction, social integration, and socialization. Culture, society, and personality mutually presuppose one another.[60] The normative concept of a legal community as an association of free and equal consociates under law, a notion that philosophical discussions still retain, is too concrete for social theory.

From the vantage point of the theory of communicative action, we can say that the subsystem "law," as a legitimate order that has become reflexive, belongs to the societal component of the lifeworld. Just as this reproduces itself only together with culture and personality structures through the flow of communicative actions, so legal actions, too, constitute the medium through which institutions of law simultaneously reproduce themselves along with intersubjectively shared legal traditions and individual competences for interpreting and observing legal rules. As part of the societal component, these legal rules constitute a higher level of legitimate orders; at the same time, however, they are also represented in the other two lifeworld components, as legal symbolism and as competences acquired via legal socialization. All three components share co-originally in the production of legal actions. Law includes all communication oriented by law, such that legal rules refer reflexively to the function of social integration directly fulfilled in the process of institutionalization. But the legal code not only keeps one foot in the medium of ordinary language, through which everyday communication achieves social integration in the lifeworld; it also accepts messages that originate there and puts these into a form that is comprehensible to the special codes of the power-steered administration and the money-steered economy. To this extent the language of law, unlike the moral communication restricted to the lifeworld, can function as a transformer in the society-wide communication circulating between system and lifeworld.

3

A Reconstructive Approach to Law I:
The System of Rights

The foregoing reflections served the propaedeutic purpose of introducing the category of law, modern law in particular, from the vantage point of the theory of communicative action. A social theory claiming to be "critical" cannot restrict itself to describing the relation between norm and reality from the perspective of an observer. Before returning in chapter 7 to this external tension between the normative claims of constitutional democracies and the facticity of their actual functioning, in this and the following chapters I want to rationally reconstruct the *self-understanding* of these modern legal orders. I take as my starting point the rights citizens must accord one another if they want to legitimately regulate their common life by means of positive law. This formulation already indicates that the system of rights as a whole is shot through with that internal tension between facticity and validity manifest in the ambivalent mode of legal validity.

As we have seen in the first chapter, the concept of individual rights plays a central role in the modern understanding of law. It corresponds to the concept of liberty or individual freedom of action: rights ("subjective rights" in German) fix the limits within which a subject is entitled to freely exercise her will. More specifically, they define the same liberties for all individuals or legal persons understood as bearers of rights. In Article 4 of the 1789 Declaration of Rights of Man and of the Citizen we read, "Political liberty consists in the power of doing whatever does not injure another. The exercise of the natural rights of every man has no other limits than those which are necessary to secure to every other man the free exercise of the same rights; and these limits are determinable only by the law."[1] Kant picks up on this proposition when he formulates his universal principle of law (or principle of right, *Rechtsprinzip*). This principle considers an act to be right or lawful as long as its guiding maxim permits one person's freedom of choice to be conjoined with everyone's freedom in accordance with a universal law. Rawls follows the same principle in formulating his first principle of justice: "each person is to have an equal right to the most extensive basic liberty compatible with a similar liberty for others."[2] The concept of a law or legal statute makes explicit the idea of equal treatment already found in the concept of right: in the form of universal and abstract laws all subjects receive the same rights.

These basic concepts and definitions explain why modern law is especially suited for the social integration of economic societies, which rely on the decentralized decisions of self-interested individuals in morally neutralized spheres of action. But law must do more than simply meet the functional requirements of a complex society; it must also satisfy the precarious conditions of a social integration that ultimately takes place through the achievements of mutual understanding on the part of communicatively acting subjects, that is, through the acceptability of validity claims. Modern law displaces normative expectations from morally unburdened individuals onto the laws that secure the compatibility of liberties.[3] These laws draw their legitimacy from a legislative procedure based for its part on the principle of popular sovereignty. The paradoxical emergence of legitimacy out of legality must be explained by means of the rights that secure for citizens the exercise of their political autonomy.

Why paradoxical? As "subjective rights," these rights enjoyed by citizens display on the one hand the same structure as all rights that grant spheres of free choice to the individual. If we disregard the different modalities in the use of these rights, then we must be able to interpret political rights, too, as subjective liberties that merely make lawful behavior a duty, and hence *leave open* the motives for conforming to norms. On the other hand, the procedure of democratic legislation must confront participants with the normative expectation of an orientation to the common good, because this procedure can draw its legitimating force only from a process in which citizens *reach an understanding* about the rules for their living together. In modern societies as well, the law can fulfill the function of stabilizing behavioral expectations only if it preserves an internal connection with the socially integrating force of communicative action.

I want to elucidate this puzzling connection between private liberties and civic autonomy with the help of the discourse concept of law. This connection involves a stubborn problem, which I will first discuss in two different contexts. Thus far no one has succeeded in satisfactorily reconciling private and public autonomy at a fundamental conceptual level, as is evident from the unclarified relation between individual rights and public law in the field of jurisprudence, as well as from the unresolved competition between human rights and popular sovereignty in social-contract theory (section 3.1). In both cases the difficulties stem not only from certain premises rooted in the philosophy of consciousness but also from a metaphysical legacy inherited from natural law, namely, the subordination of positive law to natural or moral law. In fact, however, positive law and postconventional morality emerge co-originally from the crumbling edifice of substantial ethical life. Kant's analysis of the form of law provides an occasion to discuss the relation between law and morality, in order to show that the principle of democracy must not be subordinated to the moral principle, as it is in Kantian legal theory (section 3.2). Only after this preliminary spadework can I ground the system of rights with the help of the discourse principle, so that it becomes clear why private and public autonomy, human rights and popular sovereignty, mutually presuppose one another (section 3.3).

3.1 Private and Public Autonomy, Human Rights and Popular Sovereignty

3.1.1

In German civil-law jurisprudence, which in Germany has been decisive for the understanding of law in general, the theory of "subjective right," as it was called, was initially influenced by the idealist philosophy of right. According to Friedrich Carl von Savigny, a legal relation secures "the power justly pertaining to the individual person: an area in which his will rules, and rules with our consent."[4] This still emphasizes the connection of individual liberties with an intersubjective recognition by legal consociates. As his analysis proceeds, however, an intrinsic value accrues to private law, independent of its authorization by a democratic legislature. Right "in the subjective sense" is legitimate per se because, starting with the inviolability of the person, it is supposed to guarantee "an area of independent rule" (*Herrschaft*) for the free exercise of the individual will.[5] For Georg Friedrich Puchta, too, law was essentially subjective right, that is, private law: "Law is the recognition of the freedom belonging equally to all human beings as subjects with the power of will."[6] According to this view, rights are negative rights that protect spheres of action by grounding actionable claims that others refrain from unpermitted interventions in the freedom, life, and property of the individual. Private autonomy is secured in these legally protected spheres primarily through contract and property rights.

In the later nineteenth century, though, awareness grew that private law could be legitimated from its own resources only as long as it could be assumed that the legal subject's private autonomy had a foundation in the moral autonomy of the person. Once law in general lost its idealist grounding—in particular, the support it had from Kant's moral theory—the husk of the "individual power to rule" was robbed of the normative core of a freedom of will that is both legitimate and worthy of protection from the start. The only bond that possessed legitimating force was the one that Kant, with the help of his "principle of right" (*Rechtsprinzips*), had tied between freedom of choice and the person's autonomous will. After this bond was severed, law, according to the positivist view, could only assert itself as a particular form that furnished specific decisions and powers with the force of de facto bindingness. After Bernhard Windscheid, individual rights were considered reflexes of an established legal order that transferred to individuals the power of will objectively incorporated in law: "Right is a power or rule of will conferred by the legal order."[7]

Rudolf von Ihering's utilitarian interpretation, according to which utility and not will makes up the substance of right,[8] was later included in this definition: "From a conceptual standpoint, individual rights are powers of law conferred on the individual by the legal order; from the standpoint of its purpose, they are means for the satisfaction of human interests."[9] The reference to gratification and interest allowed private rights to be extended beyond the class of negative liberties. In certain instances an individual right yields not only a right on the part of person A to something protected from the interference of third parties, but also a right, be it absolute or relative, to a share in organized services. Finally, Hans Kelsen characterized individual rights in general as interests objectively protected by law and as freedoms of choice (or "*Wollendürfen*" in Windscheid's sense) objectively guaranteed by law. At the same time, he divested the legal order of the connotations of John Austin's command theory, which had been influential up to that point in the German version of August Thon. According to Kelsen, individual entitlements are not just authorized by the will of someone with the power to command, but possess normative validity: legal norms establish prescriptions and permissions having the character of an "ought." This illocutionary "ought," however, is understood not in a deontological but in an empirical sense, as the actual validity that political lawgivers confer on their decisions by coupling enacted law with penal norms. The coercive power of state sanctions qualifies the lawgivers' will to become the "will of the state."

In Kelsen's analysis the moral content of individual rights expressly lost its reference, namely, the free will (or "power to rule") of a person who, from the moral point of view, *deserves* to be protected in her private autonomy. To this extent, his view marks the counterpart of that private-law jurisprudence stemming from Savigny. Kelsen detached the legal concept of a person not only from the moral person but even from the natural person, because a fully self-referential legal system must get by with its self-produced fictions. As Luhmann will put it after taking a further naturalistic turn, it pushes natural persons out into its environment. With individual rights, the legal order itself creates the logical space for the legal subject as bearer of these rights: "If the legal subject . . . is allowed to remain as a point of reference, then this occurs in order to keep the judgment that 'a legal subject or person "has" subjective rights' from becoming the empty tautology 'there are subjective rights.' . . . For to entitle or to obligate the person would then be to entitle rights, to obligate duties, in short, to 'norm' norms."[10] Once the moral and natural person has been uncoupled from the legal system, there is nothing to stop jurisprudence from conceiving rights along purely functionalist lines. The doctrine of rights hands on the baton to a systems theory that rids itself by methodological fiats of all normative considerations.[11]

The transformation of private law under National Socialism[12] certainly provoked moral reactions in postwar Germany, which decried the so-called "legal dethronement" (*objektiv-rechtliche Entthronung*) and concomitant hollowing out of the moral substance of rights. But the natural-law-based restoration of the connection between private and moral autonomy soon lost its power to convince. "*Ordo*"-liberalism[13] only rehabilitated the individualistically truncated understanding of rights—the very conception that invited a functionalist interpretation of private law as the framework for capitalist economic relations:

The idea of "subjective right" carries on the view that private law and the legal protection grounded in it ultimately serve to maintain the individual's freedom in society, [in other words, the view] that individual freedom is one of the foundational ideas for the sake of which private law exists. For the idea of "subjective right" expresses the fact that private law is the law of mutually independent legal consociates who act according to their own separate decisions.[14]

In opposition to the threat posed by a functionalist reinterpretation of this conception, Ludwig Raiser has drawn on social law in an attempt to correct the individualistic approach and thus restore to private law its moral content. Rather than going back to Savigny's conceptual framework, Raiser is led by the welfare-state materialization of private law to *restrict* a concept of "subjective right," which he preserves without alteration, to the classical liberties. In continuity with previous views, these rights are meant to secure "the self-preservation and individual responsibility of each person within society." But they must be supplemented with social rights: "From an ethical and political standpoint, more is required than a recognition of this [private] legal standing. Rather, it is just as important that one also integrate the individual by law into the ordered network of relationships that surround him and bind him with others. In other words, one must develop and protect the legal institutions in which the individual assumes the *status of member*."[15] "Primary" rights are too weak to guarantee protection to persons in those areas where they "are integrated into larger, transindividual orders."[16] However, Raiser's rescue attempt does not start at a sufficiently abstract level. It is true that private law has undergone a reinterpretation through the paradigm shift from bourgeois formal law to the materialized law of the welfare state.[17] But this reinterpretation must not be confused with a revision of the basic concepts and principles themselves, which have remained the same and have merely been *interpreted* differently in shifting paradigms.

Raiser does remind us of the intersubjective character of rights, though, something the individualistic reading had rendered unrecognizable. After all, such rights are based on the reciprocal recognition of cooperating legal persons. Taken by themselves, rights do not necessarily imply the atomism—the isolation of legal subjects from one another—that Raiser wants to correct. The citizens who mutually grant one another equal rights are one and the same individuals as the private persons who use rights strategically and encounter one another as potential opponents, but the two roles are not identical:

A right, after all, is neither a gun nor a one-man show. It is a relationship and a social practice, and in both those essential aspects it is seemingly an expression of connectedness. Rights are public propositions, involving obligations to others as well as entitlements against them. In appearance, at least, they are a form of social cooperation—not spontaneous but highly organized cooperation, no doubt, but still, in the final analysis, cooperation.[18]

At a conceptual level, rights do not immediately refer to atomistic and estranged individuals who are possessively set against one another. On the contrary, as elements of the legal order they presuppose collaboration among subjects who recognize one another, in their reciprocally related rights and duties, as free and equal citizens. This mutual recognition is constitutive for a legal order from which actionable rights are derived. In this sense "subjective" rights emerge co-originally with "objective" law, to use the terminology of German jurisprudence. However, a statist understanding of objective law is misleading, for the latter first issues from the rights that subjects mutually acknowledge. In order to make clear the intersubjective structure of relations of recognition that underlies the legal order as such, it is not enough to append social rights additively. Both the idealist beginnings and the positivist offshoots of German civil-law jurisprudence from Savigny to Kelsen misjudge this structure.

As we have seen, private-law theory (as the doctrine of "subjective right") got started with the idea of morally laden individual rights, which claim normative independence from, and a higher legitimacy than, the political process of legislation. The freedom-securing character of rights was supposed to invest private law with a moral authority both independent of democratic lawmaking and not in need of justification within legal theory itself. This sparked a development that ended in the abstract subordination of "subjective" rights to "objective" law, where the latter's legitimacy finally exhausted itself in the legalism of a political domination construed in positivist terms. The course of this discussion, however, concealed the real problem connected with the key position of private rights: the source from whence enacted law may draw its legitimacy is not successfully explained. To be sure, the source of all legitimacy lies in the democratic lawmaking process, and this in turn calls on the principle of popular sovereignty. But the legal positivism, or *Gesetzespositivismus*, propounded in the Weimar period by professors of public law does not introduce this principle in such a way that the intrinsic moral content of the classical liberties—the protection of individual freedom emphasized by Helmut Coing—could be preserved. In one way or another, the intersubjective meaning of legally defined liberties is overlooked, and with it the relation between private and civic autonomy in which both moments receive their full due.

3.1.2

Trusting in an idealist concept of autonomy, Savigny could still assume that private law, as a system of negative and procedural rights that secure freedom, is legitimated on the basis of reason, that is, of itself. But Kant did not give an entirely unequivocal answer to the question of the legitimation of general laws that could supposedly ground a system of well-ordered egoism. Even in his *Rechtslehre* (*Metaphysical Elements of Justice*), Kant ultimately fails to clarify the relations among the principles of morality, law (or right), and democracy (if we can call what Kant sees as constituting the republican mode of government a principle of democracy). All three principles express, each in its own way, the same *idea of self-legislation.* This concept of autonomy was Kant's response to Hobbes's unsuccessful attempt to justify a system of rights on the basis of the participants' enlightened self-interest alone, without the aid of moral reasons.

If one looks back at Hobbes from a Kantian perspective, one can hardly avoid reading him more as a theoretician of a bourgeois rule of law without democracy than as the apologist of unlimited absolutism; according to Hobbes, the sovereign can impart his commands only in the language of modern law. The sovereign guarantees an order in internal affairs that assures private persons of equal liberties according to general laws: "For supreme commanders can confer no more to their civil happiness, than that being preserved from foreign and civil wars, they may quietly enjoy that wealth which they have purchased by their own industry."[19]

For Hobbes, who clearly outfits the status of subjects with private rights, the problem of legitimation naturally cannot be managed *within* an already established legal order, and hence through political rights and democratic legislation. This problem must be solved immediately with the constitution of state authority, in a single blow, as it were; that is, it must be conjured out of existence for the future. Certainly Hobbes wants to explain why absolutist society is justified as an instrumental order from the perspective of all participants, if only they keep to a strictly purposive-rational calculation of their own interests. This was supposed to make it unnecessary to design a rule of law, that is, to elaborate regulations for a legitimate *exercise* of political authority. The tension between facticity and validity built into law itself dissolves if legal authority per se can be portrayed as maintaining an ordered system of egoism that is favored by all the participants anyhow: what appears as morally right and legitimate then issues spontaneously from the self-interested decisions of rational egoists or, as Kant will put it, a "race of devils." The utilitarian grounding of the bourgeois order of private law—that this type of market society makes as many people as possible well off for as long as possible[20]—bestows material justice on the sovereignty of a ruler who by definition can do nothing unlawful.

However, to carry out his intended demonstration, Hobbes must do more than simply show why such an order equally satisfies the interests of all participants ex post facto, that is, from the standpoint of readers who already find themselves in a civil society. He must in addition show why such a system could be *preferred* in the same way by each isolated, purposive-rational actor while still in the state of nature. Because Hobbes ascribes the same success-oriented attitude to the parties in the state of nature as private law ascribes to its addressees, it seems reasonable to construe the original act of association along the lines of an instrument available in private law, the contract—specifically, to construe this act as a civil contract in which all the parties jointly agree to install (but not to bind) a sovereign. There is one circumstance Hobbes does not consider here. Within the horizon of their individual preferences, the subjects make their decisions from the perspective of the first-person singular. But this is not the perspective from which parties in a state of nature are led, on reflection, to trade their natural, that is, mutually conflicting but unlimited, liberties for precisely those civil liberties that general laws at once limit and render compatible. Only under two conditions would one expect subjects in the state of nature to make a rationally motivated transition from their state of permanent conflict to a cooperation under coercive law that demands a partial renunciation of freedom on the part of everyone.

On the one hand, the parties would have to be capable of understanding what a social relationship based on the principle of reciprocity even *means.* The subjects of private law, who are at first only virtually present in the state of nature, have, *prior to all* association, not yet learned to "take the perspective of the other" and self-reflexively perceive themselves from the perspective of a second person. Only then could their own freedom appear to them not simply as a natural freedom that occasionally encounters factual resistance but as a freedom constituted through mutual recognition. In order to understand what a contract is and know how to use it, they must already have at their disposal the sociocognitive framework of perspective taking between counterparts, a framework they can acquire only in a social condition not yet available in the state of nature. *On the other hand,* the parties who agree on the terms of the contract they are about to conclude must be capable of distancing themselves in yet another way from their natural freedoms. They must be capable of assuming the *social* perspective of the first-person plural, a perspective always already tacitly assumed by Hobbes and his readers but withheld from subjects in the state of nature. On Hobbesian premises, these subjects may not assume the very standpoint from which each of them could first judge whether the reciprocity of coercion, which limits the scope of each's free choice according to general laws, lies in the equal interest of all and hence can be willed by all the participants. In fact, we find that Hobbes does acknowledge in passing the kinds of moral grounds that thereby come into play; he does this in those places where he recurs to the Golden Rule—*Quod tibi fieri non vis, alteri ne feceris*—as a natural law.[21] But morally impregnating the state of nature in this way contradicts the naturalism presupposed by the intended goal of Hobbes's demonstration, namely, to ground the construction of a system of well-ordered egoism on the sole basis of the enlightened self-interest of any individual.[22]

The empiricist question—how a system of rights can be explained by the interlocking of interest positions and utility calculations of accidentally related rational actors—has never failed to hold the attention of astute philosophers and social scientists. But even the modern tools of game theory have yet to provide a satisfactory solution. If for no other reason, Kant's reaction to the *failure* of this attempt continues to deserve consideration.

Kant saw that rights cannot for their part be grounded by recourse to a model taken from private law. He raised the convincing objection that Hobbes failed to notice the structural difference between the social contract, which serves as a model for legitimation, and the private contract, which basically regulates exchange relationships. In fact, one must expect something other than a merely egocentric attitude from the parties concluding a social contract in the state of nature: "the contract establishing a civil constitution . . . is of so unique a kind that . . . it is in principle essentially different from all others in what it founds."[23] Whereas parties usually conclude a contract "to some determinate end," the social contract is "an end in itself." It grounds "the right of men [to live] under public coercive law, through which each can receive his due and can be made secure from the interference of others."[24] In Kant's view the parties do not agree to appoint a sovereign to whom they cede the power to make laws. Rather, the social contract is unique in not having any specific content at all; it provides instead the model for a kind of sociation ruled by the principle of law. It lays down the performative conditions under which rights acquire legitimate validity, for "right is the limitation of each person's freedom so that it is compatible with the freedom of everyone, insofar as this is possible in accord with a general law."[25]

Under this aspect, the social contract serves to *institutionalize* the single "innate" right to equal liberties. Kant sees this primordial human right as grounded in the autonomous will of individuals who, as moral persons, have at their prior disposal the social perspective of a practical reason that tests laws. On the basis of this reason, they have *moral*—and not just prudential—grounds for their move out of the condition of unprotected freedom. At the same time, Kant sees that the "single human right" must differentiate itself into a *system of rights* through which both "the freedom of every member of society as a human being" as well as "the equality of each member with every other as a subject" assume a positive shape.[26] This happens in the form of "public laws," which can claim legitimacy only as acts of the public will of autonomous and united citizens: establishing public law "is possible through no other will than that belonging to the people collectively (because all decide for all, hence each for himself); for only to oneself can one never do injustice."[27] Because the question concerning the legitimacy of freedom-securing laws must find an answer *within* positive law, the social contract establishes the principle of law by binding the legislator's political will-formation to conditions of a *democratic procedure*; under these conditions the results arrived at in conformity with this procedure express per se the concurring will or rational consensus of all participants. In this way, the morally grounded primordial human right to equal liberties is intertwined in the social contract with the principle of popular sovereignty.

The human rights grounded in the moral autonomy of individuals acquire a positive shape solely through the citizens' political autonomy. The principle of law seems to mediate between the principle of morality and that of democracy. But it is not entirely clear how the latter two principles are related. Kant certainly introduces the concept of autonomy, which supports the whole construction, from the prepolitical viewpoint of the morally judging individual, but he explicates this concept along the lines of the universal-law version of the Categorical Imperative, drawing in turn on the model of a public and democratic self-legislation borrowed from Rousseau. From a conceptual standpoint, the moral principle and the democratic principle reciprocally explain each other, but the architectonic of Kant's legal theory conceals this point. If one accepts this reading, then the principle of law cannot be understood as the middle term between the principles of morality and democracy, but simply as the reverse side of the democratic principle itself: because the democratic principle cannot be implemented except in the form of law, both principles must be realized *uno actu.* How these three principles are related certainly remains unclear, which stems from the fact that in Kant, as in Rousseau, there still is an unacknowledged *competition* between morally grounded *human rights* and the *principle of popular sovereignty.*

But what significance can such a discussion of the history of political ideas have for a systematic treatment of private and public autonomy? Before going any further, I insert an excursus intended to clarify the impact of modern political theory.

3.1.3 Excursus

The two ideas of human rights and popular sovereignty have determined the normative self-understanding of constitutional democracies up to the present day. We must not look on the idealism anchored in our constitutional principles simply as a closed chapter in the history of political ideas. On the contrary, this history of political theory is a necessary element and reflection of the tension between facticity and validity built into law itself, between the positivity of law and the legitimacy claimed by it. This tension can be neither trivialized nor simply ignored, because the rationalization of the lifeworld makes it increasingly difficult to rely only on tradition and settled ethical conventions to meet the need for legitimating enacted law—a law that rests on the changeable decisions of a political legislator. Here let me briefly recall the rationality potential, at work in both cultural and socialization processes, that has increasingly made itself felt in the law since the first great codifications of private and public law at the end of the eighteenth century.

The classical, primarily Aristotelian, doctrine of natural law, whose influence extended well into the nineteenth century, as well as Thomas Aquinas's remodeled Christian version, still reflected an encompassing societal ethos that extended through all social classes of the population and clamped the different social orders together. In the vertical dimension of the components of the lifeworld, this ethos ensured that cultural value patterns and institutions sufficiently overlapped with the action orientations and motives fixed in personality structures. At the horizontal level of legitimate orders, it allowed the normative elements of ethical life, politics, and law to intermesh. In the train of developments I interpret as the rationalization of the lifeworld, this clamp sprang open. As the first step, cultural traditions and processes of socialization came under the pressure of reflection, so that actors themselves gradually made them into topics of discussion. To the extent that this occurred, received practices and interpretations of ethical life were reduced to mere conventions and differentiated from conscientious decisions that passed through the filter of reflection and independent judgment. In the process, the use of practical reason reached that point of specialization with which I am concerned in the present context. The modern ideas of *self-realization* and *self-determination* signaled not only different issues but two different kinds of discourse tailored to the logics of *ethical* and *moral* questions. The respective logics peculiar to these two types of questions were in turn manifested in philosophical developments that began in the late eighteenth century.

What was considered "ethics" since the time of Aristotle now assumed a new, subjectivistic sense. This was true of both individual life histories and of intersubjectively shared traditions and forms of life. In connection with, and in reaction to, a growing autobiographical literature of confessions and self-examinations—running from Rousseau through Kierkegaard to Sartre—a kind of reflection developed that altered attitudes toward one's own life. To put it briefly, in place of exemplary instructions in the virtuous life and recommended models of the good life, one finds an increasingly pronounced, abstract demand for a conscious, self-critical appropriation, the demand that one responsibly take possession of one's own individual, irreplaceable, and contingent life history. Radicalized interiority is burdened with the task of achieving a self-understanding in which self-knowledge and existential decision interpenetrate. Heidegger used the formulation "thrown project" to express the expectation of this probing selection of factually given possibilities that mold one's identity.[28] The intrusion of reflection into the life-historical process generates a new kind of tension between the consciousness of contingency, self-reflection, and liability for one's own existence. To the extent that this constellation has an ever broader impact on society through prevailing patterns of socialization, *ethical-existential* or *clinical discourses* become not only possible but in a certain sense unavoidable: the conflicts springing from such a constellation, if they are not resolved consciously and deliberately, make themselves felt in obtrusive symptoms.

Not only the conduct of personal life but also the transmission of culture is increasingly affected by the type of discourse aimed at self-understanding. In connection with, and in reaction to, the rise of the hermeneutical and historical sciences, the appropriation of our own intersubjectively shared traditions became problematic starting with Schleiermacher and continuing through Droysen and Dilthey up to Gadamer. In place of religious or metaphysical self-interpretations, history and its interpretation have now become the medium in which cultures and peoples find their self-reassurance. Although philosophical hermeneutics got its start in the methodology of the humanities, it responds more broadly to an insecurity provoked by historicism—to a reflexive refraction affecting the public appropriation of tradition in the first-person plural.[29] During the nineteenth century, a posttraditional identity first took on a definite shape under a close affiliation between historicism and nationalism. But this was still fueled by a dogmatism of national histories that has since been in the process of disintegration. A pluralism in the ways of reading fundamentally ambivalent traditions has sparked a growing number of debates over the collective identities of nations, states, cultures, and other groups. Such discussions make it clear that the disputing parties are expected to consciously choose the continuities they want to live out of, which traditions they want to break off or continue. To the extent that collective identities can develop only in the fragile, dynamic, and fuzzy shape of a decentered, even fragmented public consciousness, *ethical-political discourses* that reach into the depths have become both possible and unavoidable.

The intrusion of reflection into life histories and cultural traditions has fostered individualism in personal life projects and a pluralism of collective forms of life. Simultaneously, however, norms of interaction have also become reflexive; in this way universalist value orientations gain ascendancy. Once again, an altered normative consciousness is reflected in the relevant philosophical theories since the end of the eighteenth century. One no longer legitimates maxims, practices, and rules of action simply by calling attention to the contexts in which they were handed down. The distinction between autonomous and heteronomous actions has in fact revolutionized our normative consciousness. At the same time, there has been a growing need for justification, which, under the conditions of postmetaphysical thinking, can be met only by *moral discourses*. The latter aim at the impartial evaluation of action conflicts. In contrast to ethical deliberations, which are oriented to the telos of my/our own good (or not misspent) life, moral deliberations require a perspective freed of all egocentrism or ethnocentrism. Under the moral viewpoint of equal respect for each person and equal consideration for the interests of all, the henceforth sharply focused normative claims of legitimately regulated interpersonal relationships are sucked into a whirlpool of problematization. At the posttraditional level of justification, individuals develop a principled moral consciousness and orient their action by the idea of self-determination. What self-legislation or moral autonomy signifies in the sphere of personal life corresponds to the rational natural-law interpretations of political freedom, that is, interpretations of democratic self-legislation in the constitution of a just society.

To the extent that the transmission of culture and processes of socialization become reflexive, there is a growing awareness of the logic of ethical and moral questions. Without the backing of religious or metaphysical worldviews that are immune to criticism, practical orientations can in the final analysis be gained only from rational discourse, that is, from the reflexive forms of communicative action itself. The rationalization of a lifeworld is measured by the extent to which the rationality potentials built into communicative action and released in discourse penetrate lifeworld structures and set them aflow. Processes of individual formation and cultural knowledge-systems offer less resistance to this whirlpool of problematization than does the institutional framework. It is here, at the level of personality and knowledge, that the logic of ethical and moral questions first asserted itself, such that alternatives to the normative ideas dominating modernity could no longer be justified in the long run. The conscious life conduct of the individual person finds its standards in the expressivist ideal of self-realization, the deontological idea of freedom, and the utilitarian maxim of expanding one's life opportunities. The ethical substance of collective forms of life takes its standards, on the one hand, from utopias of nonalienated, solidary social life within the horizon of traditions that have been self-consciously appropriated and critically passed on. On the other hand, it looks to models of a just society whose institutions are so constituted as to regulate expectations and conflicts in the equal interest of all; the social-welfare ideas of the progressive increase and just distribution of social wealth are just further variants of this.

One consequence of the foregoing considerations is of particular interest in the present context: to the extent that "culture" and "personality structures" are charged with ideals of the above sort, a law robbed of its sacred foundation also comes under duress; as we have seen, the third component of the lifeworld, "society" as the totality of legitimate orders, is more intensely concentrated in the legal system the more the latter must bear the burden of fulfilling integrative functions for society as a whole. The changes just sketched in the two other components can explain why modern legal orders must find their legitimation, to an increasing degree, only in sources that do not bring the law into conflict with those posttraditional ideals of life and ideas of justice that first made their impact on persons and culture. Reasons that are convenient for the legitimation of law must, on pain of cognitive dissonances, harmonize with the moral principles of universal justice and solidarity. They must also harmonize with the ethical principles of a consciously "projected" life conduct for which the subjects themselves, at both the individual and collective levels, take responsibility. However, these ideas of self-determination and self-realization cannot be put together without tension. Not surprisingly, social-contract theories have responded to the modern ideals of justice and the good life with answers that bear different accents.

3.1.4

The aim of the excursus was to explain why human rights and the principle of popular sovereignty still constitute the sole ideas that can justify modern law. These two ideas represent the precipitate left behind, so to speak, once the normative substance of an ethos embedded in religious and metaphysical traditions has been forced through the filter of posttraditional justification. To the extent that moral and ethical questions have been differentiated from one another, the discursively filtered substance of norms finds expression in the two dimensions of self-determination and self-realization. Certainly one cannot simply align these two dimensions in direct correspondence with human rights and popular sovereignty. Still, there exist affinities between these two pairs of concepts, affinities that can be emphasized to a greater or lesser degree. If I may borrow a terminological shorthand from contemporary discussions in the United States, "liberal" traditions conceive human rights as the expression of moral self-determination, whereas "civic republicanism" tends to interpret popular sovereignty as the expression of ethical self-realization. From both perspectives, human rights and popular sovereignty do not so much mutually complement as compete with each other.

Frank Michelman, for example, sees in the American constitutional tradition a tension between the impersonal rule of law
founded on innate human rights and the spontaneous self-organization of a community that makes its law through the sovereign will
of the people.[30] This tension, however, can be resolved from one
side or the other. Liberals invoke the danger of a "tyranny of the
majority" and postulate the priority of human rights that guarantee
the prepolitical liberties of the individual and set limits on the
sovereign will of the political legislator. The proponents of a civic
republicanism, on the contrary, emphasize the intrinsic,
noninstrumentalizable value of civic self-organization, so that human rights have a binding character for a political community only
as elements of their own consciously appropriated tradition.
Whereas on the liberal view human rights all but impose themselves on our moral insight as something given, anchored in a
fictive state of nature, according to republicans the ethical-political
will of a self-actualizing collectivity is forbidden to recognize anything that does not correspond to its own authentic life project. In
the one case, the moral-cognitive moment predominates, in the
other, the ethical-volitional. By way of contrast, Rousseau and Kant
pursued the goal of conceiving the notion of autonomy as unifying
practical reason and sovereign will in such a way that the idea of
human rights and the principle of popular sovereignty would
mutually interpret one another. Nevertheless, these two authors
also did not succeed in integrating the two concepts in an evenly
balanced manner. On the whole, Kant suggests more of a liberal
reading of political autonomy, Rousseau a republican reading.

Kant obtains the "universal principle of law" by applying the
moral principle to "external" relations. He begins his *Elements of
Justice* with the one right owed to each human being "by virtue of
his humanity," that is, the right to equal individual liberties backed
by authorized coercion. This primordial right regulates "internal
property"; applying this to "external property" yields the private
rights of the individual (which then become the starting point for
Savigny and the German civil-law jurisprudence subsequent to
Kant).[31] This system of natural rights, which "one cannot give up
even if one wanted to,"[32] belongs "inalienably" to each human
being. It is legitimated, prior to its differentiation in the shape of

positive law, on the basis of moral principles, and hence independently of that political autonomy of citizens first constituted only
with the social contract. To this extent the principles of private law
enjoy the validity of moral rights already in the state of nature;
hence "natural rights," which protect the human being's private
autonomy, precede the will of the sovereign lawgiver. At least in this
regard, the sovereignty of the "concurring and united will" of the
citizens is constrained by morally grounded human rights. To be
sure, Kant did not interpret the binding of popular sovereignty by
human rights as a constraint, because he assumed that no one
exercising her autonomy as a citizen *could* agree to laws infringing
on her private autonomy as warranted by natural law. But this
means that political autonomy must be explained on the basis of an
internal connection between popular sovereignty and human rights.
The construct of the social contract is meant to accomplish just this.
However, in following a path of justification that *progresses* from
morality to law, the construction of Kant's *Rechtslehre* denies to the
social contract the central position it actually assumes in Rousseau.

Rousseau starts with the constitution of civic autonomy and
produces a fortiori an internal relation between popular sovereignty and human rights. Because the sovereign will of the people
can express itself only in the language of general and abstract laws,
it has directly *inscribed* in it the right of each person to equal
liberties, which Kant took as a morally grounded human right and
thus *put ahead of* political will-formation. In Rousseau, then, the
exercise of political autonomy no longer stands under the proviso
of innate rights. Rather, the normative content of human rights
enters into the very mode of carrying out popular sovereignty. The
united will of the citizens is bound, through the medium of general
and abstract laws, to a legislative procedure that excludes per se all
nongeneralizable interests and only admits regulations that guarantee equal liberties for all. According to this idea, the procedurally
correct exercise of popular sovereignty simultaneously secures the
substance of Kant's original human right.

However, Rousseau does not consistently carry through with this
plausible idea, because he owes a greater debt to the republican
tradition than does Kant. He gives the idea of self-legislation more
of an ethical than a moral interpretation, conceiving autonomy as

the realization of the consciously apprehended form of life of a particular people. As is well known, Rousseau imagines the constitution of popular sovereignty through the social contract as a kind of existential act of sociation through which isolated and success-oriented individuals *transform* themselves into citizens oriented to the common good of an ethical community. As members of a collective body, they fuse together into the macrosubject of a legislative practice that has broken with the particular interests of private persons subjected to laws. Rousseau takes the excessive ethical demands on the citizen, which are built into the republican concept of community in any case, to an extreme. He counts on political virtues that are anchored in the ethos of a small and perspicuous, more or less homogenous community integrated through shared cultural traditions. The single alternative would be state coercion: "Now the less the individual wills relate to the general will, that is to say customary conduct to the laws, the more repressive force has to be increased. The Government, then, in order to be good, should be relatively stronger as the people becomes more numerous."[33]

However, if the practice of self-legislation must feed off the ethical substance of a people who already *agree in advance* on their value orientations, then Rousseau cannot explain how the postulated orientation of the citizens toward the common good can be mediated with the differentiated interest positions of private persons. He thus cannot explain how the normatively construed common will can, without repression, be mediated with the free choice of individuals. This would require a genuinely moral standpoint that would allow individuals to look beyond what is good *for them* and examine what lies equally in the interest of each. In the final analysis, the ethical version of the concept of popular sovereignty must lose sight of the universalistic meaning of Kant's principle of law.

Apparently the normative content of the original human right cannot be fully captured by the grammar of general and abstract laws alone, as Rousseau assumed. The substantive legal equality[34] that Rousseau took as central to the legitimacy claim of modern law cannot be satisfactorily explained by the *semantic* properties of general laws. The form of universal normative propositions says nothing about their validity. Rather, the claim that a norm lies equally in the interest of everyone has the sense of rational acceptability: all those possibly affected should be able to accept the norm on the basis of good reasons. But this can become clear only under the *pragmatic* conditions of rational discourses in which the only thing that counts is the compelling force of the better argument based on the relevant information. Rousseau thinks that the normative content of the principle of law lies simply in the semantic properties of *what* is willed; but this content could be found only in those pragmatic conditions that establish *how* the political will is formed. So the sought-for internal connection between popular sovereignty and human rights lies in the normative content of the very *mode of exercising political autonomy,* a mode that is not secured simply through the grammatical form of general laws but only through the communicative form of discursive processes of opinion- and will-formation.

This connection remains hidden from Kant and Rousseau alike. Although the premises of the philosophy of the subject allow one to bring reason and will together in a concept of autonomy, one can do so only by ascribing this capacity for self-determination to a subject, be it the transcendental ego of the *Critique of Practical Reason* or the people of the *Social Contract.* If the rational will can take shape only in the individual subject, then the individual's moral autonomy must reach through the political autonomy of the united will of all in order to secure the private autonomy of each in advance via natural law. If the rational will can take shape only in the macrosubject of a people or nation, then political autonomy must be understood as the self-conscious realization of the ethical substance of a concrete community; and private autonomy is protected from the overpowering force of political autonomy only by the nondiscriminatory form of general laws. Both conceptions miss the legitimating force of a discursive process of opinion- and will-formation, in which the illocutionary binding forces of a use of language oriented to mutual understanding serve to bring reason and will together—and lead to convincing positions to which all individuals can agree without coercion.

However, if discourses (and, as we will see, bargaining processes as well, whose procedures are discursively grounded) are the site where a rational will can take shape, then the legitimacy of law ultimately depends on a communicative arrangement: as participants in rational discourses, consociates under law must be able to examine whether a contested norm meets with, or could meet with, the agreement of all those possibly affected. Consequently, the sought-for internal relation between popular sovereignty and human rights consists in the fact that the system of rights states precisely the conditions under which the forms of communication necessary for the genesis of legitimate law can be legally institutionalized. The system of rights can be reduced neither to a moral reading of human rights nor to an ethical reading of popular sovereignty, because the private autonomy of citizens must neither be set above, nor made subordinate to, their political autonomy. The normative intuitions we associate conjointly with human rights and popular sovereignty achieve their *full* effect in the system of rights only if we assume that the universal right to equal liberties may neither be imposed as a moral right that merely sets an external constraint on the sovereign legislator, nor be instrumentalized as a functional prerequisite for the legislator's aims. The co-originality of private and public autonomy first reveals itself when we decipher, in discourse-theoretic terms, the motif of self-legislation according to which the addressees of law are simultaneously the authors of their rights. The substance of human rights then resides in the formal conditions for the legal institutionalization of those discursive processes of opinion- and will-formation in which the sovereignty of the people assumes a binding character.

3.2 Moral Norms and Legal Norms: On the Complementary Relation between Natural Law and Positive Law

3.2.1

We have analyzed two lines of theoretical development—that of civil-law jurisprudence and that of rational natural law—and found difficulties that can be explained by similar deficits: the internal relation between "subjective" rights and "objective" law, on the one side, and between private and public autonomy, on the other, discloses itself only when we take both the intersubjective structure of rights and the communicative structure of self-legislation seriously and explicate them appropriately. Before I can attempt to do this and introduce the system of rights from a discourse-theoretic standpoint, however, the relation between law and morality must be explained. The difficulties analyzed above are not due exclusively to the false course set by the philosophy of consciousness. They also follow from the fact that modern natural law, in preserving the distinction between natural and positive law, assumed a burden of debt from traditional natural law. It holds on to a duplication of the concept of law that is sociologically implausible and has normatively awkward consequences. Rather than subordinate positive law to natural law or morality, I start with the assumption that at the postmetaphysical level of justification, legal and moral rules are *simultaneously* differentiated from traditional ethical life and appear *side by side* as two different but mutually complementary kinds of action norms. In accordance with this, the concept of practical reason must be understood so abstractly that it can assume a specifically different meaning depending on which kind of norm is at issue: the meaning of a moral principle, on the one hand, and that of a principle of democracy, on the other. If one thereby avoids a moralistic constriction of the concepts of reason and autonomy, then the Kantian principle of law loses its mediating function; instead, it serves to clarify the formal aspects under which legal rules differ from moral ones. Human rights, too, which are inscribed in citizens' practice of democratic self-determination, must then be conceived from the start as rights in the juridical sense, their moral content notwithstanding.

In his "Introduction to the Metaphysics of Morals," Kant proceeds differently.[35] He starts with the basic concept of the moral law and obtains juridical laws from it by way of *limitation*. Moral theory supplies the overarching concepts: will and free choice, action and incentive, duty and inclination, law and legislation serve in the first place to characterize moral judgment and action. In the legal theory, these basic moral concepts undergo limitations in three dimensions. According to Kant, the concept of law does not refer primarily to free will but to the *free choice* of the addressees; furthermore, it pertains to the *external relations* of one person to another; finally, it is furnished with the *coercive power* that one person is entitled to exercise with respect to another in the case of infringement. Under these three aspects, the principle of law sets limits on the moral principle. Thus limited, moral legislation is *reflected* in juridical legislation, morality in legality, duties of virtue in legal duties, and so forth.

This construction is guided by the Platonic intuition that the legal order imitates the noumenal order of a "kingdom of ends" and at the same time embodies it in the phenomenal world. More specifically, the Platonic legacy lives on in the duplication of law into natural and positive law. By this I mean the intuition that the ideal community of morally accountable subjects—the unlimited communication community from C. S. Peirce and Josiah Royce to Karl-Otto Apel[36]—enters through the medium of law into the arena of historical time and social space and acquires the concrete, spatiotemporally situated shape of a legal community. This intuition is not entirely false, for a legal order can be legitimate only if it does not contradict basic moral principles. In virtue of the legitimacy components of legal validity, positive law has a reference to morality inscribed within it. But this moral reference must not mislead us into ranking morality above law, as though there were a hierarchy of norms. The notion of a higher law (i.e., a hierarchy of legal orders) belongs to the premodern world. Rather, autonomous morality and the enacted law that depends on justification stand in a *complementary relationship*.

From a sociological point of view, both of these emerged simultaneously from that encompassing societal ethos in which traditional law and a conventional ethic were still intertwined with each other. Once the sacred foundations of this network of law, morality, and ethical life were shaken, processes of differentiation set in. At the level of cultural knowledge, legal questions separated from moral and ethical questions, as we have seen. At the institutional level, positive law separated from the customs and habits that were devalued to mere conventions. To be sure, moral and legal questions refer to the same problems: how interpersonal relationships can be legitimately ordered and actions coordinated with one another through justified norms, how action conflicts can be consensually resolved against the background of intersubjectively recognized normative principles and rules. But they refer to these same problems in different ways. Despite the common reference point, morality and law differ prima facie inasmuch as posttraditional morality represents only a form of cultural *knowledge*, whereas law has, in addition to this, a binding character at the institutional level. Law is not only a symbolic system but an action system as well.

The empirically informed view that modern legal orders are a coeval complement of autonomous morality no longer fits with the platonistic notion that law and morality are related by a kind of imitation—as if the same geometric figure were simply projected on a different level of presentation. Hence we must not understand basic rights or *Grundrechte*, which take the shape of constitutional norms, as mere imitations of moral rights, and we must not take political autonomy as a mere copy of moral autonomy. Rather, norms of action *branch out* into moral and legal rules. From a normative point of view, this corresponds to the assumption that moral and civic autonomy are co-original and can be explained with the help of a parsimonious discourse principle that merely expresses the meaning of postconventional requirements of justification. Like the postconventional level of justification itself—the level at which substantial ethical life dissolves into its elements—this principle certainly has a normative content inasmuch as it explicates the meaning of impartiality in practical judgments. However, despite its normative content, it lies at a level of abstraction that is *still neutral* with respect to morality and law, for it refers to action norms in general:

D: Just those action norms are valid to which all possibly affected persons could agree as participants in rational discourses.

This formulation contains some basic terms that require elucidation. The predicate "valid" (*gültig*) pertains to action norms and all the general normative propositions that express the meaning of such norms; it expresses normative validity in a nonspecific sense that is still indifferent to the distinction between morality and legitimacy. I understand "action norms" as temporally, socially, and substantively generalized behavioral expectations. I include among "those affected" (or involved) anyone whose interests are touched by the foreseeable consequences of a general practice regulated by the norms at issue. Finally, "rational discourse" should include *any* attempt to reach an understanding over problematic validity claims insofar as this takes place under conditions of communication that enable the free processing of topics and contributions, information and reasons in the public space constituted by illocutionary obligations. The expression also refers indirectly to bargaining processes insofar as these are regulated by discursively grounded procedures.

Naturally, to conceive (D) with sufficient abstraction, it is important that we not limit a fortiori the kinds of issues and contributions and the sorts of reasons that "count" in each case. The moral principle first results when one specifies the general discourse principle for those norms that can be justified if and *only* if equal consideration is given to the interests of all those who are possibly involved. The principle of democracy results from a corresponding specification for those action norms that appear in legal form. Such norms can be justified by calling on pragmatic, ethical-political, and moral reasons—here justification is not restricted to moral reasons alone. To anticipate analyses in the following chapter, the required kinds of reasons result from the logic of the question at issue in each case. With moral questions, humanity or a presupposed republic of world citizens constitutes the reference system for justifying regulations that lie in the equal interest of all. In principle, the decisive reasons must be acceptable to each and everyone. With ethical-political questions, the form of life of the political community that is "in each case our own" constitutes the reference system for justifying decisions that are supposed to express an authentic, collective self-understanding. In principle, the decisive reasons must be acceptable to all members sharing "our" traditions and strong evaluations. Oppositions between interests require a rational balancing of competing value orientations and interest positions. Here the totality of social or subcultural groups that are directly involved constitute the reference system for negotiating compromises. Insofar as these compromises come about under fair bargaining conditions, they must be acceptable in principle to all parties, even if on the basis of respectively different reasons.

In my previous publications on discourse ethics, I have not sufficiently distinguished between the discourse principle and the moral principle. The discourse principle is only intended to explain the point of view from which norms of action can be *impar-*

tially justified; I assume that the principle itself reflects those symmetrical relations of recognition built into communicatively structured forms of life in general. To introduce such a discourse principle already presupposes that practical questions can be judged impartially and decided rationally. This is not a trivial supposition; its justification is incumbent on a theory of argumentation, which I will sketch provisionally in the next chapter. This investigation leads one to distinguish various types of discourse (and their corresponding sorts of reasons) according to the logic of the question at issue; it also leads to a distinction between discourse and procedurally regulated bargaining. Specifically, one must show for each type which rules would allow pragmatic, ethical, and moral questions to be answered.[37] We might say that these various rules of argumentation are so many ways of operationalizing the discourse principle. For the justification of moral norms, the discourse principle takes the form of a universalization principle. To this extent, the moral principle functions as a rule of argumentation. Starting with the general presuppositions of argumentation as the reflective form of communicative action, one can attempt to elucidate this principle in a formal-pragmatic fashion.[38] I cannot go into this here. For the application of moral norms to particular cases, the universalization principle is replaced by a principle of appropriateness. We will deal with this later in regard to legal discourses of application.[39] The two principles express different aspects of the same moral principle, which requires that the interests of each person be given equal consideration. In the present context, however, I am primarily concerned with the ways in which one can distinguish the principle of democracy from that of morality.

Caution is necessary here. At this juncture, one must not succumb to the ingrained prejudice suggesting that morality pertains only to social relationships for which one is personally responsible, whereas law and political justice extend to institutionally mediated spheres of interaction.[40] Discourse theory conceives of morality as an authority that crosses the boundaries between private and public spheres; these boundaries vary throughout history anyhow, depending on social structure. If we construe the universalist claim of the moral principle intersubjectively, then we must relocate ideal role taking, which, according to Kant, each individual undertakes privately, to a public practice implemented by all persons in common. Besides, allocating the jurisdictions of morality and law according to private and public spheres of action is counterintuitive in any event, for the simple reason that the will-formation of the political legislator has to include the moral aspects of the matter in need of regulation. Indeed, in complex societies, morality can become effective beyond the local level only by being translated into the legal code.

To obtain sufficiently selective criteria for the distinction between the principles of democracy and morality, I start with the fact that the principle of democracy should establish a procedure of legitimate lawmaking. Specifically, the democratic principle states that only those statutes may claim legitimacy that can meet with the assent (*Zustimmung*) of all citizens in a discursive process of legislation that in turn has been legally constituted. In other words, this principle explains the performative meaning of the practice of self-determination on the part of legal consociates who recognize one another as free and equal members of an association they have joined voluntarily. Thus the principle of democracy lies at *another level* than the moral principle.

Whereas the moral principle functions as a rule of argumentation for deciding moral questions rationally, the principle of democracy already presupposes the possibility of valid moral judgments. Indeed, it presupposes the possibility of *all* the types of practical judgments and discourses that supply laws with their legitimacy. The principle of democracy thus does not answer the question whether and how political affairs in general can be handled discursively; that is for a theory of argumentation to answer. On the premise that rational political opinion- and will-formation is at all possible, the principle of democracy only tells us how this can be institutionalized, namely, through a system of rights that secures for each person an equal participation in a process of legislation whose communicative presuppositions are guaranteed to begin with. Whereas the moral principle operates at the level at which a specific form of argumentation is *internally* constituted, the democratic principle refers to the level at which interpenetrating forms of argumentation are *externally* institutionalized. At this latter level, provisions are made for an effective participation in discursive processes of opinion- and will-formation, which take place in forms of communication that are themselves legally guaranteed.

One way we can distinguish the principles of democracy and morality is by their different levels of reference. The other is by the difference between legal norms and other action norms. Whereas the moral principle extends to any norm for whose justification moral arguments are both necessary and sufficient, the democratic principle is tailored to legal norms. These rules differ from the simple, more or less quasi-natural norms of interaction we find in everyday life. The legal form in which these norms are clad is a relatively recent product of social evolution. In contrast to naturally emergent rules, whose validity can be judged solely from the moral point of view, legal norms have an artificial character; they constitute an intentionally produced layer of action norms that are reflexive in the sense of being applicable to themselves. Hence the principle of democracy must not only establish a procedure of legitimate lawmaking, it must also *steer the production of the legal medium itself.* The democratic principle must specify, in accordance with the discourse principle, the conditions to be satisfied by individual rights in general, that is, by any rights suitable for the constitution of a legal community and capable of providing the medium for this community's self-organization. Thus, along with the system of rights, one must also create the *language* in which a community can understand itself as a voluntary association of free and equal consociates *under law.*

Corresponding to the two ways in which we have distinguished the principles of democracy and morality, then, are two tasks the required system of rights is supposed to solve. It should institutionalize the communicative framework for a rational political will-formation, and it should ensure the very medium in which alone this will-formation can express itself as the common will of freely associated legal persons. To specify this second task, we must precisely define the formal characteristics of the medium of law.

3.2.2

In what follows, I want to elucidate the formal characteristics of law by means of the complementary relation between law and morality. This elucidation is part of a *functional* explanation and not a normative justification of law. The legal form is in no way a principle one could "justify," either epistemically or normatively. As already mentioned, Kant characterized the legality, or juridical form, of behavior through three abstractions referring to the addressees, and not the authors, of law. Law abstracts, first, from the capacity of the addressees to bind their will of their own accord, because it assumes that *free choice* is a sufficient source of law-abiding behavior. Second, the law abstracts from the complexities that action plans owe to their lifeworld contexts; it restricts itself to the *external relation* of interactive influence that typical social actors exert on one another. Third, we have already seen that law abstracts from the *kind of motivation*; it is satisfied with action that outwardly conforms to rules, however such conformity might arise.

The specifically limited status of the legal person corresponds to the modes of action constrained by law in this way. Moral norms regulate interpersonal relationships and conflicts between natural persons who are supposed to recognize one another both as members of a concrete community and as irreplaceable individuals.[41] Such norms are addressed to persons who are individuated through their life histories. By contrast, legal norms regulate interpersonal relationships and conflicts between actors who recognize one another as consociates in an abstract community first produced by legal norms themselves. Although they, too, are addressed to individual subjects, these subjects are individuated not through personal identities developed over a lifetime but through the capacity to occupy the position of typical members of a legally constituted community. From the perspective of the addressee, then, one abstracts in a legal relation from the person's capacity to bind her will through normative insights as such; it is sufficient to expect that she have the capacity for making purposive-rational decisions, that is, the capacity for freedom of choice.[42] The further aspects of legality issue from this reduction of the free (and authentic) will of a morally (and ethically) accountable person to the free choice of a legal subject oriented toward her own preferences. Only matters pertaining to external relations can be legally regulated at all. This is because rule-conformative behavior must, if necessary, be enforced. This explains in turn why the legal form has an atomizing effect, which naturally does not negate the intersubjective bases of law as such.

Up to this point, Kant's concept of legality is a helpful guide to analyzing the formal characteristics of law. However, we must not follow him in conceiving the aspects of legality as limitations of morality. I suggest instead that we explain these aspects in terms of the complementary relation between law and morality. This is suggested by a sociological approach as well: the constitution of the legal form became necessary to offset deficits arising with the collapse of traditional ethical life. From that point on, an autonomous morality supported by reason alone is concerned only with correct judgments. With the transition to a postconventional level of justification, moral consciousness detaches itself from customary practices, while the encompassing social ethos shrinks to mere convention, to habit and customary law.

A principled, postconventional morality takes a critical approach that challenges all quasi-natural, received action orientations backed by institutions and motivationally anchored through patterns of socialization. As soon as the possible options along with their normative background are exposed to the searching gaze of such a morality, they fall into the whirlpool of problematization. Specialized for questions of justice, a principled morality views *everything* through the powerful but narrow lens of universalizability. Its telos consists in the impartial judgment of morally relevant action conflicts, and hence it facilitates a knowledge that is meant to orient one's action but does not thereby *dispose* one to act rightly. Sublimated into knowledge, this morality is, like all knowledge, represented at the cultural level. It exists in the first instance only as the meaning content of cultural symbols that can be understood and interpreted, handed down and critically developed. Naturally, this type of cultural knowledge also refers to *possible* actions, but of itself it no longer maintains any contact, so to speak, with the motivations that lend moral judgments their practical thrust, nor with the institutions that ensure that justified moral expectations are actually fulfilled. A morality thus withdrawn into the cultural system maintains only a virtual relation to action as long as it is not actualized by motivated actors *themselves.* The latter must be disposed to act according to conscience. A principled morality thus depends on socialization processes that meet it halfway by engendering the corresponding agencies of conscience, namely, the correlative superego formations. Aside from the weak motivating force of good reasons, such a morality becomes effective for action only through the internalization of moral principles in the personality system.

The move from knowledge to action remains uncertain, on account of the vulnerability of the moral actor's precarious, highly abstract system of self-control, and in general on account of the vicissitudes of socialization processes that promote such demanding competences. A morality that depends on the accommodating substrate of propitious personality structures would have a limited effectiveness if it could not engage the actor's motives in *another* way besides internalization, that is, precisely by way of an institutionalized legal system that *supplements* postconventional morality in a manner effective for action. Law is two things at the same time: a system of knowledge and a system of action. We can understand it just as much as a text that consists of normative propositions and interpretations, as we can view it as an institution, that is, as a complex of normatively regulated action. Because motivations and value orientations are interwoven with each other in law as an action system, legal norms have the immediate effectiveness for action that moral judgments as such lack. At the same time, legal institutions differ from naturally emergent institutional orders in virtue of their comparatively high degree of rationality; they give firm shape to a system of knowledge that has been doctrinally refined and coupled with a principled morality. Because law is simultaneously established this way at the levels of culture and society, it can *offset* the weaknesses of a morality that exists primarily as knowledge.

The person who judges and acts morally must independently appropriate this moral knowledge, assimilate it, and put it into practice. She is subject to unprecedented (a) cognitive, (b) motivational, and (c) organizational demands, from which the person as legal subject is *unburdened*.

(a) Postconventional morality provides no more than a procedure for impartially judging disputed questions. It cannot pick out a catalog of duties or even designate a list of hierarchically ordered norms, but it expects subjects to form their own judgments. Moreover, the communicative freedom they enjoy in moral discourses leads only to fallible insights in the contest of interpretations.

Problems of norm justification do not present the real difficulties. Normally, the basic principles themselves—entailing such duties as equal respect for each person, distributive justice, benevolence toward the needy, loyalty, and sincerity—are not disputed. Rather, the abstractness of these highly generalized norms leads to problems of application as soon as a conflict reaches beyond the routine interactions in familiar contexts. Complex operations are required to reach a decision in cases of this sort. On the one hand, one must uncover and describe the relevant features of the situation in light of competing but somewhat indeterminate norm candidates; on the other hand, one must select, interpret, and apply the norm most appropriate to the present case in the light of a description of the situation that is as complete as possible. Thus, problems of justification and application in complex issues often overtax the individual's analytical capacity. This *cognitive indeterminacy* is absorbed by the facticity of the genesis of law. The political legislature decides which norms count as law, and the courts settle contests of interpretation over the application of valid but interpretable norms in a manner at once judicious and definitive for all sides. The legal system deprives legal persons in their role of addressees of the power to define the criteria for judging between lawful and unlawful. Parliamentary legislative procedures, judicial decision making, and the doctrinal jurisprudence that precisely defines rules and systematizes decisions represent different ways that law complements morality by relieving the individual of the cognitive burdens of forming her own moral judgments.

(b) However, a principled morality encumbers the individual not only with the problem of deciding action conflicts but also with expectations (*Erwartungen*) regarding her strength of will. On the one hand, in conflict situations she is supposed to be willing to seek a consensual solution, that is, to enter discourses or to carry out imaginary discourses in an advocatory fashion. On the other hand, she is supposed to find the strength to act according to moral insights, if necessary against her own immediate interests, and hence reconcile duty and inclination. The actor is supposed to achieve harmony between herself as author of moral "oughts" and herself as their addressee. In addition to the cognitive indeterminacy of principled judgment, then, there is the *motivational uncer-*

tainty about action guided by known principles. This is absorbed by the facticity of the law's enforcement. To the extent that moral cognition is not sufficiently anchored in the motives and attitudes of its addressees, it must be supplemented by a law that enforces norm-conformative behavior while leaving motives and attitudes open. Coercive law overlays normative expectations with threats of sanctions in such a way that addressees may restrict themselves to the prudential calculation of consequences.

The problem of weakness of will also gives rise to the further problem of what can be reasonably expected (*Zumutbarkeit*). A principled morality directs individuals to examine the validity of norms under the presupposition that everyone in fact observes, or at least externally complies with, valid norms. However, if precisely those norms are valid that deserve the rationally motivated agreement of all under the condition that actual compliance with the norm is *universal*, then no one *can reasonably be expected* to abide by valid norms insofar as this condition is not fulfilled. Each must be able to expect (*erwarten*) that everyone will observe valid norms. Valid norms represent reasonable expectations only if they can actually be enforced against deviant behavior.

(c) A third problem, that of the imputability of obligations, or accountability, results from the universalistic character of postconventional morality. This problem arises especially in regard to positive duties, which often—and increasingly so, as a society becomes more complex—require cooperation or organization. For example, the unmistakable duty to preserve even anonymous neighbors from starvation conspicuously contrasts with the fact that millions of inhabitants of the First World allow hundreds of thousands in poverty-stricken areas of the Third World to perish. Even charitable aid can be transmitted only along organized paths; the convoluted route taken by food, medicine, clothing, and infrastructures far exceeds the initiative and range of individual action. As many studies have shown, a structural improvement would require no less than a new economic world order. Similar problems that can only be managed by institutions arise in one's own region, and even in one's very neighborhood. The more that moral consciousness attunes itself to universalistic value orientations, the greater are the discrepancies between uncontested moral demands, on the one hand, and organizational constraints and resistances to change, on the other. Thus the moral demands that can be fulfilled only through anonymous networks and organizations first find clear addressees only within a system of rules that can be reflexively applied to itself. Law alone is reflexive *in its own right;* it contains secondary rules that serve the production of primary rules for guiding behavior. It can define jurisdictional powers and found organizations—in short, produce a system of accountabilities that refers not only to natural, legal persons but to fictive, legal subjects, such as corporations and public agencies.

Similar to the problems of reasonable expectability, weakness of will, and decidability, the question of the moral division of labor[43] announces the limits of a postconventional morality, the point where supplementation by law becomes functionally necessary. A further problem results from the fact that the postconventional level of justification removes the foundation for traditional modes of legitimating institutions. As soon as the more demanding moral standards can no longer be naively established, an impulse to raise questions arises, putting pressure on devalued traditional institutions to justify themselves. But the morality that supplies the criteria for the disillusioning assessment of existing institutions does not itself offer any *operative* means for their reconstruction. To this end, positive law stands in reserve as an action system able to take the place of other institutions.

To be sure, the law recommends itself not only for the reconstruction of quasi-natural institutional complexes that have fallen into disrepair as a result of their loss of legitimation. In the course of social modernization, a *new* kind of organizational need arises, which can only be managed constructively. Traditional spheres of interaction, such as the family or school, are *refashioned* at their institutional base, whereas formally organized action systems, such as markets, businesses, and administrations, are first *created* through legal regulation. The capitalist economy or bureaucratic agencies first come to exist in the legal medium in which they are institutionalized.

Despite what the previously examined problems might suggest, of course, the need of morality for compensation is not enough to explain the specific achievements of the legal code that are required to answer the growing need for regulation and organization in increasingly complex societies. The real proportions become evident only when one turns things around and also views morality from the vantage point of the legal system. A principled morality whose effectiveness was based solely on socialization processes and individual conscience would remain restricted to a narrow radius of action. Through a legal system with which it remains internally coupled, however, morality can spread to *all* spheres of action, including those systemically independent spheres of media-steered interactions that unburden actors of all moral expectations other than that of a general obedience to law. In less complex societies, socially integrating force inheres in the ethos of a form of life, inasmuch as this integral ethical life binds all the components of the lifeworld together, attuning concrete duties to institutions and linking them with motivations. Under conditions of high complexity, moral contents can spread throughout a society along the channels of legal regulation.

3.3 A Discourse-Theoretic Justification of Basic Rights: The Discourse Principle, the Legal Form, and the Democratic Principle

We can now tie the various strands of argument together, in order to introduce a system of rights that gives *equal weight* to both the private and the public autonomy of the citizen. This system should contain precisely the basic rights that citizens must mutually grant one another if they want to legitimately regulate their life in common by means of positive law. As in social-contract theories, these rights should be introduced first of all from the perspective of a nonparticipant. We have already taken a number of steps that prepare for this. We began by recalling the doctrinal history of civil law from Savigny to Kelsen in order to show that a legitimacy based on legality is rather puzzling. We then went on to interpret the concept of civic autonomy in discourse-theoretic terms; this brought out the internal connection between human rights and popular sovereignty. Finally, we investigated the complementary relation between law and morality so as to clarify the formal characteristics that distinguish legal norms from general norms of action. Interestingly enough, this legal form itself already gives rise to the privileged position that rights occupy in modern legal orders.

The legal medium as such presupposes rights that define the status of legal persons as bearers of rights. These rights are tailored to the freedom of choice of typical social actors; that is, they define liberties that are granted conditionally. The one aspect of this—that the actor's self-interested choice is released from the obligatory contexts of a shared background—is only the obverse side of the other aspect, namely, the coordination of action through coercible laws that impose external constraints on the range of options. This explains the significance of laws that distribute and safeguard individual liberties while rendering them compatible with the same liberties of others.

Such rights guarantee a private autonomy that can also be described as liberation from the obligations of what I call "communicative freedom." Along with Klaus Günther, I understand "communicative freedom" as the possibility—mutually presupposed by participants engaged in the effort to reach an understanding—of responding to the utterances of one's counterpart and to the concomitantly raised validity claims, which aim at intersubjective recognition.[44] Communicative action involves obligations that are *suspended* by legally protected liberties.

Communicative freedom exists only between actors who, adopting a performative attitude, want to reach an understanding with one another about something and expect one another to take positions on reciprocally raised validity claims. The fact that communicative freedom depends on an intersubjective relationship explains why this freedom is coupled with illocutionary obligations. One has the possibility of taking a yes or no position to a criticizable validity claim only if the other is willing to justify the claim raised by her speech act, should this be necessary. Communicatively acting subjects commit themselves to coordinating their action plans on the basis of a consensus that depends in turn on their reciprocally taking positions on, and intersubjectively recognizing, validity claims. From this it follows that only those reasons count that all the participating parties *together* find acceptable. It is in each case the *same* kinds of reasons that have a rationally motivating force for those involved in communicative action. By contrast, the actor who simply decides as she wishes is not concerned whether the reasons that are decisive *for her* could also be accepted by others. In the case of purposive-rational behavior, agent-relative reasons suffice. This is why we can understand the private autonomy of a legal subject essentially as the negative freedom to withdraw from the public space of illocutionary obligations to a position of mutual observation and influence. Private autonomy extends as far as the legal subject does *not* have to give others an account or give publicly acceptable reasons for her action plans. Legally granted liberties entitle one to *drop out of* communicative action, to refuse illocutionary obligations; they ground a privacy freed from the burden of reciprocally acknowledged and mutually expected communicative freedoms.

The Kantian principle of law, which holds that each person has a right to individual liberties, can then be understood as calling for the constitution of a legal code that provides rights that immunize legal subjects against the expectations of communicative freedom. To be sure, the principle of law requires not just the right to liberties in general but the right of each person to equal liberties. The liberty of *each* is supposed to be compatible with equal liberty for *all* in accordance with a universal law. It is at this point that the legitimacy claim of positive law comes into play, a claim we could disregard as long as we considered only the formal characteristics of law. In the Kantian formulation of the principle of law, the "general law" carries the weight of legitimation. The Categorical Imperative is always already in the background here: the form of a general law legitimates the distribution of liberties, because it implies that a given law has passed the universalization test and been found worthy in the court of reason. In Kant this results in a subordination of law to morality, a move incompatible with the idea of an autonomy realized in the *medium of law itself.*

The idea of self-legislation *by citizens*, that is, requires that those subject to law as its addressees can at the same time understand themselves as authors of law. We cannot meet this requirement simply by conceiving the right to equal liberties as a morally grounded right that the political legislator merely has to enact. Insofar as we have a concept of legality already at our disposal, we can certainly convince ourselves as morally judging persons of the validity of the original human right. But *as* moral legislators, we are not identical with the legal subjects on whom, as addressees, this right is *bestowed*. Even if each legal subject realizes, in the role of moral person, that she herself could have given herself certain basic rights, this moral approval in hindsight will not do; it by no means eliminates the paternalism of the "rule of law" characteristic of political heteronomy. It is only participation in the practice of *politically autonomous* lawmaking that makes it possible for the addressees of law to have a correct understanding of the legal order as created by themselves. Legitimate law is compatible only with a mode of legal coercion that does not destroy the rational motives for obeying the law: it must remain possible for everyone to obey legal norms on the basis of insight. In spite of its coercive character, therefore, law must not *compel* its addressees to adopt such motives but must offer them the option, in each case, of foregoing the exercise of their communicative freedom and not taking a position on the legitimacy claim of law, that is, the option of giving up the performative attitude to law in a particular case in favor of the objectivating attitude of an actor who freely decides on the basis of utility calculations.

The idea of self-legislation by citizens, then, should not be reduced to the *moral* self-legislation of *individual* persons. Autonomy must be conceived more abstractly, and in a strictly neutral way. I have therefore introduced a discourse principle that is initially indifferent vis-à-vis morality and law. The discourse principle is intended to assume the shape of a principle of democracy only by way of legal institutionalization. The principle of democracy is what then confers legitimating force on the legislative process. The key idea is that the principle of democracy derives from the interpenetration of the discourse principle and the legal form. I understand this interpenetration as a *logical genesis of rights*, which one can reconstruct in a stepwise fashion. One begins by applying the discourse principle to the general right to liberties— a right constitutive for the legal form as such—and ends by legally institutionalizing the conditions for a discursive exercise of political autonomy. By means of this political autonomy, the private autonomy that was at first abstractly posited can retroactively assume an elaborated legal shape. Hence the principle of democracy can only appear as the heart of a *system* of rights. The logical genesis of these rights comprises a circular process in which the legal code, or legal form, and the mechanism for producing legitimate law—hence the democratic principle—are *co-originally* constituted.

My presentation moves from the abstract to the concrete. Specificity results inasmuch as the external perspective initially taken by the theorist is, in the course of elaboration, internalized in the system of rights. This system should contain precisely the rights citizens must confer on one another if they want to legitimately regulate their interactions and life contexts by means of positive law. What is meant by the expressions "positive law" and "legitimately regulate" should be clear by now. To arrive at the system of rights, then, we need the concept of the "legal form," which stabilizes behavioral expectations in the manner already discussed, and the "discourse principle," in light of which the legitimacy of legal norms can be tested. With these we have what we need to introduce the three categories of rights in abstracto that generate the legal code itself by defining the status of legal persons:

1. Basic rights that result from the politically autonomous elaboration of the *right to the greatest possible measure of equal individual liberties.*

These rights require the following as necessary corollaries:

2. Basic rights that result from the politically autonomous elaboration of the *status of a member* in a voluntary association of consociates under law.

3. Basic rights that result immediately from the *actionability* of rights and from the politically autonomous elaboration of individual *legal protection.*

These three categories of rights result simply from the application of the discourse principle to the medium of law as such, that is, to the conditions for the legal form of a horizontal association of free and equal persons. They must not yet be understood in the sense of *Abwehrrechte,* that is, liberal rights against the state, because they only regulate the relationships among freely associated citizens *prior to* any legally organized state authority from whose encroachments citizens would have to protect themselves. In fact, the above basic rights guarantee what we now call the *private autonomy* of legal subjects only in the sense that these subjects reciprocally recognize each other in their role of *addressees* of laws and therewith grant one another a status on the basis of which they can claim rights and bring them to bear against one another. Only with the next step do legal subjects also become *authors* of their legal order, to be exact, through the following:

4. Basic rights to equal opportunities to participate in processes of opinion- and will-formation in which citizens exercise their *political autonomy* and through which they generate legitimate law.

This category of rights is reflexively applied to the constitutional interpretation and the further political development or elaboration of the basic rights abstractly identified in (1) through (4). For political rights ground the status of free and equal active citizens. This status is self-referential insofar as it enables citizens to change and expand their various rights and duties, or "material legal status," so as to interpret and develop their private and civic autonomy simultaneously. Finally, with a view toward this goal, the rights listed thus far *imply* the following:

5. Basic rights to the provision of living conditions that are socially, technologically, and ecologically safeguarded, insofar as the current circumstances make this necessary if citizens are to have equal opportunities to utilize the civil rights listed in (1) through (4).

In the following I will limit my comments to the four absolutely justified categories of civil rights; the category of social and ecological rights, which can be justified only in relative terms, I postpone to the final chapter. In keeping with this introductory sketch, the following interpretation of civil rights should clarify the internal relation between human rights and popular sovereignty and dissolve the paradox in the emergence of legitimacy from legality.

(1) Norms appearing in the form of law entitle actors to exercise their rights or liberties. However, one cannot determine which of these laws are legitimate simply by looking at the *form* of individual rights. Only by bringing in the discourse principle can one show that *each person* is owed a right to the greatest possible measure of *equal* liberties that are mutually compatible. According to this

principle, just those regulations are legitimate that satisfy the requirement that the rights of each be compatible with equal rights for all. In fact, Kant's principle of law coincides with this general right to equal liberties. It simply holds that a legal code should be set up in the form of *legitimately distributed* rights that guarantee the protection of the private autonomy of legal subjects. Naturally, with these rights alone the legal code is not yet completely institutionalized. To render this code applicable within a determinate legal community, one must demarcate the bounds of membership and provide legal remedies for cases of rights violations.

(2) Unlike moral rules, legal rules do not norm possible interactions between communicatively competent subjects *in general* but the interaction contexts of a concrete society. This follows simply from the concept of the positivity of law, that is, from the facticity of making and enforcing law. Legal norms stem from the decisions of a historical legislature; they refer to a geographically delimited legal territory and to a socially delimitable collectivity of legal consociates, and consequently to particular jurisdictional boundaries. These limitations in historical time and social space result simply from the fact that legal subjects cede their authorizations to use coercion to a legal authority that monopolizes the means of legitimate coercion and if necessary employs these means on their behalf. Every earthly monopoly on violence, even that of a world government, has finite dimensions, which remain provincial in comparison with the future and the universe. Hence the establishment of a legal code calls for rights that regulate membership in a *determinate* association of citizens, thus allowing one to differentiate between members and nonmembers, citizens and aliens. In communities organized as national states, such rights assume the form of rights that define membership in a state. The external aspects of such membership, which depend on the recognition of a government in accordance with international law, are not our concern at this point. Internally, membership status forms the basis for ascribing the rights and duties that together constitute the status of citizen. From the application of the discourse principle, it follows that each person must be protected from a unilateral deprivation of membership rights but must in turn have the right to renounce the status of a member. The right to emigrate implies that member-

ship must rest on an (at least tacit) act of agreement on the member's part. At the same time, immigration, that is, the expansion of the legal community through the inclusion of aliens who seek rights of membership, requires a regulation in the equal interest of members and applicants.

(3) The legal institutionalization of the legal code requires, finally, guaranteed legal remedies through which any person who feels her rights have been infringed can assert her claims. The coercive character of law requires in cases of conflict special procedures for interpreting and applying existing law in a binding manner. Legal persons can file suits, and thus mobilize the sanctions connected with their rights, only if they have free access to independent and effectively functioning courts that decide disputes impartially and authoritatively according to the law. In light of the discourse principle, one can then justify basic rights of due process that provide all persons with equal legal protection, an equal claim to a legal hearing, equality in the application of law, and thus equal treatment before the law.

In summary, we can say that the general right to equal liberties, along with the correlative membership rights and guaranteed legal remedies, establishes the legal code as such. In a word, there is no legitimate law without these rights. To be sure, with this legal institutionalization of the legal medium we do not yet have the familiar liberal basic rights. Aside from the fact that at this level we still are not dealing with an organized state authority against which such rights would have to be directed, the basic rights inscribed in the legal code itself remain *unsaturated,* so to speak. They must be *interpreted* and *given concrete shape* by a political legislature in response to changing circumstances. The legal code cannot be established in abstracto but only in such a way that citizens who want to legitimately regulate their living together by means of positive law grant one other *specific* rights. On the other hand, these particular rights actually function to establish a legal code only if they can be seen as explicating the legal categories mentioned above. In this sense, the classic liberal rights—to personal dignity; to life, liberty, and bodily integrity; to freedom of movement, freedom in the choice of one's vocation, property, the inviolability of one's home, and so on—are interpretations of, and ways of working out, what we might call a "general right to individual liberties," however these may be specified. Similarly, the prohibition against extradition, the right to political asylum, and everything pertaining to the rights and duties of citizens (i.e., their material legal status) specify membership in a voluntary association of free and equal legal persons. Finally, the guarantees of equal protection and legal remedies are interpreted through procedural guarantees and basic legal standards. These include the prohibitions against retroactive punishment, double jeopardy, and ad hoc courts, as well as the guarantee of an independent judiciary, and so on.

We must hold on to *two* things: on the one hand, the first three categories of rights are unsaturated placeholders for the specification of particular basic rights; they are thus more like legal principles that guide the framers of constitutions. On the other hand, these framers must, without prejudice to their sovereignty, orient themselves by the above-mentioned principles insofar as they make use of the legal medium at all. For these principles give teeth to what Hobbes and Rousseau found so important: the rationalizing character of the legal form as such.

(4) In the genesis of rights so far, we have admittedly brought the discourse principle into the legal form only from the outside, as it were, that is, from the vantage point of the political theorist. The philosopher *tells* citizens which rights they *should* acknowledge mutually if they are legitimately to regulate their living together by means of positive law. This explains the abstract nature of the legal categories discussed so far. We must now make that change in perspective necessary if citizens are to be capable of applying the discourse principle *for themselves*. For *as* legal subjects they achieve autonomy only by both understanding themselves as, and acting as, authors of the rights they submit to as addressees. To be sure, as *legal* subjects, they may no longer choose the medium in which they can actualize their autonomy. They no longer have a choice about which language they might want to use. Rather, the legal code is given to legal subjects in advance as the only language in which they can express their autonomy. The idea of self-legislation must be realized in the medium of law itself. Hence the conditions under which citizens can judge whether the law they make is legitimate (in

light of the discourse principle) must in turn be legally guaranteed. This end is served by the basic political rights to participate in processes that form the legislator's opinion and will.

After this change in perspective, we can no longer ground equal communicative and participatory rights from *our vantage point.* The citizens themselves become those who deliberate and, acting as a constitutional assembly, decide how they must fashion the rights that give the discourse principle legal shape as a principle of democracy. According to the discourse principle, just those norms deserve to be valid that could meet with the approval of those potentially affected, insofar as the latter participate in rational discourses. Hence the desired political rights must guarantee participation in all deliberative and decisional processes relevant to legislation and must do so in a way that provides each person with equal chances to exercise the communicative freedom to take a position on criticizable validity claims. Equal opportunities for the political use of communicative freedoms require a legally structured deliberative praxis in which the discourse principle is applied. Just as communicative freedom prior to any institutionalization refers to appropriate occasions for the use of language oriented toward mutual understanding, so also do political rights— in particular, entitlements to the *public use* of communicative freedom—call for the legal institutionalization of various forms of communication and the implementation of democratic procedures. These are meant to guarantee that all formally and procedurally correct outcomes enjoy a presumption of legitimacy. Rights of equal participation for each person thus result from a symmetrical juridification of the communicative freedom of all citizens. And this freedom in turn *requires* forms of discursive opinion- and will-formation that enable an exercise of political autonomy in accordance with political rights.

If one introduces the system of rights in this way, then one can understand how popular sovereignty and human rights go hand in hand, and hence grasp the co-originality of civic and private autonomy. The scope of citizens' public autonomy is not restricted by natural or moral rights just waiting to be put into effect, nor is the individual's private autonomy merely instrumentalized for the purposes of popular sovereignty. Nothing is given prior to the citizen's practice of self-determination other than the discourse principle, which is built into the conditibns of communicative association in general, and the legal medium as such. If the discourse principle is to be implemented as the democratic principle with the help of equal communicative and participatory rights, then the legal medium must be enlisted. To be sure, the establishment of the legal code as such already implies liberty rights that beget the status of legal persons and guarantee their integrity. But as soon as the legal medium is used to institutionalize the exercise of political autonomy, these rights become necessary enabling conditions; as such, they cannot *restrict* the legislator's sovereignty, even though they are not at her disposition. Enabling conditions do not impose any limitations on what they constitute.

Taken simply for themselves, neither the discourse principle nor the legal form (of interactive relationships) suffices to ground any right. The principle of discourse can assume the shape of a principle of democracy through the medium of law only insofar as the discourse principle and the legal medium interpenetrate and *develop* into a system of rights that brings private and public autonomy into a relation of mutual presupposition. Conversely, every exercise of political autonomy signifies both an interpretation and specific elaboration of these fundamentally "unsaturated" rights by a historical legislator. This also holds for the political rights made use of in this process. The principle that all "governmental authority derives from the people" must be *specified* according to circumstances in the form of freedoms of opinion and information; the freedoms of assembly and association; the freedoms of belief, conscience, and religious confession; entitlements to participate in political elections and voting processes; entitlements to work in political parties or citizens' movements, and so forth. In the constitution-making acts of a legally binding interpretation of the system of rights, citizens make an originary use of a civic autonomy that thereby constitutes itself in a performatively self-referential manner. Thus we can understand the catalogs of human and civil rights found in our historic constitutions as context-dependent readings of the *same* system of rights.

This system of rights, however, is not given to the framers of a constitution in advance as a natural law. Only in a particular constitutional interpretation do these rights first enter into consciousness at all. In fact, when citizens interpret the system of rights in a manner congruent with their situation, they merely explicate the performative meaning of precisely the enterprise they took up as soon as they decided to legitimately regulate their common life through positive law. An enterprise of this sort presupposes no more than the concept of legal form and an intuitive understanding of the discourse principle. If talk of "the" system of rights means anything, then, it refers to the points where the various explications of the given self-understanding of such a practice converge (*übereinstimmen*). Even "our" theoretical introduction to civil rights in abstracto is exposed ex post facto as an artifice. No one can credit herself with access to a system of rights in the singular, independent of the interpretations she already has historically available. "The" system of rights does not exist in transcendental purity. But two hundred years of European constitutional law have provided us with a sufficient number of models. These can instruct a generalizing reconstruction of the intuitions that guide the intersubjective practice of self-legislation in the medium of positive law. The character of constitutional foundings, which often seal the success of political revolutions, deceptively suggests that norms outside of time and resistant to historical change are simply "stated." The technical priority of the constitution to ordinary laws belongs to the systematic elucidation of the rule of law, but it only means that the content of constitutional norms is *relatively* fixed. As we will see, every constitution is a living project that can *endure* only as an ongoing interpretation continually carried forward at all levels of the production of law.

By securing both private and public autonomy in a balanced manner, the system of rights operationalizes the tension between facticity and validity, which we first encountered as a tension between the positivity and the legitimacy of law. Both moments combine in the mutual penetration of legal form and discourse principle, as well as in the Janus faces that law turns toward its addressees on the one side and its authors on the other. On the one side, by way of coercible laws that render equal liberties compatible, the system of rights unleashes the self-interested choice of individual subjects oriented by personal preferences. On the other side, in the practice of legislation, it mobilizes and unifies the communicative freedom of citizens presumptively oriented to the common good. Here the tension between facticity and validity flares up anew; indeed, it is concentrated in the seemingly paradoxical circumstance that basic political rights must institutionalize the public use of communicative freedom *in the form* of individual rights. The legal code leaves no other alternative; communicative and participatory rights must be formulated in a language that leaves it up to autonomous legal subjects whether, and if necessary how, they want to make use of such rights. It is left to the addressees' free choice: whether or not they want to engage their free will as authors, shift their perspective from their own interests and success to mutual understanding over norms acceptable to all, and make public use of their communicative freedom.

We lose sight of this difference if we limit ourselves to a merely semantic analysis of rights. If a person is entitled to a right, then she has a corresponding claim to X and can assert this claim against other persons. At this analytical level, one can distinguish negative from positive rights, but this does not get at the specific character of the legal form.[45] Only at the pragmatic level do we catch sight of those aspects of validity we analyzed in connection with Kant's key notions of freedom of choice, external relation, and authorized coercion. Under these aspects, we can see how the individual bearer of rights and beneficiary of liberties is simultaneously related to a public use of communicative freedom: these entitlements encourage one to make use of them in an other-regarding attitude, but they must *also* be such that one *can* take them at face value, that is, understand them merely as granting individual liberties. Unlike morality, law cannot *obligate* its addressees to use individual rights in ways oriented to reaching understanding, even if political rights *call for* precisely this kind of public use. Of course even the fact of this ambiguity has a good normative sense.[46]

The emergence of legitimacy from legality admittedly appears as a paradox only on the premise that the legal system must be imagined as a circular process that recursively feeds back into and legitimates *itself.* This is already contradicted by the evidence that democratic institutions of freedom disintegrate without the initiatives of a population *accustomed* to freedom. Their spontaneity cannot be compelled simply through law; it is regenerated from traditions and preserved in the associations of a liberal political culture. Legal regulations can, to be sure, take precautions that keep down the costs of the civic virtues that are called for, ensuring that only small price hikes are necessary. The discourse-theoretic understanding of the system of rights directs our attention to both sides. On the one side, the burden of legitimation shifts from citizens' qualifications to legally institutionalized procedures of discursive opinion- and will-formation. On the other side, the juridification of communicative freedom also means that the law must draw on sources of legitimation that are not at its disposal.

4

A Reconstructive Approach to Law II: The Principles of the Constitutional State

The reconstruction of law functions as an explication of meaning. With the system of rights, we have assured ourselves of the presuppositions that members of a modern legal community must take as their starting point if they are to consider their legal order legitimate but cannot base this legitimacy on religious or metaphysical arguments. However, the legitimacy of rights and the legitimation of lawmaking processes are not the only question. There is also the question of the legitimacy of a political order and the legitimation of the exercise of political power. The basic rights reconstructed in our thought experiment are constitutive for every association of free and equal consociates under law; these rights reflect the horizontal association of citizens *in statu nascendi*, as it were. But the self-referential act that legally institutionalizes civic autonomy is still incomplete in essential respects; it cannot stabilize itself. The moment of a reciprocal conferral of rights remains a metaphorical event. It can perhaps be recalled and ritualized, but it cannot become permanent unless state power is established and put to work. If the interpenetration of private and public autonomy brought about in the system of rights is to be rendered permanent, then the process of juridification must not limit itself to the liberty of private persons and the communicative freedom of citizens. It must extend immediately to that political power *already presupposed* with the medium of law, a power to which the making as well as the enforcing of law owe their binding character. The co-original constitution and conceptual interpenetration of law and political power call for a more extensive legitimation, one requiring legal channels for the sanctioning, organizing, and executive powers of the state itself. This is the idea of government by law (section 4.1). I will clarify this idea in terms of the conditions that must be respectively satisfied for, first, the generation of communicative power (section 4.2) and, second, for the use of an administrative power bound to communicative power (section 4.3).

4.1 The Internal Relation between Law and Politics

4.1.1

The law presents itself as a system of rights only as long as we consider it in terms of its specific function of stabilizing behavioral expectations. These rights can take effect and be enforced only by organizations that make collectively binding decisions. Conversely, these decisions owe their collective bindingness to the legal form in which they are clad. This *internal connection of law with political power* is reflected in the above-noted implications that "subjective" rights have for "objective" law.

The right to equal liberties assumes concrete shape in basic rights, which, as positive law, are backed by the threat of sanctions and can be enforced against norm violations or opposing interests. To this extent they presuppose the sanctioning power of an organization that possesses the means of legitimate force so as to ensure that legal norms are observed. This concerns one aspect of the state, the fact that it keeps a force in reserve as a kind of backing for its power to command.

The equal rights of membership in a voluntary association of citizens presupposes a spatiotemporally delimited collectivity with which members can identify and to which they can attribute their actions as parts of a whole. Such a collectivity can constitute itself as a legal community only if it possesses a central authority acting on behalf of all the members. This concerns a second aspect of the state, its protective capacity to preserve itself from both external enemies and internal disorder.

The equal right to individual legal protection assumes concrete shape in basic rights that ground claims to an independent and impartial judiciary. These rights thus presuppose the establishment of a state-organized system of courts whose authority in deciding disputes relies on the sanctioning power of the state and whose administration and further development of the law draw on the organizational capacity of the state.

Finally, the equal right to political self-determination assumes concrete shape in civil rights that ground equal claims to participation in democratic legislative processes. The latter must in turn be established with the help of governmental power. In addition, political will-formation set up as a legislature depends on an executive power that can carry out and implement adopted programs. This concerns the central aspect that differentiates the state as a public institution for the bureaucratic exercise of political power. The powers of the state acquire firm institutional shape in the organized offices of a public administration. The scale of this state apparatus varies with the degree to which a society makes use of the legal medium to deliberately influence its reproductive processes. This dynamic of action-upon-self is accelerated by social entitlements, that is, claims to the satisfaction of social, cultural, and ecological preconditions for the equal opportunity to utilize private liberties and participatory political rights.

In short, the state becomes necessary as a sanctioning, organizing, and executive power because rights must be enforced, because the legal community has need of both a collective self-maintenance and an organized judiciary, and because political will-formation issues in programs that must be implemented. To be sure, these are not just functionally necessary supplements to the system of rights but *implications* already contained in rights. In this context, German jurisprudence speaks of the "objective" legal implications of "subjective" rights. Political power is not externally juxtaposed to law but is rather *presupposed* by law and itself established in the form of law. Political power can develop only through a legal code, and it is, in the legal sense of the word, constituted in the form of basic rights. This led nineteenth-century German constitutionalism to conceive "government by law" in a way that made too direct a connection between rights of individual liberty and organized state power.[1] In the German tradition, government by law, or the *Rechtsstaat,* is only supposed to guarantee the private autonomy and legal equality of citizens. In contrast, discourse theory explains how private and public autonomy are internally related. The law receives its full normative sense neither through its legal *form* per se, nor through an a priori moral *content*, but through a *procedure* of lawmaking that begets legitimacy. In this respect, the material concept of the legal statute found in the early liberal constitutionalism (represented by Robert von Mohl and his contemporaries) offers a better entry into the democratic idea of government by law. These authors understood the "legal statute" as a general and abstract rule brought about with the approval of the people's representative body in a procedure characterized by discussion and publicity. The idea behind government by law requires that the collectively binding decisions of an authority that must make use of the law to fulfill its own functions are not only cast in the form of law but are for their part legitimated by statutes enacted in accordance with that procedure. It is not the legal form as such that legitimates the exercise of governmental power but only the bond with *legitimately enacted* law. At the posttraditional level of justification, as we would say today, the only law that counts as legitimate is one that could be rationally accepted by all citizens in a discursive process of opinion- and will-formation.

Of course, this has the converse effect that the civic exercise of political autonomy is incorporated in the state: the legislature is constituted as a branch *within* the state. With the conceptual move from the horizontal association of consociates who reciprocally accord rights to one another to the vertical organization of citizens within the state, the practice of self-determination is institutionalized in a number of ways. It appears as informal opinion-formation in the political public sphere, as participation inside and outside political parties, as participation in general elections, as deliberation and decision making in parliamentary bodies, and so on. A popular sovereignty that is internally laced with individual liberties is interlaced a second time with governmental power, and in such a way that the principle that "all governmental authority derives from the people" is realized through the communicative presuppositions and procedures of an institutionally differentiated opinion- and will-formation. According to the discourse-theoretic conception of government by law, popular sovereignty is no longer embodied in a visibly identifiable gathering of autonomous citizens. It pulls back into the, as it were, "subjectless" forms of communication circulating through forums and legislative bodies. Only in this anonymous form can its communicatively fluid power bind the administrative power of the state apparatus to the will of the citizens. As we will see, in the democratic rule of law, political power is differentiated into communicative power and administrative power. Because popular sovereignty no longer concentrates in a collectivity, or in the physically tangible presence of the united citizens or their assembled representatives, but only takes effect in the circulation of reasonably structured deliberations and decisions, one can attribute a harmless meaning to the proposition that there cannot be a sovereign in the constitutional state.[2] But this interpretation must be carefully defined so as not to divest popular sovereignty of its radical-democratic content.

When, in the following, we reconstruct the internal relation between law and political power, we must be careful from the start to avoid a misunderstanding. This investigation is not concerned with the gap between norm and reality, and thus does not yet approach power as a *social* facticity able to make ideas look foolish. As in the previous chapter, our attention is directed rather at the tension between facticity and validity *inside* the law. This initially appeared in the dimension of legal validity (as the tension between the positivity and the legitimacy of law) and inside the system of rights (as the tension between private and public autonomy). These perspectives broaden when we introduce the idea of the constitutional state. From rights we move over to a constitutionally organized authority whose exercise is supposed to be bound to legitimate law. Once law is reflexively applied to the political power it tacitly presupposes, of course, the tension between facticity and validity shifts to another dimension: it reappears in constitutionally organized political power itself. State power is based on a threat of sanctions backed by instruments of force held in reserve; at the same time, however, it is *authorized* by legitimate law. As is the case in legal validity, the two moments of coercion and claim to normative validity are also combined in the collective binding force of political decisions, though in the opposite way. Whereas the law inherently claims normative validity regardless of its positivity, power is at the disposition of a political will as a means for achieving collective goals, regardless of the normative constraints that authorize it. Thus, if one views it empirically, law often only provides the form that political power must *make use of.* From a normative point of view, only *this* facticity of a power external to law, and illegitimate insofar as it instrumentalizes law, seems to invert things. In any case, the challenge posed by this social facticity is not our theme at the moment. Conceptual analysis reveals only that tension between facticity and validity found in political power per se inasmuch as the latter is internally connected with law, in relation to which it must legitimate itself. This conceptual relation must not be confused with the opposition between norm and reality. As we will see in chapter 8, this opposition is only accessible to an approach that shifts from conceptual to empirical analysis.

4.1.2

The complex of law and political power characterizes the transition from societies organized by kinship to those early societies already organized around states, out of which in turn developed the ancient empires and the civilizations associated with them. Of course, the interpenetration of law and political power did not become a problem *as such* until traditional religious legitimations became increasingly problematic in the transitional societies of the early-modern period. Only with Machiavelli do we begin to see a state power conceived in naturalistic terms, one in the process of breaking away from contexts shaped by sacred traditions. This power was viewed as a potential that power holders could calculate from strategic points of view and deploy in a purposive-rational way. Philosophers of modern natural law were confronted with the evidence of this new administrative power concentrated in a state with a monopoly on the instruments of legitimate force. This influenced their choice of concepts for explaining the interplay between state-sanctioned law and juridically organized power. Hobbes operates, on the one hand, with the *rule structure* of contractual relationships and laws and, on the other hand, with the de facto *power to command* enjoyed by a sovereign whose will could defeat every other will on earth. A state is then established on the basis of a civil contract, according to which the sovereign takes on the functions of legislation and casts his imperatives in the form of general laws. The ruler's will is channeled through statutes, but this does not essentially alter the substantial nature of a will grounded on naked decision. The ruler submits to the reason sublimated in the abstract form of legal statutes only in order to use it for his own sovereign purposes. In this construction, the facticity of a quasi-natural power to command comes into *direct* contact with the rule structure of laws that grant subjects their freedom of action. One can still find traces of this antagonism even in Kant and Rousseau, although with them the rule structure of law (and democratic procedure) is conceived as the core of a new kind of autonomy; general and abstract laws manifest a practical reason that is supposed to govern the sovereign decisions of the united people. Kant's rather paternalistic ideas for piecemeal liberal reform still betray a Hobbesian respect for the natural fact of political power, the impenetrable, decisionistic core of politics that separates law from morality.[3]

The conceptual framework of modern natural law, as developed in the tradition of the philosophy of the subject, blocks an adequate sociological perception of the cohesion of kinship societies through prepolitical institutions; in fact, the complex of law and political power was able to *join forces* with this prepolitical substratum for a long time. The phenomena that first consistently appeared in modernity—the conglomeration of administrative power, the positivization of law, and the emergence of legal authority—conceal the beginnings of a kind of political authority that initially emerged in the context of traditional societies. In tribal societies, which were the seedbed for early state formations, the prestige-based *social power* of chieftains, priests, members of privileged families, and so forth, joined forces with *recognized behavioral norms* whose obligatory force stemmed from mythic powers, hence from a sacred background consensus. Together they formed a syndrome that already made institutions of conflict resolution and collective will-formation possible before the evolutionary step to state-organized power was taken. For this reason, the state complex of law and politics could arise on an archaic foundation of social integration that the modern constructs of the "state of nature" did not take into consideration. For the following presentation of the genesis of law and politics, I choose an abstract model that, for purposes of conceptual reconstruction, highlights only a few relevant aspects of an overwhelming abundance of anthropological material.

(a) To begin with, I will construct two types of conflict resolution and collective will-formation that make use neither of state-sanctioned law nor of legally formed political power, but present the elements from which law and political power can be mutually constituted.

I assume with Parsons that social interactions linked together in space and time are subject to conditions of double contingency.[4] Actors expect each other in principle to be able to decide one way as well as the other. Thus every social order with relatively stable behavior patterns must rely on mechanisms of action coordination—in general, on influence and mutual understanding. Should coordination fail, anomic action sequences ensue that the actors themselves experience as problems. Coordination problems of this kind typically take two forms. They have to do either with the regulation of a conflict caused by the clash of individual action orientations or with the choice and cooperative realization of collective goals (in other words, they concern either the regulation of interpersonal conflicts or the pursuit of collective goals and programs).[5] In the simplest case, several actors are fighting over the same good and want to settle this conflict nonviolently; or a group of actors encounter a challenge they would like to master cooperatively. In the first case, the participants face the question, "According to which rules should we live together?" In the second case, the question is, "Which goals do we want to achieve and in which ways?" Conflict resolution refers to the stabilization of behavioral expectations in the case of disagreement, collective will-formation to the choice and effective realization of consensual goals. Parsons speaks of "pattern maintenance" and "goal attainment."[6]

Simple interactions fall along a continuum defined by the pure types of value-oriented and interest-governed action. In the one case, interpersonal action coordination takes place through value consensus; in the other, through the balance of interests. In most situations, these motives constitute a melange; however, depending on which of these aspects is thematized, the actors themselves have to adopt different attitudes: either the performative attitude of an actor oriented toward reaching understanding or the objectivating attitude of an actor oriented to consequences that are evaluated in the light of his own preferences.

Problems of action coordination are perceived differently depending on the actor's perspective (see table 1). Under the conditions of value-oriented action, actors seek, or rely on, consensus; under the conditions of interest-governed action, they strive for a balance of interests or compromise. The practice of *reaching understanding* differs from that of *bargaining* with respect to its intended aim: the desired agreement is understood in one case as consensus, in the other as a negotiated agreement or contract. In the former case, appeal is made to the consideration of norms and values; in the latter, to that of interest positions.

"Consensus" and "arbitration" are labels for two types of conflict resolution. Under the conditions of norm-governed action, there is the prospect that parties involved in a conflict can reach a settlement by ascertaining, on the basis of an existing value consensus, what one *ought* to do in the disputed case. Corresponding to the structure of this solution is the use of moral authorities (e.g., priests) and their corresponding decision procedures (e.g., oracles). Under the conditions of interest-governed action, there is the prospect that parties involved in a conflict can reach a settlement by achieving a balance among their interests—normally in the form of compensations for disadvantages—on the basis of their factual power positions and the corresponding threat potentials. Corresponding to the structure of this solution is the use of a mediator who gets negotiations going and moves them along, though he cannot make any binding decisions because he does not stand *above* the parties.[7] The categories of "authority" and "compromise," on the other hand, stand for two principles of will-formation in the light of which disagreements about goal attainment can be resolved. Either individual persons or families enjoy sufficient prestige to render authoritative interpretations of shared value commitments; or the disputing parties reach a tolerable compromise, again on the basis of their factual power. The label "power of command with organization" is meant to recall the fact that the cooperative realization of goals requires an organized division of

Table 1
Elementary types of conflict resolution and collective will-formation

Mode of action coordination	Problems		
	Regulation of interpersonal conflicts	Pursuit of collective goals:	
		Goal setting	Implementation
Value orientation	Consensus	Decision by authority	Power of command with organized division of labor
Interest position	Arbitration	Compromise	

labor available on command.

It is no accident that the four problem-solving strategies derived above can be illustrated in tribal institutions of conflict resolution and collective will-formation. The data from the anthropology of law need not concern us here.[8] What matters for our further reflections is simply the fact that techniques of "arbitration" and "compromise" depend on a kind of social power that has emerged either from prestige differentials among stratified family groups or from the differentiation (whether for war or peace) of the roles of elders, priests, and chiefs. This social power is distributed according to a status system connected with institutions that are anchored in religious worldviews and magical practices. Only the other two techniques—conflict resolution through consensus and an authoritatively guided, collective will-formation—depend *directly* on a normative complex in which custom, morality, and law still symbiotically interpenetrate.

Taking these assumptions as a point of departure, the *co-original constitution of binding law and political power* can be represented as a two-stage model. The first stage is characterized by the position of a chieftain or king who assumes the role of a royal judge and therewith monopolizes the functions of conflict resolution. The second stage involves the legal institutionalization of an administrative staff that makes collective will-formation possible in the organized form of a state.[9]

(b) A leader who at first enjoys just a superior reputation and de facto social power can concentrate in his hands the hitherto dispersed functions of conflict resolution as he takes on the administration of sacred goods and makes himself the exclusive interpreter of the norms the community recognizes as holy and morally obligatory. Because sacred law represents a source of justice from which power can legitimate itself, *normative authority* accrues to the status of this judge-king: the authority of sacred law, still interwoven with custom and morality, devolves on the position of its appointed interpreter. The de facto power that initially qualified a prestigious person to assume such a position is thereby transformed into legitimate power. This reshaping of social power into political power cannot take place, though, without a simultaneous transformation of sacred law into binding law. That is, in the hands of a power holder who is thus authorized, the practice of conflict resolution is readjusted to norms that, exceeding mere moral obligation, enjoy the *affirmative validity* of *actually enforced* law. The quasi-natural social power of the judge-king was backed by physical resources from which the administration of justice could now borrow threats of sanction: prepolitical power provided a new kind of backing to the inherited law living from sacred authority alone, thereby transforming it into binding law sanctioned by the ruler. These two *simultaneous* processes go hand in hand: the authorization of power by sacred law and the sanctioning of law by social power are effected *uno actu*. In this way political power and binding law emerge as the two components that make up a legally organized political order (see figure 1).

In the second stage of our model, the co-original components of binding law and political power join up in the institutionalization of offices that provides the exercise of political authority with an administrative staff—in a word, that makes state-organized authority (*Herrschaft*) possible. Not only does law now legitimate political power, power can make use of law as a means of organizing political rule. By virtue of this instrumental function of binding law, the political authority of the ruler acquires the capacity to make legally binding decisions. At this stage, we can begin to speak of the form of government organized as a state with administrative power at its disposal. This is characterized by the function of realizing collective goals through legally binding decisions. At the same time, a state-

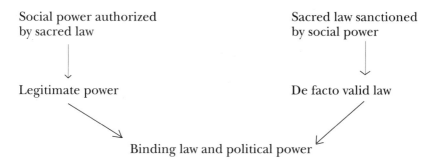

Figure 1
The constitution of law and politics.

organized penal system provides the acts of the judiciary with a coercive character. Only in virtue of this instrumental function of political power are courts transformed into organs of a state. Law thus owes to the state its function of stabilizing behavioral expectations that are generalized in temporal, social, and substantive respects. We therefore distinguish the functions that law and power fulfill *for each other* from the *intrinsic functions* the legal and power codes fulfill for society as a whole.[10]

As soon as law bestows a legal form on the exercise of political power, it serves to constitute a binary power code (table 2). Whoever possesses power can give commands to others. To this extent law functions as a means of organizing governmental authority. Conversely, insofar as power procures the observance of court decisions, it serves to constitute a binary legal code. Courts decide what counts as legal or illegal. To this extent, power serves to establish the judiciary as a branch of the state.

Only in modernity can political domination develop into legal authority in forms of positive law. The contribution of political power to the intrinsic function of law, hence to the stabilization of behavioral expectations, is to engender a *legal certainty* that enables the addressees of law to calculate the consequences of their own and others' behavior. From this point of view, legal norms must assume the form of comprehensible, consistent, and precise specifications, which normally are formulated in writing; they must be made known to all addressees, hence be public; they may not claim retroactive validity; and they must regulate the given set of circumstances or "fact situation" in terms of general features and connect

Table 2
The functional connection between the codes of law and power

	Functions	
Codes	Intrinsic functions	Functions for each other
Power	Realization of collective goals	Political institutionalization of law
Law	Stabilization of behavioral expectations	Legal organization of the exercise of political power

these with legal consequences in such a way that they can be applied to all persons and all comparable cases in the same way.[11] These requirements are met by a codification that provides legal rules with a high degree of consistency and conceptual explication. This is the task of a jurisprudence that works through the legal corpus in a rigorous fashion, making it the subject of doctrinal refinement and systematization.

The contribution that law makes to the intrinsic function of administrative power, on the other hand, is especially evident in the development of secondary rules in H. L. A. Hart's sense. These include not only power-conferring norms that furnish government institutions with their special jurisdictions or even constitute these institutions to begin with, but also organizational norms that lay down procedures according to which legal programs come into being and are dealt with administratively or judicially. Law by no means exhausts itself in behavioral norms but increasingly serves to organize and regulate state power. It functions as a system of constitutive rules that not only guarantee the private and public autonomy of citizens but generate government institutions, procedures, and official powers.

4.1.3

This analysis of the relationships between the codes of law and power could suggest the misleading picture of an evenly balanced, *self-contained* exchange between law and political power. From the selective viewpoint of functionalist analysis, the law in fact is completely defined by two things, its contribution to the constitution of the power code and the fulfillment of its own functions. From this perspective, it appears as though a self-stabilizing circular process can sustain itself between positive law and political power. As a matter of fact, however, the early-modern secularization of law soon made it clear that the legal form as such does not suffice to legitimate the exercise of political power. Certainly political power owes its normative authority solely to that fusion with law that I have presented in the foregoing model. However, this reconstruction also shows that law has a legitimating force only so long as it can function as a resource of justice. Just as political power keeps instruments of coercion in reserve as a ready resource of force, so must the law *remain* present as a resource of justice. But this source dries up if the law is made available for *just any* reasons of state.

In the Europe of the seventeenth and eighteenth centuries, when the positivization of law was already in full swing, philosophers of rational natural law saw themselves confronted with what Weber described as "legal authority" (*legale Herrschaft*). In this situation, the idea of government by law had the critical sense of uncovering the contradiction built into the established legal orders of the time: a normatively unjustified privileging of the most powerful interests certainly *can* be concealed in forms of legal authority. In this respect, rational natural law denounced the contradiction between, on the one hand, law as an organizational form of *every* government that can actually maintain itself and, on the other hand, law as a condition for the legitimacy of *the particular* political order that appeals to the authority of legitimate laws. In traditional societies, a more or less plausible connection could be forged between the actually established laws and the law claimed as legitimate so long as the conditions of the following scenario were satisfied, at least on the whole.

Against the background of acknowledged religious worldviews, the law initially possessed a sacred foundation; this law, normally interpreted and managed by theologian-lawyers, was widely accepted as a reified component of a divine order of salvation or as part of a natural world order, and as such it was not at the disposal of human beings. Even political authorities were, in their capacity of supreme judges, subordinated to this natural law. The law bureaucratically enacted by the ruler, "positive" law in the premodern sense, based its authority on the ruler's legitimacy (which was mediated by judicial authority anyway), on his interpretation of a pregiven legal order, or on custom. In the last case, customary law was secured in turn by the authority of tradition. However, as soon as the transition to modernity unraveled the binding religious worldview into a passel of subjective "gods and demons" and the law lost its metaphysical dignity and inviolability, this secular constellation was altered from the ground up.

Conventionalized law separated from postconventional morality and came to depend on the resolutions of a political legislator who could program both the judiciary and the administration without being bound himself by any norms other than those of "natural reason." As a result, a legitimation gap opened up in the circuit between instrumentally conceived power and instrumentalized law, a gap that natural law wanted to close—indeed had to close—with its recourse to practical reason. This is because the evolutionarily successful complex of law and politics, which made possible the transition to state-organized societies, depended on certain constitutive conditions, and these were violated to the extent that political power could no longer legitimate itself through a sacred tradition and an *intrinsically* legitimate law. Reason was supposed to replace the sacred resources of justice as these gradually dried up. To some extent even modern natural law remained caught in the dogmatic spell of the traditional construction of political authority as legitimated through a suprapositive law. Social-contract theories did not overcome the idea of an original antagonism between law and power. After the canopy of sacred law had collapsed, leaving behind as ruins the two pillars of politically enacted law and instrumentally employed power, reason alone was supposed to provide a substitute for sacred, self-authorizing law, a substitute that could give back true authority to a political legislator who was pictured as a power holder.

A very different perspective opens up with the discourse-theoretic concept of political autonomy. This concept explains why the production of legitimate law requires that the communicative freedom of citizens be mobilized. According to this explanation, legislation depends on the generation of another type of power, namely, on the *communicative power* that, as Hannah Arendt says, no one is really able to "possess": "Power springs up between men when they act together, and it vanishes the moment they disperse."[12] According to this model, both law and communicative power have their co-original source in the "opinion upon which many publicly were in agreement."[13] This reading of political autonomy necessitates a differentiation in the concept of political power. If the sources of justice from which the law itself draws its legitimacy are not to run dry, then a jurisgenerative communicative power must underlie the administrative power of the government. This concept, introduced dogmatically by Hannah Arendt, naturally requires further clarification.

So far we have examined the public use of unhindered communicative freedom only in *cognitive* terms, as enabling rational opinion- and will-formation: the free processing of information and reasons, of relevant topics and contributions is meant to ground the presumption that results reached in accordance with correct procedure are rational. But discursively produced and intersubjectively shared beliefs have, at the same time, a *motivating* force. Even if this remains limited to the weakly motivating force of good reasons, from this perspective, the public use of communicative freedom also appears as a generator of power potentials. This can be illustrated with the model of taking a yes or no position toward a simple speech-act offer. The *shared belief* that is produced, or even just reinforced, between speaker and hearer by the intersubjective recognition of a validity claim raised in a speech act implies a tacit acceptance of obligations relevant for action; to this extent, such acceptance creates a new social fact. By mobilizing citizens' communicative freedom for the formation of political beliefs that in turn influence the production of legitimate law, illocutionary obligations of this sort build up into a potential that holders of administrative power should not ignore.

In contrast to Weber, who sees the fundamental phenomenon of power as the probability that in a social relationship one can assert one's own will against opposition, Arendt views power as the potential of a *common will* formed in noncoercive communication.

She opposes "power" (*Macht*) to "violence" (*Gewalt*); that is, she opposes the consensus-achieving force of a communication aimed at reaching understanding to the capacity for instrumentalizing another's will for one's own purposes: "Power corresponds to the human ability not just to act but to act in concert."[14] A communicative power of this kind can develop only in undeformed public spheres; it can issue only from structures of undamaged intersubjectivity found in nondistorted communication. It arises where opinion- and will-formation instantiate the productive force of the "enlarged mentality" given with the unhindered communicative freedom each one has "to make public use of one's reason at every point." This enlargement is accomplished by "comparing our judgment with the possible rather than the actual judgments of others, and by putting ourselves in the place of any other man."[15]

Arendt conceives political power neither as a potential for asserting one's own interests or for realizing collective goals, nor as the administrative power to implement collectively binding decisions, but rather as an *authorizing* force expressed in "jurisgenesis"—the creation of legitimate law—and in the founding of institutions. It manifests itself in orders that protect political liberty; in resistance against the forms of repression that threaten political liberty internally or externally; and above all in the freedom-founding acts that bring new institutions and laws "into existence."[16] It emerges in its purest form in those moments when revolutionaries seize the power scattered through the streets; when a population committed to passive resistance opposes foreign tanks with their bare hands; when convinced minorities dispute the legitimacy of existing laws and engage in civil disobedience; when the sheer "joy of action" breaks through in protest movements. Again and again, it is the same phenomenon, *the close kinship of communicative action with the production of legitimate law*, that Arendt tracks down in different historic events and whose exemplar she found in the constitution-making force of the American Revolution.

In contrast to the constructions of modern natural law, the basic distinction between "power" and "violence" aligns power with law. In the natural-law tradition, the transition from the state of nature to society was supposed to be characterized by the fact that the parties to the social contract renounce liberties rooted in the physical strength of each individual. They transfer their unrestricted liberties to a state authority, which gathers up the scattered anarchic potentials for violence and puts them to work for the disciplinary enforcement of legally restricted liberties. Here the law arising from the renunciation of natural violence serves to channel a legitimate force identified with power. Arendt's distinction between power and violence negates this connection. Law joins forces *from the outset* with a communicative power that engenders legitimate law. This abrogates the classical task of finding a substitute for resources of justice that once flowed from a self-legitimating natural law—a substitute that could supply merely factual violence with the authority of a force whose reign bears the trappings of legitimate power. Arendt must instead explain how the united citizens produce legitimate law through the formation of communicative power, as well as how they legally secure this practice, that is, the exercise of their political autonomy. The conceptual kinship between lawmaking and this kind of power formation again makes it clear, in retrospect, why the system of rights responding to this question must appear immediately *as* positive law and may not claim for itself any moral validity that would be prior to the citizens' will-formation or based on natural law.

To be sure, with the concept of communicative power, we get hold of only the *emergence* of political power, not the administrative employment of *already* constituted power, that is, the process of exercising power. Nor does this concept explain the struggle for access to administrative power. Arendt emphasizes that the employment of, as well as the competition to acquire and preserve, power depends on the communicative formation and renewal of this power. Objecting to sociological theories that restrict themselves to phenomena of *power allocation* and *competition for power*, she rightly observes that no political authority can expand the resources of its power as it wishes. Communicatively produced power is a scarce resource, which organizations compete for and officials manage, but which none of them can produce:

[What holds a political body together is its current power potential.] . . . What first undermines and then kills political communities is loss of power and final impotence; and power cannot be stored up and kept in reserve for emergencies, like the instruments of violence, but exists only in its actualization. . . . Power is actualized only where word and deed have not parted company, where words are not empty and deeds not brutal.[17]

Now, the agreement between words and deeds may be the yardstick for a regime's legitimacy. But this does not yet explain the change in aggregate condition that communicative power must undergo before it can assume, in the form of administrative power, those sanctioning, organizing, and executive functions that the system of rights depends on and presupposes, as already shown.

The concept of communicative power requires a differentiation in the concept of political power. Politics cannot coincide as a whole with the practice of those who talk to one another in order to act in a politically autonomous manner. The exercise of political autonomy implies the discursive formation of a common will, not the implementation of the laws issuing therefrom. The concept of the political in its full sense *also* includes the use of administrative power within the political system, as well as the competition for access to that system. The constitution of a power code implies that an administrative system is steered through authorizations for rendering collectively binding decisions. This leads me to propose that we view law as the medium through which communicative power is translated into administrative power. For the transformation of communicative power into administrative has the character of an *empowerment* within the framework of statutory authorization. We can then interpret the idea of the constitutional state in general as the requirement that the administrative system, which is steered through the power code, be tied to the lawmaking communicative power and kept free of illegitimate interventions of social power (i.e., of the factual strength of privileged interests to assert themselves). Administrative power should not reproduce itself on its own terms but should only be permitted to regenerate from the conversion of communicative power. In the final analysis, this transfer is what the constitutional state should regulate, though without disrupting the power code by interfering with the self-steering mechanism of the administrative system. In sociological terms, the idea of government by law illuminates only the political side of balancing the three major forces of macrosocial integration: money, administrative power, and solidarity.

Before I can go into the principles of the constitutional state, I must state the conditions under which communicative power can take shape. In doing so, I start with the logic of the types of questions that structure opinion- and will-formation in a democratic legislature.

4.2 Communicative Power and the Genesis of Law

4.2.1

Rights of political participation refer to the legal institutionalization of a public opinion- and will-formation terminating in decisions about policies and laws. This public process is supposed to take place in forms of communication that, as we will now see, instantiate the discourse principle in a double respect. This principle has, to begin with, the *cognitive sense* of filtering reasons and information, topics and contributions in such a way that the outcome of a discourse enjoys a presumption of rational acceptability; democratic procedure should ground the legitimacy of law. The discursive character of opinion- and will-formation in the political public sphere and in parliamentary bodies, however, also has the *practical sense* of establishing relations of mutual understanding that are "violence-free" in Arendt's sense and that unleash the generative force of communicative freedom. The communicative power of shared convictions issues only from structures of undamaged intersubjectivity. This *interpenetration of discursive lawmaking and communicative power formation* ultimately stems from the fact that in communicative action reasons also have a motivational force. This interpenetration becomes necessary primarily because concrete, particular communities that want to regulate their life in common by means of law cannot fully separate the question concerning the normative regulation of behavioral expectations from questions concerning collective goal setting. That is, they cannot separate these to the degree this would be possible in the idealized community of morally responsible persons. Political questions differ from moral ones.

In contrast to morality, law does not regulate interaction contexts *in general* but serves as a medium for the self-organization of legal communities that maintain themselves in their social environment under particular historical conditions. As a result, concrete matters and teleological points of view migrate into law. Whereas moral rules, aiming at what lies in the equal interest *of all*, express a universal will pure and simple, laws also give expression to the particular wills of members of a particular legal community. Moreover, whereas the morally autonomous will remains in some sense virtual because it states only what could be rationally accepted by each, a legal community's political will, which of course should accord with moral insights, also expresses an intersubjectively shared form of life, existing interest positions, and pragmatically chosen ends. Political issues are such that in the medium of law, the normative regulation of behavior is also open for the evaluation and pursuit of collective goals. This expands the spectrum of reasons relevant for political will-formation: in addition to moral reasons, we find ethical and pragmatic ones. The focus thereby shifts from opinion- to will-formation.

The more concrete the matter in need of regulation and the more concrete the character of legal propositions, the more the acceptability of norms *also* expresses the self-understanding of a historical form of life, the balance between competing group interests, and an empirically informed choice among alternative goals. The teleological points of view that find their way into legal contents through these volitional components become more pronounced to the extent that a society concentrates the pursuit of collective goals in the state, for this also determines how much the legislature must program the expanded policy fields and growing organizational capacities of the state. Even in the *liberal model*, in which the pursuit of collective goals is generally moved from the government (restricted to enforcing rights) over to market mechanisms and voluntary associations,[18] law cannot be kept free of the political aims implemented in tax legislation and military protection. At the same time, the consideration of collective goals must not wreck the legal form, and therewith the intrinsic function of law; it must not permit law to be *absorbed* into politics. Otherwise the tension between facticity and validity, displayed in its pure form in modern law, would have to disappear. Legitimacy would be assimilated to the positivity of an imitation of substantial ethical life if, as in the *institutional model,* law were obligated to articulate pregiven "concrete orders" (in Carl Schmitt's sense).[19] Nevertheless, the relatively concrete character of law (in comparison to morality) concerns not only (a) the content and (b) the meaning of legal validity, but also (c) the mode of legislation.

(a) Deontological approaches in moral theory rule out a teleological reading of moral imperatives from the start. They rightly insist that one would misunderstand the meaning of the moral "ought" if one saw it only as expressing the attractive character of certain goods. We "ought" to obey moral precepts, because we know they are right and not because we hope to realize certain ends by doing so—even if the end were that of the highest personal happiness or the collective weal. Justice questions concern the claims contested in interpersonal conflicts. We can judge these impartially in light of valid norms. To be valid, such norms must survive a universalization test that examines what is equally good for all. Just as "true" is a predicate for the validity of assertoric sentences, so is "just" a predicate for the validity of the universal normative sentences that express general moral norms. For this reason, justice is not one value among others. Values always compete with other values. They state which goods specific persons or collectivities strive for or prefer under specific circumstances. Only from the perspective of the given individual or group can values be temporarily ranked in a transitive order. Thus values claim relative validity, whereas justice poses an absolute validity claim: moral precepts claim to be valid for each and every person. Moral norms, of course, embody values or interests, but only such as are universalizable in view of the particular matter at issue. This claim to universality excludes a teleological reading of moral imperatives, that is, a reading in terms of the *relative* preferability of specific values or interests.

However, in grounding and applying legal norms, such a reference to collective goals and goods does come into play; legal norms usually do not display the high degree of abstraction found in moral norms.[20] In general, they do not say what is equally good for all human beings; they regulate the life context of the citizens of a concrete legal community. This does not just involve the regulation of typically recurrent action conflicts from the standpoint of justice. The need for regulation is not found exclusively in problem situations that call for a moral use of practical reason. The medium of law is also brought to bear in problem situations that require the cooperative pursuit of collective goals and the safeguarding of collective goods. Hence discourses of justification and application also have to be open to a *pragmatic* and an *ethical-political use of practical reason.* As soon as rational collective will-formation aims at concrete legal programs, it must cross the boundaries of justice discourses and include problems of value (that depend on the clarification of collective identity) and the balancing of interests.

Of course, expanding the spectrum of justification this way must not lead us to deny the structural similarity that the system of rights in general establishes between morality and law. It must be possible to interpret even ordinary legislation as serving to realize and specify the system of rights elaborated in the constitution. Both moral and legal rules are "general" in at least two respects. First of all, they are general insofar as they address an indeterminate number of persons, while admitting no exceptions and excluding both privileges and discrimination in their application. This has to do with equality before the law. Whereas moral norms are directed to every person, legal norms address only the members of the legal community. But this still does not give the "generality" in the *content* of legal statutes a different sense per se. Ideally, legal rules, too, regulate a matter in the equal interest of all those affected and to that extent give expression to generalizable interests. Nonetheless, the equal consideration of all interests means something different in the law than it does in morality.

The material or substantive equality in law—which accords equal treatment to equal cases—is not wholly a question of justice, because the material regulated by laws often does not allow the degree of abstraction that pares things down to moral questions of justice alone. Legal material touches on collective goals and goods in a way that allows questions bearing on the concrete form of life to arise, if not questions of shared identity as well. In that case, however, the participants must not only clarify what is equally good for every citizen but also determine who they are as members of a political community and how they would like to live. Moreover, the goals they choose in the light of strong evaluations confront them with the question of how they can best achieve these goals. The sphere of justice questions thus expands to take in problems of achieving self-understanding and questions of the rational choice of means—and naturally problems of balancing interests that cannot be generalized but call instead for fair compromises. Only if a law expresses a reasonable consensus in view of *all* these aspects and problem types does it qualify as substantively general in the sense of material equality of treatment.

This substantive sense of equal treatment represents the normative standard for good laws insofar as these laws are not deployed simply for purposes of legal certainty—"as the most reliable and exact means of steering the course of social action"—but are adopted for the reasonable regulation of interaction in an intersubjectively shared form of life. In that case, laws are adopted "as the legal form of action for realizing democratic political decisions" and "as a means . . . for safeguarding areas of individual liberty and control."[21] However, if substantive legal equality is measured against such a complex set of criteria, then the meaning of the normative validity of statutes also does not coincide with the rightness of moral rules, which is measured against criteria of justice alone.

(b) In the dimension of legal validity (*Rechtsgeltung*), the moment of normative validity (*Gültigkeit*) or rational acceptability is combined with the fact of social recognition or acceptance, if for no other reason than because legal norms are enforced. Legal validity has the illocutionary meaning of a declaration: the state authority declares that an enacted norm has been sufficiently justified and is typically actually obeyed as well. In the present context, however, we are concerned simply with a differentiation within the normative validity dimension that is constitutive of the legitimacy of law.

According to discourse theory, moral norms can appear with a purely cognitive validity claim because the principle of universalization provides a rule of argumentation that makes it possible to decide moral-practical questions rationally. Their limited sphere of validity notwithstanding, legal norms, too, claim to *be in accord* with moral norms, that is, not to violate them. But moral reasons do not have *enough* selectivity here. Legal norms are valid, although they can be justified not only with moral but also with pragmatic and ethical-political reasons; if necessary, they must represent the outcome of a fair compromise as well. In justifying legal norms, we must use the entire breadth of practical reason. However, these *further* reasons have a relative validity, one that depends on the context. A collective self-understanding can be authentic only within the horizon of an existing form of life; the choice of strategies can be rational only in view of accepted policy goals; a compromise can be fair only in relation to given interest positions. The corresponding reasons count as valid relative to the historical, culturally molded identity of the legal community, and hence relative to the value orientations, goals, and interest positions of its members. Even if one assumes that in the course of a rational collective will-formation attitudes and motives change in line with the arguments, the facticity of the existing context cannot be eliminated; otherwise ethical and pragmatic discourses, as well as compromises, would lack an object. On account of this relation to the *de facto substratum of a legal community's will,* a volitional moment enters into the normative validity dimension—and not just into the socially binding character—of legal norms. As used for the validity component of legal validity, the expression "legitimacy" designates the specific kind of prescriptive validity (*Sollgeltung*) that distinguishes law from "morality." Valid moral norms are "right" in the discourse-theoretic sense of just. Valid legal norms indeed harmonize with moral norms, but they are "legitimate" in the sense that they additionally express an authentic self-understanding of the legal community, the fair consideration of the values and interests distributed in it, and the purposive-rational choice of strategies and means in the pursuit of policies.

(c) The teleological element comes out not only in the content and meaning of the validity of laws but also in the contingencies of the legislative process. Moral norms, which regulate a reasonable common life among rationally capable subjects in general, are surely not just "discovered" but partly "constructed" at the same time.[22] Yet the moment of construction appears more strongly in legal norms, with the help of which we give a reasonable structure to a concrete form of life. The more norms aim at specific forms of life and life circumstances, the less important is the passive moment of insight in comparison to active shaping and design. The reasons that justify moral rules lead to rationally motivated *consensus* (*Einverständnis*); the grounding of legal norms serves a rationally motivated *agreement* (*Vereinbarung*). In the one case, we convince ourselves of which duties we *have*, in the other, of which obligations we *ought* to enter into or *take on.* Rawls draws the distinction in this context between natural duties and obligations we voluntarily enter into. Obligations "arise as a result of our voluntary acts. . . . Further, the content of obligations is always defined by an institution or practice the rules of which specify what it is that one is required to do." By contrast, natural duties have the feature "that they hold between persons irrespective of their institutional relationships; they obtain between all as equal moral persons."[23]

The idea of self-legislation, which implies moral autonomy at the level of the individual will, takes on the meaning of political autonomy at the level of collective will-formation. Political autonomy is not simply a result of applying the discourse principle to a different kind of action norm and giving this principle itself a legal shape with the system of rights. It is not just the legal form alone that distinguishes political from moral self-legislation, but the contingency of the form of life, of the goals and interest positions establishing the identity of the self-determining political will in advance. Although the morally good will is fully absorbed, as it were, into practical reason, even the rationally grounded political will retains a certain contingency insofar as it rests on context-dependent reasons. This explains why the common ground of shared beliefs, achieved discursively in different political arenas, also generates communicative power.

4.2.2

The comparatively greater weight of the volitional moment in the lawmaking process follows from the logic of nonmoral issues and the context-dependence of the nonmoral reasons entering into the political legislator's opinion- and will-formation. If we want to trace out the forms of communication that guarantee the discursive character of a practice of self-determination, we must concentrate on the cognitive side and identify the relevant issues dealt with in legislative processes.

Martin Kriele sees the fruitfulness of a discourse approach in the fact "that it makes us aware of what is already presupposed in every discourse, namely the possibility of reason, which depends on observing the rules of discourse. This awareness also has a political function: to defend the form of government guided by public discussion—hence the democratic constitutional state—against political theories that fundamentally challenge its philosophical basis."[24] Kriele believes "that political and legal argument makes sense only if one presupposes this thought," even if the idealizing presuppositions of argumentation in general "cannot be established in political practice."[25] With this restriction, Kriele reminds us that the logic of discourse must not be too quickly identified with constitutional procedures. An *unmediated* application of discourse ethics (or of an unclarifed concept of discourse) to the democratic process leads to muddled analyses; these then offer skeptics pretexts for discrediting the project of a discourse theory of law and politics at its inception.[26] Hence differentiations are necessary.

According to the discourse principle, the validity of every kind of action norm in general depends on the agreement of those participating "in rational discourses" as affected parties. To the extent that the discourse principle is applied to norms of action that regulate simple interactions for an indefinitely large circle of addressees, questions arise for which a specific type of discourse is appropriate, namely, moral argumentation. If the discourse principle is applied to norms of action that can take the form of law, political issues of various sorts come into play. Different types of discourse and forms of negotiation or bargaining correspond to the logic of these issues.

A collectivity is confronted with the question "What ought we to do?" when certain problems that must be managed cooperatively impose themselves or when action conflicts requiring consensual solutions crop up. Handling these questions in a rational way demands an opinion- and will-formation that leads to justified decisions about the pursuit of collective goals and the normative regulation of life in common. In the case of goal attainment, the collectivity understands itself as a quasi subject capable of purposive action; in the case of conflict resolution, as a community whose members reach an understanding about what behavior they can legitimately expect of one another. As soon as the codes of law and power are set up, deliberation and decision making take on the differentiated form of *political* opinion- and will-formation. On the one hand, the collectivity that deliberates and decides separates from those parts or agencies that act for it, that is, that can apply and carry out approved programs. On the other hand, the collectivity composed of members of society transforms itself into one composed of legal consociates who, as enfranchised citizens, exercise their autonomy within a system of rights in need of interpretation and elaboration. Law not only confers a certain form on conflict-regulating norms; it also imposes certain limits on the realization of collective goals. The programs translated into the language of law have either themselves the form of statutory law (if necessary, they can also take the form of special legislation and private bills or various regulatory directives), or they link up with existing law. In deliberations over policies and laws, the basic question "What ought we to do?" is differentiated according to the kind of material in need of regulation. The meaning of "ought" remains unspecified as long as the relevant problem and the aspect under which it can be solved are undetermined. I want to specify these aspects along the lines of pragmatic, ethical, and moral issues. The standpoints of expediency, goodness, and justice each define a different use of practical reason. These correspond to different types of discourse, which I can only outline in broad strokes here.[27]

Pragmatic questions pose themselves from the perspective of an actor seeking suitable means for realizing goals and preferences that are already given. The goals themselves can also become problematic. In that case, the issue is no longer simply that of rationally selecting means but one of weighing goals rationally in the light of accepted value preferences. Even here the actor's will is still fixed by interests or value orientations, remaining open to further determinations only with regard to alternative means or goals. The rationally justified choice of techniques or strategies of action calls for comparisons and weighings that the actor, supported by observations and prognoses, can carry out from the standpoint of efficiency or other decision rules. The value-oriented weighing of goals and the purposive-rational choice of means lead to hypothetical recommendations that interrelate perceived causes and effects according to value preferences and chosen ends. These directives have the semantic form of conditional imperatives. Ultimately, they borrow their validity from the empirical knowledge they take in. They are justified in *pragmatic discourses*. In these, the outcome turns on arguments that relate empirical knowledge to given preferences and ends and that assess the (usually uncertain) consequences of alternative choices according to previously accepted maxims or decision rules.

Of course, as soon as the orienting values themselves become problematic, the question "What ought we to do?" takes one beyond the horizon of purposive rationality. Sometimes conflicting preferences express oppositions between interests that cannot be defused at the level of discourse. At other times, however, the contested interest positions and value orientations are so interwoven with a community's intersubjectively shared form of life that serious decisions about values touch on an unclarified collective self-understanding. *Ethical-political questions* pose themselves from the perspective of members who, in the face of important life issues, want to gain clarity about their shared form of life and about the ideals they feel should shape their common life. The "existential" question of who I am and would like to be, which is posed in the singular, is repeated in the plural—and is thus given a different meaning.[28] The identity of a group refers to the situations in which the members can utter an emphatic "we"; it is not an ego identity writ large but rather supplements the individual's identity. How we make our native traditions and forms of life our own by selectively developing them determines who we recognize ourselves to be in these cultural transmissions—who we are and would like to be as citizens. Serious value decisions result from, and change with, the politicocultural self-understanding of a historical community. Enlightenment over this self-understanding is achieved through a hermeneutics that critically appropriates traditions and thereby assists in the intersubjective reassurance or renovation of authentic life orientations and deeply held values.[29]

Ethical questions are answered with clinical advice based on a reconstruction of the form of life that has been brought to awareness while being critically probed and appropriated. This advice combines descriptive and normative components. That is, the description of identity-shaping traditions is combined with the normative projection of an exemplary way of life justified through reflection on, and evaluation of, its formative processes. The imperative sense of this advice can be understood as an "ought" that does not depend on subjective ends or preferences but states which value orientations and practices are in the long run and on the whole "good for us." Advice of this sort is grounded in *ethical discourses.* In these, the outcome turns on arguments based on a hermeneutic explication of the self-understanding of our historically transmitted form of life. Such arguments weigh value decisions in this context with a view toward an authentic conduct of life, a goal that is absolute *for us.*

Up to now we have examined processes of rational political willformation under two aspects. On the one hand, deliberative processes serve to specify and weigh collective goals as well as to construct and select programs and strategies suitable for achieving these goals. On the other hand, the value horizon in which these tasks of goal attainment are posed can in turn be included in the process of rational will-formation inasmuch as this process involves achieving self-understanding through the critical appropriation of tradition. In pragmatic discourses, we test the expediency of strategies under the presupposition that we know what we want. In ethical-political discourses, we reassure ourselves of a configuration of values under the presupposition that we do not yet know what we *really* want. In this kind of discourse, we can justify programs insofar as they are expedient and, taken as a whole, good for us. An adequate justification of policies and laws must, however, consider yet a further aspect, that of justice. Whether we should want and accept a program also depends on whether the corresponding practice is *equally* good *for all.* This shifts the meaning of the question "What ought we to do?" yet again.

In *moral questions,* the teleological point of view from which we handle problems through goal-oriented cooperation gives way entirely to the normative point of view from which we examine how we can regulate our common life in the equal interest of all. A norm is just only if all can will that it be obeyed by each in comparable situations. Moral precepts have the semantic form of categorical or unconditional imperatives. The imperative sense of these precepts can be understood as an "ought" that depends neither on subjective ends and preferences nor on the (for us) absolute goal of a good, or not misspent, way of life. Here what one "ought" to do has the sense that the corresponding practice is just. Such duties are rationally justified in *moral discourses*. In these, the outcome turns on arguments showing that the interests embodied in contested norms are unreservedly universalizable. In moral discourse, the ethnocentric perspective of a particular collectivity expands into the comprehensive perspective of an unlimited communication community, all of whose members put themselves in each individual's situation, worldview, and self-understanding, and together practice an ideal role taking (as understood by G. H. Mead).

The principle of universalization compels the participants in discourse to examine contested norms in view of *foreseeably typical* cases, in order to determine whether the norms could meet with the considered agreement of all those affected. Moral rules pass this test only if they are stated in a general, decontextualized form; hence they can be applied *directly* only to the standard situations that have already been considered in their antecedent clause. However, because *discourses of justification* cannot take into consideration *ex ante* all the possible constellations of future cases, the application of norms calls for an argumentative clarification in its own right. In such *discourses of application*, impartiality of judgment is achieved not through yet a further use of the universalization principle but through a principle of appropriateness. I will come back to this proposal advanced by Klaus Günther in connection with the analysis of judicial decision making.

4.2.3

In the discursively structured opinion- and will-formation of a legislature, lawmaking is interwoven with the formation of communicative power. We can clarify this connection with the help of a highly abstract process model that starts with pragmatic issues, advances along the branches of compromise formation and ethical discourse to the clarification of moral questions, and ends with a judicial review of norms. As we go through this sequence, the constellation of reason and will changes. In moving from technical or strategic recommendations through clinical advice to moral precepts, the shifting illocutionary meaning of "ought" is accompanied by changes in the concept of will that informs each of these imperatives.

In pragmatic recommendations, an "ought" relative to given ends and values is directed toward the *free choice* (*Willkür*) of actors who make intelligent decisions on the basis of hypothetically presupposed interests and value preferences. These interests and preferences themselves remain external to pragmatic discourses in which the rational choice between possible alternatives is justified. The validity of pragmatic recommendations therefore does not depend on whether the directives are actually adopted and followed. In such discourse itself, there is no *internal* relationship between reason and will, between practical deliberation and acceptance of the results.

In clinical advice, an "ought" relative to the telos of our own good life is addressed to the *resolve* of a collectivity that wants to assure itself of an authentic way of life. In such processes of achieving self-understanding, the roles of participant in argumentation and member of a historical community overlap. Here genesis and validity can no longer be separated as they can with programs and strategies projected along purposive-rational lines. Insights promoted in ethical-political discourses can change a group's hermeneutically clarified self-understanding and, along with this, its identity as well; in justifying serious value decisions, acts of resolve are induced by insights, for here arguments meet up with the striving for an authentic way of life. On the other hand, such hermeneutically enlightened resolutions also express the affirmation of a form of life in the light of critically appropriated traditions. Reason and will reciprocally determine each other in ethical discourses, for these discourses remain embedded in the context they thematize. In achieving hermeneutic self-understanding, those taking part in argumentation cannot work themselves free of the form of life in which they de facto find themselves.

In contrast, entry into moral discourse demands that one step back from all contingently existing normative contexts. Such discourse takes place under communicative presuppositions that require a break with everyday taken-for-granted assumptions; in particular, it requires a hypothetical attitude toward the relevant norms of action and their validity claims. The categorical "ought" of moral norms is directed toward the *autonomous will* of actors who are prepared to be rationally bound by insight into what all could will. Unlike free choice and resolve, this will is freed from the heteronomous features of contingent interests and value orientations, particular sociocultural forms of life, and identity-shaping traditions. The autonomous will is *entirely* imbued with practical reason. We can also say that the command of reason is internalized. Admittedly, the price for the rationality of the autonomous will is that it can assert itself in the social world of action only with the weak motivational force of good reasons. In the discursive will-formation of the political legislator, however, this motivation deficit is offset by legal institutionalization.

Hence the constellation of reason and will varies depending on the pragmatic, ethical, and moral aspects of a matter in need of regulation. These constellations explain the problem with which the discursive formation of a common political will begins. For the sake of simplicity, let us assume that in a parliament political questions initially arise in the pragmatic form of a purposive-rational choice of collective goals and strategies according to established value preferences. Our process model starts with the pragmatic justification of general programs that must be further explicated and implemented by the executive branch. Such justification depends primarily on a correct interpretation of the situation and the appropriate description of the problem at stake, as well as on the flow of relevant and reliable information, on the efficient (and, if necessary, theoretically guided) processing of this information, and so on. In this *first stage* of opinion- and will-formation, a certain expert knowledge is requisite, which is naturally fallible and rarely value-neutral, that is, uncontested. With the political evaluation of expertise and counterexpertise, viewpoints that depend on preferences already come into play. These preferences involve interest positions and value orientations that begin to compete openly with one another in the *second stage*; then the descriptions, prognoses, and action alternatives are supposed to ground a choice between competing proposals for handling the problem on the agenda. In this stage, the problematic value orientations themselves are up for discussion, which necessitates a change in the level of discourse. Pragmatic discourses extend only to the construction of possible programs and estimation of their consequences. They do not include the formation of the reasonable will that adopts the program only in a further step, by *making its own* the goals and values hypothetically presupposed by the program.

In the ideal case, which we assume in our model, a procedural decision is first made about the level at which the controversy should be *continued* with arguments. How this is decided depends on the aspect under which the matter in need of regulation permits further clarification. There are *three alternatives.* It may be that a morally relevant issue is immediately at stake. Consider, for example, questions of social policy, of tax law, or of the organization of educational and health-care systems, where the distribution of social wealth, life opportunities, and chances for survival in general are at stake. In any case, such moral issues call for discourses that submit the contested interests and value orientations to a universalization test within the framework set by the system of rights as it has been constitutionally interpreted and elaborated. In other cases, it may be that an ethically relevant issue is at stake. Consider, for example, ecological questions concerning the protection of the environment and animals, questions of traffic control and city planning; or consider questions of immigration policy, the protection of cultural and ethnic minorities, or any question touching on the political culture. Such questions call for discourses that push beyond contested interests and values and engage the participants in a process of self-understanding by which they become reflectively aware of the deeper consonances (*Übereinstimmungen*) in a common form of life.

In complex societies, however, it is often the case that even under ideal conditions neither of these alternatives is open. This is the case, namely, whenever it turns out that all the proposed regulations touch on the diverse interests in respectively different ways without any generalizable interest or clear priority of some one value being able to vindicate itself. In these cases, there remains the alternative of bargaining, that is, negotiation between success-oriented parties who are willing to cooperate.[30] *Bargaining* aims at compromises the participants find acceptable under three conditions. Such compromises provide for an arrangement that (a) is more advantageous to all than no arrangement whatever, (b) excludes free riders who withdraw from cooperation, and (c) excludes exploited parties who contribute more to the cooperative effort than they gain from it. Bargaining processes are tailored for situations in which social power relations cannot be neutralized in the way rational discourses presuppose. The compromises achieved by such bargaining contain a negotiated agreement (*Vereinbarung*) that balances conflicting interests. Whereas a rationally motivated consensus (*Einverständnis*) rests on reasons that convince all the parties *in the same way*, a compromise can be accepted by the different parties each for its own *different* reasons. However, the discursive chain of a rational will-formation would snap at such points of compromise if the discourse principle could not be brought to bear at least indirectly on bargaining processes.

This is not possible in a direct way, that is, within bargaining itself, because the parties resort to threats and promises, thereby introducing a bargaining power into their interaction. This power can rob their shared language of its illocutionary binding energies and restrict the use of language to the more or less cunning realization of perlocutionary effects:

To bargain is to engage in communication for the purpose of *forcing* or *inducing* the opponent to accept one's claim. To achieve this end, bargainers rely on threats and promises that will have to be executed outside the assembly itself. Bargaining power does not derive from the "power of the better argument," but from material resources, manpower and the like. Statements asserted in a process of bargaining are made with a claim to being credible, in the sense that bargainers must try *to make* their opponents *believe* that the threats and promises would actually be carried out.[31]

The discourse principle, which is supposed to secure an uncoerced consensus, can thus be brought to bear only indirectly, namely, through procedures that *regulate* bargaining from the standpoint of fairness. In this way, non-neutralizable bargaining power should at least be disciplined by its equal distribution among the parties. More specifically, the negotiation of compromises should follow procedures that provide all the interested parties with an equal opportunity for pressure, that is, an equal opportunity to influence one another during the actual bargaining, so that all the affected interests can come into play and have equal chances of prevailing. To the extent that these conditions are met, there are grounds for presuming that negotiated agreements are fair.

Such procedures define the equal consideration of the interests of each participant as a problem of procedurally correct *agreements* among power holders. Thus it is not a matter of mutual understanding among discourse participants who make use of their communicative freedom to adopt positions toward criticizable validity claims in order to mutually *convince* one another of their arguments. From a normative perspective, however, fair compromise formation does not stand on its own, for the procedural conditions under which actual compromises enjoy the presumption of fairness must be justified in moral discourses. Moreover, bargaining first becomes permissible and necessary when only particular—and no generalizable—interests are involved, something that again can be tested only in moral discourses.[32] Fair bargaining, then, does not destroy the discourse principle but rather indirectly presupposes it.

So compromise formation cannot simply replace moral discourses; this is why political will-formation cannot be reduced to compromise. This applies mutatis mutandis to ethical-political discourses as well, for their results must at least be compatible with moral principles. A fundamentalist self-understanding, for example, often privileges value choices that subordinate individual rights to collective goals and thus favor nonegalitarian regulations. Only under the conditions of postmetaphysical thinking do ethical-political discourses lead to regulations that lie per se in the equal interest of all members. So only the compatibility of all discursively achieved or negotiated programs with what is morally justifiable ensures that the discourse principle has been thoroughly applied. Rational political will-formation appears in the process model as a network of discourses and negotiations that can be linked up to one another via multiple pathways. However, transfers occur *at least* along the paths shown in figure 2.

Political will-formation terminates in resolutions about policies and legal programs that must be formulated in the language of law. This ultimately makes a judicial review necessary in which the new programs are examined for their fit with the existing legal system.

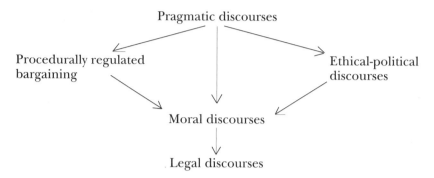

Figure 2
A process model of rational political will-formation.

The political legislature may use its lawmaking powers only to justify legal programs that—insofar as they do not immediately interpret and elaborate the system of rights—are compatible with this system and can link up with the corpus of established laws. From this *legal or juridical* standpoint, all resolutions have to be tested for coherence. The consistency of law must be preserved for the sake of legal certainty, if for no other reason. As we shall see, in a constitutional state the internal review of norms by the legislature can be subjected to further review (*Revision*) by a court that scrutinizes enacted legislation for its conformity with the constitution.[33]

4.3 Principles of the Constitutional State and the Logic of the Separation of Powers

4.3.1

Having completed these preparatory reflections, we can pull the various strands of argumentation together in order to justify the principles of government by law from a discourse-theoretic point of view. As we have seen, binding law and political power form a complex in which each fulfills a function for the other. At the same time, this complex opens up the possibility that law will be instrumentalized for the strategic deployment of power. To counter such instrumentalization, the idea of government by law requires the state apparatus to be organized in such a way that any use of publicly authorized power must be legitimated in terms of legitimately enacted law. Certainly the codes of law and power must always work for each other if each is to fulfill its own function. But these exchange relationships feed on a legitimate lawmaking that, as we have seen, goes hand in hand with the formation of communicative power. As a result, the concept of political power must be carefully differentiated. In the system of public administration, there is concentrated a power that must always regenerate itself anew out of communicative power. Thus the law is not only constitutive for the power code that steers administrative processes. It represents at the same time the medium for transforming communicative power into administrative power. The idea of the constitutional state can therefore be expounded with the aid of principles according to which legitimate law is generated from communicative power and the latter in turn is converted into administrative power via legitimately enacted law.

As already shown, the discursively structured opinion- and will-formation of the political legislature should proceed in forms of communication that allow the question "What ought we to do?" to be answered rationally under various aspects. In light of this premise, I will develop the principles of the constitutional state from the perspective of the legal institutionalization of the network of discourses and negotiation that I have just presented with the help of a simplified process model.

In the *principle of popular sovereignty*, according to which all governmental authority derives from the people, the individual's right to an equal opportunity to participate in democratic will-formation is combined with a legally institutionalized practice of civic self-determination. This principle forms the hinge between the system of rights and the construction of a constitutional democracy. By starting with discourse theory, we arrive at (a) a special interpretation of the principle of popular sovereignty. This reading yields (b) the principle of comprehensive legal protection for individuals, which is guaranteed by an independent judiciary; (c) the principles requiring that administration be subject to law and to judicial review (as well as to parliamentary oversight[34]); and (d) the principle of the separation of state and society, which is intended to prevent social power from being converted directly into administrative power, that is, without first passing through the sluices of communicative power formation.

(a) Read in discourse-theoretic terms, the principle of popular sovereignty states that all political power derives from the communicative power of citizens. The exercise of public authority is oriented and legitimated by the laws citizens give themselves in a discursively structured opinion- and will-formation. If we first view this practice as a problem-solving process, then it owes its legitimating force to a *democratic procedure* intended to guarantee a rational treatment of political questions. The rational acceptability of results achieved in conformity with procedure follows from the institutionalization of interlinked forms of communication that, ideally speaking, ensure that all relevant questions, issues, and contributions are brought up and processed in discourses and negotiations on the basis of the best available information and arguments. This legal institutionalization of specific procedures and conditions of communication is what makes possible the effective utilization of equal communicative freedom and at the same time *enjoins* the pragmatic, ethical, and moral use of practical reason or, as the case may be, the fair balance of interests.

We can also consider the principle of popular sovereignty directly in terms of power. In that case, it demands that legislative powers be transferred to the totality of citizens, who alone can generate communicative power from their midst. Justified and binding decisions about policies and laws demand, on the one hand, that deliberation and decision making take place face to face. On the other hand, at the level of direct and simple interactions, not all the citizens can join in the shared exercise of such a practice. A solution to this problem is provided by the *parliamentary principle* of establishing representative bodies for deliberation and decision making. The composition and operation of these parliamentary bodies must then be regulated according to criteria that are set in accordance with their assigned responsibilities. Questions of fundamental significance arise in regard to the mode of election and status of representatives (their immunities, whether or not they are bound by an imperative mandate, their dependence on congressional party blocks); in regard to the mode of decision making in such bodies (e.g., the *principle of majority rule*, repeated readings of a bill); and even in regard to the organization of work (e.g., the formation and power of committees). These procedural questions must be regulated in the light of the discourse principle in such a way that the necessary communicative presuppositions of pragmatic, ethical, and moral discourses, on the one hand, and the conditions for fair bargaining, on the other, can be sufficiently fulfilled.

Furthermore, the logic of discourse yields the principle of *political pluralism* both inside and outside representative bodies. Parliamentary opinion- and will-formation must remain anchored in the informal streams of communication emerging from public spheres that are open to all political parties, associations, and citizens. After Kant it was above all John Stuart Mill and John Dewey who analyzed the principle of publicity and the role an informed public opinion should have in feeding and monitoring parliament.[35] Only the principles of the *guaranteed autonomy of public spheres* and *competition between different political parties*, together with the parliamentary principle, exhaust the content of the principle of popular sovereignty. Consequently, this principle demands a discursive structuring of public networks and arenas in which anonymous circuits of communication are detached from the concrete level of simple interactions. An informal opinion-formation that prepares and influences political decision making is relieved of the institutional constraints of formal proceedings programmed to reach decisions. These arenas must certainly be constitutionally protected in view of the space they are supposed to make available for free-floating opinions, validity claims, and considered judgments. On the whole, though, they cannot be organized like corporate bodies.

(b) Although the political communications of citizens extend to all affairs of public interest, they ultimately issue in the decisions of legislative bodies. Political will-formation aims at legislation for at least two reasons. On the one hand, the system of rights that citizens have mutually accorded one another can be interpreted and developed only through laws. On the other hand, the administration that has to act as a part for the whole can be programmed and controlled only through laws. The legislative power that in principle rests with the citizenry as a whole is in fact exercised by parliamentary bodies that *justify and adopt* laws in accordance with democratic procedures. Laws form the foundation for individual legal claims; these result from the *application* of legal statutes to individual cases, be these self-executing laws or laws implemented along administrative paths. From the actionability of these claims follow the guarantee of legal remedies and the *principle of guaranteeing comprehensive legal protection for each individual.*

To be sure, dividing the authority to make and apply law into two different branches of government, institutionally independent of one another and having distinct staffs, is not immediately obvious. Classical Athens offers only one of several examples showing that popular assemblies or parliaments sometimes reserve judicial functions for themselves. Certainly there are pragmatic reasons that make it reasonable to separate the judicial from the legislative branch once the administration of justice becomes largely professionalized as a result of the academic institutionalization of jurisprudence and the doctrinal refinement of law. But from a normative and systematic point of view, the decisive reasons lie elsewhere. For one, the justification and the application of norms involve respectively different logics of argumentation. This difference is reflected in the communicative forms of justification and application discourses, which must be legally institutionalized in different ways. In legal discourses of application, a decision must be reached about which of the valid norms is appropriate in a given situation whose relevant features have been described as completely as possible. This type of discourse requires a constellation of roles in which the parties (and if necessary government prosecutors) can present all the contested aspects of a case before a judge who acts as the impartial representative of the legal community. Furthermore, it requires a distribution of responsibilities according to which the court must justify its judgment before a broad legal public sphere. By contrast, in discourses of justification there are in principle only participants. The second decisive reason for separate branches is that to enforce its decisions—and execute the law—the judiciary enlists the means of repression provided by the state apparatus. Because it thus has administrative power at its disposal, the judiciary must be separated from the legislature and prevented from programming itself. This explains the *principle of binding the judiciary to existing law.*

We might note, finally, that the principle of legal protection, in combination with the basic rights of due process, yields all the further principles pertaining to the specific tasks, mode of operation, and protected status of an independent judiciary that must apply the law in a way that guarantees both the certainty of law and the rational acceptability of court decisions.[36]

(c) The *principle of the legality of administration* clearly brings out the central meaning of the separation and balancing of powers.[37] Beyond the different logics of argumentation respectively characterizing the justification and application of norms, the institutional differentiation displayed in the separate branches of government has the purpose of binding the use of administrative power to democratically enacted law in such a way that administrative power regenerates itself solely from the communicative power that citizens engender in common. We have already examined, from the viewpoint of power, how laws bind a judiciary that must rely on means of repression. What is most noticeable from this same point of view, however, is the relation of the legislative branch to an executive branch whose activity is *subject to the law.* This requirement of statutory authorization (*Gesetzesvorbehalt*) has the effect of nullifying regulations, ordinances, agency rules and guidelines, orders, and other administrative acts that contradict a legal statute.[38] The *priority of laws* legitimated in democratic procedures has the cognitive meaning that the administration does not have its own access to the normative premises underlying its decisions. In practical terms, this means that administrative power may not be used to intervene in, or substitute for, processes of legislation and adjudication.

The utilization of administrative power on the part of the legislature and judiciary is unobjectionable only insofar as this resource is necessary for the institutionalization of the corresponding discourses. To the extent that administrative power goes to establish and organize the making and applying of law, it operates in such a way as to provide *enabling conditions.* Conversely, if the administration takes on functions that go much beyond the implementation of legal programs, then legislative and adjudicative processes become subject to *restricting conditions.* Such interventions or substitutions violate the communicative presuppositions of legislative and legal discourses and disturb the argumentation-guided processes of reaching understanding that alone can ground the rational acceptability of laws and court decisions. Empowering the executive to issue binding regulations therefore requires special legal norms that regulate the administration. Thus administrative law in particular highlights the *principle of prohibiting arbitrariness in domestic affairs.*[39]

Note, too, that the constitution of an executive authority has the effect that the liberties resulting from the right to equal freedom of action acquire the *additional* meaning of liberal *rights against the state* enjoyed by private legal subjects. The rights that citizens at first reciprocally accord each other only in the horizontal dimension of citizen-citizen interactions must now, once an executive branch has been formed, also extend to the vertical dimension of citizen-state relationships. From a historical perspective, these "liberal" (in the narrower sense) basic rights in fact make up the core of human-rights declarations. The system of rights—initially grounded in rational natural law—grew out of these.[40] The improvement of parliamentary controls on administration and above all the system of *administrative courts* point in the same direction; both of these supplement the legislator's *ex ante* control with one that is ex post facto. In principle, every case of administrative action or inaction can be contested in court by seeking a nullification or mandatory injunction. Moreover, in cases in which individual legal subjects (and also associations) feel that the executive branch (or a third party) has infringed on their basic rights, constitutional jurisdiction allows them to lodge constitutional complaints.

(d) In the German constitutional-law tradition, the *principle of separation of state and society* has been interpreted too concretely along the lines of a liberal *Rechtsstaat.* In general terms, however, this principle refers to the legal guarantee of a social autonomy that also grants each person, as enfranchised citizen, equal opportunities to make use of his rights to political participation and communication. The model of the bourgeois constitutional state is not by any means the only one corresponding to this principle. According to that model, the state limits itself to guaranteeing external and internal security. It is supposed to leave all other functions to a self-regulating economic society that has been largely freed of government regulation in the expectation that just living conditions will spontaneously result from the free play of the ends and preferences of individuals whose autonomy has been secured by private law.[41]

Read in more general terms, however, the principle of separation of state and society requires a civil society, that is, a network of voluntary associations and a political culture that are sufficiently detached from class structures. In this regard, the relation between social power and democracy is problematic, a point I will return to later. Civil society is expected to absorb and neutralize the unequal distribution of social positions and the power differentials resulting from them, so that social power comes into play only insofar as it *facilitates* the exercise of civic autonomy and does not *restrict* it. I use the term "social power" as a measure for the possibilities an actor has in social relationships to assert his own will and interests, even against the opposition of others. Social power can both facilitate and restrict the formation of communicative power, though it does so differently than administrative power. As facilitative, the disposition over social power means that the necessary material conditions for an autonomous exercise of equal liberties and communicative freedoms are satisfied. In political bargaining, for example, the involved parties must be able to make their threats or promises credible in light of their social power. As restrictive, the disposition over social power provides some parties with a privileged opportunity to influence the political process in such a way that their interests acquire a priority not in accord with equal civil rights. Businesses, organizations, and pressure groups can, for example, transform their social power into political power by way of such interventions, whether they do so directly by influencing the administration or indirectly by manipulating public opinion.[42]

In organizational terms, the principle that social power should be blocked from directly seizing administrative power finds expression in the principle of the democratic accountability that occupants of political offices have vis-à-vis voters and parliaments. Representatives must periodically stand for reelection; the responsibility of the incumbent Administration and its members for their own decisions and for those of subordinate officials corresponds to the oversight and impeachment powers enjoyed by parliamentary bodies.

The idea that the state can, as *pouvoir neutre*, rise above the pluralism of civil society was always ideological.[43] But in the face of the huge power potentials anchored in deep-seated social structures, even a political process *emerging* from civil society must gain the measure of autonomy necessary to keep the administrative system, whether as executive authority or as sanctioning power, from sinking to the level of one party among others. One danger, for example, is that the state, as a participant in corporate arrangements, might betray the claim that the implementation of legitimately enacted programs will realize political justice. In view of more recent trends in criminal law (such as plea bargaining in criminal proceedings[44]), the principle of separation of state and society continues to be relevant.

The principles of the constitutional state developed in (a) through (d) fit together into an architectonic resting on a single idea: the organization of the constitutional state is ultimately supposed to serve the politically autonomous self-organization of a community that has constituted itself with the system of rights as an association of free and equal consociates under law. The institutions of the constitutional state are supposed to secure an effective exercise of the political autonomy of socially autonomous citizens. Specifically, such institutions must accomplish two things. On the one hand, they must enable the communicative power of a rationally formed will to emerge and find binding expression in political and legal programs. On the other hand, they must allow this communicative power to circulate throughout society via the reasonable application and administrative implementation of legal programs, so that it can foster social integration through the stabilization of expectations and the realization of collective goals. Government by law is designed to spell out the system of rights in terms of a constitutional order in which the legal medium can become effective as a power transformer that reinforces the weakly integrating currents of a communicatively structured lifeworld. I would like to highlight two aspects: on the one hand, the constitutional state institutionalizes the public use of communicative freedom (sec. 4.3.2); on the other hand, it regulates the conversion of communicative into administrative power (sec. 4.3.3).

4.3.2

Depending on the issue, the various types of discourse and bargaining fill different roles for a rational political will-formation. These types are realized in the corresponding forms of communication; and the latter must in turn be legally institutionalized if the citizens' claim to the exercise of their political rights is to be guaranteed. The sociological concept of "institutionalization" pertains to normatively expected behavior: institutions let members of a social collectivity know what behavior they may demand of one another when and in which situations. One can also institutionalize procedures that stipulate the rules a cooperative effort should follow in managing specific tasks. For example, procedural norms regulate the concluding of contracts, the founding of an association, or decision making in self-governing bodies. Parliamentary deliberations and wage negotiations are also set up with the help of such legal procedures. We should carefully distinguish between forms of communication—or types of communication processes—and the legal procedures in which they can be institutionalized.

Bargaining is a special form of communication. Here we find no internal form, or logical pattern, of argumentation that corresponds to the external form of communication. The procedures intended to secure the fairness of possible compromises regulate, among other things, the right to participation, the choice of delegates, and hence the composition of delegations. If necessary they extend to such matters as the moderation and length of negotiation; they also stipulate the kinds of issues and contributions, the admissibility of sanctions, and so forth. These and similar questions are regulated with a view to ensuring that all the relevant interests are given equal consideration and all parties are furnished with equal power; here the exchange of arguments is geared to the most rational pursuit of preferences on the part of each side. Compromise procedures are intended to avert the danger that asymmetrical power structures and unequally distributed threat potentials could prejudice the outcome of bargaining. Another danger is that compromise procedures will be applied to moral or ethical questions, so that these get *redefined* into strategic questions without anyone's noticing or calling attention to the fact. As difficult as the institutionalization of bargaining systems of this sort might be, compromise procedures always pertain to the regulation of strategic interactions.

The types of procedures that regulate discourses (for example, court procedures) are a different matter. Here, institutionally devised legal procedures encounter a "procedure" of an entirely different kind, namely, argumentation processes obeying a logic of their own. When we examine the model of court procedures, we will have to clarify in detail how procedural law facilitates and institutionalizes legal discourses of application without intervening in, and thereby regulating, the argumentation as such. Legal procedures define, protect, and structure only the spaces in which argumentation is supposed to take place. By virtue of its comparatively high degree of rationality, judicial deliberation and decision making offer the most thoroughly analyzed case of an intermeshing of two types of procedure; here we find just that intersection of institutional procedure and an argumentation process whose *internal* structure eludes legal institutionalization. This intersection of two quite different "procedures"—legal and argumentative—shows that the universe of law can open itself from the inside, as it were, to argumentation processes through which pragmatic, ethical, and moral reasons find their way into the language of law without either inhibiting the argumentation game or rupturing the legal code. Although the *embeddedness of different types of argumentation in legal procedures* leaves the inner logic of such discourses intact, legal institutionalization subjects them to specific temporal, social, and substantive constraints. For example, procedural norms regulate participation and the distribution of roles in discursive processes of opinion- and will-formation; they limit the spectrum of admissible topics, questions, and arguments; and they link argumentation to decision making. In this way the instrument of law is reflexively deployed so that discourses for making and applying law can be socially expected in specific places at specific times.

Due to their idealizing content, the universal presuppositions of argumentation can only be approximately fulfilled. Moreover, because there is no criterion independent of the argumentative process, one can judge only from the participant's perspective whether these demanding presuppositions have been sufficiently fulfilled in a given case. This by itself warrants an openness to the possibility that provisionally justified views might have to be revised in the light of new information and arguments. The legal procedure offsets this fallibilism by demanding timely, unambiguous, and binding decisions. This is because legal procedures allow one to monitor adherence to procedural norms from an observer's perspective. Thus the legal code gives a socially binding character to procedurally correct results; it supplies a procedural rationality of its own that compensates for the weaknesses of its complement, the procedural rationality inherent in the process of argumentation. Legal institutionalization thus has the sense of grafting a quasi-pure procedural justice, as Rawls puts it, onto discourses and their imperfect procedural rationality. In this way the logic of argumentation is not frozen but put to work for the production of reasonable decisions having the force of law.

The *majority rule* used for deciding substantive questions in courts, parliaments, or self-governing agencies exemplifies an important feature of the legal procedures that regulate institutionalized deliberations. Majority rule retains an internal relation to the search for truth inasmuch as the decision reached by the majority only represents a caesura in an ongoing discussion; the decision records, so to speak, the interim result of a discursive opinion-forming process. To be sure, in that case the majority decision must be premised on a competent discussion of the disputed issues, that is, a discussion conducted according to the communicative presuppositions of a corresponding discourse. Only then can its content be viewed as the rationally motivated yet fallible result of a process of argumentation that has been interrupted in view of institutional pressures to decide, but is in principle resumable. Doubts about the legitimacy of majority decisions on matters with irreversible consequences are revealing in this regard. Such doubts are based on the view that the outnumbered minority give their consent to the empowerment of the majority only with the proviso that they themselves retain the opportunity in the future of winning over the majority with better arguments and thus of revising the previous decision. Hence the dissenting opinion attached to the justification of a Supreme Court ruling, for example, is meant to record arguments that in similar cases might convince the majority of a future panel of judges.[45] To be sure, majority decisions on questions that have been treated discursively certainly do not draw their legitimating force from the changeability of majority proportions per se.[46] The latter is necessary, though, if majority rule is not to undermine the legitimating force of an argumentation process meant to ground the reasonable *presumption* that fallible decisions are right. Note, too, that it is appropriate to qualify the majority, depending on the matter at issue. Majority decisions are generally constrained by basic rights protecting the minority, for in exercising their political autonomy citizens must not violate the system of rights that first constitutes this autonomy.[47] Majority rule plays a different role in compromises; in bargaining, voting results provide indicators for a given distribution of power.[48]

The *democratic procedure* that institutionalizes the forms of communication necessary for a rational political will-formation must take various conditions of communication into account at the same time. Legislation is carried out in a complex network that includes processes of reaching understanding as well as bargaining. Here pragmatic and legal discourses, which open and conclude our process model,[49] are best understood as matters requiring expert opinion. If we disregard how the input and processing of such information is organized, then the rational character of parliamentary deliberations is to be sought primarily in the fair balancing of interests, the clarification of ethical self-understanding, and the moral justification of regulations. Beyond the pragmatic question of what we *can do* with regard to programs and strategies whose goals are already settled, political opinion- and will-formation must first of all respond to three questions: the question underlying compromise formation, that is, how we *can reconcile* competing preferences; the ethical-political question of who we are and who we seriously *want to be*; and the moral-practical question of how we *ought to act* in accordance with principles of justice. In negotiations that involve the balancing of interests, an *aggregated* will can develop from the coordination and adaptation of different preferences; in hermeneutical discourses of self-understanding, an *authentic* will can arise from shared value orientations; and in moral discourses of justification and application, an *autonomous* will can emerge from shared insights. In each of these negotiations and discourses, respectively different kinds of arguments count. The process of argumentation in each case is in turn carried out in a different form of communication, at least insofar as forms of communication reflect the required patterns of argumentation. At first glance, all of these communicative forms display similar— namely, egalitarian—surface structures. Only a differentiated examination reveals deep structures that require the satisfaction of different conditions in each case. This is shown by the consequences that the individual forms of communication have for the understanding of the *representative system* and, more generally, for the relation between parliament and public opinion.

Members of parliaments are normally chosen in elections that are free, equal, and secret. This procedure has an obvious meaning for the delegation of representatives who receive a mandate to *negotiate compromises*. Participation in a fairly regulated bargaining practice calls for the equal representation of all those affected; it is meant to ensure that all the relevant interests and value orientations can be brought to bear with equal weight in the bargaining process. For example, whereas the mandate is narrowly circumscribed for wage negotiations, the mandate given to representatives of a people remains rather diffuse, even if we could view parliamentary proceedings exclusively in terms of bargaining; this is because general elections bundle together a wide range of interests with a value-generalizing effect. As long as we fully equate politics with the balancing of current interests represented by elected officials, the classical discussions over imperative and free mandates, or about whether the representative system mirrors a hypothetical or empirical popular will, lose their point of reference.

A difference between the empirical and hypothetical popular will can appear only when the preferences entering into the political process are viewed not as something merely given but as inputs that, open to the exchange of arguments, can be discursively changed.[50] An element of reason that alters the meaning of representation only comes into play with a logic intrinsic to political opinion- and will-formation. When members of parliament are elected as participants in discourses conducted by representatives or deputies, the election does not mean, in the first instance, that just voting power has been delegated. The social limitation of representative bodies, then, is in a peculiar tension with the free access that a representative discourse would actually have to require by reason of their communicative presuppositions.

Ethical-political discourses must satisfy the communicative conditions for achieving hermeneutic self-understanding on the part of collectivities. They should enable an authentic self-understanding and lead to critical revision or confirmation of (aspects of) a disputed identity. The consensus (*Konsens*) issuing from a successful search for collective self-understanding neither expresses a merely negotiated agreement (*Vereinbarung*), as in compromises, nor is it a rationally motivated consensus (*Einverständnis*), like the consensus on facts or questions of justice. It expresses two things at once: self-reflection and resolve on a form of life. For ethical-political discourses, this would ideally require that the conditions of systematically undistorted communication be satisfied, thereby protecting the participants from repression, yet without tearing them from their genuine contexts of experience and interests. Discourses for achieving self-understanding require that the cultural traditions formative of one's own identity be dealt with in a manner at once anxiety-free, reflexive, and open to learning. In the present context, it is especially important that there be no nonparticipants in processes of self-reassurance; in principle, the taking of yes/no positions cannot be delegated to others. *All* members must be able to take part in the discourse, even if not necessarily in the same way. Each must have fundamentally equal chances to take a position on all relevant contributions with a yes or no. Hence these discourses, which for technical reasons must be conducted by representatives, must not be construed in terms of the deputy, or proxy, model; they simply form the organized midpoint or focus of the society-wide circulation of informal communication. Discourses conducted by representatives can meet the condition of equal participation on the part of all members only if they remain porous, sensitive, and receptive to the suggestions, issues and contributions, information and arguments that flow in from a discursively structured public sphere, that is, one that is pluralistic, close to the grass roots, and relatively undisturbed by the effects of power.

The communicative presuppositions of *moral discourses*, under which each participant can adopt the perspective of all the rest, yield similar consequences. Whoever takes part in moral argumentation must be able to assume that certain pragmatic presuppositions are sufficiently fulfilled, that is, that the practice of reaching understanding is public, is universally accessible, is free of external and internal violence, and permits only the rationally motivating force of the better argument. Given the improbability of this form of communication, moral discourses of justification are, as a rule, carried out in an advocatory fashion. But that does not make things any easier regarding the composition and character of the bodies responsible for conducting representative discourses of justification. Here representation can only mean that the selection of members of parliament should provide for the broadest possible spectrum of interpretive perspectives, including the views and voices of marginal groups. Unlike the case of ethical-political questions, in moral discussions the circle of those possibly affected is not even limited to members of one's own collectivity. The moral point of view under which policies and laws are subjected to a sensitive universalization test demands all the more that institutionalized deliberations be open to the input of information, the pressure of problems, and the potential for stimulating suggestions found in public opinion. At the same time, the moral point of view transcends the boundaries of every concrete legal community, giving one some distance from the ethnocentrism of one's immediate surroundings.

The political balancing of interests requires the election of delegates who are charged with the tasks of compromise formation; the mode of election must provide for a fair representation and aggregation of the given interests and preferences. Achieving collective self-understanding and moral justification demands the election of competent participants in representative discourses (instead of spokespersons for group interests); the mode of election must ensure, via choice of personnel, that all the relevant perspectives and voices are included. Moreover, the logic of discourses concerned with self-understanding and justice yields compelling normative grounds for publicity requirements that keep institutionalized opinion- and will-formation open to the informal circulation of general political communication. In view of the principles of government by law, what is at stake here is the constitutional meaning of a *normative concept of the public sphere.*[51] The political will-formation organized as a legislative branch of government would destroy the basis of its own rational functioning if it were to block up the spontaneous sources of autonomous public spheres or shut itself off from the input of free-floating issues, contributions, information, and arguments circulating in a civil society set apart from the state. Parliamentary bodies should work within the parameters of what, in some sense, is a "subjectless" public opinion, which naturally cannot form in a vacuum but only against the background of a liberal political culture. Whereas the system of rights explicates the conditions under which people can unite in an association of free and equal citizens, the political culture of a population expresses how they intuitively understand the system of rights in their historically specific life context. The principles of government by law can become the driving force behind the dynamic project of realizing an association of free and equal persons only if they are contextualized in the history of a nation of citizens in such a way that they connect with these citizens' motives and mentalities.[52]

In this communication model, the *relation between parliament and the public sphere* takes a form different from that found in the classical representative or plebiscitary views of democracy. In accordance with the tenet of *stat pro ratione voluntas* ("the will stands in the place of reason"), the *plebiscitary theory* starts with the voluntarist assumption that there exists a popular will expressing the current general interest and that, under the conditions of democratic self-determination, this will largely converges with the empirical popular will. By contrast, the *representation theory* inverts Hobbes's *auctoritas non veritas facit legem* ("authority not truth makes law"). That is, it starts with the rationalist assumption that the hypothetical common good can be ascertained through deliberation only at the level of representative bodies set off from the empirical popular will. Carl Schmitt's reconstruction of bourgeois parliamentarianism integrated both conceptions in a peculiar fashion. He conceived the plebiscitary force of a presumably homogeneous, empirical popular will as the root from which the parliament's discursive opinion- and will-formation sprouts forth:

The parliament of the bourgeois constitutional state is . . . the place where a public discussion of political opinions takes place. Majority and minority, ruling party and opposition search for the correct decision by discussing arguments and counterarguments. As long as parliament represents the nation's culture [*Bildung*] and reason, uniting in itself the total intelligence of the people, a genuine discussion can arise, i.e., in public dialogue the genuine total will of the people can take shape as a *volonté générale.* The people itself cannot discuss . . ., it can only acclaim, elect, and say Yes or No to the questions set before it.

This is supposed to yield the basic idea of parliamentarianism: "The parliament represents the entire nation as such, and in this capacity, through public discussions and public decisionmaking, it enacts laws, i.e., norms that are reasonable, just, and general, which determine and regulate the total life of the state."[53]

Oddly enough, in this text Schmitt relies on a well-known statement of Marx that contradicts his own thesis. Marx of course realized that early liberalism in no way wanted to *reserve* public discussion for parliamentary bodies:

The parliamentary regime lives by discussion; how shall it forbid discussion? . . . The struggle of the orators on the platform evokes the struggle of the scribblers of the press; the debating club in parliament is necessarily supplemented by debating clubs in the salons and taverns. . . . The parliamentary regime leaves everything to the decision of majorities; how shall the great majorities outside parliament not want to decide? When you play the fiddle at the top of the state, what else is to be expected but that those down below dance?[54]

Hence Ernst Fraenkel can counter Schmitt not only with empirical arguments. Without moving outside a liberal theory of the political process, he can argue that discursive opinion- and will-formation is by no means limited to parliament. Rather, the communication circulating in the various arenas of the political public sphere, of political parties and organizations, and of parliamentary bodies and Government leaders are intermeshed with, and reciprocally influence, one another.[55]

This thought can be better explained only in a communication model that frees itself of overly concrete notions of "the people" as an entity. This model instead takes a *structuralist approach* to the manner in which institutionalized opinion- and will-formation is linked with informal opinion building in culturally mobilized public spheres. This linkage is made possible neither by the homogeneity of the people and the identity of the popular will, nor by the identity of a reason that is supposedly able simply to *discover* an underlying homogeneous general interest.[56] The discourse-theoretic conception is at cross-purposes with the classical views. If the communicatively fluid sovereignty of citizens instantiates itself in the power of public discourses that spring from autonomous public spheres but take shape in the decisions of *democratic, politically accountable* legislative bodies, then the pluralism of beliefs and interests is not suppressed but unleashed and recognized in revisable majority decisions as well as in compromises. The unity of a completely proceduralized reason then retreats into the discursive structure of public communication. This reason refuses to concede that a consensus is free of coercion, and hence has legitimating force, unless the consensus has come about under the fallibilist proviso and on the basis of an anarchic, unfettered communicative freedom. In the vertigo of this freedom, there is no longer any fixed point outside that of democratic procedure itself, a procedure whose meaning is already implicit in the system of rights.

4.3.3

The classical separation of powers is explained by differentiating governmental functions: whereas the legislature justifies and passes general programs and the judiciary resolves action conflicts on this statutory basis, the administration is responsible for implementing legal programs that are not self-executing but need to be carried out. By rendering authoritative decisions about what is legal and illegal in individual cases, the judiciary treats existing law as law, namely, from the normative standpoint of stabilizing behavioral expectations. The administration processes the teleological contents of existing law insofar as the latter puts policies in statutory form and steers the administrative realization of collective goals. From the standpoint of the logical division of labor in argumentation, juristic discourses serve to apply norms, whereas the rationality of administrative activity is secured mainly through pragmatic discourses.

Pragmatic discourses are tailored to the choice of technologies and strategies that, under the given circumstances (such as limited resources, deadlines, resistances in acceptance, and other restrictions), are suitable for realizing the values and goals previously set by the legislature:

Administration is the process of realizing stated values in a world of contingent facts. The legitimating ideals of administration are accuracy and efficiency. Administrators are to discover and undertake those actions that will be instrumental to the achievement of specified ends, without, of course, forgetting that no particular goal or end exhausts the collective demand for a good life. Administrators are to do the job assigned in a cost-effective fashion. Because values are specified, administration is oriented toward facts—some concrete or historical, What is the world like? some probabilistic, What actions in that world will cause it to conform to the goals that have been stated?. Answering these sorts of questions implies an investigative turn of mind. Doing so efficiently generally requires division of labor and hierarchical control—in short, bureaucracy. . . . it surely makes a difference to the maintenance of the possibility of liberal autonomy (and to democratic participation) that officials have discretion bounded by stated and general policies, structured by hierarchical authority, exercised in a procedurally regular fashion, and reviewed for rough conformity to some paradigm of instrumental rationality.[57]

The functional separation of powers grounded in the logic of argumentation yields a specification of tasks for the administration. Exemplary for this specification, however, are neither the government ministers and bureaucrats who draft legislative proposals nor the self-governing bodies of German municipal law, but rather the type of midlevel administration concerned exclusively with instrumental problems of implementation. The competent fulfillment of this function plays an important role in legitimating the administration in a constitutional democracy. But its legitimation is not exhausted in this.

That is, another perspective is provided by a theory of power, which accounts for the functional separation of powers as a way to secure both the priority of democratic legislation and the recoupling of administrative power with communicative power. Politically autonomous citizens can understand themselves as authors of the law to which they submit as private subjects only if legitimately generated law also determines the *direction* in which political power circulates. This is manifested at the level of the incumbent Administration, for example, through the electorate's empowerment of the leadership personnel chosen in general elections. Above all, however, it depends on the principle of legality of administration, which requires the administration to remain subject to parliamentary oversight and judicial review. This control pertains to two aspects of administrative activity: the professional character of the law's implementation; and the observance of normative responsibilities that guarantee the legality of execution and therewith meet the requirement that administrative interventions have a statutory basis (*Gesetzesvorbehalt*). The rationality of a specialized and competent fulfillment of tasks by experts is no protection against a *paternalistic* self-empowerment and self-programming on the part of administrative agencies.[58] The logic of separated powers demands instead that the administration be empowered to carry out its tasks as professionally as possible, yet only under normative premises not at its disposal: the executive branch is to be limited to *employing* administrative power according to the law.

This binding of the administration by laws must not be confused with another kind of mechanism for limiting power. The regional and functional division of administrative power in a federally structured administration or the subdivision of the executive branch into special and universal administrative agencies follows the pattern of "checks and balances," the splitting and spreading of administrative powers through different official channels within the framework of an already established functional separation of powers. This *spreading out* of administrative power is only indirectly coupled with the logic of the separation of powers, namely, insofar as the internal decentralization of the administrative apparatus has delaying, blocking, and moderating effects that open the administration as a whole to external controls.

To the extent that the law should normatively be a source of legitimation and not just a medium for the exercise of political authority, administrative power must remain bound to communicatively generated power. A functional separation of powers can serve as the link coupling the administrative power involved in goal attainment with the communicative power that generates law because the constitutional state has a twofold task: it must not only evenly divide and distribute political power but also strip such power of its violent substance by rationalizing it. The legal rationalization of force must not be conceived as taming a quasi-natural domination whose violent core is and always remains uncontrollably contingent. Rather, law is supposed to dissolve this irrational substance, converting it into a "rule of law" in which alone the politically autonomous self-organization of the legal community expresses itself. In tracing the exercise of political authority back to the citizens' exercise of political autonomy, the modern natural law operating with Rousseau's and Kant's idea of self-legislation seeks to unify practical reason and sovereign will in a way that removes any quasi-natural substance of domination from the authority of a democratic government.

For this reason, the *concept of the legal statute* as democratic law forms the cornerstone in the modern natural-law constructions of the bourgeois constitutional state. If the legal statute is understood as a general norm that acquires validity from the approval of the people's representatives in a procedure characterized by discussion and publicity, then it unifies two moments: the power of an intersubjectively formed will and the reason inherent in the legitimating procedure. Democratic law, then, is characterized by "the fact that legal decisions of whatever content are combined with quite definite procedural presuppositions."[59] Democratic genesis, not a priori principles to which the content of norms would have to correspond, provides the statute with its justice: "The justice of a law is guaranteed by the particular procedure by which it comes about."[60] The priority of the constitution over legislation is thoroughly compatible with this, for a constitution that interprets and elaborates the system of rights contains "nothing other than the principles and conditions of the ineliminable (*unaufhebbaren*) legislative process."[61]

At least in Germany, the liberal doctrine of separated powers originally relied on a narrow interpretation of this concept of democratic law. It characterized laws in terms of the semantic form of abstract and general normative propositions and considered the principle of administrative legality to be fulfilled if the implementation was limited strictly to concretizing the general contents of the norm according to the circumstances. On this reading, a law owes its legitimacy not to the democratic procedure but to its grammatical form. This semanticist abstraction suggests an interpretation of the separation of powers in terms of the "logic of subsumption." According to this view, binding the legislature to the constitution and the administration to enacted law is governed by the extensional logic that subordinates species to genera, that is, special to general norms: one must be able to subsume decrees, local ordinances, and generally binding regulations under the statute just as one can subsume ordinary laws under constitutional norms. This would allow one to operationalize the logic of the separation of powers as a set of more or less inclusionary relationships. This explanation, at once both economical and elegant, still has a certain suggestive power even today. Yet the objections that it has also provoked are aimed not so much at the logic underlying the doctrine of separated powers as at its *liberal interpretation* (in the sense of the German "liberal" tradition).

The classical scheme for separate branches of government becomes less tenable the more laws lose the form of conditional programs and assume instead the shape of goal-oriented programs. As a rule, these "materialized" laws, too, appear as general norms formulated without proper nouns and directed to an indeterminate number of addressees. However, they contain general clauses and vague statutory language, or set concrete policies (analogous to special legislation) that leave the administration considerable room for discretion. Due to the developments leading to state interventionism, more and more areas of law have been materialized, with the result that an administration geared for planning, services, and policymaking is increasingly unable to limit itself to simply implementing general and sufficiently determinate norms in a technical manner unburdened of normative questions. This development has been well documented and much discussed in regard to the Federal Republic of Germany.[62] But it holds just as much for the United States and other comparable countries:

When Congress requires the newer administrative agencies, under statutes such as the Water Quality Act, the Air Quality Act, the Consumer Product Safety Act, the Occupational Safety and Health Act, the Motor Vehicle Safety Act, or the Toxic Substances Act, to make trade-offs between the need for public health or safety and the need for employment, product diversity, and a vibrant economy, it seems clear that administrators must make value choices that outrun any definition of technical or professional competence. Administrative discretion to choose among competing social values thus undermines . . . the transmission belt . . . model of administrative legitimacy.[63]

This sort of objection only makes it clear, however, that the "transmission belt model" for the implementation of general laws does not specify the principle of administrative legality with sufficient abstraction, in two respects. On the one hand, the principles of the constitutional state must be introduced independently of any historical legal order and of any *concrete form of institutionalization*. This level of analysis—at which I have been working thus far—only requires necessary forms of institutionalization *in general*; it does not address the realization of principles in particular political institutions. Constituting different branches of government and abstractly separating their functions does not yet mean a sociological differentiation between just as many organizations. Thus one response to the expanded discretionary leeway of welfare-state bureaucracies, for example, was to build new forms of participation and arenas for deliberation into the decision-making process of the administration itself, so as to avert the danger of an improper self-programming. The affected clients received new procedural rights vis-à-vis the officials: "Rather than imposing new decisional criteria or priorities on administrators, courts required that decisions be taken only after listening to the views or evidence presented by interests that traditionally had not been presented in the administrative process. All of these techniques tended to broaden, intensify, or redefine the participation of affected parties in the administrative process."[64] Certainly the introduction of quasi-judicial hearings and other forms of participation in the administrative process conjured up new dangers, which Mashaw discusses under the labels of "overintrusion" and "underprotection." But even this critique relies on normative standards borrowed from the logic of separated powers.

The principles must be formulated with sufficient abstraction, and not just independently of their varying institutional forms. The semantic concept of a general norm, which anchored the logic of the separation of powers, also prejudges too much. This approach cannot adequately explain how the legal statute functions like a hinge in the construction of a constitutional state with separate branches of government. Rather, one must turn one's attention to the discourses and negotiations in which the legislature's will is formed, as well as to the potential of reasons and arguments by which laws are legitimated. From the vantage point of discourse theory, the functions of the legislature, judiciary, and administration can be differentiated according to forms of communication and the corresponding patterns of argumentation. Laws can regulate the transformation of communicative into administrative power inasmuch as they come about according to a democratic procedure, ground a comprehensive legal protection guaranteed by impartial courts, and *shield* from the implementing administration the sorts of reasons that support legislative and judicial decision making. These normative reasons belong to a universe in which legislature and judiciary share the work of justifying and applying norms. An administration limited to pragmatic discourses must not change anything *in this* universe by its contributions; at the same time, it draws therefrom the normative premises that have to underlie its own empirically informed, purposive-rational decision making.

From this argumentation-theoretic perspective, the division of powers and responsibilities among authorities that respectively make, apply, and implement laws follows from the *distribution of the possibilities for access to different sorts of reasons* and to the corresponding forms of communication that determine how these reasons are dealt with. Political legislators alone enjoy unlimited access to normative, pragmatic, and empirical reasons, including those constituted through the results of fair compromises, though they have this access only within the framework of a democratic procedure designed for the justification of norms. The judiciary cannot make whatever use it likes of the reasons packaged in, and linked to, statutes; these same reasons play a different role when the courts, with an eye to the coherence of the legal system as a whole, employ them in a discourse of application aimed at decisions consistent over time. In contrast to the legislature and judiciary, finally, the administration is not permitted to deal with normative reasons in either a constructive or reconstructive manner. The norms fed into the administration bind the pursuit of collective goals to pregiven premises and keep administrative activity within the horizon of purposive rationality. They empower officials to select technologies and strategies only under the proviso that—in contrast to subjects of private law—they do not follow their own interests or preferences.

The talk of "legislature," "judiciary," and "administration" suggests an overly concrete understanding led astray by inherited forms of institutionalization. Such a view misses the level of abstraction at which we have sketched the discourse-theoretic specification of the *functions* of legislation, application, and implementation. Only when one approaches these functions at an abstract level, in terms of the disposition over different kinds of admissible arguments and corresponding forms of communication, can one assess the adequacy of the various ways in which the principles implied by the logic of separated powers have been institutionalized. For example, insofar as the implementation of programmatic goals requires the administration to perform organizational tasks that at least implicitly require a further development of law, the legitimation basis of traditional administrative structures no longer suffices. The logic of the separation of powers must then be realized in new structures, say, by setting up the corresponding forms of participation and communication or by introducing quasi-judicial and parliamentary procedures, procedures for compromise formation, and so on.[65] I will treat this in greater detail in the last chapter.

5

The Indeterminacy of Law and the Rationality of Adjudication

I have introduced the system of rights and the principles of the constitutional state in connection with issues familiar from modern natural law. The shift in perspective undertaken in the course of this analysis, from contractarian theories to discourse theory, did not imply any change in the level of abstraction. The occasional illustrative allusions to the legal systems of the German Federal Republic or the United States reminded us, however, that constitutional rights and principles, while indeed defined in abstracto, can only be found in historical constitutions and political systems. They are interpreted and embodied in concrete legal orders—at the level of cultural symbolism in constitutional law, at the level of the action system in the corresponding institutions and processes. Such matters are the object of comparative law and political science; they are not our topic of discussion, though they do touch on it indirectly. Different legal orders not only represent different ways of realizing the same rights and principles; they can also reflect different paradigms of law. By the latter I mean the exemplary views of a legal community regarding how the system of rights and constitutional principles can be actualized in the *perceived* context of a given society.

A *paradigm of law* draws on a model of contemporary society to explain how constitutional rights and principles must be conceived and implemented if in the given context they are to fulfill the functions normatively ascribed to them. A "social model of law" (to use Franz Wieacker's term) represents something like the implicit social theory of the legal system, and hence the image this system forms of its social environment. Thus the legal paradigm determines how basic rights and constitutional principles are to be understood and how they can be realized in the context of contemporary society. The two most successful paradigms in the history of modern law, which are still competing today, are those of bourgeois formal law and welfare-state "materialized" law. In taking the perspective of discourse theory, I intend to sharpen the contours of a third legal paradigm, which provides a specific interpretation of the other two and goes beyond them. I start with the assumption that the legal systems emerging at the end of the twentieth century in mass welfare-state democracies are appropriately understood in proceduralist terms. Before discussing the paradigm issue, however, in this and the next chapter I extend the approach I have taken so far. Up to now I have examined law from a philosophical standpoint, introducing constitutional rights and principles from the standpoint of discourse theory. I would now like to make this approach plausible from the perspective of legal theory proper, that is, in view of the legal system *in the narrow sense.*

A double demarcation recommends itself for modern legal systems. Taken as an action system, law includes the totality of interactions regulated by legal norms. Luhmann, for example, defines law in this *broad sense* as the social subsystem specialized for stabilizing behavioral expectations. It includes all social communications that refer to law.[1] We can distinguish this from the legal system *in the narrow sense.* This includes all interactions that are not only oriented to law, but are also geared to produce new law and reproduce law as law. To institutionalize the legal system in this sense requires the self-application of law in the form of secondary rules that constitute and confer the official powers to make, apply, and implement law. The legislative, judicial, and administrative "powers" of government differ, from an analytic point of view, according to these functions.

Naturally, from an empirical standpoint one can see that in our type of society this production and reproduction of law involves various institutions that simultaneously fulfill several functions. In constitutional democracies, political legislation is considered to have the central function. Today this involves more than just political parties, electorates, parliamentary bodies, and Government leaders. It also involves the courts insofar as they interpret and develop law, and administrative agencies insofar as they exercise a rather broad discretion. In truth, the function of applying laws is performed not only by courts inside the horizon of legal doctrine and the public of legal experts, but implicitly by administrations as well. Finally, the function of implementing laws is exercised not only by the administration, but indirectly by the courts as well. To some extent these legal functions are even delegated by the government to quasi-public or private bodies.

I take the legal system in the broad sense to include all legally regulated action systems; reflexive law constitutes a core area for the production of legal acts by private persons, whereas material legal norms immediately direct behavior in various ways. Moreover, a stratification exists between formally organized spheres of interaction that are legally constituted and those spheres that, primarily regulated through extralegal institutions, merely have an overlay of law. In formally organized spheres like the economy or the state apparatus, most interactions are guided by law and, even from the actor's perspective, referred to law, whereas in spheres like the family, neighborhood, or educational system it is only in cases of conflict that the law emerges from the background and enters the awareness of the actors.[2]

These remarks should suffice to roughly locate the legal system in the narrow sense. A discourse theory of law must first of all prove itself at this level. Unlike a philosophical theory of justice, *legal theory* moves within the compass of particular legal orders. It draws its data from established law (*geltenden Recht*), from statutes and precedents, doctrinal commentaries, political contexts of legislation, historical legal sources, and so forth. Unlike philosophy, legal theory cannot afford to ignore those aspects that result from the internal connection between law and political power—primarily the question of the legal licensing of the government's application of legitimate force.[3] Like jurisprudence (*Rechtsdogmatik*), legal theory privileges the judge's perspective. This is due to the functional status the judiciary has inside the legal system in the narrow sense. Because all legal communications refer to actionable claims, court decisions provide the perspective from which the legal system is analyzed. The choice of this perspective implies only a *methodological* commitment, not a restriction of the analysis to processes of adjudication. Legal theory also extends to legislation and administration, hence to all the subsystems reflexively concerned with the production and reproduction of law, as well as to the legal system in the broad sense. Legal theory differs from the doctrinal work of jurisprudence in that it claims to achieve a theory of the legal order as a whole. It also takes the perspectives of the other participants into consideration by including the roles of the political legislator and the administrator, or of private legal persons and citizens, besides that of the judge.[4] As we will see in Ronald Dworkin's concept of law as a medium securing the integrity of society as a whole, even the collective self-understanding of the legal community comes into view this way. Nevertheless, legal theory remains first of all a *theory of adjudication* and legal discourse.

Within this sphere of adjudication, the immanent tension in law between facticity and validity manifests itself as a tension between the principle of legal certainty and the claim to a legitimate application of law, that is, to render correct or right decisions. I begin by discussing four exemplary views of law that provide different solutions for this problem of rationality in adjudication (sec. 5.1). Of particular interest is Dworkin's proposal, to meet the claim to rational decision making through a rational reconstruction of the law of the land. The ideal demands he makes on the required theory have set off a lively discussion (sec. 5.2). Frank Michelman's objections to Dworkin's solipsistic approach clear the way to an intersubjective theory of legal discourse. However, the thesis that Robert Alexy proposes in this context, that legal discourse should be conceived as a special case of moral discourse, does not quite match the complex relation between the judiciary and legislation (sec. 5.3).

5.1 Hermeneutics, Realism, and Positivism

5.1.1

When a theory of justice takes a directly normative approach and attempts to justify the principles of a well-ordered society by operating beyond existing institutions and traditions, it faces the problem of how its abstract idea of justice can be brought into contact with reality. What arises as a subsequent problem for such a philosophical approach poses the first challenge for a legal theory operating from the start within the sphere of existing law (*geltenden Rechts*). We have already seen how the tension between facticity and validity is inherent in the category of law itself and appears in the two dimensions of legal validity. On the one hand, established law guarantees the enforcement of legally expected behavior and therewith the certainty of law. On the other hand, rational procedures for making and applying law promise to legitimate the expectations that are stabilized in this way; the norms *deserve* legal obedience. Such legitimacy should allow a law-abiding behavior that, based on respect for the law, involves more than sheer compliance. Both guarantees, certainty and legitimacy, must be simultaneously redeemed at the level of judicial decision making. It is not enough that conflicting claims are transformed into legal claims and decided in an effectively binding manner after hearings in court. In order to fulfill the socially integrative function of the legal order and the legitimacy claim of law, court rulings must satisfy simultaneously the conditions of *consistent decision making* and *rational acceptability*. Because these conditions do not easily harmonize, two sets of criteria must be reconciled in the practice of adjudication.

On the one hand, the principle of legal certainty demands decisions that can be consistently rendered within the framework of the existing legal order. An existing law is the product of an opaque web of past decisions by the legislature and the judiciary, and it can include traditions of customary law as well. This institutional history of law forms the background of every present-day practice of decision making. The positivity of law also reflects the contingencies of this original context of emergence. On the other hand, the claim to legitimacy requires decisions that are not only consistent with the treatment of similar cases in the past and in accord with the existing legal system. They are also supposed to be rationally grounded in the matter at issue so that all participants can accept them as rational decisions. Judges decide actual cases within the horizon of a present future, and their opinions claim validity in the light of rules and principles that are here and now accepted as legitimate. To this extent, the justifications must be emancipated from the contingencies of their historical genesis. In hard cases, this switch in perspective from history to systematics is explicitly carried out in the transition from the internal justification of a verdict that relies on given premises to the external justification of the premises themselves.[5] As is the case with laws, court decisions, too, are "creatures of both history and morality: what an individual is entitled to have, in civil society, depends on both the practice and the justice of its political institutions."[6]

The rationality problem thus consists in this: how can the application of a contingently emergent law be carried out with both internal consistency and rational external justification, so as to guarantee simultaneously *the certainty of law* and its *rightness?* If one assumes that the natural-law option, which simply subordinated positive law to suprapositive standards, is no longer available, then there are, to begin with, three well-known alternatives for treating this central question in legal theory: (a) legal hermeneutics, (b) legal realism, and (c) legal positivism.

(a) In opposition to the conventional model of legal decision as subsuming a case under the pertinent rule, legal hermeneutics has the merit of having revived the Aristotelian insight that no rule is able to regulate its own application.[7] If we consider a case to be a state of affairs falling under a rule, then such a case is constituted only by being described in terms of the norm applied to it. At the same time, the norm acquires a more concrete meaning precisely in virtue of its application to a corresponding state of affairs, which is thereby transformed into a case. A norm always "takes in" a complex lifeworld situation only in a selective manner, in view of the criteria of relevance prescribed by the norm itself. At the same time, the single case constituted by the norm never exhausts the vague semantic contents of a general norm but rather selectively instantiates them. This circular description indicates a methodological problem that every legal theory has to elucidate. Hermeneutics proposes a process model as its solution.

Interpretation begins with an evaluatively shaped preunderstanding that establishes a prior relation between norm and circumstances and opens the horizon for further relational connections.

The initially diffuse preunderstanding becomes more articulate to the extent that under its direction the norm and the circumstances reciprocally specify each other and constitute the case by making the norm more concrete.[8] Hermeneutics adopts a distinct position in legal theory when it solves the rationality problem in adjudication by contextualizing reason in the historical nexus of a received tradition. According to this solution, the preunderstanding of the judge is shaped by the shared topoi of an ethical tradition. This preunderstanding steers the flexible connections between norms and states of affairs in the light of received, and historically corroborated, principles. The rationality of a decision is ultimately supposed to be measured against the "standards provided by customs that have not yet coalesced into norms," that is, against "jurisprudential maxims that precede law."[9] The hermeneutics that transforms topoi into legal principles holds onto the legitimacy claim raised in judicial decision making. The indeterminacy of a circular process of interpretation can be gradually reduced by referring to principles. But these principles can be legitimated only from the effective history (*Wirkungsgeschichte*) of those inherited forms of law and life in which judges contingently find themselves.

(b) In a pluralistic society in which various belief systems compete with each other, recourse to a prevailing ethos developed through interpretation does not offer a convincing basis for legal discourse. What counts for one person as a historically proven topos is for others ideology or sheer prejudice. Realist theories of law respond to just this state of affairs. They do not contest the descriptive value of hermeneutical methodology, but arrive at a different assessment of the preunderstanding that steers the process of interpretation. In the selectivity that characterizes judicial decisions, extralegal backgrounds come into play that can and should only be elucidated by empirical analyses. These external factors explain how judges fill out the discretionary leeway they enjoy in their decisions; such factors enable one to *predict* judicial decisions on historical, psychological, or sociological grounds. The legal skepticism this engenders is obvious. Insofar as the outcome of a court procedure can be explained on the basis of the judge's interest position and social background, her political attitudes and personality structures, or through ideological traditions, power constellations, and economic pressures inside and outside the legal system, the practice of decision making is no longer internally determined, that is, guided by the selectivity of procedure, case, and legal basis. Legal hermeneutics already softened up the inner logic of law by embedding it in tradition and thereby relativizing it. That logic now completely disappears in a "realistic" description of the causal process of adjudication.

From the standpoint of Legal Realism, the *Freirechtsschule* ("Free-Law" School), and Interest Jurisprudence,[10] one can no longer clearly distinguish law and politics in terms of structural features. If, however, legal decision making can be assimilated to naked power processes, then it no longer makes sense to hold that consistent decisions based on a system of sufficiently determinate norms can secure legal certainty. The law produced in the past loses its dominance over current decisions, because these lie predominantly in the judge's discretion. At best, the legitimacy claim of law can preserve its meaning insofar as judges, like future-oriented politicians, make their decisions on the basis of value orientations they consider reasonable. Law is then conceived as an instrument for behavioral control that can be deployed for reasonable political goals, that is, goals justified on utilitarian or welfare-economic grounds.[11] The participants' idealistic notion, that all (or most) cases can be decided on the basis of established law both consistently and rightly, has been subjected by realist theories to a disillusioning critique. This critique relies on an observer's point of view. From a participant's point of view, however, judicial decision making can hardly operate without idealizing suppositions. A flat revocation of any guarantees of legal certainty leads to the conclusion that the legal system must ultimately give up the idea of satisfying the very function of law, to stabilize expectations. The realists cannot explain how the functionally necessary accomplishments of the legal system are compatible with a radical skepticism on the part of legal experts.

(c) Against this, legal positivism wants to account for the function of stabilizing expectations, but without having to support the legitimacy of the legal decision on the contestable authority of customary ethical traditions. In contrast to realist schools of thought, such theoreticians as Hans Kelsen and H. L. A. Hart have worked out the internal normative character of legal rules and the systematic construction of a system of rules. This system is supposed to facilitate the consistency of rule-bound decisions and render the law largely independent of politics. In contrast to hermeneuticists, positivists emphasize the closed character and autonomy of a legal system impermeable to extralegal principles. Thus the rationality problem is resolved in a way that gives priority to a narrowly conceived institutional history purged of any suprapositive validity basis. A "basic norm" or "rule of recognition" enables one to determine unambiguously which norms belong to valid law (*geltenden Recht*) at a given point in time.

An *autonomous* legal system of this sort is differentiated into primary rules for regulating behavior and secondary rules for the self-referential production of norms. If we presuppose that law is autonomous in this way, then the validity of legal regulations is measured solely by the observance of legally stipulated procedures of lawmaking. This legitimation through the legality of the lawmaking procedure privileges the pedigree—namely, the correct process of enactment—over the rational justification of a norm's content: rules are valid because they are properly enacted by the competent institutions. The legitimation of the legal order as a whole shifts to its origin, that is, to a basic norm or rule of recognition that legitimates everything without itself being capable of rational justification; as part of a historical form of life, it must be factually accepted as settled custom. Hart makes this plausible by drawing on Wittgenstein's concept of a language game. Like the grammar of a language game, the rule of recognition is rooted in a practice that, though described externally as a fact, is taken by the participants themselves as self-evidently valid.[12]

Tying the validity of law to its genesis allows only an asymmetrical solution to the rationality problem. Reason or justice is to a certain extent subordinated to history. Hence the positivist reading of judicial decision making privileges the certainty guarantee at the expense of the rightness guarantee. The priority of legal certainty is evident in the positivist treatment of "hard cases." In these cases, the hermeneutical problem becomes especially clear: how can the appropriateness of unavoidably selective decisions be justified? Positivism plays down this problem, analyzing its effects as symptoms of an unavoidable vagueness in ordinary language. Hart traces the need to interpret legal norms back to the fundamentally open structure of natural languages and arrives at a decisionistic conclusion. Insofar as existing norms do not suffice for an exact specification of cases, judges must decide according to their own discretion. Judges fill out their discretionary leeway with extralegal preferences and orient their decisions, if necessary, by moral standards no longer covered by the authority of law.

5.1.2

Ronald Dworkin's theory of law can be seen as an attempt to avoid the deficits of the realist, positivist, and hermeneutical solutions. Specifically, Dworkin turns to a deontological concept of rights to explain how judicial decision making can simultaneously satisfy the requirements of legal certainty and rational acceptability. In opposition to realism, Dworkin holds on to both the necessity and the possibility of rule-bound, consistent decisions that guarantee a sufficient measure of legal certainty. In opposition to positivism, he maintains the necessity and possibility of "single right" decisions legitimated with respect to their content (and not just formally through procedures) in light of recognized principles. In referring to the hermeneutical role of a preunderstanding determined by principles, however, Dworkin does not leave the judge wholly at the mercy of the historical authority of self-evident topoi. Rather, the judge's recourse to a preunderstanding obligates her to critically appropriate an institutional history of law that always reveals the traces of practical reason. Courts decide who is entitled to which "political" rights; among such rights Dworkin includes rights that enjoy positive validity and at the same time deserve recognition according to standards of justice.

The thesis that such rights "exist" depends on a historically embodied practical reason that extends through history, so to speak. Instantiated in the moral point of view, this reason is articulated in the principle of equal concern and respect for each person. Dworkin's basic norm tallies with Kant's principle of right and Rawls's first principle of justice, according to which each person has a right to equal liberties. To be sure, Dworkin raises the objection against Rawls that the parties in the original position can agree on this principle only because the basic right to equal concern and respect already regulates the parties' admission to the original position, and hence belongs to the conditions of rational agreements in general. For Dworkin this basic right cannot be grounded on further principles and thus enjoys the status of a "natural right of all men and women . . . [which] they possess . . . simply as human beings with the capacity to make plans and give justice."[13] To avoid natural-law connotations, one can also understand this as an explanation of the deontological character of basic rights in general. This kind of moral meaning is transmitted to institutionally binding, or "political," rights and confers a moment of unconditionality on individual legal claims. Dworkin understands rights as "trumps" in a game in which individuals defend their justified claims against disadvantages resulting from collective policies: "It follows from the definition of a right that it cannot be outweighed by all social goals. We might, for simplicity, stipulate not to call any political aim a right unless it has a certain threshold weight against collective goals in general."[14] Certainly it is not the case that all rights have absolute validity, but each right imposes limits on cost-benefit analysis in the realization of collective goals. These limits are ultimately justified by the principle of equal respect for each person.

Dworkin's theory of rights is premised on the claim that moral arguments play a role in adjudication because positive law has unavoidably absorbed a moral content. This premise harbors no surprise for a discourse theory starting with the assumption that moral reasons enter into law via the democratic procedure of legislation (and through the fairness conditions of compromise formation).[15] Nevertheless, this point requires some explanation inasmuch as moral contents, once *translated* into the legal code, undergo a change in meaning that is specific to the legal form.

Excursus on the Moral Content of Law

The legal meaning of moral contents and the range of variation in their specific weights are most evident in the sphere of primary rules that regulate behavior. If we follow Bernhard Peter's proposed classification and divide these nonprocedural rules into repressive and restorative precepts and prohibitions on the one hand, and "prices" and transfers on the other,[16] then it becomes clear that moral contents vary over a wide spectrum. They may shrink to just the minimal expectation of obedience to legal norms as such. An indication for the relative weight of the moral content of various norms is the strength of citizens' reactions to the corresponding violations. These reactions include both informal disapproval or reproaches as well as court-imposed sanctions. The way in which penalties are categorized (from crimes to mere minor offenses), as well as the division between criminal and civil offenses (which justify claims for compensation), can be understood as the doctrinal weighting of moral content. The basic offenses of criminal law, such as murder and manslaughter, physical injury, unlawful restraint, theft, and so forth, are regarded as morally reprehensible, whereas sentencing a person to provide restitution for damage she has caused normally implies disapproval of the deed but not contempt for the culprit.

The situation is different with reactions to rewards or costs allotted on the basis of behavior, such as subsidies, fees, various taxes, and so on, or with reactions to income transfers and payments based on welfare criteria independent of behavior. Laws tied to policies of redistributive taxation and resource allocation, as well as to policies of redistribution and provision of collective goods, are directed in a morally neutral way to addressees who are assumed to be oriented primarily by cost-benefit calculations or simply by "need." Failures in the behavioral control intended by the legislator are not "reproachable." The validity of legal norms involving "prices" or transfers does not have strong moral connotations. However, such legal programs do not necessarily or even normally lack all moral content, because they result from morally justified policies. The moral standards that the legislator uses to justify these policies shape the content of the law that provides the forms in which these policies are carried out. Thus policy arguments, which Dworkin distinguishes from arguments of principle, may well become morally relevant.

Intermediate procedural norms that furnish quasi-public bodies, such as universities, professional associations, agencies, and the like, with specific powers occupy a middle position between morally laden and largely nonmoralized rules. The exercise of these powers (e.g., conducting labor actions, negotiating compromises, setting down business procedures) follows rules and formal requirements that occasionally extend to morally relevant behavior, such as duties to inform and duties of care, exclusion of improper tactics, and so on. Even in private law, "good faith" or liability for unintended consequences plays a role. Interestingly enough, such formal requirements cannot completely explicate the moral substance of what Durkheim called the noncontractual bases of contracts; this substance cannot be fully captured in the legal form. This concerns above all the capacity for moral judgment, which if it does not actually guide should at least accompany the authority to produce and apply legal norms. This interpretation might be problematic for norms that confer legal powers in the core area of private law. It does gain a certain plausibility, however, in view of areas where public powers of lawmaking and organization are delegated to bearers who are "private" in name only (e.g., parties involved in wage agreements or board members chosen according to industrial relations law).

Naturally, as a *standard for legitimate law,* morality has its primary abode in the political will-formation of the lawgiver and in the political communication of the public sphere. Even the abovementioned examples for morality *in the law* show only that moral contents are translated into the legal code and furnished with a different mode of validity. Overlapping contents do not blur the boundary between law and morality, which are irreversibly differentiated at the postconventional level of justification. As long as the *difference between the languages* of morality and law is maintained, the migration of moral contents into law does not signify any *immediate* moralization of law. When Dworkin speaks of arguments of principle justifying judicial decisions externally, in most cases he has legal principles in mind in any case, that is, standards that result from the application of the discourse principle to the legal code. The system of rights and constitutional principles are certainly indebted to practical reason, but they are due in the first instance to the special shape this reason assumes in the principle of democracy. The moral content of constitutional rights and principles is also explained by the fact that the basic norms of both law and morality, which are grounded in the same discourse principle, *substantively* intersect.

5.1.3

However Dworkin himself may conceive the relation between law and morality in detail, his theory of rights at least requires a deontological understanding of legal validity claims. With this he breaks out of the circle that ensnares legal hermeneutics in its turn toward the historically proven topoi of a received ethos. Dworkin gives the hermeneutical approach a constructivist turn. He begins by criticizing legal positivism, in particular (a) its neutrality thesis and (b) its assumption that a legal system is autonomously closed. He then goes on to develop (c) his methodological ideas regarding constructive interpretation.

(a) To begin with, Dworkin disputes the assumption that law is legitimated by the mere legality of the legislative procedure. Legal discourse is independent of morality and politics only in the sense that moral principles and political policies must also be translated into the neutral language of law and connected to the legal code. Beneath this unity of the code, however, one finds that legitimate law involves a complex notion of validity. This explains why landmark decisions and important precedents usually admit reasons of extralegal origin, hence pragmatic, ethical, and moral considerations, into legal discourse.

With the help of well-known precedents taken primarily from American law, Dworkin analyzes how judges manage to cope with indeterminate legal situations through reference to the background of political policies and moral principles. They arrive at well-grounded decisions by juristically processing arguments of policy and of principle. Such external justifications are possible because existing law itself has already incorporated teleological contents and moral principles; most important, it has absorbed the supporting reasons of the political legislature. These reasons can once again emerge, as it were, when higher courts rule on hard cases. To be sure, in the process of adjudication, arguments of principle enjoy priority over arguments of policy: policy arguments have their genuine place in the legislative process, and they make their way into juristic discourse through this process. Adjudication is geared to the application of legal norms that stabilize expectations; it considers legislative policies and goals in the light of principles, for "arguments of principle justify a political decision by showing that the decision respects or secures some individual or group right."[17] In general, political policies, too, are already justified in the light of principles and existing rights, but only arguments of principle that refer to the system of rights can preserve the internal connection between the decision about an individual case and the normative substance of the legal order as a whole.

(b) Dworkin next draws on the distinction between "rule" and "principle" to explain the inadequacy of the conception of law on which Hart based his autonomy thesis. Rules are concrete norms sufficiently specified for application to typical cases (for example, stipulations for drawing up wills), whereas principles represent general legal standards in need of interpretation (such as human rights and equal treatment). Both rules and principles are norms that claim to be deontologically valid; that is, they have an obligatory character. The distinction between these types of norms must not be confused with that between norms and policies. Neither rules nor principles have a teleological structure. Contrary to what legal methodologies tend to suggest when they refer to "weighing values" (*Güterabwägung*), principles must not be understood as optimizing prescriptions, because that would eradicate their deontological character.[18] Rules and principles both serve as arguments in the justification of decisions, though each has a different status in the logic of argumentation. Rules always contain an antecedent "if" clause, specifying the typical situational features that constitute the conditions of application, whereas principles either appear with an unspecified validity claim or are restricted in their applicability only by general conditions that require interpretation. This explains the characteristic difference that Dworkin highlights, namely, the difference in how rules and principles behave in cases of collision. A conflict between rules can only be resolved in one of two ways, either by introducing an exception clause or by declaring one of the conflicting rules to be invalid. Such an all-or-nothing decision is not necessary when principles conflict. Although the particular principle that happens to be appropriate for a given issue certainly enjoys priority, the *recessive* principles do not thereby lose their validity but only their contextual relevance. Depending on the case to be decided, one of the prima facie relevant principles takes precedence over the others. Because the appropriate principle can change from case to case, different transitive orders are set up between the same principles without thereby affecting their validity.

Positivism arrives at a false thesis of autonomy, because it conceives the law as a closed system of application-specific rules that in case of collision require all-or-nothing decisions lying in the judge's discretion. From Dworkin's perspective, positivists are forced to reach decisionistic conclusions only because they start with a *one-dimensional* conception of law as a system of rules without principles. Lacking a notion of principles, they conceive all collisions as collisions between rules. These then generate an indeterminacy in the legal situation that can be eliminated solely in a decisionistic manner. As soon as principles—and the higher-level justification of rule applications in the light of principles—are admitted and recognized as *normal* components of legal discourse, both aspects disappear: the closed character of the rule system and the irresolvability of conflicts between rules.

(c) By analyzing the roles that arguments of principle and of policy play in legal discourse, and by uncovering a stratum of higher-level norms inside the legal system itself, Dworkin gets a handle on the posttraditional level of justification that positive law requires. Contrary to what legal positivism assumes, after modern law emancipated itself from sacred foundations and extricated itself from religious-metaphysical contexts, it did not simply become contingent. Contrary to what legal realism assumes, law does not lack an internal structure of its own; it is not simply at the disposition of political policies. As deontological, rights contain a moment of inviolability that refers to a rational dimension and encourages the search for "single right" answers based on principles. Contrary to what legal hermeneutics assumes, these principles are not merely historically proven topoi that can be drawn from the tradition of an ethical community. As a result, the practice of interpretation requires a point of reference beyond settled legal traditions. Dworkin explains this standard of practical reason *methodologically* in terms of constructive interpretation. He explains it *substantively* by postulating a legal theory that can rationally reconstruct and systematize the existing body of norms.

As in the history of science, so also in the institutional history of a legal system one can distinguish internally accessible aspects from external ones. From the internal perspective, in systematically recapitulating an issue, one casts a critical light on the history of received arguments; in the light of present evidence, one will then distinguish unconvincing approaches from productive ones, dead ends and mistakes from learning processes and temporary solutions. To be sure, different lines of reconstruction retrospectively disclose themselves, depending on the underlying paradigm. Paradigms, however, cannot be chosen at will but depend on hermeneutical starting points not at our disposal. But the paradigmatic preunderstanding is not beyond correction, either; it is tested and modified in the very process of interpretation. Even at the end, though, the conception that guides the reconstruction—whether of science or law—harbors a certain prejudicial force; it is not neutral. For this reason, the paradigm must be justified as the model that best captures the subject matter of science or law.

This is precisely the point of Dworkin's "Empire of Law." A legal system that consists of rules and principles secures via discursive adjudication the integrity of relations of mutual recognition that guarantee equal concern and respect to each citizen. Referring to my critique of Gadamer,[19] Dworkin characterizes his critical-hermeneutical procedure as a "constructive interpretation" that makes the rationality of the interpretive process explicit by referring to a paradigm or "purpose":

Constructive interpretation is a matter of imposing purpose on an object or practice in order to make of it the best possible example of the form or genre to which it is taken to belong. . . . We would then say that all interpretation strives to make an object the best it can be, as an instance of some assumed enterprise, and that interpretation takes different forms in different contexts only because different enterprises engage different standards of value or success.[20]

By following such a procedure of constructive interpretation,[21] each judge should be able in principle to reach an ideally valid decision in each case by undergirding her justification with a "theory," thereby compensating for the supposed "indeterminacy of law." This theory of law is supposed to rationally reconstruct the given legal order in such a way that existing law can be justified on the basis of an ordered set of principles and thereby displayed as a more or less exemplary embodiment of valid law in general.[22]

5.2 Dworkin's Theory of Law

5.2.1

To solve the problem of how judicial reasoning can simultaneously satisfy the principle of legal certainty and the legitimacy claim of law, Dworkin looks to an ambitious theory that enables one, especially in hard cases, to justify the individual decision by its coherence with a rationally reconstructed history of existing law. As a standard for a statement's validity, coherence is weaker than the analytic truth secured by logical deduction but stronger than mere freedom from contradiction. Coherence between statements is established by substantial arguments (in Toulmin's sense), and hence by reasons that have the pragmatic property of bringing about a rationally motivated agreement among participants in argumentation.[23]

Legal discourse typically involves normative arguments that, when rules collide, justify the choice of the appropriate norm for the given case in the light of principles. Dworkin is also interested in these principles because they possess a recognizable deontological content that removes them from the contingency of arbitrary enactments or derogations. For example, where constitutional rights and principles are interpreted and elaborated or where other moral contents find their way into positive law and therewith "draw support from the official acts of legal institutions," a change in such legal regulations must not affect their normative content. It "hardly makes sense to speak of principles like these as being 'overruled' or 'repealed.'"[24] Though principles must not be ontologized into something like moral facts, their deontological force gives them a status in argumentation that explains why the resources of justification available in legal discourse allow one to go beyond internal justification and ground the premises themselves.[25]

According to Dworkin, legal principles and the legislator's political policies compatible with such principles supply the argumentative means for reconstructing the bulk of existing law to the point where it can be considered normatively justified. Dworkin calls for the construction of a theory of law, not a theory of justice. The task does not consist in the philosophical construction of a well-ordered society whose basic institutions would embody principles of justice. Rather, it consists in *discovering* valid principles and policies in the light of which a given, *concrete* legal order can be justified in its essential elements such that all the individual decisions fit into it as parts of a coherent whole. As Dworkin realizes, such a task could be performed only by a judge whose intellectual capacities would compare to the physical strength of Hercules. "Judge Hercules" has two components of ideal knowledge at his disposal: he knows all the valid principles and policies necessary for justification, and he has a complete overview of the dense web of arguments tying together the scattered elements of existing law. Both components set boundaries for theory construction. The open terrain that Hercules covers with his superhuman capacity for argumentation is indicated, on the one hand, by the possible variations in the hierarchical rankings of principles and policies and, on the other hand, by the necessity of critically sifting through the bulk of positive law and correcting "mistakes." Indeed, Hercules is supposed to discover the coherent set of principles that would justify the institutional history of a given legal system "in the way fairness requires."[26]

But only a just legal system that resulted from an ongoing learning process could be completely justified in this retrospective way: "In any case, therefore, Hercules must expand his theory to include the idea that a justification of institutional history may display some part of that history as mistaken."[27] At the same time, Hercules must not equate the role of the theoretician who *re*constructs an existing body of legal norms with that of a *con*structive legislator who generates norms. Not all the elements of the legal order, however, bind the judge to the same extent; they vary in the degree to which they permit a probing, corrective evaluation. The contingency of the original contexts, and hence the scope for a retrospectively altered assessment, increases as one moves from the constitutional framework through individual constitutional norms, ordinary statutes, and common laws to precedents, commentaries, and other legal sources. Dworkin is quite convincing when he discusses the perspectives from which precedents, for example, receive different weights for current decisions, so that Hercules may "disregard some part of institutional history as a mistake."[28] A reconstructive legal theory of this sort should be sufficiently selective always to allow precisely one right decision stating which claims a party may assert in the framework of the existing legal order, that is, to which rights a party is objectively entitled. The theory of Judge Hercules reconciles the rationally reconstructed decisions of the past with the claim to rational acceptability in the present, it reconciles history with justice. It dissolves the "tension between judicial originality and institutional history.... [J]udges must make fresh judgments about the rights of the parties who come before them, but these political rights reflect, rather than oppose, political decisions of the past."[29]

5.2.2

A postulated legal theory of this sort is in the grip of strong idealizations. It is supposed to reconcile the positivity of the legal order with the legitimacy of actionable claims and thereby cope with that tension between facticity and validity already evident in the very meaning of legal validity. The theory requires a Hercules for its author; this ironic attribution makes no secret of the ideal demands the theory is supposed to satisfy. Dworkin's proposal has thus set off a widespread controversy. The central question up for debate is this: do the ideal demands express a regulative idea by which judges must orient themselves if they want to do justice to the telos inscribed in all modern adjudication? Or, on the contrary, do these demands hold up a false ideal as the standard for judicial decision making?

(a) The so-called Critical Legal Studies movement (CLS) takes up issues in legal realism. Rather than pass off critical legal investigations to social-scientific observers, however, it carries out such investigations, as does Dworkin, from the participant perspective of judges themselves.[30] The realists shook three dogmas of legal theory: the assumption that rights exist; the assumption that actual cases can be consistently decided in agreement with the body of existing law; and thus the central assumption that court decisions are as a rule rational, that is, sufficiently determined by statutory guidelines, precedents, prevailing doctrines, and so on. Dworkin's theory of law gives these three assumptions a less vulnerable constructivist reading. The deontological character of noninstru-mentalizable rights manifests itself in the fact that they constitute "threshold weights" against political policies and collective goods. Such rights can be elaborated only in discourses guided by a legal theory. In the process, some elements of existing law, including Supreme Court decisions of the past, can prove in retrospect to be mistaken. Only a positive law justified on the basis of principles allows "single right" decisions. From the CLS perspective, of course, this recourse to a theoretical background is what, today more than ever, exposes the new form of rationalism to realist objections.

Because flesh-and-blood judges fall considerably short of the ideal figure of Hercules, the recommendation that one orient oneself in everyday work by this figure would only accommodate a desire to endorse legal decisions that are in fact determined by interest positions, political attitudes, ideological biases, or other external factors. Judges select principles and policies and construct their own legal theories from these in order to "rationalize" deci-sions, that is, to conceal the prejudices with which they compensate for the objective indeterminacy of law.[31]

Dworkin could respond to this by explicating a premise left more or less in the background. To the extent that the critics can actually prove from convincing case studies that court decisions are better explained by extralegal factors than by the legal situation, the facts speak against the existing practice. But the internal indeterminacy of law does not, as the critics think, result from the structure of law itself. Rather, it stems, on the one hand, from the judge's failure to develop the best theory possible and, on the other, from the institutional history of a legal order that, to a greater or lesser degree, resists rational reconstruction. Constructive interpretation can issue in success only to the extent that a piece of "existing reason," however fragmentary, has been deposited in the history out of which a concrete legal order has emerged. As an American, Dworkin has more than two centuries of ongoing constitutional development behind him; as a liberal, he favors a rather optimistic assessment and finds the development of American law to be driven mainly by learning processes. Someone not sharing such confidence or standing in other political and legal-historical contexts, however, need not renounce the regulative ideal embodied in Hercules as long as existing law offers at least some historical basis for a rational reconstruction.

With the concept of "integrity," Dworkin attempts to show that *all* modern legal orders refer to the idea of government by law; they secure an unshakable point of reference for critical hermeneutics even where the traces of practical reason in one's own institutional history are rather faint. Dworkin's basic standard of "integrity" indicates the political ideal of a community in which persons associated under law recognize one another as free and equal. It is a principle that obligates citizens—just as it does legislative, adjudicative, and administrative bodies—to realize the basic norm of equal concern and equal respect for each person in the practices and arrangements of society: "It insists that people are members of a genuine political community only when they accept that their fates are linked in the following strong way: they accept that they are governed by common principles, not just by rules hammered out in political compromise."[32] When a political community constitutes itself as such, the founding act of constitution making means that the citizens grant themselves a system of rights that secures their private and public autonomy. At the same time, they expect one another to join in the political process, which Dworkin describes as "a theater of debate about which principles the community should accept as a system." The ideal demands on a theoretically informed administration of justice reflect a regulative idea that the judge finds in the nation's constitution (or its equivalent): "An association of principle is not automatically a just community; its conception of equal concern may be defective or it may violate rights of its citizens or citizens of other nations. . . . But the model of principle satisfies the conditions of a true community better than any other model of community that is possible for people who disagree about justice and fairness to adopt."[33]

With this answer to a first round of criticism, Dworkin derives the idealizations built into Hercules' theory from a regulative idea that is not immediately tailored to the rationality problem facing the adjudication process. Rather, this idea emerges from a normative self-understanding of constitutional orders and penetrates the political reality of constitutionally structured processes. The judge's obligation to decide the individual case in the light of a theory that justifies law as a whole on a principled basis reflects a *prior* obligation of citizens, one attested to by the act of founding the constitution: an obligation to maintain the integrity of a life in common by following principles of justice and respecting one another as members of an association of free and equal persons. Still, this political ideal itself might express a false idealization. Constitutional practice could thus deceive itself in a manner fraught with consequences, burdening institutions with wholly unsolvable tasks.

(b) In the next round, then, critics attempt to furnish proof that Dworkin expects his Hercules to carry out an *unrealizable* program. For example, in a well-known case study, Duncan Kennedy endeavors to show that the development of American private law and its associated judicial practice revolve around two incompatible principles. On the one hand, the principle of freedom of contract, and hence the liberal vision of society as a regulated competition between private persons acting in a purposive-rational manner, is upheld. On the other hand, one finds the good-faith principle with its protections on a reciprocally obligating contract relationship, and hence the contrary vision of an association based on mutual concern and solidarity.[34] Protagonists of CLS generalize the results of this and similar studies into the thesis that existing law in general is shot through with *contradictory* principles and policies; consequently, every attempt at a rational reconstruction is doomed to failure: "Ultimately, the radical indeterminacy thesis asserts that law is not a rule system but chaos. The amalgamated contradictions form a structure that can yield no—however idealized—decision practice that would guarantee equal treatment and justice."[35]

Dworkin addresses this objection only with the cursory remark that the critics overlook the crucial difference between principles that collide in a particular case and principles that contradict one another; otherwise they would have to notice that Hercules' theoretical efforts only begin at the point where the critics conclude their hastily generalized historical studies with a skeptical view of rules.[36] Klaus Günther has added further precision to Dworkin's point by turning to a theory of argumentation that distinguishes between discourses of justification and of application.

If one assumes that the cases typical for present-day adjudication involve not only application-specific rules but principles as well, then one can easily show why collisions are quite probable—and yet do not betray a deeper-lying incoherence in the legal system itself. Except for those norms whose "if" clauses specify application conditions in such detail that they apply only to a few highly typified and well-circumscribed standard situations (and cannot be applied elsewhere without hermeneutical difficulties), *all* norms are *inherently* indeterminate. Precisely the norms that Dworkin calls "rules," which require all-or-nothing decisions in cases of conflict, are the exceptions to this. The coherence of a legal system is in fact endangered if conflicting rules of *this latter* sort provide contradictory prescriptions, each claiming equal validity, for the same class of cases. All other norms—and not just constitutional rights and principles that justify the legal system as a whole—remain indeterminate in their references to situations and have need of *additional* specifications in the individual case. Because such norms are only prima facie candidates for application, one must first enter a discourse of application to test whether they apply to a given situation (whose details could not have been anticipated in the justification process) or whether, their validity notwithstanding, they must give way to another norm, namely, the "appropriate" one. Only if a valid norm proves to be the single appropriate one in the case at hand does that norm ground a singular judgment that can claim to be right. That a norm is prima facie valid means merely that it has been impartially *justified;* only its impartial *application* leads to a valid decision about a case. The validity of the general norm does not yet guarantee justice in the individual case.

The impartial application of a norm closes the gap that normally had to remain open in the norm's impartial justification because of the unforeseeability of future situations.[37] Discourses of application concern not the norm's validity but its *appropriate reference to a situation.* Because each norm selects only specific features of an individual case situated in the lifeworld, the application discourse must determine which descriptions of the facts are significant and exhaustive for interpreting the situation in a disputed case; it must also determine which of the prima facie valid norms is the appropriate one once all the significant features of the situation have been apprehended as fully as possible:

> It is pointless to ask here whether the participants in a discourse have a full description of the situation first and then all the norms that are prima facie applicable or, the other way around, whether they obtain a description of the situation only in the light of a preunderstanding of the possibly applicable norms. . . . The participants know with which norms a prima facie applicable norm will collide in a situation only after they have related all the relevant features of a description of that situation to applicable norms.[38]

We can think of the hermeneutical process of norm application as weaving together a description of the circumstances and a concretization of general norms. What finally decides the issue is the meaning equivalence between the description of facts making up part of the interpretation of the situation and the description of facts that sets out the descriptive component of the norm, that is, its application conditions. Günther summarizes this complex interrelationship quite clearly: the justification of a singular judgment must be based on the set of all appropriate normative reasons that happen to be relevant for the case at hand in view of a complete interpretation of the situation.[39]

Thus if the "collision" between norms being weighed in the interpretive process led one to infer a "contradiction" within the system of norms itself, then one would be confusing the norm's "validity," which it enjoys in general insofar as it is justified, with its "appropriateness" for application in particular cases. If instead one explains the indeterminacy of valid norms in terms of argumentation theory, then a contest of norms competing as prima facie candidates for application in a given case makes good methodological sense: "The collision of norms cannot be reconstructed as a conflict of validity claims because colliding norms or competing semantic variants enter a relation with one another only in a concrete situation. A discourse of justification would have to abstract from just this situational dependency of collision problems. . . . What other norms or semantic variants are possibly applicable can only be known in the particular situation itself."[40]

(c) With Günther's elegant proposal, however, the ideally justified coherence of the legal system takes on a different meaning. The postulated legal theory still has the task of rationally reconstructing existing law so as to allow precisely one right decision for each new case. But now the theory merely provides guidelines for a *flexible* set of principles and policies that are transitively ordered only in each application discourse referring to a particular case. The relations among valid norms *changes* depending on the relevant constellation of features of the case to be decided. In this way, the indeterminacy of legal norms that are valid but only prima facie applicable—an indeterminacy stemming from the division of labor between justification and application—is reflected in the degrees of freedom enjoyed by a mobile set of principles. The latter enter into a specific order of relations with one another only when it becomes clear how the currently appropriate norm refers to the situation: "If every valid norm must be coherently complemented by all the other norms applicable in a situation, then the meaning of the norm [subtly] changes in every situation. In this way we depend on *history*, since it alone provides us with the unforeseeable situations that compel us to adopt at each point a *different* interpretation of the set of all valid norms."[41]

Evidently, this coherence theory of law can avoid the indeterminacy supposedly due to the contradictory structure of the legal system only at the cost of the theory itself becoming somehow indeterminate. Yet how can such a theory inform a decision-making practice intended to guarantee the certainty of law? In criticism of Dworkin's version of the coherence theory, it has been objected that a rational reconstruction of past decisions requires their revision from case to case, which would amount to a retroactive interpretation of existing law. This "ripple effect argument"[42] applies all the more to Günther's interpretation of Dworkin's coherence theory, namely, to the "ripple effect" that engulfs the system of legal norms as each successive case brings on a further coherent interpretation. The element of surprise in each new case now seems to draw theory itself into the vortex of history. The problem is obvious: the political legislator must adaptively react to historical processes, even though the law exists to erect walls of stable expectations against the pressure of historical variation.

As an opening response to this objection, one might call the concept of legal certainty into question. If, contrary to the positivist view, a legal system does not consist solely of "rules," that is, norms with built-in application procedures, then it cannot guarantee that court decisions will have the degree of predictability conditional programs make possible. The classical concept of legal certainty—whose rational implications Lon Fuller, for example, has analyzed[43]—requires a rule structure that a complex and self-referential legal system constructed of rules, principles, and polices can no longer accommodate. Hence legal certainty, which is based on the knowledge of unambiguously conditioned behavioral expectations, is itself a principle that must be weighed against other principles in the case at hand. By way of compensation, the postulated legal theory makes possible "single right" decisions guaranteeing the certainty of law *at a different level*. Procedural rights guarantee each legal person the claim to a fair procedure that in turn guarantees not certainty of outcome but a discursive clarification of the pertinent facts and legal questions. Thus affected parties can be confident that in procedures issuing in judicial decisions only relevant reasons will be decisive, and not arbitrary ones. If we view existing law as an ideally coherent system of norms, then this *procedure-dependent certainty of law* can satisfy the expectations of a legal community intent on its integrity and oriented toward principles, such that each is guaranteed the rights to which she is entitled.

The following proposal goes farther in answering the problem of retroactivity.[44] If deciding a case in the light of a prioritized norm means that one exhaustively reviews an entire system of valid norms in the course of considering all the relevant circumstances of the case at hand and if this system is in constant movement because the priority relations can change with each new situation, then the orientation toward such a demanding ideal will, as a rule, overtax even professional adjudication. Hence, in actual practice the complexity of this task is reduced by the *paradigmatic legal understanding* prevailing at the time. In the place of the ideal, we find paradigms

in which norms we consider valid here and now have been ranked in a transitive order. Since such a ranking cannot be constructed without referring to possible application situations, these paradigms contain generalized descriptions of specific kinds of situations. Usually we fall back on such rankings, which are more or less systematized, when we solve typical foreseeable cases of collision. They form a background context in which our current assessments of the situation and the corresponding prima facie moral judgments are embedded. Together with other knowledge that orients one in a culture, these paradigms belong to the form of life in which we find ourselves.[45]

Some historical examples for such legal ideologies are the paradigms of bourgeois formal law and welfare-state materialized law. In the first case, law crystallizes around the rights of the private market participant, in the second case, around the entitlements of clients of welfare agencies. Such paradigms relieve Hercules of the hypercomplex task of surveying an unordered set of prima facie valid principles and norms that must be related directly with the naked eye, as it were, to the relevant features of a situation apprehended as fully as possible. The outcome of a procedure then becomes predictable for the parties as well insofar as the pertinent paradigm determines a background understanding that legal experts *share* with all citizens.

It is admittedly somewhat ironic that legal certainty increases precisely in virtue of an element that, although moderating the ideal demands on legal theory, is the most susceptible to ideological distortions. Paradigms harden into ideologies insofar as they systematically close themselves off from the perception of radically new situations and resist different interpretations of rights and principles, interpretations that press for acknowledgment in the light of radically new historical experiences. We will consider some examples of this later. A further methodological objection arises for "closed" paradigms. The latter stabilize themselves through professionally and judicially institutionalized monopolies on interpretation and permit only internal revision according to their own standards. Here realist skepticism finds a fresh target: in contrast to the required ideal coherence of established law, coherent case interpretations inside a *fixed* legal paradigm remain fundamentally underdetermined, for they compete with equally coherent interpretations of the same case in alternative paradigms. This is sufficient incentive for a *proceduralist understanding of law* to distinguish a level at which reflexive legal paradigms can open up *for one another* and *prove themselves* against a variety of competing interpretations mobilized for the case at hand. I come back to this in the last chapter.

5.3 The Theory of Legal Discourse

5.3.1

The objections discussed so far are directed against the meaning and feasibility of an ideal legal theory intended to facilitate the best possible judicial interpretation of a legal community's rights and duties, institutional history, and political structure. These objections are premised on the theory's having a single author: the current judge who has taken Hercules as a model. Dworkin's replies to his critics, or the replies he could have given, already arouse some initial doubts about the tenability of this *monological* approach. For the criterion of "integrity" that governs the judge's rational reconstruction of existing law expresses an idea that the judiciary, together with the political legislature, *merely borrows* from the founding of the constitution and from the ongoing constitutional practice of engaged citizens. Who represents the authority of the constitution best, the citizenry as a whole or the judge? Dworkin swings back and forth between the perspective of citizens, from which judicial duties are legitimated, and the perspective of a judge, who claims to be in a privileged position in virtue of her expertise. In the end, the judge must rely only on herself, should her own interpretation happen to deviate from all others: "We want our officials to treat us as tied together in an association of principle, and we want this for reasons that do not depend on any identity of conviction among these officials. . . . Our reasons endure when judges disagree, at least in detail, because each judge still confirms and reinforces the principled character of our association by striving, in spite of the disagreement, *to reach his own* opinion."[46] These statements presuppose that the judge is exceptionally qualified, both by reason of her professional knowledge and skills and thanks to her personal virtues, to act as the citizens' *representative* in securing the integrity of the legal community. What is more, in virtue of the fact that each judge is subjectively convinced of arriving at the "single right" decision on the basis of her theory, the practice of adjudication is supposed to secure the autonomous association of citizens oriented by principles: "The judge represents integrity—self-government—to the community, not of it."[47]

However, precisely the standpoint of integrity would have to free Hercules from the solitude of a monologically conducted theory construction. This is because Dworkin, like Parsons, conceives law as a means of social integration, indeed as a medium that sustains the self-understanding of a solidary community, albeit in a highly abstract form. The relations of reciprocal recognition established in concrete forms of life through communicative action can be generalized in complex societies only through law: "I argued that a community of principles, which take integrity to be central to politics . . . assimilates political obligations to the general class of associative obligations. . . . A general commitment to integrity expresses a concern by each for all."[48] However, the mechanism for expanding relations of mutual recognition among natural persons into the abstract juridical relationship of mutual recognition among legal persons is supplied by a reflexive form of communicative action, namely, the practice of argumentation demanding that each participant adopt the perspective of everyone else. Dworkin himself recognizes this procedural core to the principle of legally secured integrity when he sees the equal right to liberty as founded in the right to equal communicative freedom.[49] That suggests that we anchor the ideal demands on legal theory in the political ideal of an "open society of interpreters of the constitution,"[50] rather than in the ideal personality of a judge who is distinguished by her virtue and her privileged access to the truth.

The monological approach becomes even less tenable if, like Günther, one considers it necessary to rely on legal paradigms that reduce complexity. The paradigmatic preunderstanding of law in general can limit the indeterminacy of theoretically informed decision making and guarantee a sufficient measure of legal certainty only if it is intersubjectively shared by *all* citizens and expresses a self-understanding of the legal community as a whole. This also holds mutatis mutandis for a proceduralist understanding of law, which reckons from the start with a discursively regulated competition among different paradigms. This is why a cooperative endeavor is required to remove the suspicion of ideology hanging over such a background understanding. The single judge must conceive her constructive interpretation fundamentally as a common undertaking supported by the public communication of citizens. Frank Michelman criticizes Dworkin's monological conception of judicial decision making along these lines:

> What is lacking is dialogue. Hercules . . . is a loner. He is much too heroic. His narrative constructions are monologous. He converses with no one, except through books. He has no encounters. He meets no otherness. Nothing shakes him up. No interlocutor violates the inevitable insularity of his experience and outlook. Hercules is just a man, after all. No one man or woman could be that. Dworkin has produced an apotheosis of appellate judging without attention to what seems the most universal and striking institutional characteristic of the appellate bench, its plurality.[51]

The above comment hints at a way out of the dilemma one faces in having to account both for the fallibility of ambitious theory constructions and for the professional character of judicial decision making. Hercules could conceive himself as a member of the interpretation community of legal experts; his interpretations would then have to follow standards recognized in the profession: "He is disciplined by a set of rules that specify the relevance and weight to be assigned to the material (e.g. words, history, intention, consequence), as well as by those that define basic concepts and that establish the procedural circumstances under which the interpretation must occur."[52] In making this proposal, Owen Fiss has in mind primarily those procedural principles and maxims of interpretation that are constitutive for the role and practice of impartial adjudication. Specifically, these are meant to ensure the independence of the judiciary, constraints on individual discretion, respect for the integrity of the disputing parties, the written justification and official signing of the judgment, its neutrality, and so on. *Professionally proven standards* are meant to guarantee the objectivity of the judgment and its openness to intersubjective review.

Naturally, the status of these rules is not unproblematic. On the one hand, they are employed in the procedural justification of judicial decision making and thus partly ground the validity of legal

judgments. On the other hand, the validity of procedural principles and maxims of interpretation is itself established by reference to proven practices and traditions of a culture of experts. To
be sure, this culture is bound by the demands of reason and
constitutional principles: "Legal interpretations are constrained by
rules that derive their authority from an interpretative community
that is itself held together by the commitment to the rule of law."[53]
From the observer's perspective, however, such standards are no
more than a self-legitimating code of professional ethics. Even
within the same legal culture, various subcultures oppose one
another over the choice of the right standards. In any event, from
an internal perspective, the mere fact that a hardly homogeneous
professional class legitimates itself is not sufficient to demonstrate
the validity (*gültig*) of the very procedural principles that ground
validity within the system (*geltungsbegründenden*). Procedural principles that secure the validity of the outcome of a procedurally fair
decision-making practice require internal justification. Nor does
recourse to enacted procedural regulations suffice; the rationality
that procedural provisions doubtless possess is a component of
existing law whose objective interpretation is not obvious but
precisely in question. One can escape this circle only by reconstructing the practice of interpretation in terms of legal theory, and
not just along narrow, doctrinal lines. The critique of Dworkin's
solipsistic theory of law must begin at the *same* level and, in the
shape of a *theory of legal argumentation*, ground the procedural
principles that henceforth bear the brunt of the ideal demands
previously directed at Hercules.

5.3.2

A theory of argumentation assuming this task cannot approach
legal discourse simply in logicosemantic terms.[54] Along such lines,
one can certainly explain the rules of inference, semantics, and
argumentation. However, the last-mentioned of these groups of
rules already point to a pragmatic conception insofar as they
involve the kinds of rules studied by Toulmin, namely, rules for
argumentatively nontrivial transitions.[55] Arguments are reasons
proffered in discourse that redeem a validity claim raised with

constative or regulative speech acts; thus they rationally motivate those taking part in argumentation to accept the corresponding descriptive or normative statements as valid. A theory of argumentation that clarifies the role and construction of particular arguments examines the argumentation game from the standpoint of the product alone; at best it provides the starting point for grounding the argumentative steps that go beyond an internal justification of legal judgments. To justify externally the premises of a decision, Dworkin calls for a comprehensive theory that, as we have seen, overtaxes the solipsistic efforts of the individual judge. This raises the question whether the ideal demands on the postulated theory might not be translated into ideal demands on a *cooperative procedure of theory formation*, that is, demands on a legal discourse that takes into account both the regulative ideal of single right decisions and the fallibility of actual decision making. A discourse theory of law, which ties the rational acceptability of judicial decisions not only to the quality of arguments but also to the structure of the argumentative process, might not solve this problem, but it at least takes it seriously. Such a theory relies on a strong concept of procedural rationality that locates the properties constitutive of a decision's validity not only in the logicosemantic dimension of constructing arguments and connecting statements but also in the pragmatic dimension of the justification process itself.

In any case, one cannot explain the rightness of normative judgments along the lines of a correspondence theory of truth, for rights are a social construction that one must not hypostatize into facts. "Rightness" means rational acceptability supported by good reasons. The validity of a judgment is certainly defined by the fact that its validity conditions are satisfied. Whether these are satisfied, however, cannot be clarified by direct access to empirical evidence or to facts given in an ideal intuition, but only discursively, precisely by way of a justification that is *carried out* with arguments. Substantial reasons can never "compel" in the sense of logical inference or conclusive evidence. The former does not suffice for justification, because it merely explicates the content of the premises, whereas the latter is not available except in the case of singular perceptual judgments, and even then it is not beyond question. Hence there is no "natural" end to the chain of possible substantial reasons; one cannot exclude the possibility that new information and better reasons will be brought forward. Under favorable conditions, we bring argumentation to a de facto conclusion only when the reasons solidify against the horizon of unproblematic background assumptions into such a coherent whole that an uncoerced agreement on the acceptability of the disputed validity claim emerges. The expression "rationally motivated agreement" takes this remainder of facticity into account: we attribute to reasons the force to "move" participants, in a nonpsychological sense, to adopt affirmative positions. To eliminate even this last remaining moment of facticity, the chain of reasons would have to be brought to a more than de facto conclusion. An internal closure, however, is to be reached only through idealization, whether this occurs in terms of a totalizing theory in which reasons systematically intermesh and mutually support one another so that the chain of arguments forms a closed circle—something the metaphysical system was once thought to accomplish—or whether it occurs in virtue of the chain of arguments approaching an ideal limit like a straight line, the vanishing point Peirce called the "final opinion."[56]

Since the absolutist ideal of the closed theory can no longer be rendered plausible under the conditions of postmetaphysical thinking, a strong theory of this sort cannot be used to elucidate the regulative ideal of the "single right" decision. Even the legal theory ascribed to Hercules would have to remain something *provisional*, a coherent order of reasons constructed *for the time being* and exposed to ongoing critique. On the other hand, the idea of an unending process of argumentation striving toward a limit requires one to specify the conditions under which this process acquires a directional character and, at least in the long run, makes progress possible in a cumulative learning process. These pragmatic process conditions ideally ensure that all the relevant reasons and information available for a given issue at a particular time are in no way suppressed, that is, that they can develop their inherent force for rational motivation. The notion of an argument is pragmatic in nature: what counts as a "good reason" manifests itself only in the role it has in an argumentation game, that is, in the contribution it makes according to the rules of the game for deciding the question whether a contested validity claim may be accepted or not. Once the concept of procedural rationality has been extended to the pragmatic dimension of the regulated contest of arguments, it allows one to *supplement* the semantic properties of reasons with properties that indirectly constitute validity, by which I mean the properties of an arrangement in which the potential of rational motivation built into good reasons is actualized. The *argumentative process* of the cooperative search for truth ideally closes the rationality gap between, on the one hand, the individual substantial reasons set out in fundamentally incomplete sequences of argument that are at most plausible and, on the other, the unconditionality of the claim to the "single right" decision.[57]

Whenever we want to convince one another of something, we always already intuitively rely on a practice in which we presume that we sufficiently approximate the ideal conditions of a speech situation specially immunized against repression and inequality. In this speech situation, persons for and against a problematic validity claim thematize the claim and, relieved of the pressures of action and experience, adopt a hypothetical attitude in order to test with reasons, and reasons alone, whether the proponent's claim stands up. The essential intuition we connect with this practice of argumentation is characterized by the intention of winning the assent of a universal audience to a problematic proposition in a noncoercive but regulated contest for the better arguments based on the best information and reasons. It is easy to see why the discourse principle requires this kind of practice for the justification of norms and value decisions: whether norms and values could find the rationally motivated assent of all those affected can be judged only from the intersubjectively enlarged perspective of the first-person plural. This perspective integrates the perspectives of each participant's worldview and self-understanding in a manner that is neither coercive nor distorting. The practice of argumentation recommends itself for such a universalized ideal role taking practiced in common. As the reflexive form of communicative action, argumentation distinguishes itself socio-ontologically, one might say, by a complete reversibility of participant perspectives that *unleashes* the higher-level intersubjectivity of the deliberating collectivity. In this way, Hegel's concrete universal is sublimated into a communicative *structure* purified of all substantive elements.

Questions of norm application touch on participants' understanding of themselves and the world in a different way than occurs in discourses of justification. In discourses of application, norms tacitly accepted as valid still refer to the interests of all those possibly affected; but with the question of which norm is the appropriate one for a given case, those general references take second place to the particular interests of the immediately affected parties. Instead, highly contextualistic interpretations of the situation come to the fore, which depend on the different self-understandings and worldviews of the actual participants. Participants in an application discourse must work their different interpretations of the same situation into a normatively rich description of the circumstances that does not simply abstract from the existing differences in perception. Once again it is a question of a sensitive, noncoercive coordination of different interpretive perspectives. Naturally, in application discourses the particular participant perspectives must simultaneously preserve the link with the universal-perspective structure that stands behind presumably valid norms in justification discourses. Hence interpretations of the individual case, which are formed in the light of a coherent system of norms, depend on the communicative form of a discourse whose socio-ontological constitution allows the perspectives of the participants and the perspectives of uninvolved members of the community (represented by an impartial judge) to be transformed into one another. This also explains why the concept of coherence employed in constructive interpretation resists purely semantic characterizations and refers to the pragmatic presuppositions of the argumentative process.

5.3.3

Two complementary avenues of thought are evident in the relevant literature on legal argumentation. One climbs from concrete questions of justifying legal decisions to a theory of legal discourse; I cannot go into this approach here.[58] The other avenue starts from above and heads downward. Robert Alexy begins with an analysis of the presuppositions and procedures of rational discourse as such. The "rules of reason," as he calls them, instantiate idealizations that must be made in the temporal, social, and substantive dimensions: endless time, unlimited participation, and perfect freedom from coercion. In rational discourse, we assume that conditions of communication obtain that (1) prevent a rationally unmotivated termination of argumentation, (2) secure both freedom in the choice of topics and inclusion of the best information and reasons through universal and equal access to, as well as equal and symmetrical participation in, argumentation, and (3) exclude every kind of coercion—whether originating outside the process of reaching understanding or within it—other than that of the better argument, so that all motives except that of the cooperative search for truth are neutralized.[59] Alexy introduces a version of Kant's universalization principle as the rule of justification for moral-practical discourses. It can be shown that this principle is rooted in the idealizing presuppositions of argumentation in general.[60] Anyone serious about participating in a practice of argumentation cannot avoid pragmatic presuppositions that require an ideal role taking, that is, presuppositions that require one to interpret and evaluate all contributions from the perspective of every other potential participant. This is how discourse ethics captures Dworkin's basic norm of equal concern and respect.

If one shares Dworkin's deontological understanding of law and follows the argumentation-theoretic considerations advanced by such authors as Aarnio, Alexy, and Günther, one will agree with two theses. First, legal discourse cannot operate self-sufficiently inside a hermetically sealed universe of existing norms but must rather remain open to arguments from other sources. In particular, it must remain open to the pragmatic, ethical, and moral reasons brought to bear in the legislative process and bundled together in the legitimacy claim of legal norms. Second, the rightness of legal decisions is ultimately measured by how well the decision process satisfies the communicative conditions of argumentation that make impartial judgment possible. Thus it is tempting to model the discourse theory of law after the better-understood discourse ethics. However, the heuristic priority of moral-practical discourses, and even the requirement that legal rules may not contradict moral norms, does not immediately imply that legal discourses should be conceived as a subset of moral argumentation. A number of objections have been raised against this "special-case thesis," which Alexy first proposed in the somewhat broader context of justification and application discourses.[61]

(a) The specific constraints governing the forensic action of parties in court seemingly prohibit one from using standards of rational discourse to assess courtroom proceedings in any way. The parties are not committed to the cooperative search for truth, and they can pursue their interest in a favorable outcome through "the clever strategy of advancing arguments likely to win consensus."[62] By way of plausible reply, one can say that each participant in a trial, whatever her motives, contributes to a discourse that *from the judge's perspective* facilitates the search for an impartial judgment. This latter perspective alone, however, is constitutive for grounding the decision.[63]

(b) The indeterminacy of the discourse procedure is more problematic; the presuppositions and procedures required for any proper process of argumentation are not selective enough to necessitate single right decisions.[64] Insofar as this objection pertains to discourse theory in general, I will not consider it here.[65] Rather, I will limit myself to the critique of the indeterminacy of legal discourses. Alexy characterizes the latter as the subset of moral-practical discourses that are bound to an existing body of legal norms. Accordingly, he supplements the universal rules of discourse with special rules and forms of argument that essentially reproduce established canons of legal interpretation. To refute the indeterminacy thesis, Alexy would have to show that these procedural principles and maxims of interpretation, which have been gathered from actual practice and systematized in textbooks, merely specify the universal requirements for moral-practical discourses in view of the connection with existing law. A brief allusion to structural similarities in the rules and forms of argument respectively deployed in the two types of discourse is not sufficient.[66]

(c) It is clear to Alexy that discursively grounded legal decisions cannot be "right" in the same sense as valid moral judgments: "The rationality of legal argumentation is thus, to the extent that it is determined by statute, relative to the rationality of legislation. Absolute rationality in legal decisionmaking would presuppose the rationality of legislation."[67] Insofar as this presupposition is not fulfilled, the harmony between law and morality assumed by Alexy has the unpleasant consequence not only of relativizing the rightness of a legal decision but of calling it into question as such. Validity claims are binarily coded and do not admit of degrees of validity: "For the rationality of an argumentative process relative to an unreasonable statute is not something inferior, but something qualitatively different from the material rationality of a decision reached according to the rules of rational practical discourse."[68] To avoid this objection, one must, like Dworkin, face the task of rationally reconstructing established law. An individual legal decision can be right only if it fits into a coherent legal system.

(d) Günther takes up this normative concept of coherence. As already shown, he draws a distinction within moral-practical discourse between justification and application and conceives legal argumentation as a special case of moral discourses of application. This relieves legal discourse of questions of justification. The "single appropriate" judgment borrows its rightness from the *presupposed* validity of norms passed by the political legislature. However, judges cannot avoid a reconstructive assessment of the norms given as valid, because they can resolve norm collisions only on the assumption "that all valid norms ultimately constitute an ideal coherent system which gives for each case exactly one right [i.e., appropriate] answer."[69] This counterfactual assumption has a heuristic value only as long as a certain amount of "existing reason" in the universe of existing law meets it halfway. According to this presupposition, then, reason must already be at work—in however fragmentary a manner—in the political legislation of constitutional democracies. But if this reason were *identical* with Kant's *morally* legislative reason, then we could hardly have any confidence in the rational reconstructibility of the established legal order, with all its contingencies. But political legislation does not rely only, not even in the first instance, on *moral* reasons, but on reasons of another kind as well.

If we follow a procedural theory, the legitimacy of legal norms is gauged by the rationality of the democratic procedure of political legislation. As already shown, this procedure is more complex than that of moral argumentation inasmuch as the legitimacy of legal statutes is determined not only by the rightness of moral judgments but, among other things, by the availability, cogency, relevance, and selection of information; by how fruitful such information proves to be; by how appropriately the situation is interpreted and the issue framed; by the rationality of voting decisions; by the authenticity of strong evaluations; and above all by the fairness of the compromises involved. No doubt one can use moral discourses of application as a model for investigating legal discourses, for both have to do with the logic of applying norms. But the more complex validity dimension of legal norms prohibits one from assimilating the legitimacy of legal decisions to the validity of moral judgments. To this extent one should not conceive legal discourse as a special case of moral discourses (of application). The procedural principles tested and confirmed in practice and the maxims of interpretation canonized in textbooks on legal method will be satisfactorily captured in a discourse theory only when the network of argumentation, bargaining, and political communications in which the legislative process occurs has been more thoroughly analyzed than it has been to date.[70]

5.3.4

Although the special-case thesis, in one version or another, is plausible from a heuristic standpoint, it suggests that law is subordinate to morality. This subordination is misleading, because it is still burdened by natural-law connotations. The thesis becomes less problematic as soon as one takes seriously the parallel differentiation of law and morality that occurs at the postconventional level of justification. As we have seen, the discourse principle then requires a duly abstract formulation, whereas the principles of morality and democracy (among others) result from the specification of the discourse principle with respect to different kinds of action norms. The principle of morality regulates informal and simple face-to-face interactions; the principle of democracy regulates relations among legal persons who understand themselves as bearers of rights. The rational discourse presupposed by the discourse principle accordingly branches out, on one side into moral argumentation, on the other into political and legal discourses that are institutionalized in legal form and include moral questions only in regard to legal norms. The system of rights that simultaneously secures citizens' private and public autonomy is interpreted and elaborated in procedures of democratic legislation and impartial norm application. Two consequences follow from this choice of conceptual strategy.

To begin with, discourses specialized for the justification and application of legal statutes do not have to be introduced simply as special cases of moral discourses of justification and application. One no longer has to bring in an extensional logic to differentiate legal from moral discourses. Legal discourses do not represent special cases of moral argumentation that, because of their link to existing law, are restricted to a subset of moral commands or permissions. Rather, they refer *from the outset* to democratically enacted law and, insofar as it is not a matter of doctrinal reflection, are themselves legally institutionalized. This means that, second, legal discourses not only refer to legal norms but, together with their institutionalized forms of communication, are themselves *embedded* in the legal system. Like democratic procedures in the area of legislation, rules of court procedure in the area of legal application are meant to compensate for the fallibility and decisional uncertainty resulting from the fact that the demanding communicative presuppositions of rational discourses can only be approximately fulfilled.

In the administration of justice, the tension between the legitimacy and positivity of law is dealt with *at the level of content*, as a problem of making decisions that are both right and consistent. This same tension, however, takes on new life at the pragmatic level of judicial decision making, inasmuch as ideal demands on the procedure of argumentation must be harmonized with the restrictions imposed by the factual need for regulation. Law must once again be applied to itself in the form of organizational norms, not just to create official powers of adjudication but to set up legal discourses as components of courtroom proceedings. Rules of court procedure institutionalize judicial decision making in such a way that the judgment and its justification can be considered the outcome of an argumentation game governed by a special program. Once again, legal procedures intertwine with processes of argumentation, and in such a way that the court procedures instituting legal discourses must not interfere with the logic of argumentation internal to such discourses. Procedural law does not regulate normative-legal discourse as such but secures, in the temporal, social, and substantive dimensions, the institutional framework that *clears the way for* processes of communication governed by the logic of application discourses. I will illustrate this by referring to the German Code of Civil Procedure and Code of Criminal Procedure.[71]

First let us consider the temporal and social restrictions on the trial proceedings. Although there is no legally stipulated limit on the length of trials, various deadlines (especially for the two stages of appeal, *Berufung* and *Revision*[72]) ensure that disputed questions are finally resolved in a timely manner. Furthermore, the distribution of social roles in the procedure sets up a symmetry between the prosecution and the defense (in criminal trials) or between plaintiff and defendant (in civil trials). This enables the court to play the role of an impartial third party during the hearing in different ways: either actively interrogating or neutrally observing. In the taking of evidence, the burdens of proof on the trial participants are more or less unambiguously regulated. The trial procedure itself is set up agonistically—more so in civil than in criminal proceedings—as a contest between parties pursuing their own interests. In criminal trials, "in order to search out the truth the court shall on its own motion extend the taking of evidence to all facts and to all means of proof that are important for the decision."[73] Yet the roles of the participants are so defined that the taking of evidence does not have the thoroughly discursive structure characterizing a cooperative search for truth. Similar to Anglo-American jury trials, however, the opportunity for strategic action is also organized in such a way that as many of the relevant facts as possible can be brought up. The court uses these as its basis for assessing evidence and reaching the legal judgment incumbent on it.

The point of the entire procedure is evident once one examines the substantive constraints imposed on the trial proceedings. These institutionally carve out an internal space for the free exchange of arguments in an application discourse. The procedures that must be observed prior to opening the main proceedings define the object of dispute, so that the trial itself can concentrate on clearly demarcated issues. The taking of evidence in face-to-face interaction, which operates under the presupposition of a methodical separation between questions of fact and questions of law, serves to determine the facts and secure the evidence. Despite the circular relationship between legal norms and the facts of the matter, and between interpretive possibilities and the reference to facts, so far the legal assessment remains largely in the background. Interestingly enough, in both criminal and civil trials, the court subsequently assesses evidence and renders its judgment "internally," that is, not in a separate procedure. It is only insofar as the court must set forth the "grounds" for its judgment before the participants and the public that procedural law touches on substantive aspects of the legal discourse in which the facts considered "proven" or "true" are normatively assessed. The court's formal justification consists in the facts of the case and the reasons for the decision: "In the actual reasons for the decision the court gives a brief summary of the considerations on which the decision is based both factually and legally (*German Code of Civil Proc.*, §313 sec.3). In addition to legal arguments this includes the assessment of evidence."[74] Hence rules of procedure standardize neither the admissible arguments nor the course of argumentation, but they do secure the space for legal discourses that become objects of the procedure only in the outcome. The outcome can be submitted to review through channels of appeal.

The institutionalized self-reflection of law promotes individual legal protection from two points of view, that of achieving justice in the individual case and that of consistency in the application and further development of law:

The *purpose of the modes of legal review* consists first of all in *obtaining, through the examination of published decisions, right and therefore just decisions* in the interest of the parties. The mere possibility of examination, moreover, compels courts to provide *careful justification.* But this is not the only purpose of these modes. Rather, there is also a *general interest* in an effective legal system. The prohibition against self-help can be effectively realized only if the parties have certain guarantees of receiving a right decision. Moreover, stages of appeal, with their *concentration of jurisdiction* in higher courts and finally only in a supreme court, leads to the urgently necessary *harmonization and further development of law.* This public interest does not play the same role in the different modes of review. It is more powerfully felt in appeals on points of law [*Revision*] than in appeals de novo [*Berufung*].[75]

The public interest in the harmonization or consistency of law highlights a concise move in the logic of adjudication: the court must decide each case in a way that preserves the coherence of the legal order as a whole.

In summary, one can say that codes of procedure provide relatively strict rules for the introduction of evidence regarding what took place. Such codes thus define the bounds within which parties can deal with the law strategically. The legal discourse of the court, on the other hand, is played out in a procedural-legal vacuum, so that reaching a judgment is left up to the judge's professional ability: "With respect to the effect of the reception of the evidence, the court decides according to its free conviction obtained from the entire trial."[76] The aim is to preserve legal discourse from external influences by moving it outside the actual procedure.

6

Judiciary and Legislature: On the Role and Legitimacy of Constitutional Adjudication

In chapter 5, Dworkin's theory of law guided our treatment of the rationality problem posed by an adjudication whose decisions must simultaneously satisfy criteria of legal certainty and of rational acceptability. Dworkin's proposals for a theory-guided, constructive interpretation of law could be defended on a proceduralist reading that transposes the idealizing demands on theory formation into the idealizing content of the necessary pragmatic presuppositions of legal discourse. We must still address the question of how such a constructive practice of interpretation can operate within the bounds of constitutionally separated powers without the judiciary's encroaching on legislative powers (and thereby also undermining the strict binding of administration by law).

Because judicial decision making is bound to law and legal statutes, the rationality of adjudication depends on the legitimacy of existing law. This legitimacy hinges in turn on the rationality of a legislative process that, under the conditions of the constitutional separation of powers, is not at the disposal of agencies responsible for the administration of justice. The constitutional aspects of politics and legislative practice represent important topics in jurisprudence, but for a theory of law keyed to legal discourse, both of these areas first open up from the perspective of adjudication. If we want to study the problematic relation between the judiciary and the legislature without abandoning the perspective of legal theory, then the jurisdiction of constitutional courts provides a methodological point of reference. It is not self-evident that constitutional courts should exist. Institutions of this sort are absent in many systems that uphold the rule of law. Where they do exist—as in the Federal Republic and the United States, the two countries I will focus on—their position in the system of constitutional powers, as well as the legitimacy of their decisions, still remains subject to an ongoing debate. As the heated controversies themselves indicate, there is need for clarification. If nothing else, the fact that theoretically quite distinct *functions* are combined in *single institutions* calls for explanation.

Of the various aspects or issues involved in this discussion, there are three that I especially want to highlight. The critique of constitutional adjudication is always made in view of the distribution of powers between the democratic legislature and the judiciary; to this extent, such critique always involves a dispute over the principle of the separation of powers. However, depending on the relevant aspect, this problem poses itself in different ways. Here I have three discourses in mind. The first leads into the contest of legal paradigms, an issue I take up in the last chapter, whereas the second continues the methodological discussions of the previous chapter. The third discourse leads into the debate over how we should understand the political process. I propose an interpretation of democratic opinion- and will-formation from the vantage point of a discourse theory of law, a discussion I continue in chapter 7 from the standpoint of democratic theory.

Under the first aspect, the critique of constitutional court decision making—a critique one hears above all in the Federal Republic—relies on a special, namely, liberal, reading of the classical scheme for separating the powers of government.[1] This view points to the development of an interventionist welfare state out of the liberal state in order to explain the unavoidable, but normatively dubious, expansion of judicial functions, which according to this view has imposed competing legislative tasks on the constitutional court (sec. 6.1). Under the second aspect, the debate over the indeterminacy of law is continued with respect to the "value jurisprudence" (*Wertejudikatur*) of the Federal Constitutional Court. The critique is directed against a methodological self-understanding cultivated by the Court, according to which the orientation by principles is equivalent to the weighing of goals, values, and collective goods (sec. 6.2). Under the third aspect, the role of the constitutional court is seen—especially in the United States—as that of protecting the democratic legislative procedure; at stake here is the renewal of a republican, hence noninstrumental, understanding of the political process as a whole (sec. 6.3).

6.1 The Dissolution of the Liberal Paradigm of Law

6.1.1

Constitutional courts normally fulfill several functions at once. Although different powers converge in the task of authoritatively interpreting the constitution and thus also preserving the coherence of the legal order, lumping these powers together inside one institution is not immediately compelling from the perspective of constitutional theory. If we take the Federal Constitutional Court as an example, we can distinguish three tasks: settling intragovernmental disputes or *Organstreitigkeiten* (including disputes between the federal government and the *Länder*); reviewing the constitutionality of norms (in what follows, we will be primarily concerned with legal statutes); and constitutional complaints. Least problematic from the standpoint of the separation of powers is the responsibility for constitutional complaints and for concrete judicial review (i.e., for cases in which a lower court suspends its proceedings and petitions the Constitutional Court to rule on the constitutionality of a law that is relevant to the particular case).[2] Here the Constitutional Court functions to preserve the consistency of law. Regardless of its authority to declare statutes invalid in these types of procedures, too, the Constitutional Court, together with the higher federal courts, represents what one might consider the reflexive apex in the hierarchy of adjudication, and, as such, it assumes the tasks of self-scrutiny for the judiciary as a whole. In a similar way, the Government leaders, as the head of the executive branch, are responsible for the administration's task of self-review. That the Constitutional Court rules on cases of intragovernmental disputes in the broader sense may be more problematic. This power touches on the separation of governmental functions, but a plausible justification for it rests on the technical requirement to settle conflicts between government agencies that depend on collaboration. Here the logic of separated powers cannot, in the final analysis, be violated by the practice of a court that lacks coercive means to enforce its decisions on a recalcitrant parliament and administration.

The competition between the Constitutional Court and the democratically legitimated legislature becomes acute primarily in the sphere of abstract judicial review. Here the question whether a statute passed by parliament is constitutional, or at least does not contradict a consistent elaboration of the system of rights, is submitted to judicial examination. Prior to adoption, this is a question that parliament must decide. Still, it is worth considering whether the legislature could not also scrutinize its decisions, exercising a quasi-judicial review of its own. This might be institutionalized, for example, in a parliamentary committee (also) staffed by legal experts. This method of internalizing self-reflection on its own decisions would have the advantage of inducing legislators to keep the normative content of constitutional principles in mind from the very start of their deliberations. This normative content is lost, for example, when, in the crush of parliamentary business, moral and ethical questions are *redefined* as negotiable questions open to compromise. In this regard, the institutional differentiation of a self-referential procedure for reviewing norms, whose operation would remain in the hands of parliament, might perhaps contribute to a more rational legislative process. This recommends itself even if one assumes, in keeping with our own analysis, that the separation of powers is primarily intended to prevent the administration from becoming independent vis-à-vis communicatively produced power.

From the vantage point of discourse theory, the logic of the separation of powers demands an asymmetry in the way the branches of government interlock: the executive branch, which is not supposed to have control over the normative grounds of legislation and adjudication, is subordinate in its activity both to parliamentary oversight and to judicial review, whereas the opposite relation, a supervision of the other two branches by the executive, is excluded. Anyone who would want to replace a constitutional court by appointing the head of the executive branch as the "Guardian of the Constitution"—as Carl Schmitt wanted to do in his day with the German president—twists the meaning of the separation of powers in the constitutional state into its very opposite.[3] If we interpret the logic of separated powers in terms of argumentation theory,[4] it is reasonable to construe legislation *self-reflexively*, in a manner similar to the self-reflexive construction of the administration of justice, and to furnish the legislature with the authority to review its own activity. As it is, the legislature does not have the power to check whether the courts, in applying the law, make use of exactly those normative reasons that appeared in the presumptively rational justification of a legal statute on the part of the legislator. On the other hand, what is known as abstract judicial review belongs without question among the functions of the legislature. Hence it is not entirely off track to reserve this function, even at a second level of appeal, to a legislative self-review that could be developed into a quasi-judicial procedure. The transfer of this power to a constitutional court requires, at the least, a complex justification: "[For] the discourse of basic rights [is] not bound to the decisions made in legislative procedures, but has priority over them. This means that the most important constraining factor for normal legal argumentation, the relatively concrete ordinary legal statute, is lacking in such discourse. In its place one finds very abstract, open, and ideologically loaded constitutional principles."[5] For Alexy, "the discourse of basic rights" pertains to all spheres of constitutional adjudication. An explicit, even if only selective, release from legally binding statutes appears most clearly in the case of abstract judicial review.

This point is illustrated by a famous controversy between Hans Kelsen and Carl Schmitt. Kelsen declared himself categorically in favor of institutionalizing a constitutional court. In support of this demand, he cited not only political considerations, which were quite plausible for the situation at the time, but interesting theoretical reasons as well. Schmitt had doubted that abstract judicial review was a question of norm application, and hence a genuine operation of judicial decision making, because one only "makes comparisons among general norms, but does not subsume one norm under another or apply one to another." The relation between the norm and the circumstances of a particular case or "fact situation" is missing.[6] To this Kelsen could only reply that the object of review is not the content of the problematic law but the constitutionality of the act of its adoption: "The fact-situation that is to be subsumed under the constitutional norm in decisions about the constitutionality of a legal statute is not the norm . . . but the production of the norm."[7] Naturally, this argument would have teeth only if one could read judicial review as a whole in proceduralist terms, as we will presently see. But then Kelsen's decisive argument again lies at the level of legal policy:

Since precisely in the most important cases of constitutional violation the parliament and the executive branch (*Regierung*) are the disputing parties, to decide the dispute it makes sense to call upon a third authority that stands apart from this conflict and is not itself involved in any way in the exercise of power, which the constitution essentially divides up between parliament and the executive. That this third authority thereby receives a certain power of its own is unavoidable. However, it makes a huge difference whether one grants an agency only that power given with the function of constitutional review, or whether one further strengthens the power of one of the chief bearers of power through the transfer of such review.[8]

However one thinks this function of interpreting the constitutionality of legislation should be *appropriately institutionalized*, constitutional jurisdiction increases the clarity of law and safeguards the coherence of the legal order.

The constitutional court, and other courts, will in any case enter into a discourse of basic rights when it is a matter not of reviewing parliamentary statutes after their adoption but simply of deciding hard cases. Whether the issue involves an individual case in which several basic rights collide, or whether in the light of one basic right ordinary statutes collide with other such rights, in quite a few cases and at every level of adjudication principles come into play that call for a "constructive" interpretation as proposed by Dworkin. To be sure, the Constitutional Court is concerned only with cases of collision; its rulings almost always deal with hard cases and subsequently become important precedents. Hence, the problem of the "indeterminacy of law" already discussed above accumulates and intensifies in constitutional jurisdiction, as it tends to do in higher courts anyway. The Federal Constitutional Court has dealt with this problem head-on (in a resolution of February 14, 1973) in reference to the Basic Law, Art. 20, Sec. 3: "The law is not identical with the totality of written laws. Besides the law enacted by state authorities, under certain conditions an additional element of law can exist that has its source in the constitutional legal order as a whole and is able to work as a corrective to the written law; the task of the judiciary is to find this element and realize it in its decisions."[9] In any case, the right interpretation is supposed to be "found" or, as it goes on to say, it is supposed to be worked out in "rational argumentation." Other formulations, however, point to a problematic self-understanding of the Constitutional Court; they assign the Court the function of further developing law through "creative legal findings." Konrad Hesse has responded to this self-understanding in a manner quite in line with the considerations in the previous chapter; he coolly notes that

decisions of the constitutional court no doubt contain a moment of creative design. But *all* interpretation has a creative character. It nonetheless remains *interpretation* even when it serves to answer questions of constitutional law and concerns norms that have the breadth and openness peculiar to constitutional law. Specifying such norms can make for greater difficulties than doing so for more detailed regulations; yet that does not alter the fact that both cases involve structurally similar processes.[10]

From this vantage point, the far-reaching powers of the Federal Constitutional Court do not *have* to endanger the logic of the separation of powers.

6.1.2

Most critics do not rely on methodological considerations but adopt a historical perspective. Examining the historical development of the legal system as a whole leads them to diagnose a constitutionally dubious shift in importance between parliaments and constitutional courts. Authors like Ernst-Wolfgang Böckenförde, Erhard Denninger, and Dieter Grimm draw out a contrast between two ideal types: the liberal arrangement, in which state and society were separate; and the circumstances of the welfare state, which no longer simply guarantees comprehensive individual legal protection but provides its citizens with a "safety net" for socially conditioned risks and losses.[11] According to the liberal model of society, the constitution was once supposed to separate a socioeconomic realm, in which individuals autonomously pursued their private happiness, from the political sphere concerned with the pursuit of the common good: "At least the constitution did not have the function of orchestrating individual well-being and the common good under one overarching idea."[12] The tasks and goals of the state were left to politics and were not supposed to become an object of constitutional regulation. Accordingly, basic rights were understood exclusively as rights against the state. Because these only ground negative claims that the state refrain from interference, they have an absolute or direct validity. This implies a strict conditioning of adjudication. Legislators, too, could manage a clear legal situation. That is, they could restrict themselves to guaranteeing public order, preventing what was perceived as "abuses" of economic liberty, and establishing general and abstract laws that precisely defined the possibilities and scope of government interventions.

In the liberal model, strict legal constraints on the judiciary and the administration led to the classical scheme for the separation of powers, which was once intended to bring the arbitrary will of an absolutist regime in line with the rule of law. The distribution of powers among the branches of government can be modeled along the temporal axis of collective decisions: judicial decision making is oriented to the past and focuses on past decisions of the political legislature that have solidified into established law; the legislature makes decisions oriented to the future and binding on future action; and the administration deals with current problems cropping up in the present. This model is governed by the premise that the democratic constitution should primarily fend off dangers that can arise in the government-citizen dimension, that is, in the relationships between the administrative apparatus, with its monopoly on the means of legitimate violence, and unarmed private persons. By contrast, the horizontal relationships among private persons, especially those intersubjective relationships constituting the common civic practice of citizens, do not have any formative effect on the liberal separation of powers. Incidentally, a positivist view of law as a recursively closed system of rules is well suited for this model.

If one takes this model as the standard of comparison, then the materialized legal order of the welfare state can appear as an upheaval, even as the corruption of the constitutional architectonic. Welfare-state law does not consist primarily of clearly defined conditional programs but facilitates political policymaking and must draw on principles in the process of adjudication. Compared to the classical separation thesis, the materialization of law results in a "remoralization" that, by admitting arguments of moral principle and of political policy into legal argumentation, *loosens* the linear binding of the judiciary to the guidelines laid down by the political legislature. The fundamental norms and principles that now penetrate all areas of the legal order demand that the individual case be interpreted constructively, in a manner sensitive to context and referring to the legal system as a whole. The context-dependence of a norm application oriented by the whole of the constitution can reinforce the freedom and responsibility of communicatively acting subjects in nonformalized spheres of action. Inside the legal system, however, it signifies increased power for the judiciary, and it enlarges the scope of judicial discretion in a way that threatens to upset the equilibrium in the normative structure of the classical constitutional state at the cost of the citizens' autonomy.[13] That is, the orientation to fundamental norms and principles means the judiciary must turn its attention from its former focus on the institutional history of the legal order and attend primarily to problems of the present and future. On the one hand (as Ingeborg Maus also fears), the judiciary encroaches on legislative powers for which it lacks democratic legitimation. On the other hand, it promotes and confirms a flexible legal structure that accommodates the autonomy of the administrative apparatus—so that the democratic legitimation of law is eroded from this side as well.

Attentive critics, such as Böckenförde, Denninger, and Maus, have reconstructed an implicit doctrine of basic rights from the pivotal decisions of the Federal Constitutional Court. This doctrine, so the interpretation goes, acknowledges that the system of rights can no longer be guaranteed on the assumed basis of an unfettered economic society spontaneously reproducing itself through autonomous, individual decisions. Rights must rather be realized through the benefits and services of an interventionist state that provides infrastructures and wards off risks—a government that at once regulates, facilitates, and compensates. Most important, in complex societies that are horizontally differentiated into networks of subsystems, the protection afforded by basic rights must extend not just to the administrative power of the state but to the social power of large organizations in general. Moreover, such protection can no longer be understood only negatively, as warding off intrusions; it also grounds affirmative claims to benefits. The decisions of the Federal Constitutional Court thus qualify basic rights as *principles of a total legal order* whose normative content structures the system of rules as a whole. This specifically German doctrine of basic rights focuses primarily on a few key ideas. These include the "reciprocal effect" (or *Wechselwirkung*) between ordinary legal statutes and fundamental rights (which remain inviolable only in their "essential content" or *Wesensgehalt*); the "implicit limits on basic rights," which hold even for those basic individual rights, such as the guarantees of human dignity, that impose affirmative duties on the state (the so-called *subjektiv-öffentliche Rechte*); the "radiating effect" (*Ausstrahlung*) of basic rights on all areas of law and their "third-party effect" (*Drittwirkung*) on the horizontal rights and duties holding between private persons; the state's mandates and obligations to provide protection, which are tasks the Court derives from the "objective" legal character of basic rights as principles of the legal order; and finally, the "dynamic protection of constitutional rights" and the links in procedural law between such rights and the "objective" content of constitutional law.[14]

I cannot go into the details of this multifaceted discussion here.[15] However, it is beyond dispute that Constitutional Court adjudication reflects a transformation in how the German judges conceive basic rights. Although basic rights originally consisted of negative or "defensive" rights (*Abwehrrechten*) that grant liberties and keep an intervening administration within the bounds of law, they have now become the architectonic principles of the legal order, thus transforming the content of individual, or "subjective," liberties (*Freiheitsrechte*) into the content of fundamental norms that penetrate and shape "objective" law, albeit in a conceptually unclarified manner. This transformation finds its methodological correspondents in "key concepts of constitutional law" (Denninger), such as the principle of proportionality, the possibility proviso (*Vorbehalt des Möglichen*), the limitation of "immediately valid" fundamental rights by a third party's fundamental rights, and the protection of basic rights through organizational and procedural provisions.[16] In cases of collision, these concepts serve to interrelate various norms with a view to the "unity and consistency of the Constitution": "With the development of key relational concepts in the light of cases and problems, the Federal Constitutional Court has acknowledged and underlined the 'open' structure of the Basic Law, within limits that must be specified."[17] To some extent, one can understand these key concepts, which have grown out of the practice of decision making itself, as procedural principles that mirror the operations of constructive interpretation as required by Dworkin, that is, the interpretation of the individual case in terms of the entirety of a rationally reconstructed legal order. Thus despite his harsh criticism of details, Denninger, too, arrives at an assessment that is quite positive overall:

In developing "key concepts," the Federal Constitutional Court has managed to supplement the "classical" legal motifs of the written German Constitution with a highly sensitive instrument whose conceptual structure and degree of complexity appear adequate to the structure of the problems at hand, especially those that demand a mediation between the microlevel (of individual action) and the macrolevel (of the system).... It is precisely the relational structure of the key concepts that makes them suitable for formulating problems of constitutional law at a level where one can avoid one-sided fixations either on negative rights against the state or on welfare-state planning. At this level one can successfully use overarching *constitutional* categories to connect the welfare state, which relies on *administrative* law in its provision of "services" and "redistribution," with the rule of law, which guarantees property [and freedom].[18]

6.1.3

Although he describes and diagnoses Federal Constitutional Court adjudication in similar terms, Böckenförde arrives at an entirely different judgment. When Denninger examines individual decisions of the Court, he detects a *trend* that could indicate a disturbing transition from a liberal style of legal authority to "political authority based on judicially sanctioned legitimacy." Here Böckenförde sees an unavoidable *dilemma*. He believes the transition from a state programmed by parliamentary legislation to a "jurisdictional state" monitored by the Constitutional Court is inexorable. The only alternative would be the restoration of a liberal understanding of law. In this context, the notion of "jurisdictio" has the premodern sense of a political authority supported by suprapositive law, to which the ruler is entitled in his adjunct role of supreme judge. Hence the term connotes an authority that *preceded* the constitutional separation between making and applying law:

In the name of giving the principles behind basic rights the force of law, it reaches the point where—in typological terms—parliament and constitutional court coordinate and converge in their development of law. The former is demoted from originary lawmaking to the provision of concrete specifications, the latter is promoted from the interpretative application of law to its creative, concrete specification. . . . To this extent the earlier qualitative difference between legislation and adjudication is leveled out. Both . . . carry on the development of law by making it more concrete, and they compete in doing so. The legislator has a [temporary] lead in this competition, but the constitutional court has [authoritative] priority. . . . The question this raises is that of the legitimation of the constitutional court.[19]

Böckenförde is convinced that the principles of the constitutional state are compatible only with a liberal understanding of basic rights as immediately valid liberties enjoyed by private persons vis-à-vis the administration. Otherwise, the functional separation of the judiciary from the legislature, and hence the democratic substance of the constitutional state, cannot, in his view, be preserved: "Whoever wants to maintain the definitive function that the popularly elected parliament has for the development of law, and wants to avoid a further remodeling of constitutional structures in favor of a 'jurisdictional state,' must also hold onto the fact that basic rights—which are actionable in court—are 'only' subjective rights or liberties vis-à-vis the state and not also norms constitutive of an objective order and binding on all spheres of law."[20]

However, these alternatives pose an unavoidable dilemma only if one takes the liberal model of the separation of state and society as normative. This mistakes the meaning of a historical paradigm. The liberal paradigm of law is certainly not a simplifying *description* of a historical starting point that we could take at face value. It tells us, rather, how the principles of the constitutional state could be realized under the hypothetically *assumed* conditions of a liberal economic society. This model stands or falls with the basic social assumptions of classical political economy, which were already shaken by Marx's critique and no longer hold for developed, postindustrial societies in the West. In other words, the principles of the constitutional state must not be confused with *one* of its context-bound historical modes of interpretation. Böckenförde himself notes this difference when he compares the interpretation of basic rights as negative rights against the state with the Kantian concept of law. What in Kant's view was supposed to secure the compatibility of each one's liberty with an equal liberty for all is, in the liberal paradigm, *attenuated* to the guarantee of private autonomy vis-à-vis the state: "According to these [basic rights interpreted as negative rights], what is compatible according to a universal law of freedom is not the freedom of one person with that of others *in general*, but only the freedom of the individual citizen with that of the state."[21] Measured against Kant's principle of law, it is only the shift to the social-welfare paradigm that again brings out the objective legal contents of individual liberties that have *always already* been implicit in the system of rights. With this shift, "the basic-rights protection afforded by courts" is increasingly transformed "into the task of mutually delimiting and coordinating colliding spheres and claims of freedom on the part of private persons."[22]

In light of a discourse theory of law, one sees the derivative character of negative rights against the state: only after a governmental authority has been constituted does the right to equal liberties, which citizens first enjoy at a horizontal level of mutual association, acquire the additional meaning of protections against an intrusive administration. As we have seen, when freely associated citizens join together in a politically autonomous legal community, there emerge certain rights that, in the first instance, have only the intersubjective meaning of securing symmetrical relations of mutual recognition. By mutually granting one another these rights, individuals acquire the status of legal subjects who are both free and equal. This original intersubjective meaning is differentiated according to "subjective" and "objective" legal contents only in view of the problem of the juridification of political power (which, however, is from the beginning tacitly presupposed for the constitution of the legal code). But it is only a particular paradigmatic understanding of law in general that causes the objective legal content apparently *to drop out* of some basic rights. This understanding stems in turn from how a particular historical situation was perceived through the lens of social theory, that is, a situation in which the liberal middle class had to grasp, on the basis of its interest position, how the principles of the constitutional state could be realized. Viewed from the standpoint of "effective history" (*wirkungsgeschichtlich*), the liberal paradigm of law represented at the time a thoroughly successful solution to this problem; today the same problem, under the altered historical circumstances that even Böckenförde recognizes, demands a different answer.

Of course, the social-welfare paradigm of law that has since been established is also no longer very convincing. However, the difficulties that Böckenförde astutely analyzes in this new paradigm are not a sufficient reason for restoring the old one.[23] In the United States, the problems that have resulted from the welfare programs of the New Deal, as well as from the sudden expansion of welfare claims sparked by the vision of the "Great Society" in the sixties and seventies, are openly acknowledged. This "rights revolution" is taken as a challenge to give a new interpretation to the principles of the constitutional state in the light of new historical experiences. For example, the partially counterproductive effects of welfare programs have led Cass Sunstein to conclude only that a new consensus must develop about how American constitutional principles can be realized under the conditions of the "regulatory" state.

As the result of an analysis of Supreme Court adjudication, Sunstein proposes a series of "background norms" that are intended to modify the paradigmatic reading of the principles of government by law:

Where there is ambiguity, courts should construe regulatory statutes so
that (1) politically unaccountable actors are prohibited from deciding
important issues; (2) collective action problems do not subvert statutory
programs; (3) various regulatory statutes are, to the extent possible,
coordinated into a coherent whole; (4) obsolete statutes are kept consistent with changing developments of law, policy, and fact; (5) procedural
qualifications of substantive rights are kept narrow; (6) the complex
systemic effects of regulation are taken into account; and, most generally,
(7) irrationality and injustice, measured against the statute's own purposes, are avoided.[24]

Sunstein's proposal, which displays parallels to Denninger's explication of key constitutional concepts, interests me at this point for
two reasons. First, it makes an exemplary contribution to the
paradigm discussion without losing sight of the original, indeed
radical-democratic meaning of the system of rights: "Notwithstanding their number and variety, the principles are united by certain
general goals. These include, above all, the effort to promote
deliberation in government, to furnish surrogates for it when it is
absent, to limit factionalism and self-interested representation,
and to help bring about political equality."[25] Second, the proposal
indicates an awareness of the difference between the principles of
the constitutional state and their paradigmatic modes of interpretation. The temptation to return to the liberal understanding of
basic rights is also due to a neglect of this difference.[26]

Through the first third of the twentieth century, the liberal
paradigm of law expressed a background consensus that was widely
shared by legal experts. It thus provided the application of law with
a context of *unquestioned* maxims of interpretation. This circumstance explains the suggestion that the law could seemingly be
applied in those days without recourse to principles and disputed
"key concepts" in need of interpretation. In fact, every legal order
justified by principles depends on a constructive interpretation
and thus on what Sunstein calls "background norms." Every important judicial decision or precedent goes beyond an interpretation
of the text of the statute and to this extent requires an external
justification:

Statutory text is the starting point, but it becomes intelligible only
because of the context and background norms that give it content.

Usually, the context is unproblematic, and the norms are so widely shared and uncontroversial that the text alone *appears* to be a sufficient base of interpretation. In many cases, however, the text, in conjunction with such norms, will produce ambiguity, overinclusiveness, or underinclusiveness; in such cases courts must look elsewhere. Contextual considerations of various sorts—including the legislative history, the statutory purpose, and the practical reasonableness of one view or another—can in these circumstances provide considerable help. But the history might itself be ambiguous—or be the work of an unrepresentative, self-interested group—and the problem of characterizing purpose in a multimember body will, in many cases, lead to the familiar problems of ambiguity, gaps, overinclusiveness, and underinclusiveness.

In such cases, courts often must resort to conspicuous or contestable background norms.[27]

To be sure, this consideration does not answer the question whether the unavoidable recourse to such background norms does not, after all, open the door for the constitutional court to engage in a politically inspired "creation of law," which, according to the logic of the separation of powers, should be reserved to the democratic legislature.

6.2 Norms versus Values: Methodological Errors in the Self-Understanding of the Constitutional Court

6.2.1

The doubts about the legitimacy of the Federal Constitutional Court are not only based on a consideration of the paradigm shift but are bound up with methodological assumptions as well. In contrast to the situation in the United States, the criticism in the Federal Republic can refer to a "doctrine of values" (*Wertordnungslehre*) developed by the Court itself, and hence can refer to a methodological self-understanding of judges that has had problematic effects on the deciding of important precedent-setting cases. The justified criticism of "value jurisprudence," though, is often directed *in an unmediated fashion* against disturbing constitutional consequences without making it clear that, in the first place, these are only the effects of a certain methodological self-understanding of the practice of the Court. The critics thereby miss the alternative of providing a correct understanding of constructive interpretation, according to which rights must not be assimilated to values.

Insofar as the charge of "value jurisprudence" applies, the Federal Constitutional Court understands the Basic Law of the Federal Republic not so much as a system of rules structured by principles, but as a "concrete order of values," in the sense of the material value ethics developed by such thinkers as Max Scheler or Nicolai Hartmann. Concurring with the wording and tenor of some important opinions of the Federal Constitutional Court, Böckenförde, too, conceives principles as values: "objective fundamental norms" are supposed to rest on "value decisions." Like Maus, he follows Alexy's proposal that we view the norms or principles thus transformed into values as optimizing prescriptions whose intensity remains open.[28] This interpretation accommodates the talk of "balancing interests" (or weighing values, *Güterabwägung*) that is common among lawyers. If principles manifest a value that one should optimally realize, and if the norms themselves do not dictate the extent to which one must fulfill this optimizing prescription, then the application of such principles within the limits of what is factually possible makes a goal-oriented weighting necessary. Because no value can claim to have an inherently unconditional priority over other values, this weighting operation transforms the interpretation of established law into the business of *realizing values* by giving them concrete shape in relation to specific cases:

Concretization is the (creative) filling out of something prescribed only as a direction or principle, something otherwise open and initially in need of being shaped through a process of specification into an executable norm. Hans Huber noted long ago that the need to concretize basic rights, understood as principles—a need following from their comprehensive validity, scope, and indeterminacy—must not be confused with the need to interpret. . . . We might add for the sake of clarity that this case-specific legislation, since it appears as interpretation of the Constitution, lies at the same level as the Constitution and thus represents constitutional legislation.[29]

Böckenförde thus takes the methodological self-understanding of the Constitutional Court at its word and criticizes it with Carl Schmitt's thesis of the "tyranny of values," without seeing that the real problem lies in the premise that assimilates legal principles to values. The problem is a conceptual one.

Principles or higher-level norms, in the light of which other norms can be justified, have a deontological sense, whereas values are teleological. Valid norms of action obligate their addressees equally and without exception to satisfy generalized behavioral expectations, whereas values are to be understood as intersubjectively shared preferences. Shared values express the preferability of goods that, in specific collectivities, are considered worth striving for and can be acquired or realized through goal-directed action. Norms of action appear with a binary validity claim and are either valid or invalid; we can respond to normative sentences, as we can to assertoric sentences, only by taking a yes or no position or by withholding judgment. By contrast, values set down preference relations telling us that certain goods are more attractive than others; hence we can assent to evaluative sentences to a greater or lesser degree. The "oughtness" of binding norms has the absolute sense of an unconditioned and universal obligation; what "one ought to do" claims to be equally good for all. The attractiveness of intersubjectively shared values has the relative sense of an estimation of goods that has become established or been adopted in cultures and forms of life: serious value choices or higher-order preferences tell us what is good for us (or for me) overall and in the long run. Different norms must not contradict one another if they claim validity for the same circle of addressees; they must fit together into a coherent complex, that is, form a system. Different values compete for priority from case to case; to the extent that they find intersubjective recognition within a culture or form of life, they form flexible configurations filled with tension.

Norms and values therefore differ, first, in their references to obligatory rule-following versus teleological action; second, in the binary versus graduated coding of their validity claims; third, in their absolute versus relative bindingness; and fourth, in the coherence criteria that systems of norms and systems of values must respectively satisfy. The fact that norms and values differ in these logical properties yields significant differences for their application as well.

Different kinds of action orientation result depending on whether I base my action in a particular case on norms or on values. The question of what I should do in a given situation is posed and answered differently in the two cases. In the light of norms, I can decide what action is commanded; within the horizon of values, which behavior is recommended. Naturally, in both cases the problem of application requires the selection of the right action. But if we start with a system of valid norms, that action is "right" that is equally good *for all*; in reference to a typical value constellation for our culture or form of life, on the other hand, that behavior is "best" that, on the whole and in the long run, is good *for us*. With principles of law or "legal values" (i.e., legally protected interests, *Rechtsgütern*), this difference is often overlooked, because positive law always holds only for a specific territory and a corresponding set of addressees. Notwithstanding this de facto restriction of the legal sphere, however, basic rights acquire a different meaning, either deontological or axiological, depending on whether one, like Dworkin, conceives them as binding legal principles or, like Alexy, as optimizable legal values. As norms, they regulate a matter in the equal interest of all; as values, they enter into a configuration with other values to comprise a symbolic order expressing the identity and form of life of a particular legal community. No doubt values or teleological contents also find their way into law, but law defined through a system of rights domesticates, as it were, the policy goals and value orientations of the legislator through the strict *priority* of normative points of view. Anyone wanting to equate the constitution with a concrete order of values mistakes its specific legal character; as legal norms, basic rights are, like moral rules, modeled after obligatory norms of action—and not after attractive goods.

From the standpoint of conceptual analysis, the terminological distinction between norms and values loses its validity *only* in those theories that claim universal validity for the highest values or goods, as in the classical versions of ethics of the good. These ontological approaches reify goods and values into entities existing in themselves; under the conditions of postmetaphysical thinking, this moral realism scarcely seems defensible. In contemporary theories of this sort, the small set of supposedly universal values or goods takes on such an abstract form that it is not difficult to recognize in them deontological principles, such as human dignity, solidarity, self-realization, and autonomy.[30] The conceptual transformation of basic rights into basic goods means that rights have been masked by teleology, concealing the fact that in contexts of justification norms and values take on *different roles in the logic of argumentation.* For this reason, postmetaphysical theories of value take into consideration the particularity of values, the flexibility of value hierarchies, and the local character of value configurations. They either trace values back to traditions and the settled value orientations of particular cultures or, if they want to emphasize the subjective and deliberate character of the choice of values, they trace them to existential decisions about metapreferences and "higher-order volitions."[31]

In the discussions among American constitutional scholars, the distinction between approaches that conceive basic rights as legal principles versus those that see them as values or goods is more clearly drawn than in the parallel German debate. For example, Paul Brest has clearly marked the opposition between "rights theories" and the approaches of either moral realism or "moral conventionalism."[32] And when John Hart Ely argues against theories of constitutional adjudication that attempt to integrate law with morality, he, too, distinguishes between the deontological understanding of law that resorts to suprapositive rights, reason, and neutral procedural principles, on the one hand, and the value-oriented approach that refers to tradition and settled consensus, on the other.[33]

A neo-Aristotelian variant of the doctrine of objective values is represented in the United States by Michael J. Perry, for example. He conceives the text of the Constitution as a founding charter that manifests the ethical self-understanding of a historical community. He thus removes the empiricist features from the moral conventionalism that sees the basic values of the Constitution as rooted in the currently dominant value consensus of the majority of the population. Like a sacred text, the Constitution founds new ideas, in the light of which the community is able to perceive its deeper aspirations and its true interests (*Interessen*): "On this view, our political life includes ongoing moral discourse with one another in an effort to achieve ever more insightful answers to the question of what are our *real* interests, as opposed to our *actual* preferences, and thus what sort of persons—with what projects, goals, ideals— ought we to be. . . . Deliberative politics is an essential instrument of self-knowledge."[34] The ethical-political discourse in which citizens achieve self-understanding finds its sharply honed expression in a value-oriented constitutional adjudication that hermeneutically appropriates the originary meaning of the Constitution by creatively actualizing that meaning in view of changing historical challenges. In a still more pronounced fashion than the German legal hermeneutics following Gadamer, Perry sees the constitutional judge in the role of a prophetic teacher, whose interpretation of the divine word of the Founding Fathers secures the continuity of a tradition that is constitutive of the community's life. To do this, the judge must neither rigidly adhere to the strict wording nor depend on majority convictions: "To 'interpret' some provisions of the Constitution is, in the main, to ascertain their aspirational meaning and then to bring that meaning to bear—that is, to answer the question of . . . what that aspiration means for the conflict at hand, what that aspiration, if accepted, requires the court to do."[35]

In fact, this kind of *value jurisprudence* raises the legitimation problem that Maus and Böckenförde analyze with respect to the decision-making practice of the Federal Constitutional Court. According to that reading, it is necessary for the court to concretize norms in a manner equivalent to implicit lawmaking, which gives constitutional adjudication the status of a competing legislation. Perry boldly draws this conclusion from his moral realist interpretation of fundamental rights, which converts such rights from deontological legal principles into teleological legal interests or goods (*Rechtsgüter*) constituting an objective order of values. These goods bind both the judiciary and the legislature to the substantial ethos (*Sittlichkeit*) of a specific form of life: "Judicial review is a deliberately countermajoritarian institution."[36]

By assuming it should strive to realize substantive values pregiven in constitutional law, the constitutional court is transformed into an authoritarian agency. For if in cases of collision *all* reasons can assume the character of policy arguments, then the fire wall erected in legal discourse by a deontological understanding of legal norms and principles collapses.

As soon as rights are transformed into goods and values in any individual case, each must compete with the others at the same level for priority. Every value is inherently just as particular as every other, whereas norms owe their validity to a universalization test. As Denninger puts it, "Values can only be relativized by other values; this process of preferring or pursuing values, however, resists attempts at logical conceptualization."[37] This is one reason why Dworkin regards rights as "trumps" that one can play against policy arguments in legal discourse. True, not every right will win out over every collective good in the justifications of concrete decisions. But a right will not prevail only when the priority of a collective good over a corresponding norm can itself be justified in the light of higher norms or principles. Because norms and principles, in virtue of their deontological character, can claim to be *universally binding* and not just *specially preferred*, they possess a greater justificatory force than values. Values must be brought into a transitive order with other values from case to case. Because there are no rational standards for this, weighing takes place either arbitrarily or unreflectively, according to customary standards and hierarchies.[38]

Insofar as a constitutional court adopts the doctrine of an objective order of values and bases its decision making on a kind of moral realism or moral conventionalism, the danger of irrational rulings increases, because functionalist arguments then gain the upper hand over normative ones. Certainly, there are a number of "principles" or collective goods that represent perspectives from which arguments can be introduced into a legal discourse in cases of norm collision: for example, the "functional capacity" of the armed forces or the judicial system, "peace" within specific domains (e.g., in labor relations), the "security of the state as guarantor of law and order," and fidelity to the principle of federalism (or the "federal comity" of government agencies, *Bundestreu*). But arguments based on such collective goods and values "count" only as much as the very norms and principles by which these goals can in turn be justified. *In the final instance*, only rights can be trump in the argumentation game. This difference is leveled out if one

counterintuitively equates legal norms and principles with interests, goals, goods, and values:

> In that case, constitutional guarantees of liberty find themselves compet-
> ing with "principles" that are opposed, not only in their content but even
> in their entire structure, such as the functional efficiency of the criminal
> justice system, the functional capacity of the Armed Forces, or the
> functional capacity of business ventures and economic sectors. . . . The
> Federal Constitutional Court transforms these (and the other) collective
> goods into immediate constitutional mandates that the legislator is
> compelled to carry out, determining in each situation what the costs are
> in terms of rights and individual liberties.[39]

By contrast, as soon as the deontological character of basic rights
is taken seriously, they are withdrawn from such a cost-benefit
analysis. This also holds for "open" norms that, unlike conditional
programs, do not refer to easily identifiable standard cases but
instead remain unspecified and thus require "concretization" in a
methodologically unobjectionable sense. These norms find their
unambiguous specification precisely in discourses of application.
In the case of a collision with other legal regulations, one does not
have to decide to what extent the competing values are respectively
optimized. As already shown, the task is rather to examine prima
facie applicable norms in order to find out which one is most
suitable to the case at hand, once the situational features of the case
have been described as exhaustively as possible from all normatively relevant points of view. In the process, one must establish a
plausible connection between the pertinent norm and the norms
that—without diminishment in their general validity—do not prevail, so that the coherence of the rule system as a whole remains
unaffected. The pertinent norm and those that give way do not
relate to each other like competing values, which, as optimizing
prescriptions, are "fulfilled" to different degrees depending on the
case. Rather, the relation is that between "appropriate" and "inappropriate" norms. Here appropriateness has the same meaning as
the validity of a singular judgment that, derived from a valid
general norm, first allows this underlying norm to become fully
"saturated."

An adjudication oriented by principles has to decide which claim
and which action in a given conflict is right—and not how to

balance interests or relate values. True, valid norms make up a flexible relational structure, in which the relations can shift from case to case; but *this* shifting is subject to the coherence proviso, which ensures that all the norms fit together into a unified system designed to admit exactly one right solution for each case. The legal validity of the judgment has the deontological character of a command, and not the teleological character of a desirable good that we can achieve to a certain degree under the given circumstances and within the horizon of our preferences. What is the best for us at a given point does not *eo ipso* coincide with what is equally good for all.

6.2.2

With respect to the legitimacy problem posed by constitutional adjudication, these methodological considerations issue in a critique of a false self-understanding and its practical effects, but they do not deny the possibility of rationally deciding constitutional questions in general. The interpretation of basic norms and principles is fundamentally no different from the interpretation of ordinary norms (unless the latter's application is conditioned for carefully defined standard situations). The application of principles does not have to generate rationality gaps any more than the application of norms does. The complex steps of a constructive interpretation certainly cannot be neatly regulated through procedural norms; they are, however, subject to scrutiny according to the procedural rationality of legally institutionalized discourses of application. In any event, rulings on constitutional complaints and the concrete constitutional review initiated by individual cases are both *limited* to the *application* of (constitutional) norms presupposed as valid. For these forms of review, the distinction between discourses that apply norms and those that justify them offers at least an argumentation-theoretic criterion for demarcating the respective tasks that the judiciary and the legislature can legitimately accomplish.

An adjudication guided by principles does not necessarily have to violate the hierarchical decision structure intended to ensure that the reasons available for decision making at *any* level are *given in advance* by the decisions of a higher-ranking authority. Maus sees the logic of the separation of powers at work in the precautionary *interruption* of an otherwise self-referentially closed circle of legitimation:

At no level of the decision process can political power simply legitimate itself through the law it has itself enacted. The legislature is legitimated both by its adherence to procedural guidelines present in the constitution and also by the current will of the people that precedes legislative action, but it is not legitimated by the ordinary statutes it has itself enacted. Only the authorities that apply [and implement] law are legitimated by ordinary law, which they therefore may not enact themselves. This structure also guarantees that ignorance of the concrete addressees of decisions is graduated across the various levels of authority in the constitutional state.[40]

The fact that the constitutional court, just like the political legislator, is bound to "procedural guidelines present in the constitution" does not imply that the judiciary competes with the legislature on an equal level. The legitimating reasons available from the constitution are given to the constitutional court in advance from the perspective of the application of law—and not from the perspective of a legislation that elaborates and *develops* the system of rights in the pursuit of policies. The court reopens the package of reasons that legitimated legislative decisions so that it might mobilize them for a coherent ruling on the individual case in agreement with existing principles of law; it may not, however, use these reasons in an implicitly legislative manner that directly elaborates and develops the system of rights.

However, as soon as a norm does not allow such a coherent application in conformity with the constitution, the question of abstract judicial review arises. This is a process that must in principle be undertaken from the legislator's perspective. As long as this review is exercised by an independent judiciary and leads only to the overturning of norms but not to mandates imposed on the legislator, pragmatic and legal-political considerations seem to support the institutional locus of authority as it exists in the Federal Republic and the United States. This then raises the further question of whether the parliament's appointment or confirmation of constitutional judges provides the required democratic legitimation for the judiciary's exercise of this function.

However one answers questions regarding the *right institutionalization* of the separation of powers, it is neither necessary nor possible to return to the liberal view of government, which holds that "basic rights are only subjective rights or liberties vis-à-vis the state and not also norms constitutive of an objective order and binding on all spheres of law."[41] This continental opposition between "subjective" rights and "objective" law is foreign to the American tradition in any case. If, under the conditions of a more or less well-established welfare-state compromise, one wants to hold on not only to government by law but to democracy as well, and thus to the idea of the legal community's self-organization, then one can no longer maintain the liberal view of the constitution as a "framework" regulating primarily the relation between administration and citizens. Economic power and social pressure need to be tamed by the rule of law no less than does administrative power. On the other hand, under the conditions of cultural and societal pluralism, the constitution must also not be conceived as a concrete legal order that imposes a priori a total form of life on society as a whole. Rather, the constitution sets down political procedures according to which citizens can, in the exercise of their right to self-determination, successfully pursue the cooperative project of establishing just (i.e., relatively more just) conditions of life. Only the *procedural conditions for the democratic genesis of legal statutes* secures the legitimacy of enacted law. If one starts with this democratic background understanding, one can also make sense of the powers of the constitutional court in a way that accords with the purpose of the separation of powers: the constitutional court should keep watch over just that system of rights that makes citizens' private and public autonomy equally possible. The classical scheme for the separation and interdependence of government branches no longer corresponds to this intention, because the function of basic rights can no longer rely on the sociological and economic assumptions built into the liberal paradigm of law. In other words, basic rights must now do more than just protect private citizens from encroachment by the state apparatus. Private autonomy is endangered today at least as much by positions of economic and social power, and it depends for its part on the manner and extent to which democratic citizens can effectively exercise their communicative and participatory rights. Hence, the constitutional court must examine the contents of disputed norms primarily in connection with the communicative presuppositions and procedural conditions of the legislative process. Such a *procedural understanding of the constitution* places the problem of legitimating constitutional review in the context of a theory of democracy. In this respect, the American discussion is more informative than the German.

The apposite conception developed by Ely adopts a skeptical attitude toward judicial activism. His approach is admittedly intended to relieve adjudication of any orientation to legal principles with moral or ethical origins. Ely proceeds on the assumption that the United States Constitution primarily regulates organizational and procedural problems and is not designed to single out and implement basic values. In his view, it is not substantive but formal regulations (like equal protection or due process) that make up the substance of the Constitution: "Our Constitution has always been substantially concerned with preserving liberty. . . . The question . . . is how that concern has been pursued. The principle answers to that . . . are by a quite extensive set of procedural protections, and by a still more elaborate scheme designed to ensure that in the making of substantive choices the decision process will be open to all on something approaching an equal basis, with the decision makers held to a duty to take into account the interests of all those their decisions affect."[42] If the Supreme Court is supposed to oversee adherence to the Constitution, then it must *in the first place* look after the procedures and organizational norms on which the legitimating effect of the democratic process depends. The Court must ensure that the "channels" for the inclusive opinion- and will-formation processes through which a democratic legal community organizes itself remain intact: "unblocking stoppages in the democratic process is what judicial review ought preeminently to be about."[43]

From this perspective, the communicative and participatory rights that are constitutive for democratic opinion- and will-formation acquire a privileged position. The principle of equal treatment is not just violated by the *content* of laws that possibly discriminate against, for example, ethnic or religious minorities, marginal groups, the handicapped, homosexuals, the elderly, youth, and so on. Rather, Ely takes a procedural view of the implicitly unequal classifications of groups that should be treated equally: such inequalities result from a political process whose *democratic procedural conditions* have been violated. Hence abstract judicial review should refer primarily to the conditions for the democratic genesis of laws. More specifically, it must start by examining the communication structures of a public sphere subverted by the power of the mass media; go on to consider the actual chances that divergent and marginal voices will be heard and that formally equal rights of participation will be effectively exercised; and conclude with the equal parliamentary representation of all the currently relevant groups, interest positions, and value orientations. Here it must also refer to the range of issues, arguments and problems, values and interests that find their way into parliamentary deliberation and are considered in the justification of approved norms. Ely gives the liberal mistrust of tyrannical majorities a surprising procedural twist. He is concerned with the de facto limits on a formally recognized pluralism and uses the classical notion of virtual representation to plead for an equal chance at participation on the part of technically represented but actually excluded or marginalized minorities. The *examination of the genesis of a norm* should also extend to the separation between the executive and legislative branches of government. Specifically, it should cover not just the administrative implementation of legal programs but also the improper passivity of a legislature that fails to make full use of its authorized powers and too easily delegates tasks to the administration: "Courts thus should ensure not only that administrators follow those legislative policy directions that do exist . . . but also that such directions are given."[44]

Ely uses this proceduralist understanding of the Constitution to justify "judicial self-restraint." In his view, the Supreme Court can retain its impartiality only if it resists the temptation to fill out its interpretive latitude with moral value judgments. Ely's skepticism is directed as much against value jurisprudence as against an interpretation oriented by principles, in the sense of Dworkin's constructive interpretation. Ely is inconsistent insofar as he must presuppose the validity of principles for his own theory; those procedural and organizational principles that should guide the Court definitely have a normative content. The concept of democratic procedure itself relies on a principle of justice entailing equal respect for all: "The argument is that the basic justice of decision-making institutions must be assessed in terms of whether all affected are treated comfortably with what philosophers call moral universalizability or reciprocity."[45] But from this it certainly does not follow that the principles grounding the legitimating force of democratic organization and procedure are, because of their merely formal nature, in need of supplementation by a substantive theory of rights.[46] Nor does it mean that *other* reasons for taking a skeptical attitude toward judicial activism have thereby lost their force.

Ely is justified in taking a skeptical view of a *paternalistic understanding* of constitutional jurisdiction. This paternalism is fed by a mistrust, widely shared among legal theorists, regarding the irrationality of legislatures that depend largely on power struggles and emotionalized majority opinions. According to this view, a creative jurisdiction of an activist Court would be justified both by its distance from politics and by the superior rationality of its professional discourse: "The methods of reasoning of other branches of government are neither structured by requirements of an articulate consistency in the elaboration of underlying principles nor secured by institutional independence in their impartial exercise."[47] In fact, legal discourses can lay claim to a comparatively high presumption of rationality, because application discourses are specialized for questions of norm application, and can thus be institutionalized within the surveyable framework of the classical distribution of roles between the involved parties and an impartial third party. For the same reasons, however, they cannot *substitute* for political discourses that, geared for the justification of norms and policies, demand the inclusion of all those affected. There is all the more need to clarify the rationality characterizing the political process. The central concept of a procedural justice of political opinion- and will-formation calls for a theory of democracy, something that Ely leaves in the background; insofar as it does appear in his analysis, it bears rather conventional features.

6.3 The Role of the Supreme Court in the Liberal, Republican, and Proceduralist Models

6.3.1

In the United States, constitutional scholars argue about the legitimacy of constitutional adjudication more from the standpoint of political science than from that of legal methodology. In the debate concerning the division of labor between the Supreme Court and the democratic legislature, differences of opinion turn primarily on how one assesses the legislative process and answers the question of how rational the Constitution requires this process to be or, even more to the point, what this rationality could and should consist in at all. In dealing with this question, legal theory also draws on a background of empirical assumptions, but it primarily addresses the normative aspect of the issue, examining how the contentious relation between these two branches of government has been viewed in the American constitutional tradition.

Frank Michelman approaches the task posed by abstract judicial review in a manner similar to Ely. That is, he assumes that when the Supreme Court intervenes in political legislation and rescinds norms passed by Congress, it can claim only a derivative authority coming from the people's right to self-determination. Here the Court should be allowed to resort only to arguments that, within the framework of a procedural understanding of the Constitution, justify an appeal to popular sovereignty as the origin of all authority for making law:

If republican constitutional possibility depends on the genesis of law in the people's ongoing normative contention, it follows that constitutional adjudicators serve that possibility by assisting in the maintenance of jurisgenerative popular engagement. Republican constitutional jurisprudence will to that extent be of the type that Lawrence Tribe calls (and criticizes as) "process-based," recalling Ely's . . . justification of judicial review as "representation reinforcing."[48]

However, the emphatic use of the adjective "republican" reveals a contrast with Ely's understanding of democracy. Michelman relies on the tradition of Aristotelian "politics" that, having come down through Roman philosophy and the political thought of the Italian Renaissance,[49] was framed in modern natural-law terms by Rousseau. Entering the American constitutional discussion via Hobbes's opponent James Harrington, this tradition presented an attractive alternative to Lockean liberalism and partly inspired the Founding Fathers' understanding of democracy.[50] J. G. A. Pocock stylizes this strand of republican thought as a form of civic humanism that, unlike modern natural law, does not draw on a legal vocabulary but on the language of classical ethics and politics.[51]

In the modern period, concepts of Roman law were used to define the *negative liberties* of citizens in order to secure the property and commercial trade of private persons against the interventions of a political authority from whose exercise those persons were excluded. By contrast, the language of ethics and rhetoric preserves the image of a political practice in which the *positive liberties* of equally entitled, participating citizens are realized.[52] The republican concept of "politics" refers not to rights of life, liberty, and property that are possessed by private citizens and guaranteed by the state, but preeminently to the practice of self-determination on the part of enfranchised citizens who are oriented to the common good and understand themselves as free and equal members of a cooperative, self-governing community. Law and legal statute are secondary in comparison to the *ethical* life context of a polis in which the virtue of active participation in public affairs can develop and stabilize. Only in this civic practice can human beings realize the telos of their species.[53] Michelman examines the debates of the writers of the United States Constitution, the text of the Constitution itself,[54] and current constitutional adjudication,[55] in an attempt to decipher traces of this republicanism, from which he wants to develop a normative concept of the political process and its *procedural conditions.* He employs a stylized opposition between the "republican" and the "liberal" paradigms to characterize not only two traditions of constitutional interpretation but also two competing trends in the constitutional reality.

The decisive difference lies in how the role of the democratic process is understood. According to the "liberal" view—here I use the shorthand accepted in the American discussion—the democratic process carries out the task of programming the government in the interest of society, where the government is represented as an apparatus of public administration, society as a system of market and labor relations among private persons. Here politics (in the sense of the citizens' political will-formation) has the function of clustering together and pushing through private interests against an administration specialized in the employment of political power for collective goals. On the republican view, however, politics involves more than just this mediating function; it should be constitutive for the social process as a whole. "Politics" is conceived as the reflexive form of substantial ethical life—as the medium in which the members of more or less naturally emergent solidary communities become aware of their dependence on one another and, acting with full deliberation, further shape and develop existing relations of reciprocal recognition into an association of free and equal citizens. With this, the liberal architectonic of state and society undergoes an important change: in addition to the hierarchical requirements of the state and the decentralized re-quirements of the market—that is, besides administrative power and individual interests—*solidarity* and the orientation to the com-mon good appear as a *third source* of social integration. In fact, this horizontal political will-formation aimed at mutual understanding or communicatively achieved consensus is even supposed to enjoy priority, both in a genetic and a normative sense. An autonomous basis in *civil society*, a basis independent of public administration and private market relations, is a precondition for civic self-deter-mination. This basis preserves political communication from being swallowed up by the state apparatus or assimilated to market structures. In the republican conception, the political public sphere acquires, along with its base in civil society, a strategic significance; it should secure the autonomy and integrating force of the citizens' communicative practices.[56] The uncoupling of political communi-cation from the socioeconomic realm is necessary for the feedback relation that couples administrative power to the communicative power emerging from political opinion- and will-formation. These competing approaches have several consequences for an assess-ment of the political process.

First, the *concepts of citizenship* differ. According to the liberal view, the status of citizens is defined primarily by negative rights against the state and other citizens. As bearers of these rights, citizens enjoy government protection as long as they pursue their private interests within the boundaries set by legal statutes, and this includes protection against government interventions that exceed statutory limits. Political rights have not only the same structure but also the same meaning as private rights that provide a space within which legal subjects are free from external compulsion. They give citizens the opportunity to assert their private interests so that, through elections, through the composition of parliamentary bodies and the selection of Government leaders, these interests finally aggregate into a political will that has an impact on the administration. In this way, citizens can, in the role of voters, supervise the exercise of governmental power so that it responds to the interests of citizens as private persons.[57]

According to the republican view, the status of citizens is not patterned on negative liberties to which these citizens can lay claim *as* private persons. Rather, civil rights—preeminently, rights of political participation and communication—are positive liberties. They guarantee not freedom from external compulsion but the possibility of participating in a common practice through which citizens can first make themselves into what they want to be: politically autonomous authors of a community of free and equal persons. To this extent, the political process does not just serve to keep government activity under the surveillance of citizens who have already acquired a prior social autonomy in the exercise of their private rights and prepolitical liberties. Nor does it function as a hinge between state and society, for administrative power is by no means autochthonous; it is not something given. Rather, governmental authority derives from the power produced communicatively in the civic practice of self-determination, and it finds its legitimation in the fact that it protects this practice by institutionalizing public liberty.[58] The state's "raison d'être" does not lie primarily in the protection of equal private rights but in the guarantee of an inclusive opinion- and will-formation in which free and equal citizens reach an understanding on which goals and norms lie in the equal interest of all. Thus more is required of the republican citizen than just an orientation to individual interest.

Second, the polemic against the classical concept of the legal person as bearer of private rights reveals a controversy about the *concept of law* itself. Whereas in the liberal view the point of a legal order is to make it possible to determine in each case which individuals are entitled to which rights, in the republican view these "subjective" rights owe their existence to an "objective" legal order that both enables and guarantees the integrity of an autonomous life based on mutual respect. In the one approach, the legal order is constructed on the basis of rights held by individual subjects; in the other approach, the objective content of the legal system is given priority. These conceptual dichotomies fail to grasp the intersubjective meaning of a system of rights that citizens mutually accord one another. From the standpoint of discourse theory, the reciprocal observance of rights and duties is grounded in symmetrical relations of recognition. To be sure, republicanism at least comes close to this concept of law, which puts the integrity of the individual and his liberties on a par with the integrity of the community in which individuals are first able to mutually recognize one another both as individuals and as members. Republicanism binds the legitimacy of laws to the democratic procedure governing their genesis, and thus maintains the internal connection between the people's practice of self-determination and the impersonal rule of law:

For republicans rights ultimately are nothing but determinations of the prevailing political will, while for liberals some rights are always grounded in a "higher law" of transpolitical reason or revelation. . . . In a republican view, a community's objective, the common good, substantially consists in the success of its political endeavor to define, establish, effectuate and sustain the set of rights (less tendentiously laws) best suited to the conditions and mores of that community, whereas in a contrasting liberal view the higher-law rights provide the transcendental structures and the curbs on power required so that pluralistic pursuit of diverse and conflicting interests may proceed as satisfactorily as possible.[59]

The right to vote, interpreted as a positive liberty, becomes the paradigm for rights in general not just because it is constitutive for political self-determination but because its structure allows one to see how inclusion in a community of equal members is connected with the individual entitlement to make autonomous contributions and take positions of one's own:

The claim is that we all take an interest in each other's enfranchisement, because (i) our choice lies between hanging together and hanging separately; (ii) hanging together depends on reciprocal assurance to all of having one's vital interests heeded by others; and (iii) in the deeply pluralized conditions of contemporary American society, such assurances are attainable . . . only by maintaining at least the semblance of a politics in which everyone is conceded a voice.[60]

Through the legislative process constituted by political rights, this structure communicates itself to *all* rights. Even when private law empowers one to pursue private, freely chosen goals, it simultaneously obligates one to stay within those boundaries of strategic action that have been agreed on in the equal interest of all.

Third, the different ways of conceptualizing citizenship and law express a deeper disagreement about the *nature of the political process*. In the liberal view, politics is essentially a struggle for positions that put one in control of administrative power. The political process of opinion- and will-formation in the public sphere and in parliament is determined by the competition of strategically acting groups to retain or acquire positions of power. Success is measured by the citizens' approval, quantified as votes, of persons and programs. In their choices at the polls, voters express their preferences. Their voting decisions have the same structure as the acts of choice made by market participants. They license access to the positions of power that political parties fight over with the same orientation to individual success. The voting input and the power output correspond to the same model of strategic action:

By contrast with deliberation, strategic interaction aims at coordination rather than cooperation. In the last analysis, it asks people to consider no one's interest but their own. Its medium is bargain, not argument. Its tools of persuasion are not claims and reasons but conditional offers of service and forbearance. Whether formally embodied in a vote or in contract, or just informally carried out in social behaviors, a strategic outcome represents not a collective judgement of reason but a vector sum in a field of forces.[61]

According to the republican view, the political opinion- and will-formation occurring in the public sphere and in parliament is governed not by market structures but by the obstinate structures of public communication oriented to mutual understanding. As a practice of civic self-legislation, politics finds its paradigm not in the market but in dialogue:

A dialogic conception envisions—or perhaps one ought to say it ideal-izes—politics as a normative activity. It imagines politics as contestation over questions of value and not simply questions of preference. It envisions politics as a process of reason not just of will, of persuasion not just of power, directed toward agreement regarding a good or just, or at any rate acceptable, way to order those aspects of life that involve people's social relations and social natures.[62]

From this point of view, there is a structural difference between the communicative power that political communication brings forth in the shape of discursively formed majority opinions and the administrative power available to the government apparatus. The parties, too, which struggle over access to positions of administra-tive power, must get involved in the deliberative style and internal logic of political discourses: "Deliberation . . . refers to a certain attitude toward social cooperation, namely, that of openness to persuasion by reasons referring to the claims of others as well as one's own. The deliberative medium is a good faith exchange of views—including participant's reports of their own understanding of their respective vital interests— . . . in which a vote, if any vote is taken, represents a pooling of judgements."[63] Hence the conflict of opinions carried out in the political arena does not have legitimat-ing force merely for the choice of political leaders, in the sense of simply authorizing access to positions of power. Rather, ongoing political discourse should shape policies; it should have binding force for the ways in which political authority is exercised. Admin-istrative power can be legitimately employed only on the basis of policies, and within the boundaries of laws, that issue from the democratic process.

Fourth, and finally, the republican understanding of politics yields a more precise definition of the *procedural conditions* that confer legitimating force on institutionalized opinion- and will-formation. These are precisely the conditions under which the political process can be presumed to generate reasonable out-comes. If represented by the liberal model of market competition, a contest of power is determined by the rational choice of optimal strategies. Given an indissoluble pluralism of prepolitical values and interests that are at best *aggregated* with equal weight in the political process, politics loses all reference to the normative core of a public use of practical reason. The republican confidence in the force of political discourses stands in contrast to this liberal skepticism about reason. Such discourses are supposed to allow participants to discuss value orientations and interpretations of needs and wants, including their prepolitical self-understandings and worldviews, and then to change these *in an insightful way.* Under discursive conditions that encourage each to adopt the perspectives of the other members or even of all other persons, rationally motivated changes in one's initial views are possible. As participants in such a discursive process of opinion- and will-formation, citizens exercise their right to political self-legislation:

Given plurality, a political process can validate a societal norm as self-given law only if (i) participation in the process results in some shift or adjustment in relevant understandings on the part of some (or all) participants, and (ii) there exists a set of prescriptive social and procedural conditions such that one's undergoing, under those conditions, such a dialogic modulation of one's understandings is not considered or experienced as coercive, or invasive, or otherwise a violation of one's identity or freedom, and (iii) those conditions actually prevailed in the process supposed to be jurisgenerative.[64]

6.3.2

If we return to the question concerning the legitimacy of constitutional review with a heightened "republican" sense for the deliberative components of the legislative process, then we can render Ely's proceduralist proposal more specific. The republican understanding of politics reminds us that the system of rights is internally related to citizens' political autonomy. From this perspective, the constitutional court must work within the limits of its authority to ensure that the process of lawmaking takes place under the legitimating conditions of *deliberative politics.* The latter is in turn bound to the demanding communicative presuppositions of political arenas that do not coincide with the institutionalized will-formation in parliamentary bodies, but rather include the political public sphere as well as its cultural context and social basis. A deliberative practice of self-legislation can develop only in the interplay between, on the one hand, the parliamentary will-formation institutionalized in legal procedures and programmed to reach decisions and, on the other, political opinion-formation along informal channels of political communication. Relevant initiatives, issues and contributions, problems and proposals come more from the *margins* than from the established center of the spectrum of opinions. "So the suggestion is that the pursuit of political freedom through law depends on 'our' [the Supreme Court's] constant reach for inclusion of the other, of the hitherto excluded—which in practice means bringing to legal-doctrinal presence the hitherto absent voices of emergently self-conscious social groups."[65]

The deliberative mode of legislation and a strict dependence of administrative activity on statutory guidelines are threatened just as much by autonomous and self-programming bureaucracies as by the privileged influence exerted by formally private social organizations. In the United States, however, the influence of *interest groups* that implement their private aims through the government apparatus at the cost of the general interest is considered the real problem, at least since the famous discussion between the Federalists and the Antifederalists. In this classical stance against the tyranny of societal powers that violate the principle of the separation of state and society, rejuvenated republicanism, too, conceives the role of the constitutional court as that of a custodian of deliberative democracy:

The American constitutional regime is built on hostility to measures that impose burdens or grant benefits merely because of the political power of private groups; some public value is required for governmental action. This norm . . . . suggests, for example, that statutes that embody mere interest-group deals should be narrowly construed. It also suggests that courts should develop interpretive strategies to promote deliberation in government—by, for example, remanding issues involving constitutionally sensitive interests or groups for reconsideration by the legislature or by regulatory agencies when deliberation appears to have been absent.[66]

Sunstein discusses some of the consequences that this guardian role has for deliberative politics. He starts with review proceedings in which the Supreme Court rejected statutes for their "discriminating classifications" on the grounds that the legislature omitted a "reasonable analysis" of the material in need of regulation. Generalizing from these cases, Sunstein arrives at a "reasoned analysis requirement" geared to the discursive mode of the legislative process: "What emerges is a jurisprudence that inspects legislation to determine whether representatives have attempted to act deliberatively."[67] The standard of judgment is the discursive character of opinion- and will-formation, in particular the question whether the legislative decision turned on reasons that can be publicly advocated or on private interests that cannot be declared in the framework of parliamentary negotiations: "One of the distinctive features of this approach is that the outcome of the legislative process becomes secondary. What is important is whether it is deliberation—undistorted by private power—that gave rise to that outcome."[68] This approach has the advantage that the Court, which does not have control over the justifying political reasons, does not have to refer to hypothetically ascribed reasons but can rely on the reasons that were actually brought forth. If one should object that retrospectively attributed or conjectured reasons should also suffice to justify a statute when the legislature's decisions were actually determined by illegitimate social pressure, then Sunstein has a convincing reply: for the citizens themselves, it makes a difference, in normative terms, whether the legitimate policies and goals that may require them to accept disadvantages are the outcome of a legitimating, deliberative process or whether, on the contrary, they merely emerge as side effects of programs and processes motivated by other, private concerns unfit for the purposes of public justification.

The republican understanding of politics yields a more ambiguous answer to the question of how aggressively the constitutional court may encroach on legislative powers. According to Sunstein's observations, the Supreme Court brings the "reasoned analysis requirement" to bear more strictly on disputed administrative measures than on legislative decisions. This restraint is justified if the rationality check refers not to the mode of the justification process but to substantive reasons that are exposed as rhetorical pretense. The Court may not arrogate to itself the role of an ideology critic vis-à-vis the political legislature; it is exposed to the same suspicion of ideology and cannot claim for itself any neutral place outside the political process. Interestingly enough, though, republicanism does not present itself as an advocate for judicial self-restraint, contrary to what its radical-democratic inspiration might lead one to expect. Rather, it pleads for judicial activism insofar as constitutional adjudication is supposed to compensate for the gap separating the republican ideal from constitutional reality. As long as deliberative politics is rejuvenated in the spirit of Aristotelian politics, this idea will depend on the virtues of citizens oriented to the common good. And this expectation of virtue pushes the democratic process, as it actually proceeds in welfare-state mass democracies, into the pallid light of an instrumentally distorted politics, a "fallen" politics.

In a different but nonetheless analogous context, Bruce Ackerman has reacted to this external tension between facticity and validity by bringing in the Supreme Court as a mediator between the ideal and the real. Ackerman makes the interesting proposal that we conceive the ups and downs of political innovation along the lines of Thomas Kuhn's model of scientific development. Just as the "normal" business of science is interrupted only in rare moments by "revolutions" that bring new paradigms on the scene, so also is politics normally the business of managers and bureaucrats whose behavior matches the liberal description of strategic market competition steered by personal interests. Only when history overheats, in "moments of constitutional excitement," do "the People" step forth from their normal civil privatism, appropriate the politics that has been bureaucratically estranged from them, and temporarily supply an unanticipated legitimacy to far-reaching innovations (as happened, for example, in the New Deal era).[69] This vitalistic reading of democratic self-determination sets the will of the people, usually slumbering through long latency periods, in opposition to the institutionalized legislation of their elected representatives. During those long intervals, the Supreme Court is supposed to act as a custodian of a currently frozen practice of self-determination locked into the routines of parliamentary business. According to Ackerman, the Court is supposed to exercise the people's right to self-determination *in a vicarious manner.* "The Court at the last appears not as representative of the People's declared will but as representation and trace of the People's absent self-government."[70] The constitutional court thus assumes the role of republican guardian of positive liberties that the citizens themselves, as *nominal* bearers of these liberties, fail to exercise. It thereby slips back, however, into just the paternalistic role that Ely strives to resist with his proceduralist understanding of the Constitution. Even Michelman, who shrinks from a constitutional-court paternalism, bridges the gap between ideal and real in a similar way: "The Court helps protect the republican state—that is, the citizens politically engaged—from lapsing into a politics of self-denial. It challenges the 'people's' self-enclosing tendency to assume their own moral completion as they now are and thus to deny to themselves the plurality on which their capacity for transformative self-renewal depends."[71]

In my opinion, it is the *exceptionalistic description* of political practice—how it really ought to be—that suggests the necessity of a pedagogical guardian or regent; the latter must exercise its regency only as long as the sovereign prefers to keep to the private realm rather than occupy the place he has inherited, the political public sphere, and appropriately fulfill its duties. The exceptionalist image of what politics should be is suggested by a republican tradition that binds the citizens' political practice to the ethos of an already integrated community. Only virtuous citizens can do politics in the right way. This *expectation of virtue* already led Rousseau to split off the citizen, who is oriented to the common good, from the private man, who would be overburdened by such ethical-political demands. The unanimity of the political legislature was supposed to be secured in advance by a substantial consensus not so much of minds as of hearts: "For Rousseau, the basis of legitimacy lies not in the free individual capable of making up his mind by weighing reasons, but rather in the individual whose will is already entirely determined, one who has made his choice."[72]

An interpretation along the lines of discourse theory, by contrast, insists on the fact that democratic will-formation does not draw its legitimating force from the prior convergence of settled ethical convictions. Rather, the source of legitimacy includes, on the one hand, the communicative presuppositions that allow the better arguments to come into play in various forms of deliberation and, on the other, procedures that secure fair bargaining conditions. Discourse theory breaks with an ethical conception of civic autonomy, and thus it does not have to reserve the mode of deliberative politics to exceptional conditions. Moreover, a constitutional court guided by a proceduralist understanding of the constitution does not have to overdraw on its legitimation credit. It can stay within its authority to apply the law—an authority clearly defined in terms of the logic of argumentation—provided that the democratic process over which it is supposed to keep watch is not described as a state of exception.

The exceptional features of the normatively privileged democratic process stem from the fact that Michelman, like other "communitarians," understands citizenship not primarily in *legal* but in *ethical terms*. According to this classical view,[73] in the political public sphere, citizens join together in seeking what is best for them as members of a particular collectivity at a given point in time. Michelman draws on the language of romanticism when he translates this striving for the collective good into the hermeneutic appropriation of "constitutive traditions." According to this view, it is only the ascribed membership in an intersubjectively shared form of life and the conscious appropriation of antecedent traditions that explain why citizens are able to achieve any consensus at all about how to solve problems on the agenda—and about what standards should define the "best" solution in each case: "Persuasive arguments and discussions seem inconceivable without conscious reference by those involved to their mutual and reciprocal awareness of being co-participants not just of this one debate, but in a more encompassing common life, bearing the imprint of a common past, within and from which the arguments and claims arise and draw their meaning."[74] Of course, the ethical particularism characteristic of an unproblematic background consensus does not sit well with the conditions of cultural and societal pluralism that distinguish modern societies.

6.3.3

We cannot carry on the discussion of the Supreme Court's activism or self-restraint in abstracto. If one understands the constitution as an interpretation and elaboration of a system of rights in which private and public autonomy are internally related (and must be simultaneously enhanced), then a rather bold constitutional adjudication is even required in cases that concern the implementation of democratic procedure and the deliberative form of political opinion-and will-formation. To be sure, we have to free the concept of deliberative politics from overly strenuous connotations that would put the constitutional court under permanent pressure to act. The court may not assume the role of a regent who takes the place of an underage successor to the throne. Under the critical gaze of a robust legal public sphere—a citizenry that has grown to become a "community of constitutional interpreters"[75]—the constitutional court can at best play the role of a tutor. There is no need to idealize this role, as self-assured constitutional scholars have done, unless one is seeking a trustee for an idealistically depicted political process. This temptation seems to follow from an *ethical constriction of political discourses* that is often but by no means necessarily linked with the concept of deliberative politics. This equating of political deliberation with processes of collective self-understanding is neither sound argumentation theory nor necessary for defending an intersubjective approach.

According to the communitarian view, there is a necessary connection between the deliberative concept of democracy and the reference to a concrete, substantively integrated ethical community. Otherwise, one supposedly cannot explain how the citizens' orientation to the common good is at all possible.[76] The individual, so the argument goes, can become aware of his membership in a collective form of life, and therewith become aware of a prior social bond not at his disposition, only in a practice exercised with others in common: "Actual participation in political action, deliberation and conflict may make us aware of our more remote and indirect connections with others, the long-range and large-scale significance of what we want and are doing."[77] In this view, the individual can get a clear sense of commonalities and differences, and hence a sense of who he is and would like to be, only in the public exchange with others who owe their identities to the same traditions and similar socialization processes. In this collective effort to achieve self-understanding, a motive for overcoming egoism and self-interest is also at work, namely, the experience that the exclusion and suppression of the few results in the alienation of all, the experience of a "causality of fate" that makes each person feel the harm of being isolated from an unavoidably shared context of communication. Hence, on the communitarian view, the only genuinely political discourses are those that have collective self-understanding as their goal.

These and similar arguments come together in the ethical interpretation of political discourse. Like Perry, Michelman conceives genuine politics as a meditation on the exceptional act of founding the constitution—and as the affirmative retrieval of this founding act. This saving *anamnesis* makes it necessary to refer to the ethical substance of one's own historical community: "The first requirement is . . . that it make sense of the centrality and constancy in American constitutional practice of the remembrance of its origins in public acts of deliberate creation; for that remembrance both deeply reflects and deeply informs American understanding of what it means for a people to be both self-governing and under law."[78] Thus Michelman models politics in general on the symbolic politics expressed, say, in bicentennial celebrations of the Declaration of Independence. He thereby accepts the gap between these ceremonial acts, essential for the political integration of a nation of citizens, and the business of everyday political life. The tension between facticity and validity, a tension that was supposed to be stabilized within the legal medium itself, once again reappears between the ideal of an ethical republic and the harsh reality of routine politics. The form of ethical-political argumentation is all that remains as the narrow bridge between originary and "fallen" politics. Where political will-formation is presented as ethical discourse, political discourse must be conducted *always* with the aim of discovering, at a given point in time and within the horizon of shared ways of life and traditions, what is best for citizens as members of a concrete community. Robert Beiner succinctly summarizes this assimilation of political judgment to the achievement of ethical self-understanding:

All political judgments are—implicitly at least—judgments about the form of collective life that is desirable for us to pursue within a given context of possibilities. The commonality of the judging subjects is internal to, or constitutive of, the judgment, not merely contingent or external to it. . . . This follows from the object of deliberation, which is directed to the very form of our relating together. . . . I can express this no better than by saying that what is at issue here is not "what should I do?" or "how should I conduct myself?" but "how are we to *be* together, and what is to be the institutional setting for that being-together?"[79]

However, this assimilation of political discourses to the clarification of collective identity does not sit well with the function of the legislative process that issues from such discourses. Legal statutes certainly contain teleological elements, but these involve more than just the hermeneutic explication of shared value orientations. By their very structure, laws are defined by the question of which norms citizens want to adopt for regulating their common life. To be sure, discourses aimed at achieving self-understanding are *also* an important component of politics. In such discourses, the participants want to get a clear understanding of themselves as members of a specific nation, as members of a local community, as inhabitants of a region, and so on; they want to determine which traditions they will continue; they strive to determine how they will treat one another and how they will treat minorities and marginal groups; in short, participants in such discourses (or in identity politics) hope to become clear about the kind of society in which they want to live. But as we have seen, these questions are subordinate to moral questions and connected with pragmatic questions. The question that has *priority* in legislative politics is how a matter can be regulated in the equal interest of all. The making of norms is primarily a justice issue, subject to principles that state what is equally good for all. Unlike ethical questions, questions of justice are not inherently related to a specific collectivity and its form of life. The law of a concrete legal community must, if it is to be legitimate, at least be compatible with moral standards that claim universal validity beyond the legal community.

Compromises make up the bulk of political decision-making processes in any case. Under conditions of cultural and societal pluralism, politically relevant goals often embody interests and value orientations that are by no means constitutive for the identity of the community at large, and hence are not constitutive for the whole of an intersubjectively shared form of life. The interests and values that conflict with one another without prospects for consensus must be balanced in a way that cannot be achieved through ethical discourses—even if the results of bargaining are subject to the proviso that they not violate a culture's consensus on basic values. The required balance of competing interests comes about as a compromise between parties that may rely on power and mutual threats. Legitimate bargaining certainly depends on the prior stipulation of fair terms, and it presupposes a willingness to cooperate, that is, to observe the rules of the game so as to arrive at results acceptable for all parties on the basis of their different preferences. Moreover, the debate over such regulations should take place according to the forms of rational discourse that neutralize power. Bargaining itself, however, may well allow for strategic interactions.

Furthermore, the deliberative mode of legislative practice is not intended simply to ensure the ethical validity of statutes. Rather, one can understand the complex validity claim of legal norms as the claim, on the one hand, to take into consideration strategically asserted particular interests in a manner compatible with the common good and, on the other hand, to bring universalistic principles of justice into the horizon of a specific form of life imbued with particular value constellations. By acquiring a binding character for a specific legal community, these principles of a "locationless" transcultural morality also take up abode in those abstract systems of action that can no longer be sufficiently integrated simply through the informal contexts of communicative action. In contrast to the ethical constriction of political discourse, the concept of deliberative politics acquires an empirical reference only when we take account of the *variety* of communicative forms, arguments, and institutionalized legal procedures.

We have already seen how legal adjudication unwraps, for the purposes of application, these variegated arguments that have already entered into the lawmaking process and provided a rational basis for the legitimacy claims of established law. In these legal discourses, moral and ethical, empirical and pragmatic reasons come into play besides doctrinal considerations immanent to law. If one looks at the democratic genesis of law from the other side— that is, from the side of legislation—one can again see the various aspects under which the syndrome of deliberative politics can be resolved, clarified, and differentiated. In legislative politics, the supply of information and purposive-rational choice of means are interwoven with the balance of interests and compromise formation; with the achievement of ethical self-understanding and preference formation; and with moral justification and tests of legal coherence. In this way, the two types of politics Michelman had opposed in a polarizing fashion rationally *interpenetrate* one another. Unlike Michelman, therefore, Sunstein draws on the origins of the American constitutional tradition to reconstruct not two different strands that display an opposition between the republican and the liberal models but an integrated concept that he calls "Madisonian Republicanism."

This concept is strong enough to ground the deliberative mode of the legislative process as a necessary condition of legitimate lawmaking, but weak enough not to lose touch with empirical theories:

There are numerous theories about legislative decisionmaking. One theory suggests that a considerable amount of legislative behavior can be explained if one assumes that members of Congress seek single-mindedly the goal of reelection. Another approach indicates that three primary considerations—achieving influence within the legislature, promoting public policy, and obtaining reelection—have more explanatory power than any single-factored approach. In the economic literature, there have been efforts to explain legislative behavior solely by reference to constituent pressures. Such interpretations have been attacked as too reductionistic.

What emerges is a continuum. At one pole are cases in which interest-group pressures are largely determinative and statutory enactments can be regarded as "deals" among contending interests. At the other pole lie cases where legislators engage in deliberation in which interest-group pressures, conventionally defined, play little or no role. At various points along the continuum a great range of legislative decisions exist where the outcomes are dependent on an amalgam of pressure, deliberation, and other factors. No simple test can distinguish cases falling at different points on the continuum.[80]

Sunstein sketches a realistic but somewhat flat picture of legislative politics. Although there is no "simple test," we can at least break up and structure the empirical continuum. Discourse theory provides conceptual tools that allow us both to analyze the observable communication flows according to the different issues and to reconstruct them in terms of the corresponding forms of communication. On a surface level, it is not easy to make out the different depth grammars that distinguish the pragmatic, ethical, and moral uses of reason, but this does not mean that the forms of politics that Michelman opposes as ideal types are in fact *indistinguishably* fused. Moreover, the rational reconstruction of a given sequence of communication with discourse-theoretic means allows one to identify deviations that have their source in effects of social and administrative power that cannot be publicly advocated.

At the same time, the necessary differentiation between politics and ethics, which republicanism fails to make sufficiently clear, does not pose any danger for the intersubjective understanding of law and politics. True, only to the extent that deliberative politics proceeds as an ethical discourse writ large does it retain its internal linkages with the received traditions of a specific historical community. Only as a process of achieving ethical self-understanding does politics generate an awareness of that bond of substantial ethical life holding the citizens together as they engage in their debates. However, because political discourses include a large portion of bargaining on the one side and the moral universalization of interests on the other, democratic procedure can no longer draw its legitimating force from any *prior* agreement provided by the political ethos of a particular community. The democratic procedure must instead look for an independent justification. This calls the communitarian reading of the republican tradition into question without touching the intersubjective core of its notion of politics. Michelman fears that once legislative politics loses its relation to a particular community and therewith the possibility of resorting to common traditions, one can save its normative sense only by referring to the "transcendent authority" of reason.[81] In fact, however, a consistent proceduralist understanding of the constitution relies on the intrinsically rational character of a democratic process that grounds the presumption of rational outcomes. Under this description, reason is embodied solely in the formal-pragmatic conditions that facilitate deliberative politics, so that we need not confront reason as an alien authority residing somewhere beyond political communication.

Our differentiated model of discourse, though more abstract than the communitarian account of dialogue, preserves quite well the individual's embeddedness in the intersubjectivity of a prior *structure* of possible mutual understanding. At the same time, the reference to an ideal audience or an ideally inclusive community extending beyond the traditional contours of any particular community encourages participants to take yes/no positions that are free from the prejudicial power of the contingent language games and particular forms of life into which they have been socialized in a merely conventional way. The discourse theory of deliberative politics introduces a *context-transcending* moment that, however, once again elicits empirical doubts: "The first criticism," Sunstein objects to himself, "would suggest that it is utopian to believe that representatives can be forced into the Madisonian model."[82] From the normative vantage point of legal theory, he can answer this objection. It is only from the different perspective afforded by a theory of democracy, however, that empirically motivated doubts develop their full force against a discourse concept of deliberative politics.

Deliberative Politics: A Procedural Concept of Democracy

The question about the conditions of a legitimating genesis of law has turned the spotlight on legislative politics, which is one part of the broad spectrum of political processes. Taking the perspective of legal theory, I have described legislative politics as a process that includes several different forms of argumentation as well as bargaining. In the demanding conditions of fair procedure and the presuppositions of communication that undergird legitimate lawmaking, the reason that posits and tests norms has assumed a procedural form. At present it is unclear how this procedural concept, so freighted with idealizations, can link up with empirical investigations that conceive politics primarily as an arena of power processes. Such investigations analyze the political sphere in terms of strategic interactions governed by interests or in terms of systemic functioning. As I understand it, this question does not imply an *opposition* between the ideal and the real, for the normative content I initially set forth for reconstructive purposes is partially inscribed in the social facticity of observable political processes. A reconstructive sociology of democracy must therefore choose its basic concepts in such a way that it can identify particles and fragments of an "existing reason" already incorporated in political practices, however distorted these may be. This approach does not need a philosophy of history to support it. It is premised simply on the idea that one cannot adequately describe the operation of a constitutionally organized political system, even at an empirical level, without referring to the validity dimension of law and the legitimating force of the democratic genesis of law.

Thus far we have taken the perspective of legal theory and pursued a tension, inhabiting the law itself, between facticity and validity. In what follows, our theme will be the *external* relation between facticity and validity, namely, the tension between the normative self-understanding of the constitutional state, as explained in discourse-theoretic terms, and the social facticity of the political processes that run their course along more or less constitutional lines. This brings us back to social theory, the dominant approach in the first two chapters. It was already clear from the internal perspective of legal theory that the system of rights takes shape in historical constitutions and is implemented in various institutions. Rather than dwell on these two levels—comparative constitutional law and the political science of institutions—I will seek out a direct transition from normative models of democracy to sociological theories of democracy. Thus far we have dealt with the generation, allocation, and exercise of political power in terms of the normative considerations that govern the constitutional state and its organization. In that context, the key question is how communicative power ought to be related to administrative and social power. Political sociology examines this same phenomenon from a different perspective.

Before going into "realist" theories of democracy in the next chapter, I would like to prepare the necessary change in perspective step by step. First I argue against a reductionist concept of democracy that eliminates the element of democratic legitimacy from power and law (sec. 7.1). After comparing different substantive models of democracy, I develop a procedural concept of democratic process. This concept, which breaks with a holistic model of society centered in the state, claims to be neutral with respect to competing worldviews and forms of life (sec. 7.2). Finally, I pursue Robert Dahl's attempt at a sociological translation and empirical testing of the procedural understanding of democracy. Here my goal is to clarify what it means to "confront" the idea of the self-organization of freely associated citizens with the reality of highly complex societies (sec. 7.3).

7.1 Normative versus Empiricist Models of Democracy

I begin by assuming that the conceptual relation between political power and law becomes empirically relevant through the conceptually unavoidable pragmatic presuppositions of legitimate lawmaking and through the institutionalization of a corresponding practice of self-governance by citizens. This assumption might be tendentious, because it excludes an empiricist approach from the start. Empiricism purges the concept of power of just that normative authority it gains through its internal connection with legitimate law. Empiricist theories of power, whether conceived at an action level or a systems level, do not ignore the normative character that permeates the legal forms for the exercise of political power, but they do reduce the latter to social power. According to one reading, "social power" expresses itself in the ability to prevail of superior interests that can be pursued more or less rationally; "political power" can then be conceived as a more-abstract and permanent form of social power that licenses access to "administrative power," that is, to various government offices. When one takes the empiricist's observer perspective, one uses *different* terms than one would from the participant perspective to describe both the claim to legitimacy expressed by the legal form of political power, as well as the need for legitimation that requires recourse to specific standards of validity: the conditions for the acceptability of law and political authority are transformed into conditions of actual acceptance, while conditions of legitimacy become conditions for the stability of a generally held belief in the government's legitimacy. As we will see, an analysis conducted with these or similar conceptual instruments allows one to subject the normative self-understanding of constitutional democracy to a rather illuminating critique.[1]

However, it is an entirely different undertaking when a theory of democracy with normative intentions merely *borrows* the objectivating view and empiricist strategy from the social sciences. This cryptonormative approach aims to demonstrate that democratic practices can be legitimated from the perspective of the participants themselves in terms of descriptive empiricist categories. Starting with the assumption that the normative validity claims of politics and law lack a cognitive meaning, such a theory attempts to explain how the individual interests of elites and citizens could nevertheless provide them with good reasons for making their contribution to the normatively demanded legitimation game of liberal mass democracies. If such a model of democracy could be justified, then our question concerning the external relation between facticity and validity would, quite elegantly, become pointless. One would no longer need to take the normative substance of the constitutional state at face value.

In section 7.1.1, I will first examine the consistency of Werner Becker's proposal for an empiricist justification of the democratic rules of the game. The unsatisfactory result will force us back to the three normative models of democracy that we have already encountered (sec. 7.1.2).

7.1.1

Becker avails himself of empiricist materials in building a normative theory of democracy, that is, one designed for purposes of justification. Just as power in general is displayed in the empirical superiority of the stronger interest or will, so also political power is displayed in the sheer stability of a political order. Legitimacy is considered a measure for stability, for the legitimacy of the state is objectively measured by de facto recognition on the part of the governed. Such legitimacy can range from mere toleration to free consent (*Zustimmung*). Here the consent that creates legitimacy is based on subjective reasons that claim to be valid inside the currently accepted "ideological frame"; but these reasons resist objective assessment. One legitimation is as good as another, so long as it sufficiently contributes to stabilizing a given political order. According to this view, even a dictatorship must be considered legitimate so long as a socially recognized framework of legitimation enables the government to remain stable. From this perspective of the theory of power, the quality of the reasons are without empirical significance: "It is an illusion of liberals and democrats to think that dictatorships can only survive under the 'protection of the bayonet.'"[2]

Becker then introduces the concept of democracy through the rules governing universal and equal suffrage, party competition, and majority rule. Of course, in the background lies an empiricist understanding of social norms, according to which the "validity" of norms only signifies their connection with sanctions effective for stability. As a result, Becker cannot define his task as that of *normatively* justifying this arrangement. Rather, his theory only aims to demonstrate that even if the participants describe themselves in empiricist categories, they can have good reasons for adhering to the rules of the game for mass democracy. This explains, in the first place, the observance of these norms by the parties that hold power: "The party in power never seeks to restrict the political activity of the citizens or parties as long as they do not attempt to overthrow the regime by violence." Correspondingly, the losers keep their peace: "The parties that lost the election never resort to violence or other illegal means to prevent the victorious party from assuming office."[3] Under these conditions, a peaceful transfer of power is secured.

Becker's justification can be reconstructed as a sequence of three steps, each of which has two parts. In each case, the first half step is an objective explanation, whereas the second consists in the attempt to translate this explanation from the observer perspective into a rational-choice explanation *for the participants themselves*. The argument aims to reach that "indifference point" where the objective explanation can also be accepted as a sufficient explanation from the participant perspective.

(a) In a pluralist democracy, legitimacy stems from a majority vote reached in elections that are free, equal, and secret. This idea is supposed to acquire its plausibility from a specifically modern worldview and self-understanding, which are grounded in what Becker calls "ethical subjectivism." On the one hand, ethical subjectivism secularizes the Judeo-Christian understanding of the equality of each individual before God and assumes the fundamental equality of all individuals. On the other hand, it replaces the transcendent origin of obligatory commands with an immanent validity; that is, it considers the validity of norms to be anchored solely in the subject's own will. In the empiricist reading, the modern understanding of freedom means, among other things, that "the validity of . . . the norms accepted by the individual human being is generated by the individual himself through his free consent."[4] The individuals themselves are the ones who deliberately produce normative validity through a free act of consent. This voluntaristic understanding of validity corresponds to a positivist view of law: law includes everything that a duly chosen political lawgiver posits as law, and only that. This view agrees with critical rationalism, in the sense that modern convictions are not rationally justified in any sense but rather express a decision or a cultural shaping that in fact has become dominant.[5]

If participating citizens want to make this explanation their own, then they are at first tempted to look for ways of grounding ethical subjectivism. They might seek this grounding in human rights, or they might look to a deontological elucidation of the moral point of view, according to which the only valid norms are those that *all* could will. But empiricism teaches them that such rationalistic escapes would lead them away from the specific insight into the irreducible contingency of what they consider normatively valid. However, precisely this awareness of contingency renders the proffered objective explanation unsatisfactory for the participants in the democratic process. They need at least a purposive-rational explanation for why the norms passed by the majority should be accepted as valid by the outvoted minority.

(b) On voluntaristic premises, the validity claim raised by majority decisions cannot be grounded by appealing to the common good, forecasts of collective utility, or practical reason, for each of these would require objective standards. Instead, Becker explains the acceptance of majority rule in terms of a domesticated struggle for power. If one presupposes, with ethical subjectivism, that each individual has equal power, then a majority of votes is an impressive numerical expression of superior strength: "If one views the matter this way, then this justification of democratic procedures is based on . . . the threat of the majority to revoke the agreement to renounce violence, when things do not go according to its will. . . . According to this view, democracy means nothing other than that one part of the people rules the other part for a set time."[6] If one considers how a threat on the part of the numerically and at least symbolically stronger party can, against the background of the latent danger of a civil war, have an intimidating effect, then temporally limited majority rule seems to recommend itself as an "acceptable solution of the power question" for the minority as well.

This Hobbesian interpretation of majority rule can also gain a certain plausibility from the participant perspective if the goal of domesticating violent disputes has priority for all. Nonetheless, the explanation remains unsatisfactory for the participants in the democratic process as long as it remains unclear how minorities can be protected from the tyranny of the majority, even a peaceful tyranny. In addition, it must be guaranteed that the disputing parties will in fact submit to majority rule.

(c) In order to protect minorities, Becker has recourse to the classical basic liberties. Majority approval for such guarantees of minority interests is explained by the current majority's fear of becoming a minority itself. This by itself should preclude the danger that tyrannical majorities could become permanent, because both the majority, with its anxiety over the loss of its power, and the minority, with its prospects for a change in power, should be motivated to observe the established rules of the game. The conditions for a transfer of power between incumbents and opposition can now be satisfied in that the competing elites split the electorate into several camps according to ideological standpoints. In doing this, the elites aim to win majorities by programmatic means—as a rule, with promises of social rewards interpreted in particular ways. Thus the process of gaining legitimation boils down to an interplay between "ideologicopolitical" and "sociopolitical" means. This interplay is partly explained by the fact that the satisfaction of societal interests by distributive measures is, in the final analysis, not something objective but rather requires a convincing interpretation.

However, this explanation of the protection of minorities and the transfer of power is tailored entirely to the interest positions of elites concerned with acquiring and maintaining power. But what these elites consider plausible will not necessarily convince the citizens. The public of citizens will hardly be moved to take part in the democratic process, or at least to tolerate it benevolently, as long as this public can be viewed only as the ideological plunder of competing parties. This public wants to be *convinced* that the one party offers the prospect of better policies than does the other party; there must be good reasons for preferring one party to the other. Here one finally reaches the point where something that looks plausible from the observer perspective can no longer be translated into an argument that looks plausible to participants in the same way. The attempt at such a translation leads, under empiricist premises, to contradictions.

(d) From the objectivating viewpoint of the empiricist model, the struggle of parties for political power lacks a validity dimension. Becker does not cease to reiterate the point that political arguments are exhausted by their *rhetorical* functions. Political arguments are intended not to be rationally acceptable but to be perlocutionarily effective: "In democracy it is not a question of ascertaining the 'objective truth' of political policies. It is rather a matter of establishing conditions for the democratic acceptability of the goals that the parties pursue. To this extent, the function of political arguments is . . . more that of advertising, or 'weapons' that circumvent the use of physical force, than that of assertions one could interpret as providing support for 'true' theories."[7] The normatively laden but vague terms of political debate have rather an emotional significance: they are intended to create mass commitments. Accordingly, political speech has "a social-psychological, not a cognitive, function."[8]

Becker must explain why citizens, and not just the elites, see through the emotional meaning of pseudoargumentative advertising—and nonetheless accept it. It is assumed that the empiricist self-description does not have deleterious effects on their motivation to participate, because enlightened citizens already have a no-nonsense view of the political process as compromise formation. But even compromises must be grounded, and what grounds the acceptance of compromises? On the one hand, there are no normative standards by which the fairness of compromises could be assessed. Social justice, for instance, is relegated to the sphere of public-relations rhetoric: "In the political reality of liberal democracies this [i.e., social justice] is a systematically superfluous idea." On the other hand, participants should still have good reasons for entering into compromises: "Under the conditions of a competitive political and social pluralism, 'social justice' simply means a fair [!] balance among the interests of social groups." This contradiction does not arise by accident. In the end, Becker must smuggle in something like "fairness" as a standard for evaluating compromises, though he cannot declare this as such: "The rules of the game for balancing interests must include 'parity of weapons'. However, contrary to what the concept of 'social justice' suggests, one does not need a unitary standard to evaluate the outcome of a balancing of interests."[9]True, bargaining partners need not accept the outcome of successful bargaining for the *same* reasons. But the prudential considerations that each side weighs from its point of view tacitly presuppose the common recognition of normative reasons. These reasons justify the procedure itself as impartial by explaining why outcomes reached in conformity with the procedure may count as fair.

In the final analysis, therefore, the chasm between what can be asserted from the perspective of an observer and what can be accepted from the perspective of participants cannot be bridged by purposive-rational considerations alone. This reflects the performative self-contradiction that ensnares an empiricist theory of democracy with normative intentions—in fact, a self-contradiction Becker already indicates in the subtitle of his book: the "decision for democracy" recommended by the book may not be understood, on the book's own premises, as a *rationally grounded* decision. If, however, it is a matter of sheer decision, then as a reader one must wonder what kind of text one is dealing with in this book. At first sight, it seems to propose a philosophical theory that explains and justifies the rules of liberal democracy. After becoming acquainted with the theory, however, one realizes that the author, if he is consistent, can understand his theory at most as an ideological *advertisement* for liberal constitutionalism.

7.1.2

To summarize the results of our analysis, we can say that if rational citizens were to describe their practices in empiricist categories, they would not have sufficient reason to observe the democratic rules of the game. Obviously, a theory with justificatory intentions must not suppress the genuinely normative sense of the intuitive understanding of democracy. Empiricist redefinitions thus do not give us a way to avoid the question of how norm and reality are related. If this is the case, then we must return to those normative models of democracy already introduced and ask whether their implicit conceptions of society offer any points of contact with available sociological analyses.

Our reflections from the standpoint of legal theory revealed that the central element of the democratic process resides in the procedure of deliberative politics. This reading of democracy has implications for the concept of society presupposed in the received models of democracy, that is, the view of society as centered in the state. The reading proposed here differs both from the liberal conception of the state as guardian of an economic society and from the republican concept of an ethical community institution-alized in the state.[10]

According to the liberal view, the democratic process is effected exclusively in the form of compromises among interests. Rules of compromise formation are supposed to secure the fairness of results through universal and equal suffrage, the representative composition of parliamentary bodies, the mode of decision making, rules of order, and so on. Such rules are ultimately justified in terms of liberal basic rights. According to the republican view, on the other hand, democratic will-formation takes the form of ethicopolitical self-understanding; here deliberation can rely on the substantive support of a culturally established background consensus shared by the citizenry. This socially integrative pre-understanding can renew itself in the ritualized recollection of the founding of the republic. Discourse theory takes elements from both sides and integrates these in the concept of an ideal procedure for deliberation and decision making. Democratic procedure, which establishes a network of pragmatic considerations, compromises, and discourses of self-understanding and of justice, grounds the presumption that reasonable or fair results are obtained insofar as the flow of relevant information and its proper handling have not been obstructed. According to this view, practical reason no longer resides in universal human rights, or in the ethical substance of a specific community, but in the rules of discourse and forms of argumentation that borrow their normative content from the validity basis of action oriented to reaching understanding. In the final analysis, this normative content arises from the structure of linguistic communication and the communicative mode of sociation.

In the present context, it is interesting that these descriptions of the democratic process also set the stage for a normative conceptualization of state and society. All we need presuppose is a type of public administration that emerged in the early-modern period with the European nation-state and developed functional ties with the capitalist economy.

According to the republican view, the citizens' opinion- and will-formation forms the medium through which society constitutes itself as a political whole. Society is, from the very start, political society—*societas civilis*—for in the citizens' practice of political self-determination the community becomes conscious of itself, as it were, and acts upon itself through the citizens' collective will. Hence democracy becomes equivalent to the political self-organization of society as a whole. This leads to an offensive *understanding of politics directed against the state apparatus.* In Hannah Arendt's political writings, one can see where republican argumentation directs its salvos: in opposition to the civil privatism of a depoliticized population and in opposition to the production of mass loyalty through parties that have become arms of the state, the political public sphere should be revitalized to the point where a regenerated citizenry can, in the forms of a decentralized self-governance, (once again) appropriate bureaucratically alienated state power. In this way society would finally develop into a political totality.

Whereas the separation of the state apparatus from society elicits a polemical response from the republican side, according to the liberal view the gap cannot be eliminated but only bridged by the democratic process. Naturally, the regulated balance of power and interests needs to be channeled by the rule of law. The democratic will-formation of self-interested citizens has comparatively weak normative connotations, and it forms only one element in a complex constitution. The constitution is supposed to curb the administration through normative provisions (such as basic rights, separation of powers, and statutory controls); in addition, the constitution is meant to motivate the state, through the competition among political parties and between incumbents and opposition, to take adequate account of societal interests and value orientations. This *state-centered understanding of politics* can forego the unrealistic assumption of a citizenry capable of collective action. It is oriented not toward the input of a rational political will-formation but toward the output of government activities that are successful on balance. Liberal argumentation aims its salvos against the potential for disruption posed by an administrative power that hinders the spontaneous social commerce of private persons. The liberal model hinges not on the democratic self-determination of deliberating citizens but on the constitutional framework for an economic society that is supposed to guarantee an essentially nonpolitical common good by satisfying personal life plans and private expectations of happiness.

Discourse theory invests the democratic process with normative connotations stronger than those found in the liberal model but weaker than those found in the republican model. Once again, it takes elements from both sides and puts them together in a new way. In agreement with republicanism, it gives center stage to the process of political opinion- and will-formation, but without understanding the constitution as something secondary; rather, as we have already seen, it conceives constitutional principles as a consistent answer to the question of how the demanding communicative forms of democratic opinion- and will-formation can be institutionalized. According to discourse theory, the success of deliberative politics depends not on a collectively acting citizenry but on the institutionalization of the corresponding procedures and conditions of communication, as well as on the interplay of institutionalized deliberative processes with informally developed public opinions. Proceduralized popular sovereignty and a political system tied into the peripheral networks of the political public sphere go together with the image of a decentered society. At any rate, this concept of democracy no longer has to operate with the notion of a social whole centered in the state and imagined as a goal-oriented subject writ large. Nor does it represent the whole in a system of constitutional norms mechanically regulating the balance of power and interests in accordance with a market model. Discourse theory drops all those motifs employed by the *philosophy of consciousness* that lead one either to ascribe the citizens' practice of self-determination to a macrosocial subject or to refer the anonymous rule of law to competing individual subjects. The former approach views the citizenry as a collective actor that reflects the whole and acts for it. In the latter approach, individual actors function as dependent variables in power processes—processes that operate blindly because beyond individual choice there can be at most aggregated, but not consciously formed and executed, collective decisions.

Discourse theory reckons with the *higher-level intersubjectivity* of processes of reaching understanding that take place through democratic procedures or in the communicative network of public spheres. Both inside and outside the parliamentary complex and its deliberative bodies, these subjectless communications form arenas in which a more or less rational opinion- and will-formation can take place for political matters, that is, matters relevant to the entire society and in need of regulation. The flow of communication between public opinion-formation, institutionalized elections, and legislative decisions is meant to guarantee that influence and communicative power are transformed through legislation into administrative power. Like the liberal model, discourse theory respects the boundaries between "state" and "society," but it distinguishes civil society, as the social basis of autonomous public spheres, from both the economic system and public administration. From a normative standpoint, this understanding of democracy requires a realignment in the relative importance of the three resources from which modern societies satisfy their needs for integration and steering: money, administration, and solidarity. The normative implications are obvious: the socially integrating force of solidarity,[11] which can no longer be drawn solely from sources of communicative action, must develop through widely diversified and more or less autonomous public spheres, as well as through procedures of democratic opinion- and will-formation institutionalized within a constitutional framework. In addition, it should be able to hold its own against the two other mechanisms of social integration, money and administrative power.

This view has implications for how one understands legitimation and popular sovereignty. On the liberal view, democratic will-formation has the exclusive function of *legitimating* the exercise of political power. Election results are the license to assume the power of governing, whereas the governing incumbents must justify the use of this power to the public and parliament. On the republican view, democratic will-formation has the significantly stronger function of *constituting* society as a political community and keeping the memory of this founding act alive with each election. The incumbent Government is not only empowered by an election between competing elites to exercise a predominantly free mandate. It is also programmed by voters to carry out certain policies. More a committee than an arm of the state, it is part of a self-governing political community and not the head of a separate branch of government. Once again, discourse theory brings another idea into play: the procedures and communicative presuppositions of democratic opinion- and will-formation function as the most important sluices for the discursive rationalization of the decisions of an administration bound by law and statute. *Rationalization* means more than mere legitimation but less than the constitution of power. The power available to the administration alters its aggregate condition as long as it remains tied in with a democratic opinion- and will-formation that does not just monitor the exercise of political power ex post facto but more or less programs it as well. Nevertheless, only the political system can "act." It is a subsystem specialized for collectively binding decisions, whereas the communicative structures of the public sphere constitute a far-flung network of sensors that react to the pressure of society-wide problems and stimulate influential opinions. The public opinion that is worked up via democratic procedures into communicative power cannot "rule" of itself but can only point the use of administrative power in specific directions.

The concept of *popular sovereignty* stems from the republican appropriation and reevaluation of the early-modern notion of sovereignty initially coupled with the absolute ruler. The state, which monopolizes the means for the legitimate application of force, is presented as a concentration of power able to overcome all the other powers of this world. This motif, which goes back to Jean Bodin, was carried over by Jean-Jacques Rousseau to the will of the united people. He fused it with the classical idea of the self-rule of free and equal persons and incorporated it in the modern concept of autonomy. Despite this sublimation, the concept of sovereignty remained bound to the notion of embodiment in the (at first even physically present) people. According to the republican view, the people, who are at least potentially present, are the bearers of a sovereignty that in principle cannot be delegated: in their sovereign character, the people cannot have others represent them. Constitutive authority is grounded in the citizens' practice of self-determination and not in their representatives. Liberalism counters this with the more realistic view that in a constitutional democracy, political authority emanating from the people is exercised only "by means of elections and voting and by specific legislative, executive, and judicial organs" (as we read, for example, in art. 20, sec. 2, of the Basic Law of the Federal Republic of Germany).

Of course, these two views exhaust the alternatives only if one dubiously conceives state and society in terms of the whole and its parts, where the whole is constituted either by a sovereign citizenry or by a constitution. By contrast, the discourse theory of democracy corresponds to the image of a decentered society, albeit a society in which the political public sphere has been differentiated as an arena for the perception, identification, and treatment of problems affecting the whole of society. Once one gives up the philosophy of the subject, one needs neither to concentrate sovereignty concretely in the people nor to banish it in anonymous constitutional structures and powers. The "self" of the self-organizing legal community disappears in the subjectless forms of communication that regulate the flow of discursive opinion- and will-formation in such a way that their fallible results enjoy the presumption of being reasonable. This is not to denounce the intuition connected with the idea of popular sovereignty but to interpret it intersubjectively.[12] Popular sovereignty, even if it becomes anonymous, retreats into democratic procedures and the legal implementation of their demanding communicative presuppositions only in order to make itself felt as communicatively generated power. Strictly speaking, this power springs from the interactions among legally institutionalized will-formation and culturally mobilized publics. The latter, for their part, find a basis in the associations of a civil society quite distinct from both state and economy alike.

Read in procedural terms, the idea of popular sovereignty refers to social-boundary conditions that, although enabling the self-organization of a legal community, are not immediately at the disposition of the citizens' will. The normative self-understanding of deliberative politics certainly requires a discursive mode of sociation *for the legal community*, but this mode does not extend to the whole of society in which the constitutionally organized political system is *embedded*. Even on its own self-understanding, deliberative politics remains part of a complex society, which, as a whole, resists the normative approach practiced in legal theory. In this regard, the discourse-theoretic reading of democracy has a point of contact with a detached social-scientific approach that considers the political system neither apex nor center nor even the structural core of society, but just *one* action system among others. On the other hand, because it provides a safety mechanism for solving problems that threaten social integration, politics must be able to communicate through the medium of law with all the other legitimately ordered spheres of action, however these happen to be structured and steered. The political system depends on the performance of other systems, such as the fiscal performances of the economic system, in more than just a trivial manner. What is more, deliberative politics is internally connected with contexts of a rationalized lifeworld that meets it halfway. This is true both for the politics governed by the formal procedures of an institutionalized opinion- and will-formation and for the politics that occurs only informally in the networks of the public sphere. It is precisely the deliberatively filtered political communications that depend on lifeworld resources—on a liberal political culture and an enlightened political socialization, above all on the initiatives of opinion-building associations. To a large extent, these resources form and regenerate spontaneously, and in any case they are not readily accessible to direct interventions of the political apparatus.

7.2 Democratic Procedure and the Problem of Its Neutrality

The discourse concept of democracy, having jettisoned received notions of a politically constituted society, is not obviously incompatible with the form and mode of operation of functionally differentiated societies. All the same, one can still ask whether and, if so, how the discursive social relations assumed for an association of free and equal citizens, and hence the self-organization of the legal community, are at all possible under the conditions for the reproduction of a complex society. For a sociologically informed resolution to this question, it is important to operationalize the procedural core of democracy at the right level. In democratic procedure, the ideal content of practical reason takes a pragmatic shape; the realization of the system of rights is measured by the forms in which this content is institutionalized. The *sociological translation* of the procedural understanding of democracy must, in regard to this normative content of the constitutional state, start neither too low nor too high.

In the introduction to his theory of democracy, Norberto Bobbio pursues a deflationary strategy.[13] He first notes some global social changes that contradict the promise of classical conceptions. First and foremost, a polycentric society of large organizations has emerged, in which influence and political power pass into the hands of collective actors and can be acquired and exerted less and less by associated individuals. In addition, competing interest groups have multiplied, making impartial will-formation difficult. Furthermore, the growth of state bureaucracies and their functions fosters the domination of experts. Finally, apathetic masses have become alienated from the elites, who become independent oligarchies that paternalize voiceless citizens. These skeptical diagnoses lead Bobbio to a cautious formulation of the democratic rules of the game: "My premise is that the only way a meaningful discussion of democracy, as distinct from all forms of autocratic government, is possible is to consider it as characterized by a set of rules . . . which establish *who* is authorized to take collective decisions and which *procedures* are to be applied."[14] Democracies satisfy the necessary "procedural minimum" to the extent that they guarantee (a) the political participation of as many interested citizens as possible, (b) majority rule for political decisions, (c) the usual communication rights and therewith the selection from among different programs and political elites, and (d) the protection of the private sphere.[15] The advantage of this minimalist definition lies in its descriptive character. It grasps the normative content of political systems as they already exist in Western-type societies organized as nation-states. For this reason, Bobbio can reach this conclusion: "The minimal content of the democratic state has not been impaired: guarantees of the basic liberties, the existence of competing parties, periodic elections with universal suffrage, decisions which are collective or the result of compromise . . . or made on the basis of the majority principle, or in any event as the outcome of open debate between the different factions or allies of a government coalition."[16]

At the same time, this operationalization by no means exhausts the normative content evident in democratic procedure when one adopts the reconstructive vantage point of legal theory. Although public controversies among several parties are mentioned as a necessary condition for the democratic mode of decision making, the proposed definition does not touch the core of a genuinely proceduralist understanding of democracy. The point of such an understanding is this: the democratic procedure is institutionalized in discourses and bargaining processes by employing forms of communication that promise that all outcomes reached in conformity with the procedure are reasonable. No one has worked out this view more energetically than John Dewey: "Majority rule, just as majority rule, is as foolish as its critics charge it with being. But it never is *merely* majority rule. . . . 'The means by which a majority comes to be a majority is the more important thing': antecedent debates, modification of views to meet the opinions of minorities. . . . The essential need, in other words, is the improvement of the methods and conditions of debate, discussion and persuasion."[17] Deliberative politics acquires its legitimating force from the discursive structure of an opinion- and will-formation that can fulfill its socially integrative function only because citizens expect its results to have a reasonable *quality*. Hence the *discursive level* of public debates constitutes the most important variable. It must not be hidden away in the black box of an operationalization satisfied with crude indicators. Before taking up a proposal that considers this aspect, I would like first to develop the concept of a two-track deliberative politics (sec. 7.2.1) and then defend this concept against communitarian and liberal objections (sec. 7.2.2).

7.2.1

Joshua Cohen has elucidated the concept of deliberative politics in terms of an "ideal procedure" of deliberation and decision making that should be "mirrored" in social institutions as much as possible. It seems Cohen has still not completely shaken off the idea of a society that is deliberatively steered *as a whole* and is thus politically constituted:

The notion of a deliberative democracy is rooted in the intuitive ideal of a democratic association in which the justification of the terms and conditions of association proceeds through public argument and reasoning among equal citizens. Citizens in such an order share a commitment to the resolution of problems of collective choice through public reasoning, and regard their basic institutions as legitimate in so far as they establish the framework for free public deliberation.[18]

In contrast to Cohen, I would like to understand the procedure from which procedurally correct decisions draw their legitimacy— a procedure I will specify more closely in what follows—as the core structure in a separate, constitutionally organized political system, but not as a model for all social institutions (and not even for all government institutions). If deliberative politics is supposed to be inflated into a structure shaping the totality of society, then the discursive mode of sociation expected in the *legal system* would have to expand into a self-organization of *society* and penetrate the latter's complexity as a whole. This is impossible, for the simple reason that democratic procedure must be embedded in contexts it cannot itself regulate.

However, Cohen plausibly characterizes the procedure itself in terms of the following postulates: (a) Processes of deliberation take place in argumentative form, that is, through the regulated exchange of information and reasons among parties who introduce and critically test proposals.[19] (b) Deliberations are inclusive and public. No one may be excluded in principle; all of those who are possibly affected by the decisions have equal chances to enter and take part. (c) Deliberations are free of any external coercion. The participants are sovereign insofar as they are bound only by the presuppositions of communication and rules of argumentation.[20] (d) Deliberations are free of any internal coercion that could detract from the equality of the participants. Each has an equal opportunity to be heard, to introduce topics, to make contributions, to suggest and criticize proposals. The taking of yes/no positions is motivated solely by the unforced force of the better argument.[21]

Additional conditions specify the procedure in view of the *political character* of deliberative processes: (e) Deliberations aim in general at rationally motivated agreement and can in principle be indefinitely continued or resumed at any time. Political deliberations, however, must be concluded by majority decision in view of pressures to decide. Because of its internal connection with a deliberative practice, majority rule justifies the presumption that the fallible majority opinion may be considered a reasonable basis for a common practice until further notice, namely, until the minority convinces the majority that their (the minority's) views are correct.[22] (f) Political deliberations extend to any matter that can be regulated in the equal interest of all. This does not imply, however, that topics and subject matters traditionally considered to be "private" in nature could be a fortiori withdrawn from discussion. In particular, those questions are publicly relevant that concern the unequal distribution of resources on which the actual exercise of rights of communication and participation depends.[23] (g) Political deliberations also include the interpretation of needs and wants and the change of prepolitical attitudes and preferences. Here the consensus-generating force of arguments is by no means based only on a value consensus previously developed in shared traditions and forms of life.[24]

Every association that institutionalizes such a procedure for the purposes of democratically regulating the conditions of its common life thereby constitutes itself as a body of citizens. It forms a particular legal community, delimited in space and time, with specific forms of life and traditions. But this distinctive cultural identity does not designate it *as* a political community of citizens. For the democratic process is governed by *universal* principles of justice that are equally constitutive for every body of citizens. In short, the ideal procedure of deliberation and decision making presupposes as its bearer an association that agrees to regulate the conditions of its common life *impartially*. What brings legal consociates together is, *in the final analysis*, the linguistic bond that holds together each communication community.[25]

This image of deliberative politics does not just omit some important internal differentiations (which I have drawn in chap. 4).

It is also silent about the relation between decision-oriented delib-erations, which are regulated by *democratic procedures*, and the informal processes of opinion-formation in the public sphere. To the extent that these procedures, unlike general elections, do not simply organize the voting that *follows* informal opinion-formation, they at least regulate the composition and operation of assemblies that "convene" for a "sitting" in which an agenda is "negotiated" and resolutions are passed if necessary. In setting up parliamentary procedures, decision-making powers (and assigned political re-sponsibilities) provide the reference point from which socially bounded and temporally limited publics are constituted. They also determine how deliberations are structured through argument and specified in regard to the matter at hand. Democratic proce-dures in such "arranged" publics structure opinion- and will-formation processes with a view to the cooperative solution of practical questions, including the negotiation of fair compromises. The operative meaning of these regulations consists less in discov-ering and identifying problems than in dealing with them; it has less to do with becoming sensitive to new ways of looking at problems than with justifying the selection of a problem and the choice among competing proposals for solving it. The publics of parliamentary bodies are structured predominantly as a *context of justification*. These bodies rely not only on the administration's preparatory work and further processing but also on the *context of discovery* provided by a procedurally unregulated public sphere that is borne by the general public of citizens.

This "weak" public is the vehicle of "public opinion."[26] The opinion-formation uncoupled from decisions is effected in an open and inclusive network of overlapping, subcultural publics having fluid temporal, social, and substantive boundaries. Within a framework guaranteed by constitutional rights, the structures of such a pluralistic public sphere develop more or less spontane-ously. The currents of public communication are channeled by mass media and flow through different publics that develop infor-mally inside associations. Taken together, they form a "wild" complex that resists organization as a whole. On account of its anarchic structure, the general public sphere is, on the one hand, more vulnerable to the repressive and exclusionary effects of unequally distributed social power, structural violence, and systematically distorted communication than are the institutionalized public spheres of parliamentary bodies. On the other hand, it has the advantage of a medium of *unrestricted* communication. Here new problem situations can be perceived more sensitively, discourses aimed at achieving self-understanding can be conducted more widely and expressively, collective identities and need interpretations can be articulated with fewer compulsions than is the case in procedurally regulated public spheres. Democratically constituted opinion- and will-formation depends on the supply of informal public opinions that, ideally, develop in structures of an unsubverted political public sphere. The informal public sphere must, for its part, enjoy the support of a societal basis in which equal rights of citizenship have become socially effective. Only in an egalitarian public of citizens that has emerged from the confines of class and thrown off the millennia-old shackles of social stratification and exploitation can the potential of an unleashed cultural pluralism fully develop—a potential that no doubt abounds just as much in conflicts as in meaning-generating forms of life. But in a secularized society that has learned to deal with its complexity consciously and deliberately, the communicative mastery of *these* conflicts constitutes the sole source of solidarity among strangers— strangers who renounce violence and, in the cooperative regulation of their common life, also concede one another the right to *remain* strangers.

7.2.2 Excursus on the Neutrality of Procedures

Deliberative politics thus lives off the interplay between democratically institutionalized will-formation and informal opinion-formation. It cannot rely solely on the channels of procedurally regulated deliberation and decision making. In discussing the objections raised against the alleged neutrality of such an "ideal procedure," we must not forget this need to supplement regulated procedures with informal communication.[27] The objections are aimed primarily at Bruce Ackerman's proposed explication. Ackerman elucidates democratic procedure by spelling out the conditions for a legitimation discourse in which a power holder must justify her more important decisions to opponents. This discourse obeys rules that should make an impartial and consistent judgment of practical questions possible.[28] In particular—and this is the bone of contention—the power holder must remain *neutral* with respect to competing and mutually incompatible conceptions of the good life: "No reason is a good reason if it requires the power holder to assert: (a) that his conception of the good is better than that asserted by any of his fellow citizens, or (b) that, regardless of his conception of the good, he is intrinsically superior to one or more of his fellow citizens."[29] Neutrality means, to begin with, the *priority* of justice over the good, and hence the fact that questions of the good life recede behind questions of justice.

However, if neutrality were in addition to require that ethical questions be *bracketed out of* political discourse in general, then such discourse would forfeit its power to rationally change prepolitical attitudes, need interpretations, and value orientations. According to this reading of "conversational restraint," practical questions that are prima facie controversial should simply not be pursued any further.[30] This amounts to treating questions of the good as "private" affairs. On this premise, however, the neutrality of procedure could be secured only by rules of avoidance (or "gag rules"[31]) and would depend on received distinctions between private and public spheres, delimitations that for their part are excluded from discussion. Such a rigid constraint, which a fortiori excludes ethical questions, would at least implicitly prejudice the agenda in favor of an inherited background of settled traditions. If we do not even present our different ethical views for discussion, then we cannot *sound out* the possibilities for reaching consensus through discourse. This leads Charles Larmore to propose a different reading of neutrality:

In particular, the ideal of political neutrality does not deny that such discussion should encompass not only determining what are the probable consequences of alternative decisions and whether certain decisions can be neutrally justified, but also clarifying one's notion of the good life and trying to convince others of the superiority of various aspects of one's view of human flourishing. This ideal demands only that so long as some view about the good life remains disputed, no decision of the state can be justified on the basis of its supposed intrinsic superiority or inferiority.[32]

The neutrality debate branches out at this point, because even this tolerant version of the neutrality thesis is contested, indeed from opposite directions.

From the *communitarian side,* one hears the radical objection that standards for an impartial judgment of practical questions in general cannot be separated from the context of specific worldviews and life projects: on this view, no presumptively neutral principle can ever be neutral in fact. Every apparently neutral procedure reflects a specific—in Ackerman's case, liberal—conception of the good life. Furthermore, a neutral procedure must not implicitly serve to realize preferred values or goals that prove to have priority from the vantage point, say, of a liberal understanding of law and politics; otherwise, it would discriminate against citizens with different conceptions and value orientations. This objection can be met if one can show that the neutrality principle is a necessary component of a practice that is without alternatives or substitutes, and in this sense *unavoidable.* A practice is "unavoidable" if it fulfills functions vital to human life and cannot be replaced by any other practice. Ackerman plays on this kind of unavoidability when he asks, "If we disdain the art of constrained conversation, how will we come to terms with each other? Is there another way beyond excommunication and brute suppression?"[33] If we find ourselves confronted with questions of conflict resolution or concerning the choice of collective goals and we want to avoid the alternative of violent clashes, then we *must* engage in a practice of reaching understanding, whose procedures and communicative presuppositions are not at our disposition.

This leads Larmore to trace the neutrality principle back to a universal rule of argumentation:

The neutral justification of political neutrality is based upon what I believe is a universal norm of rational dialogue. When two people disagree about some specific point, but wish to continue talking about the more general problem they wish to solve, each should prescind from the beliefs that the other rejects, (1) in order to construct an argument on the basis of his other beliefs that will convince the other of the truth of the disputed belief, or (2) in order to shift to another aspect of the problem, where the possibilities of agreement seem greater. In the face of disagreement, those who wish to continue the conversation should retreat to neutral ground, with the hope either of resolving the dispute or of bypassing it.[34]

Once an ethical disagreement is uncovered, "neutral dialogue" requires a transition to that higher level of abstraction characteristic of justice discourses, where participants examine what lies in the equal interest of all concerned. In Larmore's approach, this transition appears as a special case of a more general postulate of rational discourse.[35]

In response to this proposal, the communitarian objection can be radicalized still further. Even if the neutrality principle could be traced back to a universal rule of argumentation, it is objected, the reconstruction of such rules must rely on the intuitive knowledge of individual participants in rational discourse, normally our own knowledge. The reason is that the conditions for the discursive vindication of a validity claim, which are always already implicitly known, can be reflexively grasped only from the participant perspective. But this method for the rational reconstruction of intuitive knowledge can have the consequence "that when individuals' conceptions of the good life conflict, they often will also have somewhat different notions of the ideal conditions under which they believe they could justify their conception to others."[36] Larmore suspects that even universal grammatical knowledge is to a certain extent interwoven with a particular linguistic ontology or with the individual's self-understanding and worldview. Even if one grants this, however, the worst one should expect is that the *explication* of our antecedently acquired practical knowledge will exhibit perspectival distortions. One need not expect that this knowledge *itself*, which is always already intuitively employed, will take as many diverse forms as there are perspectives. The ever fallible and possibly even false *reconstruction* does not touch the always already *functioning* knowledge.[37] For this reason, we may assume that the know-how informing argumentative practices represents a point of convergence where participants, however diverse their backgrounds, can at least intuitively meet in their efforts to reach an understanding. In all languages and in every language community, such concepts as truth, rationality, justification, and consensus, even if interpreted differently and applied according to different criteria, play *the same grammatical role*.[38] At any rate, this is true for modern societies that, with positive law, secularized politics, and a principled morality, have made the shift to a postconventional level of justification and expect their members to take a reflexive attitude toward their own respective cultural traditions.[39] Of course, as soon as practical knowledge is transformed into explicit knowledge about rules and presuppositions of rational discourse, and as soon as this explicit knowledge is in turn translated into institutionalized procedures of deliberation and decision making, differences of interpretation can come into play in the course of this explicative process. These also appear in the differences between historical constitutions that interpret and elaborate the system of rights in different ways.

The nonrestrictive reading of the neutrality thesis is also exposed to objections from the *liberal side*. The liberal objections are directed against the opening of political discourse to whatever questions and arguments any party wants to bring forward. They dispute the thesis, proposed primarily by feminists, that *any* topic that at least one participant considers publicly relevant must also be a valid item for public discussion. These feminist authors fear that the liberal version of the neutrality principle makes it possible to keep from the agenda precisely those concerns hitherto designated as "private" according to rather conventional standards. Examples are not hard to find:

> Until quite recently, feminists were in the minority in thinking that domestic violence against women was a matter of common concern and thus a legitimate topic of public discussion. The great majority of people considered this issue to be a private matter between what was assumed to be a fairly small number of heterosexual couples. . . . Then feminists formed a subaltern counterpublic from which we disseminated a view of domestic violence as a widespread systematic feature of male-dominated societies. Eventually, after sustained discursive contestation, we succeeded in *making* it a common concern.

Examples of this sort lead Nancy Fraser to this conclusion: "Only participants themselves can decide what is and what is not of common concern to them."[40] This thesis has aroused the misgiving that *removing the topical or thematic limits on political discussion* will undermine the legal protection of the private sphere and endanger the personal integrity of the individual. Thus J. D. Moon, for example, speaks of a "bias against privacy." Individual private rights safeguard a sphere in which private persons are absolved of the obligation to account publicly for everything they do. If this sphere is no longer *antecedently* delimited, then the following dilemma seems to arise: "We appear to require unconstrained discourse in order to settle what the boundaries of the private should be, but such discourse itself violates those boundaries because it rests on a demand for unlimited self-disclosure."[41] The dilemma dissolves as soon as we clarify the confusions bound up with the two conceptual pairs, "private versus public" matters and "constrained versus unconstrained" discourses.

We must distinguish *procedural* constraints on public discourses from a constraint or limitation on the *range of topics* open to public discourse. The tolerant version of the neutrality principle means that not only informal but also procedurally regulated opinion- and will-formation should be open to ethically relevant questions of the good life, of collective identity, and of need interpretation. For example, political legislators who enact norms defining the crime of "spousal abuse" will accordingly be able to include the corresponding topics and contributions in their debates without thereby detracting from the impartiality of the legislative procedure. Making something that so far has been considered a private matter a topic for public discussion does not yet imply any *infringement* of individual rights. Again, we must draw the distinction between public and private matters in two respects: accessibility and *thematization,* on the one hand, and the *regulation of powers* and responsibilities, on the other. To talk about something is not necessarily the same as meddling in another's affairs. Certainly the intimate sphere must be protected from intrusive forces and the critical eyes of strangers, but not everything reserved to the decisions of private persons is withdrawn from public thematization and protected from criticism. Rather, every affair in need of political regulation should be publicly discussed, though not every legitimate object of public discussion will in fact be politically regulated. (And not every political regulation touches private responsibilities.) With the help of these distinctions, one can easily show that liberal misgivings about opening up an unrestricted spectrum of public issues and topics are not justified so long, at least, as the personal integrity of the individual is preserved.

The system of rights calls for the simultaneous and complementary realization of private and civic autonomy. From a normative standpoint, these two forms of autonomy are co-original and reciprocally presuppose each other, because one would remain incomplete without the other. But how private and public powers and responsibilities must be divided up in particular cases in order to adequately realize civil rights depends on the historical circumstances and, as we will see, on *perceived* social contexts. A sphere for a privately autonomous pursuit of individual interests and life plans cannot be delimited *once and for all* from the public sphere oriented to "the common weal," any more than the "intimate sphere" can be delimited like a core inside the wider private sphere. This sort of boundary drawing—which is often a difficult process to undertake, as the pornography debate shows—must be a legitimate object of political debate. But the *thematization* of these "boundary questions" does not by itself imply any encroachment on existing *powers* and responsibilities. This becomes especially clear if one keeps in mind that deliberative politics proceeds along two tracks that are at different levels of opinion- and will-formation, the one constitutional, the other informal.

Because the general public sphere is "unconstrained" in the sense that its channels of communication are not regulated by procedures, it is better suited for the "struggle over needs" and their interpretation.[42] Whether it is the question of spousal abuse or the question of day-care facilities for the children of working parents, it is usually a long road, involving dogged efforts at staging public "actions," before such initially "private" matters even begin to acquire the status of recognized political issues. And it is a long road until the controversial contributions on such issues—contributions that depend on competing interpretations of self and world, or on different "visions of the good life"—adequately articulate the needs of those affected. Only after a public "struggle for recognition" can the contested interest positions be taken up by the responsible political authorities, put on the parliamentary agenda, discussed, and, if need be, worked into legislative proposals and binding decisions. And only the *regulation* of a newly defined criminal offense or the *implementation* of a social program intervenes in the sphere of private life and changes formal responsibilities and existing practices.

7.3 The Sociological Translation of the Concept of Deliberative Politics

Following this excursus on the meaning, role, and status of democratic procedures, we are better equipped to deal with the question of where and how these procedures can find a place in the life of a complex society. To get at the procedural understanding of the democratic process, Robert Dahl chooses indicators that more fully capture the normative content of democratic procedures than does Bobbio's proposed operationalization. I will first present Dahl's approach (sec. 7.3.1), in order to gain a perspective from which I can then clarify the critical impact of a reconstructive sociology of democracy (sec. 7.3.2).

7.3.1

Dahl begins by liberating the intuitive understanding of democratic self-determination from the substantialism of the Aristotelian tradition:

Our common good, then—the good and interests we share with others—rarely consists of specific objects, activities, and relations; ordinarily it consists of the practices, arrangements, institutions, and processes that, in Traditionalist's terms again, promote the well-being of ourselves and others—not, to be sure, of "everyone" but of enough persons to make the practices, arrangements, etc. acceptable. . . . These would include . . . the general features of the democratic process.[43]

Dahl then lists five postulates that specify a procedure for reaching binding decisions that lie in the equal interest of all. Such a procedure should guarantee (a) the inclusion of all those affected; (b) equally distributed and effective opportunities to participate in the political process; (c) an equal right to vote on decisions; (d) an equal right to choose topics and, more generally, to control the agenda; and (e) a situation that allows all the participants to develop, in the light of sufficient information and good reasons, an articulate understanding of the contested interests and matter in need of regulation.[44] The last requirement aims at the level of information and the discursive character of will-formation: "Each citizen ought to have adequate and equal opportunities for discovering and validating . . . the choice on the matter to be decided that would best serve the citizen's interests. . . . Insofar as a citizen's good or interests requires attention to a public good or general interest, then citizens ought to have the opportunity to acquire an understanding of these matters."[45] Public discussions are especially meant to serve this end. Dahl, too, is concerned with those "methods and conditions" of political will-formation that Dewey had considered "*the* problem of the public."[46]

To date, the five criteria mentioned above have not been *sufficiently* satisfied by any actual political order. To be sure, unavoidable social complexity makes it necessary to apply the criteria in a differentiated fashion. Among other things, it requires the delegation of decision-making powers and the sensitive modification of decision procedures—in general the legal and organizational reduction of complexity. But this does not present any obstacle in principle to an "approximate" implementation of the procedure.[47] Thus one can conceive the existing pluralist democracies as systems in which democratic procedures do not just have the *nominal* form of *rights* of political participation and communication, but have *actually* been implemented in the form of practices, even if only selectively. Dahl sees these "polyarchies" as characterized by a range of effective rights and institutions that since the American and French Revolutions have gradually gained acceptance in a growing number of modern states. According to Dahl's classification, in 1930 fifteen European and six non-European states fit this description; he calculates that the number of such political systems approximately doubled by the end of the seventies.

Drawing on results of modernization research, Dahl uses his longitudinal sample to identify social indicators of "modern, dynamic, pluralist" societies favorable to democratization. These "MDP" societies display well-known features: a relatively high per capita income, long-run growth in per capita wealth, a market-based mode of production with shrinking primary and secondary sectors, a relatively high degree of urbanization, a high level of education, a decreasing infant-mortality rate, an increasing average life expectancy, and so on. Dahl interprets the statistical correlations among these indicators in terms of the *favorable social conditions* for the domestication of social power and the constitutional channeling of the state's monopoly on force: "An MDP society disperses power, influence, authority, and control away from any single center toward a variety of individuals, groups, associations, and organizations. And . . . it fosters attitudes and beliefs favourable to democratic ideas. Though these two features are independently generated, they also reinforce each other."[48] Thus democratization is fostered not simply by the polycentric distribution of power emerging in functionally differentiated societies; the decentering of power must be associated with a liberal political culture supported by corresponding patterns of political socialization. Only in the framework of such a political culture can the conflictual tensions among competing forms of life, identities, and worldviews be tolerated and handled without violence.

In Dahl's view, the most important *bottleneck* to advances beyond the present level of democratization lies in the specialization of the technical steering knowledge used in policymaking and administration. Such specialization keeps citizens from taking advantage of politically necessary expertise in forming their own opinions. The chief danger consists in the technocratic variant of a paternalism grounded in the monopolization of knowledge. Privileged access to the sources of relevant knowledge makes possible an inconspicuous domination over the colonized public of citizens cut off from these sources and placated with symbolic politics. Dahl thus sets his hopes on the technical possibilities of telecommunications; with the term "minipopulus," he proposes a type of deliberation and decision making that, at once functionally specialized and decentralized, proceeds through specially informed assemblies of representatives.[49] The abstract and somewhat utopian tenor of this recommendation oddly contrasts with the intention and structure of the investigation.

Dahl wanted to show that the idea and procedure of deliberative politics do not have to be externally imposed on the reality of developed societies, because this type of politics has had a secure hold on the institutions of such societies for a long time. He falls short of this goal, because he does not plausibly integrate the normative arguments that justify democratic procedures with the empirical analysis of their implementation, however incomplete that implementation might be. I see one reason for this in Dahl's

brand of sociological analysis: as long as social structure is apprehended solely by means of such classifications as the statistical
distribution of income, school attendance, and refrigerators, this
sociology lacks a *language* for the kind of descriptions that would
allow one to conceive favorable constellations and trends as indicators of rational potentials already at work in society itself, potentials
that can be taken up and developed by the political system. The
diagnosis that in complex societies paternalistic monopolies on
knowledge hinder further democratization is, however, a suitable
bridge for connecting the deliberative structures of the constitutionally organized political system with deeper processes of social
reproduction.

As already shown, the production of legitimate law through
deliberative politics represents a problem-solving procedure that
needs and assimilates knowledge in order to program the regulation of conflicts and the pursuit of collective goals. Politics steps in
to fill the functional gaps opened when other mechanisms of social
integration are overburdened. In doing this, it makes use of the
language of law. For law is a medium through which the structures
of mutual recognition already familiar from simple interactions
and quasi-natural solidarities can be transmitted, in an abstract but
binding form, to the complex and increasingly anonymous spheres
of a functionally differentiated society. However, the law is internally structured in such a way that a constitutional system, if it is to
provide a substitute for the integration taking place beneath the
threshold of formal law, must do so *at a reflexive level.* Social integration accomplished by democratic means must pass through a
discursive filter. Where other regulators—for example, the coordination patterns operating through settled values, norms, and
routines for reaching understanding—fail, politics and law raise
these quasi-natural problem-solving processes above the threshold
of consciousness, as it were. In filling in for social processes whose
problem-solving capacities are overtaxed, the political process
solves the *same kind* of problems as the processes it replaces. This
becomes clear if, following Bernard Peters's proposal, one classifies the standards for assessing general problems of societal integration according to the different aspects of validity: truth, normative
rightness, and authenticity. These correspond to the points of view

that allow one to distinguish the illocutionary binding forces of action oriented toward reaching an understanding.[50]

In regard to a society's integration, the activities of collective or individual actors must first of all be coordinated in such a way that their different accomplishments and contributions to a positively evaluated result fit together. These problems of *functional coordination* require a cognitive orientation to circumstances and events in the objective world. Results are judged according to the standards of technical and economic rationality. The conditions of success can thereby be described from either of two perspectives. From the viewpoint of the participating actors, success appears as the realization of collective goals, whereas from the observer perspective it appears as the maintenance of a given system or as the attunement of different systems to one another. The concept of functional coordination generalizes the concrete form of cooperation exemplified by the division of labor. It is neutral with respect to the differences between social and system integration. By contrast, the two further forms of integration belong only to social integration.

These pertain either to the *moral regulation of conflicts* or to the *ethical safeguarding of identities and forms of life*. Problems of balancing conflicting claims call for a normative orientation to legitimate orders of the social world. Problems of expressive identity formation call for an orientation to shared conceptions of the good life and the interpretation of needs. Results are judged according to the standards of moral and ethical rationality, respectively. Together with the standards of efficiency and rational decision making, these standards provide criteria for judging the success of societal integration in general. Peters derives from this a complex concept of "social rationality" that makes it possible to evaluate a society's reproduction as a more or less successful problem-solving process.[51] Consequently, the observable stability of an order is *not* a sufficient indicator of the rationality of a solution.

According to this proposal, societies are to be viewed in general as problem-solving systems, in which success or failure is measured against criteria of rationality. If we adopt this conception (which goes back to Karl Deutsch and others), then we see that democratic procedure and the discursive mode of sociation found in the legal community are simply reflexive refinements and specializations of a *general* mode of operation of social systems. Democratic procedures make the production of legitimate law depend on a presumptively reasonable treatment of problems that correspond, in the kind of issues they pose, to precisely those problems that have always already been dealt with unconsciously, so to speak, in less-specialized areas of society. For the centerpiece of deliberative politics consists in a network of discourses and bargaining processes that is supposed to facilitate the rational solution of pragmatic, moral, and ethical questions—the very problems that accumulate with the failure of the functional, moral, or ethical integration of society elsewhere.

Given the need for functional coordination that arises today in complex societies, the simple model of a division of labor between experts and laypersons no longer suffices. Rather, this need can be met only through indirect forms of regulatory action (i.e., steering) on the part of the administrative system. Dahl has recognized the danger that these "cognitive" problems of functional coordination displace other, namely, moral and ethical, problems and overburden the problem-solving capacity of democratic procedures. Various symptoms of such a *cognitive overburdening* of deliberative politics lend support to the assumption, by now widely accepted, that discursive opinion- and will-formation governed by democratic procedures lacks the complexity to take in and digest the *operatively necessary* knowledge. The required steering knowledge no longer seems capable of penetrating the capillaries of a communication network whose structures are predominantly horizontal, osmotically permeable, and egalitarian. Such evidence, however, should not lead one to forget the other fact that the uncoupling of administrative action from parliamentary control and the displacement of pertinent topics from public arenas did not take place *without resistance*. In changing constellations, the "democratic question" in one version or another has continually returned to the agenda. Dahl might even have considered his own investigation as one more instance of the drive to reinvigorate public discussion. That these countertendencies should arise is by no means accidental, if one assumes that the very medium of law, to which political power is internally linked, requires the supposition that law has a democratic genesis—and that this partly counterfactual supposition also has empirical effects. On this premise, the deployment of political power, even for cognitively quite demanding steering processes, *is still* subject to constraints that result directly from the juridical form of collectively binding decisions. In a political system under the pressure of societal complexity, these constraints manifest themselves in a growing cognitive dissonance between the validity suppositions of constitutional democracy and the way things actually happen in the political process.

7.3.2

Having taken our cue from Dahl, our first attempt at analyzing the implementation of democratic procedures in modern societies has yielded mixed results. On the one hand, deliberative politics loses much of its off-putting and unrealistic appearance if one views it as a reflexively organized learning process that *removes the burden* on latent processes of societal integration while *continuing* these processes within an action system specialized for this relief work. On the other hand, in complex societies the gap between the need for coordination and the lack of actual societal integration, the gap politics and law is meant to close, only seems to grow increasingly wider the more the administrative system has to accept tasks that increasingly overburden the costly deliberative mode of decision making. In this overburdening, one begins to notice how much the reality of complex societies resists the normative claims invested in the institutions of the constitutional state. As decision theory demonstrates, the democratic process is consumed "from within" by the shortage of functionally necessary resources; as systems theory maintains, "on the outside" it runs up against the complexity of opaque and recalcitrant functional systems. Both inside and out, the inertial moments of society—what Sartre once called the *inerte*—seemingly "become independent" (*verselbständigen*) in relation to the deliberative mode of a consciously and autonomously (*autonom*) effected sociation. However, if such reifying tendencies were an unavoidable feature of complex societies, then it would be pointless for Dahl to inquire into the conditions for a *more extensive* democratization of the existing political system. In the face of such contradictory evidence, the distinction between "democracies" and mere "polyarchies" would be tendentious.

To begin with, we must clarify in what sense society can become "independent" or "reified." This diagnosis obviously does not refer to that trivial resistance offered by stubborn everyday problems and by deficits in our attempts to resolve them. After all, the political system is especially designed to cope with these. From the participant perspective, the normal moments of inertia are perceived as differences between norm and reality, gaps that challenge us to deal with practical questions in the first place. Nor may we contrast an *independent* society-become-second-nature with the fact that associated citizens must adopt the demanding communicative presuppositions of discourse in their exercise of civic autonomy. We would misunderstand the discursive character of public opinion- and will-formation if we thought we could hypostatize the normative content of general presuppositions of rational discourse into an ideal model of purely communicative social relations.[52]

In everyday life, the mutual understanding between communicatively acting subjects is measured against validity claims that— against the massive background of an intersubjectively shared lifeworld—call for the taking of yes/no positions. Such claims are open to criticism and contain, together with the risk of dissent, the *possibility* of discursive vindication as well. In this sense, communicative action *refers to* a process of argumentation in which those taking part justify their validity claims before an ideally expanded audience. Participants in argumentation proceed on the idealizing assumption of a communication community without limits in social space and historical time. Moreover, as Karl-Otto Apel has formulated it, such participants must presuppose the possibility of an ideal community "within" their real social situation: "Anyone who engages in argument always already presupposes two things: first, a real communication community whose member he has himself become through a process of socialization, and second, an ideal communication community that would in principle be capable of adequately understanding the meaning of his arguments and judging their truth in a definitive manner."[53] Admittedly, this formulation could mislead one into thinking the "ideal communication community" has the status of an *ideal* rooted in the universal presuppositions of argumentation and able to be approximately realized. Even the equivalent concept of the "ideal speech situation," though less open to misunderstanding, tempts one to improperly hypostatize the system of validity claims on which speech is based. The counterfactual presuppositions assumed by participants in argumentation indeed open up a perspective allowing them to go beyond local practices of justification and to transcend the provinciality of their spatiotemporal contexts that are inescapable in action and experience. This perspective thus enables them to do justice to the meaning of *context-transcending* validity claims. But with context-transcending validity claims, they are not themselves transported into the beyond of an ideal realm of noumenal beings. In contrast to the projection of ideals, in the light of which we can identify *deviations*, "the idealizing presuppositions we always already have to adopt whenever we want to reach mutual understanding do not involve any kind of correspondence or comparison between idea and reality."[54]

On the other hand, it is legitimate to use such a projection for a thought experiment.[55] The essentialist misunderstanding is replaced by a methodological fiction in order to obtain a foil against which the substratum of *unavoidable* societal complexity becomes visible. In this harmless sense, the ideal communication community presents itself as a model of "pure" communicative sociation. In this community, the only available mechanism of self-organization is the instrument of discursive opinion and will-formation, and by using such means the community is supposed to be able to settle all conflicts without violence. The community even solves the "stubborn" problems of societal integration communicatively, in the final analysis through rational discourse—yet without the aid of politics and law.[56] This thought experiment must also not be misunderstood. It refers to concrete societies that are situated in space and time and already differentiated. Hence it does not detach discursive processes of reaching understanding from the bases of communicative action but reckons on their being situated in lifeworld contexts. In short, it does not abstract from the "finitude" of communicative social relations. Thus the conditions that *enable* communicative sociation must not be mistaken for contingently imposed *constraints*. In this way, we avoid the individualistic fallacy, according to which one experiences the effects of others simply as limits on one's individual freedom. Instead, the possibilities for affecting others, when legitimately regulated and based on an assumed consensus, *authorize* the exercise of a socially constituted freedom. Settled but intersubjectively recognized norms, so long as they at least *can* be problematized, do not make themselves felt in the manner of external compulsions. The same holds for the symbolism of the language and culture, as well as for the grammar of the forms of life, in which socially related individuals find themselves. All of these operate as enabling conditions. Lifeworld contexts certainly constrain actors' latitude for action and interpretation, but only in the sense that they open up a horizon for *possible* interactions and interpretations.

As soon as we conceive intentional social relations as communicatively mediated in the sense proposed, we are no longer dealing with disembodied, omniscient beings who exist beyond the empirical realm and are capable of context-free action, so to speak. Rather, we are concerned with finite, embodied actors who are socialized in concrete forms of life, situated in historical time and social space, and caught up in networks of communicative action. In fallibly interpreting a given situation, such actors must draw from resources supplied by their lifeworld and not under their control. This does not deny the contingency of given traditions and forms of life any more than it does the pluralism of existing subcultures, worldviews, and interest positions. On the other hand, actors are not simply *at the mercy* of their lifeworld. For the lifeworld can in turn reproduce itself only through communicative action, and that means through processes of reaching understanding that depend on the actors' responding with yes or no to criticizable validity claims. *The normative fault line that appears with this ability to say no* marks the finite freedom of persons who have to be *convinced* whenever sheer force is not supposed to intervene. Yet, even under such ideal conditions, discourses and bargaining can develop their problem-solving force only insofar as the problems at hand are sensitively perceived, adequately described, and productively answered in the light of a reflexive, posttraditional transmission of culture. Reaching mutual understanding through discourse indeed guarantees that issues, reasons, and information are handled reasonably, but such understanding still depends on contexts characterized by a capacity for learning, both at the cultural and the personal level. In this respect, dogmatic worldviews and rigid patterns of socialization can block a discursive mode of sociation.

Against the background of such a model of *purely communicative social relations*, then, Peters is interested in the moments of inertia inherent in the complexity of processes of opinion- and will-formation—inertias that become especially evident when these processes are supposed to satisfy the communicative presuppositions of rational discourse. For this issue, the idealizations of pure communication provide a suitable foil for bringing out the *functionally necessary* resources for communication in general. This is because the ideal model does not take account of the information and decision costs of the communication process itself. It does not consider the limited capacities for cognitive processing afforded by simple horizontal networks of communication; in particular, it abstracts from the unequal distribution of attention, competences, and knowledge within a public. It also ignores attitudes and motives at cross-purposes to the orientation to mutual understanding and is thus blind to egocentrism, weakness of will, irrationality, and self-deception on the part of participants. In light of this strong idealization, the insights of systems theory and decision theory have an especially easy time displaying the facticity of a world that is *not* set up this way.

In the world we know, communications and decisions trivially take up a certain space and time of their own, they consume an energy of their own, they require a separate expenditure of organizational capacities, and so on. The selection of topics and contributions, which is made under time pressure, gives rise to additional costs in terms of missed or postponed decisions. Furthermore, the unavoidable division of labor in the production and diffusion of knowledge results in an unequal distribution of information and expertise. In addition, the communications media intervene with a selectivity of their own in this social distribution of knowledge. The structures of the public sphere reflect unavoidable asymmetries in the availability of information, that is, unequal chances to have access to the generation, validation, shaping, and presentation of messages. Besides these systemic constraints, there are the accidental inequalities in the distribution of individual abilities. The resources for participating in political communications are in general narrowly limited. This is evident whether one examines the time available to individuals and the episodic attention to topics and issues with histories of their own; the readiness and ability to make one's own contribution to these topics; or the opportunistic attitudes, affects, prejudices, and so on, that detract from a rational will-formation.

These sketchy indications could be fleshed out with the help of an extensive literature. The only question is what they *mean* in the present context. To begin with, they illustrate deviations from the model of purely communicative social relations. Although these deviations certainly vary in degree and extent depending on the circumstances, by their very character they make us aware of *unavoidable* moments of inertia—specifically, the scarcity of those functionally necessary resources on which processes of deliberative opinion- and will-formation significantly depend. Even under favorable conditions, no complex society could ever correspond to the model of purely communicative social relations. But we should also not forget that this model is merely a methodological fiction intended to display the unavoidable inertial features of societal complexity, hence the underside of communicative social relations—an underside that, even to the participants themselves, remains largely hidden in the shadow of the idealizing presuppositions of communicative action. Yet the model owes its fictive character to the fact that it assumes a society without law and politics and projects the democratic idea of self-organization onto society as a whole. With the procedural concept of democracy, however, this idea takes the shape of a self-organizing *legal* community. According to this latter view, the discursive mode of sociation is to be implemented through the medium of law alone. And the law as such already incorporates those features from which the model of "pure" sociation abstracts.

By its very nature, positive law serves to reduce social complexity. This has been brought home to us (above) by means of the "deidealizations" in virtue of which legal rules can compensate for the cognitive indeterminacy, motivational insecurity, and limited coordinating power of moral norms. I have explained the complementary relation between law and morality as a way of compensating for the weaknesses of an action coordination based on practical reason alone.[57] From this viewpoint, however, the basic rights and principles of government by law can be understood as so many steps toward reducing the unavoidable complexity evident in the necessary deviations from the model of pure communication. We can see this reduction of complexity still more clearly when such rights and principles are spelled out in constitutional law and when procedures of deliberative politics are institutionalized (with majority rule, representative bodies, checks and balances, interlinking of oversight and review powers, etc.). Certainly all institutional or organizational mechanisms are also established to reduce complexity; in the form of constitutional regulations, however, these mechanisms (such as immunities and privileges) have at the same time the reflexive character of *countersteering measures* against a social complexity that *infiltrates* the normative presuppositions of government by law. This kind of complexity-preserving countersteering is already at work in the way that informal public opinion plays off against institutionalized, procedurally regulated opinion- and will-formation.[58] The communication circulating in the public sphere is especially vulnerable to the selective pressure of social inertia; the influence thus generated, however, can be converted into political power only if it passes through the sluices of democratic procedure and penetrates the constitutionally organized political system in general.

It would be naive to overlook the fact that the constitutionally regulated circulation of power in the political system itself is likewise subject to the pressure of social complexity. However, the objections that systems theory and decisions theory raise against the presupposition of a discursive mode of sociation in the *legal* community take on a different status once one considers that the institutions of the constitutional state, viewed sociologically, have the character of a *countersteering* preservation of complexity. This raises the question of how much the normative countersteering of constitutional institutions can compensate for the communicative, cognitive, and motivational limitations on deliberative politics and the conversion of communicative into administrative power. One must ask how much the social facticity of these unavoidable inertial features, even when they are *already taken into consideration* in the formal structure of the constitutional state, provide a point where *illegitimate* power complexes that are independent of the democratic process can crystallize. One must investigate the degree to which, in particular, the power concentrated in social subsystems, in large organizations and public administrations, inconspicuously settles into the systemic infrastructure of the normatively regulated circulation of power, and one must investigate how effectively the *unofficial* circulation of this unlegitimated power encroaches on the constitutionally regulated circulation of power.

8

Civil Society and the Political Public Sphere

In the early postwar period, the sociological study of democracy led to a theory of pluralism that still linked normative models of democracy with so-called "realist" approaches, that is, with economic theory on the one hand and systems theory on the other. If one disregards for the moment the recent revival of institutionalist approaches,[1] then one can hardly avoid the impression that as democratic theory has developed, the idealistic content of normative theories has been evaporating under the sun of social science. It was, in any case, only the liberal model of democracy—hence the normatively least demanding—that offered sociology a point of contact. The sociological enlightenment seems to recommend a disillusioning, if not downright cynical, view of the political process. It primarily focuses our attention on places where normatively "illegitimate" power forces its way into the constitutionally regulated circulation of power. If one takes the administrative system— or the "state apparatus"—as the point of reference, then the political public sphere and the parliamentary complex represent the input side, where the social power of organized interests enters the legislative process. On its output side, the administration again encounters the resistence of social subsystems and large organizations that bring their power into the implementation process. The autonomy of social power vis-à-vis the democratic process fosters in turn endogenous tendencies in the administrative complex to become increasingly autonomous. Thus an increasingly independent administrative power joins forces with a social power affecting both the input and the output side. Together they form a countercirculation that cuts across the "official" circuit of democratic decision making steered by communicative power. To be sure, most of the descriptions of these countermovements operate with empiricist concepts of power that level out the normative distinctions we have introduced from a reconstructive point of view. In particular, the construct of "communicative power" must appear tendentious in light of empiricist folklore. Political sociology usually either takes an action-theoretic approach, conceiving "power" as the capacity of actors to have their way against the opposing will of others, or it follows systems theory and splits power up into the power code of a specific, namely political, system on the one hand and, on the other, a general organizational power or, more accurately, the autopoietic capacity of systems to organize and reproduce themselves. I would like to show that the normative defeatism to which both lines of political sociology lead is not simply a result of sobering evidence but of misguided conceptual strategies as well. These strategies lose sight of what political power owes specifically to its formal constitution in legal terms.

After a global overview of theoretical developments, I first pursue Jon Elster's revisions of the economic theory of democracy. These speak for the empirical relevance of the procedural concept of deliberative politics (sec. 8.1). I then discuss Helmut Willke's concept of supervision, which is meant to explain how a decentered society that has allegedly disintegrated into autopoietic functional systems can cope with challenges to society as a whole. From the criticism of this proposal, and stimulated once again by the work of Bernard Peters, I develop a sociological model that focuses on the empirical weight of the constitutionally prescribed, hence official, circulation of power (sec. 8.2). This weight depends primarily on whether civil society, through resonant and autonomous public spheres, develops impulses with enough vitality to bring conflicts from the periphery into the center of the political system (sec. 8.3).

8.1 Sociological Theories of Democracy

8.1.1

The early *theory of pluralism* already relied on an empiricist concept of power. Pluralist theory employs an instrumentalist understanding of politics—according to which political and administrative power represent merely different manifestations of social power— to build a bridge between the liberal model of democracy introduced above and empirical science. Social power is measured in terms of the ability of organized interests to have their way. Moving up through party competition and general elections, social power is converted into a political power distributed between the incumbent Government and the opposition. This political power is in turn employed within the framework of constitutionally allocated powers and authorities so that, via the legislative process and administrative apparatus, the policies emerging from the channeled interplay of social forces can be converted into binding decisions and programs to be implemented. Moving back down in the opposite direction, administrative power is deployed to affect parliamentary will-formation and the interplay of organized interests. These interests, for their part, also get the chance to have a direct influence on policy formation and the use of administrative power. According to this model, a circular process is established that connects the clients' social power with the parties' acquisition of political power, the legitimation process with governmental services and administrative operations, and this implementation process again with the clients' initial claims. For the normative evaluation of these processes, the decisive assumption is that social power is more or less equally distributed among the relevant social interests. Only then can the balance of social forces and pressures keep political power circulating in such a way that the political system copes with the submitted claims as effectively as possible and satisfies social interests as equally as possible.

The sociological account of pluralism managed to link up with the normative model of liberalism by means of a simple substitution, namely, by replacing the individual citizens and their individual interests with large organizations and organized interests.[2] It assumed that all politically relevant collective actors enjoy roughly equal opportunites to influence the decision-making processes that concern them; that the members of the organizations determine the politics of pressure groups and parties; and that the latter in turn are pushed by multiple memberships into a readiness for compromise and the integration of interests. Under these conditions, pluralist democracies should project the social balance of power onto the distribution of political power in such a way that politics remains sensitive to a broad spectrum of values and interests.[3]

After these assumptions were falsified, pluralist theory was revised along lines already evident in the work of Joseph Schumpeter. Because the composition of interest groups is in fact highly selective, because members are largely inactive and have little influence on organizational policy, it was now assumed that power struggles are essentially conducted by elites. A further assumption also proved untenable: that politicians and administrators depend on a variety of collective actors having approximately equal weight in the competition for political influence. What remained was a *theory of political elites* that essentially reduced the role of the democratic process to plebiscites between competing leadership teams, and thus to the recruitment of personnel and the selection of leaders.[4] Naturally, from a normative standpoint, the theory still had to explain how "a politics basically initiated by elites [can] also satisfy the interests of nonelites."[5] With this question, a remnant of normative expectations was shifted from the input side to the output side of the administrative system. Because the unspecific and highly aggregated trust of masses of passive voters no longer can determine the policies of the competing leadership groups, only the *rationality* of the elites themselves, capable of decision and ready for innovation, can guarantee that the administration functions more or less in the equal interest of all. This gives rise to the image of an administrative system that, operating relatively independently of society, *procures* the necessary mass loyalty and determines political goal functions more or less by itself. From a normative standpoint, this poses the problem of the conditions under which the state apparatus, if not actually steered by societal interests, at least develops sufficient sensitivity *for* these interests. A self-programming political system must assume, on its own, the task of articulating publicly relevant needs and wants, latent conflicts, repressed problems, nonorganizable interests, and so forth.

Since the late sixties, though, the evidence for a more cautious assessment has mounted. The administrative system apparently can operate self-consciously only within extremely narrow limits; its operations seem to follow a more reactive style of politics dictated less by planning than by avoiding crisis. On the output side, the "active state" quickly reaches the limits of its steering (or regulatory) capacity, because social systems and large organizations stubbornly resist direct interventions. On the input side, the room for initiative on the part of Government leaders and parties is also restricted by the unpredictability of independent voters—whether enlightened or mobilized by populist movements—whose party ties are becoming increasingly loose. As politics grows ever more bleak, established parties have to fear the withdrawal of legitimation through protest votes and nonvoting. Both legitimation deficits and steering deficits push politics into a kind of incrementalism that can hardly be distinguished from quietism.

This has led to a fork in theoretical developments. *Systems theory* cuts the last remaining ties with normative models, essentially limits itself to the self-referential problems of an autopoietic political system, and once again takes up the organizational problems of the classical theory of the state, translating them into steering problems. By contrast, the *economic theory of democracy* presupposes a methodological individualism and focuses mainly on the process of legitimation. From the viewpoint of systems theory, the mode of operation of the political system is gauged by a rationality of self-reflexive steering that has lost all traces of the normative content of democracy (beyond an alternating allocation of power between the incumbent Government and the opposition). From the viewpoint of economic theory, this normative content is equivalent to the rational-choice behavior of those participating in the democratic process. Meanwhile, it is evident that both approaches, each in its own way, have pushed the normative weight reduction too far. Problems arising within the theories have led to revisions that are suggestive, though not always consistently carried through.

The *economic theory of democracy* attempted to capture empirically some of the normative intuitions of liberalism by demonstrating the rationality of the behavior of voters and politicians.[6] According to this model, in casting their ballots, voters translate a more or less enlightened self-interest into claims on the political system, whereas politicians who want to gain or hold office *exchange* these votes against the offer of specific policies. The transactions between rationally choosing voters and political elites supposedly yield decisions that are rational insofar as they take into account the aggregation of individual interests of equal weight. More recently, the discussion over the "voter's paradox" has inaugurated a certain shift. On the premise of exclusively self-interested behavior, the fact that citizens bother to vote at all could only be explained by a hypothesis that soon proved false: the level of voter turnout does not vary with the voters' expectation that a single vote possibly could decide a head-to-head race. Consequently, proponents expanded the egocentric rational-choice model by bringing in the concept of a metapreference, so that the model could include ethical, albeit self-regarding, considerations.[7] In the end, however, the empirical evidence spoke against all models that were premised on egocentric decision making (however expanded) and that disregarded how changes in interests and value orientations relate to social context.[8] The most recent revisions consider, for example, the "laundering" effect of institutional arrangements that give priority to normative reasons. In this way, institutionalized procedures can foster "responsible" political action: "To act responsibly, then, is for the agent to evaluate his or her own actions by methodically taking the critical perspectives, simultaneously and in the *futurum exactum*, of the expert, the generalized other, and of himself or herself. By assuming this triple perspective, the actor validates the criteria of action substantively, socially, and temporally."[9] With the perspective of Mead's "generalized other," Claus Offe approaches the concept of an opinion- and will-formation that, as I will show, explodes the conceptual framework of an empiricist theory of action.

Systems theory immediately abandons the notion of individual and collective agency. In the face of immense complexes of increasing organizational density, it resolutely concludes that society should be conceived as a network of autonomous subsystems, each of which is encapsulated in its own semantics and has all the other systems for its environment. Only the modes of operation internal to each system, and not the intentions or interests of participating actors, are decisive for interactions between such systems.[10] This choice of conceptual strategy results, on the one hand, in the rejection of a hierarchical concept of society centered in the state. Even the political system, which is specialized for generating collectively binding decisions, must assert itself opportunistically, without possibilities of privileged access, against all the other functional systems (including the legal system). On the other hand, the state-centered understanding of politics that was already present in the liberal model emerges in full force. That is, systems theory ascribes the opinion- and will-formation dominated by party competition to a public of citizens and clients that, cut off from its lifeworld roots in civil society, political culture, and socialization, is incorporated in the political system. Here the administration does not just consist in the complex with the highest organizational density. It also sets in motion a circulation running counter to the "official" circuit of power: the administration predominantly programs itself by steering the legislative process through its bill proposals, by extracting mass loyalty from the citizenry through parties that have become arms of the state, and by making direct contact with its clients.[11] With the increase in social complexity, the balance tips in favor of this informal circulation, so that the question of "how political responsibility under such conditions is even possible" becomes meaningless.[12] A systems theory that has banned everything normative from its basic concepts remains insensitive to the inhibiting normative constraints imposed on a constitutionally channeled circulation of power. Through its keen observations of how the democratic process is hollowed out under the pressure of functional imperatives, systems theory certainly makes a contribution to the theory of democracy. But it offers no framework for its *own* theory of democracy, because it divides politics and law into different, recursively closed systems and analyzes the political process essentially from the perspective of a self-programming administration.

The "realism" that systems theory gains with this selective approach comes at the cost of a disturbing problem. According to systems theory, all functional systems achieve their autonomy by developing their own codes and their own semantics, which no longer admit of mutual translation. They thereby forfeit the ability to communicate directly with one another and as a result can only "observe" each other. This autism especially affects the political system, which also self-referentially closes itself off from its environment. In the face of this autopoietic encapsulation, one can scarcely explain how the political system should be able to integrate society as a whole, even though it is specialized for regulatory activities that are meant not only to rectify disturbances in functional systems but also to achieve an "environment-friendly" coordination among systems drifting apart. It is not clear how one should reconcile the autonomy of the different functional systems and the political system's task of holding them together: "The heart of the problem lies in the improbability of successful communication among autonomous, self-referentially operating unities."[13]

The history of the "realistic" approaches leads, on the one hand, to an economic theory of democracy that would inform us about the instrumental features of democratic will-formation and, on the other hand, to a systems theory that would inform us about the impotence of this will-formation. Both approaches operate with concepts of power that are insensitive to the empirical relevance of the constitution of power under the rule of law, because they screen out the internal relation between law and political power. This deficit ultimately stands behind the questions that Elster and Willke so instructively pursue. Elster's revisions lead to an unexpected rehabilitation of the concept of deliberative politics.

8.1.2

Rational choice theory still revolves around the Hobbesian problem. It cannot explain how strategic actors are capable of stabilizing their social relations solely on the basis of rational decisions. We do not need to go into the details of the penetrating self-criticism here.[14] What interests me is how Elster handles the difficulties this theory encounters when it is applied to political processes. First of all, in this context it is unrealistic to start with a model that assumes that opportunities and preferences can be treated as something given; both of these change in the political process itself. Moreover, the individual preferences expressed in opinion polls do not reliably reflect the actual preferences of the individuals polled, if by "preferences" one means the preferences they *would* express after weighing the relevant information and arguments. For the political transformation of values and attitudes is not a process of blind adaptation but the result of a constructive opinion- and will-formation. Elster designates this as the "autonomous" formation of preferences: "autonomy is for desires what judgement is for beliefs."[15] Moreover, it is especially unrealistic to assume that all social behavior is strategic action and can thus be explained as though it were the result of egocentric utility calculations. The explanatory power of this sociological model is obviously limited: "While there is always a risk of self-serving behavior, the extent to which it is actually present varies widely. Much of the social choice and public choice literature, with its assumption of universally opportunistic behavior, simply seems out of touch with the real world, in which there is a great deal of honesty and sense of duty. If people always engaged in opportunistic behavior when they could get away with it, civilization as we know it would not exist."[16]

This and similar considerations led Elster years ago to broaden the rational-choice framework by including socioethical commitments and moral reasons among preferences. In addition, he described the democratic process as a mechanism that changes preferences through public discussions.[17] What matters most to him are the procedural aspects of such a rational will-formation.[18] To render this idea fruitful, he had to make two drastic revisions in the rational-choice model.

First, he expanded the theory by adding an additional action type. Besides *strategic* or purposive-rational action, which is oriented to consequences (under conditions of incomplete information) and steered by the individual's own preferences, there is also *norm-regulated* action. The latter is an elementary action type, because it is not reducible to strategic action.[19] In reply to the argument that norms serve only to justify opportunistic action after the fact, Elster maintains that no one could deal strategically with norms in a particular case if he could not count on the intersubjective recognition of norms in general. To this extent, the social validity of norms enjoys a logical priority over the advantages one might gain by pretending to orient oneself to such norms. Equally unconvincing is the further objection that norm-conformative behavior is actually a purposive-rational avoidance of internalized sanctions (such as feelings of shame and guilt). Dealing rationally with the consequences of a behavior that by presupposition is irrational does not explain how this behavior (as the result of the antecedent internalization of a behavioral norm) comes about in the first place: one cannot rationally resolve to act irrationally.

However, Elster still clings to empiricist premises when he introduces the new action type. As he describes it, norm-regulated action differs from strategic action only by the lack of an orientation to expected consequences. Purposive rationality is what *homo oeconomicus* has over *homo sociologicus*.[20] Norms and value orientations seem to elude rational assessment; they merely ground counterfactually maintained behavioral expectations that are immune to learning. As a result, Elster splits the moral or ethical sphere into two domains, one cognitive and rational, the other emotive and irrational. He either strips *moral* norms of their obligatory character, in line with utilitarianism, and classifies them as decision rules for purposive-rational action; or he admits them as binding norms, in the sense of a rigid ethics of conviction, but strips them of any rational character.

As long as normativity and rationality exclude each other like this, the rationally motivated coordination of action can only take the form of a negotiated agreement among strategically oriented actors. The process of rational agreement becomes equivalent to "bargaining"—the negotiation of compromises. Indeed, such bargaining, which requires a willingness to cooperate on the part of strategic actors, is connected with norms that take the form of empirical constraints or irrational self-bindings. To this end, Elster develops a parallelogram of forces that explains normatively regulated bargaining processes as a *combination* of rational calculations of success with social norms that contingently steer from behind.[21]

However, this empiricist way of introducing value orientations proves deficient if it is supposed to explain how participants can rationally change their preferences in the course of political will-formation. Nor does it explain how new options can open up in a "convincing" manner. The political process involves more than compromises based on credible threats. This is why Elster introduces "argumentation" as a further mechanism besides "bargaining" for solving problems of collective action: "Rational argumentation on the one hand, threats and promises on the other, are the main vehicles by which the parties seek to reach agreement. The former is subject to criteria of validity, the latter to criteria of credibility."[22] With "criteria of validity," a new kind of communication and action coordination comes into play. Whereas parties can agree to a negotiated compromise for different reasons, the consensus brought about through argument must rest on identical reasons able to convince the parties *in the same way*. The consensus-generating force of such reasons is displayed in the idea of impartiality that governs practical discourses.[23]

This step necessitates a revision of the first revision. With the idea of the impartial assessment of interest positions and action conflicts, those norms previously considered irrational are partly drawn into the vortex of argumentation. If Elster wants an additional mechanism of action coordination—not only the reciprocal influence exerted by actors oriented to success but also the communication among persons engaged in argument for the purposes of reaching understanding—then he must acknowledge a rational core to norms and value orientations and correspondingly enlarge his concept of rationality. This he can do with the help of the deontological concept of justice or practical reason, in the light of which rights can be justified.[24] It follows that the task of politics is not merely to eliminate inefficient and uneconomical regulations but also to establish and guarantee living conditions in the equal interest of all citizens.[25]

With these basic conceptual revisions in place, Elster undertakes an empirical analysis of the discussions conducted in the constitutional assemblies of Philadelphia (1776) and Paris (1789–1791). His analysis starts from the theoretically motivated distinction between "bargaining" and "arguing," where argumentation includes, according to our terminology, not only justice arguments but also ethical-political arguments referring to the "general welfare" of the nation. Elster goes on, by way of a comparative analysis of the first two modern constitutional processes, to examine the assumption that a parliamentary opinion- and will-formation of this kind cannot be adequately explained on the empiricist premises of a balance of interests steered exclusively by power. Rather, discourses and bargaining processes intertwine in such processes, though compromise formation often takes place spontaneously and to this extent does not satisfy the fairness conditions of *regulated* bargaining.[26] Elster's Storr Lectures permit two interpretations, depending on whether one refers to their obvious message or to the analysis of the role played by certain types of arguments selected from the debates. Read from the first perspective, Elster reconstructs a piece of legal history. He reaches the conclusion that "the will of the constitutional lawgiver" was to enact a system of rights that under the perceived circumstances was intended to guarantee the citizens' political autonomy by institutionalizing an *impartial* opinion- and will-formation. In this respect, Elster's contribution (at least implicitly) tests the discourse-theoretic reading of the constitutional state against its historical background.

His explicit goal, however, is to rationally reconstruct patterns of argument in order to show that the decisions of the political lawgiver were, to a certain extent, rationally motivated, namely, by rational discourse and mutual understanding in combination with a success-oriented exercise of influence.[27] Elster investigates primarily the interaction of these two mechanisms. In the process it turns out, not surprisingly, that the actual course of the debates deviates from the ideal procedure of deliberative politics. At the same time, however, presuppositions of rational discourse have a steering effect on the course of debate. The communicative presuppositions for a deliberative contest of opinions are institutionalized in such parliamentary bodies at least effectively enough that the democratic procedure filters arguments and gives legitimacy-producing reasons a privileged chance to come into play.

For example, not all interests can be publicly advocated. Hence the publicity of political communications (emphasized by Kant), in connection with the expectation that proponents are consistent in their utterances and explain their proposals coherently, already exerts a salutary procedural force. Under this condition, concealing publicly indefensible interests behind pretended moral or ethical reasons necessitates self-bindings that either on the next occasion expose a proponent as inconsistent or, in the interest of maintaining his credibility, lead to the inclusion of others' interests.[28]

These and similar considerations suggest that one should seek the conditions for a rational political will-formation not only at the individual level of the orientations and decisions of single actors but also at the social level of institutionalized processes of deliberation and decision making. These can be seen as arrangements that have an effect on the preferences of participants; they screen the topics and contributions, information and reasons in such a way that, ideally, only the "valid" inputs pass through the filter of fair bargaining and rational discourses. With this, the perspective shifts from rational-choice theory to discourse theory: "These institutions [i.e., of the United States Constitution] were designed to play the role of 'congealed' or 'sedimented' virtue, which thus made the *actual practice* of these virtues, such as truthfulness, wisdom, reason, justice and all kinds of exceptional moral qualities, to some extent dispensable—on the part of both the rulers and the ruled."[29] To the degree that practical reason is implanted in the very forms of communication and institutionalized procedures, it need not be embodied exclusively or even predominantly in the heads of collective or individual actors. Elster's investigation provides some support for the assumption that the discursive level of observable political communication is a standard for the effectiveness of a "proceduralized reason" of this sort. The results of deliberative politics can be understood as communicatively generated power that competes, on the one hand, with the social power of actors with credible threats and, on the other hand, with the administrative power of officeholders.

8.2 A Model of the Circulation of Political Power

Systems theory does not have to deny the phenomenon of a communicative power generated within the parliamentary complex—nor that of an influence acquired in the political public sphere—but it describes the phenomena in a way that a fortiori exposes communicative power as impotent. From this viewpoint, once the law is fully positivized, the political system should be able to forego independent sources of legitimate law. As with all functional systems, politics, too, has become an autonomous, recursively closed circuit of communication furnished with its own code. In connection with the legal system responsible for securing legality, such a contingent, self-referential politics draws everything it needs for legitimacy from itself. The need for legitimation can be met paternalistically through lines of connection that, running from the ritualized confrontation between the incumbent Government and the opposition, reach via party competition into the loose network of the voting public. However, Luhmann's depiction of the self-legitimation of a politics anchored in the state apparatus begins to fall apart if systems theory is confronted with the task of "conceiving the theory of the state from the perspective of an ethically responsible and responsive society."[30]

In section 8.2.1, I present an immanent critique of Willke's innovative attempt to develop such a theory of the state; in section 8.2.2, I then develop from this a model suitable for a sociologically informed use of the concept of deliberative politics.

8.2.1

In his *Philosophy of Right* (secs. 250–56), Hegel assigned the corporations the important task of mediating between civil society and the powers of the state. In light of the current neocorporatism debate, Willke is led to a view that reads like a modern systems-theoretic version of the Hegelian *Ständestaat*—only without its monarchical head. Concerted actions, round-table arrangements, and the various kinds of coordinating committees that arise in the gray areas between state and society are described by Willke as symptomatic bargaining systems. These systems should allow politics in a decentered society to assume the role of a therapeutically trained supervisor that preserves the encompassing social unity that the state itself can no longer represent. On the one hand, Willke, like Luhmann, sees that the political system has become one subsystem among others. No longer able to claim social primacy, it is relieved of the function of integrating society as a whole. On the other hand, through the back door, Willke reintroduces the state as guarantor of a neocorporatist social integration.

As surprising as this answer might be, the question is the logical result of the "autopoietic turn" taken by systems theory. Indeed, the logic of the functional differentiation of society implies that the separate subsystems are reintegrated at a higher level of society. If the decentered society could no longer preserve its unity somewhere, it would not profit from the growth in the complexity of its parts and would be, as a whole, the victim of their gains in differentiation. The society converted to "autopoiesis" actually seems to lead to this dead end, for the functional systems take the last step to autonomy via their own specialized semantics that, with all their advantages, have the consequence of breaking off a direct exchange of information with their corresponding environments. Each functional system forms its own picture of society. Subsystems no longer command a shared language in which the unity of society could be represented for all of them in *the same way*. Non-code-specific mutual understanding is passé. As a result, each system becomes insensitive to the costs it generates for other systems. There is no longer any place where problems relevant for the reproduction of society *as a whole* could be perceived and dealt with. The special languages like money or administrative power wear down ordinary language—as the functional systems do the lifeworld—so much that neither the one nor the other presents a sounding board that would be sufficiently complex for thematizing and treating society-wide problems. Under these conditions, the political public sphere cannot provide such a sounding board, because, together with the public of citizens, it is hitched to the power code and placated with symbolic politics.

On the other hand, the trends toward social disintegration pose a challenge especially for politics and law. In a sense, these trends revive a shock that both have experienced once before in the rise of religious pluralism and loss of an overarching religious legitimacy. The question of how the unity of society can be secured now that the state can no longer represent it is, to be sure, no longer posed today *directly* as a question of legitimation. The standard of "legitimacy" pertains only to legal and political questions; it cannot be applied to problems affecting *society as a whole*. Nevertheless, the routine business of procuring legitimation is burdened by problems of macrosocial irrationality, because law and politics have assumed a kind of surety for the cohesion of the entire system. In any case, Willke diagnoses the return of a legitimation problem that is at least *induced* through the inadequate integration of the whole of society, even if this problem is *measured* not in the specific systemic terms of "legitimacy" but by a "total system rationality." This kind of societal rationality should now be managed precisely through politically mediated processes of attunement (*Abstimmungs-*

prozesse) among different functional systems. Willke's neocorporatist vision "aims at shaping intersystem relationships among autonomous, active, and interdependent subsystems that no longer submit to the primacy of one part [namely, politics]. Hence they do not derive total system rationality from the validity of the universal but from the reflexive attunement of the particular."[31] According to his diagnosis, the political systems in Western societies are already on the road to a "supervisory" state.[32] The following three points summarize the description of a society that would be both integrated by, and under the guardianship of, an intersystemic balance of this sort:

(a) The supervisory state looks to nonhierarchical bargaining systems for an attunement among sociofunctional systems that either suffer disturbances in their operations and performance and need "developmental aid," or burden their environment with externalities and must be prodded to "show consideration." However, the manner in which self-referential systems can be induced to structural transformations is already fixed by these systems' own structures. For this reason, the supervisory state must pursue an "options policy" that goes beyond incentives. This kind of policy is a familiar idea in economic planning. To steer a given system, an options approach first considers that system's mode of operation and degrees of freedom and then exerts influence on the system's self-steering through suitable changes in the context. The extensively researched difficulties in such policy fields as health care, technology, and science provide plausible evidence for the limits of direct state interventions; instead of this, the approach taken in business consultation is considered exemplary as a strategy that implicates the various operationally closed systems in a "productive and self-binding interrelationship."[33]

(b) Even the politics that "counsels" systems must avail itself of the language of law, though no longer in the form of conditional or goal programs but as "reflexive" law.[34] Politics provides the manipulated systems with new "forms" for their own setting of priorities, so that the set of preferences internal to the system receives a different weight. Each system should play its own melody but with a new rhythm. To this end, an individualistic civil law must be transposed to the level of collective actors and converted from personal references to system relations. Examples are found in the legal protection pertaining to the new collective goods of the "risk society": protection from environmental destruction; protection from radiation poisoning or lethal genetic damage; and, in general, protection from the uncontrolled side effects of large technological operations, pharmaceutical products, scientific experimentation, and so forth. Law must not implement goals in the form of targets; rather, through "relational programs," it should induce and enable the system that is causing the danger to steer itself in a new direction. In this way, the law functions as a catalyst for self-monitored modifications.

(c) Though social integration would, according to this view, shift from the level of democratic opinion- and will-formation to the level of intersystemic monitoring, the "essential content" of a constitutional democracy transposed from persons to systems is supposed to remain intact. Willke speaks of the "establishment of societal discourses" and even of the "attunement of autonomous actors through rational discourses."[35] For the attunement processes follow the guidelines set by (democratic?) procedures that regulate the communication among the decentered units: "Consensus is required as a framework consensus regarding the foundations and bounds of dissent, so that dissent, taken continually further, does not lead to the system's dissolution." At this point, Willke adds "that consensus is needed only as the continually reconstituted imaginary line, which is no sooner fixed than differences and dissent can fasten on it to dissolve it"; thus, even the idealizing moment in the discourse concept of truth and validity is captured in the language of systems theory.[36] Of course, this formulation, which Willke's simulation of democratic consensus borrows from the intersubjectivistic vocabulary of a different theoretical tradition, can have only a metaphorical meaning under the changed premises.

On the one hand, unlike the communicative practice of citizens, the "conversation" of functional systems no longer deals with norms, values, and interests. Rather, it is restricted to the cognitive goal of enhancing systemic self-reflection. Exchanges among experts who instruct one another about the operation of their respective functional sectors is supposed to overcome the specific blindness of self-enclosed systems. As the examples drawn from management literature show, this exchange resembles more a continuing-education program in which the training leader or moderator prompts the managers coming from various branches to act as consultants for one another's business problems. On the other hand, the "conference rules" governing the conversation forfeit the universalistic content of democratic procedure; the set of functional systems "in need of therapy" at a given point cannot claim to be representative.

Willke's interesting proposal for solving theoretically acute problems of macrosocial integration runs into difficulties that deserve comment, because they reveal the true proportions of the legitimation problem suppressed by systems theory.

In reply to (a) above: In its classical form, the Hobbesian problem was posed as the question of how the confluence of the egocentric perspectives of self-interested actors could yield an order that encouraged individuals to consider the interests of others. This problem, which rational choice theory still chips away at, reappears for systems theory in a different form. A self-stabilizing order must now be explained by the cognitive attunement of system perspectives. The practical dimension of action coordination has disappeared in the approach taken by systems theory, so that a reasonable "altruism" for the intercourse of functional systems becomes meaningless. In the purely epistemic version, however, the Hobbesian problem is posed still more sharply, because the egocentrism of clashing perspectives is no longer determined simply by each person's own preferences and value orientations but by each system's own *grammar for interpreting the world*. Unlike individuals in the state of nature, autopoietic systems no longer share a common world. To this extent, the problem of successful communication among independent and self-referentially operating units, each with its own perspective on the world, corresponds almost exactly to the familiar phenomenological problem of constructing an intersubjectively shared world from the egological achievements of transcendental monads. No more than Husserl (or later, Sartre) solved this problem of intersubjectivity,[37] has systems theory managed to explain how autopoietically closed systems could, inside the circuit of self-referential steering, be induced to go beyond pure self-reference and autopoiesis.[38]

The reflexive spiral of the reciprocal observation of the other's self-observations does not escape the circle in which both external observation and self-observation are always a system's own observation; it does not penetrate the darkness of mutual opacity.[39] To "understand" the mode of operation and the self-reference of another system and not just "observe" it, to be able not just to form a "picture" of this according to their own respective codes, the systems involved would have to have available an at least partially shared language. But this is excluded ex hypothesi:

Successful communication presupposes that the parts present one another with reciprocally relevant information in such a way that it can be "read," i.e., can be understood even in the context of basic criteria that are different and foreign. The challenge is to establish compatibility between different "language games," whereby different realities and projections of the world are linked with the "language." *It is thus true even of complex societies that the deep structure of their order is bound to the grammar of the transfer of comprehensible information.*[40]

The "transference rules" making up such a grammar, however, cannot be given simply by the grammatical rules of an ordinary language circulating throughout society. Rather, following the model of international private law, they must first be constructed as collision norms that, from the perspective of each system, set up bridges of mutual understanding with other systems. But to the extent that the involved systems generate such rules for themselves, they have not yet overcome their semantic perspectivism. At best they have created the basis for a new stage of development. The required *intermeshing of perspectives* must, therefore, *wait for* a new system of rules to emerge.

In the end, Willke has to conjure the conditions for the intersubjectivity of possible mutual understanding out of the hat of social evolution: "A new kind of rule comes into play here. For the first time, these rules are no longer anchored in subsystems but arise at the level of [whole] systems from the active and intentional interplay of the parts, which want [!] to combine into an emergent total system. This type of rule is the material from which decentralized context-steering can develop as procedures of political supervision."[41] From the reciprocal observation and mutual groping of semantically closed systems, therefore, a language is supposed to *emerge* that simulates exactly what ordinary language—namely, the natural language from which the special semantics were originally differentiated—always already achieves. Willke's auxiliary construct of an emergent language is even less convincing in that the law, with its required "relational programs," must already link up with the ordinary linguistic achievements by which "comprehensible information" is transferred throughout society. If one follows the discussions in the analytical philosophy of language, it is at any rate not surprising that ordinary language functions as the "ultimate metalanguage." It forms the open medium of a language that circulates throughout society and can be translated into and from every specialized code.

In reply to (b): The supervisory state is supposed to ward off the "danger of absolutizing subsystem rationality at the expense of the rationality of the whole."[42] This goal exceeds the reach of any one system, including the political system; it makes internal political legitimation depend on a successful context steering that is no longer under political control. This steering must instead proceed through corporate bargaining, that is, through institutions of intersystemic attunement and coordination. Even if politics should manage, without cognitive dissonance, to *extend* its own code-specific criteria of legitimacy by adding the standards of a comprehensive societal rationality that govern "supervision," this would shift the basis of decision making in such a way that the political system would no longer be able to attribute all the decisions in need of legitimation *solely to itself*. But this implies an interruption of the internal process of *self*-legitimation. Intersystemic supervision is still effected in the forms of law. But when lawmaking powers are delegated to bargaining networks infected by the dynamics *specific* to different social systems operating self-referentially beyond politics, the reproduction of law and politics falls under the shadow of a "dual power" ambiguously divided between state administration and social units. The more the public administration gets involved in "societal discourses" of the new kind, the less it can satisfy the constitutional imperatives of the official circulation of power. The same neocorporatism that is supposed to cope with the dangers of macrosocial disintegration and keep the new kind of legitimation problem in check disturbs the process of self-legitimation inside the political system. This objection would be off target only if the envisioned change in the type of legal regulation could be kept within the boundaries of democracy.

The more collective actors, sociofunctional systems, and large organizations act in place of individuals, the more clearly the basis for assigning responsibility for the consequences of actions shifts—and the less it seems possible to rely on rights for safeguarding those collective goods of the "risk society" that are worth protecting. For this reason, Willke considers it obsolete to anchor law in an individualistically designed system of rights. The "relational programs" he calls for are instead designed for the autopoietic reproduction and self-steering of systems; they no longer refer to the private and public autonomy of socialized individuals. Nevertheless, such a restructuring of law is by no means intended to abandon the idea of the constitutional state but only to interpret it differently. On this premise, a formally correct legal regulation of the bargaining networks would suffice to secure their legitimacy as well. Willke even insists that

democracy can be preserved in highly complex societies only if this idea [of the constitutional state] is generalized for society as a whole. Furthermore, society must be specifically constituted in a way that permits and promotes the guarantee of the autonomy and differences of citizens as much as the autonomy and differences of its functional systems. The latter is *not just* an end in itself for the preservation of the achieved degree of functional differentiation but *in addition* serves to generalize the constitutional protection of the citizen.[43]

In fact, this formulation reveals more than a break with just one historical—indeed, historically obsolete—reading of constitutional democracy. With the "idea of a society-wide, consensually institutionalized and binding constitution" that stretches "from its citizens as natural persons to include their organizations, corporate actors, and functional systems,"[44] the systems-theoretic adaptation of the Hegelian *Ständestaat* takes the place of the democratic constitutional state and undermines its individualistic basis of legitimation. This is already evident in simple examples. Neocorporatist bargaining networks can attune the growing complexity of each functional system with the others only by simultaneously stimulating this growth; yet there is no preestablished harmony between, on the one hand, this growth in the complexity of systems that are "entitled to take part in the arrangement" and, on the other, the realization of citizens' constitutional rights. Certainly one can often justify a high level of systemic differentiation even from a normative standpoint. And as long as rising complexity in public administration and the capitalist economy was paralleled by the increasing inclusion of citizens, one could assume, all in all, that gains in functional differentiation coincided with normative progress in the realization of equal rights. However, these parallels were a matter of contingent, and hitherto in no way linear, correlations. Moreover, there are many indications of *counter*developments. To name just one of these, in the fragmented societies of today's economically interdependent OECD-world, the prosperity and security enjoyed by a majority of the population is increasingly accompanied by the segmentation of a neglected and powerless underclass that is disadvantaged in practically every respect. Conflicts arise between the neocorporatistically negotiated policies and the constitutional protection of underorganized parts of the population at the periphery of society. These conflicts arise not only as the result of an unequal distribution of social rewards but also because the loss of collective goods affects different social classes selectively.

Hence the idea of government by law is vitiated if sociofunctional systems are constitutionally released from their instrumental role and promoted to "ends in themselves." The "autonomy and differences" of citizens must then compete with that of systems for legal protection, even within the "official" circulation of power. The constitutional structure of the political system is preserved only if government officials hold out against corporate bargaining partners and maintain the asymmetrical position that results from their obligation to represent the whole of an absent citizenry, whose will is embodied in the wording of statutes. Even in attunement processes, the bonds of delegation must not tear away from actual decision making. Only in this way is the connection with the public of citizens preserved, the public that is both entitled and *in the position* to perceive, identify, and publicly thematize the social intolerability of deficient or disturbed functional systems. Indeed, only in the corporatist arrangements do these systems supposedly first learn to overcome their specific blindnesses and observe themselves as subsystems in a larger system. Hence they depend on affected clients as citizens to instruct them about their external costs and the negative effects of their internal failures. If the discourse of experts is not coupled with democratic opinion- and will-formation, then the experts' perception of problems will prevail at the citizens' expense. However, every difference of interpretation of this sort must, from the standpoint of the public of citizens, be seen as further confirmation of a systems paternalism that endangers legitimacy.

In reply to (c): This narrowly cognitivist, managerial account of neocorporatist steering discourses is explained by the fact that the attunement among systems gives rise exclusively to problems of functional coordination. Here the knowledge relevant for steering, provided by various groups of experts, is supposed to be worked into policies and translated into corresponding legal programs by legal scholars enlightened by systems theory. This conception is based on the unrealistic assumption that one can separate the professional knowledge of specialists from values and moral points of view. As soon as specialized knowledge is brought to politically relevant problems, its unavoidably normative character becomes apparent, setting off controversies that polarize the experts themselves. This by itself shows that problems of functional coordination, when handled politically, are *intertwined* with the moral and ethical dimensions of social integration. It is against the life-historical background of violated interests and threatened identities that the effects of deficient system integration are first experienced as pressing problems. Therefore, it is counterproductive, not only from the viewpoint of legitimacy but also from a cognitive viewpoint, for attunement processes between governmental and societal actors to become independent vis-à-vis the political public sphere and parliamentary will-formation. From both viewpoints, it is advisable that the enlarged knowledge base of a planning and supervising administration be shaped by deliberative politics, that is, shaped by the publicly organized contest of opinions between experts and counterexperts and monitored by public opinion.

8.2.2

The concept of a society of autonomous subsystems constituted as "estates" faces the objections analyzed in (a) through (c) above. These objections all point in the same direction: the integration of a highly complex society cannot be carried out in a systems-paternalistic fashion, that is, in a manner that bypasses the communicative power of the public of citizens. Semantically closed systems cannot be induced to invent on their own the common language necessary for the perception and articulation of the relevant issues and standards of evaluation that apply to society as a whole. For such tasks, an ordinary language is available, circulating throughout society and lying beneath the threshold of the special codes. In the peripheral networks of the political public sphere and in the parliamentary complex, this ordinary language is, in any case, already in demand for dealing with macrosocial problems. This fact alone makes it impossible to conceive politics and law as autopoietically closed systems. The constitutionally structured political system is internally differentiated into spheres of administrative and communicative power and remains open to the lifeworld. For institutionalized opinion- and will-formation depends on supplies coming from the informal contexts of communication found in the public sphere, in civil society, and in spheres of private life. In other words, the political action system is embedded in lifeworld contexts.

Paragovernmental bargaining arrangements lacking effective ties to the parliamentary complex and the public sphere give rise to legitimation problems. Because they are specialized for questions of functional coordination, such corporatist networks are also no match cognitively for the pressure of accumulating problems. Moreover, the concentration on steering problems distorts the proportion between traditional and new administrative tasks. The tasks of social integration (in its specific sense of maintaining order, income redistribution and social welfare, the protection of collective identities and the transmission of a shared political culture) still have a place second to none on the political agenda. A fixation on highly organized social complexes gives rise to a one-sided picture. Functionally differentiated societies certainly involve more than a multiplicity of self-referentially closed sub-systems. The systems paradigm corresponds most closely to the capitalist economy and to the public administration specialized in planning and welfare. However, the inner logic with which many highly organized spheres, such as the educational system or science, oppose direct interventions is due not at all to a specific code or a steering medium analogous to money but to the logic of the special questions addressed in these spheres. Besides, the "constitutionalization" of action systems, which is the purpose of the "context-steering" strategies of a supervisory state, means something different in communicatively integrated spheres, such as the family or school, than it does in systemically integrated large organizations or networks (such as markets). In the former case, the legal constitution is only *superimposed* on an existing normative infrastructure; in the latter, it aids in the functional coordination of social relationships that are legally *created*. Finally, participatory forms of administration that bring implementing agencies into discourses with their clients (taken seriously as citizens) have a different sense than do neocorporatist bargaining arrangements. These differences must not disappear in the gray-on-gray descriptions of systems theory.

If we want to answer the questions posed at the end of the last chapter, then we must find a route other than those of systems theory and rational-choice theory. Elster's reconstructive analysis of the constitution-making process directs our attention to the procedural rationality of democratic opinion- and will-formation; however, what we see there does not extend beyond the production of communicative power. From a perspective broadened by systems theory, Willke concentrates on an administration overburdened with steering problems, problems that on his analysis can be solved only by circumventing communicative power. But this diagnosis underestimates what a multifunctional ordinary language can achieve precisely in virtue of its lack of specialization. Ordinary language is the medium of communicative action through which the lifeworld reproduces itself; in it, too, the components of the lifeworld interpenetrate one another. The action systems specialized for cultural reproduction (education) or socialization (family) or social integration (such as law) are not totally separated in their operation. Through the shared code of ordinary language, each of these systems also concomitantly satisfies the functions of the other two and thus maintains a relation to the totality of the lifeworld. The core private spheres of the lifeworld, which are characterized by intimacy and hence by protection from publicity, structure encounters between relatives, friends, acquaintances, and so on, and link together the members' life histories at the level of face-to-face interactions. The public sphere has a complementary relation to this private sphere, from which the public, as the bearers of the public sphere, is recruited.

The lifeworld forms, as a whole, a network composed of communicative actions. Under the aspect of action coordination, its *society* component consists of the totality of legitimately ordered interpersonal relationships. It also encompasses collectivities, associations, and organizations specialized for specific functions. *Some* of these functionally specialized action systems become independent vis-à-vis socially integrated spheres of action, that is, spheres integrated through values, norms, and mutual understanding. Such systems develop their own codes, as the economy does with money and the administration does with power. Through the legal institutionalization of steering media, however, these systems remain anchored in the society component of the lifeworld. The language of law brings ordinary communication from the public and private spheres and puts it into a form in which these messages can also be received by the special codes of autopoietic systems—and vice versa. Without this transformer, ordinary language could not circulate throughout society.

In the following discussion, I make use of Bernard Peters's model to give a more precise form to, and seek a tentative answer to, the question of whether and how a constitutionally regulated circulation of power might be established.[45] According to Peters's proposal, processes of communication and decision making in constitutional systems display the following features: they lie along a center-periphery axis, they are structured by a system of "sluices," and they involve two modes of problem solving. The core area of the political system is formed by the familiar institutional complexes of administration (including the incumbent Government), judicial system, and democratic opinion- and will-formation (which includes parliamentary bodies, political elections, and party competition). Hence this center, distinguished from the periphery in virtue of formal decision-making powers and actual prerogatives, is internally organized as a "polyarchy." Within the core area, to be sure, the "capacity to act" varies with the "density" of organizational complexity. The parliamentary complex is the most open for perceiving and thematizing social problems, but it pays for this sensitivity with a lesser capacity to deal with problems in comparison to the administrative complex. At the edges of the administration, a kind of *inner* periphery develops out of various institutions equipped with rights of self-governance or with other kinds of oversight and lawmaking functions delegated by the state (universities, public insurance systems, professional agencies and associations, charitable organizations, foundations, etc.). The core area as a whole has an *outer* periphery that, roughly speaking, branches into "customers" and "suppliers."

On the side of implementation, for different policy fields, complex networks have arisen among public agencies and private organizations, business associations, labor unions, interest groups, and so on; these networks fulfill certain coordination functions in more or less opaque social sectors. One should distinguish this type of clientele bargaining from the "supplier" groups, associations, and organizations that, before parliaments and through the courts, give voice to social problems, make broad demands, articulate public interests or needs, and thus attempt to influence the political process more from normative points of view than from the standpoint of particular interests. The spectrum extends from organizations representing clearly defined group interests; through associations (with goals recognizably defined by party politics) and cultural establishments (such as academies, writers' associations, and "radical professionals"); up to "public-interest groups" (with public concerns, such as the protection of the environment, the testing of products, and the protection of animals) and churches or charitable organizations.[46] These opinion-forming associations, which specialize in issues and contributions and are generally designed to generate public influence, belong to the civil-social infrastructure of a public sphere dominated by the mass media. With its informal, highly differentiated and cross-linked channels of communication, this public sphere forms the real periphery. Naturally, as the debate over corporatist bargaining shows, the distinction between output-oriented "customers" and input-oriented "suppliers" is not a sharp one. But the actually observable fusion between influencing the implementation of policies that have already been adopted, on the one hand, and influencing the formulation and adoption of policies, on the other hand, is not in agreement with constitutional principles.[47]

After a descriptive overview, Peters introduces two explanatory elements: the "sluice model" and the two modes of problem solving that determine the direction in which communication flows. If binding decisions are to be carried out with authority, they must pass through the narrow channels of the core area:

> However, the legitimacy of decisions depends on processes of opinion- and will-formation at the periphery. The center is a system of sluices through which many processes in the sphere of the political-legal system must pass, but the center controls the direction and the dynamics of these processes only to a limited degree. Changes can start just as much at the periphery as at the center. . . . The idea of democracy is ultimately based on the fact that political processes of will-formation, which in the schema here sketched have a peripheral or intermediary status, are supposed to be decisive for political development. This is not predecided by the present schema.[48]

This sociological translation of the discourse theory of democracy implies that binding decisions, to be legitimate, must be steered by communication flows that start at the periphery and pass through the sluices of democratic and constitutional procedures situated at the entrance to the parliamentary complex or the courts (and, if necessary, at the exit of the implementing administration as well). That is the only way to exclude the possibility that the power of the administrative complex, on the one side, or the social power of intermediate structures affecting the core area, on the other side, become independent vis-à-vis a communicative power that develops in the parliamentary complex.

To be sure, the normal business of politics, at least as it is routinely conducted in Western democracies, cannot satisfy such strong conditions. The countercirculation cutting across the "official" circulation of power certainly involves more than just a contradictory, disdainful social facticity. Many of these communications flowing in the opposite direction serve to relieve the burden of unavoidable complexity from the official circulation by breaking problems down into smaller components. Peters takes this circumstance into account with the help of a second explanatory element. For the most part, operations in the core area of the political system proceed according to routines. Courts deliver judgments, bureaucracies prepare laws and process applications, parliaments pass laws and budgets, party headquarters conduct election campaigns, clients exert influence on "their" administrations—and all these processes follow established patterns. From a normative standpoint, the only decisive question concerns which power constellations these patterns reflect and how the latter can be *changed*. This in turn depends on whether the settled routines remain open to renovative impulses from the periphery. In cases of conflict, that is, processing matters according to the usual conventions is eclipsed by *another* mode of operation.

This latter mode of operation is characterized by a consciousness of crisis, a heightened public attention, an intensified search for solutions, in short, by *problematization*. In cases in which perceptions of problems and problem situations have taken a conflictual turn, the attention span of the citizenry enlarges, indeed in such a way that controversies in the broader public sphere primarily ignite around the normative aspects of the problems most at issue. The pressure of public opinion then necessitates an extraordinary mode of problem solving, which favors the constitutional channels for the circulation of power and thus actuates sensibilities for the constitutional allocation of *political responsibilities*. True, even during the "normal" course of business, parliaments and courts attempt normatively to limit the discretion enjoyed by an administration operating largely in a goal-oriented manner. But in cases of conflict, the constitutional scheme for regulating access to normative reasons acquires a sharper profile. Only in this way can parliaments and courts—the two branches of government that alone are *formally* empowered to deal with normative reasons in a constructive or reconstructive manner—also *actually determine* the direction in which communication circulates. When conflicts become this intense, the political lawgiver has the last word. To be sure, considerable evidence shows that by itself the parliamentary complex usually lacks the strength "to turn cases into cases of conflict." Institutions that decide under time pressure have a weak capacity to detect latent problems, which are apprehended either insufficiently or not at all by settled routines. And they have little initiative to stage newly emergent problems in a successful and dramatic manner.

The distinction between normal and extraordinary modes of posing and solving problems, however, can be rendered fruitful for a sociological translation and realistic interpretation of the discourse·concept of democracy only if we introduce two further assumptions. The illegitimate independence of social and administrative power vis-à-vis democratically generated communicative power is averted to the extent that the periphery has both (a) a specific set of capabilities and (b) sufficient occasion to exercise them. The first assumption, (a), refers to the capacities to ferret out, identify, and effectively thematize latent problems of social integration (which require political solutions); moreover, an activated periphery must then introduce them via parliamentary (or judicial) sluices into the political system in a way that *disrupts* the latter's routines. The second assumption, (b), is less problematic. As we have seen, the links between decentered, increasingly autonomous social sectors loosen in the course of progressive functional differentiation. There is thus a growing need for integration that renders crises permanent, stimulates the public sphere, and makes accelerated learning processes necessary.

The problematic assumption is (a). It places a good part of the normative expectations connected with deliberative politics on the peripheral networks of opinion-formation. The expectations are directed at the capacity to perceive, interpret, and present society-wide problems in a way that is both attention-catching and innovative. The periphery can satisfy these strong expectations only insofar as the networks of noninstitutionalized public communication make possible more or less *spontaneous* processes of opinion-formation. Resonant and autonomous public spheres of this sort must in turn be anchored in the voluntary associations of civil society and embedded in liberal patterns of political culture and socialization; in a word, they depend on a rationalized lifeworld that meets them halfway. The development of such lifeworld structures can certainly be stimulated, but for the most part they elude legal regulation, administrative control, or political steering. Meaning is a scarce resource that cannot be regenerated or propagated as one likes. Here I take "meaning" as something like a limiting value for social spontaneity. Like all empirical variables, this one, too, is conditioned. But the conditions lie in lifeworld contexts that limit *from within* the capacity of associated citizens to organize their common life for themselves. What ultimately enables a legal community's discursive mode of sociation is not simply at the disposition of the members' will.

8.3 Civil Society, Public Opinion, and Communicative Power

Up to now, I have generally dealt with the public sphere as a communication structure rooted in the lifeworld through the associational network of civil society. I have described the political public sphere as a sounding board for problems that must be processed by the political system because they cannot be solved elsewhere. To this extent, the public sphere is a warning system with sensors that, though unspecialized, are sensitive throughout society. From the perspective of democratic theory, the public sphere must, in addition, amplify the pressure of problems, that is, not only detect and identify problems but also convincingly and *influentially* thematize them, furnish them with possible solutions, and dramatize them in such a way that they are taken up and dealt with by parliamentary complexes. Besides the "signal" function, there must be an effective problematization. The capacity of the public sphere to solve problems *on its own* is limited. But this capacity must be utilized to oversee the further treatment of problems that takes place inside the political system. I can provide only a broad estimate of the extent to which this is possible. I start by clarifying the contested concepts of the public sphere (sec. 8.3.1) and civil society (sec. 8.3.2). This allows me in sec. 8.3.3 to sketch some barriers and power structures inside the public sphere. These barriers, however, can be overcome in critical situations by escalating movements (sec. 8.3.4). I then summarize those elements the legal system must take into consideration when it forms its picture of a complex society like ours (sec. 8.3.5).

8.3.1

The public sphere is a social phenomenon just as elementary as action, actor, association, or collectivity, but it eludes the conventional sociological concepts of "social order." The public sphere cannot be conceived as an institution and certainly not as an organization. It is not even a framework of norms with differentiated competences and roles, membership regulations, and so on. Just as little does it represent a system; although it permits one to draw internal boundaries, outwardly it is characterized by open, permeable, and shifting horizons. The public sphere can best be described as a network for communicating information and points of view (i.e., opinions expressing affirmative or negative attitudes); the streams of communication are, in the process, filtered and synthesized in such a way that they coalesce into bundles of topically specified *public* opinions. Like the lifeworld as a whole, so, too, the public sphere is reproduced through communicative action, for which mastery of a natural language suffices; it is tailored to the *general comprehensibility* of everyday communicative practice. We have become acquainted with the "lifeworld" as a reservoir for simple interactions; specialized systems of action and knowledge that are differentiated within the lifeworld remain tied to these interactions. These systems fall into one of two categories. Systems like religion, education, and the family become associated with general reproductive functions of the lifeworld (that is, with cultural reproduction, social integration, or socialization). Systems like science, morality, and art take up different validity aspects of everyday communicative action (truth, rightness, or veracity). The public sphere, however, is specialized in neither of these two ways; to the extent that it extends to politically relevant questions, it leaves their specialized treatment to the political system. Rather, the public sphere distinguishes itself through a *communication structure* that is related to a third feature of communicative action: it refers neither to the *functions* nor to the *contents* of everyday communication but to the *social space* generated in communicative action.

Unlike success-oriented actors who mutually observe each other as one observes something in the objective world, persons acting communicatively encounter each other in a *situation* they at the same time constitute with their cooperatively negotiated interpretations. The intersubjectively shared space of a speech situation is disclosed when the participants enter into interpersonal relationships by taking positions on mutual speech-act offers and assuming illocutionary obligations. Every encounter in which actors do not just observe each other but take a second-person attitude, reciprocally attributing communicative freedom to each other, unfolds in a linguistically constituted public space. This space stands open, in principle, for potential dialogue partners who are present as bystanders or could come on the scene and join those present. That is, special measures would be required to prevent a third party from entering such a linguistically constituted space. Founded in communicative action, this spatial structure of simple and episodic encounters can be expanded and rendered more permanent in an abstract form for a larger public of present persons. For the public infrastructure of such *assemblies*, performances, presentations, and so on, architectural metaphors of structured spaces recommend themselves: we speak of forums, stages, arenas, and the like. These public spheres still cling to the concrete locales where an audience is physically gathered. The more they detach themselves from the public's physical presence and extend to the virtual presence of scattered readers, listeners, or viewers linked by public media, the clearer becomes the abstraction that enters when the spatial structure of simple interactions is expanded into a public sphere.

When generalized in this way, communication structures contract to informational content and points of view that are uncoupled from the thick contexts of simple interactions, from specific persons, and from practical obligations. At the same time, context generalization, inclusion, and growing anonymity demand a higher degree of explication that must dispense with technical vocabularies and special codes. Whereas the *orientation to laypersons* implies a certain loss in differentiation, uncoupling communicated opinions from concrete practical obligations tends to have an *intellectualizing* effect. Processes of opinion-formation, especially when they have to do with political questions, certainly cannot be separated from the transformation of the participants' preferences and attitudes, but they can be separated from putting these dispositions into action. To this extent, the communication structures of the public sphere *relieve* the public *of the burden of decision making*, the postponed decisions are reserved for the institutionalized political process. In the public sphere, utterances are sorted according to issue and contribution, whereas the contributions are weighted by the affirmative versus negative responses they receive. Information and arguments are thus worked into focused opinions. What makes such "bundled" opinions into *public opinion* is both the controversial way it comes about and the amount of approval that "carries" it. Public opinion is not representative in the statistical sense. It is not an aggregate of individually gathered, privately expressed opinions held by isolated persons. Hence it must not be confused with survey results. Political opinion polls provide a certain reflection of "public opinion" only if they have been preceded by a focused public debate and a corresponding opinion-formation in a mobilized public sphere.

The diffusion of information and points of view via effective broadcasting media is not the only thing that matters in public processes of communication, nor is it the most important. True, only the broad circulation of comprehensible, attention-grabbing messages arouses a sufficiently inclusive participation. But the rules of a *shared* practice of communication are of greater significance for structuring public opinion. Agreement on issues and contributions *develops* only as the result of more or less exhaustive controversy in which proposals, information, and reasons can be more or less rationally dealt with. In general terms, the *discursive level* of opinion-formation and the "quality" of the outcome vary with this "more or less" in the "rational" processing of "exhaustive" proposals, information, and reasons. Thus the success of public communication is not intrinsically measured by the requirement of inclusion either[49] but by the formal criteria governing how a qualified public opinion comes about. The structures of a power-ridden, oppressed public sphere exclude fruitful and clarifying discussions. The "quality" of public opinion, insofar as it is measured by the procedural properties of its process of generation, is an empirical variable. From a normative perspective, this provides a basis for measuring the legitimacy of the influence that public opinion has on the political system. Of course, actual influence coincides with legitimate influence just as little as the belief in legitimacy coincides with legitimacy. But conceiving things this way at least opens a perspective from which the relation between actual influence and the procedurally grounded quality of public opinion can be empirically investigated.

Parsons introduced "influence" as a symbolically generalized form of communication that facilitates interactions in virtue of conviction or persuasion.[50] For example, persons or institutions can enjoy a reputation that allows their utterences to have an influence on others' beliefs without having to demonstrate authority or to give explanations in the situation. "Influence" feeds on the resource of mutual understanding, but it is based on advancing trust in beliefs that are not currently tested. In this sense, public opinion represents political potentials that can be used for influencing the voting behavior of citizens or the will-formation in parliamentary bodies, administrative agencies, and courts. Naturally, political *influence* supported by public opinion is converted into political *power*—into a potential for rendering binding decisions—only when it affects the beliefs and decisions of *authorized* members of the political system and determines the behavior of voters, legislators, officials, and so forth. Just like social power, political influence based on public opinion can be transformed into political power only through institutionalized procedures.

Influence develops in the public sphere and becomes the object of struggle there. This struggle involves not only the political influence that has already been acquired (such as that enjoyed by experienced political leaders and officeholders, established parties, and well-known groups like Greenpeace and Amnesty International). The reputation of groups of persons and experts who have acquired their influence in special public spheres also comes into play (for example, the authority of religious leaders, the public visibility of literary figures and artists, the reputation of scientists, and the popularity of sports figures and movie stars). For as soon as the public space has expanded beyond the context of simple interactions, a differentiation sets in among organizers, speakers, and hearers; arenas and galleries; stage and viewing space. The *actors' roles* that increasingly professionalize and multiply with organizational complexity and range of media are, of course, furnished with unequal opportunities for exerting influence. But the political influence that the actors gain through public communication must *ultimately* rest on the resonance and indeed the approval of a lay public whose composition is egalitarian. The public of citizens must be *convinced* by comprehensible and broadly interesting contributions to issues it finds relevant. The public audience possesses final authority, because it is *constitutive* for the internal structure and reproduction of the public sphere, the *only* place where actors can appear. There can be no public sphere without a public.

To be sure, we must distinguish the actors who, so to speak, emerge from the public and take part in the reproduction of the public sphere itself from actors who occupy an already constituted public domain in order to use it. This is true, for example, of the large and well-organized interest groups that are anchored in various social subsystems and affect the political system *through* the public sphere. They cannot make any manifest use in the public sphere of the sanctions and rewards they rely on in bargaining or in nonpublic attempts at pressure. They can capitalize on their social power and convert it into political power only insofar as they can advertise their interests in a language that can mobilize convincing reasons and shared value orientations—as, for example, when parties to wage negotiations inform the public about demands, strategies, or outcomes. The contributions of interest groups are, in any case, vulnerable to a kind of criticism to which contributions from other sources are not exposed. Public opinions that can acquire visibility only because of an undeclared infusion of money or organizational power lose their credibility as soon as these sources of social power are made public. Public opinion can be manipulated but neither publicly bought nor publicly blackmailed. This is due to the fact that a public sphere cannot be "manufactured" as one pleases. Before it can be captured by actors with strategic intent, the public sphere together with its public must have developed as a structure that stands on its own and reproduces itself *out of itself.* This lawlike regularity governing the formation of a public sphere remains latent in the constituted public sphere— and takes effect again only in moments when the public sphere is mobilized.

The political public sphere can fulfill its function of perceiving and thematizing encompassing social problems only insofar as it develops out of the communication taking place among *those who are potentially affected*. It is carried by a public recruited from the entire citizenry. But in the diverse voices of this public, one hears the echo of private experiences that are caused throughout society by the externalities (and internal disturbances) of various functional systems—and even by the very state apparatus on whose regulatory activities the complex and poorly coordinated subsystems depend. Systemic deficiencies are experienced in the context of individual life histories; such burdens accumulate in the lifeworld. The latter has the appropriate antennae, for in its horizon are intermeshed the private life histories of the "clients" of functional systems that might be failing in their delivery of services. It is only for those who are immediately affected that such services are paid in the currency of "use values." Besides religion, art, and literature, only the spheres of "private" life have an existential language at their disposal, in which such socially generated problems can be *assessed in terms of one's own life history*. Problems voiced in the public sphere first become visible when they are mirrored in personal life experiences. To the extent that these experiences find their concise expression in the languages of religion, art, and literature, the "literary" public sphere in the broader sense, which is specialized for the articulation of values and world disclosure, is intertwined with the political public sphere.[51]

As both bearers of the political public sphere and as *members of society*, citizens occupy two positions at once. As members of society, they occupy the roles of employees and consumers, insured persons and patients, taxpayers and clients of bureaucracies, as well as the roles of students, tourists, commuters, and the like; in such complementary roles, they are especially exposed to the specific requirements and failures of the corresponding service systems. Such experiences are first assimilated "privately," that is, are interpreted within the horizon of a life history intermeshed with other life histories in the contexts of shared lifeworlds. The communication channels of the public sphere are linked to private spheres— to the thick networks of interaction found in families and circles of friends as well as to the looser contacts with neighbors, work colleagues, acquaintances, and so on—and indeed they are linked in such a way that the spatial structures of simple interactions are expanded and abstracted but not destroyed. Thus the orientation to reaching understanding that is predominant in everyday practice is also preserved for a *communication among strangers* that is conducted over great distances in public spheres whose branches are quite complex. The threshold separating the private sphere from the public is not marked by a fixed set of issues or relationships but by *different conditions of communication*. Certainly these conditions lead to differences in the accessibility of the two spheres, safeguarding the intimacy of the one sphere and the publicity of the other. However, they do not seal off the private from the public but only channel the flow of topics from the one sphere into the other. For the public sphere draws its impulses from the private handling of social problems that resonate in life histories. It is symptomatic of this close connection, incidentally, that a modern bourgeois public sphere developed in the European societies of the seventeenth and eighteenth centuries as the "sphere of private persons come together as a public." Viewed historically, the connection between the public and the private spheres is manifested in the clubs and organizational forms of a reading public composed of bourgeois private persons and crystallizing around newspapers and journals.[52]

8.3.2

This sphere of civil society has been rediscovered today in wholly new historical constellations. The expression "civil society" has in the meantime taken on a meaning different from that of the "bourgeois society" of the liberal tradition, which Hegel conceptualized as a "system of needs," that is, as a market system involving social labor and commodity exchange. What is meant by "civil society" today, in contrast to its usage in the Marxist tradition, no longer includes the economy as constituted by private law and steered through markets in labor, capital, and commodities. Rather, its institutional core comprises those nongovernmental and noneconomic connections and voluntary associations that anchor the communication structures of the public sphere in the society component of the lifeworld. Civil society is composed of those more or less spontaneously emergent associations, organizations, and movements that, attuned to how societal problems resonate in the private life spheres, distill and transmit such reactions in amplified form to the public sphere. The core of civil society comprises a network of associations that institutionalizes problem-solving discourses on questions of general interest inside the framework of organized public spheres.[53] These "discursive designs" have an egalitarian, open form of organization that mirrors essential features of the kind of communication around which they crystallize and to which they lend continuity and permanence.[54]

Such associations certainly do not represent the most conspicuous element of a public sphere dominated by mass media and large agencies, observed by market and opinion research, and inundated by the public relations work, propaganda, and advertising of political parties and groups. All the same, they do form the organizational substratum of the general public of citizens. More or less emerging from the private sphere, this public is made of citizens who seek acceptable interpretations for their social interests and experiences and who want to have an influence on institutionalized opinion- and will-formation.

One searches the literature in vain for clear definitions of civil society that would go beyond such descriptive characterizations.[55] S. N. Eisenstadt's usage reveals a certain continuity with the older theory of pluralism when he describes civil society as follows:

Civil society embraces a multiplicity of ostensibly "private" yet potentially autonomous public arenas distinct from the state. The activities of such actors are regulated by various associations existing within them, preventing the society from degenerating into a shapeless mass. In a civil society, these sectors are not embedded in closed, ascriptive or corporate settings; they are open-ended and overlapping. Each has autonomous access to the central political arena, and a certain degree of commitment to that setting.[56]

Jean Cohen and Andrew Arato, who have presented the most comprehensive study on this topic, provide a catalog of features characterizing the civil society that is demarcated from the state, the economy, and other functional systems but coupled with the core private spheres of the lifeworld:

(1) *Plurality*: families, informal groups, and voluntary associations whose plurality and autonomy allow for a variety of forms of life; (2) *Publicity*: institutions of culture and communication; (3) *Privacy*: a domain of individual self-development and moral choice; (4) *Legality*: structures of general laws and basic rights needed to demarcate plurality, privacy, and publicity from at least the state and, tendentially, the economy. Together, these structures secure the institutional existence of a modern differentiated civil society.[57]

The *constitution of this sphere through basic rights* provides some indicators for its social structure. Freedom of assembly and freedom of association, when linked with freedom of speech, define the scope for various types of associations and societies: for voluntary associations that intervene in the formation of public opinion, push topics of general interest, and act as advocates for neglected issues and underrepresented groups; for groups that are difficult to organize or that pursue cultural, religious, or humanitarian aims; and for ethical communities, religious denominations, and so on. Freedom of the press, radio, and television, as well as the right to engage in these areas, safeguards the media infrastructure of public communication; such liberties are thereby supposed to preserve an openness for competing opinions and a representative diversity of voices. The political system, which must remain sensitive to the influence of public opinion, is intertwined with the public sphere and civil society through the activity of political parties and general elections. This intermeshing is guaranteed by the right of parties to "collaborate" in the political will-formation of the people, as well as by the citizens' active and passive voting rights and other participatory rights. Finally, the network of associations can assert its autonomy and preserve its spontaneity only insofar as it can draw support from a mature pluralism of forms of life, subcultures, and worldviews. The constitutional protection of "privacy" promotes the integrity of private life spheres: rights of personality, freedom of belief and of conscience, freedom of movement, the privacy of letters, mail, and telecommunications, the inviolability of one's residence, and the protection of families circumscribe an untouchable zone of personal integrity and independent judgment.

The tight connection between an autonomous civil society and an integral private sphere stands out even more clearly when contrasted with totalitarian societies of bureaucratic socialism. Here a panoptic state not only directly controls the bureaucratically desiccated public sphere, it also undermines the private basis of this public sphere. Administrative intrusions and constant supervision corrode the communicative structure of everyday contacts in families and schools, neighborhoods and local municipalities. The destruction of solidary living conditions and the paralysis of initiative and independent engagement in overregulated yet legally uncertain sectors go hand in hand with the crushing of social groups, associations, and networks; with indoctrination and the dissolution of cultural identities; with the suffocation of spontaneous public communication. Communicative rationality is thus destroyed *simultaneously* in both public and private contexts of communication.[58] The more the bonding force of communicative action wanes in private life spheres and the embers of communicative freedom die out, the easier it is for someone who monopolizes the public sphere to align the mutually estranged and isolated actors into a mass that can be directed and mobilized in a plebiscitarian manner.[59]

Basic constitutional guarantees alone, of course, cannot preserve the public sphere and civil society from deformations. The communication structures of the public sphere must rather be kept intact by an energetic civil society. That the political public sphere must in a certain sense reproduce and stabilize itself from its own resources is shown by the odd *self-referential character of the practice of communication in civil society*. Those actors who are the carriers of the public sphere put forward "texts" that always reveal the same subtext, which refers to the critical function of the public sphere in general. Whatever the manifest content of their public utterances, the performative meaning of such public discourse at the same time actualizes the function of an undistorted political public sphere as such. Thus, the institutions and legal guarantees of free and open opinion-formation rest on the unsteady ground of the political communication of actors who, in making use of them, at the same time interpret, defend, and radicalize their normative content. Actors who know they are involved in the *common* enterprise of reconstituting and maintaining structures of the public sphere as they contest opinions and strive for influence differ from actors who merely use forums that already exist. More specifically, actors who support the public sphere are distinguished by the *dual orientation* of their political engagement: with their programs, they directly influence the political system, but at the same time they are also reflexively concerned with revitalizing and enlarging civil society and the public sphere as well as with confirming their own identities and capacities to act.

Cohen and Arato see this kind of "dual politics" especially in the "new" social movements that simultaneously pursue offensive and defensive goals. "Offensively," these movements attempt to bring up issues relevant to the entire society, to define ways of approaching problems, to propose possible solutions, to supply new information, to interpret values differently, to mobilize good reasons and criticize bad ones. Such initiatives are intended to produce a broad shift in public opinion, to alter the parameters of organized political will-formation, and to exert pressure on parliaments, courts, and administrations in favor of specific policies. "Defensively," they attempt to maintain existing structures of association and public influence, to generate subcultural counterpublics and counterinstitutions, to consolidate new collective identities, and to win new terrain in the form of expanded rights and reformed institutions:

> On this account, the "defensive" aspect of the movements involves preserving *and developing* the communicative infrastructure of the lifeworld. This formulation captures the dual aspect of movements discussed by Touraine as well as Habermas's insight that movements can be the carriers of the potentials of cultural modernity. This is the sine qua non for successful efforts to redefine identities, to reinterpret norms, and to develop egalitarian, democratic associational forms. The expressive, normative and communicative modes of collective action . . . [also involve] efforts to secure *institutional* changes within civil society that correspond to the new meanings, identities, and norms that are created.[60]

In the self-referential mode of reproducing the public sphere, as well as in the Janus-faced politics aimed at the political system and the self-stabilization of public sphere and civil society, the space is provided for the extension and radicalization of existing rights: "The combination of associations, publics, and rights, when supported by a political culture in which independent initiatives and movements represent an ever-renewable, legitimate, political option, represents, in our opinion, an effective set of bulwarks around civil society within whose limits much of the program of radical democracy can be reformulated."[61]

In fact, the *interplay* of a public sphere based in civil society with the opinion- and will-formation institutionalized in parliamentary bodies and courts offers a good starting point for translating the concept of deliberative politics into sociological terms. However, we must not look on civil society as a focal point where the lines of societal self-organization as a whole would converge. Cohen and Arato rightly emphasize the *limited scope for action* that civil society and the public sphere afford to noninstitutionalized political movements and forms of political expression. They speak of a structurally necessary "self-limitation" of radical-democratic practice:

First, a robust civil society can develop only in the context of a liberal political culture and the corresponding patterns of socialization, and on the basis of an integral private sphere; it can blossom only in an already rationalized lifeworld. Otherwise, populist movements arise that blindly defend the frozen traditions of a lifeworld endangered by capitalist modernization. In their forms of mobilization, these fundamentalist movements are as modern as they are antidemocratic.[62]

Second, within the boundaries of the public sphere, or at least of a liberal public sphere, actors can acquire only influence, not political power. The influence of a public opinion generated more or less discursively in open controversies is certainly an empirical variable that can make a difference. But public influence is transformed into communicative power only after it passes through the filters of the institutionalized *procedures* of democratic opinion- and will-formation and enters through parliamentary debates into legitimate lawmaking. The informal flow of public opinion issues in beliefs that have been *tested* from the standpoint of the generalizability of interests. Not influence per se, but influence transformed into communicative power legitimates political decisions. The popular sovereignty set communicatively aflow cannot make itself felt *solely* in the influence of informal public discourses—not even when these discourses arise from autonomous public spheres. To generate political power, their influence must have an effect on the democratically regulated deliberations of democratically elected assemblies and assume an authorized form in formal decisions. This also holds, mutatis mutandis, for courts that decide politically relevant cases.

Third, and finally, the instruments that politics has available in law and administrative power have a limited effectiveness in functionally differentiated societies. Politics indeed continues to be the addressee for all unmanaged integration problems. But political steering can often take only an indirect approach and must, as we have seen, leave intact the modes of operation internal to functional systems and other highly organized spheres of action. As a result, democratic movements emerging from civil society must give up holistic aspirations to a self-organizing society, aspirations that also undergirded Marxist ideas of social revolution. Civil society can directly transform only itself, and it can have at most an indirect effect on the self-transformation of the political system; generally, it has an influence only on the personnel and programming of this system. But in no way does it occupy *the position* of a macrosubject supposed to bring society as a whole under control and simultaneously act for it. Besides these limitations, one must bear in mind that the administrative power deployed for purposes of social planning and supervision is not a suitable medium for fostering emancipated forms of life. These can *develop* in the wake of democratization processes but they cannot be *brought about* through intervention.

The self-limitation of civil society should not be understood as incapacitation. The knowledge required for political supervision or steering, a knowledge that in complex societies represents a resource as scarce as it is desirable, can certainly become the source of a new systems paternalism. But because the administration does not, for the most part, itself produce the relevant knowledge but draws it from the knowledge system or other intermediaries, it does not enjoy a natural monopoly on such knowledge. In spite of asymmetrical access to expertise and limited problem-solving capacities, civil society also has the opportunity of mobilizing counterknowledge and drawing on the pertinent forms of expertise to make *its own* translations. Even though the public consists of laypersons and communicates with ordinary language, this does not necessarily imply an inability to differentiate the essential questions and reasons for decisions. This can serve as a pretext for a technocratic incapacitation of the public sphere only as long as the political initiatives of civil society fail to provide sufficient expert knowledge along with appropriate and, if necessary, multi-level translations in regard to the managerial aspects of public issues.

8.3.3

The concepts of the political public sphere and civil society introduced above are not mere normative postulates but have empirical relevance. However, additional assumptions must be introduced if we are to use these concepts to translate the discourse-theoretic reading of radical democracy into sociological terms and reformulate it in an empirically falsifiable manner. I would like to defend the claim that *under certain circumstances* civil society can acquire influence in the public sphere, have an effect on the parliamentary complex (and the courts) through its own public opinions, and compel the political system to switch over to the official circulation of power. Naturally, the sociology of mass communication conveys a skeptical impression of the power-ridden, mass-media-dominated public spheres of Western democracies. Social movements, citizen initiatives and forums, political and other associations, in short, the groupings of civil society, are indeed sensitive to problems, but the signals they send out and the impulses they give are generally too weak to initiate learning processes or redirect decision making in the political system in the short run.

In complex societies, the public sphere consists of an intermediary structure between the political system, on the one hand, and the private sectors of the lifeworld and functional systems, on the other. It represents a highly complex network that branches out into a multitude of overlapping international, national, regional, local, and subcultural arenas. Functional specifications, thematic foci, policy fields, and so forth, provide the points of reference for a substantive differentiation of public spheres that are, however, still accessible to laypersons (for example, popular science and literary publics, religious and artistic publics, feminist and "alternative" publics, publics concerned with health-care issues, social welfare, or environmental policy). Moreover, the public sphere is differentiated into levels according to the density of communication, organizational complexity, and range—from the *episodic* publics found in taverns, coffee houses, or on the streets; through the *occasional* or "arranged" publics of particular presentations and events, such as theater performances, rock concerts, party assemblies, or church congresses; up to the *abstract* public sphere of isolated readers, listeners, and viewers scattered across large geographic areas, or even around the globe, and brought together only through the mass media. Despite these manifold differentiations, however, all the partial publics constituted by ordinary language remain porous to one another. The one text of "the" public sphere, a text continually extrapolated and extending radially in all directions, is divided by internal boundaries into arbitrarily small texts for which everything else is context; yet one can always build hermeneutical bridges from one text to the next. Segmented public spheres are constituted with the help of exclusion mechanisms; however, because publics cannot harden into organizations or systems, there is no exclusion rule without a proviso for its abolishment.

In other words, boundaries inside the universal public sphere as defined by its reference to the political system remain permeable in principle. The rights to unrestricted inclusion and equality built into liberal public spheres prevent exclusion mechanisms of the Foucauldian type and ground a *potential for self-transformation.* In the course of the nineteenth and twentieth centuries, the universalist discourses of the bourgeois public sphere could no longer immunize themselves against a critique from within. The labor movement and feminism, for example, were able to join these discourses in order to shatter the structures that had initially constituted them as "the other" of a bourgeois public sphere.[63]

The more the audience is widened through mass communications, the more inclusive and the more abstract in form it becomes. Correspondingly, the *roles of the actors* appearing in the arenas are, to an increasing degree, sharply separated from the roles of the spectators in the galleries. Although the "success of the actors in the arena is ultimately decided in the galleries,"[64] the question arises of how autonomous the public is when it takes a position on an issue, whether its affirmative or negative stand reflects a process of becoming informed or in fact only a more or less concealed game of power. Despite the wealth of empirical investigations, we still do not have a well-established answer to this cardinal question. But one can at least pose the question more precisely by assuming that public processes of communication can take place with less distortion the more they are left to the internal dynamic of a civil society that emerges from the lifeworld.

One can distinguish, at least tentatively, the more loosely organized actors who "emerge from" the public, as it were, from other actors merely "appearing before" the public. The latter have organizational power, resources, and sanctions available *from the start*. Naturally, the actors who are more firmly anchored in civil society and participate in the reproduction of the public sphere also depend on the support of "sponsors" who supply the necessary resources of money, organization, knowledge, and social capital. But patrons or "like-minded" sponsors do not necessarily reduce the authenticity of the public actors they support. By contrast, the collective actors who merely enter the public sphere from, and utilize it for, a specific organization or functional system have *their own* basis of support. Among these political and social actors who do not have to obtain their resources from other spheres, I primarily include the large interest groups that enjoy social power, as well as the established parties that have largely become arms of the political system. They draw on market studies and opinion surveys and conduct their own professional public-relations campaigns.

In and of themselves, organizational complexity, resources, professionalization, and so on, are admittedly insufficient indicators for the difference between "indigenous" actors and mere users. Nor can an actor's pedigree be read directly from the interests actually represented. Other indicators are more reliable. Thus actors differ in how they can be identified. Some actors one can easily identify from their functional background; that is, they represent political parties or pressure groups; unions or professional associations; consumer-protection groups or rent-control organizations, and so on. Other actors, by contrast, must first *produce* identifying features. This is especially evident with social movements that initially go through a phase of self-identification and self-legitimation; even after that, they still pursue a self-referential "identity politics" parallel to their goal-directed politics—they must continually reassure themselves of their identity. Whether actors merely use an already constituted public sphere or whether they are involved in reproducing its structures is, moreover, evident in the above-mentioned sensitivity to threats to communication rights. It is also shown in the actors' willingness to go beyond an interest in self-defense and take a universalist stand against the open or concealed exclusion of minorities or marginal groups. The very existence of social movements, one might add, depends on whether they find organizational forms that produce solidarities and publics, forms that allow them to fully utilize and radicalize existing communication rights and structures as they pursue special goals.[65]

A third group of actors are the journalists, publicity agents, and members of the press (i.e., in the broad sense of *Publizisten*) who collect information, make decisions about the selection and presentation of "programs," and to a certain extent control the entry of topics, contributions, and authors into the mass-media-dominated public sphere. As the mass media become more complex and more expensive, the effective channels of communication become more centralized. To the degree this occurs, the mass media face an increasing pressure of selection, on both the supply side and the demand side. These selection processes become the source of a new sort of power. This *power of the media* is not sufficiently reined in by professional standards, but today, by fits and starts, the "fourth branch of government" is being subjected to constitutional regulation. In the Federal Republic, for example, it is both the legal form and the institutional structure of television networks that determine whether they depend more on the influence of political parties and public interest groups or more on private firms with large advertising outlays. In general, one can say that the image of politics presented on television is predominantly made up of issues and contributions that are professionally produced as media input and then fed in via press conferences, news agencies, public-relations campaigns, and the like. These official producers of information are all the more successful the more they can rely on trained personnel, on financial and technical resources, and in general on a professional infrastructure. Collective actors operating outside the political system or outside large organizations normally have fewer opportunities to influence the content and views presented by the media. This is especially true for messages that do not fall inside the "balanced," that is, the centrist and rather narrowly defined, spectrum of "established opinions" dominating the programs of the electronic media.[66]

Moreover, before messages selected in this way are broadcast, they are subject to *information-processing strategies* within the media. These are oriented by reception conditions as perceived by media experts, program directors, and the press. Because the public's receptiveness, cognitive capacity, and attention represent unusually scarce resources for which the programs of numerous "stations" compete, the presentation of news and commentaries for the most part follows market strategies. Reporting facts as human-interest stories, mixing information with entertainment, arranging material episodically, and breaking down complex relationships into smaller fragments—all of this comes together to form a syndrome that works to depoliticize public communication.[67] This is the kernel of truth in the theory of the culture industry. The research literature provides fairly reliable information on the institutional framework and structure of the media, as well as on the way they work, organize programs, and are utilized. But, even a generation after Paul Lazarsfeld, propositions concerning the *effects of the media* remain controversial. The research on effect and reception has at least done away with the image of passive consumers as "cultural dopes" who are manipulated by the programs offered to them. It directs our attention to the *strategies of interpretation* employed by viewers, who communicate with one another, and who in fact can be provoked to criticize or reject what programs offer or to synthesize it with judgments of their own.[68]

Even if we know something about the internal operation and impact of the mass media, as well as about the distribution of roles among the public and various actors, and even if we can make some reasonable conjectures about who has privileged access to the media and who has a share in media power, it is by no means clear how the mass media intervene in the diffuse circuits of communication in the political public sphere. The *normative reactions* to the relatively new phenomenon of the mass media's powerful position in the competition for public influence are clearer. Michael Gurevitch and Jay G. Blumler have summarized the tasks that the media *ought* to fulfill in democratic political systems:

1. surveillance of the sociopolitical environment, reporting developments likely to impinge, positively or negatively, on the welfare of citizens;

2. meaningful agenda-setting, identifying the key issues of the day, including the forces that have formed and may resolve them;

3. platforms for an intelligible and illuminating advocacy by politicians and spokespersons of other causes and interest groups;

4. dialogue across a diverse range of views, as well as between power-holders (actual and prospective) and mass publics;

5. mechanisms for holding officials to account for how they have exercised power;

6. incentives for citizens to learn, choose, and become involved, rather than merely to follow and kibitz over the political process;

7. a principled resistance to the efforts of forces outside the media to subvert their independence, integrity and ability to serve the audience;

8. a sense of respect for the audience member, as potentially concerned and able to make sense of his or her political environment.[69]

Such principles orient the professional code of journalism and the profession's ethical self-understanding, on the one hand, and the formal organization of a free press by laws governing mass communication, on the other.[70] In agreement with the concept of deliberative politics, these principles express a simple idea: the mass media ought to understand themselves as the mandatary of an enlightened public whose willingness to learn and capacity for criticism they at once presuppose, demand, and reinforce; like the judiciary, they ought to preserve their independence from political and social pressure; they ought to be receptive to the public's concerns and proposals, take up these issues and contributions impartially, augment criticisms, and confront the political process with articulate demands for legitimation. The power of the media should thus be neutralized and the tacit conversion of administrative or social power into political influence blocked. According to this idea, political and social actors would be allowed to "use" the public sphere only insofar as they make convincing contributions to the solution of problems that have been perceived by the public or have been put on the public agenda with the public's consent. In a similar vein, political parties would have to participate in the opinion- and will-formation from the public's own perspective, rather than patronizing the public and extracting mass loyalty from the public sphere for the purposes of maintaining their own power.[71]

The sociology of mass communication depicts the public sphere as infiltrated by administrative and social power and dominated by the mass media. If one places this image, diffuse though it might be, alongside the above normative expectations, then one will be rather cautious in estimating the chances of civil society having an influence on the political system. To be sure, this estimate pertains only to a *public sphere at rest*. In periods of mobilization, the structures that actually support the authority of a critically engaged public begin to vibrate. The balance of power between civil society and the political system then shifts.

8.3.4

With this I return to the central question of who can place issues on the agenda and determine what direction the lines of communication take. Roger Cobb, Jennie-Keith Ross, and Marc Howard Ross have constructed models that depict how new and compelling issues develop, from the first initiative up to formal proceedings in bodies that have the power to decide.[72] If one suitably modifies the proposed models—inside access model, mobilization model, outside initiative model—from the viewpoint of democratic theory, they present basic alternatives in how the public sphere and the political system influence each other. In the first case, the initiative comes from officeholders or political leaders, and the issue continues to circulate inside the political system all the way to its formal treatment, while the broader public is either excluded from the process or does not have any influence on it. In the second case, the initiative again starts inside the political system, but the proponents of the issue must mobilize the public sphere, because they need the support of certain groups, either to obtain formal consideration or to implement an adopted program successfully. Only in the third case does the initiative lie with forces at the periphery, outside the purview of the political system. With the help of the mobilized public sphere, that is, the pressure of public opinion, such forces compel formal consideration of the issue:

The outside initiative model applies to the situation in which a group outside the government structure 1) articulates a grievance, 2) tries to expand interest in the issue to enough other groups in the population to gain a place on the public agenda, in order to 3) create sufficient pressure on decision makers to force the issue onto the formal agenda for their serious consideration. This model of agenda building is likely to predominate in more egalitarian societies. Formal agenda status, . . . however, does not necessarily mean that the final decisions of the authorities or the actual policy implementation will be what the grievance group originally sought.[73]

In the normal case, issues and proposals have a history whose course corresponds more to the first or second model than to the third. As long as the informal circulation of power dominates the political system, the initiative and power to put problems on the agenda and bring them to a decision lies more with the Government leaders and administration than with the parliamentary complex. As long as in the public sphere the mass media prefer, contrary to their normative self-understanding, to draw their material from powerful, well-organized information producers and as long as they prefer media strategies that lower rather than raise the discursive level of public communication, issues will tend to start in, and be managed from, the center, rather than follow a spontaneous course originating in the periphery. At least, the skeptical findings on problem articulation in public arenas accord with this view.[74] In the present context, of course, there can be no question of a conclusive empirical evaluation of the mutual influence that politics and public have on each other. For our purposes, it suffices to make it plausible that in a perceived crisis situation, the *actors in civil society* thus far neglected in our scenario *can* assume a surprisingly active and momentous role.[75] In spite of a lesser organizational complexity and a weaker capacity for action, and despite the structural disadvantages mentioned earlier, at the critical moments of an accelerated history, these actors get the chance to *reverse* the normal circuits of communication in the political system and the public sphere. In this way they can shift the entire system's mode of problem solving.

The communication structures of the public sphere are linked with the private life spheres in a way that gives the civil-social periphery, in contrast to the political center, the advantage of greater sensitivity in detecting and identifying new problem situations. The great issues of the last decades give evidence for this. Consider, for example, the spiraling nuclear-arms race; consider the risks involved in the peaceful use of atomic energy or in other large-scale technological projects and scientific experimentation, such as genetic engineering; consider the ecological threats involved in an overstrained natural environment (acid rain, water pollution, species extinction, etc.); consider the dramatically progressing impoverishment of the Third World and problems of the world economic order; or consider such issues as feminism, increasing immigration, and the associated problems of multiculturalism. Hardly any of these topics were *initially* brought up by exponents of the state apparatus, large organizations, or functional systems. Instead, they were broached by intellectuals, concerned citizens, radical professionals, self-proclaimed "advocates," and the like. Moving in from this outermost periphery, such issues force their way into newspapers and interested associations, clubs, professional organizations, academies, and universities. They find forums, citizen initiatives, and other platforms before they catalyze the growth of social movements and new subcultures.[76] The latter can in turn dramatize contributions, presenting them so effectively that the mass media take up the matter. Only through their controversial presentation in the media do such topics reach the larger public and subsequently gain a place on the "public agenda." Sometimes the support of sensational actions, mass protests, and incessant campaigning is required before an issue can make its way via the surprising election of marginal candidates or radical parties, expanded platforms of "established" parties, important court decisions, and so on, into the core of the political system and there receive formal consideration.

Naturally, there are other ways in which issues develop, other paths from the periphery to the center, and other patterns involving complex branchings and feedback loops. But, in general, one can say that even in more or less power-ridden public spheres, the power relations shift as soon as the perception of relevant social problems evokes a *crisis consciousness* at the periphery. If actors from civil society then join together, formulate the relevant issue, and promote it in the public sphere, their efforts can be successful, because the endogenous mobilization of the public sphere activates an otherwise latent dependency built into the internal structure of every public sphere, a dependency also present in the normative self-understanding of the mass media: the players in the arena owe their influence to the approval of those in the gallery. At the very least, one can say that insofar as a rationalized lifeworld supports the development of a liberal public sphere by furnishing it with a solid foundation in civil society, the authority of a position-taking public is strengthened in the course of escalating public controversies. Under the conditions of a *liberal* public sphere, informal public communication accomplishes two things in cases in which mobilization depends on crisis. On the one hand, it prevents the accumulation of indoctrinated masses that are seduced by populist leaders. On the other hand, it pulls together the scattered critical potentials of a public that was only abstractly held together through the public media, and it helps this public have a political influence on institutionalized opinion- and will-formation. Only in *liberal* public spheres, of course, do subinstitutional political movements—which abandon the conventional paths of interest politics in order to boost the constitutionally regulated circulation of power in the political system—take this direction. By contrast, an authoritarian, distorted public sphere that is brought into alignment merely provides a forum for plebiscitary legitimation.[77]

This sense of a reinforced demand for legitimation becomes especially clear when subinstitutional protest movements reach a high point by escalating their protests. The last means for obtaining more of a hearing and greater media influence for oppositional arguments are acts of civil disobedience. These acts of nonviolent, symbolic rule violation are meant as expressions of protest against binding decisions that, their legality notwithstanding, the actors consider illegitimate in the light of valid constitutional principles. Acts of civil disobedience are directed simultaneously to two addressees. On the one hand, they appeal to officeholders and parliamentary representatives to reopen formally concluded political deliberations so that their decisions may possibly be revised in view of the continuing public criticism. On the other hand, they appeal "to the sense of justice of the majority of the community," as Rawls puts it,[78] and thus to the critical judgment of a public of citizens that is to be mobilized with exceptional means. Independently of the current object of controversy, civil disobedience is also always an implicit appeal to connect organized political will-formation with the communicative processes of the public sphere. The message of this subtext is aimed at a political system that, as constitutionally organized, may not detach itself from civil society and make itself independent vis-à-vis the periphery. Civil disobedience thereby refers to its own origins in a civil society that in crisis situations actualizes the normative contents of constitutional democracy in the medium of public opinion and summons it against the systemic inertia of institutional politics.

This *self-referential character* is emphasized in the definition that Cohen and Arato have proposed, drawing on considerations raised by Rawls, Dworkin, and me:

Civil disobedience involves illegal acts, usually on the part of collective actors, that are public, principled, and symbolic in character, involve primarily nonviolent means of protest, and appeal to the capacity for reason and the sense of justice of the populace. The aim of civil disobedience is to persuade public opinion in civil and political society . . . that a particular law or policy is illegitimate and a change is warranted. Collective actors involved in civil disobedience invoke the utopian principles of constitutional democracies, appealing to the ideas of fundamental rights or democratic legitimacy. Civil disobedience is thus a means for reasserting the link between civil and political society . . . , when legal attempts at exerting the influence of the former on the latter have failed and other avenues have been exhausted.[79]

This interpretation of civil disobedience manifests the self-consciousness of a civil society confident that at least in a crisis it can increase the pressure of a mobilized public on the political system to the point where the latter switches into the conflict mode and neutralizes the unofficial countercirculation of power.

Beyond this, the justification of civil disobedience[80] relies on a *dynamic understanding* of the constitution as an unfinished project. From this long-term perspective, the constitutional state does not represent a finished structure but a delicate and sensitive—above all fallible and revisable—enterprise, whose purpose is to realize the system of rights *anew* in changing circumstances, that is, to interpret the system of rights better, to institutionalize it more appropriately, and to draw out its contents more radically. This is the perspective of citizens who are actively engaged in realizing the system of rights. Aware of, and referring to, changed contexts, such citizens want to overcome in practice the tension between social facticity and validity. Although legal theory cannot adopt this participant perspective as its own, it can reconstruct the paradigmatic *understanding* of law and democracy that guides citizens whenever they form an idea of the structural constraints on the self-organization of the legal community in their society.

8.3.5

From a reconstructive standpoint, we have seen that constitutional rights and principles merely explicate the performative character of the self-constitution of a society of free and equal citizens. The organizational forms of the constitutional state make this practice permanent. Every historical example of a democratic constitution has a double temporal reference: as a historic document, it recalls the foundational act that it interprets—it marks a beginning in time. At the same time, its normative character means that the task of interpreting and elaborating the system of rights poses itself *anew* for each generation; as the project of a just society, a constitution articulates the horizon of expectation opening on an ever-present future. From this perspective, as an *ongoing* process of constitution making set up for the long haul, the democratic procedure of legitimate lawmaking acquires a privileged status. This leads to the pressing question of whether such a demanding procedure can be implemented in complex societies like our own and, if it can, how this can be done effectively, so that a constitutionally regulated circulation of power actually prevails in the political system. The answers to this question in turn inform our own paradigmatic understanding of law. I note the following four points for elucidating such a historically situated understanding of the constitution.

(a) The constitutionally organized political system is, on the one hand, specialized for generating collectively binding decisions. To this extent, it represents only one of several subsystems. On the other hand, in virtue of its internal relation to law, politics is responsible for problems that concern society as a whole. It must be possible to interpret collectively binding decisions as a realization of rights such that the structures of recognition built into communicative action are transferred, via the medium of law, from the level of simple interactions to the abstract and anonymous relationships among strangers. In pursuing what in each case are particular collective goals and in regulating specific conflicts, politics simultaneously deals with general problems of integration. Because it is constituted in a legal form, a politics whose mode of operation is functionally specified still refers to society-wide problems: it carries on the tasks of social integration at a reflexive level when other action systems are no longer up to the job.

(b) This asymmetrical position explains the fact that the political system is subject to constraints on two sides and that corresponding standards govern its achievements and decisions. As a functionally specified action system, it is limited by other functional systems that obey their own logic and, to this extent, bar direct political interventions. On this side, the political system encounters limits on the effectiveness of administrative power (including legal and fiscal instruments). On the other side, as a constitutionally regulated action system, politics is connected with the public sphere and depends on lifeworld sources of communicative power. Here the political system is not subject to the external constraints of a social environment but rather experiences its internal dependence on enabling conditions. This is because the conditions that make the production of legitimate law possible are ultimately not at the disposition of politics.

(c) The political system is vulnerable on both sides to disturbances that can reduce the *effectiveness* of its achievements and the *legitimacy* of its decisions, respectively. The regulatory competence of the political system fails if the implemented legal programs remain ineffective or if regulatory activity gives rise to disintegrating effects in the action systems that require regulation. Failure also occurs if the instruments deployed overtax the legal medium itself and strain the normative composition of the political system. As steering problems become more complex, irrelevance, misguided regulations, and self-destruction can accumulate to the point where a "regulatory trilemma" results.[81] On the other side, the political system fails as a guardian of social integration if its decisions, even though effective, can no longer be traced back to legitimate law. The constitutionally regulated circulation of power is nullified if the administrative system becomes independent of communicatively generated power, if the social power of functional systems and large organizations (including the mass media) is converted into illegitimate power, or if the lifeworld resources for spontaneous public communication no longer suffice to guarantee an uncoerced articulation of social interests. The independence of illegitimate power, together with the weakness of civil society and the public sphere, can deteriorate into a "legitimation dilemma," which in certain circumstances can combine with the steering trilemma and develop into a vicious circle. Then the political system is pulled into the whirlpool of legitimation deficits and steering deficits that reinforce one another.

(d) Such crises can at most be explained historically. They are not built into the structures of functionally differentiated societies in such a way that they would intrinsically compromise the project of self-empowerment undertaken by a society of free and equal subjects who bind themselves by law. However, they are symptomatic of the peculiar position of political systems as asymmetrically embedded in highly complex circulation processes. Actors must form an idea of this context whenever, adopting the performative attitude, they want to engage successfully as citizens, representatives, judges, or officials, in realizing the system of rights. Because these rights must be interpreted in various ways under changing social circumstances, the light they throw on this context is refracted into a spectrum of changing legal paradigms. Historical constitutions can be seen as so many ways of construing one and the *same* practice—the practice of self-determination on the part of free and equal citizens—but like every practice this, too, is situated in history. Those involved must start with their *own current* practice if they want to achieve clarity about what such a practice means *in general.*

9

Paradigms of Law

Since the great codifications of the eighteenth century, if not before, the established law in such countries as France and Germany has assumed tangible form primarily in texts: the propositions in the statute books tell us which norms are valid. These propositions provide the basis of adjudication, and they provide the perspective from which legal doctrine strives to interpret law. Legal theory and legal history cultivate a more objectivating approach in their understanding of legal texts and rule systems, albeit in different directions. As we have seen, by generalizing and abstracting from the adjudication of cases, legal theory gains distance without giving up the participant perspective as such. By contrast, the objectivating gaze of the historian focuses on the social contexts in which the law, as a system of action, is embedded—and from which the implicit background assumptions of adjudication and contemporary legal doctrine are nourished. Adopting this observer perspective discloses those connections that, latent for the participants themselves, functionally link a legal system with its social environment—and also link it through the image legal scholars have of their society. It then becomes clear that experts interpret individual propositions not only in the context of the legal corpus as a whole but also within the horizon of a currently dominant preunderstanding of contemporary society. To this extent, the interpretation of law is also an answer to the perceived challenges of the present social situation.

In some prominent places, the text of the law itself reveals these implicit diagnoses of the times, for example, in the "bill of rights" section of constitutions that have emerged from political upheavals or revolutions. In contrast to the professionally formulated or developed law of legal scholars, even the style and wording of these declarations display an emphatic statement of will from citizens who are reacting to concrete experiences of repression and humiliation. Most articles in a bill of rights resonate with a suffered injustice that is negated word for word, as it were.[1] What is obvious in those rare moments of a revolutionary founding of a constitution remains implicit in the everyday work of the legislature and the judiciary and so must be laboriously deciphered by the historian. Parliaments and courts can pursue the goal of realizing rights only in a context that their members interpret in view of actually allowed but limited possibilities of action. One can understand what actors respond to, and have responded to, with their decisions and reasons only if one recognizes their *implicit image of society* and only if one knows which structures, achievements, potentials, and dangers they ascribe to their own society at the time, in the light of their task of realizing the system of rights.

As early as 1931, Otto Kahn-Freund examined the "social ideal" of the Supreme Labor Court (*Reichsarbeitsgerichts*) from the perspective of ideology critique.[2] Two decades later, Franz Wieacker introduced the equivalent concept of the "social model" for descriptive purposes when he deciphered the liberal paradigm of law in the classical statute books of private law. His aim was "to disclose the social model of a given legal order and how that model changes; its secret design, so to speak, which is initially concealed by the literary, humanistic, and conceptual continuity of the scientific tradition."[3] In elaborating the paradigm of bourgeois formal law, Wieacker's famous study simultaneously clarified the background in contrast to which the "materialization" of law during the last one hundred years could emerge—a trend, already bemoaned by Max Weber, that fully asserted itself only with the development of the social-welfare state at the end of the Second World War. This *social transformation of law* was initially thought of as a process in which a new instrumental understanding of law, one related to social-welfare conceptions of justice, was superimposed on the liberal model of law. German jurisprudence has perceived this long-standing process, which dissolved the classical unity and systematic organization of the only legal order that appeared rational, as a "crisis of law."

At the beginning of the fifties, constitutional scholars hotly debated the place and import of the social-welfare provisions in the architectonic of the *Grundgesetz* (Basic Law) of the German Federal Republic. One side contested what the other fiercely maintained. The dispute concerned the choice between two competing legal paradigms. The tacit assumption that these two paradigms exhausted the alternatives was questioned only after the dysfunctional side effects of the successfully implemented welfare state became pressing political issues. For legal scholars, an especially disturbing aspect of the newly invoked "crisis of the welfare state" was the "insensitivity" of the growing state bureaucracies to restrictions on their clients' individual self-determination—a weakness of the social-welfare paradigm that symmetrically corresponds to the "social blindness" of the liberal paradigm. Since the seventies, the paradigm discussion has become more or less "reflexive." The vivid awareness of the paradigm shift has made it impossible for any paradigmatic understanding to maintain its naïveté as a background knowledge that orients us merely *intuitively*. Thus the dispute over the correct paradigm of law has become an explicit theme in legal doctrine.

Today legal practice privileges neither the conditional programs of bourgeois formal law nor the purposive programs of welfare law. At the same time, the expansion of organizational and procedural norms by no means relieves the legislator of the burden of regulating complex matters and recalcitrant functional spheres. The opaque and inconsistent structure of such a legal order has thus stimulated the *search for a new paradigm* beyond the familiar alternatives.[4] The tentative answers that readers are left with at the end of Dieter Grimm's study "The Future of the Constitution" typify the aporias afflicting contemporary debates. As we will see, Grimm's study addresses the structural reasons for the steering deficits and the diminishing binding force of constitutional law. It concludes by asking whether the idea of the constitution has any future at all: "Once the Constitution no longer succeeds in bringing all public authorities into its regulatory framework, one also must expect that it will no longer cover every sphere of state action. Whether a *different understanding of the Constitution* can absorb this loss of validity, or whether the Constitution will atrophy into a partial order, remains an open question at this point."[5] In Germany, the legal profession seems to be confronted with two alternatives. Either it must articulate a convincing understanding of law that is connected with a constitutional project tailored for complex societies,[6] or it must altogether abandon a normative understanding of law. The latter alternative would mean giving up the expectation that law can transform the weak force of uncoerced, intersubjectively shared convictions into a socially integrating power that is ultimately capable of overcoming every instance of sheer violence in whatever form it disguises itself.[7]

In concluding this study, I want to examine whether the proceduralist understanding of law developed in the previous chapters can help support the first alternative. To begin, I explain how the materialization of law has taken place in several areas of private law and in the social-welfare transformation of classical liberties. The paradigm shift shows that the private autonomy connected with the status of legal persons in general must be realized in different ways as the social context changes (sec. 9.1). The development of the welfare state endangers the guarantees for the individual's autonomous conduct of life; I deal with these problems by drawing on the dialectic of legal and factual equality. The unintended effects of juridification draw attention to the internal relation between private and public autonomy. The undesirable effects of welfare-state provisions can be countered by a politics of qualifications for citizenship. This politics grounds entitlements only in relation to a citizenship status that simultaneously guarantees private and public autonomy (sec. 9.2). The changed catalog of governmental tasks and the expanded functional sphere of the administration also give rise to problems for the separation of powers. The self-programming of an independent administration and the unauthorized delegation of powers can be met by shifting the functional separation of powers into the administrative system itself—through new elements of participation and control, including domain-specific public spheres (sec. 9.3).

9.1 The Materialization of Private Law

9.1.1

Expressions like "social ideal," "social model," "social vision," and even simply "theory" have become generally accepted ways of referring to a social epoch's paradigmatic understanding of law. Such expressions refer to those implicit ideas or images of one's own society that provide a perspective for the practices of making and applying law. These images orient the project of realizing an association of free and equal citizens. However, the historical studies of changes in legal paradigms—as well as doctrinal contributions to the paradigm debate—are limited to professional interpretations of existing law. A paradigm is discerned primarily in important court decisions and usually equated with the *judge's* implicit image of society. For example, Friedrich Kübler, relying on the phenomenological sociology of knowledge, speaks of the "social construction of reality" that underlies judgments of facts in legal discourse, that is, how factual courses of events and the functioning of social action systems are described and evaluated: "The 'facts' are mutually related behavioral expectations and motivations, human interactions, small particles from the great stream of richly interwoven social events. More precisely, they are not these sequences of events themselves but the ideas the court forms of these events."[8] Henry J. Steiner calls judges' implicit theory of society a "social vision." It forms the context whenever judges, in justifying their decisions, ascertain facts and relate these to norms: "By social vision . . . I mean perceptions of courts about society (its socioeconomic structure, patterns of social interaction, moral goals, and political ideologies), about social actors (their character, behavior, and capacities), and about accidents (their causes, volume and toll)." Steiner goes on to explain this concept with reference to American adjudication on accident law:

The concept then includes courts' understanding about matters as varied as the incidence and social costs of accidents, the operation of market pricing mechanisms, the capacity of individuals for prudent behavior, the bureaucratic rationality of business forms, the effects of standard clauses in contracts, and ideologies of growth or distribution in the nineteenth century or today. Social vision embraces not only empirical observations (the number of auto accidents), but also evaluative characterizations of events (the absence of free choice in a given context) and feelings of disapproval or empathy towards what is described (a "sharp" bargain, or a "tragic" loss).[9]

Lately, the phenomenon of an unavoidable background understanding of society has come to represent more than the object of descriptive legal history. Legal commentators and practitioners themselves have become aware of this phenomenon. Today, adjudication can no longer have a naive attitude toward its own social model. Because the paradigmatic legal understanding has lost the innocence of an orienting knowledge that operates behind the actors' backs, it invites a self-critical justification. Even specialized doctrinal commentary can no longer evade the question about the "correct" paradigm, now that this reflexive impulse has been felt. Hence Kübler's initially descriptive approach to the issue takes a constructivist turn when he concludes "that it is increasingly urgent that private law explain and justify its relations to society as a whole, that is, its emergence from and functioning in society." The reason is that "the conventional attempts at explanation," whether those of the liberal or of the social-welfare model, "are no longer sufficiently convincing."[10] The desired paradigm should satisfy the best description of complex societies; it should illuminate once again the original idea of the self-constitution of a community of free and equal citizens; and it should overcome the rampant particularism of a legal order that, having lost its center in adapting to the *uncomprehended* complexity of the social environment, is unraveling bit by bit. In addition, the fixation on the judge's image of society suggests that jurisprudence has to solve this task on its own.

However, the historian's decision to make use of the more readily available data of black-letter law and its application, although certainly a reasonable research technique, must not mislead one into identifying the paradigm inscribed in a specific legal system with the conceptual economy of its professional custodians. Otherwise one is easily led to conclude that simply through interdisciplinary cooperation with the social sciences, a critical jurisprudence can isolate the constructive function "of the judicial ideas summarized by the notion of a 'theory'" and then develop this into a paradigmatic legal understanding that makes a strictly *theoretical claim.* On this view, the required paradigm would result from a legal and social-scientific clarification of the "natural" theories of judges. It would even have the format of a theory, specifically, "as the set of ideas, resting on shared convictions, about the course of social processes, about behavior patterns and integrating mechanisms that constitute the polity." Such a theory would have a "guiding role: it determines how the law is understood and construed; it stipulates which places, in which direction, and to what extent statutory law (*Gesetzesrecht*) is to be supplemented and modified by doctrinal commentary and judge-made law (*Richterrecht*); and this means: it bears part of the responsibility for the future of social existence."[11]

Kübler emphasizes the methodological gains that appropriate legal paradigms can yield for judicial decision making: they reduce the complexity of the task of deciding the individual case both consistently and rationally, that is, the task of deciding in the light of a coherently ordered system of rules. He also sees that the required "theory" not only facilitates the self-understanding of the legal profession but in addition fulfills legitimation functions for the courts in dealing with their clients. In view of the civil-law decisions Kübler has in mind, the required "theory" is supposed to render the basic constructions "comprehensible to all, . . . so that it can bring about agreement over the functional conditions for the practice of private law."[12] At this point, if not sooner, one naturally begins to have doubts about whether the dispute over the correct legal paradigm can be conducted solely as a dispute among experts—or whether a paradigm can have the format of a legal and social theory at all.

Of course, it is no less one-sided to shift the focus of discussion without further ado from the courts to the population in general, that is, to the totality of the courts' clients. In this vein, Lawrence Friedman defends the thesis that the structural transformation of society is converted into the transformation of law itself via the legal culture—which is to say, through a change in the paradigmatic legal understanding of the whole population: "legal culture here means the ideas, opinions, values, and attitudes about law, that people carry about with them in their heads. If you ask, which people? the answer is: whichever people you like, whatever group, and at whatever level of generality."[13] From this legal-sociological point of view, the transformation of legal culture and legal consciousness acquires a quasi-natural character; Friedman's proposal does not do justice to the fact that the competition between the two problematic paradigms has by now become an explicit issue in its own right. This latter development is, after all, the result of the mobilization of law by courts and democratic legislatures, which for their parts are certainly not acting in a vacuum. The mobilizing force of adjudication and legislation reminds us that the population supposedly has the role of author, is a public of citizens—and does not just play the role of client.

As long as they function as a kind of latent background knowledge, paradigms of law have a hold on the minds of all actors—the consciousness of citizens and clients no less than that of legislators, judges, and administrators. The exhaustion of the social-welfare paradigm gave rise to legal problems that no doubt imposed themselves first on legal experts, leading them to study the social models inscribed in the law. No doubt the doctrinal attempts to escape the alternatives of either fixating on the welfare state or returning to bourgeois formal law also fostered a reflexive understanding of law, if they did not create it outright: as soon as the constitution is conceived as a demanding process of realizing rights, the task of historically situating this project arises. But in that case *all* the involved actors must form an idea of how the normative content of the democratic state can be effectively and fully exploited within the horizon of existing social structures and perceived developmental tendencies. The dispute over the correct paradigmatic understanding of the legal system, a subsystem reflected in the whole of society as one of its parts, is essentially a political dispute. In a constitutional democracy, this dispute concerns all participants, and it must not be conducted only as an esoteric discourse among experts apart from the political arena. In virtue of their prerogatives and, more generally, their professional experience and knowledge, members of the judiciary and legal experts participate in this contest of interpretations in a privileged way; but they cannot use their professional authority to impose one view of the constitution on the rest of us. The public of citizens must itself find such a view convincing.

9.1.2

As the disciplinary origins of the above-mentioned authors indicates, the paradigm shift was first noticed and discussed within private law. This was no accident, especially in Germany. Here, private law developed as a domain of judge-made law and jurisprudence inside the framework of a constitutional monarchy. In the course of the nineteenth century, and hence up to the codification of the Civil Code in 1900,[14] private law, untouched by the formative influence of a constitutional democracy, achieved the systematic closure of an independent and self-contained area of law. Premised on the separation of state and society, doctrinal refinement proceeded on the assumption that private law, by organizing a depoliticized economic society withdrawn from state intrusion, guaranteed the *negative* freedom of legal subjects and therewith the principle of legal freedom. Public law, on the contrary, was allocated by a division of labor to the sphere of the authoritarian state in order to keep a rein on an administration that reserved to itself the right to intervene. At the same time, public law was also to guarantee the citizens' *positive* legal status via individual legal protection. No doubt the materialization of private law—in the sense of a rather authoritarian exercise of duties of social protection—was already beginning to develop. But only with the establishment of the Weimar Republic did the political bases for the assumed autarky of private law finally disappear. It was then no longer possible "to contrast private law as the realm of individual freedom with public law as the field in which state coercion has effect."[15] The end of the substantive priority of private law over constitutional law, which only sealed the de facto dissolution of an ideologically maintained "private law society" (Franz Böhm), has been perceived by German civil-law jurisprudence as an "overpowering" of private law by principles of public law and as the "destruction" of the independent edifice of a unified legal system.

The priority of the democratic constitution over private law meant that the normative content of basic rights henceforth had to unfold within private law itself through an active legislature and courts: "According to constitutional law, the legislator of private law has the task of *converting* the content of basic rights into a differentiated and more concrete law that is immediately binding for participants in a private-legal relationship. It is in principle incumbent on the legislature to attend to the various modifications required to realize the influence of basic rights on private law."[16] As this process was accelerated after the Second World War through the adjudication of the Federal Constitutional Court, neither complaints about the disintegration of the legal corpus nor attempts at redefinition sufficed to fit the changed legal situation into the received categories. Already on the defensive, civil-law jurisprudence was stimulated particularly by these developments to reflect on those nonlegal background assumptions that had provided tacit underlying premises for the now-wavering division between private and public law.

Since the nineteenth century, a similar social transformation can also be observed in the law of societies with other legal traditions but comparable to Germany. In these countries, too, such changes provided an incentive for studying, primarily in private law, the eclipse and replacement of the liberal legal model by the social-welfare model.[17] The welfare state obviously posed a challenge for private law, even apart from the reasons peculiar to the development of German law. We will see that the social changes leading to an awareness of the paradigm shift make it necessary to conceive the *relation* between private and political autonomy no longer as an opposition but as a nexus of reciprocal connections. This task admittedly confronts civil law, which is tailored to the negative status of legal subjects, with greater problems than it does public law, which keeps all aspects of citizenship in view from the start. This is shown in one of the early attempts to use new systematic concepts for clarifying the confusion caused by the overlapping of private and public law.

According to classical private law, individual self-determination, in the sense of the negative freedom to do as one pleases, is sufficiently guaranteed by a certain set of rights and institutions. These included not only personal rights and protection from torts, but above all freedom of contract (especially in the exchange of goods and services) and property rights (with the guarantees of use and disposal, including inheritance) allied with institutional guarantees for marriage and family. This situation was fundamentally changed through the emergence of new areas of law (such as labor law, social legislation, and commercial law) as well as by the materialization of contract law, tort law, and property law. In many cases, principles that hitherto could be allocated either to private law or to public law merged and combined. The *whole* of private law now appeared to go beyond the goal of safeguarding individual self-determination, in order to serve the realization of social justice: "In this way, subsistence guarantees for all persons and protections for the weak acquired, even in private law, a rank equal to the pursuit of individual interests."[18] Under this description, socioethical considerations found their way into areas of law that until then had their overall consistency in the normative goal of guaranteeing private autonomy. The additional goal of social justice now seemed to demand new ways of construing formally equal but materially different legal relationships, whereby the same legal categories and institutions could fulfill different social functions.

To reorganize the disparate areas of law, Ludwig Raiser has borrowed from sociological role theory. He distinguishes "spheres" or domains of action whose "public" or "political" content stands in inverse proportion to the level of legal protection granted to the individual. According to this reading, the level of protection decreases the more the individual is caught up in social interdependencies through her social roles or, to put this in a different theoretical language, the more strongly her range of options is determined by functional systems and large organizations whose processes the individual cannot influence:

Whereas the public law regulating the police, industry, labor, or the civil service categorizes me according to my professional activity, I encounter the norms of private law as producer or consumer, as head of a household, as homeowner, as member of a sports club and professional association, or as commuter, having in each case particular rights and duties appropriate to these different situations. The institutions of private law that I thereby use—such as contract, property and possession, membership, tortious liability—may be the same, nevertheless they change their function and their legal valuation depending on the typical situation and the publicity content of the affected domain.[19]

For this reason, Raiser demarcates a sphere of private life in the narrow sense (the domestic sphere of home, family and marriage, as well as the domains of leisure and consumption, private associations, etc.) from a private sphere in a broad sense, which is characterized by typified group interests. Here individuals in their client roles depend, for example, on employment and tenancy or on transportation and supply companies. By contrast, the social sphere is dominated by interactions among corporate enterprises, large organizations, associations, and intermediary structures of all sorts, which have an influence on individuals' decisions through the exercise of economic and social power. This theory of spheres, which is also reflected in the adjudication of the Federal Constitutional Court,[20] has a certain descriptive value. Its real intention is to emphasize the ethical core of private rights with the help of a sociological concept of the "private sphere."

The principle of legal freedom, which was initially connected with classical private law, requires "that the individual is due the highest possible degree of freedom to do as he or she pleases, relative to the legal and factual possibilities."[21] This principle coincides with Kant's universal human right, the right to the greatest possible degree of equal individual liberty. Because the options available to legal subjects should be restricted by prohibitions or commands as little as possible, the principle of legal freedom directly *guarantees* the negatively defined latitude for the pursuit of one's own interests. At the same time, however, it *enables* an autonomous conduct of life in the ethical sense of pursuing one's own conception of the good, which is the sense associated with "independence," "self-responsibility," and the "free development" of one's personality. One realizes the positive freedom of the ethical person by consciously living out one's individual life. Such freedom is manifested in those core private domains where, at the level of simple interactions, the life histories of members of an intersubjectively shared lifeworld are intertwined with common traditions. As ethical, this freedom escapes legal regulation, but it is made possible by legal freedom. Indeed, the classical liberties of private law—rights protective of personality and the individual, the freedom to enter contracts, property rights, the right of private association—are what protect that innermost sphere where the ethical person can emerge from the shell of the legal subject and document, so to speak, the metalegal, indeed ethical, value of legal freedom.[22]

In spite of its phenomenological power, though, the theory of spheres is unsatisfactory. This is not just because its spatial model of life spheres, whose "public" and "political" content is hardly operationalizable, oversimplifies complex functional interrelationships. The real weakness of the theory lies in the fact that in place of legal criteria for assessing and systematically demarcating areas of law, it substitutes vague social indicators. This displacement, moreover, insinuates a false assumption: that the domain in which the classical idea of private autonomy had validity was *curtailed* by the competing, politically enforced claim of social justice, that is, the idea of "the individual's social membership and his consequent social responsibility."[23] This curtailment is even assumed to have favored a deeper, socioethical conception of personality that, strictly speaking, cannot be accommodated by legal concepts. In fact, however, the changes in private law are explained by a *changed paradigmatic understanding* of the same normative concept of private autonomy.

What the liberal model of law *assumed* about the functioning of the market mechanism and about the economy as a power-free sphere proved incorrect. As a result, to enforce the principle of legal freedom under the changed social conditions as they are *perceived* in the social-welfare model, it is necessary to "materialize" existing rights and create new types of rights. The idea of private autonomy, expressed in the right to the greatest possible degree of equal liberty, did not change at all. What did change were the perceived social contexts in which each individual's private autonomy was supposed to be equally realized. With her private autonomy, the individual as such is guaranteed the status of a legal person. But this status is by no means grounded only in the protection of a sphere of private life in the sociological sense, even if it is primarily in this sphere that legal freedom can *prove* itself as making ethical freedom possible. The status of a private legal subject is constituted by all those rights that relate to action and condition and that issue from the political elaboration of the principle of legal freedom—no matter in which social sphere. For this reason, legally demarcating an "inviolable domain of private life-plans" can only mean that restrictions in this domain must be justified by especially weighty reasons on a case-by-case basis.[24] But it does not mean that every right that can serve the private pursuit of an autonomous life refers to the protection of a private sphere conceived in sociological terms and privileged from an ethical perspective.

Most important, restrictions on the classical liberties in the "social" sphere (as distinct from broader or narrower private spheres) certainly cannot be traced back to the interference of *other* legal principles (such as social justice or social responsibility). What appears as a restriction is only the flip side of the enforcement of *equal* individual liberties for all. This is because private autonomy, in the sense of this universal right to equal liberties, implies a universal right of equality, that is, the right to equal treatment according to norms that guarantee substantive legal equality. This may produce *actual* restrictions for one or another party in comparison to the status quo ante. If so, such restrictions are not limitations on the principle of legal freedom, but arise as a result of abolishing privileges that are incompatible with the equal distribution of individual liberties required by this principle.

9.1.3

The social-welfare model emerged from the reformist critique of bourgeois formal law. According to this model, an economic society institutionalized in the form of private law (above all through property rights and contractual freedom) was separated from the sphere of the common good, the state, and left to the spontaneous workings of market mechanisms. This "private-law society" was tailored for the autonomy of legal subjects who, primarily as market participants, would seek and find their happiness by pursuing their own particular interests as rationally as possible. The interpenetration of the principle of legal freedom with the universal right to equality grounded the normative expectation that social justice could be concomitantly established by defining spheres of individual liberty, that is, by guaranteeing a negative legal status connected with a claim to corresponding individual legal protection. For the right of *each person* to do as she pleases within the framework of laws is legitimate only under the condition that these laws guarantee *equal* treatment in the sense of substantive legal equality. This seemed to be already guaranteed through the formal universality of legal statutes, that is, through the type of conditional legal program privileged by bourgeois formal law. In any case, this legal form was typical for the norms of bourgeois private law that confer powers and impose prohibitions. (It was also typical for the corresponding individual rights that impose certain interventionary duties on an administration bound by law.) However, the expectation of social justice—as achievable via the private-legal elaboration of the principle of legal freedom— was thereby implicitly linked with the demarcation of nondiscriminatory *conditions for the actual exercise* of liberties granted by the legal norms regulating contracts, property, inheritance, and association. This expectation tacitly relied on certain social-theoretic assumptions or factual suppositions. Primarily, it depended on economic assumptions about equilibrium in market processes (with entrepreneurial freedom and consumer sovereignty). Corresponding to these were sociological assumptions about the distribution of wealth and an approximately equal distribution of social power, which was supposed to secure equal opportunities for exercising the powers conferred by private law. If freedom in "the capacity to have and acquire" is to satisfy justice expectations, then an equality of "legal capacity" must exist.

Thus the social-contract model of bourgeois formal law soon proved to be vulnerable to empirical criticism. This led to a reformist practice, which, however, was based not on a change in the normative premises but only on a more abstract reading of them. Under the conditions of an organized capitalism dependent on the government's provision of public infrastructure and planning, and with a growing inequality in economic power, assets, and social situations, the *objective legal content* of subjective private rights—that is, their substantive implications for public law— merely became visible. In such a changed social context, the universal right to equal individual liberties could no longer be guaranteed through the negative status of the legal subject. Rather, it proved necessary, on the one hand, to specify the content of existing norms of private law and, on the other, to introduce a new category of basic rights grounding claims to a more just distribution of social wealth (and a more effective protection from socially produced dangers). From a normative point of view, both the materialization of private law and the new category of social entitlements are *justified in a relative sense*, namely, in relation to an absolutely justified equal distribution of individual liberties. Materialization results from the fact "that legal freedom, that is, the legal permission to do as one pleases, is worthless without actual freedom, the real possibility of choosing between the permitted alternatives." Social entitlements, on the other hand, are due to the fact "that under the conditions of modern industrial society the actual freedom of a large number of rights-bearers does not have its material basis in an environment they control, but essentially depends on government activities."[25] We might also note that the democratic constitution links private law to the expanded catalog of basic rights, establishing a connection that binds the legislator and, what is more, has left its mark on the decisions of the Constitutional Court, supported by the doctrine that basic rights have a "radiating effect" (*Ausstrahlung*) or "third-party effect" (*Drittwirkung*).[26]

Changes in the classical areas of property law and contract law serve as prime examples of the materialization of bourgeois formal law. Thus, on the one hand, property guarantees have been extended beyond material property to include all entitlements and rights affecting income (such as membership rights, pension rights, and pension eligibility). As a result, in many areas "public surrogates for property" have taken over the role that property law played in safeguarding freedom. On the other hand, the social duties of property pertain to any object that stands "in a social relation or a social function." More specifically, the binding power of property as a basic right has been reduced "to a relatively narrow core of what is most personal" (consider, for example, the co-determination rights that employees have vis-à-vis management; takings and similar expropriative interventions; and the separation of usufruct).[27] Horst Bethge sees the property guarantee as that liberty "whose explicit social duties have progressed the farthest, not only in a negative sense but in an actively positive sense as well."[28]

Doctrinal legal commentary has been just as dramatic in its assessment of changes in contract law that in effect recast exchange relationships from an observer point of view. This shift is evident in the consideration of de facto contractual relations, the duty of suppliers to enter contracts for the delivery of essential goods and services, safeguards on good faith, the doctrines of mistaken intention and positive breach of contract; it is especially clear in the controls imposed on framing and entering into contracts, as well as in the corresponding obligations to provide information and advice and to exercise due care. As in the case of property law, here, too, the declared purpose of the regulations is to provide compensation for "market failure" to those in weaker market positions (employees, tenants, consumers, etc.). Typical conditions of good faith, self-binding commitments, obligations to fulfill a contract, and so on, are understood as social-welfare protections. As materialized in this way, contract law no longer allows the "rightness" of contractual terms to depend entirely on the fiction of the free declaration of intention linked with the freedom to enter into contracts. Even the "law that governs entry into contracts belongs to that part of private law that adjusts for systemic advantages and dependencies. This compensatory law does not rely on the fiction that the subjects entering into the contract are equal, but instead makes structural advantages in information, power, and authority accessible to empirical analysis and legally binding evaluation."[29]

I mention the above as examples of the further development of law initiated primarily in the adjudication process. These examples are relevant here because of their underlying premises, which reveal a changed perception and interpretation of social processes. Statutory limitations on property, as well as judicial interventions into the framing and concluding of contracts, seek to compensate for asymmetries in economic power positions.[30] The principle of an equal opportunity to exercise liberties is used to justify this goal both critically, with reference to a rejected social model (market failure), and constructively in view of a new model, that of the welfare state. This new background understanding has two components: on the one hand, there emerges the image of an increasingly complex society of functionally specified domains of action that push individual actors into the marginal position of "clients," handing them over to the contingencies of independently operating systems. On the other hand, there is the expectation that these contingencies can be normatively domesticated with the deployment of administrative power, that is, through the redistributive measures of a welfare state that is becoming active in either a preventative or reactive manner.

Using the example of American adjudication on accident law, Steiner has supplied convincing evidence for the paradigm shift to be observed in the United States: "What this common law change does express is not a radical shift in political or legal premises, but rather a trend in liberal thought from the vision and ideology of a more individualist society stressing a facilitative state framework for private activity to the vision and ideology of a more managerial, redistributive, and welfare state."[31] If we list the combinations of features with which cases of liability in business transactions were once described—*and therewith interpreted*—from a liberal viewpoint and compare these features with how such cases are described and interpreted today in view of welfare regulations, we obtain the following table:

The Liberal View	*Today's View*
unique	statistical
individual, personal	category, impersonal
concrete, anecdotal	generalized, purged of detail
occasional, random	recurrent, systemic
isolated conduct	part of an activity
unforeseeable (in the particular)	predictable (in the aggregate)
wait and see, fatalism	manageable, planning through insurance and regulation

If one reads the table in the given sequence (from top to bottom), then the difference in the patterns of interpretation appears as a change in perspective that an observer makes in moving from the action level to the system level of description: on the left side, the individual actor in her natural, that is, contingently changing environment, provides the point of reference; with her individual liberty, she also has the responsibility for the consequences of her decisions. On the right side, the statistically described interrelationships of a system constitute the point of reference; here the doubly contingent decisions of the involved parties together with their consequences are taken as dependent variables. If, on the contrary, one reads the table in reverse order (from the bottom up), then the difference in patterns of interpretation appears as a shift in the actor's perspective: according to the liberal market model, society represents the result of spontaneous forces and thus is something like a "second nature" that resists the influence of individual actors. From the vantage point of the regulatory welfare state, however, society loses precisely this quasi-natural character. As soon as system conditions vary beyond a certain level determined by the "limits of social tolerance," the state is held accountable for crisis conditions perceived to result from its own steering deficits.

The social-welfare model appears in different versions, depending on whether one naively credits the state with a wide range of possibilities for direct political intervention in a society at its disposal, or whether one conceives it more realistically as one system among several, which must restrict itself to a narrow range of indirect steering inputs. However, as long as the administration remains bound by individual rights—so that not all normative constraints on its activities are surrendered in favor of mere compliance with "systemic imperatives"—both readings of the social-welfare model assume a competition between two agents, the state and those subject to it, who dispute each other's scope for action. One might say this model *pays for* the expanding agency of the state at the expense of the autonomous status of individual actors. Whether one is dealing with the active "interventionary" state or the ironic "supervisory" state, what is awarded to the state in capacities for social regulation seemingly must be *taken*, in the form of private autonomy, from individuals caught in their systemic dependencies. From this point of view, the administration and private actors are involved in a zero-sum game: what the one gains in competence the other loses. According to the liberal model, the subjects of private law who once acted within the framework of their equally distributed liberties were limited only by the contingencies of the quasi-natural social situation. Today they run up against the paternalistic provisions of a superior political will that, attempting to influence and shape these social contingencies, intervenes with the intention of enhancing the opportunities for an equal use of legal freedoms.

Welfare-state paternalism has raised the disturbing question whether the new paradigm is compatible with the principle of legal freedom at all. This question has become more acute in view of the juridification effects arising from certain properties of administrative power as the medium for state interventions, properties that are hardly neutral. The welfare state provides services and apportions life opportunities; by guaranteeing employment, security, health care, housing, minimum income, education, leisure, and the natural bases of life, it grants each person the material basis for a humanly dignified existence. But with such overwhelming provisions, the welfare state obviously runs the risk of impairing individual autonomy, precisely the autonomy it is supposed to promote by providing the factual preconditions for the equal opportunity to exercise negative freedoms. For this reason, Hans H. Rupp objects to the prevailing interpretation of social entitlements as rights that secure personal freedom by guaranteeing a "fair share":

Having a share [*Teilhabe*] is the antithesis of having property [*Eigenhabens*] in the liberal sense. The former makes personal decision, self-realization, and individual responsibility equivalent to the individual's merely passive participation in prefabricated pieces of the gross national product. It limits the individual's "freedom" to the right of receiving one's due share and using it according to directions. This "fair share" interpretation . . . has nothing to do with securing the conditions for the genesis of personal freedom through civil rights.[32]

It is certainly true that the welfare state may not *reduce* the task of securing the material basis of private autonomy to the bureaucratic provision of security and benefits. However, the rhetoric of the "Western-liberal conception of freedom" achieves very little by itself. For the justified critique that the welfare paradigm levels against bourgeois formal law precludes a return to the liberal paradigm. At the same time, the weaknesses of the social-welfare model might be explained by the fact that it is still too closely attached to the premises of its liberal counterpart.

That is, both paradigms share the *productivist image* of a capitalist industrial society. In the liberal view, the private pursuit of personal interests is what allows capitalist society to satisfy the expectation of social justice, whereas in the social-welfare view, this is precisely what shatters the expectation of justice. Both views are fixated on the normative implications of how a legally protected negative status functions in a given social context. This means that both are fixated on the question of whether it suffices to guarantee private autonomy through individual liberties, or whether on the contrary the *conditions for the genesis* of private autonomy must be secured by granting welfare entitlements. Both views lose sight of the internal relation between private and *political* autonomy, and thus lose sight of the democratic meaning of a community's self-organization. The still-unresolved dispute between these two parties is focused on specifying the material preconditions for the equal status of legal persons as addressees of the legal order. These persons are autonomous, however, only insofar as they can at the same time understand themselves as authors of the law to which they are subject as addressees.

In justifying the system of rights, we saw that the autonomy of citizens and the legitimacy of law *refer* to each other. Under postmetaphysical conditions, the only legitimate law is one that emerges from the discursive opinion- and will-formation of equally enfranchised citizens. The latter can in turn adequately exercise their public autonomy, guaranteed by rights of communication and participation, only insofar as their private autonomy is guaranteed. A well-secured private autonomy helps "secure the conditions" of public autonomy just as much as, conversely, the appropriate exercise of public autonomy helps "secure the conditions" of private autonomy. This mutual dependency, or circular reinforcement, is manifested in the genesis of valid law. This is because legitimate law reproduces itself only in the forms of a constitutionally regulated circulation of power, which should be nourished by the communications of an unsubverted public sphere rooted in the core private spheres of an undisturbed lifeworld via the networks of civil society. With this conception, the burden of normative expectations in general shifts from the level of *actors'* qualities, competences, and opportunities to the *forms of communication* in which an informal and noninstitutionalized opinion- and will-formation can develop and interact with the institutionalized deliberation and decision making inside the political system. In place of the zero-sum game between the competing initiatives of private and governmental actors, we reckon instead with the more or less intact forms of communication found in the private and public spheres of the lifeworld, on the one hand, and those in political institutions, on the other.

This does not mean that the law's internal references to actors are disregarded; law is not converted over to anonymous systems that serve as surrogates for individual bearers of rights. Rather, all rights ultimately stem from the system of rights that free and equal legal subjects would mutually accord to one another. The reference to the communicative relations from which political power arises, the reference to the forms of communication on which the generation of legitimate law depends and through which it is reproduced—this reference directs our attention to those structures of mutual recognition that, as preserved in the legal order, are stretched like a skin around society as a whole. A legal order *is* legitimate to the extent that it equally secures the co-original private and political autonomy of its citizens; at the same time, however, it *owes* its legitimacy to the forms of communication in which alone this autonomy can express and prove itself. In the final analysis, the legitimacy of law depends on undistorted forms of public communication and indirectly on the communicational infrastructure of the private sphere as well. This is the key to a proceduralist understanding of law. After the formal guarantee of private autonomy has proven insufficient, and after social intervention through law also threatens the very private autonomy it means to restore, the only solution consists in thematizing the connection between forms of communication that *simultaneously* guarantee private and public autonomy *in the very conditions from which they emerge.*

9.2 The Dialectic of Legal and Factual Equality: The Feminist Politics of Equality

So far the contours of the proceduralist legal paradigm that is supposed to lead us out of the cul-de-sac of the social-welfare model have remained vague. Let me begin with three premises: (a) the way back that neoliberalism advertises as a "return of civil society and its law"[33] is blocked; however, (b) the call for the "rediscovery of the individual" is provoked by a welfare-state juridification that threatens to twist the declared goal of restoring private autonomy into its opposite;[34] finally, (c) the social-welfare project must neither be simply continued along the same lines nor be broken off, but must be pursued at a higher level of reflection.[35] The intention is to tame the capitalist economic system, that is, to "restructure" it socially and ecologically in such a way that the deployment of administrative power can be simultaneously brought under control. From the standpoint of effectiveness, this means training the administration to employ mild forms of indirect steering; from the standpoint of legitimacy, it means linking the administration to communicative power and immunizing it better against illegitimate power. This path to realizing the system of rights under the conditions of a complex society cannot be adequately characterized in terms of a specific legal form—reflexive law—that the procedural paradigm of law would privilege in a manner similar to the way the liberal and welfare paradigms once favored their corresponding legal forms—formal and material law.[36] Rather, the choice of the respective legal form must in each case remain bound to the original meaning of the system of rights, which is to secure the citizens' private and public autonomy *uno actu*: each legal act should at the same time be understood as a contribution to the politically autonomous elaboration of basic rights, and thus as an element in an ongoing process of constitution making. I will flesh out the details of this background understanding by first examining, from the perspective of private law, some dilemmas of law in the welfare state.[37]

9.2.1

In the area of private law, we find a number of proposals for escaping welfare-state paternalism. One line of thought directs attention to the actionability of rights. This approach starts with the observation that materialized law, because of its complex references to typical social situations, requires conflicting parties to have a high level of competence.[38] Rights can become socially effective only to the extent that the affected parties are sufficiently informed and capable of actualizing, in the relevant cases, the legal protection guaranteed by the basic right of due process. The competence to mobilize the law already depends in general on formal education, social background, and other variables (such as gender, age, previous courtroom experience, and the kind of social relationship affected by the conflict). But the access barriers are even higher for utilizing materialized law, which requires laypersons to dissect their everyday problems (regarding work, leisure and consumption, housing, illness, etc.) into highly specialized legal constructions that are abstractly related to real-life contexts. This makes it reasonable to require a compensatory approach to legal protection, which strengthens the vulnerable clients' legal knowledge, their capacity to perceive and articulate problems, their readiness for conflict, and in general their ability to assert themselves. In addition to conventional measures, such as forms of legal insurance and legal aid, the countervailing power of social interests can be promoted by developing *collective modes of implementing law*. Naturally, class-action suits or community complaints, as well as the creation of ombudspersons, arbitration boards, and such, will counteract the disempowerment of overburdened clients only if collective legal protection, besides relieving the strain on individuals through competent representation, also *involves* them in the organized perception, articulation, and assertion of their own interests. If the above proposals are not to further exacerbate the loss of voice in the welfare state, then affected citizens must experience the organization of legal protection as a political process, and *they themselves* must be able to take part in the construction of countervailing power and the articulation of social interests. Participation in legal procedures could then be interpreted as collaboration in the process of realizing rights, thus linking positive legal status with the status of active citizenship. Paul Häberle has extended this democratic-process view of participation to the realization of social entitlements in general. He sets his hopes on the elaboration of a "status activus processualis" (active procedural status).[39] Even if one should not overburden and misuse procedural law as an ersatz theory of democracy, this proposal for correcting Georg Jellinek's venerable status theory (*Statuslehre*) at least reminds us of the internal relation between private and public autonomy.

The school of thought inspired by Rudolf Wiethölter's proposals prefers a different approach to making up for the impairments in negative liberty that result from the deployment of materialized law for welfare-state purposes.[40] In this approach, too, organization and procedure are supposed to strengthen the individual's positive legal status, only this time not by way of collective implementation but in *forms of cooperative will-formation*. The legislature is supposed to make procedures and organizational forms available for the internal constitutionalization of different spheres of action; modeled after self-governing bodies and arbitration boards, these forms are intended to enable involved parties to manage their own affairs and resolve conflicts by themselves. In this way, the individual's private autonomy could be supplemented or replaced by a kind of *social autonomy*. Taking this perspective, Eberhard Schmidt observes that materialized law is already being "overlaid" by "procedural" law:

> If the golden age of private autonomy was tied to the developmental needs of a bourgeoisie still confident of the self-regulating powers of free enterprise; and if subsequent endeavors that were fixated on acts of substantive distribution essentially sprang from the attempt to administer, through some kind of representation, the interests of those excluded from the earlier model; then we find ourselves today in a situation that is characterized less and less by a bitter class antagonism, a situation in which one can see instead a constantly intensifying mutual dependence among stratified social groups.

The growing interdependence of action systems is accompanied by a "growing capacity for articulation on the part of those involved." Schmidt continues:

> This capacity—and this is fundamentally new—is developed not at the individual level but in a solidaristic fashion. For the sphere of production one need only consider the union movement. In this area we have for a long time been accustomed to the fact that standard definitions of the needs for protection and income are neither left to individual practice nor regulated by the state. . . . That wage agreements can occasionally even replace coercible law exemplifies the fact that social autonomy is conceded to have priority over state heteronomy in this area.[41]

However, the concept of social autonomy, like that of active procedural status, reduces private and public autonomy to a common denominator too quickly. The right to free collective bargaining is certainly a good example of the internal constitutionalization of a nongovernmental subsystem specialized for conflict resolution; the example also shows how the positive legal status of association members can be furnished with quasi-political rights of participation and assimilated to active citizenship. On the other hand, this same right to collective bargaining provides examples of how individual self-determination can be undermined by collective powers. The willingness of the legislature to transfer lawmaking authority to the bargaining parties and restrict itself to complementary tasks does not imply an *unqualified* gain in autonomy for the individual employees. Spiros Simitis has studied a range of legal phenomena apropos of this issue: rigid and gender-specific age limits, protective norms for women employees, regulations governing part-time work, the internal protection of computerized information, workplace safety regulations and, more generally, the legal elaboration of the so-called normal work relation. Simitis's investigations show that the instruments of the labor-management contract and the wage agreement—not unlike the labor law passed by the political legislator—satisfy social claims at the cost of dictating schemata and behavioral patterns from above. These normative controls can have the effect of *normalizations that restrict freedom.* For example, they unreasonably restrict the private life plans of beneficiaries insofar as they promote traditional social roles instead of involving the affected persons themselves in the interpretation, differentiation, or reorganization of these patterns:

Statutes and wage agreements do not build bridges for the employee's self-determination. On the contrary, they institutionalize heteronomy for the sake of better protecting the individual employee. As long as the statute and wage agreement do not perceive the employee as an individual but as part of a collectivity, they cannot fulfill their task of establishing standards that counteract the consequences of dependence in the workplace. The result: statutes and wage agreements introduce a *colonization of employee behavior* that, scarcely detectable at first, increasingly spreads and solidifies.[42]

Thus the internal constitutionalization of labor relations does not by itself yield greater autonomy: "thus, regardless of whether it concerns legislation or collective bargaining, the individual agreement is without exception suppressed in favor of a regulation that is oriented not by the expectations of the individual employee but by the situation of a specific group of employees, if not that of employees in general."[43]

Naturally, Simitis does not style himself an advocate for a backward-looking neoliberalism, for the causes that have led to welfare-state regulations will not disappear through deregulation.[44] But these and similar analyses draw attention to problems of equal status and equal treatment, problems that are not immediately solved by the effective implementation of existing procedural rights or by the introduction of new ones. One cannot specify the correct relation between material and legal equality with a view to individual private rights alone. If private and public autonomy are co-original, then this relation can, *in the final analysis*, be specified only by the citizens themselves.

9.2.2

Discourse theory explains the legitimacy of law by means of procedures and communicative presuppositions that, once they are legally institutionalized, ground the supposition that the processes of making and applying law lead to rational outcomes. The norms passed by the political legislature and the rights recognized by the judiciary prove their "rationality" by the fact that addressees are treated as free and equal members of an association of legal subjects. In short, this rationality is proven in the equal treatment of legal persons who at the same time are protected in their integrity. This consequence is juristically expressed in the requirement of equal treatment. Although this includes equality in applying the law, that is, the equality of citizens *before* the law, it is equivalent to the broader principle of substantive legal equality, which holds that what is equal in all relevant respects should be treated equally, and what is unequal should be treated unequally. But what counts in each case as the *"relevant respects"* requires justification. Robert Alexy thus interprets the equality principle as a rule that assigns the burden of argument (in discourses of justification and application).[45] The reasons are either themselves normative or are based on normative reasons. They are good or "weighty" reasons if they "count" under discursive conditions and are, in the final analysis, rationally acceptable for the public of citizens as authors of the legal order. Legitimate law closes the circle between the private autonomy of its addressees, who are treated equally, and the public autonomy of enfranchised citizens, who, as equally entitled authors of the legal order, must ultimately decide on the criteria of equal treatment.

These criteria are by no means indifferent to how one draws the boundary between private and public spheres. One can view the historical dispute between the welfare and liberal paradigms as a dispute over this boundary as well, and thus over the respective criteria of equal treatment. Now that the dispute has become reflexive, neither paradigm can claim to be dominant any longer. It must therefore be decided from case to case whether and in which respects factual (or material) equality is required for the legal equality of citizens who are both privately and publicly autonomous. The proceduralist paradigm gives normative emphasis precisely to this double reference that the relation between legal and factual equality has to private and public autonomy. And it privileges all the arenas where disputes over the essentially contestable criteria of equal treatment must be discursively carried out if the circulation of power in the political system is to stay the course set by constitutional regulation.

The social-welfare critique of bourgeois formal law directs attention to the dialectic between the legal and factual freedom of the *addressees* of law, and hence focuses primarily on the implementation of basic social rights. Factual equality is gauged by the observable social effects that legal regulations have for those affected, whereas legal equality refers to the latter's power to decide freely according to their own preferences within the legal framework. The principle of legal freedom engenders factual inequalities, since it not only permits but facilitates the differential use of the same rights by different subjects; it thereby fulfills the legal presuppositions for the autonomous pursuit of private life plans. To this extent, legal equality cannot coincide with factual equality. On the other hand, the requirement of equal legal treatment is contradicted by those inequalities that discriminate against specific persons or groups by actually reducing their opportunities to utilize equally distributed individual liberties. Insofar as welfare compensations establish equal opportunities to make equal use of legal

powers, compensation for material inequalities in life circumstances and power positions helps realize legal equality. To this
extent, the dialectic between legal and factual equality has been an
inconspicuous motor of legal development for quite some time.

This relation grows into a *dilemma*, however, when welfare regulations, employing criteria of equal treatment in an attempt to
secure an actual equality in living situations and power positions,
achieve this goal only under conditions or with instruments that, as
far as the presumptive beneficiaries are concerned, also severely
limit the vulnerable areas in which individuals can autonomously
pursue a private life plan. In his examination of the examples
mentioned above, Simitis has illuminated the critical point "where
the possible gain in the material capacity to act changes into a new
dependency."[46] This point is reached when statutory regulations on
work and family life *force* employees or family members to conform
their behavior to a "normal" work relation or a standard pattern of
socialization; when the recipients of other compensations *pay* for
these with dependence on normalizing intrusions by employment
offices, welfare agencies, and housing authorities, or when they
must accept court decisions that directly intervene in their lives; or
when collective legal protection, the right to unionize, and so on,
provide an effective representation of interests only at the cost of
the freedom to decide by organization members, who are condemned to *passive followership* and conformity. Each of these critical
cases concerns the same phenomenon: satisfying the material
preconditions for an equal opportunity to exercise individual
liberties alters living situations and power positions in such a way
that the compensation for disadvantages is associated with forms of
tutelage that convert the intended *authorization* for the use of
freedom into a *custodial supervision.*

As is also clear in the case of social legislation,[47] materialized law
is stamped by an ambivalence of guaranteeing freedom and taking
it away, an ambivalence that results from the dialectic of legal and
factual equality and hence issues from the structure of this process
of juridification. Still, it would be rash to describe this structure
itself as *dilemmatic.*[48] For the criteria by which one can identify the
point where empowerment is converted into supervision are, even
if context-dependent and contested, not arbitrary.

These criteria express a clear normative intuition, which is interpreted differently in different political cultures and in view of changing social situations. According to the discourse-theoretic reading of the system of rights, positive law, because it depends on the decisions of a legislature, must split up the autonomy of legal persons into the complementary relation between private and public autonomy, so that the addressees of enacted law can at the same time understand themselves as authors of lawmaking. Both sides of autonomy are essentially incomplete elements that refer to their respective complement. This nexus of reciprocal references provides an intuitive standard by which one can judge whether a regulation promotes or reduces autonomy. According to this standard, enfranchised citizens must, in exercising their public autonomy, draw the boundaries of private autonomy in such a way that it sufficiently qualifies private persons for their role of citizen. This is because communication in a public sphere that recruits private persons from civil society depends on the spontaneous inputs from a lifeworld whose core private domains are intact. At the same time, the normative intuition that private and public autonomy reciprocally presuppose each other informs public dispute over the criteria for securing the equal autonomy of private persons, that is, criteria that specify what material preconditions of legal equality are required at a given time. These criteria also determine when a regulation results in formal legal discrimination or welfare-state paternalism. A legal program proves to be discriminating if it is insensitive to how actual inequalities have side effects that in fact restrict the use of equally distributed liberties. And it proves to be paternalistic if it is insensitive to the freedom-restricting side effects of the state's compensations for those inequalities.

The recognition of claims to social benefits (and protection from ecological or technological threats) is justified in relative terms; such recognition is indirectly related to the guarantee of personal self-determination as a necessary condition for political self-determination. In this sense, Ulrich Preuss justifies welfare rights by the purpose of securing an autonomous citizenship status:

[Today] the inescapable starting point for citizenship qualifications is the equal freedom of each citizen regardless of his or her quite different natural talents, capacities, and capabilities. . . . Not only does each individual have an interest in this, . . . but democratic society as a whole depends on the citizens' decisions having a certain quality, however that quality is defined. For this reason society also has an interest in the good quality of enfranchised citizens: specifically, it has an interest in their being informed, in their capacity to reflect and to consider the consequences of their politically relevant decisions, in their will to formulate and assert their interests in view of the interests of their fellow citizens as well as future generations. In short, it has an interest in their "communicative competence" . . . . The unequal distribution of basic goods diminishes the quality of civic virtues and thus, as a result, the rationality that can be attained by collective decisions as well. For this reason, a policy of compensating for the unequal distribution of social goods can be justified as a "politics of qualifications for citizenship."[49]

Of course, this interpretation must not end up functionalizing *all* basic rights for the democratic process, since negative liberties also have an intrinsic value.[50]

9.2.3

The welfare paradigm of law is oriented exclusively toward the problem of the just distribution of socially produced life opportunities. By reducing justice to *distributive* justice, it misses the freedom-guaranteeing meaning of legitimate rights: indeed, the system of rights only spells out what those who participate in the self-organization of a community of free and equal citizens must always already implicitly presuppose. The idea of a just society is connected with the promise of emancipation and human dignity. The distributive aspect of equal legal status and equal treatment—the just distribution of social benefits—is simply what *results* from the universalistic character of a law intended to guarantee the freedom and integrity of each. The normative key is autonomy, not well-being. In a legal community, *no one* is free as long as the freedom of one person must be purchased with another's oppression. The distribution of compensations only follows from an equal distribution of rights, which in turn results from the mutuality of recognizing all as free and equal members. Under this aspect of equal respect, subjects have a claim to equal rights. The complementary mistake of the liberal paradigm lies in reducing justice to an equal distribution of rights, as though this were a distribution of goods—thereby assimilating rights to goods that one can divide up and possess. It is equally mistaken to see rights as collective goods that one consumes in common. Rights can be "enjoyed" only insofar as one *exercises* them. Moreover, individual self-determination manifests itself in the exercise of those rights derived from *legitimately produced* norms. For this reason the equal distribution of rights cannot be detached from the public autonomy that enfranchised citizens can exercise only in common, by taking part in the practice of legislation.

The complementary blind spots of the social-welfare and liberal paradigms of law stem from the same error: both paradigms misunderstand the legal "constitution" of freedom as "distribution" and assimilate it to the model of the equal distribution of acquired or allocated goods. Iris Marion Young has convincingly criticized this error:

What does distributing a right mean? One may talk about having a right to a distributive share of material things, resources, or income. But in such cases it is the good that is distributed, not the right. . . . Rights are not fruitfully conceived as possessions. Rights are relationships, not things; they are institutionally defined rules specifying what people can *do* in relation to one another. Rights refer to *doing* more than *having*, to social relationships that enable or constrain action.[51]

Injustice means primarily the constraint of freedom and the violation of human dignity. It can, though, express itself in discrimination that withholds from the "oppressed" and "subordinated" what enables them to exercise their private and public autonomy:

Justice should refer not only to distribution, but also to the institutional conditions necessary for the development and exercise of individual capacities and collective communication and cooperation. Under this conception of justice, injustice refers primarily to two forms of disabling constraints, oppression and domination. While these constraints include distributive patterns, they also involve matters which cannot easily be assimilated to the logic of distribution: decisionmaking procedures, division of labor and culture.[52]

It is no accident that this critique arises in the context of a *feminist theory of law* that rejects the welfare paradigm. The feminist discussion, which has made the most progress in the United States, focuses on developments in law where the dialectic of legal and factual equality has intensified in an interesting way. The problems connected with the equal treatment of men and women makes one aware that the sought-for liberation should not be understood simply in terms of welfare benefits in the sense of a just social share. Rights can empower women to shape their own lives autonomously only to the extent that these rights also facilitate equal participation in the practice of civic self-determination, because only women themselves can clarify the "relevant aspects" that define equality and inequality for a given matter. Feminism insists on the emancipatory meaning of equal legal treatment because feminist critique is aimed at structural dependencies concealed by a paradigm geared to social redistribution: "Domination consists in institutional conditions which inhibit or prevent people from participation in determining their actions or the conditions of their actions. Welfare capitalist society creates specifically new forms of domination. Increasingly the activities of everyday work and life come under rationalized bureaucratic control, subjecting people to the discipline of authorities and experts in many areas of life."[53] As long as these colonizing dependencies are not overcome, a politics of "preferential treatment," however well-intentioned, heads in the wrong direction, for it suppresses the voices of those who alone could *say* what the currently relevant reasons are for equal or unequal treatment.[54]

I would like to start with the feminist charter that was adopted in Houston, Texas, in 1977 by two thousand delegates of diverse social, ethnic, and regional backgrounds. If one considers this catalog of demands[55] from the standpoint of legal theory, one recognizes the historical layers of the *still-outstanding* concerns of the feminist movement. (a) The *liberal* demands refer, on the one hand, to a more extensive inclusion of women (abolition of all gender discrimination in education and employment; increased representation of women in elective and appointive public offices). On the other hand, these demands refer to the implementation of basic rights, either in social domains that can be considered spheres of "special power relations" in a new sense (governmental support for battered women and displaced homemakers; the revision of criminal and family laws regarding marital support) or in view of new legal definitions (reproductive freedom, pornography, consensual homosexual activity, etc.). (b) These stand alongside *social-welfare* demands (an adequate standard of living for all individuals, including income transfers labeled as wages, not welfare, for indigent homemakers with dependent children; federally funded child-care services accessible to families at all income levels, with adequate opportunity for parental involvement). The last clause can already be understood as the result of disappointing experiences with the effects of implementing social-welfare demands. (c) A *reflexive attitude* toward the successes of feminist reforms is also expressed by a demand such as that for full employment, with increased opportunities for flexible and part-time schedules. The contemporaneity of the noncontemporaneous revealed by this agenda from the days of the political struggle for the Equal Rights Amendment gives one some idea of the nearly two-hundred-year-long learning process. In the present context, it is especially interesting that this learning process reflects a typical transformation of the paradigmatic understanding of law.

The classical feminism stemming from the nineteenth century understood the equality of women primarily as equal access to existing educational institutions and occupational systems, to public offices, parliaments, and so forth. The rhetoric of implementing formal rights was intended to uncouple the acquisition of social status as much as possible from gender and to guarantee women equal opportunities in the competition for education, jobs, income, social standing, influence, and political power, regardless of the outcome. Liberal politics was supposed to bring about the inclusion of women in a society that hitherto had denied them fair chances to compete. The difference between the sexes supposedly would lose its social relevance, once the differential access to the relevant spheres was overcome. Opponents of this liberal feminism stubbornly resisted the neutralization of the "natural" arrangement, that is, the traditional role of the (bourgeois) wife, who, according to (thoroughly modern) notions of a patriarchal division of labor, should remain bound to the private sphere of household life. The two sides respectively accused each other of a "cult of the household" and a "preoccupation with self-realization."[56] Of course, to the extent that the formal equality of women was implemented in important social spheres, the dialectic of legal and factual equality was also felt, leading to special regulations primarily in welfare law, labor law, and family law. Good examples are found in the protective norms pertaining to pregnancy and maternity, or custody rights in divorce cases. Such norms and rights cluster around the clear biological differences connected with reproduction. The same holds for special regulations in the criminal law dealing with sex offenses. In these areas, the feminist legislation followed the social-welfare program of promoting equality in women's legal status via compensations for disadvantages, whether "natural" or "social."

Since the late sixties, the lines of debate have become confused (in such countries as the United States and the Federal Republic). Since then a reawakening feminist movement does not just direct public attention to unsatisfied social-welfare or liberal demands for equal treatment; it focuses above all on the *ambivalent consequences* of more or less *successfully implemented* programs. Welfare-state paternalism has in many cases assumed a literal meaning. This has occurred, for example, to the extent that legal provisions for pregnancy and maternity have only increased the risk of women losing their jobs; to the extent that protective labor laws have generally reinforced segregation in the labor market or the overrepresentation of women in lower wage brackets; to the extent that a liberalized divorce law has confronted women with the burdening effects of divorce; or to the extent that neglected interdependencies between regulations of welfare, labor, and family law have led to the further accumulation of gender-specific disadvantages through negative-feedback loops. To the extent that such things have occurred, a materialization of law directed at the real discrimination against women has had the opposite effect.

The statistical findings on the "feminization of poverty" have been alarming, and not simply in the United States.[57] Today trends familiar in Western societies are repeating themselves in an accelerated and acute form in the new states of the Federal Republic. In these areas, women are, once again, far more severely affected than men by "modernization losses."

From a juristic point of view, one reason for this reflexively generated discrimination lies in the *overgeneralized classifications* used to label disadvantaging situations and disadvantaged groups of persons. What is meant to promote the equal status of women in general often benefits only one category of (already privileged) women at the cost of another category, because gender-specific inequalities are correlated in a complex and obscure manner with membership in other underprivileged groups (social class, age, ethnicity, sexual orientation, etc.). However, an important role is played by the fact that legislation and adjudication arrive at "false" classifications, not because they are altogether blind to contexts, but because their perception of context is guided by an *outmoded paradigmatic understanding of law.* This is the more or less unarticulated issue common to the various currents of radical feminism since the seventies. The feminist movement objects to the premise underlying both the social-welfare and the liberal politics of equality, namely, the assumption that the equal entitlement of the sexes can be achieved within the existing institutional framework and within a culture dominated and defined by men.

Each special regulation intended to compensate for the disadvantages of women in the labor market or the workplace, in marriage or after divorce, in regard to social security, health care, sexual harassment, pornography, and so forth, rests on an interpretation of differences in gender-specific living situations and experiences. To the extent that legislation and adjudication in these cases are oriented by traditional interpretive patterns, regulatory law consolidates the existing *stereotypes of gender identity.* In producing such "normalizing effects," legislation and adjudication themselves become part of the problem they are meant to solve:

At the most basic level, traditional approaches have failed to generate coherent or convincing *definitions of difference.* All too often, modern equal-protection law has treated as inherent and essential differences that are cultural and contingent. Sex-related characteristics have been both over- and undervalued. In some cases, such as those involving occupational restrictions, courts have allowed biology to dictate destiny. In other contexts, such as pregnancy discrimination, they have ignored woman's special reproductive needs. The focus on whether challenged classifications track some existing differences between the sexes has obscured the disadvantages that follow from such differences. . . . We must insist not just on equal treatment but on woman's treatment as equal. Such a strategy will require substantial changes in our legal paradigms.[58]

An extreme example is the discussion surrounding the question whether, and in what capacity, women should serve in the military. The dispute primarily concerns the symbolic implications of exclusion—for instance, the question whether women can command the same respect as citizens that men do, if women are exempt from an obligation that is central to citizenship. The problematic use of gender stereotypes to determine relevant differences is a more tangible matter in civilian occupations. As long as the "normal work relation" of the fully employed male serves as the standard for "deviations" that need to be offset, women are forced by compensatory regulations to adapt to institutions that *structurally* disadvantage them: "A more satisfactory theoretical framework for employment litigation would take neither gender nor jobs as fixed. The question should not be simply whether women are, or are not, 'like men' with respect to a given occupation. Of greater significance is whether that occupation can be redefined to accommodate biological differences and whether gender as a social construct can be redefined to make those differences less occupationally relevant."[59] The pressure toward assimilation that is exerted on women by both the social-welfare and the liberal politics of equality—a pressure felt precisely where these programs succeed—ultimately stems from the fact that gender differences are not conceived as relationships involving two *equally* problematic variables and *in need of interpretation*. Differences are instead seen as deviations from supposedly unproblematic male standards. Of course, the two legal paradigms, which concur in their premises, lead to different consequences. Whereas the social-welfare paradigm makes special legal allowances for divergences and freezes them as such, the liberal market model tends to ignore and trivialize actual inequalities.[60]

Today the discussion revolves around the appropriate definition of gender-dependent differences. Even if only a thin line separates "relational feminism" from the praise of "women's nature," the thematic shift from assimilation to difference does not *automatically* imply a return to traditionalist role definitions: "From their perspective, gender inequality stemmed less from denial of opportunities available to men than from devaluation of functions and qualities associated with women."[61] Feminist critique misses its real target, however, if it locates the mistake in the "sameness/differ-ence approach" as such and hence in the dialectic of legal and factual equality driven by the imperative of equal treatment. This is true of approaches that, in rejecting the conventional paradig-matic understanding of rights, also throw out the idea of realizing rights *in any way*.[62] The theory of rights is not necessarily connected with an individualistic contraction of the concept of rights.[63] If one starts with an intersubjective concept of rights, the real source of error is easily identified: *public discussions must first clarify* the aspects under which differences between the experiences and living situ-ations of (specific groups of) women and men become relevant for an equal opportunity to take advantage of individual liberties. Institutionally defined gender stereotypes must not be assumed without question. Today these social constructions can be formed only in a conscious, deliberate fashion; they require *the affected parties themselves* to conduct public discourses in which they articu-late the standards of comparison and justify the relevant aspects. Appealing to the pragmatist tradition, Martha Minow holds on to the concept of rights and the publicly conducted dialectic of legal and factual equality: "Interpreting rights as features of relation-ships, contingent upon negotiation within a community commit-ted to this mode of solving problems, pins law not on some force beyond human control but on human responsibility for the pat-terns of relationships promoted or hindered by this process. In this way the notion of rights as tools in continuing communal discourse helps to locate responsibility in human beings for legal action and inaction."[64]

Gender identity and gender relations are social constructions that crystallize around biological differences yet vary historically. In women's struggle for equality, as well as in the transformation of the paradigmatic understanding of the corresponding legal pro-grams, one can observe that the rights meant to guarantee the autonomous pursuit of a personal life project for women cannot be adequately formulated at all unless the relevant aspects for defin-ing equal and unequal treatment are convincingly articulated and justified beforehand. The classification of gender roles and gen-der-related differences touches elementary layers of a society's cultural self-understanding. Radical feminism has emphasized the fallible, essentially contestable character of this self-understanding. Therefore, competing views about the identity of the sexes and their relation to each other must be open to public discussion. Even the feminist avant-garde does not have a monopoly on definition. Like intellectuals in general, spokeswomen can be sure they do not prejudge anything and that they treat no one as an inferior only when all those affected have an effective opportunity to voice their demands for rights on the basis of concrete experiences of violated integrity, discrimination, and oppression. The concrete relations of recognition mirrored in the mutual attribution of rights always emerge from a "struggle for recognition"; this struggle is motivated by the suffering incurred by, and the indignation against, concrete cases of disrespect.[65] As Axel Honneth has shown, experiences of insults to human dignity are what must be articulated in order to attest to those aspects under which equals should be treated equally and unequals treated unequally in the given context. This contest over the interpretation of needs cannot be delegated to judges and officials, nor even to political legislators.

The important consequence of this for our purposes is the following: no regulation, however sensitive to context, can *adequately* concretize the equal right to an autonomous private life unless it simultaneously strengthens the position of women in the political public sphere and thereby augments participation in forms of political communication that provide the sole arenas in which citizens can clarify the relevant aspects that define equal status. The insight into this connection between private and public autonomy underlies the reservations that contemporary feminism has with regard to an instrumental model of politics oriented exclusively to results; it explains the importance that feminism places on "identity politics," that is, on the consciousness-raising effected in the political process itself. According to this proceduralist understanding, the realization of basic rights is a process *that secures the private autonomy of equally entitled citizens only in step with the activation of their political autonomy.* This legal paradigm is incompatible with projections of a universally binding "identity of the sexes in a just society," whether this be androgynous or, under the banner of femininity or motherhood, stamped by a gender dualism understood in essentialist terms. On the other hand, the proceduralist understanding of law opens a perspective for the determinate negation of injustices that can be identified here and now:

Although we cannot know a priori what the good society will be, we know more than enough about what it will not be to provide a current agenda. It will not be a society with wide gender disparities in status, power and economic security. Nor will it be a society that limits women's reproductive freedom, tolerates substantial poverty, violence, and racial injustice, or structures its workplace without regard to family needs. Finally, and most fundamentally, it will not be a society that denies many of its members substantial power over the terms of their daily existence. To realize its full potential, feminism must sustain a vision concerned not only with relations between men and women but also with relations among them. The commitment to sexual equality that gave birth to the women's movement is necessary but not sufficient to express the values underlying that movement.[66]

9.3 Crisis Theories and the Proceduralist Understanding of Law

Up to this point I have discussed the procedural paradigm of law in regard to the realization of rights. However, the new legal understanding also, indeed primarily, pertains to the problem of how constitutional democracy can be consolidated in complex societies. As we have seen, the transition to the social-welfare model was justified by the fact that rights can be violated not only by the administration's unlawful intrusions but also by its withholding of services necessary for the actual exercise of rights. The structural transformation of society reawakened an awareness of the implicit content of the universal right to equal liberties. This did not bring new normative viewpoints into play:

The assumption characterizing the [liberal] paradigm of formal law, that only an individualistic justice would guarantee social solidarity, that only the freedom of contract would ensure an effective and just protection of good faith, proved untenable. Hence the fact that positive duties to provide certain benefits increasingly appeared beside negative rights against intrusion did not imply any fundamental transformation in the idea of a law grounded in the principle of reciprocity.[67]

What did change, though, was the peculiarly ambivalent effect of the new kind of social entitlements. Such rights unambiguously reinforce private autonomy only insofar as the entitled persons do not simply come to enjoy benefits that are dispensed paternalistically but are themselves involved in the interpretation of the standards by which legal equality can be established in the face of actual inequalities. This condition is fulfilled at an abstract level by the democratic legitimation of the legislature and the constitutional separation of powers. But concrete examples, say, from the domain of the feminist politics of equality, make one suspicious of such a straightforward answer. With the growth and qualitative transformation of governmental tasks, the need for legitimation changes; the more the law is enlisted as a means of political steering and social planning, the greater is the burden of legitimation that must be borne by the *democratic genesis* of law.

To be sure, concrete particularities and goal orientations have always migrated into law by way of legislators' political programs. Even bourgeois formal law had to be open for collective goals, such as those found in policies having to do with the military and taxation. In such cases, however, the pursuit of collective goals had to be subordinate to the main function of law (i.e., the norming of behavioral expectations) in a way that made it possible to interpret politics in general as a realization of rights. Because law has a structure of its own and is not arbitrarily malleable, this requirement held even for the collectively binding decisions of an active state that employed the law to influence social processes. The constitutive conditions of law and political power would be violated if policy formation were to make use of the form of law for *whatever purpose it pleased*, thereby destroying the internal function of law. Even in the welfare state, law must not be completely reduced to politics if the internal tension between facticity and validity, and hence the normativity of law, is not to be extinguished: "Law becomes an instrument of politics, yet at the same time [the very medium of law] stipulates the procedural conditions under which politics may have law at its disposition."[68] The constraints imposed on politics by the form of law are structural and not, as neoliberalism fears, quantitative. The *sheer quantity* of politics ends up overburdening the legal medium only if the political process violates the procedural conditions of legitimate lawmaking that are spelled out by constitutional principles; ultimately, this is to violate the democratic procedure for a politically autonomous elaboration of the system of rights. Policies that are adopted in a manner that does not conform to the conditions for the democratic genesis of law are merely cloaked in juridical form. When this occurs, one also loses the criteria by which these policies can be normatively assessed. In the execution of such programs, standards of effectiveness that govern the deployment of administrative power *take the place* of standards for the legitimacy of legal regulation. In fact, this danger seems to grow as the state is expected to take on an increasing number of tasks. Then the law, having been *instrumentalized* for political goals and deprived of its internal structure, degenerates in the eyes of an independent administrative system into one more means for solving problems of functional integration—and only for solving such problems.[69] On this premise, "the categorial difference between the two standards [is] not developed but reinterpreted in an empiricist fashion. *Legitimate* political opinion- and will-formation, as well as *efficient* implementation, [are] modeled as two equivalent conditions of possibility for successfully changing social structures through political planning."[70]

In fact, however, legitimation problems cannot be reduced to the inefficiency of administrative steering. Legitimation deficits result from disturbances in the democratic genesis of law, regardless of how such problems might be bound up with the effects of unsolved steering problems. To regard legitimation problems simply as a dependent variable in steering problems is falsely to assume that law, as mobilized by the active state, is handed over to opportunistic efforts to reconcile competing values in an arbitrary way. This picture is an artifact of a false paradigmatic understanding of law. Insofar as it has descriptive content, it simply results from a confusion that can be cleared up with the proceduralist understanding of law: wherever normative standards become contingent, regulatory law has been uprooted from the soil of legitimate lawmaking. For such standards can develop only in those public forums where individuals have the chance to recount their lived experiences of repression and disrespect—and to argue for criteria in the light of which like cases can be treated alike and different cases differently. To the extent that institutionalized deliberation and decision making loses contact with an uncoerced process of need articulation, it lacks parameters that it cannot generate of its own accord. Then the dialectic of legal and factual equality coalesces into a second nature; it is at the mercy of the shifting values that issue contingently from the adaptation processes of a largely self-programming administration. Government agencies that instrumentalize the law to achieve collective goals become, in concert with their most powerful clients, an independent administration of collective goods that does not monitor the selection of the goals themselves against the project of realizing non-instrumentalizable rights.

Such trends toward the independence of illegitimate power are unmistakable today. But it is problematic to describe these trends in a way that not only registers how the constitutional state is undermined but presents this as the *unavoidable* result of structural changes in state and society. In this third section, I first recall some familiar views of the crisis of the constitutional state and delve into the functionalist background understanding that gives these crisis diagnoses their fatalistic tenor (sec. 9.3.1). Taking the perspective provided by the proceduralist paradigm, I then attempt to explain the diagnosed "decline in the constitution's binding force" (sec. 9.3.2). I close with some brief remarks on the meaning of the "project" of a self-organizing legal community (sec. 9.3.3).

9.3.1

The central issues in the contemporary critique of law are the diminishing binding force of parliamentary statutes and the threat to the principle of separated powers in a state burdened with a growing set of tasks that are qualitatively new. As long as the classical administration could concentrate on the tasks of ordering an economic society left to economic self-regulation, in principle the need for intervention arose only if this order was disturbed— an order permanently established by constitutional law and guaranteed by the constitutional state.[71] The general and abstract statute, which precisely delineated typical "fact situations" and offenses in specific legal terms and linked them with unequivocally defined legal consequences, was tailored for these cases that required intervention. For the liberal meaning of the legal order

was to protect the legal freedom of the citizen against encroachments of a state apparatus restricted to preserving the public order.
But as soon as the administration was enlisted by the social-welfare
legislature for tasks of planning and political regulation, the statute
in its classical form could no longer adequately program administrative practice. Supplementary to the classical administration
(*Eingriffsverwaltung*), whose activity was characterized as reactive,
bipolar, and selective,[72] there arose administrations whose practice
was entirely different. The "service" administration (*Leistungsver-
waltung*) of the regulatory state, which assumes tasks of providing
basic services and infrastructure, planning, and risk prevention—
hence the tasks of political planning and regulation in the widest
sense—acts in a future-oriented and expansive manner; moreover,
its interventions affect the relationships among citizens and social
groups at an ever more concrete level. Modern administrative
practice displays "such a high degree of complexity, situational
dependency, and uncertainty that it cannot be completely anticipated in the imagination [of the legislature] nor, consequently,
conclusively determined at a normative level. Here the classical
type of legal norm breaks down to a large extent. For this norm is
a conditional program that defines offenses by listing those conditions under which the state is entitled to intervene; in the legal
consequences it stipulates the measures the state may employ."[73]
The spectrum of legal forms has expanded to include special
legislation, experimental temporary laws, and broad regulatory
directives involving uncertain prognoses; the influx of blanket
clauses, general clauses, and indefinite statutory language into the
vocabulary of the legislator has sparked the discussion over the
"indeterminacy of law" that worries American as much as German
jurisprudence.[74]

Here I am interested in how the materialization of law has
affected the functional separation of powers.[75] I have already
discussed in some detail the criticism of the judicial development
of law, which, having expanded into an implicit legislation, endangers the rationality of adjudication as well as the basis of judicial
legitimacy.[76] Still more disturbing is the lack of constitutional
controls on administrative activity. The formerly authoritarian
relation between the administration and its clients was long ago

replaced, even in Germany, by a juridified relation monitored by the courts and binding on both sides. In addition, the area covered by judicial review of the administration has been broadened by expanding the requirement of statutory authorization (*Gesetzes-vorbehalt*).[77] But this does not sufficiently compensate for weaknesses in the binding force of regulatory law, because in fulfilling its regulatory tasks the administration often does not even need to intervene in the technical legal sense:

> Where there is no intervention, no statutory authorization is required; where no statutory authorization is required, there are no statutory controls; and where there are no statutory controls on the administration, there is no review of legality by the courts. But the deficit even extends into the domain of intervention itself. Requiring statutory authorization no longer has the effect of protecting basic rights when it is the legislature itself that changes social relations and structures affecting large social groups whose basic rights collide.[78]

In such domains the administration programs itself in a self-referential fashion, guided by such maxims as the proportionality principle or reasonableness and hardship clauses. These clauses, which are familiar from adjudication, indicate that the administration is no longer allowed to deal with statutory guidelines in the normatively neutral way that was once required.

These problems are aggravated by the expansion of the temporal horizon in which the state's social policies, and especially its preventive activity, must unfold. Whether actively or by omission, the state is increasingly involved in the production of new risks connected with science and technology. Risks such as those arising from nuclear technology or genetic engineering pose the problem of taking precautions for the sake of future generations. This problem requires—naturally on the part of the legislature, too—an enlarged perspective in which interests are perceived through the eyes of the other. In general, the dangers of the "risk society"[79] make such high demands on the analytic and prognostic abilities of experts, as well as on their readiness to act and the reaction time of the precautionary administration, that the problems of statutory control and legal certainty afflicting the regulatory state are dramatically exacerbated. On the one hand, such complex activities have a dynamic character insofar as they reach far into the future, are dependent on prognoses, and require self-correction; the preventive norms of the legislature can only partially regulate these activities and link them to the democratic process. On the other hand, the imperative legal instruments for classical prevention, geared more to material risks than to potential threats to large groups of people, are failing. In view of the discretionary latitude that the increasingly prevention-oriented administration must surmount by referring to contested technical considerations, even a dynamic reading of basic rights and the protection they afford does not guarantee sufficient legal protection: "merely granting procedural standing in place of clear substantive entitlements does not by any means improve the situation of those affected."[80] In this context, Denninger observes that "the accent has shifted from a system based on a *certainty of law* [*Rechtssicherheit*] to one based on a *security of legal values* [*Rechtsgütersicherheit*]" that "modifies and dissolves" individual legal protection.[81] In addition, the welfare-state dialectic of empowerment and tutelage is accelerated insofar as constitutional control of the state's duty to protect has the effect of building up and arming the constitutional state to the point where it becomes the "security state" (*Sicherheitsstaat*)[82]: "This is especially true of the transformation of the boundary conditions of constitutional freedom that occurs when a society produces so many security risks that it is able to protect threatened constitutional values only by considerably expanding the surveillance apparatus."[83]

The independence of administrative power vis-à-vis a marginalized legislature, however, is not the only effect of the growth in regulatory tasks. This growth involves the state in bargaining with social subsystems, large organizations, associations, and such, which, to a considerable extent, resist legal imperatives (effected through sanctions, fees, or financial incentives). Such systems and organizations are open only to persuasive means: "There is no duty to obey that corresponds to indirect measures for redirecting behavior. . . . Policies thus become the topic of negotiations in which the private addressees can have their willingness to comply honored by the state. . . . State and society meet at the same level."[84] State sovereignty is undermined to the extent that powerful corporations are involved in the exercise of political authority without being legitimated for this and without submitting to the usual responsibilities incumbent on government authorities. As already mentioned, social actors equipped with paraconstitutional bargaining power are increasingly difficult to contain within the constitutional framework. Even the political parties, which, according to the German Basic Law, Article 21, are entitled to "participate in forming the political will of the people," have now become an independent power cartel integrating all branches of government—a cartel that is not provided for in the Constitution, and for good reason. Once acting as catalysts in the conversion of public opinion into communicative power, parties have taken possession of the core areas of the political system without fitting into the functional separation of powers. They exercise paragovernmental integrative functions, indeed in three ways: (a) through their powers to recruit personnel, powers that extend to the administration, judiciary, mass media, and other social sectors; (b) by shifting political decisions from committees with formal responsibility to the back rooms of informal agreements and interparty arrangements; and (c) by instrumentalizing the public sphere to gain access to administrative positions.

How one formulates and assesses this or that crisis diagnosis is open to dispute. But these diagnoses point to crisis tendencies in the constitutional state, to which the proper response is neither appeasement[85] nor a return to the liberal understanding of government by law. But the conclusion that the complexity of new governmental tasks inevitably overburdens the legal medium as such is not compelling. The socially integrating force of law would be structurally overburdened only if the crisis of the constitutional state were to prove *hopelessly insoluble.* I suspect that the suggestion of an aporia is an artifact; it results from an understanding of law that is biased toward functionalism and fixated on administrative processes.

This latter interpretation is based on a certain periodization of the growing complexity of governmental tasks. According to this scheme, the state had to specialize initially in the classical task of preserving order, later in the just distribution of social compensations, and finally in the management of collective risks. The tasks of taming absolutist state power, overcoming the poverty generated by capitalism, and taking precautions against the risks created by science and technology provide the epochal themes and goals: legal certainty, social welfare, and prevention. The ideal-typical forms of government—the constitutional state (*Rechtsstaat*), the social-welfare state (*Sozialstaat*), and the security state (*Sicherheits-staat*)—are supposed to be tailored for these goals. The German names for these ideal types already suggest that only the historical formation represented by the *Rechtsstaat* maintained a close relationship with law as such. The legally constrained administration of the liberal state does its business by means of law, whereas the regulatory activity of the welfare state and the indirect steering of the preventive state must rely increasingly on other resources: on money and economically valuable infrastructural activity, as well as on information and technical expertise. Only the classical administration of the liberal period can adequately solve its tasks with the normative instruments of law; the administrations of the welfare and security states rely on expanded monetary resources and a new knowledge base—and must, in adapting to a cognitive basis for action, distance themselves from the normative instruments of law.

This analytical perspective might be fruitful if one is interested in the functional conditions for effective administration. But the results of a functionalist analysis must not be precipitously translated into legal paradigms. The trend toward technical matter-of-factness that is perceived from this point of view simply means that the pressing problems are less and less of a legal nature; it does not mean that the corresponding administrative practice will increasingly escape legal regulation. The growth of complexity does not automatically imply a shift from the normative to the cognitive. This is merely suggested by the way the problems that are prominent in each period are designated. According to this designation, only the liberal state can solve its problem—namely, to establish legal certainty—by means of the legal medium. The conditions for effective governmental action *coincide* with the essential conditions of legitimacy (secured through formal law) only in view of a contingent complementarity between a legally restricted administration and liberal economic society. In the subsequent periods, it becomes clear that the conditions for effectiveness by no means have to coincide with conditions of legitimacy. This disjunction creates conflicting goals for administrations that are bound by constitutional principles and at the same time engaged in programming and regulation. But these conflicts do not *automatically* give rise to the irrelevance of law; nor do they subvert constitutional norms. Rather, a different analytical perspective recommends itself for answering the question of how legal freedom and equality can be guaranteed in a different way. If one starts by asking how the system of rights can be realized in view of the growing complexity of administration, the sociological periodization of administrative types turns out to be too crude. From the vantage point of legal doctrine, new risks to legal certainty do not pose any *new* problems but at most exacerbate the old ones—problems already familiar from the development of the welfare state, that is, those posed by the diminishing binding power of regulatory law. Preventive norms create a *new* problem only in regard to a long-overdue extension of individual to collective legal protection.

For our purposes, it is more important that independent administrative power cannot be detached from constitutional norms *without consequences*. That is, a self-programming administration has to give up the neutrality in dealing with normative reasons that was intended by the classical separation of powers. In this respect, a trend toward matter-of-factness is precisely what we do not observe. To the extent that the administration assumes tasks of political legislation and autonomously develops its own programs in the process of implementation, it must decide on its own how to justify and apply norms. These normative questions, however, cannot be decided from the standpoint of effectiveness, but demand that normative reasons be dealt with rationally. An administration operating in the cognitive style lacks the communicative presuppositions and procedures for doing this. The technocratic denial and empiricist redefinition of normative questions in no way leads to a matter-of-fact treatment of administrative problems. Rather, it results in opportunistic or unreflective ways of reconciling value complexes without the guidance of reasonable criteria. The symptoms of an erosion of the constitutional state no doubt signal crisis tendencies. But what these tendencies reveal is not so much that constitutional principles place aporetic demands on an increasingly complex governmental activity, as that such principles are *insufficiently institutionalized.*

9.3.2

Legal paradigms make it possible to diagnose situations so as to guide action. They illuminate the horizon of a given society in view of the project of realizing the system of rights. To this extent, they primarily have a world-disclosive function. Paradigms open up interpretive perspectives from which the principles of the constitutional state (in a specific interpretation) can be related to the social context as a whole. They throw light on the restrictions and possibilities for realizing basic rights, which, as unsaturated principles, require further interpretation and elaboration. Hence the proceduralist paradigm, like all others, also contains both normative and descriptive components.

On the one hand, the *discourse theory of law* conceives constitutional democracy as institutionalizing—by way of legitimate law (and hence by also guaranteeing private autonomy)—the procedures and communicative presuppositions for a discursive opinion- and will-formation that in turn makes possible (the exercise of political autonomy and) legitimate lawmaking. The *communication theory of society*, on the other hand, conceives the constitutionally organized political system as one among several subsystems. This system can serve as backup surety for problems of overall social integration. It does so through an interplay of institutionalized opinion- and will-formation with informal processes of public communication. The political system can succeed at this insofar as it is embedded, through a public sphere based in civil society, in a lifeworld context shaped by a liberal political culture and corresponding socialization patterns. Finally, a specific *conception of law* establishes the relationship between the normative and the empirical analyses. According to this conception, legal communication can be conceived as a medium through which the structures of recognition built into communicative action are transferred from the level of simple interactions to the abstract level of organized relationships. The web of legal communication is even capable of embracing complex societies as a whole. The proceduralist legal paradigm, I should add, results from a contest of paradigms. It presupposes that the welfare and liberal models of law construe the realization of rights *in overly concrete terms* and *conceal* the internal relation between private and public autonomy, a relation that must be interpreted from case to case. Under these premises the above-mentioned crisis tendencies appear in a different light, and the changed assessment yields different practical recommendations.

The central problem is considered to be an instrumentalization of law for purposes of political regulation, which overtaxes the structure of the legal medium and dissolves the bonds linking politics to the realization of non-instrumentalizable rights. From a proceduralist viewpoint, however, this problem can no longer be reduced to the replacement of one type of law by another. The spread of regulatory law only presents the *occasion* for the dissolution of a specific historical form of the constitutional separation of powers. Today the political legislator must choose from among formal, material, and procedural law, according to the matter that requires regulation. This makes it necessary to institutionalize the principle of separated powers in a different way. Choosing among alternative legal forms reflexively does not permit one to privilege just one of these forms. We can no longer focus on the abstract, general statute as though it were the sole support for the institutional separation of the legislative, adjudicative, and executive branches of government. Even during the so-called liberal period, the *institutional* separation of powers by no means fully coincided with the *functional* separation. To be sure, the differences emerged more clearly as the welfare state developed. In speaking of "legislature," "judiciary," and "administration" in overly concrete terms, one disguises the logic of a functional separation of powers, which, at a different level of abstraction, governs the availability of various sorts of reasons and how these are dealt with. This logic requires the institutionalization of various discourses and corresponding forms of communication that, *regardless in which local context*, open up possibilities of access to the corresponding sorts of reasons. A reflexive approach to urgent problems, to the choice of the appropriate type of law, and to the requisite reasons has consequences both for the democratic genesis of legal programs and for their further treatment. What is puzzling in the present situation is the broad diffusion of actual access to normative reasons that, in the classical scheme of separated powers, were reserved to the parliamentary lawgiver and the judiciary. I can offer only a few brief remarks on this here.

(a) Dealing with the law reflexively requires that *parliamentary legislators* first make metalevel decisions: whether they should decide at all; who could decide in their place; and, assuming they do want to decide, what the consequences will be for the further legitimate processing of their broad legal programs. In simple cases, the uncontrolled shift of legislative powers to courts and administrations is encouraged by the indecisiveness of a legislature that does not fully exercise its authority and refuses to regulate the matters that call for legal statutes. Other cases pose the considerably more difficult question of whether the parliamentary legislature can, by decentralizing legislative powers, relieve itself of decisions that it could not make with sufficient specificity by itself. But if it does employ regulatory law—generally, these are the problematic cases—it must take precautions that legitimately compensate for the weak binding force of such law in the judiciary and administration.

Whereas the legislature interprets and elaborates—and creates—rights as it pursues its policies, the *judiciary* strives to reach coherent decisions in the particular case. In adjudicating cases, it may mobilize only the reasons that have already been given to it by "statute and law" (*Gesetz und Recht*). As we have seen, this holds even for the constructive interpretations of a constitutional court that would see its role in more restrictive terms according to a proceduralist understanding of judicial review. On this view, the ˅ procedural conditions of the democratic process are what primarily deserve protection. These conditions acquire an importance that throws a different light on many hard cases in which different norms collide. In the proceduralist paradigm, the vacancies left by the private-market participant and the client of welfare bureaucracies are filled by enfranchised citizens who participate in political discourses in order to address violated interests and, by articulating new needs, to collaborate in shaping standards for treating like cases alike and different cases differently. To the extent that legal programs are in need of further specification by the courts— because decisions in the gray area between legislation and adjudication tend to devolve on the judiciary, all provisos notwithstanding—juristic discourses of application must be visibly supplemented by elements taken from discourses of justification.

Naturally, these elements of a quasi-legislative opinion- and will-formation require another kind of legitimation than does adjudication proper. The additional burden of legitimation could be partly satisfied by additional obligations for courts to justify opinions before an enlarged critical forum specific to the judiciary. This requires the institutionalization of a legal public sphere that goes beyond the existing culture of experts and is sufficiently sensitive to make important court decisions the focus of public controversies.

(b) The weak binding power of regulatory law, however, demands compensations primarily in the area of *administration*, where officials can no longer restrict their activity to a normatively neutral, technically competent implementation of statutes within the framework of normatively unambiguous responsibilities. According to the expertocratic model, the administration had to make only pragmatic decisions. Naturally, it never obeyed this ideal. In the modern service administration, however, problems accumulate that require the weighing of collective goods, the choice between competing goals, and the normative evaluation of individual cases. These can be treated rationally only in discourses of justification and application that cannot be contained within the professional confines of a normatively neutral task fulfillment. Consequently, procedural law must be enlisted to build a *legitimation filter* into the decisional processes of an administration still oriented as much as ever toward efficiency. To this extent, my image of the democratically "besieged" fortress of the state apparatus was misleading.[86] Insofar as the administration cannot refrain from appealing to normative reasons when it implements open legal programs, it should be able to carry out these steps of administrative lawmaking in forms of communication and according to procedures that satisfy the conditions of constitutional legitimacy. This implies a "democratization" of the administration that, going beyond special obligations to provide information, would supplement parliamentary and judicial controls on administration from within. But whether the participation of clients, the use of ombudspersons, quasi-judicial procedures, hearings, and the like, are appropriate for such a democratization, or whether other arrangements must be found for a domain so prone to interference and dependent on efficiency, is, as always with such innovations, a question of the interplay of institutional imagination and cautious experimentation. Of course, participatory administrative practices must not be considered simply as surrogates for legal protection but as procedures that are *ex ante* effective in legitimating decisions that, from a normative point of view, substitute for acts of legislation or adjudication.

Naturally, this does not make reactive controls on the administration superfluous. Such provisos as an expanded requirement of statutory authorization, more dynamic constitutional protections, and collective forms of legal protection are intended to prevent *individual legal protection* from being undermined, something we discussed in connection with the tasks of preventive government. Legal remedies remain ineffective as long as those affected are not willing or able to exercise their rights. The proceduralist paradigm directs the legislature's attention to the *conditions for mobilizing* law. With a high level of social differentiation and a corresponding fragmentation of the knowledge and consciousness of potentially endangered groups, precautions are required that "also enable the individual to develop interests, perceive these in common with others, and bring them to bear in the governmental decisionmaking process."[87]

(c) These considerations do not yet touch on the *neocorporatist relation* the administration has to those organizations and subsystems whose social power and complex internal structure render them largely inaccessible to legal imperatives and thus distinguish them from other clients. We have seen that the architectonic of the constitutional state suffers damage if in such bargaining processes the state is content to occupy the position of one participant among many. When faced with political decisions relevant to the whole of society, the state must be able to perceive, and if necessary assert, public interests as it has in the past. Even when it appears in the role of an intelligent adviser or supervisor who makes procedural law available, this kind of lawmaking must remain linked to legislative programs in a transparent, comprehensible, and controllable way. There is no patented recipe for this. Once again, in the final analysis, the only thing that serves as a "palladium of liberty" against the growth of independent, illegitimate power is a suspicious, mobile, alert, and informed public sphere that affects the parliamentary complex and secures the *sources from which legitimate law can arise.*

This brings us to the core of the proceduralist paradigm: according to Ingeborg Maus's formulation, "the universal combination and reciprocal mediation of legally institutionalized and noninstitutionalized popular sovereignty" is the key to the democratic genesis of law.[88] Here the social substratum for the realization of the system of rights consists neither in spontaneous market forces nor in the deliberate measures of the welfare state but in the currents of communication and public opinion that, emerging from civil society and the public sphere, are converted into communicative power through democratic procedures. The fostering of autonomous public spheres, an expanded citizen participation, curbs on the power of the media, and the mediating function of political parties that are not simply arms of the state are of central significance for this. The well-known proposals to insert plebiscitary elements into the constitution (direct popular vote, petitions for a referendum, etc.), as well as the proposals to introduce democratic procedures at a grassroots level (in the nomination of candidates, will-formation inside the party, etc.), are meant to counteract the subversion of the *political public sphere* by power. The attempts at a stronger constitutional regulation of the *power of the media* have the same intent. The mass media must be kept free from the pressure of political and other functional elites; they must be capable of raising and maintaining the discursive level of public opinion-formation without constraining the communicative freedom of critical audiences.[89] In the proceduralist paradigm, the public sphere is not conceived simply as the back room of the parliamentary complex, but as the impulse-generating periphery that *surrounds* the political center: in cultivating normative reasons, it affects all parts of the political system without intending to conquer it. Passing through the channels of general elections and various forms of participation, public opinions are converted into a communicative power that authorizes the legislature and legitimates regulatory agencies, while a publicly mobilized critique of judicial decisions imposes more-intense justificatory obligations on a judiciary engaged in further developing the law.

The criticism of the assimilation of *political parties* into the state apparatus is directed primarily against an established practice that reduces the competition of party platforms for voters' approval to an instrument for personnel recruitment and the distribution of public offices. This criticism objects to a conflation of two different functions that, for good reasons, parties exercise simultaneously. As catalysts of public opinion, they are called to collaborate in political will-formation and political education (with the goal of promoting the qualifications required for citizenship). At the same time, as recruiting machines they select personnel and dispatch leadership groups into the political system. To the extent that the parties have themselves become an integral part of this very system, the two functions are no longer kept separate. In the eyes of power holders inside the administrative system, parties do not exercise their privileges in collaboration with civil society but treat the public sphere as the system's environment, from which they extract mass loyalty. In contrast to this, the public of citizens should have the opportunity to recognize itself not in the person of a chancellor or president, that is, the chief administrator, but in democratic party leaders. The latter would have to distinguish themselves in the contest over the appropriate interpretation of needs and promotion of relevant issues, in the dispute over the correct description of problems and the best proposals for their solution. As long as democratic competition does not provide such leaders with a higher reputation than the bonus of office gives to holders of administrative power, politics has not yet laid aside its false appearance of sanctity. For in a constitutional democracy, as the dwelling of a self-organizing legal community, the symbolic location of discursively fluid sovereignty remains *empty*.[90]

9.3.3

Under the conditions of postmetaphysical thinking—for which no plausible alternatives exist, despite fundamentalist reactions against the losses incurred by modernization—the state has lost its sacred substance. This secularization of the spiritual bases of governmental authority, by now long under way, suffers from a deficit in implementation that is overdue. If this deficit is not met by more-extensive democratization, the constitutional state itself will be endangered. We could gather further evidence for this thesis if we were to go beyond our limited focus on national societies and, as an epoch of decolonization draws to a close, broaden our view to take in the international order of the world society. The legitimations enlisted by the allies for the Gulf War provide evidence of a progressive denationalization of international law.[91] This example reflects the trends toward the dissolution of the sovereignty of the nation-state. Against the horizon of an emerging global public sphere, such trends could signal the beginning of a new universalist world order.[92] In view of the pressing problems mentioned in the preface, this is naturally no more than a hope—indeed a hope born of desperation.

If one counters such reformist perspectives with the usual arguments referring to complexity, then one conflates legitimacy and efficiency. Moreover, one fails to realize that the institutions of government by law were always already set up not only to reduce complexity but also to maintain it through countersteering so as to stabilize the tension inherent in law between facticity and validity. At the same time, when I infer from the proceduralist legal paradigm certain consequences for understanding the "crisis of the constitutional state," I am certainly not offering anything original at the level of particular details. But this paradigm can provide a certain coherence to the reform efforts that are either under discussion or already under way.

If a utopia is equivalent to the ideal projection (*Entwurf*) of a concrete form of life, then the constitution taken as a project (*Projekt*) is neither a social utopia nor a substitute for such. This project is, in fact, just the "opposite from the utopia in which collective reason and secularized omnipotence are unified and institutionalized in the state: rather, it implies the idea of civil society and its capacity to regulate itself in discursive processes and through clever institutionalization."[93] Ulrich Preuss defines "constitution" as the establishment of a fallible learning process through which a society gradually overcomes its inability to engage in normative reflection on itself: "A society is constituted when it is confronted with itself in suitable institutional forms and normatively guided processes of adjustment, resistance, and self-correction."[94] The procedural paradigm is not distinguished from the two earlier paradigms by its being "formal" in the sense of "empty" or "poor in content." In pointing to civil society and the political public sphere, it forcefully singles out points of reference from which the democratic process acquires a different weight and a role previously neglected in the realization of the system of rights. In complex societies, the scarcest resources are neither the productivity of a market economy nor the regulatory capacity of the public administration. It is above all the resources of an exhausted economy of nature and of a disintegrating social solidarity that require a nurturing approach. The forces of social solidarity can be regenerated in complex societies only in the forms of communicative practices of self-determination.

The project of realizing the system of rights—a project specifically designed for the conditions of our society, and hence for a particular, historically emergent society—cannot be merely formal. Nevertheless, this paradigm of law, unlike the liberal and social-welfare models, no longer favors a particular ideal of society, a particular vision of the good life, or even a particular political option. It is "formal" in the sense that it merely states the necessary conditions under which legal subjects in their role of enfranchised citizens can reach an understanding with one another about what their problems are and how they are to be solved. The procedural paradigm is certainly connected with the self-referential expectation of shaping not only the self-understanding of elites who deal with law as experts but that of *all* participants. But this expectation does not aim at indoctrination and has nothing totalitarian about it—to anticipate an objection that, though far-fetched, is leveled against discourse theory again and again. For the new paradigm is up for discussion under its own conditions: to the extent that it would shape the horizon of a preunderstanding within which everyone could take part in the interpretation of the constitution, each sharing the labor in her own way, every perceived historical change in the social context would have to be conceived as a challenge to reexamine the legal paradigm itself. Certainly this understanding, like the rule of law itself, retains a dogmatic core: the idea of autonomy according to which human beings act as free subjects only insofar as they obey just those laws they give themselves in accordance with insights they have acquired intersubjectively. This is "dogmatic" only in a harmless sense. It expresses a tension between facticity and validity, a tension that is "given" with the fact of the symbolic infrastructure of sociocultural forms of life, which is to say that *for us*, who have developed our identity in such a form of life, it cannot be circumvented.

Postscript (1994)

There is a sense in which an author first learns what he has said in a text from the reactions of his readers. In the process, he also becomes aware of what he meant to say, and he gains an opportunity to express more clearly what he wanted to say. I find myself in this position hardly one year after the appearance of my book—and after reading an array of intelligent, mainly sympathetic, and in any case instructive reviews. Certainly the interpreter enjoys the advantage of understanding a text better than the author himself, but on the occasion of a new printing, the author may be permitted to take the role of an interpreter and attempt to recapitulate the core idea that informs the whole book as he sees it. This also allows him to clear up some of the objections that have been raised in the meantime.

1

Modern law is formed by a system of norms that are coercive, positive, and, so it is claimed, freedom-guaranteeing. The formal properties of coercion and positivity are associated with the claim to legitimacy: the fact that norms backed by the threat of state sanction stem from the changeable decisions of a political lawgiver is linked with the expectation that these norms guarantee the autonomy of all legal persons equally. This expectation of legitimacy is intertwined with the facticity of making and enforcing law. This connection is in turn mirrored in the ambivalent mode of legal validity. Modern law presents itself as Janus-faced to its addressees: it leaves it up to them which of two possible approaches they want to take to law. Either they can consider legal norms merely as commands, in the sense of factual constraints on their personal scope for action, and take a *strategic* approach to the calculable consequences of possible rule violations; or they can take a *performative* attitude in which they view norms as valid precepts and comply "out of respect for the law." A legal norm has validity whenever the state guarantees two things at once: on the one hand, the state ensures average compliance, compelled by sanctions if necessary; on the other hand, it guarantees the institutional preconditions for the legitimate genesis of the norm itself, so that it is always at least possible to comply out of respect for the law.

What grounds the legitimacy of rules that can be changed at any time by the political lawgiver? This question becomes especially acute in pluralistic societies in which comprehensive worldviews and collectively binding ethics have disintegrated, societies in which the surviving posttraditional morality of conscience no longer supplies a substitute for the natural law that was once grounded in religion or metaphysics. The democratic procedure for the production of law evidently forms the only postmetaphysical source of legitimacy. But what provides this procedure with its legitimating force? Discourse theory answers this question with a simple, and at first glance unlikely, answer: democratic procedure makes it possible for issues and contributions, information and reasons to float freely; it secures a discursive character for political will-formation; and it thereby grounds the fallibilist assumption that results issuing from proper procedure are more or less reasonable. Two considerations provide prima facie grounds in favor of a discourse-theoretic approach.

From the standpoint of *social theory*, law fulfills socially integrative functions; together with the constitutionally organized political system, law provides a safety net for failures to achieve social integration. It functions as a kind of "transmission belt" that picks up structures of mutual recognition that are familiar from face-to-face interactions and transmits these, in an abstract but binding form, to the anonymous, systemically mediated interactions among strangers. Solidarity—the third source of societal integration besides money and administrative power—arises from law only indirectly, of course: by stabilizing behavioral expectations, law simultaneously secures symmetrical relationships of reciprocal recognition between abstract bearers of individual rights. These structural similarities between law and communicative action explain why discourses, and thus reflexive forms of communicative action, play a constitutive role for the production (and application) of legal norms.

From the standpoint of *legal theory*, the modern legal order can draw its legitimacy only from the idea of self-determination: citizens should always be able to understand themselves also as authors of the law to which they are subject as addressees. Social-contract theories have construed the autonomy of citizens in the categories of bourgeois contract law, that is, as the private free choice of parties who conclude a contract. But the Hobbesian problem of founding a social order could not be satisfactorily resolved in terms of the fortuitous confluence of rational choices made by independent actors. This led Kant to equip the parties in the state of nature with genuinely moral capacities, as Rawls would later do with parties in the original position. Today, following the linguistic turn, discourse theory provides an interpretation of this deontological understanding of morality. Consequently, a discursive or deliberative model replaces the contract model: the legal community constitutes itself not by way of a social contract but on the basis of a discursively achieved agreement.

The break with the tradition of rational natural law is incomplete, however, as long as *moral* argumentation remains the exemplar for constitution-making discourse. Then, as we find in Kant, the autonomy of citizens coincides with the free will of moral persons, and morality or natural law continues to make up the core of positive law.[1] This model is still based on the natural-law image of a hierarchy of legal orders: positive law remains subordinate to, and is oriented by, the moral law. In fact, however, the relation between morality and law is much more complicated.

The argument developed in *Between Facts and Norms* essentially aims to demonstrate that there is a conceptual or internal relation, and not simply a historically contingent association, between the rule of law and democracy. As I have shown in chapter 9, this relation is also evident in the dialectic between legal and factual equality, a dialectic that first called forth the social-welfare paradigm in response to the liberal understanding of law and that today recommends a proceduralist self-understanding of constitutional democracy. The *democratic process* bears the entire burden of legitimation. It must simultaneously secure the private and public autonomy of legal subjects. This is because individual private rights cannot even be adequately formulated, let alone politically implemented, if those affected have not first engaged in public discussions to clarify which features are relevant in treating typical cases as alike or different, and then mobilized communicative power for the consideration of their newly interpreted needs. The proceduralist understanding of law thus privileges the communicative presuppositions and procedural conditions of democratic opinion- and will-formation as the sole source of legitimation. The proceduralist view is just as incompatible with the Platonistic idea that positive law can draw its legitimacy from a higher law as it is with the empiricist denial of any legitimacy beyond the contingency of legislative decisions. To demonstrate an internal relation between the rule of law and democracy, then, we must explain why positive law cannot simply be subordinated to morality (sec. 2); show how popular sovereignty and human rights presuppose each other (sec. 3); and make it clear that the principle of democracy has its own roots independent of the moral principle (sec. 4).

2

2.1

Certainly, morality and law both serve to regulate interpersonal conflicts, and both are supposed to protect the autonomy of all participants and affected persons equally. Interestingly enough, however, the positivity of law forces autonomy to *split up* in a way that has no parallel in morality. Moral self-determination is a unitary concept, according to which each person obeys just those norms that he considers binding according to his own impartial judgment. By contrast, the self-determination of citizens appears in the dual form of private and public autonomy. Legal autonomy does not coincide with freedom in the moral sense. It includes two further moments: the free choice of rationally deciding actors as well as the existential choice of ethically deciding persons.

In the first instance, individual rights have the character of *releasing* legal persons from moral precepts in a carefully circumscribed manner and granting agents the scope for legitimate free choice. With these rights, modern law as a whole upholds the principle that whatever is not explicitly prohibited is permitted. Whereas in morality an inherent symmetry exists between rights and duties, legal *duties* only result as consequences of the protection of *entitlements*, which are conceptually prior. However, private autonomy does not simply mean free choice within legally secure boundaries; it also forms a protective cover for the individual's ethical freedom to pursue his own existential life project or, in Rawls's words, his current conception of the good.[2] A moral dimension first appears in the autonomy that enfranchised citizens as co-legislators must exercise in common so that everyone can equally enjoy individual liberties. Unlike the moral autonomy that is *equivalent* to the capacity for rational self-binding, then, the autonomy of the legal person includes three different components: the jointly exercised autonomy of citizens, and the capacities for rational choice and for ethical self-realization.

The exercise of legal autonomy divides into the public use of communicative liberties and the private use of individual liberties. This differentiation is explained by the positivity of a law that stems from the collectively binding decisions of lawmaking (and law-applying) agencies. Hence conceptually it requires at least a provisional separation of roles between authors who make (and apply) valid law and addressees who are subject to law. However, if the autonomy of the legal person involves more than autonomy in the moral sense, then positive law cannot be conceived as a special case of morality.

2.2

Other reasons also preclude a hierarchical conception of natural and positive law. Moral and legal prescriptions each have different reference groups and regulate different matters. The *moral* universe, which is unlimited in social space and historical time, encompasses *all* natural persons in their life-historical complexity. To this extent, it refers to the moral protection of the integrity of fully individuated persons. By contrast, a spatiotemporally localized *legal community* protects the integrity of its members only insofar as they acquire the status of bearers of individual rights.

Morality and law also differ in their extensions. The matters that are in need of, and capable of, legal regulation are at once narrower and broader in scope than morally relevant concerns: they are narrower inasmuch as legal regulation has access only to external, that is, coercible, behavior; they are broader inasmuch as law, as a means for organizing political rule, provides collective goals or programs with a binding form and thus is not *exhausted* in the regulation of interpersonal conflicts. Policies and legal programs have a greater or lesser moral weight from case to case, for the matters in need of legal regulation certainly do not raise moral questions *only*, but also involve empirical, pragmatic, and ethical aspects, as well as issues concerned with the fair balance of interests open to compromise. Thus the opinion- and will-formation of the democratic legislature depends on a complicated network of discourses and bargaining—and not simply on moral discourses. Unlike the clearly focused normative validity claim of moral commands, the legitimacy claim of legal norms, like the legislative practice of justification itself, is supported by different types of reasons.[3]

In summary, we can say that law has a more complex structure than morality because it (1) simultaneously unleashes and normatively limits individual freedom of action (with its orientation toward each individual's own values and interests) and (2) incorporates collective goal setting, so that its regulations are too concrete to be justifiable by moral considerations alone. As an alternative to the natural-law subordination of law to morality, it makes sense to view actionable positive law as a functional complement to morality: it *relieves* the judging and acting person of the considerable cognitive, motivational, and—given the moral division of labor often required to fulfill positive duties—organizational demands of a morality centered on the individual's conscience. Law, as it were, compensates for the functional weaknesses of a morality that, from the observer perspective, frequently delivers cognitively indeterminate and motivationally unstable results. This *complementary* relation, however, by no means implies that law enjoys moral neutrality. Indeed, moral reasons enter into law by way of the legislative process. Even if moral considerations are not selective enough for the legitimation of legal programs, politics and law are still supposed to be compatible with morality—on a common postmetaphysical basis of justification.[4]

The doubling of law into natural and positive law suggests that historical legal orders are supposed to *copy* a pregiven suprasensible order. The discourse-theoretic concept of law steers between the twin pitfalls of legal positivism and natural law: if the legitimacy of positive law is conceived as procedural rationality and ultimately traced back to an appropriate communicative arrangement for the lawgiver's rational political will-formation (and for the application of law), then the inviolable moment of legal validity need not disappear in a blind *decisionism* nor be preserved from the vortex of temporality by a moral *containment*. The leading question of modern natural law can then be reformulated under new, discourse-theoretic premises: what rights must citizens mutually grant one another if they decide to constitute themselves as a voluntary association of legal consociates and legitimately to regulate their living together by means of positive law? The performative *meaning* of this constitution-making practice already contains *in nuce* the entire content of constitutional democracy. The system of rights and the principles of the constitutional state can be developed from what it means to carry out the practice that one has gotten into with the first act in the self-constitution of such a legal community.

If we have to undertake this reconstruction of law without the support of a higher or prior law enjoying moral dignity, then the foregoing considerations lead to two problems: section 3 raises the question of how we should conceive the equal guarantee of private and public autonomy if we situate liberty rights, conceived as human rights, in the same dimension of positive law as political rights; section 4 confronts us with the question of how we should understand the standard for the legitimacy of law, the discourse principle, if the *complementarity* of law and morality prohibits us from *identifying* it with the moral principle.

3

The internal relation between the rule of law and democracy can be explained at a conceptual level by the fact that the individual liberties of the subjects of private law and the public autonomy of enfranchised citizens make each other possible. In political philosophy, this relation is typically presented in such a way that the private autonomy of members of society is guaranteed by human rights (the classical rights to "life, liberty, and property") and an anonymous *rule of law*, whereas the political autonomy of enfranchised citizens is derived from the principle of popular sovereignty and takes shape in democratic *self-legislation*. In the tradition, however, the relation between these two elements is marked by an unresolved *competition*. The *liberalism* going back to Locke has, at least since the nineteenth century, invoked the danger of tyrannical majorities and postulated a priority of human rights in relation to popular sovereignty, whereas the *civic republicanism* reaching back to Aristotle has always granted priority to the political "liberty of the ancients" over the unpolitical "liberty of the moderns." Even Rousseau and Kant missed the intuition they wanted to articulate. Human rights, which for Kant are summarized in the "original" right to equal individual liberties, must neither be merely imposed on the sovereign legislator as an external constraint nor be instrumentalized as a functional requisite for the sovereign's legislative aims.

Human rights might be quite justifiable as *moral* rights, yet as soon as we conceive them as elements of *positive* law, it is obvious that they cannot be paternalistically imposed on a sovereign legislator. The addressees of law would not be able to understand themselves as its authors if the legislator were to discover human rights as pregiven moral facts that merely need to be enacted as positive law. At the same time, this legislator, regardless of his autonomy, should not be able to adopt anything that violates human rights. For solving this dilemma, it now turns out to be an advantage that we have characterized law as a unique kind of medium that is distinguished from morality by its formal properties.

A constitution-making practice requires more than just a discourse principle by which citizens can judge whether the law they enact is legitimate. Rather, the very forms of communication that are supposed to make it possible to form a rational political will through discourse need to be legally institutionalized themselves. In assuming a legal shape, the discourse principle is transformed into a principle of democracy. For this purpose, however, the legal code as such must be available, and establishing this code requires the creation of the status of possible legal persons, that is, of persons who belong to a voluntary association of bearers of actionable individual rights. Without this guarantee of private autonomy, something like positive law cannot exist at all. Consequently, without the classical rights of liberty that secure the private autonomy of legal persons, there is also no *medium* for legally institutionalizing those conditions under which citizens can first make use of their civic autonomy.

Subjects who want to legitimately regulate their living together by means of positive law are no longer free to choose the medium in which they can realize their autonomy. They participate in the production of law only as *legal subjects*; it is no longer in their power to decide which language they will use in this endeavor. Consequently, the desired internal relation between "human rights" and popular sovereignty consists in the fact that the requirement of legally institutionalizing self-legislation can be fulfilled only with the help of a code that *simultaneously* implies the guarantee of actionable individual liberties. By the same token, the equal distribution of these liberties (and their "fair value") can in turn be satisfied only by a democratic procedure that grounds the supposition that the outcomes of political opinion- and will-formation are reasonable. This shows how private and public autonomy reciprocally presuppose one another in such a way that neither one may claim primacy over the other.

The critique of liberalism entailed by this idea has roused defenders of the primacy of human rights. Otfried Höffe, for example, has objected to the demotion of *human* rights (whose universal validity he wants to ground anthropologically) to mere *basic legal* rights.[5] If one wants to speak of "law" only in the sense of positive law, then in fact one must distinguish between *human* rights as morally justified norms of action and human *rights* as positively valid constitutional norms. Such basic constitutional rights have a differ-

ent status—but not necessarily a different meaning—from moral
norms. As enacted actionable norms, constitutional rights are valid
within a particular legal community. But this status does not
contradict the universalistic meaning of the classical liberties that
include all persons as such and not only all members of a legal
community. Even as basic legal rights, they extend to all persons
insofar as the latter simply reside within the jurisdiction of the legal
order: to this extent, everyone enjoys the protection of the constitution. In the Federal Republic of Germany, for example, the legal
status of aliens, displaced foreigners, and stateless persons has at
least approached the status of citizens because of the human-rights
meaning of these basic rights; these groups enjoy the same legal
protection and have, according to the letter of the law, similar
duties and entitlements.[6]

The discrepancy between, on the one hand, the human-rights
content of classical liberties and, on the other, their form as positive
law, which initially limits them to a nation-state, is just what makes
one aware that the discursively grounded "system of rights" points
beyond the constitutional state in the singular toward the
globalization of rights. As Kant realized, basic rights require, by
virtue of their semantic content, an international, legally administered "cosmopolitan society." For actionable rights to issue from
the United Nations Declaration of Human Rights, it is not enough
simply to have international courts; such courts will first be able to
function adequately only when the age of individual sovereign
states has come to an end through a United Nations that *can not only
pass but also act on and enforce its resolutions.*[7]

In defending the primacy of human rights, liberals follow the
plausible intuition that legal persons ought to be protected from
the state's abuse of its monopoly on violence (*Gewalt*). Thus
Charles Larmore believes that at least *one* individual right—which
is morally grounded—has to precede and constrain democratic
will-formation: "No one should be forcibly compelled to submit to
norms whose validity cannot be made evident to reason."[8] On a
harmless reading, the argument holds that persons who want to
constitute themselves as a legal community have *eo ipso* accepted a
concept of positive law that includes the expectation of legitimacy.
In that case, the need for justification is one of the semantic
implications of this concept of law and thus is part of the practice

of constitution making as such. On a stronger reading, however, the argument expresses the special assumption that the impersonal rule of law is as fundamental as the violence of the Leviathan it is supposed to enchain.

However, this liberal motif, which is explained by obvious historical experiences, does not do justice to the constitutive connection between law and politics.[9] It conflates popular sovereignty with the monopoly on violence and misses the inherently technical, and in any case nonrepressive, meaning of an administrative power (*Macht*) appearing in the form of law—insofar as this power is exercised within the framework of democratic laws. Above all, it misses the constitutive meaning that an intersubjectively exercised civic autonomy has for every political community. To do justice to both democratic self-determination and the rule of law requires a two-stage reconstruction. First, one starts with the horizontal sociation of citizens who, recognizing *one another* as equals, mutually accord rights to one another. Only then does one advance to the constitutional taming of the power (*Gewalt*) presupposed with the medium of law. By proceeding in two steps, one sees that the liberal rights protecting the individual against the state apparatus, with its monopoly on violence, are by no means *originary* but rather emerge from a transformation of individual liberties that were at first *reciprocally* granted. The individual rights linked with the legal code as such acquire only secondarily the negative meaning of delimiting a private sphere that is supposed to be free from arbitrary administrative interference. Rights against the state arise only as a *consequence* of the process of differentiation in which a self-governing association of consociates under law becomes a legal community organized around a state. Such rights arise co-originally with the constitutional principle of legality of administration; hence in the conceptual construction of the system of rights, they do not have the fundamental position that Larmore gives them in order to ground the primacy of human rights.

4

Positive law can no longer derive its legitimacy from a higher-ranking moral law but only from a procedure of presumptively rational opinion- and will-formation. Using a discourse-theoretic approach, I have more closely analyzed this democratic procedure that lends legitimating force to lawmaking under conditions of social and ideological pluralism.[10] In doing so, I started with a principle that I cannot justify here, namely, that the only regulations and ways of acting that can claim legitimacy are those to which all who are possibly affected could assent as participants in rational discourses.[11] In the light of this "discourse principle," citizens test which rights they should mutually accord one another. *As* legal subjects, they must anchor this practice of self-legislation in the medium of law itself; they must legally institutionalize those communicative presuppositions and procedures of a political opinion- and will-formation in which the discourse principle is applied. Thus the establishment of the legal code, which is undertaken with the help of the universal right to equal individual liberties, must be *completed* through communicative and participatory rights that guarantee equal opportunities for the public use of communicative liberties. In this way, the discourse principle acquires the legal shape of a democratic principle.

Contrary to what Onora O'Neill seems to assume, here the counterfactual idea that a norm deserves universal assent is by no means absorbed and neutralized by the facticity that attends the legal institutionalization of public discourse.[12] Albrecht Wellmer rightly emphasizes that the

concept of the legitimacy of law also has a *counterfactual* application . . . . Admittedly, it lies within the logic of the modern concept of legitimacy that the common nature of any decision-making process must as far as possible be realized *in actual fact*—that is, insofar as all those affected are ultimately to be accorded an equal right to participate in the collective processes by which the common will is formed: this is the idea of democracy. But if legitimate laws are to be such that all those affected would have been capable of passing them collectively, and if all those affected are—in principle—to have an equal right to participate in the collective decision-making process, then it goes without saying that the settling of normative questions by means of public argument must play a central part in any attempt to realize the possibility of legitimate law . . . and to ensure that the law is acknowledged as legitimate. To argue in favor of a legal norm—or a system of legal norms—means in this case the attempt to provide reasons which convince all other affected persons why all people of good will and discernment should necessarily be able to deem it to be equally in the interests of all that this norm or these norms should prevail in society.[13]

To be sure, this tension between facticity and validity is already built into moral discourse, as it is in the practice of argumentation in general; in the medium of law, it is simply intensified and operationalized.

Wellmer, however, wants to reserve the idea of universal rational acceptability for explaining the legitimacy of *law* and not have it extend to the validity of *moral* norms. He believes it is a mistake for discourse ethics to carry over the connection between normative validity and real discourse, which is present in the special case of legal validity, to the validity of moral commands. In this context, we cannot concern ourselves with this objection itself,[14] but it does draw our attention to a demarcation problem that the discourse theory of law and morality in fact poses. If, unlike Wellmer, one does not bring in the discourse principle exclusively to explain the principle of democracy, but employs it more generally to explicate the meaning of the impartial assessment of normative questions of *every kind*, then one runs the risk of blurring the boundary between the postconventional justification of norms of action in general and the justification of moral norms in particular. In my view, the discourse principle must be situated at a level of abstraction that is still neutral vis-à-vis the distinction between morality and law. On the one hand, it is supposed to have a normative content sufficient for the impartial assessment of norms of action as such; on the other hand, it must not coincide with the moral principle, because it is only subsequently differentiated as the moral principle and the democratic principle. Therefore, it must be shown to what extent the discourse principle does not already exhaust the content of the discourse-ethical principle of universalization (U). Otherwise, the moral principle that was merely concealed in the discourse principle would once again, as in natural law, be the sole source of legitimation in law.

It is important to note that the two key concepts in the proposed formulation of the discourse principle (D) remain indeterminate: "Only those norms of action are valid to which all possibly affected persons could assent as participants in rational discourses." This formula does not specify the different "norms of action" (and corresponding normative statements) nor the different "rational discourses" (on which, incidentally, bargaining depends insofar as its procedures must be discursively justified). This provides enough latitude, however, for deriving the democratic and moral principles by appropriately specifying the discourse principle. Whereas the democratic principle is applied only to norms that display the formal properties of legal norms, the moral principle—according to which valid norms are in the equal interest of all persons[15]—signifies a restriction to the kind of discourse in which *only* moral reasons are decisive. The moral principle does not specify the type of norm, whereas the democratic principle does not specify the forms of argumentation (and bargaining). That explains two asymmetries. First, whereas moral discourses are specialized for a single type of reason, and moral norms are furnished with a corresponding mode of normative validity that is sharply focused, the legitimacy of legal norms is supported by a broad spectrum of reasons, including moral reasons. Second, whereas the moral principle, as a rule of argument, serves exclusively in the formation of *judgments*, the principle of democracy structures not only knowledge but, at the same time, the institutional *practice* of citizens.

Note that if one defines the relation between morality and law this way and no longer uses the common label of "rightness" to identify the legitimacy claim of legal norms with the claim to moral justice,[16] then one can leave open the further question of whether there are *moral* grounds for entering a legal order in the first place—the problem that rational natural law posed as the transition from the state of nature to civil society. The positive law that we find in modernity as the outcome of a societal learning process has formal properties that recommend it as a suitable instrument for stabilizing behavioral expectations; there does not seem to be any functional equivalent for this in complex societies. Philosophy makes *unnecessary* work for itself when it seeks to demonstrate that it is not simply functionally recommended but also morally required that we organize our common life by means of positive law, and thus that we form legal communities. The philosopher should be satisfied with the insight that in complex societies, law is the only medium in which it is possible reliably to establish morally obligated relationships of mutual respect even among strangers.

5

Law is not a narcissistically self-enclosed system, but is nourished by the "democratic *Sittlichkeit*" of enfranchised citizens and a liberal political culture that meets it halfway.[17] This becomes clear when one attempts to explain the paradoxical fact that legitimate law can arise from mere legality. The democratic procedure of lawmaking relies on citizens' making use of their communicative and participatory rights *also* with an orientation toward the common good, an attitude that can indeed be politically called for but not legally compelled. Like all individual rights, the form of political rights is also such that they merely grant spheres for free choice and only make legal behavior into a duty. Despite this structure, however, they can open up the sources of legitimation in discursive opinion- and will-formation only if citizens do not exclusively use their communicative liberties *like* individual liberties in the pursuit of personal interests, but rather use them *as* communicative liberties for the purpose of a "public use of reason." Law can be preserved as legitimate only if enfranchised citizens switch from the role of private legal subjects and take the perspective of participants who are engaged in the process of reaching understanding about the rules for their life in common. To this extent, constitutional democracy depends on the motivations of a population *accustomed* to liberty, motivations that cannot be generated by administrative measures. This explains why, in the proceduralist paradigm of law, the structures of a vibrant civil society and an unsubverted political public sphere must bear a good portion of the normative expectations, especially the burden of a normatively expected democratic genesis of law.

  Not surprisingly, this brings out the skeptic in both the social scientist and the legal scholar. As an empiricist, the former teaches us about powerless ideas that always look foolish in the face of interests; as a pragmatist, the latter teaches us about the hardened conflicts that can be dealt with only by calling on the backing of a substantial state power. It is precisely the discourse-theoretic approach that introduces a realistic element insofar as it shifts the conditions for a rational political opinion- and will-formation from the level of *individual* or group motivations and decisions to the *social* level of institutionalized processes of deliberation and decision making. With this move, a *structuralist* point of view comes into play: democratic procedures and their corresponding communicative arrangements can function as a filter that sorts out issues and contributions, information and reasons in such a way that only the relevant and valid inputs "count." Nevertheless, one must still answer the question of how a demanding self-understanding of law that, pace Kant, is not designed for a "race of devils" is at all compatible with the functional conditions of complex societies.

It was just this skepticism that led me to focus on the tension between facticity and validity in the first place.[18] A reconstructive legal theory follows a methodology premised on the idea that the counterfactual self-understanding of constitutional democracy finds expression in unavoidable, yet factually efficacious idealizations that are presupposed by the relevant practices. The first act of a constitution-making practice already drives the wedge of an expansive idea into societal complexity. In the light of this idea of the self-constitution of a community of free and equal persons, established practices of making, applying, and implementing law cannot avoid being exposed to critique and self-critique. In the form of individual rights, the energies of free choice, strategic action, and self-realization are simultaneously released and channeled by compelling norms, about which citizens must reach an understanding by following democratic procedures and publicly exercising their legally guaranteed communicative liberties. The paradoxical achievement of law thus consists in the fact that it reduces the conflict potential of unleashed individual liberties through norms that can coerce only so long as they are recognized as legitimate on the fragile basis of unleashed communicative liberties. A force that otherwise stands opposed to the socially integrating force of communication is, in the form of legitimate coercion, thus converted into the means of social integration itself. Social integration thereby takes on a peculiarly reflexive shape: by meeting its need for legitimation with the help of the productive force of communication, law takes advantage of a permanent risk of dissensus to spur on legally institutionalized public discourses.

Appendix I

Popular Sovereignty as Procedure (1988)

In view of its impressive historical influence, the French Revolution can "scarcely be compared with any other historical event."[1] This one undisputed statement explains why almost any other statement is subject to debate. In our day a new controversy has arisen: whether the Great Revolution has ceased to be relevant.

Under the banner of postmodern farewells, we are now also supposed to distance ourselves from that exemplary event whose effects have been felt for the last two hundred years. The eminent Leipzig historian of the Revolution, Walter Markov, still claimed in 1967 that "The French Revolution has been experienced by no subsequent generation as a self-contained episode or museum piece."[2] At that time François Furet and Denis Richet had just published an impressive analysis of the Revolution in terms of the *histoire des mentalités*.[3] A decade later, when the self-criticism of the Left in Paris developed into the more extreme poststructuralist critique of reason, Furet could laconically conclude that "the French Revolution has ended."[4] Furet wanted to escape the hold of a "testamentary historiography" that conceived the French Revolution as the action-orienting origin of the present. He declared the French Revolution finished, so that the "contamination of the past" by narcissistic reference to the present would stop.

This impulse toward a more dispassionate, scholarly approach must not be confused with the most recent attempt to faith heal an allegedly contaminated present by normalizing and leveling out another, *negatively* charged past. The clocks of collective memory keep different time in France and Germany. In France, liberal and socialist interpretations of the Revolution have determined the nation's self-understanding. In contrast, since the initial enthusiasm of the Revolution's contemporaries died down, we Germans have constantly been suspicious of the terrorist consequences of the "ideas of 1789." This was not only true of the earlier Prussian self-understanding of the German nation. Traces of a conservative, even aggressively hostile, historiography were still to be found on this side of the Rhine up to 1945.[5] International differences in reception history do not, by themselves, say anything about the truth of a thesis, but the same thesis takes on a different significance in different contexts. Furet was responding to the tradition in which the French Revolution stands as a model alongside the Bolshevik revolution. This dialectical relation supports his thesis of the end of the French Revolution—and simultaneously relativizes it.[6]

A nonhistorian cannot contribute much to that controversy. Instead, I want to take the perspective of political theory and address the question of whether the orienting power of the French Revolution is exhausted. I am concerned with the normative issue of whether the shift in mentality that occurred during the French Revolution still represents, in some respects, an unclaimed heritage. Can we read the "revolution in ideas" of 1789 in a way that might still inform our own needs for orientation?

1

1.1

We can discuss the question concerning the still promising aspects of the French Revolution from various points of view.

(a) In France, the Revolution in part made possible, in part only accelerated, the development of a mobile bourgeois society and a capitalist economic system. It furthered processes that had occurred in other countries without a revolutionary reorganization of political authority and the legal system. Since then, this economic and social modernization has become not only permanently crisis-ridden but overtly secular as well. Today, with its dysfunctional side effects, we are more aware of the dangers; we now experience the inexorable development of productive forces and the global expansion of Western civilization more as threats. One can no longer coax an unredeemed promise from the production-centered capitalist project. The workers' social utopia is exhausted.

(b) Something similar holds for the rise of the modern state apparatus. As Alexis de Tocqueville already saw, the French Revolution by no means signified an innovation in the development of state bureaucracies. At most, it accelerated trends that were already under way. Today, the integrative capabilities of the state continue to diminish under the pressure of regional movements, on the one hand, and worldwide corporations and transnational organizations, on the other. Where the ethos of instrumental rationality still survives, it hardly finds any support in the unpredictable organizational accomplishments of self-programming government administrations.

(c) We find a genuine product of the French Revolution, however, in the nation-state that could require universal conscription of its patriotic citizens. With national consciousness, a new form of social integration developed for enfranchised citizens who were released from the bonds of estates and corporations. This French model also guided the last generation of states emerging from decolonization. But, with their multiethnic societies, the superpowers of the United States and the Soviet Union have never fit into the nation-as-state scheme. And the contemporary heirs of the European system of states, having taken nationalism beyond its limits, find themselves on the path to a postnational society.

(d) There seems to be only one remaining candidate for an affirmative answer to the question concerning the relevance of the French Revolution: the ideas that inspired constitutional democracy. Democracy and human rights form the universalist core of the constitutional state that emerged from the American and French Revolutions in different variants. This universalism still has its explosive power and vitality, not only in Third World countries and the Soviet bloc, but also in European nations, where constitutional patriotism acquires new significance in the course of an identity transformation. This, at least, is the opinion recently expressed by Rudolf von Thadden at the German-French meeting in Belfort:

"With immigration at seven to eight percent, nations run the risk of changing their identity; soon they will no longer be able to understand themselves as monocultural societies, if they do not provide any points of integration beyond pure ethnic descent. In these circumstances it becomes urgent that we return to the idea of the citizen as the *citoyen*, which is at once more open and less rigid than the traditional idea of ethnic belonging."[7]

Of course, if the institutionalization of equal liberties were the only still promising idea, it would suffice, as many believe, to draw upon the heritage of the American Revolution: we could emerge from the shadows of the *terreur*.

Von Thadden does not draw this conclusion. Moreover, it is unlikely that the occasion of his speech (the opening of the celebration of the two-hundredth anniversary of the Great Revolution) is enough to explain why he reaches back to specifically French ideas. In the spirit of Jean-Jacques Rousseau, he contrasts the *citoyen* with the *bourgeoisie*; in line with the republican tradition, he links civil rights and participation with fraternity or solidarity. One can still hear the echoes of the old revolutionary slogans in what he says: "The Europe of citizens that we must build needs the forces of fraternity, of mutual aid and solidarity, so that the weak, the needy, and the unemployed are also able to accept the European Community as an advance over existing conditions. This appeal for the promotion of fraternity, connected with the idea of citizenship, must be the central message of the celebration of the two-hundredth anniversary of the French Revolution."[8]

Unlike the American Revolution, which was, so to speak, the *outcome* of events, the French Revolution was *carried forward* by its protagonists in the consciousness of a revolution. Furet also sees in the consciousness of revolutionary practice a new modality of historical action. One could even say that the bourgeois revolutions—the Dutch, English, and American—became aware of themselves *as* revolutions only in the French Revolution. Neither capitalistic economic trade (a, above), nor the bureaucratic form of legal authority (b), nor even national consciousness (c) and the modern constitutional state (d) had to emerge from a radical change experienced *as* revolution. "France, however, is the country that invents democratic culture through the Revolution and reveals to the world one of the foundational postures of conscious historical action."[9] Our current posture has two features: we still appeal to the readiness to act and to the political-moral orientation to the future, on the part of those who want to rebuild the existing order; at the same time, however, we have lost our confidence that conditions can be changed by revolution.

1.2

The revolutionary consciousness gave birth to a new mentality, which was shaped by a new time consciousness, a new concept of political practice, and a new notion of legitimation. The historical consciousness that broke with the traditionalism of nature-like continuities; the understanding of political practice in terms of self-determination and self-realization; and the trust in rational discourse, through which all political authority was supposed to legitimate itself—each of these is specifically modern. Under these three aspects, a radically this-worldly, postmetaphysical concept of the political penetrated the consciousness of a mobilized population.

Of course, looking back over the last two hundred years can arouse the suspicion that this understanding of politics has become so far removed from its intellectual and cultural origins that the revolutionary consciousness has ceased to be relevant at all. Is it not precisely the revolutionary signature, specifically inscribed on the years between 1789 and 1794, that has faded?

(a) The revolutionary consciousness was expressed in the conviction that a new beginning could be made. This reflected a change in historical consciousness.[10] Drawn together into a single process, world history became the abstract system of reference for a future-oriented action considered capable of uncoupling the present from the past. In the background lay the experience of a break with tradition: the threshold to dealing reflexively with cultural transmissions and social institutions was crossed. The process of modernization was experienced as the acceleration of events that were open, as it were, to single-minded collective intervention. The current generation saw itself burdened with responsibility for the fate of future generations, while the example of past generations lost its binding character. Within the enlarged horizon of future possibilities, the topicality of the present moment acquired excessive prominence in contrast to the normativity of an existing reality that merely protruded into the present. Hannah Arendt associated this emphatic confidence with our "natality," the moving affection that is always aroused on seeing a newborn infant and that brings the expectation of a better future.

This vitality, however, lost its revolutionary form long ago. For the reflexive liquefaction of traditions has by now become permanent; the hypothetical attitude toward existing institutions and given forms of life has become the norm. The Revolution has itself slipped into tradition: 1815, 1830, 1848, 1871, and 1917 represent the caesurae of a history of revolutionary struggles, but also a history of disappointments. The Revolution dismisses its dissidents, who no longer rebel against anything except the Revolution itself. This self-destructive dynamic is also rooted in a concept of progress, already discredited by Walter Benjamin, that dedicates itself to the future without remembering the victims of past generations. On the other hand, the effects of student revolts and new social movements in Western-style societies lead one to suspect that the cultural dynamic unleashed by the French Revolution is having an effect in the less-conspicuous value transformations of broad strata of the population, whereas the esoteric consciousness of contemporary relevance, penetrating continuity, and violated normativity has retreated into areas of post-avant-gardist art.

(b) Revolutionary consciousness was further expressed in the conviction that emancipated individuals are jointly called to be authors of their destiny. In their hands lies the power to decide about the rules and manner of their living together. As citizens, they give *themselves* the laws they want to obey, thereby producing their own life context. This context is conceived as the product of a cooperative practice centered in conscious political will-formation. A radically this-worldly politics understands itself as the expression and confirmation of the freedom that springs simultaneously from the subjectivity of the individual and the sovereignty of the people. At the level of political theory, individualist and collectivist approaches, which respectively give priority to the individual and the nation, have no doubt competed with one another from the beginning. But political freedom has always been conceived as the freedom of a subject that determines and realizes itself. Autonomy and self-realization are the key concepts for a practice with an immanent purpose, namely, the production and reproduction of a life worthy of human beings.[11]

This holistic concept of political practice has also lost its luster and motivating power. As the equal participation of all citizens in political will-formation was laboriously institutionalized according to the rule of law, the contradictions built into the concept of popular sovereignty itself became manifest. The people from whom all governmental authority is supposed to derive does not comprise a subject with will and consciousness. It only appears in the plural, and *as* a people it is capable of neither decision nor action as a whole. In complex societies, even the most earnest endeavors at political self-organization are defeated by resistant elements originating in the stubborn systemic logics of the market and administrative power. At one time, democracy was something to be asserted against the despotism palpably embodied in the king, members of the aristocracy, and higher-ranking clerics. Since then, political authority has been depersonalized. Democratization now works to overcome not genuinely political forms of resistance but rather the systemic imperatives of differentiated economic and administrative systems.

(c) Revolutionary consciousness was expressed, finally, in the conviction that the exercise of political domination could be legitimated neither religiously (by appeal to divine authority) nor metaphysically (by appeal to an ontologically grounded natural law). From now on, a politics radically situated in this world should be justifiable on the basis of reason, using the tools of postmetaphysical theorizing. Doctrines of rational natural law, that is, social-contract theories, were proposed with this purpose in mind. Such theories translated the Aristotelian concept of political authority—the self-rule of free and equal persons—into the basic concepts of the philosophy of the subject. In doing so, they finally satisfied the demands of individual freedom as well as those of universal justice. Revolutionary practice could thus be understood as a theoretically informed realization of human rights; the Revolution itself seemed to be derived from principles of practical reason. This self-understanding also explains the influence of the "sociétés de penser" and the active role of the "ideologues."

This intellectualism did not just awaken the suspicion of conservative opponents. The assumption that political will-formation is immediately receptive to theory, that it can be guided by a prior consensus on moral principles, had consequences that were unfortunate for democratic theory and disastrous for political practice. Theory must cope with the tension between sovereign will-formation and the apodictic insight of reason; practice must deal with the false apotheosis of reason, such as that manifested in the cult of the supreme being and the emblems of the French Revolution.[12] In the name of an authoritarian reason prior to every actual process of mutual understanding, a dialectic of spokespersons unfolded that blurred the difference between morality and tactics and ended by justifying "virtuous terror." Hence, thinkers from Carl Schmitt to Hermann Lübbe, from Cochin to Furet, have denounced the discourse that converts power into word; that is, they have portrayed it as a mechanism that inevitably gives rise to the consensually veiled domination of intellectual spokespersons—in other words, avant-gardism.[13]

1.3

Our review seems to suggest that the mentality created by the French Revolution became both permanent and trivial: no longer surviving today as revolutionary consciousness, it has forfeited its explosive utopian power and much of its rhetorical power as well. But has this transformation of form also depleted its energies? The *cultural* dynamic released by the French Revolution has obviously *not* come to a standstill. Today, for the first time, this dynamic has created the conditions for a cultural activism stripped of all high-cultural privileges and stubbornly eluding administrative manipulation. To be sure, the highly diversified pluralism of these activities, which are not confined by socioeconomic class, is opposed to the revolutionary self-understanding of a more or less homogeneous nation. Nevertheless, the cultural mobilization of the masses goes back to this source. In urban centers one can discern the emerging contours of a social intercourse characterized by both socially de-differentiated forms of expression and individualized lifestyles. The ambiguous physiognomy is not easy to decipher. One is not quite sure whether this "culture society" reflects only the commercially and strategically "exploited power of the beautiful"—a semantically desiccated, privatistic mass culture—or whether it might provide receptive ground for a revitalized public sphere where the ideas of 1789 could finally take root.

In what follows, I must leave this question open and restrict myself to normative arguments. My aim is simply to determine how a radically democratic republic might even be *conceived* today, assuming we can reckon on a resonant political culture that meets it halfway. A republic of this sort is not a possession we simply accept as our fortunate inheritance from the past. Rather it is a project we must carry forward in the consciousness of a revolution both permanent and quotidian. I am not speaking of a trivial continuation of the revolution by other means. One can already learn from Büchner's *Danton* how soon the revolutionary consciousness became enmeshed in the aporias of revolutionary instrumentalism. Melancholy is inscribed in the revolutionary consciousness—a mourning over the failure of a project that *nonetheless cannot be relinquished*. One can explain both the failure and this unrelinquishable character by the fact that the revolutionary project overshoots the revolution itself; it eludes the revolution's own concepts. Hence I will endeavor to translate the normative content of this unique revolution into our own concepts. In view of the double anniversary of the years 1789 and 1949—and stung by *other* "anniversaries"—a leftist in the Federal Republic must consider this undertaking an imperative: the principles of the Constitution will not take root in our souls until reason has assured itself of its orienting, future-directed contents. It is only as a historical project that constitutional democracy points beyond its legal character to a normative meaning—a force at once explosive and formative.

From the viewpoint of political theory, history is a laboratory for arguments. The French Revolution comprised in any case a chain of events fortified with arguments: the Revolution robed itself in the discourses of modern natural law. And it left behind prolix traces in the political ideologies of the nineteenth and twentieth centuries. From the distance available to later generations, the ideological struggles between democrats and liberals, between socialists and anarchists, between conservatives and progressives—to summarize loosely—display basic patterns of argumentation that are still instructive today.

2

2.1

The *dialectic between liberalism and radical democracy* that was intensely debated during the French Revolution has exploded worldwide. The dispute has to do with how one can reconcile equality with liberty, unity with variety, or the right of the majority with the right of the minority. Liberals begin with the legal institutionalization of equal liberties, conceiving these as rights held by individual subjects. In their view, human rights enjoy normative priority over democracy, and the constitutional separation of powers has priority over the will of the democratic legislature. Advocates of egalitarianism, on the other hand, conceive the collective practice of free and equal persons as sovereign will-formation. They understand human rights as an expression of the sovereign will of the people, and the constitutional separation of powers *emerges* from the enlightened will of the democratic legislature.

Thus the starting constellation is already characterized by Rousseau's answer to John Locke. Rousseau, the forerunner of the French Revolution, understands liberty as the autonomy of the people, as the equal participation of each person in the practice of *self-legislation*. Immanuel Kant, as a philosophical contemporary of the French Revolution who admitted that Rousseau first "set him straight," formulates this point as follows:

> The legislative authority can be attributed only to the united will of the people. Because all right and justice is supposed to proceed from this authority, it can do absolutely no injustice to anyone. Now, when someone prescribes for another, it is always possible that he thereby does the other an injustice, but this is never possible with respect to what he decides for himself (for *volenti non fit injuria*—"he who consents cannot receive an injury"). Hence, only the united and consenting will of all—that is, a general and united will of the people by which each decides the same for all and all decide the same for each—can legislate.[14]

The point of this reflection is the unification of practical reason and sovereign will, of human rights and democracy. A rational structure is inscribed in the autonomy of the legislative practice itself, so that the reason that legitimates political authority no longer has to rush ahead of the sovereign will of the people and anchor human rights in a imaginary state of nature, as it did in Locke. Because it can express itself only in general and abstract laws, the united will of the citizens must perforce exclude all nongeneralizable interests and admit only those regulations that guarantee equal liberties to all. The exercise of popular sovereignty simultaneously secures human rights.

Through Rousseau's Jacobin disciples, this idea kindled practical enthusiasm and provoked liberal opposition. The critics insisted that the fiction of the unified popular will could be realized only at the cost of masking or suppressing the heterogeneity of individual wills. In fact, Rousseau had already imagined the constitution of the popular sovereign as something like an existential act of sociation through which isolated individuals were transformed into citizens oriented toward the common good. These citizens comprise the members of a collective *body*; they are the subject of a legislative practice that has been freed from the individual interests of private persons who are merely passively subjected to legal statutes. All the radical varieties of Rousseauianism labor under this moral overburdening of the virtuous citizen. The assumption of republican virtues is realistic only for a polity with a normative consensus that has been secured in advance through tradition and ethos: "Now the less the individual wills relate to the general will, that is to say customary conduct to the laws, the more repressive force has to be increased."[15] Liberal objections to Rousseauianism can thus draw on Rousseau himself: modern societies are not homogeneous.

2.2

The opponents emphasize the diversity of interests that must be brought into balance and the pluralism of opinions that must be brought into a majority consensus. In fact, the critique leveled against the "tyranny of the majority" appears in two different variants. The classical liberalism of Tocqueville understands popular sovereignty as a principle of equality that needs to be limited. It is the fear the *bourgeoisie* have of being overpowered by the *citoyen*: if the constitutional regime with its separation of powers does not *set boundaries* on the democracy of the people, then the prepolitical liberties of the individual are in danger. With this, of course, liberal theory falls back into its earlier difficulties: the practical reason incorporated in the constitution once again comes into conflict with the sovereign will of the political masses. The problem Rousseau sought to solve with the concept of self-legislation reappears. A democratically enlightened liberalism must therefore hold on to Rousseau's intention.

At this end of the political spectrum, the critique led not to a limitation but to a redefinition of the principle of popular sovereignty: such sovereignty should express itself only under the discursive conditions of an internally differentiated process of opinion- and will-formation. In 1848—hence before John Stuart Mill, in his "On Liberty" (1859), united equality and liberty in the idea of the discursive public sphere—the German democrat Julius Fröbel issued a flyer in which he conceived the idea of a total will *along completely nonutilitarian lines*. This will should emerge from the free will of all citizens through discussion and voting: "We seek the social republic, that is, the state in which the happiness, freedom, and dignity of each individual are recognized as the common goal of all, and the perfection of the law and power of society springs from the *mutual understanding* and agreement *of all its members*."[16]

A year earlier Fröbel had published *System der socialen Politik* (System of Social Politics),[17] in which he connects the principle of free discussion with majority rule in an interesting way. He assigns to public discourse the role that Rousseau ascribed to the supposedly universalizing force of the mere *form* of the legal statute. The normative meaning of the validity of laws that deserve general assent cannot be explained by the semantic properties of abstract and general laws. Instead, Fröbel has recourse to the communicative conditions under which opinion-formation oriented to truth can be combined with majoritarian will-formation. At the same time, he holds on to Rousseau's concept of autonomy: "A law exists only for the one who has made it himself or agreed to it; for everyone else it is a command or an order" (p. 97). Hence laws require the justified assent of all. The democratic legislature, however, decides by majority. Consensus and majority rule are compatible only if the latter has an internal relation to the search for truth: public discourse must mediate between reason and will, between the opinion-formation of all and the majoritarian will-formation of the representatives.

A majority decision may come about only in such a way that its content is regarded as the rationally motivated but *fallible* result of an attempt to determine what is right through a discussion that has been brought to a *provisional* close under the pressure to decide: "The discussion allows convictions as they have developed in the minds of different human beings to have an effect on one another, it clarifies them and enlarges the circle in which they find recognition. The . . . practical specification of law results from the development and recognition of the theoretical legal consciousness already present in the society, but it can . . . succeed in one way only, namely that of voting and deciding according to the majority" (p. 96). Fröbel interprets the majority decision as a *conditional* consensus, as the consent of the minority to a practice that conforms to the will of the majority: "Certainly one does not require that the minority, by resigning their will, declare their opinion to be incorrect; indeed, one does not even require that they abandon their aims, but rather . . . that they forego the practical application of their convictions, until they succeed in better establishing their reasons and procuring the necessary number of affirmative votes" (pp. 108f.).

2.3

Fröbel's position shows that the normative tension between equality and liberty can be resolved as soon as one renounces an *overly concrete reading of the principle of popular sovereignty.* Unlike Rousseau, who focused on the mere form of general law, Fröbel does not imbue the sovereign will of a collectivity with practical reason but anchors the latter in a procedure of opinion- and will-formation that determines when a political will not identical with reason has the presumption of reason on its side. This preserves Fröbel from a normative devaluation of pluralism. Public discourse mediates between reason and will: "For the progress of knowledge, a unity of convictions would be a misfortune; in the affairs of society, a unity of aims is a necessity" (p. 108). The majoritarian production of a unified will is compatible with the "principle of the equal validity of the personal will of each" only in connection with the principle "of reducing error on the way to conviction" (p. 105). And the latter principle can be asserted against tyrannical majorities only in public discourses.

Fröbel therefore proposes popular education, a high level of education for all, as well as the freedom to express "theoretical" opinions and to campaign (*Propaganda*). He is also the first to recognize the constitutional significance of parties and of their political struggles for the majority of votes conducted with the instruments of "theoretical propaganda." Only open structures of communication can prevent the ascendancy of avant-garde parties. Only "parties" and not "sects" should exist: "The party wants to validate its separate aims in the state, the sect wants to use its separate aims to overcome the state. The party seeks to come to power in the state, the sect seeks to impose its own form of existence on the state. By coming to power in the state, the party seeks to dissolve into it, whereas the sect, by dissolving the state into itself, seeks to come to power" (p. 277). Fröbel stylizes the loose parties of his day as free associations that specialize in bringing influence to bear, primarily through arguments, on the process of public opinion- and will-formation. They represent the organizational core of an enfranchised public citizenry that, engaged in a multivocal discussion and deciding by majority, occupies the seat of the sovereign.

Whereas with Rousseau the sovereign *embodied* power and the legal monopoly on power, Fröbel's public is no longer a body. Rather, it is only the medium for a multivocal process of opinion-formation that substitutes mutual understanding for power and rationally motivates majoritarian decisions. Party competition in the political public sphere thus serves to establish the Rousseauian act of the social contract for the long run, in the form of a "legal and permanent revolution," as Fröbel puts it. Fröbel's constitutional principles strip the constitutional order of everything substantial. Strictly postmetaphysical, they delineate not "natural rights" but simply the procedure of opinion- and will-formation that secures equal liberties via general rights of communication and participation:

> With the constitutional compact the parties make an agreement to have their opinions affect one another through free discussion alone and to forego the implementation of any theory until it has the majority of citizens on its side. With the constitutional compact the parties agree to the following: to determine the unity of aims according to the majority of those supporting the theory; but to leave publicity for the theory to the freedom of each individual; and to give further shape to their constitution and legislation according to the outcome of all the individual efforts as shown by the votes. (p. 113)

Whereas the first three articles of the constitution establish the conditions and procedures of a rational democratic will-formation, the fourth article rules out the unchangeability of the constitution as well as every *external* limitation on proceduralized popular sovereignty. Human rights do not *compete* with popular sovereignty; they are identical with the constitutive conditions of a self-limiting practice of publicly discursive will-formation. The separation of powers is then explained by the logic of application and supervised implementation of laws that have been enacted through such a process.

3

3.1

The discourse over liberty and equality is carried on at another level in the *dispute between socialism and liberalism.* This dialectic, too, was already built into the French Revolution: it appeared when Jean-Paul Marat opposed the formalism of legal statutes and spoke of "legal tyranny," when Jacques Roux complained that the equality of legal statutes was aimed against the poor, and when François Babeuf, appealing to an equal satisfaction of the needs of each, criticized the institutionalization of equal liberties.[18] This discussion first acquired clear contours in early socialism.

In the eighteenth century, the critique of social inequality was directed against the social effects of political inequality. Legal arguments, that is, arguments based on modern natural law, provided a sufficient basis to plead for the equal liberties of constitutional democracy and bourgeois private law in opposition to the ancien régime. However, as constitutional monarchy and the Code Napoléon were implemented, social inequalities of *another* kind came to light. The inequalities connected with political privilege were replaced by ones that first appeared in the process of institutionalizing equal liberties according to private law. The social effects of the unequal distribution of a nonpolitical economic power were now at issue. When Karl Marx and Friedrich Engels denounced the bourgeois legal order as the juridical expression of unjust relations of production, they were borrowing arguments from political economy, thereby enlarging the concept of the political itself. No longer was just the organization of the state open to our control but the arrangement of society as a whole.[19]

With this change in perspective, a functional relationship between class structure and the legal system came into view. This connection made it possible to criticize legal formalism, and thus to criticize the substantive inequality of rights that were formally equal (i.e., equal according to their literal meaning). However, this same shift in perspective simultaneously made it difficult to see the problem that arises for political will-formation once the social is politicized. Marx and Engels, satisfied with allusions to the Paris Commune, more or less put aside questions of democratization. The philosophical background of these authors could also partly explain their blanket rejection of legal formalism (in fact a rejection of the legal sphere as a whole). Specifically, one could argue that they read Rousseau and Hegel too much through the eyes of Aristotle; that they failed to appreciate the normative substance of Kantian universalism and the Enlightenment; and that their idea of a liberated society was too concrete. They conceived socialism as a historically privileged form of concrete ethical life (*Sittlichkeit*) and not as the set of necessary conditions for emancipated forms of life about which participants *themselves* would have to reach an understanding.

The expanded concept of the political was not matched by a deeper understanding of the functional modes, forms of communication, and institutional conditions of egalitarian will-formation.

The holistic notion of a politicized society of workers remained central. The early socialists were still confident that the convivial forms of life of freely associated workers would emerge spontaneously from properly organized production processes. Faced with the complexity of developed, functionally differentiated societies, this idea of workers' self-governance had to fail—and fail even if the workers' social utopia was imagined, with Marx, as a realm of freedom to be established on the basis of an ongoing, systemically regulated realm of necessity. Even Lenin's strategy, the seizure of power by professional revolutionaries, could not make up for the lack of political theory. The practical effects of this deficit are evident in those aporias that to this day still grip bureaucratic socialism, with its political avant-garde frozen into *nomenklatura*.

3.2

On the other hand, achieving the social-welfare compromise has been a disappointing experience for the reformist unions and parties that operate within the framework of constitutional democracy. That is, they had to be content with an adjusted version of bourgeois liberalism and forego the redemption of radical democratic promises. The intellectual kinship between reformism and left liberalism (between Eduard Bernstein and Friedrich Naumann, still the godsons of the social-liberal coalition) rests on the shared goal of universalizing basic rights from a social-welfare perspective.[20] Normalizing the status of dependent wage labor through participatory political and social rights is supposed to provide the mass of the population with the opportunity to live in security, social justice, and growing prosperity. On the basis of a capitalist growth that is both domesticated and nurtured, the parties in power are supposed to operate the levers of administrative power so as to implement these goals via interventions. According to orthodox Marxism, social emancipation was to be achieved through a political revolution that took possession of the state apparatus only to smash it to pieces. Reformism can bring about social pacification solely by way of social-welfare interventions, but in doing so parties are absorbed into an expanding state apparatus. As parties become arms of the state, political will-formation shifts into a political system that is largely self-programming. To the extent that it succeeds in *extracting* mass loyalty from the public sphere, the political system becomes independent of the democratic sources of its legitimation. Thus the flip side of a halfway successful welfare state is a mass democracy in which the process of legitimation is *managed* by the administration. At the programmatic level, this is associated with resignation: both the acceptance of the scandalous "natural fate" imposed by the labor market and the renunciation of radical democracy.

This explains the relevance of the *discourse between anarchism and socialism* that has been carried on since the nineteenth century. What was already practiced in the petit bourgeois revolution of the sansculottes finally received rational justification and partial theoretical elaboration in anarchist social criticism and the idea of council democracy. Here the techniques of self-organization (such as permanent consultation, imperative mandates, rotation of offices, and interlocking powers) were probably less important than the organizational form itself: the model of the voluntary association.[21] Such associations displayed only a minimal degree of institutionalization. The horizontal contacts at the level of face-to-face interactions were supposed to coalesce into an intersubjective practice of deliberation and decision making strong enough to maintain all the *other* institutions in the fluid condition of the founding phase, more or less preserving them from coagulation. This anti-institutionalism coincided with the classical liberal idea that associations could support a public sphere in which the communicative practices of opinion- and will-formation would occur, guided of course by argumentation. When Donoso Cortes complained that liberalism erroneously made discussion into the principle of political decision, and when Carl Schmitt likewise denounced the liberal bourgeoisie as the discussing class, both had the anarchistic, hence *power-dissolving*, consequences of public discussion in view. The same motive still drives the numerous disciples of Schmitt in their shadowboxing with the intellectual instigators of a "European civil war."

In contrast to the individualistic, natural-*law* construct of the state of nature, the organizational form of voluntary association is a *sociological* concept that allows one to think of spontaneously emergent, domination-free relationships in noncontractualist terms. Then one no longer needs to conceive of domination-free society as an instrumental and hence prepolitical order established on the basis of contracts, that is, through the self-interested agreements of private persons oriented toward success. A society integrated through associations instead of through markets would be a political, yet nevertheless domination-free, order. The anarchists trace spontaneous sociation back to a different impulse than does modern natural law, that is, not to the interest in the useful exchange of goods but rather to the willingness to solve problems and coordinate action through mutual understanding. Associations differ from formal organizations in that the purpose of the union has not yet become functionally autonomous vis-à-vis the associated members' value orientations and goals.

3.3

This anarchist projection of a society made up entirely of horizontal networks of associations was always utopian; today it is still less workable, given the regulatory and organizational needs of modern societies. Media-steered interactions in the economic and administrative systems are defined precisely by the uncoupling of organizational functions from members' orientations. From the actor's perspective, this uncoupling manifests itself as an inversion of ends and means; processes of utilization and administration appear to acquire a fetishistic life of their own. But the anarchist's suspicion can be given a methodological turn; indeed it can be turned critically against both sides: against the system-blindness of a normative theory of democracy that disregards the bureaucratic expropriation of the grassroots level, and against the fetishizing gaze of a systems theory that dismisses all normative considerations. By methodological fiat, systems theory excludes the possibility of communication in which a society could examine itself as a whole.[22]

The classical theories of democracy start with the assumption that society has an effect or influence on itself through the sovereign legislature. The people program the laws, and these in turn program the implementation and application of law, so that through the collectively binding decisions of administration and judiciary the members of society receive the benefits and regulations that they themselves have programmed in their role of citizens. This *idea of an action-upon-self programmed by laws* appears plausible only on the supposition that society as a whole can be represented as an association writ large, which governs itself through the media of law and political power. Today we know better, now that sociological analyses have enlightened us about the actual circulation of power. We also know that as an organizational form, an association lacks the complexity necessary to structure the social fabric as a whole. But this is not my concern here. I am interested, rather, in the conceptual analysis of the reciprocal constitution of law and political power. Such an analysis already shows that, in the medium proper to action-upon-self programmed by laws, there exists *an opposing, self-programming circulation* of power.

Before law and political power can take on *their own* functions, namely, stabilization of behavioral expectations and collectively binding decisions, they must fulfill functions for each other. Thus law, which borrows its coercive character from power, first bestows on power the legal form that provides power with its binding character. Each of these two codes requires its own perspective: law requires a normative perspective, and power an instrumental one. From the perspective of law, policies as well as laws and decrees have need of normative justification, whereas from the perspective of power they function as means for and constraints upon the reproduction of power. The perspective of legislation and adjudication yields a normative approach to law; the perspective of preserving power yields a corresponding instrumental approach. From the perspective of power, the circulation of normative action-upon-self programmed through laws acquires the opposite character of a self-programming circulation of power: the administration programs itself by steering the behavior of the voting public, preprogramming the executive branch (*Regierung*) and legislature, and functionalizing the judiciary.

As the welfare state develops, the opposing element that is already *conceptually* present in the medium of legal-administrative action-upon-self also begins to have an empirical effect that gradually increases in strength. By now it is clear that the administrative instruments for implementing social-welfare programs are by no means a passive medium without properties of its own, as it were. To an increasing degree, the interventionist state has contracted into a subsystem steered by power and centered in itself; to an increasing degree, it has displaced legitimation processes into its environment. In fact, this process has progressed to the point where we would do well to consider modifications in the normative idea of a self-organizing society. I thus propose that we make a distinction in the concept of the political itself, consonant with the duality of normative and instrumental perspectives.[23]

We can distinguish between *communicatively generated* power and *administratively employed* power. In the political public sphere, then, two contrary processes encounter and cut across each other: the communicative generation of legitimate power, for which Arendt sketched a normative model, and the political-systemic acquisition of legitimacy, a process by which administrative power becomes reflexive. How these two processes—the spontaneous forming of opinion in autonomous public spheres and the organized extraction of mass loyalty—interpenetrate, and which overpowers which, are empirical questions. What primarily interests me is this: insofar as this distinction comes to have any empirical relevance, the normative understanding of a democratic self-organization of the legal community must also change.

4

4.1

The first question concerns the mode of action-upon-self. Because the administrative system must translate all normative inputs into its own language, one must explain how this system can be programmed at all through the policies and laws emerging from processes of public opinion- and will-formation. The administration obeys its own rationality criteria as it operates according to law; from the perspective of employing administrative power, what counts is not the practical reason involved in applying norms but the effectiveness of implementing a given program. Thus the administrative system primarily deals with the law instrumentally. Normative reasons, which justify adopted policies and enacted norms in the language of law, are regarded in the language of administrative power as rationalizations appended to decisions that were previously induced. Naturally, because of its juridical character, political power still depends on normative reasons. Normative reasons thus constitute the means by which communicative power makes itself felt. The indirect measures by which the administration manages the economy illustrate how influence can be brought to bear on self-regulating mechanisms (e.g., "help to self-help"). Perhaps we can apply this model to the relation between the democratic public sphere and the administration. Communicatively generated legitimate power can have an effect on the political system insofar as it assumes responsibility for the pool of reasons from which administrative decisions must draw their rationalizations. If the normative arguments appended by the system have been discursively invalidated by counterarguments from prior political communication, then it is simply not the case that "anything goes," that is, anything feasible for the political system.

The next question concerns the possibility of democratizing opinion- and will-formation themselves. Normative reasons can achieve an indirect steering effect only to the extent that the political system does not, for its part, steer the very production of these reasons. Now, democratic procedures are meant to institutionalize the forms of communication necessary for a rational will-formation. From this standpoint, at least, the institutional framework in which the legitimation process occurs today can be submitted to critical evaluation. With some institutional imagination, moreover, one can think of how existing parliamentary bodies might be supplemented by institutions that would allow affected clients and the legal public sphere to exert a stronger pressure for legitimation on the executive and judicial branches. The more difficult problem, however, is how to ensure the autonomy of the opinion- and will-formation that have already been institutionalized. After all, these generate communicative power only to the extent that majority decisions satisfy the conditions stated by Fröbel, that is, only insofar as they come about discursively.

The assumed internal relation between political will-formation and opinion-formation can secure the expected rationality of decision making only if parliamentary deliberations do not pro-

ceed according to ideologically *pregiven* assumptions. Elitist interpretations of the principle of representation respond to this requirement by shielding organized politics from a forever-gullible
popular opinion. In normative terms, however, this way of defending rationality against popular sovereignty is contradictory: if the
voters' opinion is irrational, then the election of representatives is
no less so. This dilemma turns our attention toward a relation
Fröbel did not discuss, that between formally structured political
will-formation and the surrounding environment of unstructured
processes of opinion-formation. The former issues in decisions
(and is also the level at which general elections are located),
whereas the latter remains informal, because it is not under any
pressure to decide. Fröbel's own assumptions compel one to
conclude that the democratic procedure can lead to a rational will-
formation only insofar as organized opinion-formation, which
leads to accountable decisions within government bodies, remains
permeable to the free-floating values, issues, contributions, and
arguments of a surrounding political communication that, as such,
cannot be *organized* as a whole.

Thus the normative expectation of rational outcomes is grounded
ultimately in the interplay between institutionally structured political will-formation and spontaneous, unsubverted circuits of communication in a public sphere that is not programmed to reach
decisions and thus is not organized. In this context, the public
sphere functions as a normative concept. Voluntary associations
represent the nodal points in a communication network that
emerges from the intermeshing of autonomous public spheres.
Such associations specialize in the generation and dissemination of
practical convictions. They specialize, that is, in discovering issues
relevant for all of society, contributing possible solutions to problems, interpreting values, producing good reasons, and invalidating others. They can become effective only indirectly, namely, by
altering the parameters of institutionalized will-formation by broadly
transforming attitudes and values. The manner in which general
voting behavior is increasingly affected by opaque mood swings in
the political culture indicates that the foregoing reflections are not
entirely out of touch with social reality. But here we must restrict
ourselves to the normative implications of this descriptive analysis.

4.2

Following Arendt's lead, Albrecht Wellmer has underscored the self-referential structure of the public practice issuing from communicative power.[24] This communicative practice bears the burden of stabilizing itself; with each important contribution, public discourse must keep alive both the meaning of an undistorted political public sphere as such and the very goal of democratic will-formation. The public sphere thereby continually thematizes itself as it operates, for the existential presuppositions of a nonorganizable practice can be secured only by this practice itself. The institutions of public freedom stand on the shifting ground of the political communication of those who, by using them, at the same time interpret and defend them. The public sphere thus reproduces itself *self-referentially*, and in doing so reveals the place to which the expectation of a sovereign self-organization of society has withdrawn. The idea of popular sovereignty is thereby desubstantialized. Even the notion that a network of associations could replace the dismissed "body" of the people—that it could occupy the vacant seat of the sovereign, so to speak—is too concrete.

This fully dispersed sovereignty is not even embodied in the heads of the associated members. Rather, if one can still speak of "embodiment" at all, then sovereignty is found in those subjectless forms of communication that regulate the flow of discursive opinion- and will-formation in such a way that their fallible outcomes have the presumption of practical reason on their side. Subjectless and anonymous, an intersubjectively dissolved popular sovereignty withdraws into democratic procedures and the demanding communicative presuppositions of their implementation. It is sublimated into the elusive interactions between culturally mobilized public spheres and a will-formation institutionalized according to the rule of law. Set communicatively aflow, sovereignty makes itself felt in the power of public discourses. Although such power originates in autonomous public spheres, it must take shape in the decisions of democratic institutions of opinion- and will-formation, inasmuch as the responsibility for momentous decisions demands clear institutional accountability. Communicative power is exercised in the manner of a siege. It influences the premises of judgment and decision making in the political system without intending to conquer the system itself. It thus aims to assert its imperatives in the only language the besieged fortress understands: it takes responsibility for the pool of reasons that administrative power can handle instrumentally but cannot ignore, given its juridical structure.

Naturally, even a proceduralized "popular sovereignty" of this sort cannot operate without the support of an accommodating political culture, without the basic attitudes, mediated by tradition and socialization, of a population *accustomed* to political freedom: rational political will-formation cannot occur unless a rationalized lifeworld meets it halfway. This thesis could appear to be just one more guise for a civic-republican ethos and its expectations of virtue that have morally overburdened citizens since time immemorial. If we are to dispel this suspicion, then we must finally argue for what neo-Aristotelian political theory slips in with its concept of ethos: we must explain how it is possible in principle for civic virtue and self-interest to intermesh. If it is to be *reasonable to expect* the political behavior that is normatively required, then the moral substance of self-legislation—which for Rousseau was concentrated in a single act—must be parceled out over many stages: the process of proceduralized opinion- and will-formation must break down into numerous smaller particles. It must be shown that political morality is exacted only in small increments.[25] Here I can illustrate this point only briefly.

Why should representatives base their decisions on correct and, as we are here assuming, more or less discursively formed judgments and not merely advance legitimating reasons as a pretext? It is because the institutions are designed in such a way that representatives normally do not want to expose themselves to the criticism of their voters. After all, voters can sanction their representatives at the next opportunity, but representatives do not have any comparable way of sanctioning voters. But why should voters base their ballot choices on, as we here assume, a more or less discursively formed public opinion, instead of ignoring the legitimating reasons? It is because normally they can choose only between the highly generalized policies and vague profiles of popular parties, and they can perceive their own interests only in the light of pregeneralized interest positions. But are not these two assumptions themselves unrealistic? Not entirely, so long as we are only normatively assessing the alternatives that are possible in principle. As we have seen, democratic procedures should produce rational outcomes insofar as opinion-formation inside parliamentary bodies remains sensitive to the results of a surrounding informal opinion-formation in autonomous public spheres. No doubt this second assumption of an unsubverted political public sphere is unrealistic; properly understood, however, it is not utopian in a bad sense. It would be realized to the extent that opinion-forming associations developed, catalyzed the growth of autonomous public spheres, and, in virtue of the natural visibility such associations enjoy, changed the spectrum of values, issues, and reasons. This would both innovatively unleash and critically filter the elements of discourse that have been channeled by the mass media, unions, associations, and parties, according to the dictates of power. In the final analysis, of course, the emergence, reproduction, and influence of such a network of associations remains dependent on a liberal-egalitarian political culture sensitive to problems affecting society as a whole—a culture that is even jumpy or in a constant state of vibration, and thus responsive.

4.3

Let us assume that complex societies would be open to such fundamental democratization. In that case, we are immediately confronted with *objections that conservatives* since Edmund Burke have repeatedly marshaled against the French Revolution and its effects.[26] In this final round of reflection, we must take up the arguments that such thinkers as Joseph de Maistre and Louis de Bonald have used to remind overly naive believers in progress of the limits of what can be done. The overextended project of a self-organizing society, so the argument goes, carelessly disregards the weight of traditions, organically developing reserves and resources that cannot be created at will. As a matter of fact, the instrumentalism underlying a practice that directly attempts to realize theory has had disastrous effects. Robespierre already set up an opposition between revolution and constitution: the Revolution exists for war and civil war, the Constitution for the victorious peace. From Marx to Lenin, the theoretically informed intervention of revolutionaries was merely supposed to complete the teleology of history driven by the forces of production. Proceduralized popular sovereignty, however, no longer has any place for such trust in a philosophy of history. Once the subject is removed from practical reason, the progressive institutionalization of procedures of rational collective will-formation can no longer be conceived as purposive action, as a kind of sublime process of production. Rather, today the controversial *realization* of universalist constitutional principles has become a permanent process that is already under way in ordinary legislation. The debates that precede decisions take place under conditions of a social and politicocultural transformation whose direction, though certainly not open to control by direct political intervention, can be indirectly accelerated or inhibited. The constitution has thus lost its static character. Even if the wording of norms has not changed, their interpretations are in flux.

Constitutional democracy is becoming a project, at once the outcome and the accelerating catalyst of a rationalization of the lifeworld reaching far beyond the political. The sole substantial aim of the project is the gradual improvement of institutionalized procedures of rational collective will-formation, procedures that cannot prejudge the participants' concrete goals. Each step along this path has repercussions on the political culture and forms of life. Conversely, without the support of the sociopolitical culture, which cannot be produced upon demand, the forms of communication adequate to practical reason cannot emerge.

Such a culturalistic understanding of constitutional *dynamics* seems to suggest that the sovereignty of the people should be relocated to the cultural dynamics of opinion-forming avant-gardes. This conjecture will fuel suspicions against intellectuals all the more: powerful in word, they grab for themselves the very power they profess to dissolve in the medium of the word. But at least one obstacle stands in the way of domination by intellectuals: communicative power can become effective only indirectly, insofar as it limits the implementation of administrative, hence actually exercised, power. And unstructured public opinion can in turn function as a siege of this sort only by way of accountable decision making organized according to democratic procedures. What is more important, the influence of intellectuals could coalesce into communicative power at all only under conditions that exclude a concentration of power. Autonomous public spheres could crystallize around free associations only to the extent that current trends toward an uncoupling of culture from class structures continue.[27] Public discourses find a good response only in proportion to their diffusion, and thus only under conditions of a broad and active participation that simultaneously has a *dispersing effect.* This in turn requires a background political culture that is egalitarian, divested of all educational privileges, and thoroughly intellectual.

There is certainly no necessity that this increasingly reflexive transmission of cultural traditions be associated with subject-centered reason and future-oriented historical consciousness. To the extent that we become aware of the intersubjective constitution of freedom, the possessive-individualist illusion of autonomy as self-ownership disintegrates. The self-assertive subject that wants to have everything at its disposal lacks an adequate relation to any tradition. Benjamin's youthful conservative sensibility detected another time consciousness in the culture revolution itself, a consciousness that turned our attention away from the horizon of our own "future presents" and back to the claims that past generations make on us. But one reservation still remains. The sobriety of a secular, unreservedly egalitarian mass culture does not just defeat the pathos of the holy seriousness that seeks to ensure social status to the prophetic alone. The fact that everyday affairs are necessarily banalized in political communication also poses a danger for the semantic potentials from which this communication must still draw its nourishment. A culture without thorns would be absorbed by mere needs for compensation; as M. Grefrath puts it, it settles over the risk society like a foam carpet. No civil religion, however cleverly adjusted, could forestall this entropy of meaning.[28] Even the moment of unconditionality insistently voiced in the context-transcending validity claims of everyday life does not suffice. *Another* kind of transcendence is preserved in the unfulfilled promise disclosed by the critical appropriation of identity-forming religious traditions, and *still another* in the negativity of modern art. The trivial and everyday must be open to the shock of what is absolutely strange, cryptic, or uncanny. Though these no longer provide a cover for privileges, they refuse to be assimilated by pregiven categories.[29]

Appendix II
Citizenship and National Identity (1990)

Until the mid eighties, history seemed to be entering that crystalline state known as *posthistoire*. This was Arnold Gehlen's term for the strange feeling that the more things change, the more they remain the same. *Rien ne va plus*—nothing really surprising can happen anymore. Locked in by systemic constraints, all the possibilities seemed to have been exhausted, all the alternatives frozen, and any remaining options drained of meaning. Since then this mood has completely changed. History is once again on the move, accelerating, even overheating. New problems are shifting the old perspectives. What is more important, new perspectives are opening up for the future, points of view that restore our ability to perceive alternative courses of action.

Three historical movements of our contemporary period, once again in flux, affect the relation between citizenship and national identity: (1) In the wake of German unification, the liberation of the East Central European states from Soviet tutelage, and the nationality conflicts breaking out across Eastern Europe, the question concerning the future of the nation-state has taken on an unexpected topicality. (2) The fact that the states of the European Community are gradually growing together, especially with the caesura that will be created when a common market is introduced in 1993, sheds light on the relation between the nation-state and democracy: the democratic processes constituted at the level of the nation-state lag hopelessly behind the economic integration taking place at a supranational level. (3) The tremendous tide of immigration from the poor regions of the East and South, with which Europe will be increasingly confronted in the coming years, lends the problem of asylum a new significance and urgency. This process exacerbates the conflict between the universalistic principles of constitutional democracy, on the one hand, and the particularistic claims to preserve the integrity of established forms of life, on the other.

These three topics offer an occasion for the conceptual clarification of some normative perspectives from which we can gain a better understanding of the complex relation between citizenship and national identity.

1 The Past and Future of the Nation-State

The events in Germany and the Eastern European states have given a new twist to a long-standing discussion in the Federal Republic about the path to a "postnational society."[1] Many German intellectuals have complained, for example, about the democratic deficits of a unification process that is implemented at the administrative and economic levels without the participation of citizens; they now find themselves accused of "postnational arrogance." This controversy over the form and tempo of political unification is fueled not only by the contrary feelings of the disputing parties but also by conceptual unclarities. One side sees the accession of the five new Länder to the Federal Republic as restoring the unity of a nation-state torn apart four decades ago. From this viewpoint, the nation represents the prepolitical unity of a community with a shared historical destiny (*Schicksalsgemeinschaft*). The other side sees political unification as restoring democracy and the rule of law in a territory where civil rights have been suspended in one form or another since 1933. From this viewpoint, what used to be West Germany was no less a nation of enfranchised citizens than is the new Federal Republic. This republican usage strips the term "nation-state" of precisely those prepolitical and ethnic-cultural connotations that have accompanied the expression in modern Europe. Dissolving the semantic connections between state citizenship and national identity honors the fact that today the classic form of the nation-state is, with the transition of the European

Community to a political union, disintegrating. This is confirmed by a glance back at its genesis in early modernity.

In modern Europe, the premodern form of *empire* that used to unite numerous peoples remained rather unstable, as shown in the cases of the Holy Roman Empire or the Russian and Ottoman empires.[2] A second, federal form of state emerged from the belt of Central European cities. It was above all in Switzerland that a *federation* developed that was strong enough to balance the ethnic tensions within a multicultural association of citizens. But it was only the third form, the centrally administered *territorial state*, that came to have a lasting formative effect on the structure of the European system of states. It first emerged—as in Portugal, Spain, France, England, and Sweden—from kingdoms. Later, as democratization proceeded along the lines of the French example, it developed into the *nation-state*. This state formation secured the boundary conditions under which the capitalist economic system could develop worldwide. That is, the nation-state provided the infrastructure for an administration disciplined by the rule of law, and it guaranteed a realm of individual and collective action free of state interference. Moreover—and this is what primarily interests us here—it laid the foundation for the ethnic and cultural homogeneity that made it possible, beginning in the late eighteenth century, to forge ahead with the democratization of government, albeit at the cost of excluding and oppressing minorities. Nation-state and democracy are twins born of the French Revolution. From a cultural point of view, they both stand under the shadow of nationalism.

This national consciousness is a specifically modern manifestation of cultural integration. The political consciousness of national membership arises from a dynamic that first took hold of the population after processes of economic and social modernization had torn people from their places in the social hierarchy, simultaneously mobilizing and isolating them as individuals. Nationalism is a form of consciousness that presupposes an appropriation, filtered by historiography and reflection, of cultural traditions. Originating in an educated bourgeois public, it spreads through the channels of modern mass communication. Both elements, its literary mediation and its dissemination through public media, lend to nationalism its artificial features; its somewhat constructed character makes it naturally susceptible to manipulative misuse by political elites.

The history of the term "nation" reflects the historical genesis of the nation-state.[3] For the Romans, *Natio* was the goddess of birth and origin. *Natio* refers, like *gens* and *populus* but unlike *civitas*, to peoples and tribes who were not yet organized in political associations; indeed, the Romans often used it to refer to "savage," "barbaric," or "pagan" peoples. In this classical usage, then, nations are communities of people of the same descent, who are integrated geographically, in the form of settlements or neighborhoods, and culturally by their common language, customs, and traditions, but who are not yet politically integrated through the organizational form of the state. This meaning of "nation" persisted through the Middle Ages and worked its way into the vernacular languages in the fifteenth century. Even Kant still wrote that "those inhabitants . . . which recognize themselves as being united into a civil whole through common descent, are called a nation (*gens*)."[4] However, in the early-modern period a competing usage arose: the nation is the bearer of sovereignty. The estates represented the "nation" over against the "king." Since the middle of the eighteenth century, these two meanings of "nation"—community of descent and "people of a state"—have intertwined. With the French Revolution, the "nation" became the source of state sovereignty, for example, in the thought of Emmanuel Sieyès. Each nation is now supposed to be granted the right to political self-determination. The intentional democratic community (*Willensgemeinschaft*) takes the place of the ethnic complex.

With the French Revolution, then, the meaning of "nation" was transformed from a prepolitical quantity into a constitutive feature of the political identity of the citizens of a democratic polity. At the end of the nineteenth century, the conditional relation between ascribed national identity and acquired democratic citizenship could even be reversed. Thus the gist of Ernest Renan's famous saying, "the existence of a nation is . . . a daily plebiscite," was already directed *against* nationalism. After 1871, Renan could rebut Germany's claims to the Alsace by referring to the inhabitants' French nationality only because he thought of the "nation" as a nation of citizens, and not as a community of descent. The nation of citizens finds its identity not in ethnic and cultural commonalities but in the practice of citizens who actively exercise their rights to participation and communication. At this juncture, the republican strand of citizenship completely parts company with the idea of belonging to a prepolitical community integrated on the basis of descent, shared tradition, and common language. Viewed from this end, the initial fusion of national consciousness with republican conviction only functioned as a catalyst.

The nationalism mediated by the works of historians and romantic writers, hence by scholarship and literature, grounded a collective identity that played a *functional* role for the notion of citizenship that originated in the French Revolution. In the melting pot of national consciousness, the ascriptive features of one's origin were transformed into just so many results of a conscious appropriation of tradition. Ascribed nationality gave way to an achieved nationalism, that is, to a conscious product of one's own efforts. This nationalism was able to foster people's identification with a role that demanded a high degree of personal commitment, even to the point of self-sacrifice; in this respect, general conscription was simply the flip side of civil rights. National consciousness and republican conviction in a sense proved themselves in the willingness to fight and die for one's country. This explains the complementary relation that originally obtained between nationalism and republicanism: one became the vehicle for the emergence of the other.

However, this social-psychological connection does not mean that the two are linked at the conceptual level. National independence and collective self-assertion against foreign nations can be understood as a collective form of freedom. This national freedom does not coincide with the genuinely political freedom that citizens enjoy within a country. For this reason, the modern understanding of this republican freedom can, at a later point, cut its umbilical links to the womb of the national consciousness of freedom that originally gave it birth. The nation-state sustained a close connection between "demos" and "ethos" only briefly.[5] Citizenship was never conceptually tied to national identity.

The concept of citizenship developed out of Rousseau's concept of self-determination. "Popular sovereignty" was initially understood as a delimitation or reversal of royal sovereignty and was judged to rest on a contract between a people and its government. Rousseau and Kant, by contrast, did not conceive of popular sovereignty as the transfer of ruling authority from above to below or as its distribution between two contracting parties. For them, popular sovereignty signified rather the transformation of authority into *self-legislation*. A historical pact, the civil contract, is replaced here by the social contract, which functions as an abstract model for the way in which an authority legitimated only through the implementation of democratic self-legislation is *constituted*. Political authority thereby loses its character of quasi-natural violence: the *auctoritas* of the state should be purged of the remaining elements of *violentia*. According to this idea, "only the united and consenting Will of all—... by which each decides the same for all and all decide the same for each—can legislate."[6]

This idea does not refer to the substantive generality of a popular will that would owe its unity to a prior homogeneity of descent or form of life. The consensus fought for and achieved in an association of free and equal persons ultimately rests only on the unity of a *procedure* to which all consent. This procedure of democratic opinion- and will-formation assumes a differentiated form in constitutions based on the rule of law. In a pluralistic society, the constitution expresses a formal consensus. The citizens want to regulate their living together according to principles that are in the equal interest of each and thus can meet with the justified assent of all. Such an association is structured by relations of mutual recognition in which each person can expect to be respected by all as free and equal. Each and every person should receive a three-fold recognition: they should receive equal protection and equal respect in their integrity as irreplaceable individuals, as members of ethnic or cultural groups, and as citizens, that is, as members of the political community. This idea of a self-determining political community has assumed a variety of concrete legal forms in the different constitutions and political systems of Western Europe and the United States.

In the language of law, though, "*Staatsbürgerschaft*," "*citoyenneté*," or "citizenship" referred for a long time only to nationality or membership in a state; only recently has the concept been enlarged to cover the status of citizens defined in terms of civil rights.[7]

Membership in a state assigns a particular person to a particular nation whose existence is recognized in terms of international law. Regardless of the internal organization of state authority, this definition of membership, together with the territorial demarcation of the country's borders, serves to delimit the state in social terms. In the democratic constitutional state, which understands itself as an association of free and equal persons, state membership depends on the principle of voluntariness. Here, the conventional ascriptive characteristics of domicile and birth (*jus soli* and *jus sanguinis*) by no means justify a person's being irrevocably subjected to that government's sovereign authority. These characteristics function merely as administrative criteria for attributing to citizens an assumed, implicit consent, to which the right to emigrate or to renounce one's citizenship corresponds.[8]

Today, though, the expressions "*Staatsbürgerschaft*" or "citizenship" are used not only to denote organizational membership in a state but also for the status materially defined by civil rights and duties. The Basic Law of the Federal Republic has no explicit parallel to the Swiss notion of active citizenship.[9] However, taking Article 33, section 1, of the Basic Law as its starting point, German legal thought has expanded the package of civil rights and duties, especially the basic rights, to generate an overall status of a similar kind.[10] In the republican view, citizenship has its point of reference in the problem of the legal community's self-organization, whereas its core consists in the rights of political participation and communication. Rolf Grawert, for example, conceives citizenship as "the legal institution through which the individual member of a state is given a collaborative role in the concrete matrix of state actions."[11] The status of citizen fixes in particular the democratic rights to which the individual can reflexively lay claim in order to *change* his material legal status.

In the philosophy of law, two contrary interpretations of this active citizenship vie with each other for pride of place. The role of the citizen is given an individualist and instrumentalist reading in the liberal tradition of natural law starting with John Locke, whereas a communitarian and ethical understanding of this role has emerged in the republican tradition of political philosophy going back to Aristotle. In the first case, citizenship is conceived along the lines of an organizational membership that grounds a legal status. In the second case, it is modeled after a self-determining ethnic-cultural community. In the first interpretation, individuals remain outside the state. In exchange for organizational services and benefits, they make specific contributions, such as voting inputs and tax payments, to the reproduction of the state. In the second interpretation, citizens are integrated into the political community like the parts of a whole, in such a way that they can develop their personal and social identity only within the horizon of shared traditions and recognized political institutions. On the liberal reading, citizens do not differ essentially from private persons who bring their prepolitical interests to bear vis-à-vis the state apparatus. On the republican reading, citizenship is actualized solely in the collective practice of self-determination. Charles Taylor describes these two competing concepts of citizen as follows:

> One [model] focuses mainly on individual rights and equal treatment, as well as a government performance which takes account of the citizen's preferences. This is what has to be secured. Citizen capacity consists mainly in the power to retrieve these rights and ensure equal treatment, as well as to influence the effective decisionmakers. . . . [T]hese institutions have an entirely instrumental significance. . . . [N]o value is put on participation in rule for its own sake. . . .
>
> The other model, by contrast, defines participation in self-rule as of the essence of freedom, as part of what must be secured. This is . . . an essential component of citizen capacity. . . . Full participation in self-rule is seen as being able, at least part of the time, to have some part in the forming of a ruling consensus, with which one can identify along with others. To rule and be ruled in turn means that at least some of the time the governors can be "us," and not always "them."[12]

The holistic model of a community that incorporates its citizens in every aspect of their lives is in many respects inadequate for modern politics. Nevertheless, it has an advantage over the organizational model, in which isolated individuals confront a state apparatus to which they are only functionally connected by membership: the holistic model makes it clear that political autonomy is an end in itself that can be realized not by the single individual privately pursuing his own interests but only by all together in an intersubjectively shared practice. The citizen's legal status is constituted by a network of egalitarian relations of mutual recognition.

It assumes that each person can adopt the participant perspective of the first-person plural—and not just the perspective of an observer or actor oriented to his own success.

Legally guaranteed relations of recognition do not, however, reproduce themselves of their own accord. Rather, they require the cooperative efforts of a civic practice that no one can be compelled to enter into by legal norms. It is for good reason that modern coercive law does not extend to the motives and basic attitudes of its addressees. A legal duty, say, to make active use of democratic rights has something totalitarian about it. Thus the legally constituted status of citizen depends on the *supportive spirit* of a consonant background of legally noncoercible motives and attitudes of a citizenry oriented toward the common good. The republican model of citizenship reminds us that constitutionally protected institutions of freedom are worth only what a population *accustomed* to political freedom and settled in the "we" perspective of active self-determination makes of them. The legally institutionalized role of citizen must be embedded in the context of a liberal political culture. This is why the communitarians insist that citizens must "patriotically" identify with their form of life. Taylor, too, postulates a shared consciousness that arises from the identification with the consciously accepted traditions of one's own political and cultural community: "The issue is, can our patriotism survive the marginalization of participatory self-rule? As we have seen, a patriotism is a common identification with an historical community founded on certain values. . . . But it must be one whose core values incorporate freedom."[13]

With this, Taylor seems to contradict my thesis that there is only a historically contingent and not a conceptual connection between republicanism and nationalism. Studied more closely, however, Taylor's remarks boil down to the statement that the universalist principles of constitutional democracy need to be somehow anchored in the political culture of each country. Constitutional principles can neither take shape in social practices nor become the driving force for the dynamic project of creating an association of free and equal persons until they are situated in the historical context of a nation of citizens in such a way that they link up with those citizens' motives and attitudes.

As the examples of multicultural societies like Switzerland and the United States demonstrate, a political culture in which constitutional principles can take root need by no means depend on all citizens' sharing the same language or the same ethnic and cultural origins. A liberal political culture is only the common denominator for a *constitutional* patriotism (*Verfassungspatriotismus*) that heightens an awareness of both the diversity and the integrity of the different forms of life coexisting in a multicultural society. In a future Federal Republic of European States, the *same* legal principles would also have to be interpreted from the perspectives of *different* national traditions and histories. One's own tradition must in each case be appropriated from a vantage point relativized by the perspectives of other traditions, and appropriated in such a manner that it can be brought into a transnational, Western European constitutional culture. A particularist anchoring of *this kind* would not do away with one iota of the universalist meaning of popular sovereignty and human rights. The original thesis stands: democratic citizenship need not be rooted in the national identity of a people. However, regardless of the diversity of different cultural forms of life, it does require that every citizen be socialized into a common political culture.

2 Nation-State and Democracy in a Unified Europe

The political future of the European Community sheds light on the relation between citizenship and national identity in yet another respect. The concept of citizenship developed by Aristotle was, after all, originally tailored for the size of cities or city-states. The transformation of populations into nations that formed states occurred, as we have seen, under the banner of a nationalism that seemed to reconcile republican ideas with the larger dimensions of modern territorial states. It was in the political forms created by the nation-state that modern trade and commerce arose. And, like the bureaucratic state, the capitalist economy, too, developed a systemic logic of its own. The markets for goods, capital, and labor obey their own logic, independent of the intentions of human subjects. Alongside the administrative power incorporated in government bureaucracies, money has become an anonymous medium of societal integration operating above the participants' heads. This *system integration* competes with the form of integration mediated by the actors' consciousnesses, that is, the *social integration* taking place through values, norms, and mutual understanding. The *political integration* that occurs through democratic citizenship represents one aspect of this general social integration. For this reason, the relation between capitalism and democracy is fraught with tension, something liberal theories often deny.

Examples from the developing countries show that the relation between the development of the democratic constitutional state and capitalist modernization is by no means linear. Nor did the social-welfare compromise, operative in Western democracies since the end of the Second World War, come about automatically. The development of the European Community manifests this same tension between democracy and capitalism in another way. Here it is expressed in the vertical divide between the systemic integration of economy and administration that emerges at the supranational level and the political integration effected only at the level of the nation-state. Hence, the technocratic shape of the European Community reinforces doubts that were already associated with the normative expectations linked with the role of the democratic citizen. Were not these expectations always largely illusory, even within the borders of the nation-state? Did not the temporary symbiosis of republicanism and nationalism merely mask the fact that the concept of the citizen is, at best, suited for the less complex relations of an ethnically homogenous and surveyable polity still integrated by tradition and custom?

Today the "European Economic Community" has become a "European Community" that proclaims the political will to form a "European Political Union." Aside from India, the United States provides the only example for a governmental structure of this sort (which at present would encompass 320 million inhabitants). The United States, though, is a multicultural society united by the same political culture and (at least for now) a single language, whereas the European Union would represent a multilingual state of different nationalities. Even if such an association were to resemble more of a Federal Republic than a federation of semisovereign individual states—a question that is still a matter of controversy—it would have to retain certain features of de Gaulle's "Europe of Father-lands." The nation-states as we know them would, even in such a Europe, *continue to have* a strong structuring effect.

However, nation-states present a problem along the thorny path to European Union not so much on account of their insuperable claims to sovereignty but because democratic processes have hith-erto functioned, imperfectly to be sure, only inside national bound-aries. To put it briefly, up to the present the political public sphere has been fragmented into national units. Hence we cannot avoid the question whether a European citizenship can even exist at all. By this I do not mean the possibility of collective political action across national boundaries but the consciousness "of an obligation toward the European common good."[14] As late as 1974, Raymond Aron answered this question with a decisive "No." At the supra-national steering level, an extensive European market will soon be set up with legal-administrative instruments. This contrasts with the very limited powers of the European Parliament, a body that will probably be scarcely visible in the political public spheres of the member states. To date, rights of political participation do not effectively extend beyond national boundaries.

The administration of justice by the European Court takes the "Five Freedoms of the Common Market" as its point of orientation and interprets as basic rights the free movement of goods, the free movement of labor, the freedom of entrepreneurial establishment, the freedom to provide services, and the free movement of capital and payments. This corresponds to the powers the Treaty of Rome conferred on the Council of Ministers and the High Commission in Article 3. These in turn are explained in terms of the goal set out in Article 9: "The Community shall be based upon a customs union which shall cover all trade in goods." The internal market and the planned establishment of an autonomous central bank serve the same end. The new level of economic interdependence should give rise to a growing need for coordination in other policy fields as well, such as environmental policy, fiscal and social policy, and educa-tional policy. This need for regulation will again be assessed primarily from the standpoint of economic rationality, according to standards of fair competition. Thus far these tasks are accom-plished by European organizations that have intermeshed to form a dense administrative network. The new functional elites are, formally speaking, still accountable to the governments and institutions in their respective countries of origin; in reality, however, they have already outgrown their national contexts. Professional civil servants form a bureaucracy that is aloof from democratic processes.

For the citizen, this translates into an ever greater gap between being passively affected and actively participating. An increasing number of measures decided at a supranational level affect the lives of more and more citizens to an ever greater extent. Given that the role of citizen has hitherto been effectively institutionalized only at the level of the nation-state, however, citizens have no promising opportunities to bring up issues and influence European decisions. M. R. Lepsius tersely states, "There is no European public opinion."[15] Does this disparity represent merely a passing imbalance that can be set right by the parliamentarization of the Brussels expertocracy? Or do these bureaucracies, oriented as they are by economic criteria of rationality, merely highlight developments already long under way and inexorably advancing even within nation-states? I allude here to the fact that economic imperatives have become independent of everything else and that politics has been absorbed into the state (*Verstaatlichung*). These developments undermine the status of citizen and contradict the republican claim associated with this status.

Taking England as his example, T. H. Marshall has studied the expansion of citizen rights and duties in connection with capitalist modernization.[16] Marshall's division of such rights into "civil," "political," and "social rights" follows a well-known legal classification. Here, liberal negative rights protect the private legal subject against illegal government infringements of freedom and property; rights of political participation enable the active citizen to take part in democratic processes of opinion- and will-formation; social rights grant clients of the welfare state a minimum income and social security. Marshall advances the thesis that the status of the citizen in modern societies has been expanded and consolidated in a succession of steps. On his analysis, negative liberty rights were first supplemented by democratic rights, and then these two classical types of rights were followed by social rights. Through this process, ever greater sections of the population have acquired their full rights of membership step by step.

Even leaving the historical details aside, this suggestion of a more or less linear development only holds for what sociologists designate by the general term "inclusion." In a society increasingly differentiated along functional lines, an ever greater number of persons acquire an ever larger number of rights of access to, and participation in, an ever greater number of subsystems. Such subsystems include markets, factories, and places of work; government offices, courts, and the military; schools, hospitals, theaters, and museums; political associations and public communications media; political parties, self-governing institutions, and parliaments. For the individual, the number of memberships therewith multiplies, and the range of options expands. However, this image of linear progress emerges from a description that remains neutral toward increases or losses in autonomy. This description is blind to the actual use made of an active citizenship status that allows individuals to play a role in democratically changing their own status. Indeed, only rights of political participation ground the citizen's reflexive, self-referential legal standing. Negative liberties and social rights can, by contrast, be conferred by a paternalistic authority. In principle, the constitutional state and the welfare state are possible without democracy. Even in countries in which all three categories of rights are institutionalized, as in the "democratic and social federal state" defined by the Basic Law, article 20, these negative and social rights are still Janus-faced.

Historically speaking, liberal rights crystallized around the social position of the private-property owner. From a *functionalist* viewpoint, one can conceive them as institutionalizing a market economy, whereas, from a *normative* viewpoint, they guarantee individual freedoms. Social rights signify, from a *functionalist* viewpoint, the installation of welfare bureaucracies, whereas, from a *normative* viewpoint, they grant compensatory claims to a just share of social wealth. It is true that both individual freedom and welfare guarantees can also be viewed as the legal basis for the social independence that first makes it possible to put political rights into effect. But these are empirical, and not conceptually necessary, relationships. Negative liberties and social rights can just as well facilitate the privatistic retreat from a citizen's role. In that case, citizenship is reduced to a client's relationships to administrations that provide services and benefits.

The syndrome of civil privatism and the exercise of citizenship from the standpoint of client interests become all the more probable the more the economy and state—which have been institutionalized through the same rights—develop their own internal systemic logics and push the citizen into the peripheral role of mere organization member. As self-regulating systems, economy and administration tend to close themselves off from their environments and obey only their internal imperatives of money and power. They explode the model of a polity that determines itself through the shared practice of the citizens themselves. The fundamental republican idea of the self-conscious political integration of a "community" of free and equal persons is obviously too concrete and simple for modern conditions. This is true, at least, if one is still thinking of a nation; the republican idea is still more problematic if one's model is an ethnically homogeneous "community of shared destiny" held together by common traditions.

Fortunately, law is a medium that allows for a much more abstract notion of civic, or public, autonomy. Today, the public sovereignty of the people has withdrawn into legally institutionalized procedures and the informal, more or less discursive opinion- and will-formation made possible by basic rights. I am assuming here a network of different communicative forms, which, however, must be organized in such a way that one can presume they bind public administration to rational premises. In so doing, they also impose social and ecological limits on the economic system, yet without impinging on its inner logic. This provides a *model of deliberative politics*. This model no longer starts with the macrosubject of a communal whole but with anonymously intermeshing discourses. It shifts the brunt of normative expectations over to democratic procedures and the infrastructure of a political public sphere fueled by spontaneous sources. Today, the mass of the population can exercise rights of political participation only in the sense of being integrated into, and having an influence on, an informal circuit of public communication that cannot be organized as a whole but is rather carried by a liberal and egalitarian political culture. At the same time, deliberations in decision-making bodies must remain porous to the influx of issues, value orientations, contributions, and programs originating from a political public sphere unsubverted by power. Only if such an interplay were to materialize between institutionalized opinion- and will-formation and informal public communications could citizenship mean more today than the aggregation of prepolitical individual interests and the passive enjoyment of rights bestowed by a paternalistic authority.

I cannot go into this model in any further detail here.[17] Yet, when we assess the chances for a future European citizenship, we can glean some empirical clues, at least, from the history of the institutionalization of civil rights (in the broad sense) in the nation-state. Clearly, the schema that presents civil rights essentially as the product of class struggle is too narrow.[18] Other types of social movements, above all migrations and wars, have also driven the development of a full-fledged citizenship status. In addition, factors that prompted the juridification of new forms of inclusion also had an impact on the political mobilization of the population, thus contributing to the activation of already existing rights of citizenship.[19] These and similar findings permit a cautiously optimistic extrapolation of the course that European development could take, so that we are not condemned to resignation from the outset.

The European market will set in motion a greater horizontal mobility and multiply the contacts among members of different nationalities. In addition to this, immigration from Eastern Europe and the poverty-stricken regions of the Third World will heighten the multicultural diversity of society. This will no doubt give rise to social tensions. But if those tensions are dealt with productively, they can foster a political mobilization that will give additional impetus to the new endogenous social movements already emergent within nation-states—I am thinking of the peace, environmental, and women's movements. These tendencies would strengthen the relevance that public issues have for the lifeworld. At the same time, there is a growing pressure of problems that can be solved only at a coordinated European level. Under these conditions, communication complexes could develop in Europe-wide public spheres. These publics would provide a favorable context both for new parliamentary bodies of regions that are now in the process of merging and for a European Parliament furnished with greater authority.

To date, in the member states the policy of the European Community is not yet an object of a legitimating public debate. By and large, national public spheres are still culturally isolated from one another. That is, they are rooted in contexts in which political questions become significant only against the background of each nation's own history. In the future, however, a common *political* culture could differentiate itself from the various *national* cultures. A differentiation could appear between a Europe-wide *political* culture and the various *national* traditions in art and literature, historiography, philosophy, and so on, which have been branching out since early modernity. Cultural elites and the mass media would have an important role to play in this process. Unlike the American variant, a European constitutional patriotism would have to grow together from various nationally specific interpretations of the same universalist principles of law. Switzerland provides an example for how a common politicocultural self-understanding can emerge by differentiation from the cultural orientations of different nationalities.

In this context, our task is less to reassure ourselves of our common origins in the European Middle Ages than to develop a new political self-consciousness commensurate with the role of Europe in the world of the twenty-first century. Hitherto, history has granted the empires that have come and gone but *one* appearance on the world stage. This is just as true of the modern states—Portugal, Spain, England, France, and Russia—as it was for the empires of antiquity. By way of exception, Europe as a whole is now being given a *second* chance. But it will be able to make use of this opportunity not on the terms of its old-style power politics but only under the changed premises of a nonimperialist process of reaching understanding with, and learning from, other cultures.

3 Immigration and the Chauvinism of Affluence: A Debate

Hannah Arendt's diagnosis—that stateless persons, refugees, and those deprived of rights would come to symbolize this century—has proved frighteningly accurate. The "displaced persons" that the Second World War left in a devastated Europe have long since been replaced by asylum seekers and immigrants flooding into a peaceful and prosperous Europe from the South and the East. The old refugee camps can no longer accommodate the flood of new immigrants. Statisticians anticipate that in coming years twenty to thirty million immigrants will come from eastern Europe alone. This problem can be solved only by the joint action of the European states involved. In the process, a dialectic that has already taken place on a smaller scale during the process of German unification would repeat itself. The transnational movements of immigrants function as sanctions that compel western Europe to fulfill a responsibility that has fallen on it with the bankruptcy of state socialism. Either Europe must make the utmost effort to quickly improve conditions in the poorer regions of central and eastern Europe or it will be flooded by asylum seekers and immigrants.

Experts are debating the capacity of the economic system to absorb these groups of people. But the readiness to politically integrate immigrants seeking economic betterment also depends on how the indigenous populations *perceive* the social and economic problems posed by immigration. This should be the sole matter for discussion. Throughout Europe, right-wing xenophobic reactions against the "corrupting influence of foreigners" has increased. The relatively deprived classes, whether they feel endangered by social decline or have already slipped into segmented marginal groups, identify quite openly with the ideologized supremacy of their own collectivity and reject everything foreign. This is the underside of a chauvinism of affluence that is on the rise everywhere. Thus the "asylum problem" also brings to light the latent tension between citizenship and national identity.

One example is the nationalistic and anti-Polish sentiments in the new German Länder. There the newly acquired status of citizenship in the Federal Republic was coupled with the hope that the Republic's frontier of affluence would move straightaway toward the Oder and Neisse Rivers. Their newly gained citizenship also gives many of them the ethnocentric satisfaction that they will no longer be treated as second-class Germans. They forget that the rights of the citizen guarantee liberty because they contain universal human rights. Article 4 of the Revolutionary Constitution of 1793, which defined "The Status of Citizen," was already quite consistent in granting *every* adult foreigner who lived for one year in France not just the right to remain within the country but also active citizenship rights.

In the Federal Republic, as in most Western legal systems, the legal status of aliens, homeless foreigners, and stateless persons has at least become more like the status of citizens. Because the architectonic of the Basic Law is defined by the idea of human rights, *every* inhabitant enjoys the protection of the Constitution. Foreigners have the same duties, entitlements, and legal protections as do native citizens; with few exceptions, they also receive equal treatment with regard to economic status. The large number of statutes that are indifferent to membership status relativizes the real significance of its absence. The human-rights component of citizenship will be strengthened through supranational rights, and especially through European Civil Rights, which might even affect the core opportunities for exercising political influence. The Federal Constitutional Court's decision of October 31, 1990, is notable in this context. Though it declared unconstitutional the right of foreigners to vote in municipal and district elections (i.e., the local voting right of foreigners), its justification at least acknowledged the principles raised by the petitioners: "Behind this view obviously stands the notion that the idea of democracy, and especially the idea of liberty contained in it, implies that a congruence should be established between the possessors of democratic political rights and those who are permanently subject to a specific government. This is the proper starting point."[20]

These trends simply mean that the normative content of a citizenship largely dissociated from national identity does not provide arguments for restrictive or obstructionist asylum and immigration policies. However, it remains an open question whether the European Community of today, in expectation of large streams of immigrants, can and ought to pursue foreigner and immigration policies as liberal as those of the Jacobins in their day. The pertinent *discussion in moral theory*, to which I restrict myself here, turns on the concept of "special duties," those special obligations that exist only within the social boundaries of a community. The state, too, forms a concrete legal community that imposes special obligations on its members. Economic immigrants, more than asylum seekers, confront members of the European states with the problem of whether one can justify the priority of special membership-based duties over universal obligations that transcend state boundaries. I will recapitulate this recent topic of philosophical discussion in five steps.

(a) *Special obligations* are owed by specific persons to other specific persons who "are close" to them as "members," such as members of one's own family, friends and neighbors, and fellow citizens of one's political community or nation. Parents have special obligations toward their children, and vice versa; consulates in foreign countries have special obligations toward their own citizens in need of protection, and these in turn have obligations toward the institutions and laws of their own land. In this context, we think primarily of positive duties, which are indeterminate insofar as they demand acts of solidarity, care, and commitment in ways that cannot be fixed in exact terms. One cannot reasonably expect that everyone should provide help on every occasion. Special obligations, which arise from the fact that one belongs to particular communities, can be understood as socially ascribing, and substantively specifying, such naturally indeterminate duties.

Utilitarians have attempted to ground special duties in the mutual benefit that members of a polity gain from one another through their reciprocal services. Even nations and states are conceived as such "mutual-benefit societies."[21] According to this model, each member can expect that the long-term profit gained through exchange relationships with the other members is proportional to the services he himself contributes in his interactions with others. On this basis, one can justify a reciprocity of special duties and rights, which prohibits, for example, the underprivileging of guest workers. Of course, this model cannot ground any duties toward members who cannot contribute as much (e.g., the handicapped, the ill, and the elderly) or toward those in need of help (e.g., foreigners seeking asylum). The instrumental ethnocentrism of reciprocal benefit expectations would suggest an immigration policy that granted entry to foreigners only if there were reasonable prospects that they would not burden the existing balance of contributions and claims (e.g., in a social-security or national-insurance system).

(b) This counterintuitive result is a reason to abandon the utilitarian approach in favor of a model that explains special duties not in terms of the reciprocal benefits of an exchange of services among those belonging to a collectivity but in terms of the coordinating capacities of a centrally established, moral division of labor.[22] For special obligations do not vary in direct proportion to the social distance between individuals, as though the claims of those who are near to us should always have priority over those who are far. This intuition applies only within the close confines of family and neighborhood. But it is misleading insofar as all those persons beyond these intimate circles are equally close and distant. Normally, we perceive these "strangers" under the category of the "other," whether they are fellow citizens of our own nation or not. Special obligations toward "others" do not result primarily from belonging to a concrete community. They issue rather from the abstract action coordination effected by *legal* institutions. By assigning particular obligations to particular categories of persons or agents, these institutions socially and substantively specify and make binding those positive duties that otherwise remain indeterminate. On this view, special duties issue from the institutionally mediated assignment of specific responsibilities to particular addressees active in a moral division of labor. In the framework of such a legally regulated moral division of labor, the social boundaries of a legal community have only the function of regulating the distribution of responsibilities. This does not mean that our obligations in general end at these boundaries. Rather, national governments also have to see to it that citizens fulfill their positive duties toward nonmembers, such as asylum seekers. Naturally, this does not yet tell us what these duties consist in.

(c) The moral point of view obligates us to assess this problem impartially, and thus not just from the one-sided perspective of an inhabitant of an affluent region but also from the perspective of immigrants who are seeking their well-being there. In other words, they seek a free and dignified existence and not just political asylum. In John Rawls's well-known thought experiment of the original position, individuals behind a "veil of ignorance" do not know the society into which they were born or their position in that society. If one applies this moral test to our problem, then the outcome for a world society is obvious:

> Behind the "veil of ignorance," in considering possible restrictions on freedom, one adopts the perspective of the one who would be most disadvantaged by the restrictions, in this case the perspective of the alien who wants to immigrate. In the original position, then, one would insist that the right to migrate be included in the system of basic liberties for the same reasons that one would insist that the right to religious freedom be included: it might prove essential to one's plan of life.[23]

Legitimate restrictions of immigration rights could at most be justified in the light of competing considerations, for example, the need to avoid social conflicts and burdens on a scale that would seriously endanger the public order or economic reproduction of society. Criteria of ethnic descent, language, or education—or even an "attestation of belonging to the cultural community" of the land of immigration, as in the case of *Statusdeutschen* ("Germans by status")—could not justify privileges in the process of immigration and naturalization.

(d) The communitarians, by contrast, point to a fact that the above-mentioned individualistic approaches overlook. Contrary to what the model of the legally regulated moral division of labor suggests, the social boundaries of a political community do not have just a *functional* meaning. Rather, they regulate one's belonging to a historical community of shared destiny and a political form of life that is constitutive for the citizens' very identity: "Citizenship is an answer to the question, 'Who am I?' and 'What should I do?' when posed in the public sphere."[24] Membership in a political community grounds special duties, behind which stands a patriotic identification. This kind of loyalty reaches beyond the validity of institutionally prescribed legal duties: "Each member recognizes a loyalty to the community, expressed in a willingness to sacrifice personal gain to advance its interests."[25] The misgivings about an exclusively moral and legal view of the problem draw support from the communitarian concept of citizenship, which we have already encountered. Such conceptions are no longer appropriate for the conditions of complex societies, but they do highlight an *ethical* component that should not be ignored.

The modern state, too, represents a political form of life that cannot be translated without remainder into the abstract form of institutions designed according to general legal principles. This form of life comprises the *politicocultural* context in which universalistic constitutional principles must be implemented, for only a population *accustomed* to freedom can keep the institutions of freedom alive. For that reason, Michael Walzer is of the opinion that the right of immigration is limited by the right of a political community to preserve the integrity of its form of life. In his view, the right of citizens to self-determination includes the right of self-assertion for each particular form of life.[26]

(e) This argument, of course, can be read in two opposed ways. On the communitarian reading, additional normative restrictions should be imposed on liberal immigration rights. In addition to the functional restrictions that result from the conditions for the reproduction of the socioeconomic system, there are restrictions that secure the ethnic-cultural substance of the particular form of life. With this the argument takes on a *particularistic* meaning, wherein citizenship is intertwined, not with a national identity, but with historically specific cultural identities. Thus Herman R. van Gunsteren, fully in the spirit of Arendt, formulates the following condition for admission to citizenship in a democratic polity:

> The prospective citizen must be capable and willing to be a member of this particular historical community, its past and future, its forms of life and institutions within which its members think and act. In a community that values autonomy and judgment of its members, this is obviously not a requirement of pure conformity. But it is a requirement of knowledge of the language and the culture and of acknowledgement of those institutions that foster the reproduction of citizens who are capable of autonomous and responsible judgment.[27]

Nonetheless, the requisite "competence to act as a member of *this* particular polity"[28] must be understood in another sense completely, namely, a *universalistic* one, as soon as the political community itself implements universalistic constitutional principles. The identity of the political community, which also must not be violated by immigration, depends primarily on the legal principles anchored in the *political culture* and not on an *ethical-cultural* form of life as a whole. It follows that one must expect only that immigrants willingly engage in the political culture of their new home, without necessarily abandoning the cultural life specific to their country of origin. The *political acculturation* demanded of them does not extend to the whole of their socialization. Rather, by importing new forms of life, immigrants can expand or multiply the perspectives from which the shared political constitution must be interpreted: "People live in communities with bonds and bounds, but these may be of different kinds. In a liberal society, the bonds and bounds should be compatible with liberal principles. Open immigration would change the character of the community, but it would not leave the community without any character."[29]

The discussion we have traced through steps (a) through (e) finally yields the following normative conclusion: the European states should agree on a liberal immigration policy. They must not circle their wagons and use a chauvinism of affluence as cover against the onrush of immigrants and asylum seekers. Certainly the democratic right to self-determination includes the right to preserve one's own *political* culture, which forms a concrete context for rights of citizenship, but it does not include the right to self-assertion of a privileged *cultural* form of life. Within the constitutional framework of the democratic rule of law, diverse forms of life can coexist equally. These must, however, overlap in a common political culture that in turn is open to impulses from new forms of life.

Only a democratic citizenship that does not close itself off in a particularistic fashion can pave the way for a *world citizenship*, which is already taking shape today in worldwide political communications. The Vietnam War, the revolutionary changes in eastern and central Europe, as well as the Gulf War, are the first *world-political* events in the strict sense. Through the electronic mass media, these events were brought instantaneously before a ubiquitous public sphere. In the context of the French Revolution, Kant made reference to the reactions of a participating public. At that time, he identified the phenomenon of a world public sphere, which today is becoming political reality for the first time in a cosmopolitan matrix of communication. Even the superpowers cannot ignore the reality of worldwide protests. The ongoing state of nature between bellicose states that have already forfeited their sovereignty has at least begun to appear obsolescent. Even if we still have a long way to go before fully achieving it, the cosmopolitan condition is no longer merely a mirage. State citizenship and world citizenship form a continuum whose contours, at least, are already becoming visible.

Notes

Translator's Introduction

1. James S. Fishkin, *Democracy and Deliberation: New Directions for Democratic Reform* (New Haven, Conn.: Yale University Press, 1991), p. 4; see also Joshua Cohen, "Deliberation and Democratic Legitimacy," in Alan Hamlin and Philip Pettit, eds., *The Good Polity* (Oxford: Blackwell, 1989), pp. 17–34; Cass R. Sunstein, "Interest Groups in American Public Law," *Stanford Law Review* 38 (1985): 29–87; John S. Dryzek, *Discursive Democracy: Politics, Policy, and Political Science* (Cambridge: Cambridge University Press, 1990); Benjamin Barber, *Strong Democracy: Participatory Politics for a New Age* (Berkeley: University of California Press, 1984).

2. Jürgen Habermas, *Strukturwandel der Öffentlichkeit: Untersuchungen zu einer Kategorie der bürgerlichen Gesellschaft* (Darmstadt: Luchterhand, 1962); the English translation appeared only recently: *The Structural Transformation of the Public Sphere: An Inquiry into a Category of Bourgeois Society*, trans. Thomas Burger with the assistance of Frederick Lawrence (Cambridge: MIT Press, 1989).

3. *The Theory of Communicative Action*, trans. Thomas McCarthy, 2 vols. (Boston: Beacon, 1984, 1987); hereafter cited as *TCA*. The German edition first appeared in 1981. For important qualifications, see his "A Reply," in Axel Honneth and Hans Joas, eds., *Communicative Action: Essays on Jürgen Habermas's "The Theory of Communicative Action*," trans. Jeremy Gaines and Doris L. Jones (Cambridge, Mass.: MIT Press, 1991), pp. 214–64. For an introduction, see Maeve Cooke, *Language and Reason: A Study of Habermas's Pragmatics* (Cambridge: MIT Press, 1994).

4. H. L. A. Hart provides a good twentieth-century statement of the duality of law in *The Concept of Law* (Oxford: Clarendon, 1961). The well-known image of the "bad man's" view of law is from Oliver Wendell Holmes, "The Path of the Law," in Holmes, *Collected Legal Papers* (New York: P. Smith, 1952), pp. 167–202, here p. 171.

5. Immanuel Kant, *The Metaphysical Elements of Justice*, trans. John Ladd (New York: Macmillan, 1965), p. 34; also p. 35 (translation slightly altered); see also his

"On the Proverb: That May Be True in Theory, but Is of No Practical Use," in Kant, *Perpetual Peace and Other Essays*, trans. Ted Humphrey (Indianapolis: Hackett, 1983), esp. pp. 71ff. The exact relation between Kant's principle of law and his moral principle is not entirely clear; see the discussion in Kenneth Baynes, *The Normative Grounds of Social Criticism: Kant, Rawls, and Habermas* (Albany: SUNY Press, 1992), chap. 1.

6. See John Rawls, "Justice as Fairness: Political not Metaphysical," *Philosophy and Public Affairs* 14 (1985): 223–51, and his more recent *Political Liberalism* (New York: Columbia University Press, 1993); Ronald Dworkin, *Law's Empire* (Cambridge: Harvard University Press, 1986). There have been some recent attempts to revive a metaphysical approach in legal philosophy, but whether they can have the same scale and confidence as did ancient and medieval systems is a further question; cf. John Finnis, *Natural Law and Natural Rights* (New York: Oxford University Press, 1980); for a critical assessment, see Raymond A. Belliotti, *Justifying Law: The Debate over Foundations, Goals, and Methods* (Philadelphia: Temple University Press, 1992), chap. 1.

7. For Habermas's elaboration on this, see his *Postmetaphysical Thinking*, trans. William Mark Hohengarten (Cambridge: MIT Press, 1992), and *Moral Consciousness and Communicative Action*, trans. Christian Lenhardt and Shierry W. Nicholsen (Cambridge: MIT Press, 1990), esp. the first two essays and the title essay. A prime example of such interdisciplinary cooperation is the current work being done in the psychology of moral development.

8. See Jürgen Habermas, "What Is Universal Pragmatics?" in Habermas, *Communication and the Evolution of Society*, trans. Thomas McCarthy (Boston: Beacon, 1979), pp. 1–68; also *TCA* 1:273–337; and the Christian Gauss Lectures, "Vorlesungen zu einer sprachtheoretischen Grundlegung der Soziologie," in Habermas, *Vorstudien und Ergänzungen zur Theorie des kommunikatives Handelns*, 2d ed. (Frankfurt: Suhrkamp, 1986), pp. 11–126; English translation forthcoming, MIT Press.

9. For a fuller account of Habermas's concept of discourse, see Thomas McCarthy, *The Critical Theory of Jürgen Habermas* (Cambridge: MIT Press, 1978), chap. 4.

10. For the most important distinctions, see Jürgen Habermas, "On the Pragmatic, the Ethical, and the Moral Employments of Practical Reason," in his *Justification and Application: Remarks on Discourse Ethics*, trans. Ciaran P. Cronin (Cambridge: MIT Press, 1993), pp. 1–18; also in *Between Facts and Norms*, chap. 3, excursus, and chap. 4, sect. 2.

11. On Habermas's concept of lifeworld, see *TCA* 2:119–52. For the members themselves the background remains largely unthematized, but the theorist can differentiate its resources into three broad components: the stock of taken-for-granted certitudes and ideas ("culture"); the norms, loyalties, institutions, and so forth, that secure group cohesion or solidarity ("society"); and the competences and skills that members have internalized ("personality"). A viable lifeworld is reproduced, then, through the cultural transmission of ideas, through forms of social integration, and through the socialization of its members.

12. See Peter L. Berger, *The Sacred Canopy: Elements of a Sociological Theory of Religion* (Garden City, N.Y.: Anchor-Doubleday, 1969).

13. On the development of subsystems, see Habermas, *TCA* 2:153–97. For helpful summaries of Habermas's account of societal rationalization, see Jane Braaten, *Habermas's Critical Theory of Society* (Albany: SUNY Press, 1991), chap. 5, and Stephen K. White, *The Recent Work of Jürgen Habermas: Reason, Justice, and Modernity* (Cambridge: Cambridge University Press, 1988), chap. 5.

14. Habermas develops his concept of media by way of a critical appropriation of Talcott Parsons; see *TCA* 2:199–299; here esp. 256–70. For Parsons's account, see "On the Concept of Political Power," in Parsons, *Sociological Theory and Modern Society* (New York: Free Press, 1967), pp. 297–354. One should note here that Habermas does not simply accept the development of such systems of money and power uncritically, as is shown by his concern with the intrusion of systemic imperatives into the lifeworld; see *TCA* 2:332–73 on the notion of "colonization." But he is also dubious of utopias that suggest one can dispense with the contribution of systemic integration in complex societies.

15. For the complications, see Thomas McCarthy, "Complexity and Democracy: The Seducements of Systems Theory," in McCarthy, *Ideals and Illusions: On Reconstruction and Deconstruction in Contemporary Critical Theory* (Cambridge: MIT Press, 1991), pp. 152–80; see also Habermas's qualifications in "Reply," pp. 250–63.

16. See John Rawls, *A Theory of Justice* (Cambridge: Harvard University Press, 1971), and *Political Liberalism*. See also the exchange between Rawls and Habermas in *Journal of Philosophy* 92, no. 3 (March 1995): 109–80.

17. For example, see Niklas Luhmann, *The Differentiation of Society*, trans. Stephen Holmes and Charles Larmore (New York: Columbia University Press, 1982); Martin Albrow, ed., *A Sociological Theory of Law*, trans. Elizabeth King and Martin Albrow (London: Routledge, 1985); *Essays on Self-Reference* (New York: Columbia University Press, 1990); *Political Theory in the Welfare State*, trans. John Bednarz (New York: de Gruyter, 1990). For a recent overview of Luhmann's approach, see his *Ecological Communication*, trans. John Bednarz (Chicago: University of Chicago Press, 1989).

18. On the association between "modern natural law" and social-contract theory, see A. P. d'Entrèves, *Natural Law: An Historical Survey* (New York: Harper, 1965), chap. 3.

19. For a helpful introduction, see Walter Buckley, *Sociology and Modern Systems Theory* (Englewood Cliffs, N.J.: Prentice-Hall, 1967); Buckley distinguishes a "process" model as well, which avoids the static implications associated with equilibrium and homeostasis.

20. Humberto R. Maturana and others contributed the seminal ideas in the theory of self-organization or "autopoiesis"; see Milan Zeleny, ed., *Autopoiesis: A Theory of Living Organization* (New York: North Holland, 1981). For applications to law, see Gunther Teubner, ed., *Autopoietic Law: A New Approach to Law and Society* (Berlin: de Gruyter, 1988).

21. Niklas Luhmann, "Operational Closure and Structural Coupling: The Differentiation of the Legal System," *Cardozo Law Review* 13 (1992): 1419–41; here p. 1424.

22. See Luhmann, *Sociological Theory of Law*, for a fuller explication.

23. More specifically, Luhmann points out that law stabilizes behavioral expectations across three dimensions: temporally, by holding them constant across time; socially, in that all members of the group hold the same expectations; and substantively, in that the abstract meanings contained in legal norms (role definitions, situational features, etc.) hold across sufficiently similar situations; see *Sociological Theory of Law*, pp. 41–82.

24. This is the point of Luhmann's concept of "structural coupling." The difficulties that autopoiesis creates for a systems analysis of regulatory law, for example, are discussed by Gunther Teubner, in Z. Bankowski, ed., *Law as an Autopoietic System*, trans. A. Bankowska and Ruth Adler (Oxford: Blackwell, 1993), chap. 5. For Habermas's earlier critique of systems theory, see his *On the Logic of the Social Sciences*, trans. Shierry W. Nicholsen and Jerry A. Stark (Cambridge: MIT Press, 1988), chap. 5, and *Legitimation Crisis*, trans. Thomas McCarthy (Boston: Beacon, 1975), chap. 1.

25. For a summary of the central arguments of the book, see the postscript; here I also draw on his "On the Internal Relation between the Rule of Law and Democracy," *European Journal of Philosophy* 3 (1995): 12–20.

26. For a brief introduction, see John Gray, *Liberalism* (Minneapolis: University of Minnesota Press, 1986); for the classic statement of twentieth-century liberalism, see F. A. Hayek, *The Constitution of Liberty* (Chicago: University of Chicago Press, 1960); for an overview of approaches to the concept of the "rule of law," see Geoffrey de Q. Walker, *The Rule of Law: Foundation of Constitutional Democracy* (Carlton: Melbourne University Press, 1988), chap. 1; for an influential formulation of the liberal view of the rule of law, see F. A. Hayek, *The Road to Serfdom* (Chicago: University of Chicago Press, 1944), chap. 6; see also Joseph Raz, "The Rule of Law and Its Virtue," in Raz, *The Authority of Law* (Oxford: Clarendon, 1979), pp. 210–29.

27. See, for example, Frank I. Michelman, "The Supreme Court 1985 Term, Foreword: Traces of Self-Government," *Harvard Law Review* 100 (1986): 4–77; also his "Political Truth and the Rule of Law," *Tel Aviv University Studies in Law* 8 (1988): 281–91; and Sunstein, "Interest Groups."

28. *Between Facts and Norms*, p. 107; Habermas's interpretation of (D) corrects his earlier view, which identified (D) simply as a principle of morality; see his "Discourse Ethics: Notes on a Program of Philosophical Justification," in *Moral Consciousness*, pp. 43–115, esp. pp. 66, 93.

29. *Between Facts and Norms*, p. 169.

30. See Roscoe Pound, "The Need of a Sociological Jurisprudence," *The Green Bag* 19 (1907): 607–15, and his "Mechanical Jurisprudence," *Columbia Law Review* 8 (1908): 605–10. Subsequent to Pound and prior to Hart, this issue

received considerable attention in the Legal Realist movement; for a historical overview, see William Twining, *Karl Llewellyn and the Realist Movement* (London: Weidenfeld and Nicolson, 1973). Since Hart, it has been the focus of debates involving the Critical Legal Studies movement; see Andrew Altman, *Critical Legal Studies: A Liberal Critique* (Princeton: Princeton University Press, 1990).

31. See the references to Michelman in note 27 above and his "Law's Republic," *Yale Law Journal* 97 (1988): 1493–1537; Cass Sunstein, "Interest Groups" and *After the Rights Revolution* (Cambridge: Harvard University Press, 1990); John Hart Ely, *Democracy and Distrust: A Theory of Judicial Review* (Cambridge: Harvard University Press, 1980); and Bruce Ackerman, *We the People*, vol. 1 (Cambridge: Harvard University Press, 1991).

32. In the American jurisprudential tradition, one finds a parallel to the European development of "materialized law" in the call for "sociological jurisprudence"; see note 30 above. The classic liberal argument against the welfare state is Hayek's *Road to Serfdom*; for a response, see Harry W. Jones, "The Rule of Law and the Welfare State," in *Essays on Jurisprudence from the Columbia Law Review* (New York: Columbia University Press, 1963), pp. 400–413.

33. His earlier critique relied more heavily on the lifeworld as the source of resistance against bureaucratic intrusion or "colonization"; see *TCA*, vol. 2, chap. 8; cf. Dryzek, *Discursive Democracy*, p. 20; also Amy Bartholomew, "Democratic Citizenship, Social Rights and the 'Reflexive Continuation' of the Welfare State," *Studies in Political Economy* 42 (1993): 141–56.

34. Habermas's lengthy reply to the participants in a symposium on the book provides still further elaboration of his central arguments and assumptions; see the *Cardozo Law Review* 17/2–3 (fall 1995). For further succinct overviews of the book, see David M. Rasmussen, "How Is Valid Law Possible?" *Philosophy and Social Criticism* 20 (1994): 21–44; Kenneth Baynes, "Democracy and the *Rechtsstaat*: Remarks on Habermas's *Faktizität und Geltung*," in Stephen White, ed., *The Cambridge Companion to Habermas* (New York: Cambridge University Press, 1995), pp. 201–32; and James Bohman, "Complexity, Pluralism, and the Constitutional State: On Habermas's *Faktizität und Geltung*," *Law and Society Review* 28 (1994): 897–930.

35. For a comparative overview, see Konrad Zweigert and Hein Kötz, *Introduction to Comparative Law*, 2d ed., trans. Tony Weir (Oxford: Clarendon, 1987), vol. 1, chaps. 11–12, 16–21; for a concise introduction to the civil-law tradition in general, see John Henry Merryman, *The Civil Law Tradition: An Introduction to the Legal Systems of Western Europe and Latin America*, 2d ed. (Stanford: Stanford University Press, 1985); also helpful are Norbert Horn, Hein Kötz, and Hans G. Leser, *German Private and Commercial Law: An Introduction*, trans. Tony Weir (Oxford: Clarendon, 1982), and B. S. Markesinis, *A Comparative Introduction to the German Law of Torts*, 2d ed. (Oxford: Clarendon, 1990). On German constitutional law, see Donald P. Kommers, *The Constitutional Jurisprudence of the Federal Republic of Germany* (Durham, N.C.: Duke University Press, 1989), and David P.

Currie, *The Constitution of the Federal Republic of Germany* (Chicago: University of Chicago Press, 1994).

36. "Objective law is the rule to which the individual must make his conduct conform; subjective right is the power of the individual that is derived from the norm." Merryman, *Civil Law Tradition*, p. 70, quoting from an unidentified civil-law textbook.

37. T. H. Marshall, "Citizenship and Social Class," in Marshall, *Class, Citizenship, and Social Development* (Garden City, N.Y.: Doubleday, 1964), p. 71.

Preface

1. W. Hassemer, "Rechtsphilosophie, Rechtswissenschaft, Rechtspolitik—am Beispiel des Strafrechts," in R. Alexy et al., eds., *Rechts- und Sozialphilosophie in Deutschland Heute, Archiv für Rechts- und Sozialphilosophie*, Beiheft 44 (1991): 130–43.

2. The contribution that discourse theory could make on this issue is sketched by K. Günther, "Möglichkeiten einer diskursethischen Begründung des Strafrechts," in H. Jung et al., eds., *Recht und Moral* (Baden-Baden, 1991), pp. 205–17.

3. J. Habermas, *Moral Consciousness and Communicative Action*, trans. C. Lenhardt and S. W. Nicholsen (Cambridge, Mass., 1990); *Justification and Application: Remarks on Discourse Ethics*, trans. C. P. Cronin (Cambridge, Mass., 1993).

4. "Law and Morality," trans. K. Baynes, in S. M. McMurrin, ed., *The Tanner Lectures on Human Values*, vol. 8 (Salt Lake City, 1988), pp. 217–79. In my opinion, Karl-Otto Apel also overextends the normative approach in his "Diskursethik vor der Problematik von Recht und Politik," in K.-O. Apel and M. Kettner, eds., *Zur Anwendung der Diskursethik in Politik, Recht und Wissenschaft* (Frankfurt am Main, 1992), pp. 29–61.

5. Rudiger Bubner continues to raise the "blindness" objection; most recently, see his "Das sprachliche Medium der Politik," in Bubner, *Antike Themen und ihre moderne Verwandlung* (Frankfurt am Main, 1992), pp. 188–202, here pp. 196ff. For the anarchism charge, see O. Höffe, *Politische Gerechtigkeit* (Frankfurt am Main, 1987), pp. 193ff.

6. See N. Luhmann, *Beobachtungen der Moderne* (Cologne, 1992), for a scientistic view; for an aesthetic view, see J. Derrida, "Force of Law: The 'Mystical Foundation of Authority'," trans. M. Quaintance, *Cardozo Law Review* 11 (1990): 919–1045.

7. These lectures on "Natural Law and Revolution" were held in October 1962; the English translation appears in J. Habermas, *Theory and Practice*, trans. J. Viertel (Boston, 1973), pp. 82–120, here p. 113 [trans. altered. Trans.].

8. K. Günther, *The Sense of Appropriateness*, trans. J. Farrell (Albany, 1993); B. Peters, *Rationalität, Recht und Gesellschaft* (Frankfurt am Main, 1991); I. Maus, *Aufklärung der Demokratietheorie* (Frankfurt am Main, 1992); B. Peters, *Die Integra-*

tion moderner Gesellschaften (Frankfurt am Main, 1993); L. Wingert, *Gemeinsinn und Moral* (Frankfurt am Main, 1993); R. Forst, *Kontexte der Gerechtigkeit* (Frankfurt am Main, 1994).

Chapter 1

1. J. Habermas, "Reconstruction and Interpretation in the Social Sciences," in Habermas, *Moral Consciousness and Communicative Action*, trans. C. Lenhardt and S. W. Nicholsen (Cambridge, Mass., 1990), pp. 21–42.

2. J. Habermas, *Justification and Application*, trans. C. P. Cronin (Cambridge, Mass., 1993).

3. N. Luhmann, "Intersubjectivität oder Kommunikation: Unterschiedliche Ausgangspunkte soziologischer Theoriebildung," *Archivo di Filosofia* 54 (1986): 51 n28.

4. B. Peters, *Rationalität, Recht und Gesellschaft* (Frankfurt am Main, 1991), pp. 33ff.

5. See chap. 3, sect. 2, in this volume.

6. In a similar fashion, Edmund Husserl took into account the fundamental role of validity claims in the constitution of the lifeworld; see J. Habermas, "Vorlesungen zu einer sprachtheoretischen Grundlegung der Soziologie," in Habermas, *Vorstudien und Ergänzungen zur Theorie des kommunikativen Handelns* (Frankfurt am Main, 1984), esp. pp. 35ff. (English translation forthcoming, Cambridge, Mass.).

7. G. Frege, *Logical Investigations*, ed. P. T. Geach, trans. P. T. Geach and R. H. Stoothoff (New Haven, Conn., 1977), p. 24. [I have changed the translation of *Vorstellungen* from "ideas" to "representations." Trans.]

8. Cf. E. Tugendhat, *Traditional and Analytical Philosophy*, trans. P. A. Gorner (Cambridge, 1982), pp. 21–34.

9. Frege, *Logical Investigations*, p. 28.

10. J. Habermas, "Peirce and Communication," in Habermas, *Postmetaphysical Thinking*, trans. W. M. Hohengarten (Cambridge, Mass., 1992), pp. 88–112.

11. C. S. Peirce, *Collected Papers*, 6 vols., ed. C. Hartshorne and P. Weiss (Cambridge, Mass., 1931–35), 5:311; cf. also K.-O. Apel, *Charles S. Peirce*, trans. J. M. Krois (Amherst, Mass., 1981); J. E. McCarthy, "Semiotic Idealism," *Transactions of the Charles S. Peirce Society* 20 (1984): 395ff.

12. J. Habermas, "Toward a Critique of the Theory of Meaning," in Habermas, *Postmetaphysical Thinking*, pp. 57–87; cf. also A. Wellmer, "Konsens als Telos sprachlicher Kommunikation," in H. J. Giegel, ed., *Kommunikation und Konsens in moderner Gesellschaften* (Frankfurt am Main, 1992), pp. 18–30.

13. J. Habermas, *The Theory of Communicative Action*, 2 vols., trans. T. McCarthy (Boston, 1984, 1987), 2:119–52 (hereafter *TCA*); see also my "Actions, Speech Acts, Linguistically Mediated Interactions and the Lifeworld," in G. Fløistad, ed., *Philosophical Problems Today*, vol. 1 (Boston, 1994), pp. 45–74.

14. J. Habermas, "Edmund Husserl über Lebenswelt, Philosophie und Wissenschaft," in Habermas, *Texte und Kontexte* (Frankfurt am Main, 1991), pp. 34–43.

15. A. Gehlen, *Man, His Nature and Place in the World*, trans. C. McMillan and K. Pillemer (New York, 1988); also his *Urmensch und Spätkultur* (Bonn, 1956).

16. Habermas, *TCA*, 2:49ff.

17. W. Benjamin, "Der Sürrealismus," in Benjamin, *Gesammelte Schriften II*, ed. R. Tiedemann and H. Schweppenhäuser (Frankfurt am Main, 1977), 3:295ff.

18. The basic concept of communicative action explains how social integration can come about through the binding forces of an intersubjectively shared language. The latter imposes pragmatic constraints on subjects who want to use the binding energies of language and compels them to step out of an egocentric orientation to their own success so as to open themselves to the public criteria of the rationality of mutual understanding. From this viewpoint, society presents itself as a symbolically structured lifeworld that reproduces itself through communicative action. Naturally, it does not follow from this that strategic interactions could not emerge *in* the lifeworld. But such interactions now have a different significance than they do in Hobbes or in game theory: they are no longer conceived as the mechanism for *generating* an instrumental order. Rather, strategic interactions find their place in a lifeworld that has already been constituted elsewhere, as it were. Those who act strategically no doubt also have a lifeworld background always behind them; but this background is neutralized in its action-coordinating force. It no longer provides a shared consensus in advance, because strategic actors encounter normative contexts, as well as other participants, only as social facts. In the objectivating attitude of an observer, they can no longer reach an understanding with others *as* second persons.

19. The usual objections against the theory of communicative action fail to appreciate this theoretical assumption of permanent dissension in modern societies; see H. J. Giegel, introduction to Giegel, *Kommunikation*, pp. 7–17.

20. I. Kant, *The Metaphysical Elements of Justice*, pt. 1 of *The Metaphysics of Morals*, trans. J. Ladd (New York, 1965), p. 36.

21. Kant, *Elements of Justice*, p. 34 [translation slightly altered. Trans.].

22. Kant, *Elements of Justice*, p. 19 [translation slightly altered. Trans.].

23. I. Kant, *The Metaphysical Principles of Virtue*, in Kant, *Ethical Philosophy*, trans. J. W. Ellington (Indianapolis, 1983), p. 38.

24. R. Dreier, "Recht und Moral," in Dreier, *Recht-Moral-Ideologie* (Frankfurt am Main, 1981), pp. 180ff, here 194ff.

25. Dreier, "Recht und Moral," p. 198. Dreier uses the expression "ethical" in a way that corresponds to my use of "moral."

26. In what follows, I draw on suggestive discussions with Lutz Wingert.

27. H. Putnam, *Reason, Truth and History* (Cambridge, 1981).

28. R. Rorty, *Objectivity, Relativism, and Truth* (Cambridge, 1991); for a critical response to Rorty, see H. Putnam, "Why Reason Can't Be Naturalized," *Synthese* 52 (1982): 1–23.

Chapter 2

1. For an overview of forms of legal criticism, see B. Peters, *Rationalität, Recht und Gesellschaft* (Frankfurt am Main, 1991), pp. 136–66.

2. A. Ferguson, *An Essay on the History of Civil Society* (Edinburgh, 1767); J. Millar, *The Origin of the Distinction of Ranks*, 3d ed. (London, 1779).

3. C. B. Macpherson, *The Political Theory of Possessive Individualism* (Oxford, 1962); W. Euchner, *Naturrecht und Politik bei John Locke* (Frankfurt am Main, 1979).

4. I. Fetscher and H. Münkler, eds., *Pipers Handbuch politischer Ideen*, vol. 3 (Munich, 1985), chap. 7, pp. 353ff.

5. K. Löwith, *Meaning in History* (Chicago, 1970).

6. S. Benhabib, *Critique, Norm and Utopia* (New York, 1986).

7. W. Lepenies, *Melancholie und Gesellschaft* (Frankfurt am Main, 1969).

8. N. Luhmann, *Ausdifferenzierung des Rechts* (Frankfurt am Main, 1981); also his *Legitimation durch Verfahren* (Neuwied, 1969).

9. G. Teubner, *Recht als autopoietisches System* (Frankfurt am Main, 1989), p. 46; for the English, see Teubner, *Law as an Autopoietic System*, trans. A. Bankowska and R. Adler, ed. Z. Bankowski (Oxford, 1993), p. 33 [hereafter *Law;* in what follows I cite both German and English editions, because the English translation has been shortened; in addition, I occasionally alter the original translation. Trans.].

10. N. Luhmann, "Normen in soziologischer Perspektive," *Soziale Welt* 20 (1969): 35.

11. N. Luhmann, *Die soziologische Beobachtung des Rechts* (Frankfurt am Main, 1986), p. 33.

12. N. Luhmann, "Juristische Argumentation," ms. 1991, p. 1. The answer that Luhmann offers is not very convincing. It goes something like this: If "information" renders the unknown known and if "redundancies" repeat what is already known, then communication can be generally understood as the routine conversion of information into redundancies. Argumentation achieves the same thing at a reflexive level. It uses reasons to secure a sufficient measure of redundancy with the help of available redundancies and thus counteracts the pressure of variation from incoming information. Correspondingly, legal argumentation deals with the need for justification arising from the pressure of variation created by new cases; in this it aims to secure the consistency of decisions over time. It thus erects a doctrinal (*dogmatische*) barrier against the cognitive adaptability of an adjudication that weighs interests in light of anticipated consequences. This proposal is implausible, however, because a doctrinal conservation of existing

law could be had with fewer risks than by restricting argumentation. Reasons have not only a redundancy function, but are double-edged from the start: they not only secure the coherence of a body of knowledge but are innovative as well, in that they interpret new things in a new way and may change the context of knowledge. For this reason, precedent-setting decisions also require a more considerable expenditure of argument than do routine decisions. One might also note here that a systems-theoretic approach cannot at all explain the intrinsic function of justification, namely, to avoid or correct mistakes, because it does not allow the analytical distinction between actual and correct legal decisions.

13. R. Mayntz, "Steuerung, Steuerungsakteure, Steuerungsinstrumente," *HiMon-DB* 70 (Gesamthochschule Siegen, 1986); cf. R. Mayntz, ed., *Implementation politischer Programme II* (Opladen, 1983).

14. R. Münch, "Die sprachlose Systemtheorie," *Zeitschrift für Rechtstheorie* 6 (1985):4–35; N. Luhmann, "Some Problems with Reflexive Law," in A. Febbrajo and G. Teubner, eds., *State, Law, Economy as Autopoietic Systems* (Milan, 1992), pp. 389–416; cf. also G. Teubner, ed., *Autopoietic Law* (Berlin, 1988).

15. G. Teubner, "Die Episteme des Rechts," in D. Grimm, ed., *Wachsende Staatsaufgaben—sinkende Steuerungsfähigkeit des Rechts* (Baden-Baden, 1990), p. 126; for the English, see Teubner, "How the Law Thinks: Toward a Constructivist Epistemology of Law," *Law and Society Review* 23 (1989): 727–57, here 738.

16. Teubner, *Recht als autopoietisches System*, pp. 109f. [this passage is not present in the English translation. Trans.].

17. Teubner, *Recht als autopoietisches System*, p. 107; *Law*, p. 86.

18. Teubner, *Recht als autopoietisches System*, p. 108; *Law*, p. 87.

19. Teubner, "Episteme," p. 27 (emphasis added); "How the Law Thinks," p. 745.

20. Teubner, *Recht als autopoietisches System*, p. 109; *Law*, p. 88.

21. See J. Habermas, "Actions, Speech Acts, Linguistically Mediated Interactions and the Lifeworld," in G. Fløistad, ed., *Philosophical Problems Today*, vol. 1 (Boston, 1994), pp. 45–74.

22. From the perspective of systems theory, society-wide circulation is a symptom of the rather archaic status of a morality that has been surpassed by functional systems; see N. Luhmann, "Ethik als Reflexionstheorie der Moral," in Luhmann, *Gesellschaftsstruktur und Semantik*, vol. 3 (Frankfurt am Main, 1990), pp. 358–448.

23. A. E. Buchanan, *Marx and Justice* (London, 1982); P. Koslowski, *Gesellschaft und Staat* (Stuttgart, 1982), chap. 6, pp. 242–92.

24. On the following, see K. Baynes, *The Normative Grounds of Social Criticism: Kant, Rawls, Habermas* (Albany, N.Y., 1992).

25. J. Rawls, *A Theory of Justice* (Cambridge, Mass., 1971). We do not need to go into the details here. See my analyses in *Justification and Application*, trans. C. P. Cronin (Cambridge, Mass., 1993), pp. 25–30 and 92–96.

26. J. Rawls, "Kantian Constructivism in Moral Theory," *Journal of Philosophy* 77 (1980): 518.

27. J. Rawls, "The Domain of the Political and Overlapping Consensus," *New York University Law Review* 64 (1989): 234.

28. Rawls also includes this among the "burdens of reason." The articles Rawls wrote between 1978 and 1983 have recently been brought together in revised form in his *Political Liberalism* (New York: Columbia University Press, 1993); for his treatment of what he now calls the "burdens of judgment," see pp. 54–58.

29. J. Rawls, "Justice as Fairness: Political not Metaphysical," *Philosophy and Public Affairs* 14 (1985): 231.

30. R. Rorty, "The Priority of Democracy to Philosophy," in Rorty, *Objectivity, Relativism, and Truth* (Cambridge, 1991), pp. 175–96; here p. 189; see also R. Bernstein, "One Step Forward, Two Steps Backward: Richard Rorty on Liberal Democracy and Philosophy," and R. Rorty, "Thugs and Theorists: A Reply to Bernstein," in *Political Theory* 15 (1987): 538–63 and 564–80, resp.

31. Rorty, "Priority," p. 180.

32. Cf. Karl-Otto Apel's critique of Rorty's position, "Zurück zur Normalität? Oder könnten wir aus der nationalen Katastrophe etwas Besonderes gelernt haben?" in Apel, *Diskurs und Verantwortung* (Frankfurt am Main, 1988), pp. 412ff.

33. R. Dworkin, "Foundations of Liberal Equality," in G. B. Peterson, ed., *The Tanner Lectures on Human Values*, vol. 11 (Salt Lake City, 1990), pp. 2f. With regard to Rawls's postmetaphysical concept of justice, he adds, "A political conception of justice, constructed to be independent of and neutral among different ethical positions people in the community hold, is perhaps more likely to prove acceptable to everyone in the community than any conception that is not neutral in this way. If we were statesmen intent on securing the widest possible agreement for some political theory, which could then serve as the basis of a truly and widely consensual government, we might well champion a political conception for that reason. . . . But we need more from a theory of justice than consensual promise; we need categorical force. Liberals insist that political decisions be made on liberal principles now, even before liberal principles come to be embraced by everyone, if they ever will be." Ibid., p. 17. Cf. also R. Dworkin, "Liberal Community," *California Law Review* 77 (1989): 479–589, here 561ff.

34. See J. Habermas, "On the Pragmatic, the Ethical, and the Moral Employments of Practical Reason," in Habermas, *Justification and Application*, pp. 1–17.

35. Cf. Peters, *Rationalität, Recht und Gesellschaft*, pp. 35ff.

36. M. Weber, *Economy and Society*, 2 vols., ed. G. Roth and C. Wittich (Berkeley, 1978), 1:31. [I occasionally alter the translations from this text. Trans.]

37. M. Weber, "Über einige Kategorien der verstehenden Soziologie," in Weber, *Methodologische Schriften* (Frankfurt am Main, 1968), pp. 196f.; the translation of this particular passage is from appendix 1 to Weber, *Economy and Society*, 2:1378; for the full article in translation, see M. Weber, "Some Categories of Interpretive Sociology," trans. E. Garber, *Sociological Quarterly* 22 (1981): 151–80; here p. 168.

38. Weber, *Economy and Society*, 1:31.

39. Weber, *Economy and Society*, 1:31.

40. Weber, *Economy and Society*, 1:34.

41. Weber, "Some Categories," p. 158. [Translation altered. Trans.]

42. Weber, *Economy and Society*, 1:311.

43. K. Eder, *Die Entstehung staatlich organisierter Gesellschaften* (Frankfurt am Main, 1976); also his *Geschichte als Lernprozeß?* (Frankfurt am Main, 1985).

44. L. Kohlberg, *Essays on Moral Development* (San Francisco, 1981).

45. W. Schluchter, *The Rise of Western Rationalism: Max Weber's Developmental History*, trans. G. Roth (Berkeley, 1981), p. 100 [translation slightly altered. Trans.]. Cf. also Schluchter's "Beiträge zur Werttheorie," in Schluchter, *Religion und Lebensführung* (Frankfurt am Main, 1988), vol. 1, pp. 165ff. Regarding Schluchter's critique of discourse ethics, see the remarks in Habermas, *Justification and Application*, pp. 163ff. (from "Morality, Society, and Ethics").

46. N. Luhmann, *A Sociological Theory of Law*, trans. E. King and M. Albrow, ed. M. Albrow (London, 1985), p. 161.

47. Weber, *Economy and Society*, 1:36.

48. J. Habermas, *The Theory of Communicative Action*, trans. T. McCarthy, 2 vols. (Boston, 1984, 1987), 1:262ff.

49. Cf. U. Wesel, *Frühformen des Rechts in vorstaatlichen Gesellschaften* (Frankfurt am Main, 1985).

50. T. Parsons, *The System of Modern Societies* (Englewood-Cliffs, N.J., 1971).

51. Parsons, *System of Modern Societies*, pp. 118f.

52. Parsons, *System of Modern Societies*, p. 97. This connection was already important for Durkheim, inasmuch as he conceived democracy as the "system based on reflection," i.e., a form of government characterized by the fact that "there is a constant flow of communication between [citizens] and the state." E. Durkheim, *Professional Ethics and Civic Morals*, trans. C. Brookfield (London, 1957), p. 91. The maturity of a democracy is measured by the level of this public communication: "Seen from this point, a democracy may, then, appear as the political system by which the society can achieve a consciousness of itself in its purest form. The more that deliberation and reflection and a critical spirit play a considerable part in the course of public affairs, the more democratic the nation. It is the less democratic when lack of consciousness, uncharted customs, the obscure sentiments and prejudices that evade investigation, predominate." Ibid., p. 89.

53. T. H. Marshall, "Citizenship and Social Class," in Marshall, *Class, Citizenship and Social Development* (Westport, Conn., 1973), pp. 65ff.

54. A. Giddens, *Profiles and Critiques in Social Theory* (London, 1982), p. 171.

55. B. S. Turner, *Citizenship and Capitalism* (London, 1986).

56. J. M. Barbalet, *Citizenship* (Stratford, Engl., 1988).

57. D. Held, "Citizenship and Autonomy," in Held, *Political Theory and the Modern State* (Oxford, 1989), pp. 214–42.

58. F. Ewald, *L'Etat Providence* (Paris, 1986).

59. The same objection can be leveled against Richard Münch's theory, which, following Parsons, works with a normatively loaded concept of the interpenetration of subsystems; see R. Münch, *Theorie des Handelns* (Frankfurt am Main, 1982); also his *Die Kultur der Moderne*, 2 vols. (Frankfurt am Main, 1986).

60. See Habermas, "Actions, Speech Acts, Linguistically Mediated Interactions."

Chapter 3

1. [The translation is that of Thomas Paine, in his *Rights of Man*. Trans.]

2. J. Rawls, *A Theory of Justice* (Cambridge, Mass., 1971), p. 60. In response to a criticism of H. L. A. Hart, "Rawls on Liberty and Its Priority," in N. Daniels, ed., *Reading Rawls* (Oxford, 1975), pp. 230–52, Rawls replaced this formulation with another one that, at least to me, does not seem to be an improvement: "Each person has an equal right to a fully adequate scheme of equal basic liberties which is compatible with a similar scheme of liberties for all." J. Rawls, "The Basic Liberties and Their Priority," in S. McMurrin, ed., *The Tanner Lectures on Human Values*, vol. 3 (Salt Lake City, 1982), p. 5.

3. E.-W. Böckenförde, "Das Bild vom Menschen in der Perspektive der heutigen Rechtsordnung," in Böckenförde, *Recht, Staat, Freiheit* (Frankfurt am Main, 1991), pp. 58–66.

4. F. C. von Savigny, *System des heutigen Römischen Rechts*, vol. 1 (Berlin, 1840), sec. 4. [For an English translation of this book, see Savigny, *System of the Modern Roman Law*, vol. 1, trans. W. Holloway (Madras, 1867). Trans.]

5. Savigny, *System*, sec. 53.

6. G. F. Puchta, *Cursus der Institutionen* (Leipzig, 1865), sec. 4.

7. B. Windscheid, *Lehrbuch des Pandektenrechts* (Frankfurt am Main, 1906), vol. 2, sec. 37. Here one might also note the affirmative reference to Ferdinand Regelsberger's definition: "We have to do with a subjective right if the legal order cedes the realization of a recognized purpose, i.e., the satisfaction of a recognized interest, to the participant and grants him legal power for this end."

8. R. von Ihering, *Geist des römischen Rechts* (Leipzig, 1888), pt. 3, p. 338.

9. L. Enneccerus, *Allgemeiner Teil des Bürgerlichen Rechts*, 15th ed. (Tübingen, 1959), sec. 72.

10. H. Kelsen, *Allgemeine Staatslehre* (Bad Homburg, 1968), p. 64.

11. J. Schmidt, "Zur Funktion der subjektiven Rechte," *Archiv für Rechts- und Sozialphilosophie* 57 (1971): 383–96.

12. B. Rüthers, *Die unbegrenzte Auslegung* (Frankfurt am Main, 1973).

13. [Associated with the so-called "Ordo Circle," this German version of liberal economic and legal thought got started before World War II and considerably

influenced postwar policies in Germany. Trans.]

14. H. Coing, "Zur Geschichte des Begriffs 'subjektives Recht'," in Coing et al., *Das subjektive Recht und der Rechtsschutz der Persönlichkeit* (Frankfurt am Main, 1959), pp. 7–23, here pp. 22–23.

15. L. Raiser, "Der Stand der Lehre vom subjektiven Recht im Deutschen Zivilrecht (1961)," in Raiser, *Die Aufgabe des Privatrechts* (Frankfurt am Main, 1977), pp. 98ff., here p. 115.

16. Raiser, "Stand der Lehre," p. 113.

17. See chapter 9 in this volume, sec. 9.1.2.

18. F. Michelman, "Justification (and Justifiability) of Law in a Contradictory World," in J. R. Pennock and J. W. Chapman, eds., *Justification*, Nomos vol. 18 (New York, 1986), pp. 71–99, here p. 91.

19. T. Hobbes, *De Cive*, chap. 13, par. 6 (trans. attributed to Hobbes, in *Man and Citizen*, ed. B. Gert [Indianapolis, 1991]); cf. J. Habermas, "The Classical Doctrine of Politics in Relation to Social Philosophy," in Habermas, *Theory and Practice*, trans. J. Viertel (Boston, 1973), pp. 41–81.

20. Hobbes, *De Cive*, chap. 13, par. 3.

21. "Whatsoever you require that others should do to you, that do ye to them." Hobbes, *Leviathan*, ed. R. Tuck (Cambridge, 1991), p. 92; cf. also pp. 117, 188.

22. Otfried Höffe likewise pursues mutatis mutandis this Hobbesian goal of demonstration. For him justice consists in limitations of freedom that are universally distributed and hence equally advantageous for all sides: "Because it is advantageous for all, natural justice has no need of moral conscience, nor of personal justice, for its implementation. It can be satisfied with self-interest as a motivating principle." O. Höffe, *Politische Gerechtigkeit* (Frankfurt am Main, 1987), p. 407. This approach is even more clearly elaborated in Höffe's *Kategorische Rechtsprinzipien* (Frankfurt am Main, 1990); Höffe, *Gerechtigkeit als Tausch?* (Baden-Baden, 1991). For a critique, see K. Günther, "Kann ein Volk von Teufeln Recht und Staat moralisch legitimieren?" *Rechtshistorisches Journal* 10 (1991): 233–67.

23. I. Kant, "On the Proverb: That May Be True in Theory, But Is of No Practical Use," in Kant, *Perpetual Peace and Other Essays*, trans. T. Humphrey (Indianapolis, 1983), p. 71.

24. Kant, "On the Proverb," p. 72 [translation slightly altered. Trans.].

25. Kant, "On the Proverb," p. 72.

26. Kant, "On the Proverb," p. 72.

27. Kant, "On the Proverb," pp. 75–76 [trans. slightly altered. Trans.].

28. Ernst Tugendhat has reconstructed this, using linguistic analysis; see his *Self-Consciousness and Self-Determination*, trans. P. Stern (Cambridge, Mass., 1986).

29. J. Habermas, "Historical Consciousness and Post-Traditional Identity: The Federal Republic's Orientation to the West," in Habermas, *The New Conservatism*,

ed. and trans. S. W. Nicholsen (Cambridge, Mass., 1989), pp. 249–67.

30. F. Michelman, "Law's Republic," *Yale Law Journal* 97 (1988): 1499f.: "I take American constitutionalism—as manifest in academic constitutional theory, in the professional practice of lawyers and judges, and in the ordinary political self-understanding of Americans at large—to rest on two premises regarding political freedom: first, that the American people are politically free insomuch as they are governed by themselves collectively, and, second, that the American people are politically free insomuch as they are governed by laws and not by men. I take it that no earnest, non-disruptive participant in American constitutional debate is quite free to reject either of those two professions of belief. I take them to be premises whose problematic relation to each other, and therefore whose meanings, are subject to an endless contestation."

31. See I. Kant, *The Metaphysical Elements of Justice*, trans. J. Ladd (New York, 1965), pp. 35, 44–45.

32. Kant, "On the Proverb," p. 82 [translation slightly altered. Trans.].

33. J.-J. Rousseau, *Of the Social Contract or Principles of Political Right*, trans. C. M. Sherover (New York, 1984), p. 55 (bk. 3, pt. 1, par. 159).

34. [According to Habermas, "substantive legal equality," or *Rechtsinhaltsgleichheit*, has two components: (a) legal statutes are applied so as to treat like cases alike and different cases differently; and (b) legal statutes regulate matters in a way that is in the equal interest of each person. Trans.]

35. Kant, *Elements of Justice*, pp. 10ff.

36. J. Royce, *The Spirit of Modern Philosophy* (Boston, 1892).

37. J. Habermas, "On the Pragmatic, the Ethical, and the Moral Employments of Practical Reason," in Habermas, *Justification and Application*, trans. C. P. Cronin (Cambridge, Mass., 1993), pp. 1–17.

38. Cf. W. Rehg, "Discourse and the Moral Point of View: Deriving a Dialogical Principle of Universalization," *Inquiry* 34 (1991): 27–48; also his *Insight and Solidarity: A Study in the Discourse Ethics of Jürgen Habermas* (Berkeley, 1994).

39. Habermas, *Justification and Application*, pp. 35–39; K. Günther, *The Sense of Appropriateness*, trans. J. Farrell (Albany, 1993). See also chap. 5 below, pp. 216ff.

40. Albrecht Wellmer does just this when he contrasts the privately applicable moral principle with a principle of justice that regulates common political will-formation; A. Wellmer, "Ethics and Dialogue: Elements of Moral Judgement in Kant and Discourse Ethics," in Wellmer, *The Persistence of Modernity*, trans. D. Midgley (Cambridge, Mass., 1991), pp. 113–231; Otfried Höffe would like to distinguish the moral standpoint from the standpoint of political justice in a similar fashion; Höffe, *Politische Gerechtigkeit*, p. 41.

41. L. Wingert, *Gemeinsinn und Moral* (Frankfurt am Main, 1993).

42. The character of this abstraction is such that it secures freedom; the status of the legal person protects the sphere in which real persons who are both morally responsible and follow their ethical conceptions of the good life can freely

develop. Insofar as the legal guarantee of individual liberties secures the space for an authentic and autonomous conduct of life, it makes sense even from a moral and ethical standpoint to reduce the legal person to a bearer of rights who is individuated by freedom of choice. Law is held up as a "protective mask" (Hannah Arendt) over the physiognomy of persons individuated through their life histories, persons who want to live conscientiously and authentically; on this, see R. Forst, *Kontexte der Gerechtigkeit* (Frankfurt am Main, 1994).

43. H. Shue, "Mediating Duties," *Ethics* 98 (1988): 687–704.

44. K. Günther, "Die Freiheit der Stellungnahme als politisches Grundrecht," in P. Koller et al., eds., *Theoretische Grundlagen der Rechtspolitik, Archiv für Rechts- und Sozialphilosophie*, Beiheft 54 (1992): 58ff.

45. On the semantic analysis of legal concepts, see H. J. Koch, *Die juristische Methode im Staatsrecht* (Frankfurt am Main, 1977), pp. 29ff.

46. Despite problematic conclusions, this represents the valid core of Albrecht Wellmer's argument in "Models of Freedom in the Modern World," *Philosophical Forum* 21 (1989/90): 227–52.

Chapter 4

1. E.-W. Böckenförde, "Entstehung und Wandel des Rechtsstaatsbegriffs," in Böckenförde, *Recht, Staat, Freiheit* (Frankfurt am Main, 1991), pp. 143–69; I. Maus, "Entwicklung und Funktionswandel der Theorie des bürgerlichen Rechtsstaats," in Maus, *Rechtstheorie und Politische Theorie im Industriekapitalismus* (Munich, 1986), pp. 11–82.

2. M. Kriele, *Einführung in die Staatslehre* (Opladen, 1980), pp. 224ff.

3. C. Langer, *Reform nach Prinzipien* (Stuttgart, 1986).

4. T. Parsons, R. F. Bales, and E. Shils, *Working Papers in the Theory of Action* (New York, 1953), pp. 63ff.

5. T. Raiser, *Rechtssoziologie* (Frankfurt am Main, 1987), pp. 275ff., 292ff.; see also H. Popitz, *Die normative Konstruktion von Gesellschaft* (Tübingen, 1980).

6. T. Parsons and E. Shils, *Toward a General Theory of Action* (New York, 1951).

7. Raiser, *Rechtssoziologie*, pp. 301ff.

8. U. Wesel, *Frühformen des Rechts in vorstaatlichen Gesellschaften* (Frankfurt am Main, 1985); L. Poposil, *Anthropologie des Rechts* (Munich, 1982).

9. On the following, cf. K. Eder, *Die Entstehung staatlich organisierter Gesellschaften* (Frankfurt am Main, 1976); J. Habermas, *Communication and the Evolution of Society*, trans. T. McCarthy (Boston, 1979), pp. 158ff.

10. On Parsons's theory of communication media, see Habermas, *The Theory of Communicative Action*, trans. T. McCarthy, 2 vols. (Boston, 1984, 1987), 2:256ff.

11. Lon Fuller considers this the basis of the morality contained in positive law: L. Fuller, *The Morality of Law* (Chicago, 1969); see also R. S. Summers, *Lon L. Fuller* (Stanford, 1984).

12. H. Arendt, *The Human Condition* (Chicago, 1958), p. 200; on the following, see J. Habermas, "Hannah Arendt: On the Concept of Power," in Habermas, *Philosophical-Political Profiles*, trans. F. G. Lawrence (Cambridge, Mass., 1985), pp. 173–89.

13. H. Arendt, *On Revolution* (New York, 1965), p. 71.

14. H. Arendt, *On Violence* (New York, 1970), p. 44.

15. In reference to Kant's *Critique of Judgment*, sec. 40, B158, Arendt explains the internal relationships among power, communicative freedom, discourse, and impartiality in her *Lectures on Kant's Political Philosophy*, ed. R. Beiner (Chicago, 1982), pp. 7–77. [The quoted texts, which are found on pp. 39 and 43, are from Kant's "What Is Enlightenment?," in Kant, *On History*, ed. L. W. Beck, trans. L. W. Beck, R. E. Anchor, and E. L. Fackenheim (Indianapolis, 1963) and *Critique of Judgment*, sec. 40, trans. J. H. Bernard (New York, 1951). Trans.]

16. Arendt, *On Violence*, p. 41.

17. Arendt, *Human Condition*, p. 200; the bracketed sentence appears only in the German edition: *Vita Activa* (Stuttgart, 1960), p. 193.

18. F. A. Hayek, *The Constitution of Liberty* (Chicago, 1960).

19. For the anthropological approach in the sociology of law, see H. Schelsky, *Die Soziologen und das Recht* (Opladen, 1980); for "concrete order" thinking in jurisprudence, see C. Schmitt, *Über drei Arten des rechtswissenschaftlichen Denkens* (Hamburg, 1934). On Schmitt, see also I. Maus, *Bürgerliche Rechtstheorie und Faschismus*, 2d ed. (Munich, 1980).

20. R. Dworkin, "Principle, Policy, Procedure," in Dworkin, *A Matter of Principle* (Cambridge, Mass., 1985), pp. 72–103.

21. E. Denninger, "Verfassung und Gesetz," *Kritische Vierteljahresschrift für Gesetzgebung und Rechtswissenschaft* 1 (1986): 300f.

22. J. Rawls, "Kantian Constructivism in Moral Theory," *Journal of Philosophy* 77 (1980): 515–72; see also J. Habermas, *Justification and Application*, trans. C. P. Cronin (Cambridge, Mass., 1993), pp. 26ff.

23. J. Rawls, *Theory of Justice* (Cambridge, Mass., 1971), pp. 113, 115.

24. M. Kriele, *Recht und praktische Vernunft* (Göttingen, 1979), p. 31.

25. Kriele, *Recht und praktische Vernunft*, p. 30.

26. H. Scheit, *Wahrheit, Diskurs, Democratie* (Freiburg, 1987), pp. 370ff.

27. On what follows, see J. Habermas, "On the Pragmatic, the Ethical, and the Moral Employments of Practical Reason," in *Justification and Application*, pp. 1–17.

28. R. Beiner, *Political Judgment* (Chicago, 1983); E. Vollrath, *Die Rekonstruktion der politischen Urteilskraft* (Stuttgart, 1977).

29. Hans-Georg Gadamer's philosophical hermeneutic clarifies the logic of these processes of achieving self-understanding; see his *Truth and Method*, 2d rev. ed., trans. J. Weinsheimer and D. G. Marshall (New York, 1990); for an analysis

geared more to ethical-political questions, see A. MacIntyre, *Whose Justice? Which Rationality?* (Notre Dame, 1988).

30. J. Elster, *The Cement of Society* (Cambridge, 1989), p. 50, defines the occasion for bargaining: "Bargaining occurs when there are several cooperative arrangements and the parties have conflicting preferences over them."

31. J. Elster, "Arguing and Bargaining," ms. 1991, p. 3 [Habermas has altered Elster's original emphasis. Trans.].

32. J. Habermas, *Legitimation Crisis*, trans. T. McCarthy (Boston, 1975), pp. 111ff.; see also my "Die Utopie des guten Herrschers," in Habermas, *Kleine politische Schriften I–IV* (Frankfurt am Main, 1981), pp. 44ff.

33. This circumstance recalls the fact that the moral and ethical discourses that are part of political will-formation do not just differ from informal, everyday moral and ethical discourses in virtue of how they are juridically institutionalized. The moral and ethical considerations entering into the justification of legal norms via legislative processes are important factors in the law's claim to legitimacy, but they do not explode the form of law. The legally channeled results of the legislature's moral and ethical deliberations have a different, indeed *specifically limited*, meaning in comparison to analogous results of everyday moral and ethical discourses. This is obvious in ethical discourses that, if they are conducted from the perspective of the first-person singular, are geared to the existential questions of my own authentic life conduct. This clinical advice is addressed to natural persons not to legal subjects. Even the everyday discourses conducted from the "we" perspective—be it a particular historical "we" or that of an unlimited communication community—leads to recommendations or imperatives that are directed to natural persons individuated in the context of their own life history. By contrast, laws that norm behavior are directed to socially typified legal persons individuated solely through their freedom of choice. As we have already seen in the analysis of the legal form, legal relationships extend to the "external aspects" of matters that can be enforceably regulated. This explains, for example, the difference between the Fifth Commandment and corresponding specifications in criminal law with regard to homicide, although both regulations can largely coincide in their *moral contents.*

34. [The German term *Kontrolle*, which Habermas uses here, refers both to judicial review and to forms of legislative oversight or control. In keeping with standard usage in United States law, I normally use two distinct terms, though occasionally I simply use "controls" or "control" in a general sense that can, depending on the context, include both legislative and judicial powers to check the administration. Trans.]

35. On J. S. Mill, see J. Hellesnes, "Toleranz und Dissens," *Zeitschrift für Philosophie* 40 (1992): 245–55; on John Dewey, see R. B. Westbrook, *John Dewey and American Democracy* (Ithaca, 1991).

36. E. Denninger, *Staatsrecht* (Reinbek, 1973), vol. 1, pp. 101ff.; K. Hesse, *Grundzüge des Verfassungsrechts der Bundesrepublik Deutschland* (Heidelberg, 1990), pp. 76ff. and 213ff.; M. Kriele, *Einführung in die Staatslehre*, pp. 104ff.

37. E. Schmidt-Assmann, "Der Rechtsstaat," in *Handbuch des Staatsrechts,* ed. J. Isensee and P. Kirchhoff, vol. 1 (Heidelberg, 1987), sec. 24, pp. 987–1043.

38. [In a narrower sense, *Vorbehalt des Gesetzes,* or *Gesetzesvorbehalt,* refers to the "requirement of specific legislative enactment," i.e., the constitutional provision that under certain conditions some of the basic rights may be restricted, but only "by or pursuant to statute" (Basic Law, art. 8, sec. 2). Habermas uses the term here in its broader sense, as referring to the principle that the executive branch may not act without statutory authority. In this passage, he also lists different types of administrative laws and actions, ranging from the more general to the more concrete, that are subject to this requirement: *Verordnungen* are agency regulations that have the force of generally binding law; *Satzungen* are laws binding inside a limited area, such as a municipality; *Vorschriften* designate internal agency guidelines; and *Maßnahmen* are more particular administrative actions that apply to just one or a few cases. Trans.]

39. P. Kunig, *Das Rechtsstaatsprinzip* (Tübingen, 1986), pp. 312ff.

40. Cf. the classical contributions in R. Schnur, ed., *Zur Geschichte der Erklärung der Menschenrechte* (Darmstadt, 1964).

41. D. Grimm, *Recht und Staat in der bürgerlichen Gesellschaft* (Frankfurt am Main, 1987); E. W. Böckenförde, ed., *Staat und Gesellschaft* (Darmstadt, 1976); D. Suhr, "Staat—Gesellschaft—Verfassung von Hegel bis heute," *Der Staat* 17 (1978): 369–95; E. W. Böckenförde, *Recht, Staat, Freiheit.*

42. See my "Further Reflections on the Public Sphere," trans. T. Burger, in *Habermas and the Public Sphere,* ed. C. Calhoun (Cambridge, Mass., 1992), pp. 421–61.

43. An ideology that in particular was widely shared by disciples of Carl Schmitt, as seen for example in W. Weber, *Spannungen und Kräfte im westdeutschen Verfassungssystem* (Stuttgart, 1951); E. Forsthoff, *Der Staat der Industriegesellschaft* (Munich, 1971).

44. On the replacement of state criminal prosecution with private settlements see W. Naucke, "Versuch über den aktuellen Stil des Rechts," *Schriften der Hermann-Ehlers-Akademie* 19 (1986).

45. B. Guggenberger and C. Offe, eds., *An den Grenzen der Mehrheitsdemokratie* (Opladen, 1984).

46. C. Gusy, "Das Mehrheitsprinzip im demokratischen Staat," in Guggenberger and Offe, pp. 61–82. Admittedly this point is more problematic for decisions about personnel.

47. G. Frankenberg and U. Rödel, *Von der Volkssouveränität zum Minderheitenschutz* (Frankfurt am Main, 1981).

48. H. J. Varain, "Die Bedeutung des Mehrheitsprinzips im Rahmen unserer politischen Ordnung," in Guggenberger and Offe, p. 56: "Many majorities are only temporary alliances. . . . But for all of them the possibility is open of dissolving and combining into new majorities. Thus one finds in majority decisions a 'soft' expression of will."

49. See figure 2 above.

50. E. Fraenkel, "Die repräsentative und plebiszitäre Komponente im demokratischen Verfassungsstaat," in Fraenkel, *Deutschland und die westlichen Demokratien* (Frankfurt am Main, 1991), pp. 153–203.

51. See appendix I, "Popular Sovereignty as Procedure," in this volume.

52. C. Taylor, "Cross-Purposes: The Liberal-Communitarian Debate," in N. Rosenblum, ed., *Liberalism and the Moral Life* (Cambridge, Mass., 1989), pp. 176ff. On the idea of a "nation of citizens," see appendix II, "Citizenship and National Identity," in this volume.

53. C. Schmitt, *Verfassungslehre* (Berlin, 1928), pp. 315f.

54. K. Marx, *The Eighteenth Brumaire of Louis Bonaparte* (New York, 1963), p. 66 [translation slightly altered. Trans.]

55. E. Fraenkel, "Parlament und öffentliche Meinung," in Fraenkel, *Deutschland,* p. 209: "The theory of 'virtual representation' and the utopia of the 'volonté générale' are both equally distant from the modern idea of an interdependence of parliament and public opinion as two independent but nevertheless indissolubly connected components."

56. Cf. my critique of Carl Schmitt's *Crisis of Parliamentary Democracy,* trans. E. Kennedy (Cambridge, Mass., 1988), in J. Habermas, "The Horrors of Autonomy: Carl Schmitt in English," in Habermas, *The New Conservatism,* ed. and trans. S. W. Nicholsen (Cambridge, Mass., 1989), pp. 128–39.

57. J. L. Mashaw, *Due Process in the Administrative State* (New Haven, Conn., 1985), p. 230.

58. On the expertocratic model of administration, see Mashaw, *Due Process,* p. 19: "By virtue of constant exposure to a single type of problem, as well as by selection of personnel with specialized training, the administrative agency could bring to bear an expertise that generalist courts and generalist legislatures could rarely hope to match. Although the agency may not have the requisite scientific knowledge or technical expertise to effect final solutions at the inception of its operations, the expertise model of administration imagines that over time experience and research will produce increasingly sound administrative judgements."

59. I. Maus, "Zur Theorie der Institutionalisierung bei Kant," in G. Göhler et al., eds., *Politische Institutionen im gesellschaftlichen Umbruch* (Opladen, 1990), pp. 358ff.; here p. 372.

60. I. Maus, "Entwicklung und Funktionswandel der Theorie des bürgerlichen Rechtsstaates," in M. Tohidipur, ed., *Der bürgerliche Rechtsstaat,* vol. 1 (Frankfurt am Main, 1978), p. 15.

61. Maus, "Zur Theorie," pp. 374f. On the transition from material to procedural natural law in Kant, see also I. Maus, *Zur Aufklärung der Demokratietheorie* (Frankfurt am Main, 1992), pp. 148ff.

62. I. Maus, "Verrechtlichung, Entrechtlichung und der Funktionswandel von Institutionen," in Maus, *Rechtstheorie und politische Theorie*, pp. 277–331.

63. Mashaw, *Due Process*, p. 22.

64. Mashaw, *Due Process*, pp. 26f.

65. A glance at the structures of local self-government (*kommunalen Selbstverwaltung*) is enough to show that a linear correlation of principles of the constitutional state with corresponding forms of its organizational realization will not work. As is well known, municipal structures cannot be forced into the classical schema for the separation of powers. Local self-government is included in the general national administration only because, from a legal viewpoint, "municipal law is at bottom organizational law and thus closely interacts with the law governing the organization of *Länder*" (D. Czybulka, *Die Legitimation der öffentlichen Verwaltung* [Heidelberg, 1989], p. 195). From a functional point of view, however, the decentralization of comprehensive powers at this grassroots level of decision making facilitates an organizational intertwining of governmental functions that is still compatible with the logic of separated powers. Although municipalities do not have legislative powers at their disposal, they do have the power to pass local ordinances (*Satzungsautonomie*). Legitimation through general elections that are more personalized, the parliamentary form of will-formation, the voluntary participation of laypersons, etc., enables local citizens to exert a comparatively strong influence on the programs and course of a universal administration, an influence that goes beyond other models of participatory administration (or "organized participation of those concerned"). It is all the more difficult to enforce the principle of separation of state and society. This type of organization remains susceptible to the informally exerted pressure of socially powerful persons or groups. I use the example of local self-government merely to recall the fact that the principles of the constitutional state are not immediately mirrored at the organizational level of political institutions or even at the level of the political process. Therefore, it is by no means the case that all those phenomena that seem to speak against the classical schema for the separation of powers in fact support objections against the underlying logic of that separation itself.

Chapter 5

1. N. Luhmann, *Ausdifferenzierung des Rechts* (Frankfurt am Main, 1981), pp. 35ff.

2. Prior to an actual conflict, actors do not have a "legal consciousness" honed to protect their own interests.

3. It is from this standpoint that Ronald Dworkin draws the distinction between "law" and "justice": "Justice is a matter of the correct or best theory of moral and political rights. . . . Law is a matter of which supposed rights supply a justification for using or withholding the collective force of the state because they are included in or implied by actual political decisions of the past." R. Dworkin, *Law's Empire* (Cambridge, Mass., 1986), p. 97.

4. Cf. R. Dreier, *Was ist und wozu Allgemeine Rechtstheorie?* (Tübingen, 1975); N. MacCormick, *Legal Reasoning and Legal Theory* (Oxford, 1978).

5. J. Wroblewski, "Legal Syllogism and Rationality of Judicial Decision," *Rechtstheorie* 5 (1974): 33–46.

6. R. Dworkin, *Taking Rights Seriously* (Cambridge, Mass., 1978), p. 87.

7. H.-G. Gadamer, *Truth and Method*, 2d. ed., trans. J. Weinsheimer and D. G. Marshall (New York, 1990).

8. W. Hassemer, "Juristische Hermeneutik," *Archiv für Rechts- und Sozialphilosophie* 72 (1986): 195ff.; see also U. Neumann, *Juristische Argumentationslehre* (Darmstadt, 1986), pp. 54ff.

9. J. Esser, *Grundsatz und Norm in der richterlichen Fortbildung des Privatsrechts*, 2nd ed. (Tübingen, 1964), p. 182; see also his *Vorverständnis und Methodenwahl in der Rechtsfindung* (Kronberg, 1972).

10. G. Ellscheid and W. Hassemer, eds., *Interessenjurisprudenz* (Darmstadt, 1974).

11. On American Legal Realism, see R. S. Summers, *Instrumentalism and American Legal Theory* (Ithaca, 1982).

12. H. L. A. Hart, *The Concept of Law* (Oxford, 1961), p. 107: "The rule of recognition exists only as a complex, but normally concordant, practice of the courts, officials, and private persons in identifying the law by reference to certain criteria. Its existence is a matter of fact."

13. Dworkin, *Taking Rights Seriously*, p. 182.

14. Dworkin, *Taking Rights Seriously*, p. 92.

15. R. Alexy, "Zur Kritik des Rechtspositivismus," in R. Dreier, ed., *Rechtspositivismus und Wertbezug des Rechts* (Stuttgart, 1990), pp. 9–26; for a contrasting view, see N. Hoerster, *Verteidigung des Rechtspositivismus* (Frankfurt am Main, 1989).

16. B. Peters, *Rationalität, Recht und Gesellschaft* (Frankfurt am Main, 1991), pp. 278f.

17. Dworkin, *Taking Rights Seriously*, p. 82.

18. Cf. R. Alexy, *Theorie der Grundrechte* (Baden-Baden, 1985), pp. 75ff.; for a criticism of this view, see K. Günther, *The Sense of Appropriateness: Application Discourses in Morality and Law*, trans. J. Farrell (Albany, 1993), pp. 212ff. [On the concept of value involved in *Güterabwägung*, see chap. 6 n28. Trans.]

19. J. Habermas, *The Theory of Communicative Action*, trans. T. McCarthy, 2 vols. (Boston, 1984, 1987) 1:130–36 (hereafter, *TCA*); see also J. Habermas, *On the Logic of the Social Sciences*, trans. S. W. Nicholsen and J. A. Stark (Cambridge, Mass., 1988), pp. 143ff.

20. R. Dworkin, *Law's Empire*, pp. 52f., 419 n2.

21. One of the few works that relates Dworkin's concept of interpretation to the European discussion, especially to the views of Gadamer, Derrida, and myself, is David C. Hoy's "Interpreting the Law: Hermeneutical and Poststructuralist Perspectives," *Southern California Law Review* 58 (1985): 135–76; see also his

"Dworkin's Constructive Optimism vs. Deconstructive Legal Nihilism," *Law and Philosophy* 6 (1987): 321–56.

22. Dworkin, *Taking Rights Seriously*, p. 66; cf. also his *Matter of Principle* (Cambridge, Mass., 1985), pt. 2.

23. S. Toulmin, *The Uses of Argument* (Cambridge, 1964); S. Toulmin, R. Rieke, and A. Janik, *An Introduction to Reasoning* (New York, 1979).

24. Dworkin, *Taking Rights Seriously*, pp. 41, 40, resp.

25. "I mean only to suppose that a particular social institution like slavery might be unjust, not because people think it unjust, or have conventions according to which it is unjust ... but just because slavery is unjust. If there are such moral facts, then a proposition of law might rationally be supposed to be true even if lawyers continue to disagree about the proposition after all hard facts are known or stipulated." Dworkin, *A Matter of Principle*, p. 138.

26. Dworkin, *Taking Rights Seriously*, p. 120.

27. Dworkin, *Taking Rights Seriously*, p. 121.

28. Dworkin, *Taking Rights Seriously*, p. 119.

29. Dworkin, *Taking Rights Seriously*, p. 87.

30. R. M. Unger, *The Critical Legal Studies Movement* (Cambridge, Mass., 1986); D. M. Trubek and J. P. Esser, "'Critical Empiricism' and American Critical Legal Studies," in C. Joerges and D. M. Trubek, eds., *Critical Legal Thought* (Baden-Baden, 1989), pp. 105–56; G. Minda, "The Jurisprudential Movements of the 1980s," *Ohio State Law Journal* 50 (1989): 599–662; J. Boyle, "The Politics of Reason: Critical Legal Theory and Local Social Thought," *Pennsylvania Law Review* 133 (1985): 685–780.

31. A. Altman, "Legal Realism, Critical Legal Studies, and Dworkin," *Philosophy and Public Affairs* 15 (1986): 202–35.

32. Dworkin, *Law's Empire*, p. 211.

33. Dworkin, *Law's Empire*, pp. 213f.

34. D. Kennedy, "Form and Substance in Private Law Adjudication," *Harvard Law Review* 89 (1976): 1688ff.

35. G. Frankenberg, "Down by Law: Irony, Seriousness, and Reason," *Northwestern University Law Review* 83 (1988): 360–97; here pp. 392–93.

36. Dworkin, *Law's Empire*, pp. 271–75.

37. K. Günther, "A Normative Conception of Coherence for a Discursive Theory of Legal Justification," *Ratio Juris* 2 (1989): 157: "When we recognize a norm as valid we do not take every individual application situation into account, as can be seen even in our ordinary use of the term 'valid.' We use this predicate even for those norms we know will interfere with universalizable interests at least in some cases. For example we all know (and could foresee in a discourse on validity) that the norm 'Do not break a promise' will collide with the norm 'Help your neighbor if he is in an emergency' at least in some cases. ... In spite of the

foreseeable possibility of their collision we would not consider the two precepts invalid. We would be astonished if a discourse on the validity of one of these norms led to the opposite result." [Translation altered; for the German, see Günther, "Ein normativer Begriff der Kohärenz für eine Theorie der juristischen Argumentation," *Rechtstheorie* 20 (1989): 168. Trans.] See also J. Habermas, *Justification and Application*, trans. C. P. Cronin (Cambridge, Mass., 1993), pp. 35ff.

38. Günther, "Ein normativer Begriff," p. 175. [For a partial English translation, see his "Normative Conception of Coherence," p. 160. Trans.]

39. K. Günther, "Universalistische Normbegründung und Normanwendung," in M. Herberger et al., eds., *Generalisierung und Individualisierung im Rechtsdenken*, *Archiv für Rechts- und Sozialphilosophie* Beiheft 45 (1992): 36–76.

40. Günther, *Sense of Appropriateness*, pp. 239–40 [translation altered. Trans.].

41. Günther, "Ein normativer Begriff," p. 182; "A Normative Conception of Coherence," p. 163 [trans. altered. Trans.].

42. K. J. Kress, "Legal Reasoning and Coherence Theories: Dworkin's Rights Thesis, Retroactivity, and the Linear Order of Decisions," *California Law Review* 72 (1984): 369–402.

43. R. S. Summers, *Lon L. Fuller* (Stanford, 1984), pp. 27ff. and 36ff.

44. In this context, I disregard institutional proposals, according to which the prohibition against retroactivity in criminal law, for example, would be extended to *disadvantageous* changes in the administration of justice. Cf. U. Neumann, "Rückwirkungsverbot bei belastenden Rechtsprechungsänderungen der Strafgerichte?" *Zeitschrift für die gesamte Staatswissenschaft* 103 (1991): 331–56.

45. Günther, "Ein normativer Begriff," p. 182; "Normative Conception," pp. 163f. See also J. Habermas, "Der Philosoph als wahrer Rechtslehrer: Rudolf Wiethölter," *Kritische Justiz* 22 (1989): 138–56.

46. Dworkin, *Law's Empire*, p. 264 (my emphasis).

47. F. Michelman, "The Supreme Court 1985 Term—Foreword: Traces of Self-Government," *Harvard Law Review* 100 (1986): 72f.

48. Dworkin, *Law's Empire*, p. 216.

49. Dworkin, *Taking Rights Seriously*, pp. 273f.; see also Günther, *Sense of Appropriateness*, pp. 282ff.

50. See the chapter with this title in P. Häberle, *Die Verfassung des Pluralismus* (Frankfurt am Main, 1980), pp. 79–105.

51. Michelman, "The Supreme Court 1985 Term," p. 76; cf. K. Günther, "Hero-Politics in Modern Legal Times," Institute for Legal Studies, series 4 (Madison, Wisc., 1990).

52. O. Fiss, "Objectivity and Interpretation," *Stanford Law Review* 34 (1982): 739–63; here 744.

53. Fiss, "Objectivity and Interpretation," p. 762.

54. A. J. Arnaud, R. Hilpinen, and J. Wróblewski, eds., *Juristische Logik und Irrationalität im Recht, Rechtstheorie* Beiheft 8 (1985).

55. Toulmin, *Uses of Argument*; Toulmin, Rieke, and Janik, *Introduction to Reasoning*.

56. K. O. Apel, *Charles S. Peirce*, trans. J. M. Krois (Amherst, Mass., 1981); see also K. O. Apel, "Sprache und Bedeutung, Wahrheit und normative Gültigkeit," *Archivo di Filosophia* 55 (1987): 51–88.

57. See my excursus on argumentation theory in *TCA*, 1:22–42.

58. Aulis Aarnio begins by conceiving legitimacy, one of the two dimensions of legal validity, as rational acceptability (*The Rational as Reasonable* [Boston, 1987], pp. 43ff.). He goes on to discuss various sorts of legal norms, arranging these categories of valid law hierarchically (pp. 61ff. and 78ff.): these are the "sources of information." Aarnio then deals with the discourse rules that govern interpretation; these constitute the "sources of rationality." Like Dworkin, he mainly emphasizes the external justification of the premises of decisions, which requires substantial reasons, to wit, principles and policies (rightness reasons vs. goal reasons). Unlike Dworkin, however, to justify these principles Aarnio does not require the construction of an encompassing theory but only coherence under the conditions of rational discourse:

[T]he justification procedure is essentially a dialogue. It is a succession of questions and answers on the basis of which different pro and contra arguments will be presented.... The addressee can rationally accept the interpretation only if the justification results in a coherent cluster of statements and if this cluster fulfills [certain] criteria [above all criteria for the connection to valid law].... This is so, because the standards of legal reasoning alone do not guarantee the coherence of the justificatory material. All reasons must also be used in a rational way. (Aarnio, p. 187)

Good reasons display their rationally motivating force only in a forum that grants a hearing to all relevant voices. Aarnio describes this forum in terms of Chaim Perelman's concept of the "ideal audience." Naturally, for legal discourse a particular ideal audience limited to the boundaries of the legal community suffices. This audience consists of rational persons who allow the unforced force of the better argument to determine whether they take a yes or no position— though only within the context of a concrete form of life they already share.

59. R. Alexy, *A Theory of Legal Argumentation*, trans. R. Adler and N. MacCormick (Oxford, 1989); Alexy, *Theorie der juristischen Argumentation*, 2d ed. (Frankfurt am Main, 1991); Alexy refers to J. Habermas, "Wahrheitstheorien," which is available in Habermas, *Vorstudien und Ergänzungen zur Theorie des kommunikativen Handelns* (Frankfurt am Main, 1984), pp. 127–83.

60. J. Habermas, "Discourse Ethics: Notes on a Program of Philosophical Justification," in *Moral Consciousness and Communicative Action*, trans. C. Lenhardt and S. W. Nicholsen (Cambridge, Mass., 1990), pp. 43–115.

61. In his afterword, Alexy indeed distinguishes the rationality of established law

from the right application of norms taken as justified. But he goes on to say, "Both aspects are contained in the claim to rightness raised in judicial decisions." Alexy, *Theorie der juristischen Argumentation*, p. 433.

62. Neumann, *Juristische Argumentationslehre*, p. 85.

63. Alexy, "Antwort auf einige Kritiker," in Alexy, *Theorie der juristischen Argumentation*.

64. A. Kaufmann, *Theorie der Gerechtigkeit* (Frankfurt am Main, 1984), pp. 35ff.; A. Kaufmann, "Recht und Rationalität," in Kaufmann et al., eds., *Rechtsstaat und Menschenwürde* (Frankfurt am Main, 1988); A. Kaufmann, *Rechtsphilosophie in der Nach-Neuzeit* (Heidelberg, 1990), pp. 28ff. and 35ff.; see also R. Alexy, "Eine diskurstheoretische Konzeption der praktischen Vernunft," and O. Weinberger, "Die Streit um die praktische Vernunft," both in R. Alexy and R. Dreier, eds., *Legal System and Practical Reason, Archiv für Rechts- und Sozialphilosophie* Beiheft 51 (1993): 11–29 and 30–46, resp.

65. Cf. R. Alexy, "Probleme der Diskurstheorie," *Zeitschrift für philosophische Forschung* 43 (1989): 81–93; J. Habermas, *Justification and Application*, pp. 54–60.

66. Alexy, *Theory of Legal Argumentation*, pp. 289–91.

67. Alexy, *Theory of Legal Argumentation*, p. 289.

68. Neumann, *Juristische Argumentationslehre*, p. 90.

69. Günther, "Normative Conception of Coherence," p. 163; "Ein normativer Begriff," p. 182 (Günther's emphasis removed).

70. To this extent one must agree with Alexy, *Theory of Legal Argumentation*, p. 289: "In order to arrive at a theory of legal discourse which would also embrace these conditions [of the rationality of legislation], the theory of general, rational, practical discourse would have to be expanded to include a theory of legislation and then a normative theory of society."

71. I am indebted to Klaus Günther for the following points.

72. [*Berufung* and *Revision* denote two separate stages or "instances" of appeal in the German court system. The first stage, *Berufung* or "appeal de novo," allows for a review both of the facts (including the introduction of new evidence) and points of law, whereas the second stage, *Revision* or "appeal for error," reviews exclusively matters of procedure and the application of law. Together with "interlocutory appeals" (*Beschwerde*), these make up the three "modes of legal review" (*Rechtsmittel*) that German law provides for appealing decisions in civil and criminal cases. Trans.]

73. *The German Code of Criminal Procedure*, trans. H. Niebler (London, 1973), §244, sec. 2; p. 119 [trans. amended. Trans.].

74. P. Arens, *Zivilprozeßrecht*, 4th ed. (Munich, 1988), p. 219 margin no. 338.

75. Arens, *Zivilprozeßrecht*, pp. 346f. margin no. 381.

76. *German Code of Criminal Proc.*, §261, p. 125.

Chapter 6

1. [The German equivalent of the U. S. Supreme Court is the Federal Constitutional Court. Depending on the context, the uncapitalized term "constitutional court" may be used generally, as referring to both the U.S. and German systems. Trans.]

2. [In the German legal system, it is possible to review the constitutionality of norms both in the abstract, i.e., simply on the request of certain other governmental powers, and in the concrete, on the occasion of a real controversy whose litigation first requires the Federal Constitutional Court to decide the constitutionality of the norm in question. In the latter case, the issue is referred to the Constitutional Court by the lower court that happens to be handling the original lawsuit. Trans.]

3. C. Schmitt, *Der Hüter der Verfassung* (Tübingen, 1931). In his sharp critique, Hans Kelsen showed that this proposal rigorously follows from Schmitt's "turn to the total state": H. Kelsen, "Wer soll der Hüter der Verfassung sein?" *Die Justiz* 6 (1931): 576–628.

4. See the end of chap. 4 in this volume, pp. 192–93.

5. R. Alexy, *Theorie der Grundrechte* (Baden-Baden, 1985), p. 501.

6. Schmitt, *Der Hüter*, p. 42.

7. Kelsen, "Wer soll der Hüter," p. 590.

8. Kelsen, "Wer soll der Hüter," p. 609.

9. *Entscheidungen des Bundesverfassungsgericht*, 34, 269 (1973), p. 304.

10. K. Hesse, *Grundzüge des Verfassungsrechts der Bundesrepublik Deutschland* (Heidelberg, 1990), p. 219.

11. E.-W. Böckenförde, *Staat, Verfassung, Demokratie* (Frankfurt am Main, 1991); E. Denninger, *Der gebändigte Leviathan* (Baden-Baden, 1990); D. Grimm, *Die Zukunft der Verfassung* (Frankfurt am Main, 1991).

12. E. Denninger, "Verfassungsrechtliche Schlüsselbegriffe," in Denninger, *Der gebändigte Leviathan*, p. 159.

13. I. Maus, "Die Trennung von Recht und Moral als Begrenzung des Rechts," *Rechtstheorie* 20 (1989): 191–210.

14. [The idea of *Wechselwirkung* reflects the idea in German constitutional law that, although basic rights, such as freedom of expression, might be subject to certain statutory restrictions, these are in turn limited by the value embodied in the basic right (as well as by the "essential content" of the right). *Drittwirkung* and *Ausstrahlung* refer to the pervasive effects that constitutional values and rights have on all areas of law. More specifically, *Drittwirkung* concerns the issue of whether basic rights protecting the individual from state encroachment also apply in areas of private law, i.e., to relationships between individuals. Finally, note that the term "objective" in this context picks up on the long-standing distinction, prevalent in the German civil-law tradition, between "subjective rights" and "objective law." Trans.]

15. H. Huber, "Die Bedeutung der Grundrechte für die sozialen Beziehungen unter den Rechtsgenossen (1955)," in Huber, *Rechtstheorie, Verfassungsrecht, Völkerrecht* (Bern, 1971), pp. 157ff.; P. Häberle, "Grundrechte im Leistungsstaat," *Veröffentlichungen der Vereinigung der Deutschen Staatsrechtslehrer* 30 (1972): 43–131; P. Häberle, ed., *Verfassungsgerichtbarkeit* (Darmstadt, 1976); E.-W. Böcken-förde, "Grundrechtstheorie und Grundrechtsinterpretation," *Neue Juristische Wochenschrift* 27 (1974): 1529ff.; H. Ridder, *Die soziale Ordnung des Grundgesetzes* (Opladen, 1975); U. K. Preuss, *Die Internalisierung des Subjekts* (Frankfurt am Main, 1979).

16. [The proportionality principle holds that authorized legislative restrictions on basic rights must be reasonable, i.e., suitable for a legitimate goal, necessary, and not excessive; the possibility proviso stipulates that rights are to be guaranteed provided it is possible for the government to do so. Trans.]

17. Denninger, *Der gebändigte Leviathan*, p. 176.

18. Denninger, *Der gebändigte Leviathan*, pp. 174f.

19. E.-W. Böckenförde, "Grundrechte als Grundsatznormen: Zur gegenwärtigen Lage der Grundrechtsdogmatik," in Böckenförde, *Staat, Verfassung, Demokratie*, pp. 189–91.

20. Böckenförde, "Grundrechte als Grundsatznormen," in *Staat, Verfassung, Demokratie*, p. 194. "Left-wing" critics of the Constitutional Court arrive at a similar neoformalist conclusion; see D. Grimm, "Reformalisierung des Rechtsstaates?" *Juristische Schulung* 10 (1980): 704–9.

21. Böckenförde, "Grundrechte als Grundsatznormen," in *Staat, Verfassung, Demokratie*, p. 189 (emphasis added).

22. Denninger, *Der gebändigte Leviathan*, p. 148.

23. E.-W. Böckenförde, "Die sozialen Grundrechte im Verfassungsgefüge," in Böckenförde, *Staat, Verfassung, Demokratie*, pp. 146–58.

24. C. R. Sunstein, *After the Rights Revolution* (Cambridge, Mass., 1990), pp. 170f.

25. Sunstein, *After the Rights Revolution*, p. 171.

26. Cf. D. Grimm, "Rückkehr zum liberalen Grundrechtsverständnis?" in Grimm, *Die Zukunft der Verfassung*, pp. 221–40.

27. Sunstein, *After the Rights Revolution*, p. 157 (emphasis added).

28. Maus, "Die Trennung von Recht und Moral," p. 199. [The following discussion of value jurisprudence involves the concept of a *Rechtsgut* (plural *Rechtgüter* or just *Güter*), which refers to legally protected interests or values. These may be interests or goods of individuals (e.g., health, liberty) or they may be collective or public goods (e.g., national security, clean air). Where I occasionally render *Rechtsgut* as "interest," the context should make it clear that the term has this special meaning, which should not be conflated with the use of "interest" in other contexts. Trans.]

29. Böckenförde, "Grundrechte als Grundsatznormen," in *Staat, Verfassung, Demokratie*, pp. 186f.

30. C. Taylor, *Sources of the Self* (Cambridge, Mass., 1989); see my critique in *Justification and Application*, trans. C. P. Cronin (Cambridge, Mass., 1993), pp. 69–76.

31. H. Frankfurt, "Freedom of the Will and the Concept of the Person," in Frankfurt, *The Importance of What We Care About* (Cambridge, 1988), pp. 11–25.

32. P. Brest, "The Fundamental Rights Controversy," *Yale Law Journal* 90 (1981): 1063–1109.

33. J. H. Ely, *Democracy and Distrust* (Cambridge, Mass., 1980).

34. M. J. Perry, *Morality, Politics, and Law* (Oxford, 1988), pp. 152f. (emphasis added).

35. Perry, *Morality*, pp. 135f.

36. Perry, *Morality*, p. 149.

37. Denninger, *Der gebändigte Leviathan*, p. 147.

38. Because there are no unambiguous units for measuring so-called legal values, Alexy's economic model of justification also does not help operationalize the weighing process; Alexy, *Theorie der Grundrechte*, pp. 143–53. Cf. K. Günther, *Sense of Appropriateness*, trans. J. Farrell (Albany, 1993), pp. 212ff.

39. Maus, "Die Trennung von Recht und Moral," pp. 197f.

40. Maus, "Die Trennung von Recht und Moral," p. 208.

41. Böckenförde, "Grundrechte als Grundsatznormen," in *Staat, Verfassung, Demokratie*, p. 194.

42. Ely, *Democracy and Distrust*, p. 100.

43. Ely, *Democracy and Distrust*, p. 117.

44. Ely, *Democracy and Distrust*, p. 133.

45. D. A. J. Richards, "Moral Philosophy and the Search for Fundamental Values in Constitutional Law," *Ohio State Law Journal* 42 (1981): 330; cf. also P. Brest, "The Fundamental Rights Controversy," pp. 1092ff.

46. L. H. Tribe, "The Puzzling Persistence of Process-Based Constitutional Theories," *Yale Law Journal* 89 (1980): 1063–80.

47. Richards, "Moral Philosophy," p. 330; cf. also Brest, "The Fundamental Rights Controversy," pp. 1105ff.

48. F. Michelman, "Law's Republic," *Yale Law Journal* 97 (1988): 1525.

49. J. G. A. Pocock, *The Machiavellian Moment* (Princeton, 1975).

50. P. W. Kahn, "Reason and Will in the Origins of American Constitutionalism," *Yale Law Journal* 98 (1989): 449–517.

51. J. G. A. Pocock, "Virtues, Rights, and Manners," *Political Theory* 9 (1981): 353–68.

52. On the concepts of "positive" and "negative" liberty, see C. Taylor, "What Is Human Agency?" in Taylor, *Human Agency and Language* (Cambridge, 1985), pp. 15–44.

53. J. Ritter, *Hegel and the French Revolution*, trans. R. D. Winfield (Cambridge, Mass., 1982).

54. F. I. Michelman, "The Supreme Court 1985 Term—Foreword: Traces of Self-Government," *Harvard Law Review* 100 (1986): 4–77.

55. F. I. Michelman, "Conceptions of Democracy in American Constitutional Argument: Voting Rights," *Florida Law Review* 41 (1989): 443–90 (hereafter, "Conceptions of Democracy: Voting").

56. See H. Arendt, *On Revolution* (New York, 1963); see also her *On Violence* (New York, 1970).

57. F. I. Michelman, "Political Truth and the Rule of Law," *Tel Aviv University Studies in Law* 8 (1988): 283: "The political society envisioned by bumper-sticker republicans is the society of private rights bearers, an association whose first principle is the protection of the lives, liberties, and estates of its individual members. In that society, the state is justified by the protection it gives to those pre-political interests; the purpose of the constitution is to ensure that the state apparatus, the government, provides such protection for the people at large rather than serves the special interests of the governors or their patrons; the function of citizenship is to operate the constitution and thereby motivate the governors to act according to that protective purpose; and the value to you of your political franchise—your right to vote and speak, to have your views heard and counted—is the handle it gives you on influencing the system so that it will adequately heed and protect *your* particular, pre-political rights and other interests."

58. Michelman, "Political Truth," p. 284: "In civic constitutional vision, political society is primarily the society not of rights-bearers, but of citizens, an association whose first principle is the creation and provision of a public realm within which a people, together, argue and reason about the right terms of social coexistence, terms that they will set together and which they understand as comprising their common good. . . . Hence, the state is justified by its purpose of establishing and ordering the public sphere within which persons can achieve freedom in the sense of self-government by the exercise of reason in public dialogue."

59. Michelman, "Conceptions of Democracy: Voting," pp. 446f.

60. Michelman, "Conceptions of Democracy: Voting," p. 484.

61. F. I. Michelman, "Conceptions of Democracy in American Constitutional Argument: The Case of Pornography Regulation," *Tennessee Law Review* 56 (1989): 293 (hereafter, "Conceptions of Democracy: Pornography").

62. F. I. Michelman, "Bringing the Law to Life: A Plea for Disenchantment," *Cornell Law Review* 74 (1989): 257.

63. Michelman, "Conceptions of Democracy: Pornography," p. 293.

64. Michelman, "Law's Republic," pp. 1526f.

65. Michelman, "Law's Republic," p. 1529; he goes on (p. 1531) as follows:

The full lesson of the civil rights movement will escape whoever focuses too sharply on the country's most visible, formal legislative assemblies—Congress, state legislatures, the councils of major cities—as exclusive, or even primary, arenas of jurisgenerative politics and political freedom. I do not mean that those arenas are dispensable or unimportant. Rather I mean the obvious points that much of the country's normatively consequential dialogue occurs outside the major, formal channels of electoral and legislative politics, and that in modern society those formal channels cannot possibly provide for most citizens much direct experience of self-revisionary, dialogic engagement. Much, perhaps most, of that experience must occur in various arenas of what we know as public life in the broad sense, some nominally political and some not: in the encounters and conflicts, interactions and debates that arise in and around town meetings and local government agencies; civic and voluntary associations; social and recreational clubs; schools public and private; managements, directorates and leadership groups of organizations of all kinds; workplaces and shop floors; public events and street life; and so on. . . . Understandings of the social world that are contested and shaped in the daily encounters and transactions of civil society at large are of course conveyed to our representative arenas. . . . [They] are, then, to be counted among the sources and channels of republican self-government and jurisgenerative politics.

66. Sunstein, *After the Rights Revolution*, p. 164.

67. C. R. Sunstein, "Interest Groups in American Public Law," *Stanford Law Review* 38 (1985): 59.

68. Sunstein, "Interest Groups," p. 58.

69. B. Ackerman, "The Storrs Lectures: Discovering the Constitution," *Yale Law Journal* 93 (1984): 1013–72. See also his *We the People*, vol. 1 (Cambridge, Mass., 1991).

70. Michelman, "Supreme Court 1985 Term," p. 65 (Michelman's emphasis removed).

71. Michelman, "Law's Republic," p. 1532.

72. B. Manin, "On Legitimacy and Political Deliberation," *Political Theory* 15 (1987): 347; cf. my critique of Rousseau in J. Habermas, *The Structural Transformation of the Public Sphere* (1962), trans. T. Burger (Cambridge, Mass., 1989), sec. 12; see also J. Habermas, "Further Reflections on the Public Sphere," in *Habermas and the Public Sphere*, ed. C. Calhoun (Cambridge, Mass., 1992), pp. 421–61.

73. See appendix II in this volume.

74. Michelman, "Law's Republic," p. 1513.

75. In the Federal Republic, the legal thought of the communitarians finds a certain parallel in P. Häberle's interpretation of constitutional law; see his *Verfassung als öffentlicher Prozeß* (Frankfurt am Main, 1978); cf. also A. Blankenagel, *Tradition und Verfassung* (Baden-Baden, 1987).

76. The communitarians also consider this relation to a community necessary for explaining the meaning of political duties. Because the observance of an

obligation going beyond current interests cannot be grounded in terms of an exchange model—an exchange of natural freedom for protection and security—they replace the contract model with the idea of an original act of mutual *promising*. As a result, democratic elections are conceived as current counterparts to a promise of the Founding Fathers. In elections, subsequent generations renew and confirm the founding generation's self-obligation that once constituted the political community: "Citizens collectively must create their political obligation and political authority through participatory voting in a democratic community." Of course, because a promise establishes an interpersonal relationship between particular individuals, this explanation must be extended to a network of such relationships, like that established in a concrete community (C. Pateman, *The Problem of Political Obligation* [Oxford, 1979], p. 174). Aside from the fact that obligations toward *other* political communities cannot be justified this way, this model begs the question, by tacitly presupposing what it claims to explain: precisely the obligatory meaning of the validity of binding norms. A glance at the speech act of "promising" can make this clear. The promise borrows the decisive normative meaning of its illocutionary force from the speaker's autonomy: the speaker can act responsibly only if he already knows what it means to *bind* one's own will. Hence, this kind of autonomy presupposes that the subject can orient his action in general by normative expectations, and thus can act from duty. Whether a "promise" is unilateral or reciprocal, such an illocutionary act generates duties that have a *specific* content, but it does not create the binding character of obligations *as such*.

77. H. Pitkin, "Justice: On Relating Private and Public," *Political Theory* 9 (1981): 344.

78. Michelman, "Law's Republic," p. 1508.

79. R. Beiner, *Political Judgment* (Chicago, 1983), p. 138.

80. Sunstein, "Interest Groups," pp. 48–49.

81. Michelman, "Conceptions of Democracy: Pornography," pp. 291f.

82. Sunstein, "Interest Groups," p. 76.

Chapter 7

1. See chap. 8, sec. 8.1, in this volume.

2. W. Becker, *Die Freiheit, die wir meinen: Entscheidung für die liberale Demokratie* (Munich, 1982), p. 61 (in subsequent quotations from this book, Becker's original emphasis has been removed).

3. Becker, *Freiheit*, p. 68.

4. Becker, *Freiheit*, p. 38.

5. Becker, *Freiheit*, p. 58.

6. Becker, *Freiheit*, p. 77.

7. Becker, *Freiheit*, p. 101.

8. Becker, *Freiheit*, p. 104; cf. pp. 155f.: "An ideological pluralism is desirable because democratic legitimation is not a matter of theoretical discussion directed toward ascertaining the 'truth' of this or that philosophical or religious view. Rather, legitimation only has to do with how such views, by being disseminated, function as ideologicopolitical means for bringing about a majority's assent to the state's guarantee of individual liberties. It would not be desirable to stage public discussions of these different or even opposed worldviews and ethical approaches in an attempt to ferret out which one is 'right' and which one is 'wrong.'"

9. Becker, *Freiheit*, p. 186f.

10. D. Held, *Models of Democracy* (Oxford, 1987). As in the previous chapter, when I refer to "liberal" conceptions of the state, I use the term in the narrow sense of the tradition going back to Locke. "Liberals" like Dworkin or Rawls cannot be confined to this tradition.

11. As in the first two chapters, I am using "solidarity" here not as a normative but as a sociological concept.

12. On the concept of popular sovereignty, see I. Maus, *Zur Aufklärung der Demokratietheorie* (Frankfurt am Main, 1992), pp. 176ff.

13. N. Bobbio, *The Future of Democracy*, trans. R. Griffin (Cambridge, 1987).

14. Bobbio, *Future*, p. 24.

15. Bobbio, *Future*, p. 56: "Parallel to the need for self-rule there is the desire not to be ruled at all and to be left in peace."

16. Bobbio, *Future*, p. 40.

17. J. Dewey, *The Public and Its Problems* (Chicago, 1954), pp. 207f. [Dewey's quote is taken from Samuel J. Tilden. Trans.]

18. J. Cohen, "Deliberation and Democratic Legitimacy," in A. Hamlin and B. Pettit, eds., *The Good Polity* (Oxford, 1989), pp. 17–34; here p. 21.

19. "Deliberation is reasoned in that parties to it are required to state their reasons for advancing proposals, supporting them or criticizing them. . . . Reasons are offered with the aim of bringing others to accept the proposal, given their disparate ends and their commitment to settling the conditions of their association through free deliberation among equals." Cohen, "Deliberation," p. 22.

20. "Their consideration of proposals is not constrained by the authority of prior norms or requirements." Cohen, "Deliberation," p. 22.

21. "The participants are substantively equal in that the existing distribution of power and resources does not shape their chances to contribute to deliberation, nor does that distribution play an authoritative role in their deliberation." Cohen, "Deliberation," p. 23.

22. "Even under ideal conditions there is no promise that consensual reasons will be forthcoming. If they are not, then deliberation concludes with voting, subject to some form of majority rule. The fact that it may so conclude does not, however,

eliminate the distinction between deliberative forms of collective choice and forms that aggregate by non-deliberative preferences." Cohen, "Deliberation," p. 23.

23. "Inequalities of wealth, or the absence of institutional measures to redress the consequences of those inequalities, can serve to undermine the equality required in deliberative arenas themselves." Cohen, "Deliberation," p. 27; cf. also J. Cohen and J. Rogers, *On Democracy* (New York, 1983), chap. 6, pp. 146ff.; W. E. Connolly, *The Terms of Political Discourse* (Lexington, Mass., 1974).

24. "The relevant conceptions of the common good are not comprised simply of interests and preferences that are antecedent to deliberation. Instead, the interests, aims and ideals that comprise the common good are those that survive deliberation, interests that, on public reflection, we think it legitimate to appeal to in making claims on public resources." Cohen, "Deliberation," p. 23.

25. Cf. Michael Walzer's treatment of integration problems created in modern societies by the growing mobility of marriage partners, residences, social status, and political loyalties. These "four mobilities" loosen ascriptive bonds to family, locality, social background, and political tradition. For affected individuals, this implies an ambiguous release from traditional living conditions that, though socially integrating and providing orientation and protection, are also shaped by dependencies, prejudices, and oppression. This release is ambivalent, because it makes an increasing range of options available to the individual, and hence sets her free. On the one hand, this is a negative freedom that isolates the individual and compels her to pursue her own interests in a more or less purposive-rational fashion. On the other hand, as positive freedom it also enables her to enter into new social commitments of her own free will, to appropriate traditions critically, and to construct her own identity in a deliberate way. According to Walzer, in the last instance only the linguistic structure of social relations prevents disintegration: "Whatever the extent of the Four Mobilities, they do not seem to move us so far apart that we can no longer *talk* with one another. . . . Even political conflict in liberal societies rarely takes forms so extreme as to set its protagonists beyond negotiation and compromise, procedural justice and the very possibility of *speech*." "The Communitarian Critique of Liberalism," *Political Theory* 18 (1990): 13f.

26. Cf. N. Fraser, "Rethinking the Public Sphere: A Contribution to the Critique of Actually Existing Democracy," in C. Calhoun, ed., *Habermas and the Public Sphere* (Cambridge, Mass., 1992), p. 134: "I shall call *weak* publics publics whose deliberative practice consists exclusively in opinion formation and does not also encompass decision making."

27. See the contributions by B. Barry et al., "Symposium on Social Justice in the Liberal State," *Ethics* 93 (1983): 328–90; see also S. Benhabib, "Liberal Dialogue versus a Critical Theory of Discursive Legitimation," in N. Rosenblum, ed., *Liberalism and the Moral Life* (Cambridge, Mass., 1989), pp. 145ff.; J. D. Moon, "Constrained Discourse and Public Life," *Political Theory* 19 (1991): 202–29.

28. B. Ackerman, *Social Justice in the Liberal State* (New Haven, Conn., 1980), p. 4:

"Whenever anybody questions the legitimacy of anyone's power, the power holder must respond not by suppressing the questioner but by giving a reason that explains why he is more entitled to the source than the questioner is"; p. 7: "The reason advanced by a power wielder must not be inconsistent with the reasons he advances to justify his other claims to power."

29. Ackerman, *Social Justice*, p. 11.

30. B. Ackerman, "Why Dialogue?" *Journal of Philosophy* 86 (1989): 16: "We should simply say *nothing at all* about [any] disagreement and put the moral ideas that divide us off the conversational agenda."

31. Cf. S. Holmes, "Gag Rules or the Politics of Omission," in J. Elster and R. Slagstad, eds., *Constitutionalism and Democracy* (Cambridge, 1988), pp. 19–58.

32. C. Larmore, *Patterns of Moral Complexity* (Cambridge, 1987), p. 47.

33. B. Ackerman, "What Is Neutral about Neutrality?" *Ethics* 93 (1983): 390.

34. Larmore, *Patterns of Moral Complexity*, p. 53; the formulation of this "norm of rational dialogue" is modified somewhat in Larmore's "Political Liberalism," *Political Theory* 18 (1990): 347.

35. Here I skip over the relevant discussion of John Rawls's concept of "overlapping consensus": J. Rawls, *Political Liberalism* (New York, 1993), pp. 133–72; see also J. Habermas, *Justification and Application*, trans. C. P. Cronin (Cambridge, Mass., 1993), pp. 92–96.

36. Larmore, *Patterns of Moral Complexity*, p. 58.

37. On the procedure of fallibly reconstructing pretheoretical knowledge, see J. Habermas, "What Is Universal Pragmatics?" in Habermas, *Communication and the Evolution of Society*, trans. T. McCarthy (Boston, 1979), pp. 1–68.

38. J. Habermas, *Postmetaphysical Thinking*, trans. W. M. Hohengarten (Cambridge, Mass., 1992), pp. 136ff.

39. Under these conditions, even religious or metaphysical worldviews lose their fundamentalistic character; without giving up their claim to truth, they must take up the fallibilistic presuppositions of secularized thought insofar as they reflect on the fact that they compete with other interpretations of the world within the *same* universe of validity claims. In this connection, John Rawls speaks of "reasonable comprehensive doctrines." On the cognitive aspects of the distinction between tradition and modernity, see my discussion of Alasdair MacIntyre in Habermas, *Justification and Application*, pp. 96–105.

40. Fraser, "Rethinking the Public Sphere," p. 129; along similar lines, see S. Benhabib, "Models of Public Space: Hannah Arendt, the Liberal Tradition, and Jürgen Habermas," in Benhabib, *Situating the Self* (Cambridge, 1992), pp. 89–120.

41. Moon, "Constrained Discourse and Public Life," p. 221.

42. N. Fraser, "Struggle over Needs: Outline of a Socialist-Feminist Critical Theory of Late Capitalist Culture," in Fraser, *Unruly Practices* (Minneapolis, 1989), pp. 161–90.

43. R. A. Dahl, *Democracy and Its Critics* (New Haven, Conn., 1989), p. 307.

44. R. A. Dahl, *A Preface to Economic Democracy* (Oxford, 1985), pp. 59f.

45. Dahl, *Democracy and Its Critics*, p. 112.

46. Dewey, *The Public and Its Problems*, p. 208.

47. Dahl, *Democracy and Its Critics*, pp. 115ff.

48. Dahl, *Democracy and Its Critics*, p. 252; see also the summary on p. 314.

49. Dahl, *Democracy and Its Critics*, pp. 339f.

50. B. Peters, *Die Integration moderner Gesellschaften* (Frankfurt am Main, 1993), chap. 2.

51. B. Peters, *Rationalität, Recht und Gesellschaft* (Frankfurt am Main, 1991), pp. 204ff.

52. On what follows, see L. Wingert, *Gemeinsinn und Moral* (Frankfurt am Main, 1993), pts. 2 and 3.

53. K.-O. Apel, "The *A Priori* of the Communication Community and the Foundations of Ethics," in Apel, *Towards a Transformation of Philosophy*, trans. G. Adey and D. Frisby (London, 1980), p. 280 [translation slightly altered. Trans.].

54. H. Brunkhorst, "Zur Dialektik von realer und idealer Kommunikationsgemeinschaft," in A. Dorschel et al., eds., *Transzendentalpragmatik* (Frankfurt am Main, 1993), p. 345.

55. For the following, I rely on Peters, *Integration*, chaps. 5 and 6.

56. This presents an alternative to the "control model" of pure social relations. As is well known, to elucidate the concept of intentional social relations, relations brought about with will and consciousness, Marx turned in *Capital* to a model that linked the legal concept of civil union—the "association of free human beings"—with the productivist motif of a cooperative community of workers. He apparently imagined the autonomy of the self-organizing society as the exercise of conscious control over, or the planned management of, the material process of production: analogous to the mastery of nature, the social subject has its own objectified learning process at its "control" or "disposition." With this subjectivist concept of autonomy, however, the core problem of social self-organization—the constitution and self-stabilization of a community of free and equal persons—disappears. It is not the common control of social cooperation that forms the core of intentionally established social relations. Rather, this core resides in a normative regulation of life in common, a regulation that rests on the agreement of all and secures inclusive, egalitarian relations of mutual recognition (and therewith the integrity of each individual). In Marx the guiding thread is not communicative practice but the control or planning of theoretically objectified social processes. See the critique of this model in my "Dogmatism, Reason, and Decision: On Theory and Practice in Our Scientific Civilization," in Habermas, *Theory and Practice*, trans. J. Viertel (Boston, 1973), pp. 253–82.

57. See chap. 3 in this volume.

58. Klaus Lüderssen develops this concept of countersteering in the context of criminal law: "Die Steuerungsfunktion des Gesetzes—Überformung oder Gegensteuerung zur Entwicklungstendenz einer Gesellschaft," in Lüderssen, *Genesis und Geltung im Recht* (Frankfurt am Main, 1993).

Chapter 8

1. U. Bermbach, "Politische Institutionen und gesellschaftlicher Wandel," in H. H. Hartwich, ed. *Macht und Ohnmacht politischer Institutionen* (Opladen, 1989), pp. 57–71; see also the following by J. G. March and J. P. Olsen: *Rediscovering Institutions* (New York, 1989); "The New Institutionalism: Organizational Factors of Political Life," *American Political Science Review* 77 (1984):734–49; "Popular Sovereignty and the Search for Appropriate Institutions," *Journal of Public Policy* 6 (1984): 341–70.

2. Cf. also N. Bobbio, *The Future of Democracy*, trans. R. Griffin (Cambridge, 1987), p. 28.

3. F. Scharpf, *Demokratietheorie zwischen Utopie und Anpassung* (Konstanz, 1970), pp. 29ff.

4. J. A. Schumpeter, *Capitalism, Socialism and Democracy*, 2d ed. (New York, 1947), pp. 269ff.; for a critique, see P. Bachrach, *The Theory of Democratic Elitism* (Washington, D.C., 1980).

5. Scharpf, *Demokratietheorie*, p. 39.

6. A. Downs, *An Economic Theory of Democracy* (New York, 1957).

7. A. Sen, "Rational Fools: A Critique of the Behavioral Foundations of Economic Theory," *Philosophy and Public Affairs* 6 (1977): 328ff.

8. J. Mansbridge, "Self-Interest in Political Life," *Political Theory* 18 (1990): 132–53. "Rational choice models need now to expand the range of motives they take into account and the contexts in which they are deployed, asking specifically in what context a model premised on one kind of motivation best predicts the behavior of certain actors" (ibid., p. 145).

9. C. Offe, "Bindings, Shackles, Brakes: On Self-Limitation Strategies," in A. Honneth et al., eds., *Cultural-Political Interventions in the Unfinished Project of Enlightenment*, trans. B. Fultner (Cambridge, Mass., 1992), p. 78.

10. For a critique, see F. W. Scharpf, "Politische Steuerung und politische Institution," in Hartwich, *Macht und Ohnmacht*, pp. 17–29. See also the exchange between Scharpf and Luhmann in *Politische Vierteljahresschrift*, vol. 30 (1989): N. Luhmann, "Politische Steuerung: Ein Diskussionsbeitrag," pp. 4–9, and F. W. Scharpf, "Politische Steuerung und politische Institution," pp. 10–21; and in the special issue, vol. 19 (1989), on "state activity," F. W. Scharpf, "Verhandlungs-systeme, Verteilungskonflikte und Pathologien der politischen Steuerung," pp. 61–67.

11. N. Luhmann, *Political Theory in the Welfare State*, trans. J. Bednarz, Jr. (New York, 1990), p. 49: "The administration drafts the bills for politics and dominates

parliamentary committees and similar institutions. Politics, with the help of its party organizations, suggests to the public what it should vote for and why. And the public exercises its influence on the administration through various channels, like interest groups and emotional appeals" [translation slightly altered. Trans.].

12. Luhmann, *Political Theory*, p. 50 [translation slightly altered. Trans.].

13. H. Willke, *Ironie des Staates* (Frankfurt am Main, 1992), p. 345.

14. T. C. Schelling, *Micromotives and Macrobehavior* (New York, 1978), pp. 225f.; H. Simon, "Rational Decision Making in Business Organizations," in *Models of Bounded Rationality*, vol. 2 (Cambridge, Mass., 1982), pp. 486f.

15. J. Elster, "The Market and the Forum," in J. Elster and A. Hylland, eds., *Foundations of Social Choice Theory* (Cambridge, 1986), p. 109.

16. J. Elster, "The Possibility of Rational Politics," in D. Held, ed., *Political Theory Today* (Oxford, 1991), p. 120.

17. Elster, "The Market and the Forum," p. 112.

18. Elster, "The Market and the Forum," p. 117: "The mere decision to engage in rational discussion does not ensure that the transactions will in fact be conducted rationally, since much depends on the structure and framework of the proceedings."

19. On what follows, see J. Elster, *The Cement of Society* (Cambridge, 1989), chap. 3.

20. "The former is supposed to be guided by instrumental rationality, while the behavior of the latter is dictated by social norms. The former is 'pulled' by the prospect of future rewards, whereas the latter is 'pushed' from behind by quasi-internal forces. The former adapts to changing circumstances. . . . The latter is . . . sticking to the prescribed behavior even if new and apparently better options become available." Elster, *Cement of Society*, p. 97.

21. Elster, *Cement of Society*, pp. 231ff.

22. J. Elster, "Arguing and Bargaining in Two Constituent Assemblies," The Storr Lectures, Yale Law School, 1991, ms., pp. 37f.

23. On the critical reception that game theory has given the concept of communicative action, see J. Johnson, "Habermas on Strategic and Communicative Action," *Political Theory* 19 (1991): 181–201.

24. "Given the fragility of instrumental thinking in politics, the chosen conception of justice cannot be a consequentialist one like utilitarianism. Rather, it must focus on the inherent rights of individuals to equal shares in decision-making and in social welfare." Elster, "The Possibility of Rational Politics," p. 116.

25. Elster, "The Possibility of Rational Politics," p. 120.

26. In response to the obvious objection that the extraordinary design of constitutional assemblies favors his hypothesis, Elster points to the equally unusual revolutionary situations triggered by legitimation crises. In the latter situations, threats—on the part of the southern states willing to secede or on the part of the king willing to intervene—were more likely to have had a polarizing effect.

27. "The process of constitution-making can illuminate the two types of speech acts I shall refer to as *arguing* and *bargaining*. To understand constitutional proceedings, we can benefit from Jürgen Habermas no less than from Thomas Schelling. . . . Although my illustrations will be mainly taken from the two constituent assemblies, much of what I shall have to say applies more broadly, to ordinary legislatures, committees and similar bodies." Elster, "Arguing and Bargaining," p. 4.

28. Elster, "Arguing and Bargaining," pp. 91f.: "Impartiality is logically prior to the attempt to exploit it (or the need to respect it) for self-interested purposes. This is not to say, however, that impartial concerns are necessarily widespread. We know from other contexts that it may take only a tiny proportion of cooperators in a population to induce everybody to behave *as if* they were cooperators. Similarly, a small group of impartially minded individuals might induce large numbers to mimic their impartiality out of self-interest. . . . Also, the norm against the expression of self-interest will be stronger in public settings than if the debates are conducted behind closed doors. A public setting will also encourage the use of precommitment through principle, with the larger audience serving as a resonance board for the claim and making it more difficult to back down."

29. C. Offe and U. K. Preuss, "Democratic Institutions and Moral Resources," in Held, ed., *Political Theory Today*, p. 149.

30. Willke, *Ironie des Staates*, p. 12.

31. Willke, *Ironie des Staates*, p. 207.

32. [In this context, the idea of "supervision" connotes a form of direction more akin to the therapist's cautious use of indirect hints than to direct forms of control. Trans.]

33. Willke, *Ironie des Staates*, p. 134.

34. G. Teubner, "Juridification—Concepts, Aspects, Limits, Solutions," in Teubner, ed., *Juridification of Social Spheres* (Berlin, 1987), pp. 3–48.

35. Willke, *Ironie des Staates*, p. 202.

36. Willke, *Ironie des Staates*, p. 49.

37. See my "Vorlesungen zu einer sprachtheoretischen Grundlegung der Soziologie," in Habermas, *Vorstudien und Ergänzungen zur Theorie des kommunikativen Handelns* (Frankfurt am Main, 1984), pp. 35–59. English translation forthcoming (Cambridge, Mass.).

38. See my excursus on Luhmann in Habermas, *Philosophical Discourse of Modernity*, trans. F. Lawrence (Cambridge, Mass., 1987), pp. 368–85.

39. Willke, *Ironie des Staates*, pp. 165f.

40. Willke, *Ironie des Staates*, pp. 345f. (emphasis added).

41. Willke, *Ironie des Staates*. p. 346.

42. Willke, *Ironie des Staates*, p. 197.

43. Willke, *Ironie des Staates*, p. 358 (emphasis added).

44. Willke, *Ironie des Staates*, p. 357.

45. B. Peters, *Die Integration moderner Gesellschaften* (Frankfurt am Main, 1993), chap. 9, sec. 2.

46. H. J. Merry, *Five Branch Government* (Urbana, Ill., 1980), p. 25; "public interest groups" were treated early on by E. E. Schattschneider, *The Semisovereign People* (New York, 1960), pp. 22ff.

47. Naturally, this is not true for democratic procedures that, for example, require administrations to publicize and justify decisions, that grant clients the right to a hearing or rights to participate, and thus do not impair the priority of legal statutes.

48. Peters, *Integration*, pp. 340f.

49. As held by J. Gerhards and F. Neidhardt, *Strukturen und Funktionen moderner Öffentlichkeit* (Berlin, 1990), p. 19.

50. T. Parsons, "On the Concept of Influence," in Parsons, *Sociological Theory and Modern Society* (New York, 1967), pp. 355–82. On the relation between "influence" and "value," and on the delimitation of these generalized forms of communication from steering media, such as money and administrative power, see J. Habermas, *The Theory of Communicative Action*, trans. T. McCarthy, 2 vols. (Boston, 1984, 1987), 2:273–82.

51. On this function of churches and religious communities, see F. S. Fiorenza, "The Church as a Community of Interpretation: Political Theology between Discourse Ethics and Hermeneutical Reconstruction," in D. S. Browning and F. S. Fiorenza, eds., *Habermas, Modernity, and Public Theology* (New York, 1992), pp. 66–91.

52. J. Habermas, *The Structural Transformation of the Public Sphere*, trans. T. Burger and F. Lawrence (Cambridge, Mass., 1989), p. 27 [trans. altered]; see Craig Calhoun's introduction to the collection edited by him: *Habermas and the Public Sphere* (Cambridge, Mass., 1992), p. 27; see also D. Goodman, "Public Sphere and Private Life: Toward a Synthesis of Current Historical Approaches to the Old Regime," *History and Theory* 31 (1992): 1–20.

53. T. Smith, *The Role of Ethics in Social Theory* (Albany, 1991), pp. 153–74.

54. On the concept of "discursive design," see J. S. Dryzek, *Discursive Democracy* (Cambridge, 1990), pp. 43ff.

55. J. Keane, *Democracy and Civil Society* (London, 1988). Antonio Gramsci introduced this concept into more recent discussion; see N. Bobbio, "Gramsci and the Concept of Civil Society," in J. Keane, ed., *Civil Society and the State* (London, 1988), pp. 73–100.

56. S. N. Eisenstadt, ed., *Democracy and Modernity* (Leiden, 1992), p. ix; in the same volume, see also L. Roniger, "Conditions for the Consolidation of Democracy in Southern Europe and Latin America," pp. 53–68.

57. J. L. Cohen and A. Arato, *Civil Society and Political Theory* (Cambridge, Mass., 1992), p. 346.

58. E. Hankiss, "The Loss of Responsibility," in J. MacLean, A. Montefiori, and P. Winch, eds., *The Political Responsibility of Intellectuals* (Cambridge, 1990), pp. 29–52.

59. See Hannah Arendt's communication-theoretic interpretation of totalitarianism in *The Origins of Totalitarianism* (New York, 1973), pp. 473–78; e.g., pp. 473–74, 475: "[Totalitarian government] presses masses of isolated men together *and* supports them in a world that has become a wilderness for them . . . , in order to set the terror-ruled movement into motion and keep it moving . . . . [It] could not exist without destroying the public realm of life, that is, without destroying, by isolating men, their political capacities. But . . . it is not content with this isolation and destroys private life as well."

60. Cohen and Arato, *Civil Society*, p. 531.

61. Cohen and Arato, *Civil Society*, p. 474.

62. The classic study on fascism by I. Bibo (*Die deutsche Hysterie* [Frankfurt am Main, 1991]) already emphasizes this double aspect. Socialism, too, was Janus-faced, looking simultaneously toward the future and the past: in the new industrial forms of trade, it wanted to rescue the old forces of social integration found in the solidary communities of a vanishing preindustrial world. See the title essay in J. Habermas, *Die nachholende Revolution* (Frankfurt am Main, 1990), pp. 179–204.

63. J. Habermas, *Strukturwandel der Öffentlichkeit* (Frankfurt am Main, 1990), pp. 15–20. For the English, see Habermas, "Further Reflections on the Public Sphere," in Calhoun, *Habermas and the Public Sphere*, pp. 425–29.

64. Gerhards and Neidhardt, *Strukturen*, p. 27.

65. Cohen and Arato, *Civil Society*, pp. 492–563.

66. M. Kaase, "Massenkommunikation und politischer Prozeß," in M. Kaase and W. Schulz, eds., *Massenkommunikation, Kölner Zeitschrift für Soziologie und Sozialpsychologie* Sonderheft 30 (1989): 97–117.

67. This is primarily true of electronic media, which are most frequently used by a broad public; it must be qualified for newspapers and other media.

68. S. Hall, "Encoding and Decoding in TV-Discourse," in Hall, ed., *Culture, Media, Language* (London, 1980), pp. 128–38; D. Morley, *Family Television* (London, 1988).

69. M. Gurevitch and G. Blumler, "Political Communication Systems and Democratic Values," in J. Lichtenberg, ed., *Democracy and the Mass Media* (Cambridge, Mass., 1990), p. 270.

70. Cf. the principles for a "regulated pluralism" of the mass media in J. B. Thompson, *Ideology and Modern Culture* (Cambridge, 1990), pp. 261ff.

71. J. Keane advocates a similar "media philosophy" in *The Media and Democracy* (Cambridge, 1991).

72. R. Cobb, J. K. Ross, and M. H. Ross, "Agenda Building as a Comparative Political Process," *American Political Science Review* 70 (1976): 126–38; R. Cobb and C. Elder, "The Politics of Agenda-Building," *Journal of Politics* (1971): 892–915.

73. Cobb, Ross, and Ross, "Agenda Building as a Comparative Political Process," p. 132.

74. S. Hilgartner, "The Rise and Fall of Social Problems," *American Journal of Sociology* 94 (1988): 53–78.

75. For a stimulating empirical analysis of social movements as "exponents of the lifeworld," see L. Rolke, *Protestbewegungen in der Bundesrepublik* (Opladen, 1987).

76. J. Raschke, *Soziale Bewegungen* (Frankfurt am Main, 1985).

77. C. Offe, "Challenging the Boundaries of Institutional Politics: Social Movements since the 1960s," in C. S. Maier, *Changing Boundaries of the Political* (Cambridge, 1987), pp. 63–106.

78. J. Rawls, *A Theory of Justice* (Cambridge, Mass., 1971), p. 364.

79. Cohen and Arato, *Civil Society*, pp. 587f. On "militant tolerance," see U. Rödel, G. Frankenberg, and H. Dubiel, *Die demokratische Frage* (Frankfurt am Main, 1989), chap. 6.

80. On the scholarly legal discussion, see R. Dreier, "Widerstandsrecht im Rechtsstaat?" in Dreier, *Recht—Staat—Vernunft* (Frankfurt am Main, 1991), pp. 39–72; T. Laker, *Ziviler Ungehorsam* (Baden-Baden, 1986).

81. G. Teubner, "Reflexives Recht: Entwicklungsmodelle des Rechts in vergleichender Perspektive," *Archiv für Rechts- und Sozialphilosophie* 68 (1982): 13ff.

Chapter 9

1. Impressive examples are provided by the detailed catalog of fundamental rights found in the constitutions of the German Länder (federal states) adopted after 1945, as well as in the April 1990 outline of a constitution for the German Democratic Republic. The latter, which was not adopted as law, was published by the "New Constitution of the GDR" Team of the *Runde Tisch* (Berlin, 1990).

2. O. Kahn-Freund, "Das soziale Ideal des Reichsarbeitsgerichts," in T. Ramm, ed., *Arbeitsrecht und Politik* (Frankfurt am Main, 1966), pp. 149ff.

3. F. Wieacker, "Das Sozialmodell der klassischen Privatrechtsgesetzbücher und die Entwicklung der modernen Gesellschaft," in Wieacker, *Industriegesellschaft und Privatrechtsordnung* (Frankfurt am Main, 1974), p. 5.

4. For an overview of the discussion, see H. D. Assmann, *Wirtschaftsrecht in der Mixed Economy* (Frankfurt am Main, 1980), chap. 2.

5. D. Grimm, "Die Zukunft der Verfassung," in Grimm, *Die Zukunft der Verfassung* (Frankfurt am Main, 1991), p. 437 (emphasis added).

6. U. K. Preuss, *Revolution, Fortschritt und Verfassung* (Berlin, 1990).

7. This conclusion suggests itself if one adopts the systems-theoretic description of the legal system as self-description; see R. Wiethölter, "Ist unserem Recht der Prozeß zu machen?" in Honneth et al., eds., *Zwischenbetrachtungen im Prozeß der Aufklärung* (Frankfurt am Main, 1989), pp. 794–812.

8. F. Kübler, *Über die praktischen Aufgaben zeitgemäßer Privatrechtstheorie* (Karlsruhe, 1975), p. 9.

9. H. J. Steiner, *Moral Argument and Social Vision in the Courts* (Madison, Wisc., 1987), p. 92.

10. F. Kübler, "Privatrecht und Demokratie: Zur Aktualität gesellschafts-theoretischer Vorstellungen in der Jurisprudenz," in F. Baur et al., eds., *Funktionswandel der Privatrechtsinstitutionen* (Tübingen, 1974), p. 719.

11. Kübler, *Über die praktischen Aufgaben*, pp. 51f.

12. Kübler, *Über die praktischen Aufgaben*, p. 60.

13. L. M. Friedman, "Transformations in American Legal Culture 1800–1985," *Zeitschrift für Rechtssoziologie* 6 (1985): 191.

14. [Habermas refers here to the German Code of Civil Law, i.e., the *Bürgerliches Gesetzbuch* or BGB. Trans.]

15. L. Raiser, *Die Zukunft des Privatrechts* (Berlin, 1971), p. 20.

16. K. Hesse, *Verfassungsrecht und Privatrecht* (Heidelberg, 1988), p. 27.

17. For the Anglo-American countries, see P. S. Atiyah, *The Rise and Fall of Freedom of Contract* (Oxford, 1979); L. M. Friedman, *Total Justice* (New York, 1985); Steiner, *Moral Argument and Social Vision*.

18. Hesse, *Verfassungsrecht*, p. 34.

19. Raiser, *Zukunft des Privatrechts*, p. 29.

20. R. Alexy, *Theorie der Grundrechte* (Baden-Baden, 1985), pp. 327–30.

21. Alexy, *Theorie der Grundrechte*, p. 317.

22. On the distinction between the moral, legal, and ethical concepts of the person, see R. Forst, *Kontexte der Gerechtigkeit* (Frankfurt am Main, 1994). A *metalegal* concept of the person is likewise involved when Konrad Hesse describes the human type on which the constitutional order of the Basic Law "depends": "It is the type of human being as 'person': a being of non-instrumentalizable value, a being destined for free development, at the same time related and bound to community and thus also called to take part in responsibly shaping human living together." Hesse, *Verfassungsrecht*, p. 43.

23. Raiser, *Zukunft des Privatrechts*, p. 9.

24. Alexy, *Theorie der Grundrechte*, p. 329.

25. Alexy, *Theorie der Grundrechte*, pp. 458f.

26. J. Köndgen, *Selbstbindung ohne Vertrag* (Tübingen, 1981); C. Joerges, "Die Überarbeitung des BGB, die Sonderprivatrechte und die Unbestimmtheit des Rechts," *Kritische Justiz* 20 (1987): 166–82. In the Federal Republic, the "seizure"

of private law by basic rights either is interpreted in the sense of binding the civil legal order to basic constitutional norms, and hence as the demand for a congruence of norms in (objective) law, or it is interpreted as the private-legal concretization of publicly protected (subjective) rights "that need to be fleshed out." See H. H. Rupp, "Vom Wandel der Grundrechte," *Archiv des öffentlichen Rechts* 101 (1976): 168ff.

[The ideas of *Drittwirkung* and *Ausstrahlung* refer to the effects that constitutional values and rights have on all areas of law. More specifically, *Drittwirkung* concerns the issue of whether basic rights protecting the individual from state encroachment also apply in areas of private law, i.e., to relationships between individuals. Trans.]

27. H. J. Papier, *Eigentumsgarantie des Grundgesetzes im Wandel* (Heidelberg, 1984), p. 27.

28. H. Bethge, "Aktuelle Probleme der Grundrechtsdogmatik," *Der Staat* 24 (1985): 369.

29. D. Hart, "Soziale Steuerung durch Vertragsabschlußkontrolle—Alternativen zum Vertragsschluß?," *Kritische Vierteljahresschrift für Gesetzgebung und Rechtswissenschaft* 1 (1986): 240f.

30. Compare the interesting justification given by the Federal Constitutional Court in its ruling of July 2, 1990 (1 BvR 26/84) on the constitutional complaint against a judgment of the Federal High Court of Justice; *Juristenzeitung* 45/14 (1990): 691ff., esp. p. 692.

31. Steiner, *Moral Argument*, p. 9; cf. Köndgen, *Selbstbindung*, pp. 19ff.

32. Rupp, "Vom Wandel," p. 180.

33. See E. J. Mestmäcker, "Wiederkehr der bürgerlichen Gesellschaft und ihres Rechts," *Rechtshistorisches Journal* 10 (1991): 177–84; see also E. J. Mestmäcker, "Der Kampf ums Recht in der offenen Gesellschaft," *Rechtstheorie* 20 (1989): 273–88.

34. S. Simitis, "Wiederentdeckung des Individuums und arbeitsrechtliche Normen," *Sinzheimer Cahiers* 2 (1991): 7–42.

35. J. Habermas, "The New Obscurity: The Crisis of the Welfare State and the Exhaustion of Utopian Energies," in Habermas, *The New Conservatism*, ed. and trans. S. W. Nicholsen (Cambridge, Mass., 1989), pp. 64–69.

36. G. Teubner, "Substantive and Reflexive Elements in Modern Law," *Law and Society Review* 17 (1983): 239ff.; see also his "Regulatorisches Recht: Chronik eines angekündigten Todes," *Archiv für Rechts- und Sozialphilosophie* Beiheft 54 (1990): 140–61; but see also E. Rehbinder, "Reflexive Law and Practice," in A. Febbrajo and G. Teubner, eds., *State, Law, Economy as Autopoietic Systems* (Milan, 1992), pp. 579–608.

37. G. Teubner, ed., *Dilemmas of Law in the Welfare State* (Berlin, 1986).

38. For a discussion of this in the area of liability law, see G. Brüggemeier, "Justizielle Schutzpolitik de lege lata," in G. Brüggemeier and D. Hart, *Soziales Schuldrecht* (Bremen, 1987), pp. 7–41.

39. P. Häberle, *Verfassung als öffentlicher Prozeß* (Frankfurt am Main, 1978).

40. R. Wiethölter, "Proceduralization of the Category of Law," in C. Joerges and D. M. Trubek, eds., *Critical Legal Thought* (Baden-Baden, 1989), pp. 501–10; in the same volume, C. Joerges, "Politische Rechtstheorie und Critical Legal Studies," pp. 597–644; also G. Brüggemeier, "Wirtschaftsordnung und Staatsverfassung—Mischverfassung des demokratischen Interventionskapitalismus—Verfassungstheorie des Sozialstaates: Drei Modelle der Verflechtung von Staat und Wirtschaft?," *Jahrbuch für Rechtstheorie und Rechtssoziologie* 8 (1982): 60–73.

41. E. Schmidt, "Von der Privat- zur Sozialautonomie," *Juristenzeitung* 35 (1980): 158.

42. Simitis, "Wiederentdeckung des Individuums," p. 11 (emphasis added); see also S. Simitis, "Juridification of Labor Relations," in G. Teubner, ed., *Juridification of Social Spheres* (Berlin, 1987), pp. 113–61.

43. Simitis, "Wiederentdeckung des Individuums," p. 10.

44. S. Simitis, "Selbstbestimmung: Illusorisches Projekt oder reale Chance?" in J. Rüsen et al., eds., *Die Zukunft der Aufklärung* (Frankfurt am Main, 1988), p. 177: "Intervention was not the result of whim or accident, and thus it cannot be easily reversed." Cf. also I. Maus, "Verrechtlichung, Entrechtlichung und der Funktionswandel von Institutionen," in G. Göhler, ed., *Grundfragen der Theorie politischer Institutionen* (Opladen, 1987), pp. 132–72.

45. Alexy, *Theorie der Grundrechte*, pp. 370, 372: "If no sufficient reason exists for permitting unequal treatment, then equal treatment is required," or "if sufficient reason exists for requiring unequal treatment, then unequal treatment is required."

46. Simitis, "Selbstbestimmung," p. 193; see also Simitis's treatment of developments in family law, which lead him to conclude (pp. 184f.):

The recognition that each family member is an individual, as well as the recognition that each member has independent interests, in no way makes it necessary to develop a detailed intervention system that would have the purpose of realizing a precise educational idea and thus would constantly require elaboration. . . . Rather, each legal regulation must be oriented by the significance that familial interaction has for the development of its members; hence, it must see its real starting point in family dynamics. The rejection of the idea that the family is a harmonious unit . . . is by no means a compelling reason to give authorities outside the family the power to make substantive decisions. To begin with, their intervention must not touch the family members' entitlement and obligation to decide what form their relations to one another must take. . . . In attempting to preserve those affected, for the sake of their self-determination, from burdens that make communication impossible or at least endanger it, one must not submit them to even more regulatory influences than before.

47. H. F. Zacher, "Juridification in the Field of Social Law," in Teubner, ed., *Juridification*, pp. 373–417.

48. As in Habermas, *The Theory of Communicative Action*, trans. T. McCarthy, 2 vols. (Boston, 1984, 1987), 2:361–73; there I proposed a distinction between law as institution and law as medium—contrasting socially integrative norms with the legal forms of the political system—which cannot be maintained. On this, see K. Tuori, "Discourse Ethics and the Legitimacy of Law," *Ratio Juris* 2 (1989): 125–43.

49. U. Preuss, "Verfassungstheoretische Überlegungen zur normativen Begründung des Wohlfahrtsstaates," in C. Sachße and H. T. Engelhardt, eds., *Sicherheit und Freiheit* (Frankfurt am Main, 1990), pp. 125f.

50. Böckenförde characterizes such a "democratic-function theory of basic rights" as follows: "Basic rights receive their meaning and their importance in principle as constituent factors of a free process . . . of democratic will-formation." See his "Basic Rights: Theory and Interpretation," in Böckenförde, *State, Society, and Liberty*, trans. J. A. Underwood (New York, 1991), p. 192.

51. I. M. Young, *Justice and the Politics of Difference* (Princeton, 1990), p. 25.

52. Young, *Justice*, p. 39.

53. Young, *Justice*, p. 76.

54. In comparison with theories that highlight distribution, the focus of feminist legal theory on power has this advantage: in emphasizing the emancipatory meaning of equal rights, one locates the normative core of the system of rights in the autonomy both of the individual and of the associated citizens. To be sure, the feminist analysis of power sometimes has the tendency to stylize the sexes as monolithic entities, similar to the way in which orthodox Marxism objectified social classes into macrosubjects. C. A. MacKinnon, *Towards a Feminist Theory of the State* (Cambridge, Mass., 1989), which is otherwise quite instructive, is not entirely free of this tendency.

55. D. L. Rhode, *Justice and Gender* (Cambridge, Mass., 1989), pp. 61f.

56. On the history of feminism in America, see Rhode, *Justice and Gender*, pt. 1.

57. Rhode, *Justice and Gender*, p. 126: "Those interrelated inequalities, coupled with shifting marriage, employment and fertility patterns, have contributed to an increasing feminization of poverty. Although official classifications of poverty are an imperfect index of actual need, they can measure relative status. Women of all ages are twice as likely as men to be poor, and women who are single parents are five times as likely. Two thirds of all indigent adults are female, and two thirds of the persistently poor live in female-headed households. Some 90 percent of single-parent families are headed by women, and half of those families are under the poverty line. Among minorities, the situation is worse; women head three quarters of all poor black families and over half of all Hispanic families."

58. Rhode, *Justice and Gender*, p. 82; emphasis added.

59. Rhode, *Justice and Gender*, pp. 97f.

60. See MacKinnon, *Towards a Feminist Theory of the State*, p. 219: "Doctrinally speaking, two alternative paths to sex equality for women exist within the

mainstream approach to sex discrimination, paths that follow the lines of the sameness/difference tension. The leading one is: be the same as men. This path is termed 'gender neutrality' doctrinally and the single standard philosophically. It is testimony to how substance becomes form in law that this rule is considered formal equality. . . . To women who want equality yet find themselves 'different', the doctrine provides an alternative route: be different from men. This equal recognition of difference is termed the special benefit rule or special protection rule legally, the double standard philosophically. It is in rather bad odor, reminiscent . . . of protective labor laws."

61. Rhode, *Justice and Gender*, p. 306.

62. MacKinnon, *Towards a Feminist Theory of the State*, chaps. 12, 13; Young, *Justice*, chap. 4; C. Smart, *Feminism and the Power of Law* (London, 1989), pp. 138–59.

63. Seyla Benhabib argues against the contextualist and skeptical interpretation of political discourse on the part of poststructuralist feminism; see her "Feminism and the Question of Postmodernism," in Benhabib, *Situating the Self* (Cambridge, 1992), pp. 203–41.

64. M. Minow, *Making All the Difference* (Ithaca, 1990), p. 309.

65. A. Honneth, *Struggle for Recognition*, trans. J. Anderson (Cambridge, 1995).

66. Rhode, *Justice and Gender*, p. 317.

67. K. Günther, "Der Wandel der Staatsaufgaben und die Krise des regulativen Rechts," in D. Grimm, ed., *Wachsende Staatsaufgaben—sinkende Steuerungsfähigkeit des Rechts* (Baden-Baden, 1990), p. 62.

68. Günther, "Wandel der Staatsaufgaben und die Krise des regulativen Rechts," p. 57. [The tense of the passage has been changed from past to present. Trans.]

69. Note that some disciples of the democratic legal positivism (*Gesetzespositivismus*) of the Weimar period were not immune to this view of law, i.e., the view of a social-welfare legislator who is insensitive to the inherent normativity of the legal form.

70. Günther, "Wandel der Staatsaufgaben und die Krise des regulativen Rechts," p. 65.

71. For a treatment of the classical administration, see D. Grimm, *Recht und Staat in der bürgerlichen Gesellschaft* (Frankfurt am Main, 1987).

72. D. Grimm, "Der Wandel der Staatsaufgaben und die Krise des Rechtsstaats," in Grimm, *Die Zukunft der Verfassung*, pp. 165f.: "It was reactive insofar as it always presupposed an external event that proved to be a disturbance; it was bipolar insofar as the activity was restricted to the relation between state and disturber; it was selective insofar it expended itself in the prevention or elimination of individual disturbances."

73. Grimm, "Wandel der Staatsaufgaben und die Krise des Rechtsstaats," *Zukunft der Verfassung*, p. 172.

74. Joerges and Trubek, eds., *Critical Legal Thought*.

75. In Germany the discussion over the generality of legal statutes is still colored by the rather extreme views found in Carl Schmitt's 1928 *Verfassungslehre*

(Constitutional Theory). This view became influential in the Federal Republic through the direct efforts of Ernst Forsthoff and indirectly through Franz Neumann. I did not escape this influence myself at the end of the fifties; see my introduction to J. Habermas, L. v. Friedeburg, C. Oehler, and F. Weltz, *Student und Politik* (Neuwied, 1961), pp. 11–55. More recently, see the historically reflective and systematically clear analysis of H. Hofmann, "Das Postulat der Allgemeinheit des Gesetzes," in C. Starck, ed., *Die Allgemeinheit des Gesetzes* (Göttingen, 1987), pp. 9–48.

76. See chaps. 5 and 6 of this volume.

77. W. Schmidt, *Einführung in die Probleme des Verwaltungsrechts* (Munich, 1982), pp. 241–61; H. Faber, *Verwaltungsrecht* (Tübingen, 1987), pp. 25ff. [On the concept of *Gesetzesvorbehalt*, see chap. 4 n38. Trans.]

78. Grimm, "Zukunft der Verfassung," *Zukunft der Verfassung*, p. 433.

79. U. Beck, *Risk Society*, trans. M. Ritter (London, 1992); see also his *Gegengifte: Die organisierte Unverantwortlichkeit* (Frankfurt am Main, 1988).

80. E. Denninger, "Der Präventions-Staat," in Denninger, *Der gebändigte Leviathan* (Baden-Baden, 1990), p. 42.

81. Denninger, "Präventions-Staat," *Der gebändigte Leviathan*, pp. 33, 35; emphasis modified.

82. J. Hirsch, *Der Sicherheitsstaat* (Frankfurt am Main, 1980).

83. D. Grimm, "Verfassungsrechtliche Anmerkungen zum Thema Prävention," in Grimm, *Zukunft der Verfassung*, p. 217.

84. Grimm, "Zukunft der Verfassung," *Zukunft der Verfassung*, pp. 420–22.

85. B. Peters, *Rationalität, Recht und Gesellschaft* (Frankfurt am Main, 1991), pp. 136ff.

86. See appendix I, "Popular Sovereignty as Procedure," in this volume.

87. D. Grimm, "Interessenwahrung und Rechtsdurchsetzung in der Gesellschaft von morgen," in Grimm, *Zukunft der Verfassung*, p. 178.

88. I. Maus, *Zur Aufklärung der Demokratietheorie* (Frankfurt am Main, 1992), pp. 203ff.; also her "Basisdemokratische Aktivitäten und rechtsstaatliche Verfassung: Zum Verhältnis von institutionalisierter und nichtinstitutionalisierter Volkssouveränität," in T. Kreuder, ed., *Der orientierungslose Leviathan* (Marburg, 1992), pp. 99–116.

89. See the decisions of the Constitutional Court that at least point toward a constitutional regulation of the "Fourth Estate": *Neue Juristische Wochenschrift* 34/33 (1981): 1774ff.; also 40/5 (1987): 239ff.; 40/47 (1987): 2987ff.; 44/14 (1991): 899ff.; see also F. Kübler, "Die neue Rundfunkordnung: Marktstruktur und Wettbewerbsbedingungen," *Neue Juristische Wochenschrift* 40/47 (1987): 2961–67.

90. Drawing on Claude Lefort's work, Ulrich Rödel, Günter Frankenberg, and Helmut Dubiel have developed this idea in *Die demokratische Frage* (Frankfurt am Main, 1989), pp. 85ff.; see also U. Rödel, ed., *Autonome Gesellschaft und libertäre Demokratie* (Frankfurt am Main, 1990).

91. J. Habermas, *The Past as Future*, trans. and ed. M. Pensky (Lincoln, Nebr., 1994), pp. 8ff.

92. R. Knieper, *Nationale Souveränität* (Frankfurt am Main, 1991).

93. Preuss, "Verfassungstheoretische Überlegungen," p. 64.

94. Preuss, "Verfassungstheoretische Überlegungen," p. 73.

Postscript

1. This interpretation of Kantian private law is contested by I. Maus, *Zur Aufklärung der Demokratietheorie* (Frankfurt am Main, 1992), pp. 148ff.

2. J. Rawls, *Political Liberalism* (New York, 1993).

3. Political questions are normally so complex that they require the simultaneous treatment of pragmatic, ethical, and moral *aspects*. To be sure, these aspects are only *analytically* distinct. Thus my attempt in chap. 4 (pp. 164ff.) to exemplify different types of discourses by ordering concrete questions in a linear fashion is misleading.

4. Naturally, one must distinguish between morally grounded rights and policies; not all legitimate political programs ground rights. Thus, on the one hand, there are strong moral grounds for an individual right to political asylum and a corresponding guarantee of legal remedies (which must not be replaced by institutional guarantees provided by the state). On the other hand, the individual has no absolute legal claim to immigration, although Western societies are indeed morally obligated to uphold a liberal immigration policy. In appendix II, pp. 513ff., I do not draw these distinctions clearly enough, but see my reply to Charles Taylor, entitled "Struggles for Recognition in the Democratic Constitutional State," in A. Gutmann, ed., *Multiculturalism* (Princeton, 1994), pp. 107–48.

5. O. Höffe, "Eine Konversion der Kritischen Theorie?" *Rechtshistorisches Journal* 12 (1993): 70–88.

6. By this I do not mean to deny the limitations that still exist, especially those deficits in German citizenship law (*Staatsbürgerrechts*) that have been discussed for some time in connection with the issues of foreigners' right to vote in local elections and "dual" citizenship; see appendix II, pp. 509ff.

7. See the afterword to J. Habermas, *The Past as Future*, trans. and ed. M. Pensky (Lincoln, Nebr., 1994), pp. 143–65.

8. C. Larmore, "Die Wurzeln radikaler Demokratie," *Deutsche Zeitschrift für Philosophie* 41 (1993): 327.

9. For the conceptual analysis, see chap. 4, sec. 4.1.

10. See pp. 157–68 and pp. 304ff. in this volume.

11. See pp. 107ff. in this volume. The idea that a norm deserves universal approval elucidates what it means for norms of action to be valid in terms of a rational acceptability that is not just local. This explication of normative validity

pertains to the process of justification, not application, of norms. Thus the comparison with a maxim of judicial decision making is out of place; see N. Luhmann, "Quod omnes tangit...," *Rechtshistorisches Journal*, 12 (1993): 36–56.

12. O. O'Neill, "Kommunikative Rationalität und praktische Vernunft," *Deutsche Zeitschrift für Philosophie* 41 (1993): 329–32.

13. A. Wellmer, "Ethics and Dialogue: Elements of Moral Judgement in Kant and Discourse Ethics," in Wellmer, *The Persistence of Modernity*, trans. D. Midgley (Cambridge, Mass., 1991), p. 194.

14. For my critique of Wellmer, see J. Habermas, *Justification and Application*, trans. C. P. Cronin (Cambridge, Mass., 1993), pp. 30ff.; see also L. Wingert, *Gemeinsinn und Moral* (Frankfurt am Main, 1993).

15. See the formulation of (U) in J. Habermas, *Moral Consciousness and Communicative Action*, trans. C. Lenhardt and S. W. Nicholsen (Cambridge, Mass., 1990), p. 120: "For a norm to be valid, the consequences and side effects that its general observance can be expected to have for the satisfaction of the particular interests of each person affected must be such that all affected can accept them freely."

16. Cf. R. Alexy, *Begriff und Geltung des Rechts* (Freiburg, 1992).

17. On the concept of democratic *Sittlichkeit*, see A. Wellmer, "Bedingungen einer demokratischen Kultur," in M. Brumlik and H. Brunkhorst, eds., *Gemeinschaft und Gerechtigkeit* (Frankfurt am Main, 1993), pp. 173–96; also in the same volume, A. Honneth, "Posttraditionale Gesellschaften," pp. 260–70.

18. See pp. 34–41 in this volume.

Appendix I

This was presented as a lecture in December, 1988, and was first published in Forum für Philosophie Bad Homburg, ed., *Die Ideen von 1789* (Frankfurt am Main, 1989), pp. 7–36.

1. E. Schulin, *Die Französische Revolution* (Munich, 1988), p. 11.

2. W. Markov, *Die Jakobinerfrage heute* (Berlin, 1967), p. 3.

3. F. Furet and D. Richet, *La Révolution* (Paris, 1965); citations are from the German translation, *Die Französische Revolution* (Frankfurt am Main, 1968); here see p. 84. An English translation is available under the title *French Revolution*, trans. S. Hardman (New York, 1970).

4. F. Furet, *Penser la Révolution française* (Paris, 1978); citations are taken from the German translation, *1789—Vom Ereignis zum Gegenstand der Geschichtswissenschaft* (Frankfurt am Main, 1980).

5. Schulin, *Die Französische Revolution*, pp. 9ff.

6. Furet himself has since adopted this relativizing view. See F. Furet, *La Révolution 1780–1880* (Paris, 1988); and his "La France Unie," in *La République du Centre* (Paris, 1988); cf. A. I. Hartig, "Das Bicentennaire—eine Auferstehung?" *Merkur* 43 (1989): 258ff.

7. R. v. Thadden, "Die Botschaft der Brüderlichkeit," *Süddeutsche Zeitung,* Nov. 26/27, 1988.

8. Ibid.

9. Furet, *1789—Vom Ereignis,* p. 34.

10. R. Koselleck, *Futures Past,* trans. K. Tribe (Cambridge, Mass., 1985); J. Habermas, *The Philosophical Discourse of Modernity,* trans. F. Lawrence (Cambridge, Mass., 1987), chap. 1.

11. C. Taylor, "Legitimation Crisis?" in Taylor, *Philosophy and the Human Sciences* (Cambridge, 1985), pp. 248–88.

12. J. Starobinski, *1789: The Emblems of Reason,* trans. B. Bray (Charlottesville, Va., 1982)

13. For an astounding agreement with Carl Schmitt, see Furet, *1789—Vom Ereignis,* pp. 197ff.

14. I. Kant, *Metaphysical Elements of Justice,* trans. J. Ladd (New York, 1965), p. 78 [translation altered. Trans.].

15. J.-J. Rousseau, *Of the Social Contract,* trans. C. M. Sherover (New York, 1984), bk. 3, chap. 1, sec. 159 (p. 55).

16. J. Fröbel, *Monarchie oder Republik* (Mannheim, 1848), p. 6.

17. J. Fröbel, *System der socialen Politik* (Mannheim, 1847; reprint, Scientia Verlag, Aalen, 1975; intralinear page numbers refer to the latter edition).

18. H. Dippel, "Die politischen Ideen der französischen Revolution," in *Pipers Handbuch der Politischen Ideen,* vol. 4 (Munich, 1986), pp. 21ff.

19. O. Negt and E. T. Mohl, "Marx und Engels—der unaufgehobene Widerspruch von Theorie und Praxis," in *Pipers Handbuch der Politischen Ideen,* vol. 4, pp. 449ff.

20. O. Kallscheuer, "Revisionismus und Reformismus," in *Pipers Handbuch der Politischen Ideen,* vol. 4, pp. 545ff.

21. P. Lösche, "Anarchismus," in *Pipers Handbuch der Politischen Ideen,* vol. 4, pp. 415ff.

22. N. Luhmann, *Political Theory in the Welfare State,* trans. J. Bednarz, Jr. (New York, 1990).

23. J. Habermas, *Die Neue Unübersichtlichkeit* (Frankfurt am Main, 1985).

24. A. Wellmer, "Hannah Arendt on Judgment: The Unwritten Doctrine of Reason," in L. May and J. Kohn, eds., *Hannah Arendt: Twenty Years Later* (Cambridge, Mass., 1996); see H. Arendt, *On Violence* (New York, 1970); J. Habermas, "Hannah Arendt: On the Concept of Power," in Habermas, *Philosophical-Political Profiles,* trans. F. Lawrence (Cambridge, Mass., 1985), pp. 173–89.

25. U. Preuß, "Was heißt radikale Demokratie heute?" in Forum für Philosophie Bad Homburg, ed., *Die Ideen von 1789* (Frankfurt am Main, 1989), pp. 37–67.

26. H. J. Puhle, "Die Anfänge des politischen Konservatismus in Deutschland," in *Pipers Handbuch der Politischen Ideen,* vol. 4, pp. 255ff.

27. H. Brunkhorst, "Die Ästhetisierung der Intellektuellen," *Frankfurter Rundschau*, November 28, 1988.

28. H. Kleger and R. Müller, eds., *Religion des Bürgers* (Munich, 1986); H. Dubiel, "Zivilreligion in der Massendemokratie," ms. 1989.

29. C. Menke-Eggers, *Die Souveränität der Kunst* (Frankfurt am Main, 1988); English translation forthcoming (Cambridge, Mass., 1996).

Appendix II

First published as a monograph by Erker-Verlag, St. Gallen, 1991. I am grateful to Ingeborg Maus and Klaus Günther for critical advice and suggestions.

1. P. Glotz, *Der Irrweg des Nationalstaats* (Stuttgart, 1990); J. Habermas, *The Past as Future*, trans. and ed. M. Pensky (Lincoln, Nebr., 1994).

2. On the following, see M. R. Lepsius, "Der europäische Nationalstaat," in Lepsius, *Interessen, Ideen und Institutionen* (Opladen, 1990), pp. 256ff.

3. See the article entitled "Nation" in *Historisches Wörterbuch der Philosophie*, vol. 6, pp. 406–14.

4. I. Kant, *Anthropology from a Pragmatic Point of View*, trans. V. L. Dowdell, rev. and ed. H. H. Rudnick (Carbondale, Ill., 1978), p. 225.

5. M. R. Lepsius, "Ethos und Demos," in Lepsius, *Interessen*, pp. 247–55.

6. I. Kant, *Metaphysical Elements of Justice*, trans. J. Ladd (New York, 1965), sec. 46, p. 78.

7. On the following, see R. Grawert, "Staatsangehörigkeit und Staatsbürgerschaft," *Der Staat* 23 (1984): 179–204.

8. P. H. Shuck and R. M. Smith, *Citizenship without Consent* (New Haven, Conn., 1985), chap. 1. Admittedly, not everywhere is the normative meaning of national citizenship consistently uncoupled from ascriptive characteristics of descent. Article 116 of the Basic Law of the Federal Republic, for example, introduces a notion of so-called *Statusdeutschen* ("German by status"), someone who belongs to the German people according to an objectively confirmed "attestation of membership in the cultural community," without being a German citizen. Such a person enjoys the privilege of being able to become a German citizen, although this is now disputed at a constitutional level.

9. R. Winzeler, *Die politischen Rechte des Aktivbürgers nach schweizerischem Bundesrecht* (Bern, 1983).

10. K. Hesse, *Grundzüge des Verfassungsrechts* (Heidelberg, 1990), p. 113, states, "In their function as subjective rights, [the basic rights] determine and secure the foundations of the individual's legal status. In their function as [objective] basic elements of the democratic constitutional order, they insert the individual into this order, which can in turn become a reality only if these rights are actualized. The status of the individual in terms of constitutional law, as grounded in and guaranteed by the basic rights laid out in the Basic Law, is a

material legal status, i.e., a status with concretely specified contents over which neither the individual nor government authorities have unlimited control. This constitutional status forms the core of the general status of citizenship that, along with the basic rights, . . . is laid down in law."

11. R. Grawert, "Staatsvolk und Staatsangehörigkeit," in J. Isensee and P. Kirchof, eds., *Handbuch des Staatsrechts* (Heidelberg, 1987), p. 685; see also pp. 684ff.

12. C. Taylor, "Cross-Purposes: The Liberal-Communitarian Debate," in N. Rosenblum, ed., *Liberalism and the Moral Life* (Cambridge, Mass., 1989), pp. 178–79.

13. Taylor, "Cross-Purposes," p. 178.

14. P. Kielmannsegg, "Ohne historisches Vorbild," *Frankfurter Allgemeine Zeitung*, December 7, 1990.

15. M. R. Lepsius, *Die Europäische Gemeinschaft* (Frankfurt am Main, 1990).

16. T. H. Marshall, *Citizenship and Social Class* (Cambridge, Mass., 1950).

17. See chap. 7, sec. 7.2, in this volume.

18. B. S. Turner, *Citizenship and Capitalism* (London, 1986).

19. J. M. Barbalet, *Citizenship* (Stratford, England, 1988).

20. *Europäische Grundrechtszeitschrift* (1990): 443.

21. R. Goodin, "What Is So Special about Our Fellow Countrymen?" *Ethics* 98 (1988): 663–86.

22. H. Shue, "Mediating Duties," *Ethics* 98 (1988): 687–704.

23. J. H. Carens, "Aliens and Citizens: The Case for Open Borders," *Review of Politics* 49 (1987): 258.

24. H. R. van Gunsteren, "Admission to Citizenship," *Ethics* 98 (1988): 732.

25. D. Miller, "The Ethical Significance of Nationality," *Ethics* 98 (1988): 648.

26. M. Walzer, *Spheres of Justice* (New York, 1983), pp. 31–63.

27. Gunsteren, "Admission to Citizenship," p. 736.

28. Gunsteren, "Admission to Citizenship," p. 736.

29. Carens, "Aliens and Citizens," p. 271.

Bibliography

Aarnio, A. *The Rational as Reasonable: A Treatise on Legal Justification.* Boston, 1987.

Ackerman, B. *Social Justice in the Liberal State.* New Haven, Conn., 1980.

————. "The Storrs Lectures: Discovering the Constitution." *Yale Law Journal* 93 (1984): 1013–72.

————. *We the People.* Vol. 1. Cambridge, Mass., 1991.

————. "What Is Neutral about Neutrality?" *Ethics* 93 (1983): 372–90.

————. "Why Dialogue?" *Journal of Philosophy* 86 (1989): 5–22.

Alexy, R. *Begriff und Geltung des Rechts.* Freiburg, 1992.

————. "Eine diskurstheoretische Konzeption der praktischen Vernunft." In R. Alexy and R. Dreier, eds., *Legal System and Practical Reason. Archiv für Rechts- und Sozialphilosophie* Beiheft 51 (1993): 11–29.

————. "Probleme der Diskurstheorie." *Zeitschrift für philosophische Forschung* 43 (1989): 81–93.

————. *Theorie der Grundrechte.* Baden-Baden, 1985.

————. *Theorie der juristischen Argumentation: Die Theorie des rationalen Diskurses als Theorie der juristischen Begründung.* 2d ed. Frankfurt am Main, 1991.

————. *A Theory of Legal Argumentation: The Theory of Rational Discourse as Theory of Legal Justification.* Translated by R. Adler and N. MacCormick. Oxford, 1989.

————. "Zur Kritik des Rechtspositivismus." In R. Dreier, ed., *Rechtspositivismus und Wertbezug des Rechts.* Stuttgart, 1990. Pp. 9–26.

Altman, A. "Legal Realism, Critical Legal Studies, and Dworkin." *Philosophy and Public Affairs* 15 (1986): 202–35.

Apel, K.-O. "The A Priori of the Communication Community and the Foundations of Ethics: The Problem of a Rational Foundation of Ethics in the Scientific Age." In Apel, *Towards a Transformation of Philosophy.* Translated by G. Adey and D. Frisby. London, 1980. Pp. 225–300.

————. *Charles S. Peirce: From Pragmatism to Pragmaticism.* Translated by J. M. Krois. Amherst, Mass., 1981.

————. "Diskursethik vor der Problematik von Recht und Politik: Können die Rationalitätsdifferenzen zwischen Moralität, Recht und Politik selbst noch durch die Diskursethik normativ-rational gerechtfertigt werden?" In K.-O. Apel and M. Kettner, eds., *Zur Anwendung der Diskursethik in Politik, Recht und Wissenschaft.* Frankfurt am Main, 1992. Pp. 29–61.

————. "Sprache und Bedeutung, Wahrheit und normative Gültigkeit." *Archivo di Filosophia* 55 (1987): 51–88.

————. "Zurück zur Normalität? Oder könnten wir aus der nationalen Katastrophe etwas Besonderes gelernt haben? Das Problem des (welt-)geschichtlichen Übergangs zur postkonventionellen Moral aus spezifisch deutscher Sicht." In Apel, *Diskurs und Verantwortung: Das Problem des Übergangs zur postkonventionellen Moral.* Frankfurt am Main, 1988. Pp. 370–474.

Arendt, H. *The Human Condition.* Chicago, 1958.

————. *Lectures on Kant's Political Philosophy.* Edited by R. Beiner. Chicago, 1982.

————. *The Origins of Totalitarianism.* New York, 1973.

————. *On Revolution.* New York, 1963.

————. *On Violence.* New York, 1970.

————. *Vita Activa.* Stuttgart, 1960.

Arens, P. *Zivilprozeßrecht.* 4th ed. Munich, 1988.

Arnaud, A. J., R. Hilpinen, and J. Wróblewski, eds. *Juristische Logik und Irrationalität im Recht. Rechtstheorie* Beiheft 8 (1985).

Assmann, H. D. *Wirtschaftsrecht in der Mixed Economy: Auf der Suche nach einem Sozialmodell für das Wirtschaftsrecht.* Frankfurt am Main, 1980.

Atiyah, P. S. *The Rise and Fall of Freedom of Contract.* Oxford, 1979.

Bachrach, P. *The Theory of Democratic Elitism: A Critique.* Washington, D.C., 1980.

Barbalet, J. M. *Citizenship: Rights, Struggle, and Class Inequality.* Stratford, Engl., 1988.

Barry, B., et al. "Symposium on Social Justice in the Liberal State." *Ethics* 93 (1983): 328–90.

Baynes, K. *The Normative Grounds of Social Criticism: Kant, Rawls, and Habermas.* Albany, N.Y., 1992.

Beck, U. *Gegengifte: Die organisierte Unverantwortlichkeit.* Frankfurt am Main, 1988.

————. *Risk Society: Towards a New Modernity.* Translated by M. Ritter. London, 1992.

Becker, W. *Die Freiheit, die wir meinen: Entscheidung für die liberale Demokratie.* Munich, 1982.

Beiner, R. *Political Judgment.* Chicago, 1983.

Benhabib, S. *Critique, Norm and Utopia: A Study of the Foundations of Critical Theory.*
New York, 1986.

———. "Feminism and the Question of Postmodernism." In Benhabib, *Situating the Self: Gender, Community and Postmodernism in Contemporary Ethics.* Cambridge, 1992. Pp. 203–41.

———. "Liberal Dialogue versus a Critical Theory of Discursive Legitimation," In N. Rosenblum, ed., *Liberalism and the Moral Life.* Cambridge, Mass., 1989. Pp. 143–56.

———. "Models of Public Space: Hannah Arendt, the Liberal Tradition and Jürgen Habermas." In Benhabib, *Situating the Self: Gender, Community and Postmodernism in Contemporary Ethics.* Cambridge, 1992. Pp. 89–120.

Benjamin, W. "Der Sürrealismus." In Benjamin, Gesammelte Schriften II: Aufsätze, Essays, Vorträge. Edited by R. Tiedemann and H. Schweppenhäuser. Frankfurt am Main, 1977. Vol. 3. Pp. 295ff.

Bermbach, U. "Politische Institutionen und gesellschaftlicher Wandel." In Hartwich, ed., *Macht und Ohnmacht politischer Institutionen.* Pp. 57–71.

Bernstein, R. "One Step Forward, Two Steps Backward: Richard Rorty on Liberal Democracy and Philosophy." *Political Theory* 15 (1987): 538–63.

Bethge, H. "Aktuelle Probleme der Grundrechtsdogmatik." *Der Staat* 24 (1985): 351–82.

Bibo, I. *Die deutsche Hysterie: Ursachen und Geschichte.* Frankfurt am Main, 1991.

Blankenagle, A. *Tradition und Verfassung: Neue Verfassung und alte Geschichte in der Rechtsprechung des Bundesverfassungsgerichts.* Baden-Baden, 1987.

Bobbio, N. *The Future of Democracy: A Defence of the Rules of the Game.* Translated by R. Griffin. Edited by R. Bellamy. Cambridge, 1987.

———. "Gramsci and the Concept of Civil Society," In Keane, ed., *Civil Society and the State.* Pp. 73–100.

Böckenförde, E.-W. "Basic Rights: Theory and Interpretation." In Böckenförde, *State, Society and Liberty: Studies in Political Theory and Constitutional Law.* Translated by J. A. Underwood. New York, 1991. Pp. 175–203.

———. "Grundrechtstheorie und Grundrechtsinterpretation." *Neue Juristische Wochenschrift* 27 (1974): 1529–38.

———. *Recht, Staat, Freiheit: Studien zur Rechtsphilosophie, Staatstheorie und Verfassungsgeschichte.* Frankfurt am Main, 1991.

———. *Staat, Verfassung, Demokratie: Studien zur Verfassungstheorie und zum Verfassungsrecht.* Frankfurt am Main, 1991.

———, ed. *Staat und Gesellschaft.* Darmstadt, 1976.

Boyle, J. "The Politics of Reason: Critical Legal Theory and Local Social Thought." *Pennsylvania Law Review* 133 (1985): 685–780.

Brest, P. "The Fundamental Rights Controversy." *Yale Law Journal* 90 (1981): 1063–109.

Brüggemeier, G. "Justizielle Schutzpolitik de lege lata." In G. Brüggemeier and D. Hart, *Soziales Schuldrecht.* Bremen, 1987. Pp. 7–41.

———. "Wirtschaftsordnung und Staatsverfassung—Mischverfassung des demokratischen Interventionskapitalismus—Verfassungstheorie des Sozialstaates: Drei Modelle der Verflechtung von Staat und Wirtschaft?" *Jahrbuch für Rechtstheorie und Rechtssoziologie* 8 (1982): 60–73.

Brumlik, M., and H. Brunkhorst, eds. *Gemeinschaft und Gerechtigkeit.* Frankfurt am Main, 1993.

Brunkhorst, H. "Die Ästhetisierung der Intellektuellen." *Frankfurter Rundschau.* November 28, 1988.

———. "Zur Dialektik von realer und idealer Kommunikationsgemeinschaft." In A. Dorschel et al., eds., *Transzendentalpragmatik.* Frankfurt am Main, 1993. Pp. 342–58.

Bubner, R. "Das sprachliche Medium der Politik." In Bubner, *Antike Themen und ihre moderne Verwandlung.* Frankfurt am Main, 1992. Pp. 188–202.

Buchanan, A. E. *Marx and Justice: The Radical Critique of Liberalism.* London, 1982.

Calhoun, C., ed. *Habermas and the Public Sphere.* Cambridge, Mass., 1992.

———. "Introduction: Habermas and the Public Sphere." In Calhoun, ed., *Habermas and the Public Sphere.* Pp. 1–50.

Carens, J. H. "Aliens and Citizens: The Case for Open Borders." *Review of Politics* 49 (1987): 251–73.

Cobb, R., and C. Elder. "The Politics of Agenda-Building." *Journal of Politics* (1971): 892–915.

Cobb, R., J. K. Ross, and M. H. Ross. "Agenda Building as a Comparative Political Process." *American Political Science Review* 70 (1976): 126–38.

Cohen, J. L., and A. Arato. *Civil Society and Political Theory.* Cambridge, Mass., 1992.

Cohen, J. "Deliberation and Democratic Legitimacy." In A. Hamlin and B. Pettit, eds., *The Good Polity: Normative Analysis of the State.* Oxford, 1989. Pp. 17–34.

Cohen, J., and J. Rogers. *On Democracy: Toward a Transformation of American Society.* New York, 1983.

Coing, H. "Zur Geschichte des Begriffs 'subjektives Recht'." In Coing et al., *Das subjektive Recht und der Rechtsschutz der Persönlichkeit.* Frankfurt am Main, 1959. Pp. 7–23.

Connolly, W. E. *The Terms of Political Discourse.* Lexington, Mass., 1974.

Czybulka, D. *Die Legitimation der öffentlichen Verwaltung: Unter Berücksichtigung ihrer Organisation sowie der Entstehungsgeschichte zum Grundgesetz.* Heidelberg, 1989.

Dahl, R. A. *Democracy and Its Critics.* New Haven, Conn., 1989.

———. *A Preface to Economic Democracy.* Oxford, 1985.

Denninger, E. *Der gebändigte Leviathan.* Baden-Baden, 1990.

———. *Staatsrecht.* Vol. 1. Reinbek, 1973.

———. "Verfassung und Gesetz." *Kritische Vierteljahresschrift für Gesetzgebung und Rechtswissenschaft* 1 (1986): 291–314.

Derrida, J. "Force of Law: The 'Mystical Foundation of Authority'." Translated by M. Quaintance. *Cardozo Law Review* 11 (1990): 919–1045.

Dewey, J. *The Public and Its Problems.* Chicago, 1954.

Dippel, H. "Die politischen Ideen der französischen Revolution." In *Pipers Handbuch der Politischen Ideen.* Vol. 4. Munich, 1986. Pp. 21ff.

Downs, A. *An Economic Theory of Democracy.* New York, 1957.

Dreier, R. "Recht und Moral." In Dreier, *Recht—Moral—Ideologie.* Vol. 1 of *Studien zur Rechtstheorie.* Frankfurt am Main, 1981. Pp. 180–216.

———. *Was ist und wozu Allgemeine Rechtstheorie?.* Tübingen, 1975.

———. "Widerstandsrecht im Rechtsstaat?" In Dreier, *Recht—Staat—Vernunft.* Vol. 2 of *Studien zur Rechtstheorie.* Frankfurt am Main, 1991. Pp. 39–72.

Dryzek, J. S. *Discursive Democracy: Politics, Policy, and Political Science.* Cambridge, 1990.

Dubiel, H. "Zivilreligion in der Massendemokratie." Unpublished ms. 1989.

Durkheim, E. *Professional Ethics and Civic Morals.* Translated by C. Brookfield. London, 1957.

Dworkin, R. "Foundations of Liberal Equality." In G. B. Peterson, ed., *The Tanner Lectures on Human Values.* Vol. 11. Salt Lake City, 1990. Pp. 1–119.

———. *Law's Empire.* Cambridge, Mass., 1986.

———. "Liberal Community." *California Law Review* 77 (1989): 479–589.

———. *A Matter of Principle.* Cambridge, Mass., 1985.

———. "Principle, Policy, Procedure." In Dworkin, *A Matter of Principle.* Pp. 72–103.

———. *Taking Rights Seriously.* Cambridge, Mass., 1978.

Eder, K. *Die Entstehung staatlich organisierter Gesellschaften: Ein Beitrag zu einer Theorie sozialer Evolution.* Frankfurt am Main, 1976.

———. *Geschichte als Lernprozeß? Zur Pathogenese politischer Modernität in Deutschland.* Frankfurt am Main, 1985.

Eisenstadt, S. N., ed. *Democracy and Modernity.* Leiden, 1992.

Ellscheid, G., and W. Hassemer, eds. *Interessenjurisprudenz.* Darmstadt, 1974.

Elster, J. "Arguing and Bargaining in Two Constituent Assemblies." The Storr Lectures, Yale Law School. Unpublished ms. 1991.

———. *The Cement of Society.* Cambridge, 1989.

———. "The Market and the Forum: Three Varieties of Political Theory." In J. Elster and A. Hylland, eds., *Foundations of Social Choice Theory.* Cambridge, 1986. Pp. 103–32.

———. "The Possibility of Rational Politics." In D. Held, ed., *Political Theory Today*. Oxford, 1991. Pp. 115–42.

Ely, J. H. *Democracy and Distrust: A Theory of Judicial Review*. Cambridge, Mass., 1980.

Enneccerus, L. *Allgemeiner Teil des Bürgerlichen Rechts*. 15th ed. Tübingen, 1959.

Esser, J. *Grundsatz und Norm in der richterlichen Fortbildung des Privatsrechts*. 2nd ed. Tübingen, 1964.

———. *Vorverständnis und Methodenwahl in der Rechtsfindung: Rationalitätsgarantien der richterlichen Entscheidungspraxis*. Kronberg, 1972.

Euchner, W. *Naturrecht und Politik bei John Locke*. Frankfurt, 1979.

Ewald, F. *L'Etat Providence*. Paris, 1986.

Faber, H. *Verwaltungsrecht*. Tübingen, 1987.

Ferguson, A. *An Essay on the History of Civil Society*. Edinburgh, 1767.

Fetscher, I., and H. Münkler, eds. *Pipers Handbuch politischer Ideen*. Vol. 3. Munich, 1985.

Fiorenza, F. S. "The Church as a Community of Interpretation: Political Theology between Discourse Ethics and Hermeneutical Reconstruction." In D. S. Browning and F. S. Fiorenza, eds., *Habermas, Modernity, and Public Theology*. New York, 1992. Pp. 66–91.

Fiss, O. "Objectivity and Interpretation." *Stanford Law Review* 34 (1982): 739–63.

Forst, R. *Kontexte der Gerechtigkeit: Politische Philosophie jenseits von Liberalismus und Kommunitarismus*. Frankfurt am Main, 1994.

Forsthoff, E. *Der Staat der Industriegesellschaft*. Munich, 1971.

Fraenkel, E. *Deutschland und die westlichen Demokratien*. Frankfurt am Main, 1990.

Frankenberg, G. "Down by Law: Irony, Seriousness, and Reason." *Northwestern University Law Review*. 83 (1988): 360–97.

Frankenberg, G., and U. Rödel. *Von der Volkssouveränität zum Minderheitenschutz*. Frankfurt am Main, 1981.

Frankfurt, H. *The Importance of What We Care About*. Cambridge, 1988.

Fraser, N. "Rethinking the Public Sphere: A Contribution to the Critique of Actually Existing Democracy." In Calhoun, ed., *Habermas and the Public Sphere*. Pp. 109–42.

———. "Struggle over Needs: Outline of a Socialist-Feminist Critical Theory of Late Capitalist Political Culture." In Fraser, *Unruly Practices: Power, Discourse, and Gender in Contemporary Social Theory*. Minneapolis, 1989. Pp. 161–90.

Frege, G. *Logical Investigations*. Edited by P. T. Geach. Translated by P. T. Geach and R. H. Stoothoff. New Haven, Conn., 1977.

Friedman, L. M. *Total Justice*. New York, 1985.

———. "Transformations in American Legal Culture 1800–1985." *Zeitschrift für Rechtssoziologie* 6 (1985): 191–205.

Fröbel, J. *Monarchie oder Republik.* Mannheim, 1848.

―――. *System der socialen Politik.* Mannheim, 1847. Reprint, Aalen, 1975.

Fuller, L. *The Morality of Law.* Chicago, 1969.

Furet, F. "La France Unie." In Furet, J. Julliard, and P. Rosanvallon, *La République du centre: La fin de l'exception Française.* Paris, 1988.

―――. *La Révolution 1780–1880.* Paris, 1988.

―――. *1789—Vom Ereignis zum Gegenstand der Geschichtswissenschaft.* Frankfurt am Main, 1980.

Furet, F., and D. Richet. *Die Französische Revolution.* Frankfurt am Main, 1968.

Gadamer, H. G. *Truth and Method.* 2d ed. Translated by J. Weinsheimer and D. G. Marshall. New York, 1990.

Gehlen, A. *Man, His Nature and Place in the World.* Translated by C. McMillan and K. Pillemer. New York, 1988.

―――. *Urmensch und Spätkultur: Philosophische Ergebnisse und Aussagen.* Bonn, 1956.

Gerhards, J., and F. Neidhardt. *Strukturen und Funktionen moderner Öffentlichkeit.* Berlin, 1990.

The German Code of Criminal Procedure. Translated by H. Niebler. London, 1973.

Giddens, A. *Profiles and Critiques in Social Theory.* London, 1982.

Giegel, H. J. Introduction to Giegel, ed., *Kommunikation und Konsens in moderner Gesellschaften.* Frankfurt am Main, 1992. Pp. 7–17.

Glotz, P. *Der Irrweg des Nationalstaats: Europäische Reden an ein deutsches Publikum.* Stuttgart, 1990.

Goodin, R. "What Is So Special about Our Fellow Countrymen?" *Ethics* 98 (1988): 663–86.

Goodman, D. "Public Sphere and Private Life: Toward a Synthesis of Current Historical Approaches to the Old Regime." *History and Theory* 31 (1992): 1–20.

Grawert, R. "Staatsangehörigkeit und Staatsbürgerschaft." *Der Staat* 23 (1984): 179–204.

―――. "Staatsvolk und Staatsangehörigkeit." In J. Isensee and P. Kirchof, eds., *Handbuch des Staatsrechts der Bundesrepublik Deutschland.* Vol. 1: *Grundlagen von Staat und Verfassung.* Heidelberg, 1987. Pp. 663–90.

Grimm, D. *Recht und Staat der bürgerlichen Gesellschaft.* Frankfurt am Main, 1987.

―――. "Reformalisierung des Rechtsstaates?" *Juristische Schulung* 10 (1980): 704–9.

―――. *Die Zukunft der Verfassung.* Frankfurt am Main, 1991.

―――, ed. *Wachsende Staatsaufgaben—sinkende Steuerungsfähigkeit des Rechts.* Baden-Baden, 1990.

Guggenberger, B., and C. Offe, eds. *An den Grenzen der Mehrheitsdemokratie: Politik und Soziologie der Mehrheitsregel.* Opladen, 1984.

Gunsteren, H. R. van. "Admission to Citizenship." *Ethics* 98 (1988): 731–41.

Günther, K. "Die Freiheit der Stellungnahme als politisches Grundrecht." In P. Koller et al., eds., *Theoretische Grundlagen der Rechtspolitik. Archiv für Rechts- und Sozialphilosophie* Beiheft 54 (1992): 58–73.

———. "Hero-Politics in Modern Legal Times." Institute for Legal Studies, University of Wisconsin at Madison. Series 4. Madison, Wisc., 1990.

———. "Kann ein Volk von Teufeln Recht und Staat moralisch legitimieren?" *Rechtshistorisches Journal* 10 (1991): 233–67.

———. "Möglichkeiten einer diskursethischen Begründung des Strafrechts." In H. Jung et al., eds., *Recht und Moral.* Baden-Baden, 1991. Pp. 205–17.

———. "A Normative Conception of Coherence for a Discursive Theory of Legal Justification." *Ratio Juris* 2 (1989): 155–66.

———. "Ein normativer Begriff der Kohärenz für eine Theorie der juristischen Argumentation." *Rechtstheorie* 20 (1989): 163–90.

———. *The Sense of Appropriateness: Application Discourses in Morality and Law.* Translated by J. Farrell. Albany, N.Y., 1993.

———. "Universalistische Normbegründung und Normanwendung." In M. Herberger et al., eds., *Generalisierung und Individualisierung im Rechtsdenken. Archiv für Rechts- und Sozialphilosophie* Beiheft 45 (1992): 36–76.

———. "Der Wandel der Staatsaufgaben und die Krise des regulativen Rechts." In D. Grimm, ed., *Wachsende Staatsaufgaben.* Pp. 51–68.

Gurevitch, M., and J. G. Blumler. "Political Communication Systems and Democratic Values." In J. Lichtenberg, ed., *Democracy and the Mass Media.* Cambridge, Mass., 1990. Pp. 269–89.

Gusy, C. "Das Mehrheitsprinzip im demokratischen Staat." In Guggenheimer and Offe, eds., *An den Grenzen der Mehrheits demokratie.* Pp 61–82.

Häberle, P. "Grundrechte im Leistungsstaat." *Veröffentlichungen der Vereinigung der Deutschen Staatsrechtslehrer* 30 (1972): 43–131.

———. *Verfassung als öffentlicher Prozeß.* Frankfurt am Main, 1978.

———. "Die Verfassung des Pluralismus." In Häberle, *Die Verfassung des Pluralismus: Studien zur Verfassungstheorie der offenen Gesellschaft.* Frankfurt am Main, 1980. Pp. 79–105.

———, ed. *Verfassungsgerichtbarkeit.* Darmstadt, 1976.

Habermas, J. "Actions, Speech Acts, Linguistically Mediated Interactions and the Lifeworld." In G. Fløistad, ed., *Philosophical Problems Today.* Vol. 1: *Willard V. Quine.* Boston, 1994. Pp. 45–74.

———. *Communication and the Evolution of Society.* Translated by T. McCarthy. Boston, 1979.

———. "Edmund Husserl über Lebenswelt, Philosophie und Wissenschaft." In Habermas, *Texte und Kontexte.* Frankfurt am Main, 1991. Pp. 34–43.

———. "Further Reflections on the Public Sphere." Translated by T. Burger. In Calhoun, ed., *Habermas and the Public Sphere*. Pp. 421–61.

———. "Hannah Arendt: On the Concept of Power." In Habermas, *Philosophical-Political Profiles*. Translated by F. G. Lawrence. Cambridge, Mass., 1985. Pp. 173–89.

———. Introduction to J. Habermas, L. v. Friedeburg, C. Oehler, and F. Weltz, *Student und Politik*. Neuwied, 1961. Pp. 11–55.

———. *Justification and Application: Remarks on Discourse Ethics*. Translated by C. P. Cronin. Cambridge, Mass., 1993.

———. "Law and Morality." Translated by K. Baynes. In S. M. McMurrin, ed., *The Tanner Lectures on Human Values*. Vol. 8. Salt Lake City, 1988. Pp. 217–79.

———. *Legitimation Crisis*. Translated by T. McCarthy. Boston, 1975.

———. *Moral Consciousness and Communicative Action*. Translated by C. Lenhardt and S. W. Nicholsen. Cambridge, Mass., 1990.

———. *Die nachholende Revolution*. Frankfurt am Main, 1990.

———. *Die Neue Unübersichtlichkeit*. Frankfurt am Main, 1985.

———. *The New Conservativism: Cultural Criticism and the Historians' Debate*. Edited and translated by S. W. Nicholsen. Cambridge, Mass., 1989.

———. *On the Logic of the Social Sciences*. Translated by S. W. Nicholsen and J. A. Stark. Cambridge, Mass., 1988.

———. *The Past as Future*. Translated and edited by M. Pensky. Lincoln, Nebr., 1994.

———. "Der Philosoph als wahrer Rechtslehrer: Rudolf Wiethölter." *Kritische Justiz* 22 (1989): 138–56.

———. *The Philosophical Discourse of Modernity*. Translated by F. Lawrence. Cambridge, Mass., 1987.

———. *Postmetaphysical Thinking: Philosophical Essays*. Translated by W. M. Hohengarten. Cambridge, Mass., 1992.

———. *The Structural Transformation of the Public Sphere: An Inquiry into a Category of Bourgeois Society*. Translated by T. Burger and F. Lawrence. Cambridge, Mass., 1989.

———. "Struggles for Recognition in the Democratic Constitutional State." Translated by S. W. Nicholsen. In A. Gutmann, ed., *Multiculturalism: Examining the Politics of Recognition*. Princeton, 1994. Pp. 107–48.

———. *Strukturwandel der Öffentlichkeit: Untersuchungen zu einer Kategorie der bürgerlichen Gesellschaft*. Darmstadt, 1962; Frankfurt am Main, 1990.

———. *Theory and Practice*. Translated by J. Viertel. Boston, 1973.

———. *The Theory of Communicative Action*. Vol. 1, *Reason and the Rationalization of Society*. Vol. 2, *Lifeworld and System: A Critique of Functionalist Reason*. Translated by T. McCarthy. Boston, 1984, 1987.

————. "Die Utopie des guten Herrschers." In Habermas, *Kleine politische Schriften I–IV.* Frankfurt am Main, 1981. Pp. 44ff.

————. "Vorlesungen zu einer sprachtheoretischen Grundlegung der Soziologie." In Habermas, *Vorstudien und Ergänzungen zur Theorie des kommunikativen Handelns.* Frankfurt am Main, 1984. Pp. 11–126.

————. "Wahrheitstheorien." In Habermas, *Vorstudien und Ergänzungen zur Theorie des kommunikativen Handelns.* Frankfurt am Main, 1984. Pp. 127–83.

Hall, S. "Encoding and Decoding in TV-Discourse." In S. Hall, ed., *Culture, Media, Language.* London, 1980. Pp. 128–38.

Hankiss, E. "The Loss of Responsibility." In J. MacLean, A. Montefiori, and P. Winch, eds., *The Political Responsibility of Intellectuals.* Cambridge, 1990. Pp. 29–52.

Hart, D. "Soziale Steuerung durch Vertragsabschlußkontrolle—Alternativen zum Vertragsschluß?" *Kritische Vierteljahresschrift für Gesetzgebung und Rechtswissenschaft* 1 (1986): 211–241.

Hart, H. L. A. *The Concept of Law.* Oxford, 1961.

————. "Rawls on Liberty and Its Priority." In N. Daniels, ed., *Reading Rawls: Critical Studies of* A Theory of Justice. Oxford, 1975. Pp. 230–52.

Hartig, A. I. "Das Bicentennaire—eine Auferstehung?: François Furet als König der Revolution." *Merkur* 43 (1989): 258–64.

Hartwich, H. H., ed. *Macht und Ohnmacht politischer Institutionen.* Opladen, 1989.

Hassemer, W. "Juristische Hermeneutik." *Archiv für Rechts- und Sozialphilosophie* 72 (1986): 195–212.

————. "Rechtsphilosophie, Rechtswissenschaft, Rechtspolitik—am Beispiel des Strafrechts." In R. Alexy et al., eds., *Rechts- und Sozialphilosophie in Deutschland Heute. Archiv für Rechts- und Sozialphilosophie* Beiheft 44 (1991): 130–43.

Hayek, F. A. *The Constitution of Liberty.* Chicago, 1960.

Held, D. "Citizenship and Autonomy." In Held, *Political Theory and the Modern State.* Oxford, 1989. Pp. 214-42.

————. *Models of Democracy.* Oxford, 1987.

Hellesnes, J. "Toleranz und Dissens." *Zeitschrift für Philosophie* 40 (1992): 245–55.

Hesse, K. *Grundzüge des Verfassungsrechts der Bundesrepublik Deutschland.* Heidelberg, 1990.

————. *Verfassungsrecht und Privatrecht.* Heidelberg, 1988.

Hilgartner, S. "The Rise and Fall of Social Problems." *American Journal of Sociology* 94 (1988): 53–78.

Hirsch, J. *Der Sicherheitsstaat.* Frankfurt am Main, 1980.

Hobbes, T. *De Cive.* In Hobbes, *Man and Citizen.* Edited by B. Gert. Indianapolis, 1991.

————. *Leviathan.* Edited by R. Tuck. Cambridge, 1991.

Hoerster, N. *Verteidigung des Rechtspositivismus.* Frankfurt am Main, 1989.

Höffe, O. *Gerechtigkeit als Tausch? Zum politischen Projekt der Moderne.* Baden-Baden, 1991.

————. *Kategorische Rechtsprinzipien: Kontrapunkte der Moderne.* Frankfurt am Main, 1990.

————. "Eine Konversion der Kritischen Theorie?" *Rechtshistorisches Journal* 12 (1993): 70–88.

————. *Politische Gerechtigkeit: Grundlegung einer kritischen Philosophie von Recht und Staat.* Frankfurt am Main, 1987.

Hofmann, H. "Das Postulat der Allgemeinheit des Gesetzes." In C. Starck, ed., *Die Allgemeinheit des Gesetzes.* Göttingen, 1987. Pp. 9–48.

Holmes, S. "Gag Rules or the Politics of Omission." In J. Elster and R. Slagstad, eds., *Constitutionalism and Democracy.* Cambridge, 1988. Pp. 19–58.

Honneth, A. "Posttraditionale Gesellschaften." In Brumlik and Brunkhorst, eds., *Gemeinschaft und Gerechtigkeit.* Pp. 260–70.

————. *Struggle for Recognition: The Moral Grammar of Social Conflicts.* Translated by J. Anderson. Cambridge, 1995.

Hoy, D. C. "Dworkin's Constructive Optimism vs. Deconstructive Legal Nihilism." *Law and Philosophy* 6 (1987): 321–56.

————. "Interpreting the Law: Hermeneutical and Poststructuralist Perspectives." *Southern California Law Review* 58 (1985): 135–76.

Huber, H. "Die Bedeutung der Grundrechte für die sozialen Beziehungen unter den Rechtsgenossen (1955)." In Huber, *Rechtstheorie, Verfassungsrecht, Völkerrecht: Ausgewählte Aufsätze 1950–1970.* Bern, 1971. Pp. 139–65.

Ihering, R. von. *Geist des römischen Rechts.* Leipzig, 1888.

Joerges, C. "Politische Rechtstheorie und Critical Legal Studies: Points of Contact and Divergences." In Joerges and Trubek, eds., *Critical Legal Thought.* Pp. 597–644.

————. "Die Überarbeitung des BGB, die Sonderprivatrechte und die Unbestimmtheit des Rechts." *Kritische Justiz* 20 (1987): 166–82.

Joerges, C., and D. M. Trubek, eds. *Critical Legal Thought: An American-German Debate.* Baden-Baden, 1989.

Johnson, J. "Habermas on Strategic and Communicative Action." *Political Theory* 19 (1991): 181–201.

Kaase, M. "Massenkommunikation und politischer Prozeß." In M. Kaase and W. Schulz, eds., *Massenkommunikation: Theorien, Methoden, Befunde. Kölner Zeitschrift für Soziologie und Sozialpsychologie* Sonderheft 30 (1989): 97–117.

Kahn, P. W. "Reason and Will in the Origins of American Constitutionalism." *Yale Law Journal* 98 (1989): 449–517.

Kahn-Freund, O. "Das soziale Ideal des Reichsarbeitsgerichts." In T. Ramm, ed., *Arbeitsrecht und Politik: Quellentexte 1918–1933.* Frankfurt am Main, 1966. Pp. 149–210.

Kallscheuer, O. "Revisionismus und Reformismus." In *Pipers Handbuch der Politischen Ideen.* Vol. 4. Munich, 1986. Pp. 545ff.

Kant, I. *Anthropology from a Pragmatic Point of View.* Translated by V. L. Dowdell. Revised and edited by H. H. Rudnick. Carbondale, Ill., 1978.

———. *The Metaphysical Elements of Justice: Part I of The Metaphysics of Morals.* Translated by J. Ladd. New York, 1965.

———. *The Metaphysical Principles of Virtue.* In Kant, *Ethical Philosophy.* Translated by J. W. Ellington. Indianapolis, 1983.

———. "On the Proverb: That May Be True in Theory, But Is of No Practical Use." In Kant, *Perpetual Peace and Other Essays.* Translated by T. Humphrey. Indianapolis, 1983. Pp. 61–92.

Kaufmann, A. *Rechtsphilosophie in der Nach-Neuzeit.* Heidelberg, 1990.

———. "Recht und Rationalität: Gedanken beim Wiederlesen der Schriften von Werner Maihofer." In Kaufmann et al., eds., *Rechtsstaat und Menschenwürde: Festschrift für Werner Maihofer zum 70. Geburtstag.* Frankfurt am Main, 1988. Pp. 11–39.

———. *Theorie der Gerechtigkeit: Problemgeschichtliche Betrachtungen.* Frankfurt am Main, 1984.

Keane, J. *Democracy and Civil Society: On the Predicaments of European Socialism, the Prospects for Democracy, and the Problem of Controlling Social and Political Power.* London, 1988.

———. *The Media and Democracy.* Cambridge, 1991.

———, ed. *Civil Society and the State: New European Perspectives.* London, 1988.

Kelsen, H. *Allgemeine Staatslehre.* Bad Homburg, 1968.

———. "Wer soll der Hüter der Verfassung sein?" *Die Justiz* 6 (1931): 576–628.

Kennedy, D. "Form and Substance in Private Law Adjudication." *Harvard Law Review* 89 (1976): 1685–778.

Kielmannsegg, P. "Ohne historisches Vorbild." *Frankfurter Allgemeine Zeitung.* December 7, 1990.

Kleger, H., and R. Müller, eds. *Religion des Bürgers: Zivilreligion in Amerika und Europa.* Munich, 1986.

Knieper, R. *Nationale Souveränität: Versuche über Ende und Anfang einer Weltordnung.* Frankfurt am Main, 1991.

Koch, H. J., ed. *Die juristische Methode im Staatsrecht: Über Grenzen von Verfassungs- und Gesetzesbindung.* Frankfurt am Main, 1977.

Kohlberg, L. *Essays on Moral Development.* San Francisco, 1981.

Köndgen, J. *Selbstbindung ohne Vertrag: Zur Haftung aus geschäftsbezogenem Handeln.* Tübingen, 1981.

Koselleck, R. *Futures Past: On the Semantics of Historical Time.* Translated by K. Tribe. Cambridge, Mass., 1985.

Koslowski, P. *Gesellschaft und Staat: Ein unvermeidlicher Dualismus.* Stuttgart, 1982.

Kress, K. J. "Legal Reasoning and Coherence Theories: Dworkin's Rights Thesis, Retroactivity, and the Linear Order of Decisions." *California Law Review* 72 (1984): 369–402.

Kriele, M. *Einführung in die Staatslehre: Die geschichtlichen Legitimitätsgrundlagen des demokratischen Verfassungsstaates.* Opladen, 1980.

―――. *Recht und praktische Vernunft.* Göttingen, 1979.

Kübler, F. "Die neue Rundfunkordnung: Marktstruktur und Wettbewerbsbedingungen." *Neue Juristische Wochenschrift* 47 (1987): 2961–67.

―――. "Privatrecht und Demokratie: Zur Aktualität gesellschaftstheoretischer Vorstellungen in der Jurisprudenz." In F. Baur et al., eds., *Funktionswandel der Privatrechtsinstitutionen: Festschrift für Ludwig Raiser zum 70. Geburtstag.* Tübingen, 1974. Pp. 697–725.

―――. *Über die praktischen Aufgaben zeitgemäßer Privatrechtstheorie.* Karlsruhe, 1975.

―――, ed. *Verrechtlichung von Wirtschaft, Arbeit und sozialer Solidarität: Vergleichende Analysen.* Frankfurt am Main, 1984.

Kunig, P. *Das Rechtsstaatsprinzip: Überlegungen zu seiner Bedeutung für das Verfassungsrecht der Bundesrepublik Deutschland.* Tübingen, 1986.

Laker, T. *Ziviler Ungehorsam: Geschichte—Begriff—Rechtfertigung.* Baden-Baden, 1986.

Langer, C. *Reform nach Prinzipien: Zur politischen Theorie Immanuel Kants.* Stuttgart, 1986.

Larmore, C. *Patterns of Moral Complexity.* Cambridge, 1987.

―――. "Political Liberalism." *Political Theory* 18 (1990): 339–60.

―――. "Die Wurzeln radikaler Demokratie." *Deutsche Zeitschrift für Philosophie* 41 (1993): 321–27.

Lepenies, W. *Melancholie und Gesellschaft.* Frankfurt am Main, 1969.

Lepsius, M. R. *Die Europäische Gemeinschaft: Beitrag zum 20. Deutschen Soziologentag.* Frankfurt am Main, 1990.

―――. *Interessen, Ideen und Institutionen.* Opladen, 1990.

Lösche, P. "Anarchismus." In *Pipers Handbuch der Politischen Ideen.* Vol. 4. Munich, 1986. Pp. 415ff.

Löwith, K. *Meaning in History.* Chicago, 1970.

Lüderssen, K. "Die Steuerungsfunktion des Gesetzes—Überformung oder Gegensteuerung zur Entwicklungstendenz einer Gesellschaft." In Lüderssen,

Genesis und Geltung im Recht. Frankfurt am Main, 1993.

Luhmann, N. *Ausdifferenzierung des Rechts: Beiträge zur Rechtssoziologie und Rechtstheorie.* Frankfurt am Main, 1981.

————. *Beobachtungen der Moderne.* Cologne, 1992.

————. "Ethik als Reflexionstheorie der Moral." In Luhmann, *Gesellschaftsstruktur und Semantik: Studien zur Wissenssoziologie der modernen Gesellschaft.* Vol. 3. Frankfurt am Main, 1990. Pp. 358–448.

————. "Intersubjectivität oder Kommunikation: Unterschiedliche Ausgangspunkte soziologischer Theoriebildung." *Archivo di Filosofia* 54 (1986): 41ff.

————. "Juristische Argumentation." Unpublished ms. 1991.

————. *Legitimation durch Verfahren.* Neuwied, 1969.

————. "Normen in soziologischer Perspektive." *Soziale Welt* 20 (1969): 28ff.

————. *Political Theory in the Welfare State.* Translated by J. Bednarz, Jr. New York, 1990.

————. "Politische Steuerung: Ein Diskussionsbeitrag." *Politische Vierteljahresschrift* 30 (1989): 4–9.

————. "Quod omnes tangit . . . " *Rechtshistorisches Journal* 12 (1993): 36–56.

————. *A Sociological Theory of Law.* Translated by E. King and M. Albrow. Edited by M. Albrow. London, 1985.

————. "Some Problems with Reflexive Law." In A. Febbrajo and G. Teubner, eds., *State, Law, Economy as Autopoietic Systems: Regulation and Autonomy in a New Perspective.* Milan, 1992. Pp. 389–416.

————. *Die soziologische Beobachtung des Rechts.* Frankfurt am Main, 1986.

MacCormick, N. *Legal Reasoning and Legal Theory.* Oxford, 1978.

MacIntyre, A. *Whose Justice? Which Rationality?.* Notre Dame, 1988.

MacKinnon, C. A. *Towards a Feminist Theory of the State.* Cambridge, Mass., 1989.

Macpherson, C. B. *The Political Theory of Possessive Individualism: Hobbes to Locke.* Oxford, 1962.

Manin, B. "On Legitimacy and Political Deliberation." Translated by E. Stein and J. Mansbridge. *Political Theory* 15 (1987): 338–68.

Mansbridge, J. "Self-Interest in Political Life." *Political Theory* 18 (1990): 132–53.

March, J. G., and J. P. Olsen. "The New Institutionalism: Organizational Factors of Political Life." *American Political Science Review* 77 (1984): 734–49.

————. "Popular Sovereignty and the Search for Appropriate Institutions." *Journal of Public Policy* 6 (1984): 341–70.

————. *Rediscovering Institutions: The Organizational Basis of Politics.* New York, 1989.

Markov, W. *Die Jakobinerfrage heute.* Berlin, 1967.

Marshall, T. H. *Citizenship and Social Class*. Cambridge, Mass., 1950. Also in Marshall, *Class, Citizenship and Social Development*. Westport, Conn., 1973. Pp. 65–122.

Marx, K. *The Eighteenth Brumaire of Louis Bonaparte*. New York, 1963.

Mashaw, J. L. *Due Process in the Administrative State*. New Haven, Conn., 1985.

Maus, I. "Basisdemokratische Aktivitäten und rechtsstaatliche Verfassung: Zum Verhältnis von institutionalisierter und nichtinstitutionalisierter Volkssouveränität." In T. Kreuder, ed., *Der orientierungslose Leviathan: Verfassungsdebatte, Funktion und Leistungsfähigkeit von Recht und Verfassung*. Marburg, 1992. Pp. 99–116.

————. *Bürgerliche Rechtstheorie und Faschismus: Zur sozialen Funktion und aktuellen Wirkung der Theorie Carl Schmitts*. 2d ed. Munich, 1980.

————. "Entwicklung und Funktionswandel der Theorie des bürgerlichen Rechtsstaats." In Maus, *Rechtstheorie und Politische Theorie im Industriekapitalismus*. Pp. 11–82. Also in M. Tohidipur, ed., *Der bürgerliche Rechtsstaat*. Vol. 1. Frankfurt am Main, 1978. Pp. 13–81.

————. *Rechtstheorie und politische Theorie im Industriekapitalismus*. Munich, 1986.

————. "Die Trennung von Recht und Moral als Begrenzung des Rechts." *Rechtstheorie* 20 (1989): 191–210.

————. "Verrechtlichung, Entrechtlichung und der Funktionswandel von Institutionen." In Maus, *Rechtstheorie und politische Theorie*. Pp. 277–331. Also in G. Göhler, ed., *Grundfragen der Theorie politischer Institutionen: Forschungsstand— Probleme—Perspektiven*. Opladen, 1987. Pp. 132–72.

————. *Zur Aufklärung der Demokratietheorie: Rechts- und demokratietheoretische Überlegungen im Anschluß an Kant*. Frankfurt am Main, 1992.

————. "Zur Theorie der Institutionalisierung bei Kant." In G. Göhler at al., eds., *Politische Institutionen im gesellschaftlichen Umbruch: Ideengeschichtliche Beiträge zur Theorie politische Institutionen*. Opladen, 1990. Pp. 358ff.

Mayntz, R., ed. *Implementation politischer Programme II: Aufsätze zur Theoriebildung*. Opladen, 1983.

————. "Steuerung, Steuerungsakteure, Steuerungsinstrumente: Zur Präzisierung des Problems." *HiMon-DB* 70. Gesamthochschule Siegen, 1986.

McCarthy, J. E. "Semiotic Idealism." *Transactions of the Charles S. Peirce Society* 20 (1984): 395–433.

McMurrin, S. M., ed. *The Tanner Lectures on Human Values*. Vol. 8. Salt Lake City, 1988.

Menke-Eggers, C. *Die Souveränität der Kunst: Ästhetische Erfahrung nach Adorno und Derrida*. Frankfurt am Main, 1988.

Merry, H. J. *Five Branch Government*. Urbana, Ill., 1980.

Mestmäcker, E. J. "Der Kampf ums Recht in der offenen Gesellschaft." *Rechtstheorie* 20 (1989): 273–88.

———. "Wiederkehr der bürgerlichen Gesellschaft und ihres Rechts." *Rechtshistorisches Journal* 10 (1991): 177–84.

Michelman, F. I. "Bringing the Law to Life: A Plea for Disenchantment." *Cornell Law Review* 74 (1989): 256–69.

———. "Conceptions of Democracy in American Constitutional Argument: The Case of Pornography Regulation." *Tennessee Law Review* 56 (1989): 291–319.

———. "Conceptions of Democracy in American Constitutional Argument: Voting Rights." *Florida Law Review* 41 (1989): 443–90.

———. "Justification (and Justifiability) of Law in a Contradictory World." In J. R. Pennock and J. W. Chapman, eds. *Justification.* Nomos vol. 18. New York, 1986. Pp. 71–99.

———. "Law's Republic." *Yale Law Journal* 97 (1988): 1493–537.

———. "Political Truth and the Rule of Law." *Tel Aviv University Studies in Law* 8 (1988): 281–91.

———. "The Supreme Court 1985 Term—Foreword: Traces of Self-Government." *Harvard Law Review* 100 (1986): 4–77.

Millar, J. *The Origin of the Distinction of Ranks.* 3d ed. London, 1779.

Miller, D. "The Ethical Significance of Nationality." *Ethics* 98 (1988): 647–62.

Minda, G. "The Jurisprudential Movements of the 1980s." *Ohio State Law Journal* 50 (1989): 599–662.

Minow, M. *Making All the Difference: Inclusion, Exclusion and American Law.* Ithaca, N.Y., 1990.

Moon, J. D. "Constrained Discourse and Public Life." *Political Theory* 19 (1991): 202–29.

Morley, D. *Family Television.* London, 1988.

Münch, R. *Die Kultur der Moderne.* 2 vols. Frankfurt am Main, 1986.

———. "Die sprachlose Systemtheorie: Systemdifferenzierung, reflexives Recht, reflexive Selbststeuerung und Integration durch Indifferenz." *Zeitschrift für Rechtssoziologie* 6 (1985): 4–35.

———. *Theorie des Handelns: Zur Rekonstruktion der Beiträge von Talcott Parsons, Emile Durkheim und Max Weber.* Frankfurt am Main, 1982.

Naucke, W. "Versuch über den aktuellen Stil des Rechts." *Schriften der Hermann-Ehlers-Akademie* 19 (1986).

Negt, O., and E. T. Mohl. "Marx und Engels—der unaufgehobene Widerspruch von Theorie und Praxis." In *Pipers Handbuch der Politischen Ideen.* Vol. 4. Munich, 1986. Pp. 449ff.

Neumann, U. *Juristische Argumentationslehre.* Darmstadt, 1986.

———. "Rückwirkungsverbot bei belastenden Rechtsprechungsänderungen der Strafgerichte?" *Zeitschrift für die gesamte Staatswissenschaft* 103 (1991): 331–56.

Offe, C. "Bindings, Shackles, Brakes: On Self-Limitation Strategies." In A. Honneth et al., eds., *Cultural-Political Interventions in the Unfinished Project of Enlightenment.* Translated by B. Fultner. Cambridge, Mass., 1992. Pp. 63–94.

————. "Challenging the Boundaries of Institutional Politics: Social Movements since the 1960s." In C. S. Maier, *Changing Boundaries of the Political.* Cambridge, 1987. Pp. 63–106.

Offe, C., and U. K. Preuss. "Democratic Institutions and Moral Resources." In D. Held, ed., *Political Theory Today.* Oxford, 1991. Pp. 143–71.

O'Neill, O. "Kommunikative Rationalität und praktische Vernunft." *Deutsche Zeitschrift für Philosophie* 41 (1993): 329–32.

Papier, H. J. *Eigentumsgarantie des Grundgesetzes im Wandel.* Heidelberg, 1984.

Parsons, T. "On the Concept of Influence." In Parsons, *Sociological Theory and Modern Society.* New York, 1967. Pp. 355–82.

————. *The System of Modern Societies.* Englewood-Cliffs, N.J., 1971.

Parsons, T., R. F. Bales, and E. Shils. *Working Papers in the Theory of Action.* New York, 1953.

Parsons, T., and E. Shils. *Toward a General Theory of Action.* New York, 1951.

Pateman, C. *The Problem of Political Obligation: A Critical Analysis of Liberal Theory.* Oxford, 1979.

Peirce, C. S. *Collected Papers.* 6 vols. Edited by C. Hartshorne and P. Weiss. Cambridge, Mass., 1931–1935. Vol. 5.

Perry, M. J. *Morality, Politics, and Law: A Bicentennial Essay.* Oxford, 1988.

Peters, B. *Die Integration moderner Gesellschaften.* Frankfurt am Main, 1993.

————. *Rationalität, Recht und Gesellschaft.* Frankfurt am Main, 1991.

Pitkin, H. F. "Justice: On Relating Private and Public." *Political Theory* 9 (1981): 327–52.

Pocock, J. G. A. *The Machiavellian Moment: Florentine Political Thought and the Atlantic Republican Tradition.* Princeton, 1975.

————. "Virtues, Rights, and Manners." *Political Theory* 9 (1981): 353–68.

Popitz, H. *Die normative Konstruktion von Gesellschaft.* Tübingen, 1980.

Poposil, L. *Anthropologie des Rechts.* Munich, 1982.

Preuss, U. K. *Die Internalisierung des Subjekts: Zur Kritik der Funktionsweise des subjektiven Rechts.* Frankfurt am Main, 1979.

————. *Revolution, Fortschritt und Verfassung: Zu einem neuen Verfassungsverständnis.* Berlin, 1990.

————. "Verfassungstheoretische Überlegungen zur normativen Begründung des Wohlfahrtsstaates." In C. Sachße and H. T. Engelhardt, eds., *Sicherheit und Freiheit: Zur Ethik des Wohlfahrtsstaates.* Frankfurt am Main, 1990. Pp. 106–32.

————. "Was heißt radikale Demokratie heute?" In Forum für Philosophie Bad Homburg, ed., *Die Ideen von 1789: In der deutschen Rezeption.* Frankfurt am Main, 1989. Pp. 37–67.

Puchta, G. F. *Cursus der Institutionen.* Leipzig, 1865.

Puhle, H. J. "Die Anfänge des politischen Konservatismus in Deutschland." In *Pipers Handbuch der Politischen Ideen.* Vol. 4. Munich, 1986. Pp. 255ff.

Putnam, H. *Reason, Truth and History.* Cambridge, 1981.

————. "Why Reason Can't Be Naturalized." *Synthese* 52 (1982): 1–23.

Raiser, L. "Der Stand der Lehre vom subjektiven Recht im Deutschen Zivilrecht (1961)." In L. Raiser, *Die Aufgabe des Privatrechts.* Frankfurt am Main, 1977. Pp. 98ff.

————. *Die Zukunft des Privatrechts.* Berlin, 1971.

Raiser, T. *Rechtssoziologie: Ein Lehrbuch.* Frankfurt am Main, 1987.

Raschke, J. *Soziale Bewegungen: Ein historisch-systematischer Grundriss.* Frankfurt am Main, 1985.

Rawls, J. "The Basic Liberties and Their Priority." In S. McMurrin, ed., *The Tanner Lectures on Human Values.* Vol. 3. Salt Lake City, 1982. Pp. 1–87.

————. "The Domain of the Political and Overlapping Consensus." *New York University Law Review* 64 (1989): 233–55.

————. "Justice as Fairness: Political Not Metaphysical." *Philosophy and Public Affairs* 14 (1985): 223–51.

————. "Kantian Constructivism in Moral Theory." *Journal of Philosophy* 77 (1980): 515–72.

————. *Political Liberalism.* New York, 1993.

————. *A Theory of Justice.* Cambridge, Mass., 1971.

Rehbinder, E. "Reflexive Law and Practice." In A. Febbrajo and G. Teubner, eds., *State, Law, Economy as Autopoietic Systems: Regulation and Autonomy in a New Perspective.* Milan, 1992. Pp. 579–608.

Rehg, W. "Discourse and the Moral Point of View: Deriving a Dialogical Principle of Universalization." *Inquiry* 34 (1991): 27–48.

————. *Insight and Solidarity: A Study in the Discourse Ethics of Jürgen Habermas.* Berkeley, 1994.

Rhode, D. L. *Justice and Gender: Sex Discrimination and the Law.* Cambridge, Mass., 1989.

Richards, D. A. J. "Moral Philosophy and the Search for Fundamental Values in Constitutional Law." *Ohio State Law Journal* 42 (1981): 319–33.

Ridder, H. *Die soziale Ordnung des Grundgesetzes.* Opladen, 1975.

Ritter, J. *Hegel and the French Revolution.* Translated by R. D. Winfield. Cambridge, Mass., 1982.

Rödel, U., ed. *Autonome Gesellschaft und libertäre Demokratie.* Frankfurt am Main, 1990.

Rödel, U., G. Frankenberg, and H. Dubiel. *Die demokratische Frage.* Frankfurt am Main, 1989.

Rolke, L. *Protestbewegungen in der Bundesrepublik.* Opladen, 1987.

Roniger, L. "Conditions for the Consolidation of Democracy in Southern Europe and Latin America." In Eisenstadt, ed., *Democracy and Modernity.* Pp. 53–68.

Rorty, R. *Objectivity, Relativism, and Truth.* Cambridge, 1991.

———. "The Priority of Democracy to Philosophy." In Rorty, *Objectivity, Relativism, and Truth.* Cambridge, 1991. Pp. 175–96.

———. "Thugs and Theorists: A Reply to Bernstein." *Political Theory* 15 (1987): 564–80.

Rousseau, J.-J. *Of the Social Contract or Principles of Political Right.* Translated by C. M. Sherover. New York, 1984.

Royce, J. *The Spirit of Modern Philosophy.* Boston, 1892.

Runde Tisch. "New Constitution of the GDR." Berlin, 1990.

Rupp, H. H. "Vom Wandel der Grundrechte." *Archiv des öffentlichen Rechts* 101 (1976): 161–201.

Rüthers, B. *Die unbegrenzte Auslegung: Zum Wandel der Privatrechtsordnung im Nationalsozialismus.* Frankfurt am Main, 1973.

Savigny, F. C. von. *System des heutigen Römischen Rechts.* Vol. 1. Berlin, 1840.

Scharpf, F. W. *Demokratietheorie zwischen Utopie und Anpassung.* Konstanz, 1970.

———. "Politische Steuerung und politische Institution." *Politischen Vierteljahresschrift* 30 (1989): 10–21.

———. "Politische Steuerung und politische Institution." In Hartwich, ed., *Macht und Ohnmacht politischer Institutionen.* Pp. 17–29.

———. "Verhandlungssysteme, Verteilungskonflikte und Pathologien der politischen Steuerung." *Politischen Vierteljahresschrift* Sonderheft 19 (1989): 61–67.

Schattschneider, E. E. *The Semisovereign People: A Realistic View of Democracy in America.* New York, 1960.

Scheit, H. *Wahrheit, Diskurs, Democratie: Studien zur "Konsensustheorie der Wahrheit."* Freiburg, 1987.

Schelling, T. C. *Micromotives and Macrobehavior.* New York, 1978.

Schelsky, H. *Die Soziologen und das Recht: Abhandlungen und Vorträge zur Soziologie von Recht, Institution und Planung.* Opladen, 1980.

Schluchter, W. "Beiträge zur Werttheorie." In Schluchter, *Religion und Lebensführung.* Frankfurt am Main, 1988. Vol. 1. Pp. 165ff.

———. *The Rise of Western Rationalism: Max Weber's Developmental History.* Translated by G. Roth. Berkeley, 1981.

Schmidt, E. "Von der Privat- zur Sozialautonomie." *Juristenzeitung* 35 (1980): 153–61.

Schmidt, J. "Zur Funktion der subjektiven Rechte." *Archiv für Rechts- und Sozialphilosophie* 57 (1971): 383–96.

Schmidt, W. *Einführung in die Probleme des Verwaltungsrechts.* Munich, 1982.

Schmidt-Assmann, E. "Der Rechtsstaat." In J. Isensee and P. Kirchhoff, eds., *Handbuch des Staatsrechts der Bundesrepublik Deutschland.* Vol. 1: *Grundlagen von Staat und Verfassung.* Heidelberg, 1987. Pp. 987–1043.

Schmitt, C. *The Crisis of Parliamentary Democracy.* Translated by E. Kennedy. Cambridge, Mass., 1988.

———. *Der Hüter der Verfassung.* Tübingen, 1931.

———. *Über drei Arten des rechtswissenschaftlichen Denkens.* Hamburg, 1934.

———. *Die Verfassungslehre.* Berlin, 1928.

Schnur, R., ed. *Zur Geschichte der Erklärung der Menschenrechte.* Darmstadt, 1964.

Schulin, E. *Die Französische Revolution.* Munich, 1988.

Schumpeter, J. A. *Capitalism, Socialism und Democracy.* 2d ed. New York, 1947.

Sen, A. "Rational Fools: A Critique of the Behavioral Foundations of Economic Theory." *Philosophy and Public Affairs* 6 (1977): 317–44.

Shuck, P. H., and R. M. Smith. *Citizenship without Consent: Illegal Aliens in the American Polity.* New Haven, Conn., 1985.

Shue, H. "Mediating Duties." *Ethics* 98 (1988): 687–704.

Simitis, S. "Juridification of Labor Relations." In Teubner, ed., *Juridification of Social Spheres,* pp. 113–61.

———."Selbstbestimmung: Illusorisches Projekt oder reale Chance?" In J. Rüsen et al., eds., *Die Zukunft der Aufklärung.* Frankfurt am Main, 1988. Pp. 165–94.

———. "Wiederentdeckung des Individuums und arbeitsrechtliche Normen." *Sinzheimer Cahiers* 2 (1991): 7–42.

Simon, H. A. "Rational Decision Making in Business Organizations." In Simon, *Models of Bounded Rationality.* Vol. 2: *Behavioral Economics and Business Organizations.* Cambridge, Mass., 1982. Pp. 474–94.

Smart, C. *Feminism and the Power of Law.* London, 1989.

Smith, T. *The Role of Ethics in Social Theory.* Albany, 1991.

Starobinski, J. *1789: The Emblems of Reason.* Translated by B. Bray. Charlottesville, Va., 1982.

Steiner, H. J. *Moral Argument and Social Vision in the Courts.* Madison, Wisc., 1987.

Suhr, D. "Staat-Gesellschaft-Verfassung von Hegel bis Heute." *Der Staat* 17 (1978): 369–95.

Summers, R. S. *Instrumentalism and American Legal Theory.* Ithaca, N.Y., 1982.

———. *Lon L. Fuller.* Stanford, 1984.

Sunstein, C. R. *After the Rights Revolution: Reconceiving the Regulatory State.* Cambridge, Mass., 1990.

———. "Interest Groups in American Public Law." *Stanford Law Review* 38 (1985): 29–87.

Taylor, C. "Cross-Purposes: The Liberal-Communitarian Debate." In N. Rosenblum, ed., *Liberalism and the Moral Life.* Cambridge, Mass., 1989. Pp. 159–82.

———. *Human Agency and Language: Philosophical Papers I.* Cambridge, 1985.

———. "Legitimation Crisis?" In Taylor, *Philosophy and the Human Sciences: Philosophical Papers II.* Cambridge, 1985. Pp. 248–88.

———. *Sources of the Self: The Making of the Modern Identity.* Cambridge, Mass., 1989.

———. "What Is Human Agency?" In Taylor, *Human Agency.* Pp. 15–44.

Teubner, G. "Die Episteme des Rechts: Zu erkenntnistheoretischen Grundlagen des reflexiven Rechts." In Grimm, ed., *Wachsende Staatsaufgaben—sinkende Steuerungsfähigkeit des Rechts.* Pp. 115–54.

———. "How the Law Thinks: Toward a Constructivist Epistemology of Law." *Law and Society Review* 23 (1989): 727–57.

———. "Juridification—Concepts, Aspects, Limits, Solutions." In Teubner, ed., *Juridification of Social Spheres,* pp. 3–48.

———. *Law as an Autopoietic System.* Translated by A. Bankowska and R. Adler. Edited by Z. Bankowski. Oxford, 1993.

———. *Recht als autopoietisches System.* Frankfurt am Main, 1989.

———. "Reflexives Recht: Entwicklungsmodelle des Rechts in vergleichender Perspektive." *Archiv für Rechts- und Sozialphilosophie* 68 (1982): 13–59.

———. "Regulatorisches Recht: Chronik eines angekündigten Todes." *Archiv für Rechts- und Sozialphilosophie* Beiheft 54 (1990): 140–61.

———. "Substantive and Reflexive Elements in Modern Law." *Law and Society Review* 17 (1983): 239–85.

———, ed. *Autopoietic Law: A New Approach to Law and Society.* Berlin, 1988.

———, ed. *Dilemmas of Law in the Welfare State.* Berlin, 1986.

———, ed. *Juridification of Social Spheres: A Comparative Analysis in the Areas of Labor, Corporate, Antitrust and Social Welfare Law.* Berlin, 1987.

Thadden, R. von. "Die Botschaft der Brüderlichkeit." *Süddeutsche Zeitung.* Nov. 26/27, 1988.

Thompson, J. B. *Ideology and Modern Culture: Critical Social Theory in the Era of Mass Communication.* Cambridge, 1990.

Toulmin, S. *The Uses of Argument.* Cambridge, 1964.

Toulmin, S., R. Rieke, and A. Janik. *An Introduction to Reasoning.* New York, 1979.

Tribe, L. H. "The Puzzling Persistence of Process-Based Constitutional Theories." *Yale Law Journal* 89 (1980): 1063–80.

Trubek, D. M., and J. P. Esser. "'Critical Empiricism' and American Critical Legal Studies: Paradox, Program, or Pandora's Box?" In Joerges and Trubek, eds., *Critical Legal Thought.* Pp. 105–56.

Tugendhat, E. *Self-Consciousness and Self-Determination.* Translated by P. Stern. Cambridge, Mass., 1986.

————. *Traditional and Analytical Philosophy: Lectures on the Philosophy of Language.* Translated by P. A. Gorner. Cambridge, 1982.

Tuori, K. "Discourse Ethics and the Legitimacy of Law." *Ratio Juris* 2 (1989): 125–43.

Turner, B. S. *Citizenship and Capitalism: The Debate over Reformism.* London, 1986.

Unger, R. M. *The Critical Legal Studies Movement.* Cambridge, Mass., 1986.

Varain, H. J. "Die Bedeutung des Mehrheitsprinzips im Rahmen unserer politischen Ordnung." In Guggenberger and Offe, eds., *An den Grenzen der Mehrheitsprinzip.* Pp. 48–60.

Vollrath, E. *Die Rekonstruktion der politischen Urteilskraft.* Stuttgart, 1977.

Walzer, M. "The Communitarian Critique of Liberalism." *Political Theory* 18 (1990): 6–23.

————. *Spheres of Justice: A Defence of Pluralism and Equality.* New York, 1983.

Weber, M. *Economy and Society: An Outline of Interpretive Sociology.* 2 vols. Edited by G. Roth and C. Wittich. Berkeley, 1978.

————. *Rechtssoziologie.* Edited by J. Winckelmann. Neuwied, 1960.

————. "Some Categories of Interpretive Sociology." Translated by E. Garber. *Sociological Quarterly* 22 (1981): 151–80.

————. "Über einige Kategorien der verstehenden Soziologie." In M. Weber, *Methodologische Schriften.* Frankfurt am Main, 1968.

Weber, W. *Spannungen und Kräfte im westdeutschen Verfassungssystem.* Stuttgart, 1951.

Weinberger, O. "Der Streit um die praktische Vernunft." In R. Alexy and R. Dreier, eds., *Legal System and Practical Reason. Archiv für Rechts- und Sozialphilosophie* Beiheft 51 (1993): 30–46.

Wellmer, A. "Bedingungen einer demokratischen Kultur." In Brumlik and Brunkhorst, eds., *Gemeinschaft und Gerechtigkeit.* Pp. 173–96.

————. "Ethics and Dialogue: Elements of Moral Judgement in Kant and Discourse Ethics." In Wellmer, *The Persistence of Modernity: Essays on Aesthetics, Ethics, and Postmodernism.* Translated by D. Midgley. Cambridge, Mass., 1991. Pp. 113–231.

————. "Hannah Arendt on Judgment: The Unwritten Doctrine of Reason." In L. May and J. Kohn, eds., *Hannah Arendt: Twenty Years Later.* Cambridge, Mass., 1996.

————. "Konsens als Telos sprachlicher Kommunikation." In H. J. Giegel, ed., *Kommunikation und Konsens in modernen Gesellschaften.* Frankfurt am Main, 1992. Pp. 18–30.

————. "Models of Freedom in the Modern World." *Philosophical Forum* 21 (1989/90): 227–52.

Wesel, U. *Frühformen des Rechts in vorstaatlichen Gesellschaften: Umrisse einer Frühgeschichte des Rechts bei Sammlern und Jägern und akephalen Ackerbauern und Hirten.* Frankfurt am Main, 1985.

Westbrook, R. B. *John Dewey and American Democracy.* Ithaca, N.Y., 1991.

Wieacker, F. "Das Sozialmodell der klassischen Privatrechtsgesetzbücher und die Entwicklung der modernen Gesellschaft." In Wieacker, *Industriegesellschaft und Privatrechtsordnung.* Frankfurt am Main, 1974.

Wiethölter, R. "Ist unserem Recht der Prozeß zu machen?" In Honneth et al., eds., *Zwischenbetrachtungen im Prozeß der Aufklärung: Jürgen Habermas zum 60. Geburtstag.* Frankfurt am Main, 1989. Pp. 794–812.

————. "Proceduralization of the Category of Law." In Joerges and Trubek, eds., *Critical Legal Thought.* Pp. 501–10.

Willke, H. *Ironie des Staates: Grundlinien einer Staatstheorie polyzentrischer Gesellschaft.* Frankfurt am Main, 1992.

Windscheid, B. *Lehrbuch des Pandektenrechts.* Vol. 2. Frankfurt am Main, 1906.

Wingert, L. *Gemeinsinn und Moral: Elemente einer intersubjektivistischen Moral Konzeption.* Frankfurt am Main, 1993.

Winzeler, R. *Die politischen Rechte des Aktivbürgers nach schweizerischem Bundesrecht.* Bern, 1983.

Wroblewski, J. "Legal Syllogism and Rationality of Judicial Decision." *Rechtstheorie* 5 (1974): 33–46.

Young, I. M. *Justice and the Politics of Difference.* Princeton, 1990.

Zacher, H. F. "Juridification in the Field of Social Law." In Teubner, ed., *Juridification of Social Spheres.* Pp. 373–417.

Index

Aarnio, Aulis, 230, 541n58
Ackerman, Bruce, xxix–xxx
  two-track model of democracy, 277–278,
    308–310, 550n28, 551n30
Action theory. *See also* Communicative
  action; Orientation to reaching
  understanding; Orientation to success
action coordination, 4, 8, 17–20, 35, 73–
  74, 83–84, 106, 119, 139–142, 338–341,
  346, 354, 511, 524n18 (*see also* Law,
  stabilization of expectations by; Social
  integration)
interest-oriented action, xix, 25–27, 69,
  83, 139–141, 159–160, 555n28 (*see also*
  Values, as action orientation)
strategic action, xii, xvi–xix, 25–27, 272–
  274, 337–339
Adjudication. *See also* Judiciary
  application discourse and, 217–221, 233–
    237, 242–243
  certainty of law in, 173, 197–199, 201–
    203, 211, 219–221, 223, 237–238
  coherence of law in, 192, 198–199, 211–
    221, 232, 236–237
  constitutional adjudication, xxix–xxx,
    239–268, 274–280, 397, 399, 430 (*see also*
    Judiciary, constitutional courts)
  indeterminacy of law in, 214, 216–219,
    223, 231, 239, 243–244, 431
  Judge Hercules/judge in, 172, 203, 207,
    211–217, 221–225, 227, 253
  legitimacy and, 198–199, 222, 224–225,
    238, 246, 252–253, 261, 264, 267, 274,
    283, 394

possibility proviso, 248, 544n16
principles of, 172, 208–211, 214, 216–217,
  219, 243, 248, 260–261, 264–266, 388
rationality problem of, 7, 197–207, 214,
  216, 238
special cases/hard cases of, 202–203, 207,
  211, 231, 233, 243, 439
theories of judicial decision making (*see*
  Theories of law)
trial proceedings, 231, 235–236
value jurisprudence, xxix, 209, 239–240,
  253–261, 265, 282, 544n28 (*see also*
  Values)
Administration
administrative power, 39–40, 75, 133–138,
  141–143, 329–331, 483–484
administrative steering, 327, 332–333,
  358–359, 430–432
bound by law, 73, 150, 173–174, 186–190,
  300, 441, 457, 483–484, 534n34, 535n38
citizens and clients and, 78, 136, 173, 270,
  335, 350, 431–432, 461, 492, 497,
  556n47
classical liberal administration, 247, 396,
  402, 430–431, 435–436
communicative power and, xxvii, 136,
  147, 149–150, 169, 187–188, 329–330,
  356–358, 483–490
discourse theory/discourses and, 169–
  170, 173–174, 186, 192, 285, 299–300,
  348, 436, 440–441
incumbent Administration, 187, 299–300,
  354, 380, 482

Rousseau, Jean-Jacques, 32
on autonomy, 100–103, 138, 189, 300,
454, 472, 474, 487
and civic republican tradition, xxv, 100–
103, 267–268, 278, 300, 466
on connection between popular
sovereignty and human rights, 94, 100–
103, 138, 300–301, 454, 472–474, 476,
495–496
ethics of, 96, 101–102, 278, 478
on law, 101–103, 126, 138, 474, 475
Roux, Jacques, 477
Royce, Josiah, 106
Rule of law. See Constitutional state, rule of
law
Rupp, Hans H., 407
Russell, Bertrand, 10

Sartre, Jean-Paul, 96, 321, 346
Savigny, Friedrich Carl von, 85–87, 89–90,
100, 118
Scheler, Max, 2, 254
Schelling, Thomas, 555n27
Schleiermacher, Friedrich, 96
Schluchter, Wolfgang, 70–71
Schmidt, Eberhard, 412
Schmitt, Carl
on constitutional adjudication, 241–243,
254, 543n3
on democracy, 184–185, 470, 480, 535n43
on law, 152–153, 563n75
Schumpeter, Joseph, 332
Searle, John, xiv
Self-determination. See also Autonomy;
Ethical discourse
of citizens, 128, 263, 268, 271, 277–278,
298, 386–387, 390, 449–451, 457, 495–
496
civic republicanism on, 268, 271, 297, 301
collective, 110, 457, 489
discursive, 98–99, 128, 157, 445
individual, 398–399, 413–414, 419,
561n46
moral discourse and, 95, 97–100, 450
political, 41, 134, 169, 263, 269–272, 297,
420, 467, 494–496, 498–499, 505, 513
right of, 134, 263, 277–278, 514
Semantics
legal form and, 102, 130, 191, 456–457
on representational thinking, 10–12

semantic generality, 11, 13–14, 17, 19,
102, 191, 311–312, 490
Separation of powers, 327, 474, 480
administration and, 173, 186–188, 193,
195, 241, 300, 430, 434, 436, 438 (see
also Administration)
classical, 186–190, 245, 537n65
discourse theoretic specification of, xxix,
191–192, 241–242
functional, 186–193, 431, 438
judiciary and, xxix, 186, 192–193, 195,
238–241, 243–244, 261–263, 265, 438
(see also Judiciary)
law and, 189–191, 245, 246, 431, 438–439,
477
legal paradigms on, xxix, xxxiii, 189–190,
239, 244–246, 250–251, 263, 297, 301,
391, 431, 438, 472
legislature and, 135, 172, 186–187, 193,
261, 438 (see also Legislature)
principle of, 191
Sieyès, Emmanuel, 494
Simitis, Spiros, 413–414, 416, 561nn.44, 46
Sluice model. See Democratic theory, core-
periphery model
Smith, Adam, 45, 57
Social complexity. See also Pluralism;
Society, complex
communication and, 52–56, 323–328
democracy and, xxx–xxxii, 315–328
legal institutions and, 47–56, 326–328,
356–357
systems theory on, xxi–xxiii, 47–56, 342–
353
Social contract theory, xx. See also Natural
law
association in, 91, 93–94, 102, 476, 480–
481, 548n76
autonomy in, 85, 449, 495–496
contract law and, 44, 92, 402, 449
discourse theory and, 134–135, 194, 449
justice and, 56–57, 62, 65, 99
on law, 44, 48, 65, 92–93, 146, 402, 449
on rights, 84, 92–93, 101, 118, 148–149,
469, 476
on state, 6, 137–138, 495–496
Social integration
archaic/preestablished means of, 8, 24,
138–139, 296, 466, 550n25, 557n62